Lecture Notes in Computer Science 2694
Edited by G. Goos, J. Hartmanis, and J. van Leeuwen

Springer
*Berlin
Heidelberg
New York
Hong Kong
London
Milan
Paris
Tokyo*

Radhia Cousot (Ed.)

Static Analysis

10th International Symposium, SAS 2003
San Diego, CA, USA, June 11-13, 2003
Proceedings

Springer

Series Editors

Gerhard Goos, Karlsruhe University, Germany
Juris Hartmanis, Cornell University, NY, USA
Jan van Leeuwen, Utrecht University, The Netherlands

Volume Editor

Radhia Cousot
École Polytechnique, STIX
91128 Palaiseau cedex, France
E-mail: radhia.cousot@polytechnique.fr

Cataloging-in-Publication Data applied for
A catalog record for this book is available from the Library of Congress

Bibliographic information published by Die Deutsche Bibliothek
Die Deutsche Bibliothek lists this publication in the Deutsche Nationalbibliographie;
detailed bibliographic data is available in the Internet at <http://dnb.ddb.de>.

CR Subject Classification (1998): D.3.2-3, F.3.1-2, D.2.8, F.4.2, D.1

ISSN 0302-9743
ISBN 3-540-40325-6 Springer-Verlag Berlin Heidelberg New York

This work is subject to copyright. All rights are reserved, whether the whole or part of the material is
concerned, specifically the rights of translation, reprinting, re-use of illustrations, recitation, broadcasting,
reproduction on microfilms or in any other way, and storage in data banks. Duplication of this publication
or parts thereof is permitted only under the provisions of the German Copyright Law of September 9, 1965,
in its current version, and permission for use must always be obtained from Springer-Verlag. Violations are
liable for prosecution under the German Copyright Law.

Springer-Verlag Berlin Heidelberg New York
a member of BertelsmannSpringer Science+Business Media GmbH

http://www.springer.de

© Springer-Verlag Berlin Heidelberg 2003
Printed in Germany

Typesetting: Camera-ready by author, data conversion by Christian Grosche, Hamburg
Printed on acid-free paper   SPIN: 10927960   06/3142   5 4 3 2 1 0

Preface

Static analysis is a research area aimed at developing principles and tools for verification and semantics-based manipulation of programs and high-performance implementations of programming languages. The series of Static Analysis symposia has served as the primary venue for presentation and discussion of theoretical, practical, and application advances in the area.

This volume contains the papers accepted for presentation at the 10th International Static Analysis Symposium (SAS 2003), which was held June 11–13, 2003 in San Diego, California, USA.

Firmly established as a leading forum in the static analysis area, SAS 2003 received 82 high-quality submissions. Each paper was carefully reviewed, being judged according to scientific quality, originality, and relevance to the symposium topics.

Following on-line discussions, the program committee met in Paris, France, at the École Normale Supérieure on March 15, 2003, and selected 25 papers. In addition to the contributed papers, this volume includes an invited paper by Manuel Hermenegildo (Technical University of Madrid and University of New Mexico) and the abstract of an invited talk by Ken McMillan (Cadence Berkeley Laboratories).

On behalf of the Program Committee and the General Chair, I would like to thank the authors of the submitted papers, and the external referees, who provided timely and significant reviews. I owe special thanks to Jacques Beigbeder from École Normale Supérieure for managing the submission site and the developers of CyberChair for the use of their software.

On this occasion, SAS was sponsored by the Association for Computing Machinery (ACM) and was held as part of the Federated Computing Research Conference (FCRC 2003). I would like to thank all organizing committee members for all their tremendous work.

April 2003   Radhia Cousot

Organization and Sponsor

The 10th International Static Analysis Symposium (SAS 2003) was sponsored by the Association for Computing Machinery (ACM) and was held as part of the Federated Computing Research Conference (FCRC 2003).

FCRC 2003 Organizing Committee

General Chair	Barbara Ryder, Rutgers University
Keynote Speaker Chair	Stuart Feldman, International Business Machines
Website Coordinator	Jack Davidson, University of Virginia
Support Travel Chair	Kathleen Fisher, AT&T Research
Past FCRC General Chair	David Johnson, AT&T Research
Student Activities Chair	John Karro, Oberlin College
ACM FCRC Coordinator	Donna Baglio, Association for Computing Machinery

Program Committee

Alex Aiken	University of California, Berkeley, USA
Radhia Cousot (Chair)	CNRS/École Polytechnique, France
Luddy Harrison	Intel Corporation, USA
Susan Horwitz	University of Wisconsin-Madison, USA
Andy King	University of Kent, UK
Giorgio Levi	University of Pisa, Italy
Michael Lowry	NASA Ames Research Center, USA
Laurent Mauborgne	École Normale Supérieure, France
Alan Mycroft	Cambridge University, UK
Germán Puebla	Technical University of Madrid, Spain
Francesco Ranzato	University of Padova, Italy
Shmuel Sagiv	Tel Aviv University, Israel
David Sands	Chalmers University of Technology and University of Göteborg, Sweden
Helmut Seidl	University of Trier, Germany
Mary Lou Soffa	University of Pittsburgh, USA
Harald Søndergard	University of Melbourne, Australia

Executive Committee

General Chair	Peter Lee, Carnegie Mellon University
Program Chair	Radhia Cousot, CNRS/École Polytechnique
Submission Website	Jacques Beigbeder, École Normale Supérieure
Website	Radhia Cousot, CNRS/École Polytechnique

Steering Committee

Patrick Cousot	École Normale Supérieure
Gilberto Filé	Università di Padova
David Schmidt	Kansas State University

Referees

Nava Aizikowitz
Krzysztof Apt
Alessandro Armando
Roberto Bagnara
Bruno Blanchet
Chiara Bodei
Howard Bowman
Andrea Bracciali
Guillaume Brat
Francisco Bueno
Peter Bunus
Daniel Cabeza
Manuel Carro
Livio Colussi
Jesus Correas
Agostino Cortesi
Patrick Cousot
Ferruccio Damiani
Marco Danelutto
Anuj Dawar
Bjorn De Sutter
Saumya K. Debray
Pierpaolo Degano
Giorgio Delzanno
Amer Diwan
Nurit Dor
Stephen A. Edwards
Rob Ennals
Peter Faber
Christian Ferdinand
Jérôme Feret
Gilberto Filé
Simon Frankau
Roberto Giacobazzi
Robert Glück
Jose M. Gomez-Perez
Roberta Gori
Susanne Graf
Jörgen Gustavsson
Jurriaan Hage
Les Hatton
Bastiaan Heeren
Nevin Heintze
Fergus Henderson

Angel Herranz-Nieva
Pat Hill
Michael Hind
Jacob Howe
Charles Hymans
Radha Jagadeesan
Bertrand Jeannet
Ranjit Jhala
Neil Johnson
Stefan Kahrs
Volker Klotz
Jens Knoop
John Kodumal
Francesco Logozzo
Alan C. Lawrence
Marina Lenisa
Francesca Levi
Donglin Liang
Sandra Loosemore
Pedro Lopez-Garcia
Lunjin Lu
Antoine Mineé
Andrea Maggiolo Schettini
Rupak Majumdar
Roman Manevich
Julio Mariño
Damien Massé
Isabella Mastroeni
Fred Mesnard
David Monniaux
Jose F. Morales
Markus Müller-Olm
Lee Naish
Härmel Nestra
Nicholas Nethercote
Karol Ostrovsky
Linda Pagli
Justin Pearson
Susanna Pelagatti
Andreas Podelski
Corrado Priami
Ganesan Ramalingam
Laura Ricci
Martin Rinard

Xavier Rival
Alexandru Salcianu
Peter Schachte
Sybille Schupp
Francesca Scozzari
Cotton Seed
Clara Segura
Peter Sestoft
Ran Shaham
Richard Sharp
Ilya Shlyakhter
Simon Frankau
Jeremy Singer
Fausto Spoto
Peter Stuckey

Zhendong Su
Martin Sulzmann
Josef Svenningsson
Walid Taha
Francesco Tapparo
Eben Upton
Arnaud Venet
Eelco Visser
Keith Wansbrough
Joe Wells
Herbert Wiklicky
Reinhard Wilhelm
Eran Yahav
Greta Yorsh
Min Zhao

Table of Contents

Static Analysis of Object-Oriented Languages

Precise Analysis of String Expressions 1
  Aske Simon Christensen, Anders Møller, and
  Michael I. Schwartzbach (BRICS, Department of Computer Science,
  University of Aarhus)

Modular Class Analysis with DATALOG 19
  Frédéric Besson and Thomas Jensen (Irisa)

Class-Level Modular Analysis for Object Oriented Languages 37
  Francesco Logozzo (STIX - École Polytechnique)

Static Analysis of Concurrent Languages

Checking Interference with Fractional Permissions 55
  John Boyland (University of Wisconsin-Milwaukee)

Message Analysis for Concurrent Languages 73
  Richard Carlsson, Konstantinos Sagonas, and Jesper Wilhelmsson
  (Computing Science Department, Uppsala University, Sweden)

Instantaneous Termination in Pure Esterel 91
  Olivier Tardieu and Robert de Simone (INRIA)

Stack Size Analysis for Interrupt-Driven Programs 109
  Krishnendu Chatterjee (University of California, Berkeley),
  Di Ma (Purdue University),
  Rupak Majumdar (University of California, Berkeley),
  Tian Zhao (University of Wisconsin, Milwaukee),
  Thomas A. Henzinger (University of California, Berkeley), and
  Jens Palsberg (Purdue University)

Invited Paper

Program Development Using Abstract Interpretation
(And the Ciao System Preprocessor) 127
  Manuel V. Hermenegildo (Technical University of Madrid and
  University of New Mexico),
  Germán Puebla, Francisco Bueno, and Pedro López-García
  (Technical University of Madrid)

Static Analysis of Functional Languages

Selective Tail Call Elimination 153
  Yasuhiko Minamide (University of Tsukuba and PRESTO, JST)

Inserting Safe Memory Reuse Commands into ML-Like Programs 171
  Oukseh Lee, Hongseok Yang, and Kwangkeun Yi
  (Korea Advanced Institute of Science and Technology)

Static Analysis of Procedural Languages

Weighted Pushdown Systems and Their Application to Interprocedural
Dataflow Analysis 189
  Thomas Reps (University of Wisconsin),
  Stefan Schwoon (Universität Stuttgart), and
  Somesh Jha (University of Wisconsin)

Client-Driven Pointer Analysis 214
  Samuel Z. Guyer and Calvin Lin (The University of Texas at
  Austin)

Abstract Interpretation of Programs as Markov Decision Processes 237
  David Monniaux (CNRS/École normale supérieure)

Static Data Analysis

A Logic for Analyzing Abstractions of Graph Transformation Systems 255
  Paolo Baldan (Dipartimento di Informatica, Università Ca' Foscari
  Venezia, Italy),
  Barbara König (Institut für Informatik, Technische Universität
  München, Germany), and
  Bernhard König (Department of Mathematics, University of
  California, Irvine, USA)

Type Systems for Distributed Data Sharing 273
  Ben Liblit, Alex Aiken, and Katherine Yelick (UC Berkeley)

Z-Ranking: Using Statistical Analysis to Counter the Impact of Static
Analysis Approximations 295
  Ted Kremenek and Dawson Engler (Stanford University)

Computer-Assisted Verification of a Protocol for Certified Email 316
  Martín Abadi (University of California, Santa Cruz) and
  Bruno Blanchet (École Normale Supérieure, Paris and
  Max-Planck-Institut für Informatik, Saarbrücken)

Invited Talk

Craig Interpolation and Reachability Analysis 336
    Ken L. McMillan (Cadence Berkeley Laboratories)

Static Linear Relation Analysis

Precise Widening Operators for Convex Polyhedra 337
    Roberto Bagnara (Department of Mathematics, University of Parma, Italy),
    Patricia M. Hill (School of Computing, University of Leeds, UK),
    Elisa Ricci, and Enea Zaffanella (Department of Mathematics, University of Parma, Italy)

Cartesian Factoring of Polyhedra in Linear Relation Analysis 355
    Nicolas Halbwachs (Verimag/CNRS),
    David Merchat (Verimag), and
    Catherine Parent-Vigouroux (Verimag/UJF)

Static Analysis Based Program Transformation

Continuation-Based Partial Evaluation without Continuations 366
    Peter Thiemann (Universität Freiburg)

Loop Transformations for Reducing Data Space Requirements of
Resource-Constrained Applications 383
    Priya Unnikrishnan, Guangyu Chen, Mahmut Kandemir (Penn State Univ),
    Mustafa Karakoy (Imperial College, London), and
    Ibrahim Kolcu (UMIST, UK)

Code Compaction of Matching Single-Entry Multiple-Exit Regions 401
    Wen-Ke Chen, Bengu Li, and Rajiv Gupta (University of Arizona)

Static Heap Analysis

Existential Heap Abstraction Entailment Is Undecidable 418
    Viktor Kuncak and Martin Rinard (MIT Laboratory for Computer Science)

Typestate Verification: Abstraction Techniques and Complexity Results ... 439
    John Field, Deepak Goyal, G. Ramalingam (IBM T.J. Watson Research Center), and
    Eran Yahav (Tel Aviv University)

Static Analysis of Accessed Regions in Recursive Data Structures......... 463
   Stephen Chong and Radu Rugina (Cornell University)

Establishing Local Temporal Heap Safety Properties with Applications to
Compile-Time Memory Management..................................... 483
   *Ran Shaham (Tel-Aviv University and IBM Haifa Research
   Laboratory),
   Eran Yahav (Tel-Aviv University),
   Elliot Kolodner (IBM Haifa Research Laboratory),, and
   Mooly Sagiv (Tel-Aviv University)*

Author Index 505

Precise Analysis of String Expressions

Aske Simon Christensen, Anders Møller*, and Michael I. Schwartzbach

BRICS**
Department of Computer Science
University of Aarhus, Denmark
{aske,amoeller,mis}@brics.dk

Abstract. We perform static analysis of Java programs to answer a simple question: which values may occur as results of string expressions? The answers are summarized for each expression by a regular language that is guaranteed to contain all possible values. We present several applications of this analysis, including statically checking the syntax of dynamically generated expressions, such as SQL queries. Our analysis constructs flow graphs from class files and generates a context-free grammar with a nonterminal for each string expression. The language of this grammar is then widened into a regular language through a variant of an algorithm previously used for speech recognition. The collection of resulting regular languages is compactly represented as a special kind of multi-level automaton from which individual answers may be extracted. If a program error is detected, examples of invalid strings are automatically produced. We present extensive benchmarks demonstrating that the analysis is efficient and produces results of useful precision.

1 Introduction

To detect errors and perform optimizations in Java programs, it is useful to know which values that may occur as results of string expressions. The exact answer is of course undecidable, so we must settle for a conservative approximation. The answers we provide are summarized for each expression by a regular language that is guaranteed to contain all its possible values. Thus we use an upper approximation, which is what most client analyses will find useful.

This work is originally motivated by a desire to strengthen our previous static analysis of validity of dynamically generated XML documents in the JWIG extension of Java [4], but it has many other applications. Consider for example the following method, which dynamically generates an SQL query for a JDBC binding to a database:

```
public void printAddresses(int id) throws SQLException {
    Connection con = DriverManager.getConnection("students.db");
```

---

* Supported by the Carlsberg Foundation contract number ANS-1069/20.
** Basic Research in Computer Science (http://www.brics.dk), funded by the Danish National Research Foundation.

```
    String q = "SELECT * FROM address";
    if (id!=0) q = q + "WHERE studentid=" + id;
    ResultSet rs = con.createStatement().executeQuery(q);
    while(rs.next()){ System.out.println(rs.getString("addr")); }
}
```

The query is built dynamically, so the compiler cannot guarantee that only syntactically legal queries will be generated. In fact, the above method compiles but the query will sometimes fail at runtime, since there is a missing space between `address` and `WHERE`. In general, it may range from tedious to difficult to perform manual syntax checking of dynamically generated queries.

Our string analysis makes such derived analyses possible by providing the required information about dynamically computed strings. We will use the term *string operations* when referring to methods in the standard Java library that return instances of the classes `String` or `StringBuffer`.

Outline

Our algorithm for string analysis can be split into two parts:

- a *front-end* that translates the given Java program into a flow graph, and
- a *back-end* that analyzes the flow graph and generates finite-state automata.

We consider the full Java language, which requires a considerable engineering effort. Translating a collection of class files into a sound flow graph is a laborious task involving several auxiliary static analyses. However, only the front-end is language dependent, hence the string analysis can be applied to other languages than Java by replacing just the front-end. The back-end proceeds in several phases:

- The starting point is the flow graph, which gives an abstract description of a program performing string manipulations. The graph only has def-use edges, thus control flow is abstracted away. Flow graph nodes represent operations on string variables, such as concatenation or substring.
- The flow graph is then translated into a context-free grammar with one nonterminal for each node. Flow edges and operations are modeled by appropriate productions. To boost precision, we use a special kind of grammar in which string operations are explicitly represented on right-hand sides. The resulting grammar defines for each nonterminal the possible values of the string expression at the corresponding flow graph node.
- The context-free grammar is then transformed into a mixed left- and right-recursive grammar using a variant of the Mohri-Nederhof algorithm [11], which has previously been used for speech recognition.
- A program may contain many string expressions, but typically only few expressions, called *hotspots*, for which we actually want to know the regular language. For this reason, we introduce the *multi-level automaton (MLFA)*, which is a compact data structure from which individual answers may be

extracted by need. Extensive use of memoization helps to make these computations efficient. An MLFA is a well-founded hierarchical directed acyclic graph (DAG) of nondeterministic finite automata.

All regular and context-free languages are over the Unicode alphabet, which we denote Σ. The core of the algorithm is the derivation of context-free grammars from programs and the adaptation of the Mohri-Nederhof algorithm [11], which provides an intelligent means of approximating a context-free language by a larger regular language. Naive solutions to this problem will not deliver sufficient precision in the analysis.

In programs manipulating strings, concatenation is the most important string operation — and in our analysis this operation is the one that we are able to model with the highest precision, since it is an inherent part of context-free grammars. We represent other string operations using less precise automata operations or character set approximations.

The translation from flow graph to multi-level automaton is linear-time. The extraction of a deterministic finite-state automaton (DFA) for a particular string expression is worst-case doubly exponential: one for unfolding the DAG and one for determinizing and minimizing the resulting automaton. In the case of a monovariant analysis, the flow graph obtained from a Java program is in the worst case quadratic in the size of the program, but for typical programs, the translation is linear.

We provide a Java runtime library with operations for selecting the expressions that are hotspots, casting a string expression to the language of a specified regular expression, and for probing regular language membership. This library serves several purposes: 1) It makes it straightforward to apply our analysis tool. 2) In the same way normal casts affect type checking, the "regexp" cast operation can affect the string analysis since the casts may be assumed to succeed unless cast exceptions are thrown. This is useful in cases where the approximations made by the analysis are too rough, and it allows explicit specification of assertions about strings that originate from outside the analyzed program. 3) Even without applying the string analysis, the operations can detect errors, but at runtime instead of at compile-time.

In Section 2, we describe related work and alternative approaches. Section 3 defines *flow graphs* as the connection between the front-end and the back-end of the analysis. In Section 4, a notion of context-free grammars extended with *operation productions* is defined, and we show how to transform flow graphs into such grammars. Section 5 explains how a variant of the Mohri-Nederhof algorithm can be applied to approximate the grammars by strongly regular grammars. These are in Section 6 translated into MLFAs that efficiently allow minimal deterministic automata to be extracted for the hotspots of the original program. Section 7 sketches our implementation for Java, and Section 8 describes examples of string analysis applications and a number of practical experiments.

We describe in what sense the algorithm is sound; however, due to the limited space, we omit proofs of correctness of the translation steps between the intermediate representations.

Contributions

The contributions in this paper consist of the following:

- Formalization of the general framework for this problem and adaptation of the Mohri-Nederhof algorithm to provide solutions.
- Development of the MLFA data structure for compactly representing the resulting family of automata.
- A technique for delaying the approximation of special string operations to improve analysis precision.
- A complete open source implementation for the full Java language supporting the full Unicode alphabet.
- A Java runtime library for expressing regular language casts and checks.
- Experiments to demonstrate that the implementation is efficient and produces results of useful precision.

Running Example

In the following sections we illustrate the workings of the various phases of the algorithm on this tricky program:

```
public class Tricky
{
  String bar(int n, int k, String op) {
    if (k==0) return "";
    return op+n+"]"+bar(n-1,k-1,op)+" ";
  }

  String foo(int n) {
    StringBuffer b = new StringBuffer();
    if (n<2) b.append("(");
    for (int i=0; i<n; i++) b.append("(");
    String s = bar(n-1,n/2-1,"*").trim();
    String t = bar(n-n/2,n-(n/2-1),"+").trim();
    return b.toString()+n+(s+t).replace(']',')');
  }

  public static void main(String args[]) {
    int n = new Random().nextInt();
    System.out.println(new Tricky().foo(n));
  }
}
```

It computes strings of the form (((((((8*7)*6)*5)+4)+3)+2)+0) in a manner suitably convoluted to challenge our analysis.

2 Related Work

As far as we know, this straightforward problem of statically determining the possible values of string expressions has not really been explored before. We therefore choose to provide a discussion explaining why it cannot readily be solved using standard techniques: abstract interpretation or set constraints.

In both of those approaches, our work in obtaining a flow graph for string operations in Java programs would essentially have to be duplicated; the differences lie in the subsequent analysis of this flow graph.

Using the standard monotone framework for abstract interpretation [7, 13], the lattice of regular languages would be used to model abstract string values and all string operations would be given an abstract semantics. The standard fixed-point iteration over the flow graph would, however, fail to provide a solution since the lattice of regular languages has infinite height. Thus, we would at some stage be required to perform a widening step. Finding an intelligent way of generalizing a regular language into a useful larger language becomes the stumbling block for this approach. Note that the context-free language defined by a grammar is in fact obtained as the fixed-point of a series of finite approximants. Thus, our application of the Mohri-Nederhof algorithm may be viewed as a technique for jumping directly to a larger regular limit point.

Using set constraints [2], strings would be represented as linear terms with a constructor for each Unicode character. With this encoding, regular tree languages coincide with regular string languages. In the standard approach, each occurrence of an expression in the flow graph would be modeled by a set variable. String operations should then be modeled through appropriate set constraints on these variables. However, several of the operations we consider cannot be captured with any degree of precision by the permitted constraint operators. In particular, concatenation is not allowed: with such an operation, set constraints would no longer define regular tree languages [6]. Thus, we are returned to the problem that we solve in this paper: the flow graph inherently defines a context-free language, which must subsequently be given a regular approximation.

A different approach is described in [17], which introduces the λ^{re}-calculus where string expressions are typed by regular languages. This calculus allows in principle limited type inference (types of recursive functions must be given explicitly), but no algorithm is provided. Intriguingly, the paper refers to the Mohri-Nederhof algorithm as a possible venue for future work. In our approach, we use flow analysis rather than type inference. Thus, λ^{re} compares to our present work as XDuce [10] does to our previous work on JWIG [3].

There is of course much work in speech recognition related to the Mohri-Nederhof algorithm, but we refer to their paper [11] for this discussion.

In our previous work on JWIG [4], we used a simple string analysis that keeps track of finite sets of strings but widens to Σ^* at the slightest provocation. We believe that this simple algorithm has been used in many other places but has not been formally published.

Some work on machine learning is vaguely related to the problem we attack [14]: regular languages are inferred not from a flow graph but from a number of examples and answers to queries. We see no way of applying these techniques to our problem.

Other program analysis techniques also extract context-free grammars from programs [15], however, their grammars usually represent possible execution traces and never string values.

Finally, we note that another well-known combination of strings and program analysis is unrelated to our work. In [8] the problem is to detect memory errors in manipulations of C-like string pointers, and the actual characters occurring in strings are irrelevant to the results.

3 Definition of Flow Graphs

A *flow graph* captures the flow of strings and string operations in a program while abstracting everything else away. The nodes in such a graph represent variables or expressions, and the edges are directed *def-use edges* that represent the possible data flow [1]. More precisely, a flow graph consists of a finite set N of nodes of the following kinds:

- Init: construction of a string value, for instance from a constant or the Integer.toString method, and is associated a symbol reg that denotes a regular language $[\![reg]\!]$ representing the possible strings.
- Join: an assignment or other join location.
- Concat: a string concatenation.
- UnaryOp: a unary string operation, for instance setCharAt or reverse, with an associated symbol op_1 denoting a function $[\![op_1]\!] : \Sigma^* \to \Sigma^*$. Non-string arguments to string operations are considered to be part of the function symbols.
- BinaryOp: a binary string operation, for instance insert, with an associated symbol op_2 denoting a function $[\![op_2]\!] : \Sigma^* \times \Sigma^* \to \Sigma^*$.

Init nodes have no incoming edges, Join nodes may have an arbitrary number of incoming edges, each UnaryOp node has exactly one incoming edge, and each Concat and BinaryOp node has an ordered pair of incoming edges that represent flow into the respective arguments. Note that our notion of flow graphs is essentially a static single assignment (SSA) form where the Join nodes correspond to Φ functions. The flow graph for the Tricky example looks as follows, see Fig. 1. The rightmost node corresponds to the single hotspot at println.

The semantics of a flow graph is defined as the least solution to a constraint system, similarly to the approach in [4]. The result is a map $F : N \to \Sigma^*$, such that $F(n)$ for every node n contains all possible values of the source program expression or variable that corresponds to n. The constraints are generated according to the following rules:

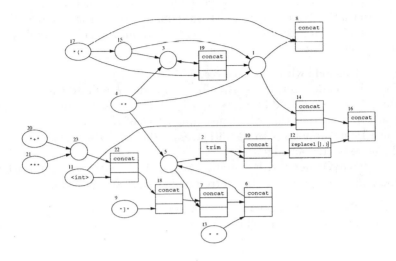

Fig. 1.

$F(n) \supseteq [\![reg]\!]$	for each Init node n
$F(n) \supseteq F(m)$	for each edge from a node m to a Join node n
$F(n) \supseteq F(m)F(p)$	for each Concat node n with edges from (m, p)
$F(n) \supseteq [\![op_1]\!](F(m))$	for each UnaryOp node n with edge from m
$F(n) \supseteq [\![op_2]\!](F(m), F(p))$	for each BinaryOp node n with edges from (m, p)

4 Construction of Context-Free Grammars

From the flow graph, we construct a special context-free grammar such that each flow graph node $n \in N$ is associated a nonterminal A_n. This grammar has the following property: For each node n, the language $\mathcal{L}(A_n)$ (that is, the language of the grammar with A_n as start nonterminal) is the same as $F(n)$.

First, we define a *context-free grammar with operation productions* as a grammar where the productions are of the following kinds:

$X \to Y$	[unit]
$X \to Y\ Z$	[pair]
$X \to reg$	[regular]
$X \to op_1(Y)$	[unary operation]
$X \to op_2(Y, Z)$	[binary operation]

where X, Y, and Z are nonterminals. The language of such a grammar is defined as one would expect: For a production $X \to reg$, X can derive all strings in $[\![reg]\!]$. For a unary operation $X \to op_1(Y)$, X can derive $[\![op_1]\!](\alpha)$ if Y can derive $\alpha \in \Sigma^*$, and similarly for binary operations. Note that the language is not necessarily context-free because of the operation productions.

The translation from flow graphs to grammars is remarkably simple: For each node n, we add a nonterminal A_n and a set of productions corresponding to the incoming edges of n:

- For an Init node with language reg, add $A_n \to reg$.
- For a Join node, add $A_n \to A_m$ for each node m with an edge to n.
- For a Concat node, add $A_n \to A_m\, A_p$ where m and p are the two nodes that correspond to the pair of incoming edges of n.
- For a UnaryOp node with operation op_1, add $A_n \to op_1(A_m)$ where m is the node having an edge to n.
- For a BinaryOp node with operation op_2, add $A_n \to op_2(A_m, A_p)$ where m and p are the two nodes that correspond to the pair of incoming edges of n.

The size of the resulting grammar is linear in the size of the flow graph. For the Tricky example it looks as follows:

$X_1 \to X_4$ $X_1 \to X_{15}$ $X_1 \to X_{19}$ $X_2 \to \text{trim}(X_5)$
$X_3 \to X_{19}$ $X_3 \to X_{15}$ $X_3 \to X_4$ $X_4 \to \text{""}$
$X_5 \to X_4$ $X_5 \to X_6$ $X_6 \to X_7\, X_{13}$ $X_7 \to X_{18}\, X_5$
$X_8 \to X_1\, X_{17}$ $X_9 \to \text{"]"}$ $X_{10} \to X_2\, X_2$ $X_{11} \to \text{<int>}$
$X_{12} \to \text{replace[],)}](X_{10})$ $X_{13} \to \text{" "}$ $X_{14} \to X_1\, X_{11}$ $X_{15} \to X_{17}$
$X_{17} \to \text{"("}$ $X_{16} \to X_{14}\, X_{12}$ $X_{18} \to X_{22}\, X_9$ $X_{19} \to X_3\, X_{17}$
$X_{20} \to \text{"+"}$ $X_{21} \to \text{"*"}$ $X_{22} \to X_{23}\, X_{11}$ $X_{23} \to X_{20}$
$X_{23} \to X_{21}$

The indices correspond to the node numbers in the flow graph. The regular language symbols are defined as expected: For example, $[\![\text{"+"}]\!] = \{+\}$ and $[\![\text{<int>}]\!]$ is specified by the regular expression `0|(-?[1-9][0-9]*)` (in Unix regexp notation).

5 Regular Approximation

We wish to approximate the grammar generated in the previous section with a regular grammar whose language contains that of the original. The central idea in our approach is based on the well-known fact that left-linear and right-linear context-free grammars effectively define regular languages [9]. This result extends to *strongly regular* grammars, as explained below.

As in the Mohri-Nederhof algorithm [11], we first find the strongly connected components of the grammar by viewing it as a graph with nonterminals as nodes and for each production an edge from the left-hand nonterminal to those on the right-hand side. For the Tricky example, the graph of Fig. 2 is obtained.

Notice the resemblance with the flow graph shown in Section 3. The two marked node groups correspond to the nontrivial strongly connected components.

The Mohri-Nederhof approximation algorithm requires that for all operation productions, the nonterminals occurring on the right-hand side belong to

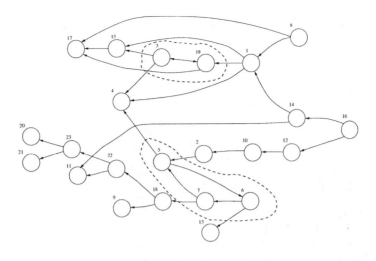

Fig. 2.

a component different from the left-hand nonterminal. For this reason, we first eliminate all cycles that contain operation productions: For each unary operation op_1 being used, we require a *character set approximation* $[\![op_1]\!]_C : 2^\Sigma \to 2^\Sigma$ where $[\![op_1]\!]_C(S)$ contains the set of characters that may occur in $[\![op_1]\!](x)$ for a string $x \in S^*$, and similarly for binary operations.

Using these approximations in a simple fixed point computation on the grammar, we find for each nonterminal X a set $C(X) \subseteq \Sigma$ containing all characters that may appear in the language of X. For each cycle we replace one operation production with $X \to r$ where r denotes the regular language $C(X)^*$. After this transformation, the strongly connected components are recomputed. For the Tricky example, neither the trim nor the replace operation occurs on a cycle.

A component M is *right-generating* if there exists a pair production $A \to B\ C$ such that A and B are in M, and M is *left-generating* if there exists a pair production $A \to B\ C$ such that A and C are in M. Each component now has one of four types: *simple* if it is neither right- nor left-generating, *left-linear* if it is right-generating but not left-generating, *right-linear* if it is left-generating but not right-generating, and *non-strongly-regular* otherwise. A context-free grammar is *strongly regular* if it has no non-strongly-regular components. The key observation of Mohri and Nederhof is that the desired approximation of the whole grammar can be obtained by a simple transformation of the non-strongly-regular components.

We adapt the Mohri-Nederhof algorithm to our form of grammar by transforming each non-strongly-regular component M into a right-linear one as follows: For each nonterminal A in M, add a fresh nonterminal A'. If A corresponds to a hotspot or is used in another component than M, then add a production $A' \to e$ where e denotes $\{\epsilon\}$. (Intuitively, A' represents substrings that may be recognized immediately after the substrings that are recognized by A.) Then replace all productions having A as left-hand side as follows:

$$
\begin{array}{lll}
A \to X & \rightsquigarrow & A \to X\ A' \\
A \to B & \rightsquigarrow & A \to B,\ \ B' \to A' \\
A \to X\ Y & \rightsquigarrow & A \to R\ A',\ \ R \to X\ Y \\
A \to X\ B & \rightsquigarrow & A \to X\ B,\ \ B' \to A' \\
A \to B\ X & \rightsquigarrow & A \to B,\ \ B' \to X\ A' \\
A \to B\ C & \rightsquigarrow & A \to B,\ \ B' \to C,\ \ C' \to A' \\
A \to reg & \rightsquigarrow & A \to R\ A',\ \ R \to reg \\
A \to op_1(X) & \rightsquigarrow & A \to R\ A',\ \ R \to op_1(X) \\
A \to op_2(X,Y) & \rightsquigarrow & A \to R\ A',\ \ R \to op_2(X,Y)
\end{array}
$$

Here, A, B, and C are nonterminals within M, X and Y are nonterminals outside M, and each R is a freshly generated nonterminal. Intuitively, when considering a specific component M we may view the nonterminals outside M as terminals. Since all cycles with operation productions already have been eliminated, the operation arguments cannot belong to M.

As a result of this transformation, the component is now right-linear, its size is proportional to the original one, and it is constructed in linear time. In contrast to Mohri and Nederhof's application where the grammar always has one fixed start nonterminal, our application requires regular approximation for all nonterminals that correspond to hotspots. By construction, the language of a hotspot nonterminal in the original grammar is always a subset of the language of the same nonterminal in the approximated grammar.

We require for each unary operation op_1 being used a conservative regular approximation (e.g. in the form of an automaton operation) $[\![op_1]\!]_R : REG \to REG$, where REG is the family of regular languages — and similarly for the binary operations. When the operations used in the grammar are replaced by their approximating counterparts, the language of each nonterminal is guaranteed to be regular.

The restriction on adding the $A' \to e$ productions is essential for our application. As an example, consider the grammar:

$$
\begin{array}{l}
S \to T\ S\ |\ \text{a} \\
T \to S\ \text{+}
\end{array}
$$

which accepts strings of the form a+a+...+a and could be constructed from a tiny recursive Java method. Without the restriction, $T' \to e$ would be added, so the resulting grammar would accept, for example, the string a+, which is an unacceptably rough approximation. Instead, the presented algorithm produces an approximation corresponding to the regular expression a(+a)*, which is the best we could hope for.

The Tricky example contains one non-strongly-regular component consisting of $\{X_5, X_6, X_7\}$, and the approximation algorithm transforms the grammar into the following:

$X_1 \rightarrow X_4$　　　　$X_1 \rightarrow X_{15}$　　　　$X_1 \rightarrow X_{19}$　　　　$X_2 \rightarrow \text{trim}(X_5)$
$X_3 \rightarrow X_{19}$　　　$X_3 \rightarrow X_{15}$　　　　$X_3 \rightarrow X_4$　　　　　$X_4 \rightarrow \texttt{""}$
$X_5 \rightarrow X_4\ X_5'$　　$X_5 \rightarrow X_6$　　　　　$X_6' \rightarrow X_5'$　　　　　$X_6 \rightarrow X_7$
$X_7' \rightarrow X_{13}\ X_6'$　　$X_7 \rightarrow X_{18}\ X_5$　　$X_5' \rightarrow X_7'$　　　　　$X_8 \rightarrow X_1\ X_{17}$
$X_9 \rightarrow \texttt{"]"}$　　　$X_{10} \rightarrow X_2\ X_2$　　　$X_{11} \rightarrow \texttt{<int>}$　　$X_{12} \rightarrow \texttt{replace[],)}(X_{10})$
$X_{13} \rightarrow \texttt{" "}$　　　$X_{14} \rightarrow X_1\ X_{11}$　　　$X_{15} \rightarrow X_{17}$　　　　$X_{16} \rightarrow X_{14}\ X_{12}$
$X_{17} \rightarrow \texttt{"("}$　　$X_{18} \rightarrow X_{22}\ X_9$　　　$X_{19} \rightarrow X_3\ X_{17}$　　$X_{20} \rightarrow \texttt{"+"}$
$X_{21} \rightarrow \texttt{"*"}$　　$X_{22} \rightarrow X_{23}\ X_{11}$　　$X_{23} \rightarrow X_{20}$　　　　$X_{23} \rightarrow X_{21}$
$X_5' \rightarrow \texttt{""}$

with again X_{16} corresponding to the hotspot. For the replace[],)] operation, the regular approximation $[\![\texttt{replace[],)}]\!]_R$ is defined as an automaton operation that transforms one automaton into another by replacing all ']' transitions by ')' transitions, where we use automata with partial transition functions. The character set approximation $[\![\texttt{replace[],)}]\!]_C$ transforms one set of characters into another by removing ']' and adding ')' if ']' occurred originally. However, it is not used in this example since the operation does not occur in a cycle.

Notice the different sources of imprecision in the regular approximation: The Mohri-Nederhof transformation handles concatenation operations that occur in non-strongly-regular components. Other string operations are handled by the regular approximations specified as automata operations. The character set approximation, which is the most rough approximation in use, is used to break cycles of operation productions.

6 Multi-level Finite Automata

As in [11], we extract automata from strongly regular grammars. However, since we consider the language of more than one nonterminal and have the special operation productions, we use a novel formalism, *multi-level finite automata (MLFA)*, with two important properties: 1) A strongly regular grammar can be translated into an equivalent MLFA in linear time, and 2) from the MLFA, we can efficiently extract a minimal deterministic (normal) automaton for each hotspot.

We define an MLFA to consist of a finite set of states Q and a set of transitions $\delta \subseteq Q \times T \times Q$ where T is a set of labels of the following kinds:

- reg
- ϵ
- (p, q)
- $op_1(p, q)$
- $op_2((p_1, q_1), (p_2, q_2))$

where each p and q are states from Q. There must exist a *level map* $\ell : Q \rightarrow \mathbb{N}$ such that:

- $(s,(p,q),t) \in \delta \Rightarrow \ell(s) = \ell(t) > \ell(p) = \ell(q)$,
- $(s, op_1(p,q), t) \in \delta \Rightarrow \ell(s) = \ell(t) > \ell(p) = \ell(q)$, and
- $(s, op_2((p_1,q_1),(p_2,q_2)), t) \in \delta \Rightarrow \ell(s) = \ell(t) > \ell(p_i) = \ell(q_i)$ for $i = 1, 2$.

That is, the states mentioned in a transition label are always at a lower level than the endpoints of the transition, and the endpoints are at the same level. The language $\overline{\mathcal{L}}$ of a single transition is defined according to its kind:

$\overline{\mathcal{L}}(reg) = [\![reg]\!]$
$\overline{\mathcal{L}}(\epsilon) = \{\epsilon\}$
$\overline{\mathcal{L}}((p,q)) = \mathcal{L}(p,q)$
$\overline{\mathcal{L}}(op_1(p,q)) = [\![op_1]\!]_R(\mathcal{L}(p,q))$
$\overline{\mathcal{L}}(op_2((p_1,q_1),(p_2,q_2))) = [\![op_2]\!]_R(\mathcal{L}(p_1,q_1), \mathcal{L}(p_2,q_2))$

Let $\overline{\delta}(q,x) = \{p \in Q \mid (q,t,p) \in T \wedge x \in \overline{\mathcal{L}}(t)\}$ for $q \in Q$ and $x \in \Sigma^*$, and let $\widehat{\delta}: Q \times \Sigma^* \to 2^Q$ be defined by:

$\widehat{\delta}(q, \epsilon) = \overline{\delta}(q, \epsilon)$
$\widehat{\delta}(q, x) = \{r \in Q \mid r \in \overline{\delta}(p,z) \wedge p \in \widehat{\delta}(q,y) \wedge x = yz \wedge z \neq \epsilon\}$ for $x \neq \epsilon$

The language $\mathcal{L}(s, f)$ of a pair $s, f \in Q$ of start and final states where $\ell(s) = \ell(f)$ is defined as $\mathcal{L}(s, f) = \{x \in \Sigma^* \mid f \in \widehat{\delta}(s, x)\}$. This is well-defined because of the existence of the level map.

A strongly regular grammar produced in the previous section is transformed into an MLFA as follows: First, a state q_A is constructed for each nonterminal A, and additionally, a state q_M is constructed for each strongly connected component M. Then, for each component M, transitions are added according to the type of M and the productions whose left-hand side are in M. For a simple or right-linear component:

$A \to B$	$\rightsquigarrow$	(q_A, ϵ, q_B)
$A \to X$	$\rightsquigarrow$	$(q_A, \Psi(X), q_M)$
$A \to X\,B$	$\rightsquigarrow$	$(q_A, \Psi(X), q_B)$
$A \to X\,Y$	$\rightsquigarrow$	$(q_A, \Psi(X), p), (p, \Psi(Y), q_M)$
$A \to reg$	$\rightsquigarrow$	(q_A, reg, q_M)
$A \to op_1(X)$	$\rightsquigarrow$	$(q_A, op_1(\Psi(X)), q_M)$
$A \to op_2(X, Y)$	$\rightsquigarrow$	$(q_A, op_2(\Psi(X), \Psi(Y)), q_M)$

For a left-linear component:

$A \to B$	$\rightsquigarrow$	(q_B, ϵ, q_A)
$A \to X$	$\rightsquigarrow$	$(q_M, \Psi(X), q_A)$
$A \to B\,X$	$\rightsquigarrow$	$(q_B, \Psi(X), q_A)$
$A \to X\,Y$	$\rightsquigarrow$	$(q_M, \Psi(X), p), (p, \Psi(Y), q_A)$
$A \to reg$	$\rightsquigarrow$	(q_M, reg, q_A)
$A \to op_1(X)$	$\rightsquigarrow$	$(q_M, op_1(\Psi(X)), q_A)$
$A \to op_2(X, Y)$	$\rightsquigarrow$	$(q_M, op_2(\Psi(X), \Psi(Y)), q_A)$

Each p represents a fresh state. The function Ψ maps each nonterminal into a state pair: If A belongs to a simple or right-linear component M, then $\Psi(A) =$

(q_A, q_M), and otherwise $\Psi(A) = (q_M, q_A)$. The essence of this construction is the standard translation of right-linear or left-linear grammars to automata [9]. The construction is correct in the sense that the language $\mathcal{L}(A)$ of a nonterminal A is equal to $\mathcal{L}(\Psi(A))$. We essentially follow Mohri and Nederhof, except that they construct an automaton for a fixed start nonterminal and do not have the unary and binary operations.

Given a hotspot from the source program, we find its flow graph node n, which in turn corresponds to a grammar nonterminal A_n that is associated with a pair of states $(s, f) = \Psi(A_n)$ in an MLFA F. From this pair, we extract a normal nondeterministic automaton U whose language is $\mathcal{L}(s, f)$ using the following algorithm:

- For each state q in F where $\ell(q) = \ell(s)$, construct a state q' in U. Let s' and f' be the start and final states, respectively.
- For each transition (q_1, t, q_2) in F where $\ell(q_1) = \ell(q_2) = \ell(s)$, add an equivalent sub-automaton from q_1' to q_2': If $t = reg$, we use a sub-automaton whose language is $[\![reg]\!]$, and similarly for $t = \epsilon$. If $t = (p, q)$, then the sub-automaton is the one obtained by recursively applying the extraction algorithm for $\mathcal{L}(p, q)$. If $t = op_1(p, q)$, the language of the sub-automaton is $[\![op_1]\!]_R(\mathcal{L}(p, q))$, and similarly for $t = op_2((p_1, q_1), (p_2, q_2))$.

This constructively shows that MLFAs define regular languages. The size of U is worst-case exponential in the size of F since the sub-automata may be duplicated. Since we subsequently determinize and minimize U, the size of the final DFA is worst-case doubly exponential, however, our experiments in Section 8 indicate that such blowups do not occur naturally. Our implementation uses memoization such that the automaton for a state pair (s, f) is only computed once. This reuse of computations is important for programs with many hotspots, especially if these involve common subcomputations.

We can now see the benefit of representing the unary and binary operations throughout all phases instead of, for instance, applying the character set approximation on all operations at an early stage: Those operations that in the flow graph do not occur in loops are modeled with higher precision than otherwise possible. For example, the insert method can be modeled quite precisely with an automaton operation, whereas that is difficult to achieve on the flow graph or grammar level.

To summarize, the whole translation from Java programs to DFAs is sound: Flow graphs are constructed such that they conservatively model the Java programs, and the regular approximation of grammars is also conservative. Both the translation from flow graphs to context-free grammars, the translation from strongly regular grammars to MLFAs, and the extraction of DFAs from MLFAs are exact. Together, this implies that if a Java program at some program point may produce a particular string during execution, then this string is guaranteed to be accepted by the automaton extracted for the program point.

7 Implementation for Java

Our implementation works for the full Java language, which makes the translation to flow graphs quite involved and beyond the scope of this paper. Hence, we settle for a rough sketch.

We use the Soot framework [18] to parse class files and compute interprocedural control flow graphs. We give a precise treatment of String, StringBuffer, and multidimensional arrays of strings. Using a null-pointer analysis, we limit proliferation of null strings. The construction of the flow graphs further requires a constant analysis, a liveness analysis, a may-must alias analysis, and a reaching definitions analysis – all in interprocedural versions that conservatively take care of interaction with external classes.

Our analysis tool is straightforwardly integrated with client analyses, such as the ones described in the next section. Furthermore, it is connected to the runtime library mentioned in Section 1 such that regexp casts are fed into the analysis and the designated hotspots are checked.

8 Applications and Experiments

We have performed experiments with three different kinds of client analyses.

Our motivating example is to boost our previously published tool for analyzing dynamically generated XML in the JWIG extension of Java [4]. This tool uses a primitive string analysis as a black box that is readily upgraded to the one developed in this work.

Another example is motivated by the Soot framework [18] that we use in our implementation. Here a string analysis can be used to improve precision of call graphs for Java programs that use reflection through the Class.forName method.

Finally, it is possible to perform syntax checking of expressions that are dynamically generated as strings, as in the example in Section 1.

In all three cases we provide a number of benchmark programs ranging from small to medium sized. Each benchmark contains many string expressions, but only few of those are hotspots. For each benchmark we report the number of lines of Java code, the total number of string expressions, the number of hotspots considered, the number of seconds to compute the MLFA, the total number of seconds to provide automata for all hotspots, and the maximal memory consumption (in MB) during this computation. The timings do not include time used by Soot to load and parse the class files, which typically takes 5-30 seconds for the programs considered. The accuracy of the analysis is explained for each kind of application. All experiments are performed on a 1 GHz Pentium III with 1 GB RAM running Linux.

8.1 Tricky

The Tricky benchmark is the example we followed in the previous sections, generating strings of the form: (((((((8*7)*6)*5)+4)+3)+2)+1)+0). The analysis runs in 0.9 seconds and uses 26 MB of memory. The regular approximation that we compute is (in Unix regexp notation) \(*<int>([+*]<int>\))* where <int> abbreviates 0|(-?[1-9][0-9]*). This is a good result, but with a polyvariant analysis, the two calls to the bar method could be distinguished and the result further sharpened to \(*<int>(*<int>\))*(\+<int>\))*.

8.2 JWIG Validity Analysis

The five smaller JWIG benchmarks are taken from the JWIG Web site. The three larger ones are a game management system (MyreKrig), a portal for a day care institution (Arendalsvej), and a system for management of the JAOO 2002 conference (JAOO). The hotspots correspond to places where strings are plugged into XML templates.

Example	Lines	Exps	Hotspots	MLFA	Total	Memory
Chat	67	86	5	0.597	0.603	34
Guess	77	50	4	0.577	0.581	34
Calendar	89	116	6	0.712	0.828	34
Memory	169	144	3	0.833	6.656	45
TempMan	323	220	9	0.845	0.890	33
MyreKrig	579	1,248	56	3.700	5.480	51
Arendalsvej	3,725	5,517	274	20.767	35.473	102
JAOO	3,764	9,655	279	39.721	86.276	107

The time and memory consumptions are seen to be quite reasonable. The precision is perfect for these ordinary programs, where only URL syntax, integers and scalar values must be checked to conform to the requirements of XHTML 1.0. We use the DSD2 schema language [12] which is expressive enough to capture these requirements on string values. Compared to our previous string analysis, we are able to validate more strings, such as dynamically built URL strings. The string analysis typically takes 10-20% of the total JWIG analysis time.

8.3 Reflection Analysis

These benchmarks are culled from the Web by searching for programs that import java.lang.reflect and selecting non-constant uses of Class.forName which also constitute the hotspots.

Example	Lines	Exps	Hotspots	MLFA	Total	Memory
Switch	21	45	1	1.155	1.338	25
ReflectTest	50	95	2	1.117	1.220	25
SortAlgorithms	54	31	1	0.997	1.214	25
CarShop	56	30	2	0.637	0.656	25
ValueConverter	1,718	438	4	4.065	4.127	36
ProdConsApp	3,496	1,909	3	12.160	13.469	80

Again, the time and memory consumptions are unremarkable. Without a client analysis, it is difficult to rate the precision. In simple cases like SortAlgorithms and CarShop we find the exact classes, and in some like ValueConverter we fail because strings originate from external sources.

8.4 Syntax Analysis

Many Java programs build string expressions that are externally interpreted, a typical example being SQL queries handled by JDBC, as the example in Section 1. At present, no static syntax checking is performed on such expressions, which is a potential source of runtime errors. We can perform such checking by approximating the allowed syntax by a regular subset which is then checked to be a superset of the inferred set of strings. For SQL, we have constructed a regular language that covers most common queries and translates into a DFA with 631 states.

The benchmarks below are again obtained from the Web. Most originate from database textbooks or instruction manuals for various JDBC bindings. The hotspots correspond to calls of executeQuery and similar methods.

Example	Lines	Exps	Hotspots	MLFA	Total	Memory	Errors	False Errors
Decades	26	63	1	0.669	1.344	27	0	0
SelectFromPer	51	50	1	1.442	1.480	27	0	0
LoadDriver	78	154	1	0.942	0.981	28	0	0
DB2Appl	105	59	2	0.736	0.784	27	0	0
AxionExample	162	37	7	0.800	1.008	29	0	0
Sample	178	157	4	0.804	1.261	28	0	0
GuestBookServlet	344	320	4	1.741	3.167	33	1	0
DBTest	384	412	5	1.688	2.387	31	1	0
CoercionTest	591	1,133	4	4.457	5.664	42	0	0

As before, the analysis runs efficiently. All hotspots except two are validated as constructing only correct SQL syntax, and encouragingly, the two remaining correspond to actual errors. The GuestBookServlet builds a string value with the construction "'" + email + "'", where email is read directly from an input field in a Web form. Our tool responds by automatically generating the shortest counterexample:

```
INSERT INTO comments (id,email,name,comment,date) VALUES (0,''','','','')
```

which in fact points to a severe security flaw.

XPath expressions [5] are other examples where static syntax checking is desirable. Also, arguments to the method Runtime.exec could be checked to belong to a permitted subset of shell commands.

Finally, we could use our technique to attack the problem of format string vulnerabilities considered in [16]. In our approach, format strings that were tainted by outside values would be recognized possibly to evaluate to illegal strings. The precision of this approach is left for future work. Compared to the use of type qualifiers, our technique is more precise for string operations but it is less flow sensitive.

9 Conclusion

We have presented a static analysis technique for extracting a context-free grammar from a program and apply a variant of the Mohri-Nederhof approximation algorithm to approximate the possible values of string expressions in Java programs. The potential applications include validity checking of dynamically generated XML, improved precision of call graphs for Java programs that use reflection, and syntax analysis of dynamically generated SQL expressions.

Our experiments show that the approach is efficient and produces results of useful precision on realistic benchmarks. The open source implementation together with documentation and all benchmark programs are available at http://www.brics.dk/JSA/.

References

[1] Alfred V. Aho, Ravi Sethi, and Jeffrey D. Ullman. *Compilers – Principles, Techniques, and Tools*. Addison-Wesley, November 1985.
[2] Alex Aiken. Introduction to set constraint-based program analysis. *Science of Computer Programming*, 35:79–111, 1999.
[3] Aske Simon Christensen, Anders Møller, and Michael I. Schwartzbach. Static analysis for dynamic XML. Technical Report RS-02-24, BRICS, May 2002. Presented at Programming Language Technologies for XML, PLAN-X, October 2002.
[4] Aske Simon Christensen, Anders Møller, and Michael I. Schwartzbach. Extending Java for high-level Web service construction. *ACM Transactions on Programming Languages and Systems*, 2003. To appear.
[5] James Clark and Steve DeRose. XML path language, November 1999. W3C Recommendation. http://www.w3.org/TR/xpath.
[6] H. Comon, M. Dauchet, R. Gilleron, F. Jacquemard, D. Lugiez, S. Tison, and M. Tommasi. Tree automata techniques and applications, 1999. Available from http://www.grappa.univ-lille3.fr/tata/.
[7] Patrick Cousot and Radhia Cousot. Abstract interpretation: a unified lattice model for static analysis of programs by construction or approximation of fixpoints. In *Proc. 4th ACM SIGPLAN-SIGACT Symposium on Principles of Programming Languages, POPL '77*, pages 238–252, 1977.
[8] Nurit Dor, Michael Rodeh, and Mooly Sagiv. Cleanness checking of string manipulations in C programs via integer analysis. In *Proc. 8th International Static Analysis Symposium, SAS '01*, volume 2126 of *LNCS*. Springer-Verlag, July 2001.
[9] John E. Hopcroft and Jeffrey D. Ullman. *Introduction to Automata Theory, Languages and Computation*. Addison-Wesley, April 1979.
[10] Haruo Hosoya and Benjamin C. Pierce. XDuce: A typed XML processing language. In *Proc. 3rd International Workshop on the World Wide Web and Databases, WebDB'00*, volume 1997 of *LNCS*. Springer-Verlag, May 2000.
[11] Mehryar Mohri and Mark-Jan Nederhof. *Robustness in Language and Speech Technology*, chapter 9: Regular Approximation of Context-Free Grammars through Transformation. Kluwer Academic Publishers, 2001.
[12] Anders Møller. Document Structure Description 2.0, December 2002. BRICS, Department of Computer Science, University of Aarhus, Notes Series NS-02-7. Available from http://www.brics.dk/DSD/.

[13] Flemming Nielson, Hanne Riis Nielson, and Chris Hankin. *Principles of Program Analysis*. Springer-Verlag, October 1999.
[14] Rajesh Parekh and Vasant Honavar. DFA learning from simple examples. *Machine Learning*, 44:9–35, 2001.
[15] Thomas Reps. Program analysis via graph reachability. *Information and Software Technology*, 40(11-12):701–726, November/December 1998.
[16] Umesh Shankar, Kunal Talwar, Jeffrey S. Foster, and David Wagner. Detecting format string vulnerabilities with type qualifiers. In *Proc. 10th USENIX Security Symposium*, 2001.
[17] Naoshi Tabuchi, Eijiro Sumii, and Akinori Yonezawa. Regular expression types for strings in a text processing language. In *Proc. Workshop on Types in Programming, TIP '02*, 2002.
[18] Raja Vallee-Rai, Laurie Hendren, Vijay Sundaresan, Patrick Lam, Etienne Gagnon, and Phong Co. Soot – A Java optimization framework. In *Proc. IBM Centre for Advanced Studies Conference, CASCON'99*. IBM, November 1999.

Modular Class Analysis with DATALOG*

Frédéric Besson and Thomas Jensen

IRISA/INRIA/CNRS
Campus de Beaulieu
F-35042 Rennes, France

Abstract. DATALOG can be used to specify a variety of class analyses for object-oriented programs as variations of a common framework. In this framework, the result of analysing a class is a set of DATALOG clauses whose least fixpoint is the information analysed for. Modular class analysis of program fragments is then expressed as the resolution of *open* DATALOG programs. We provide a theory for the partial resolution of sets of open clauses and define a number of operators for reducing such open clauses.

1 Introduction

One of the most important analyses for object-oriented languages is *class analysis* that computes an (over-)approximation of the set of classes that an expression can evaluate to at run-time [1,3,12,23,24]. Class analysis forms the foundation for static *type checking* for OO programs aimed at guaranteeing that methods are only invoked on objects that implement such a method. It is also used for building a precise call graph for a program which in turn enables other optimisations and verifications. For example, the information deduced by class analysis can in certain cases be used to replace virtual method invocations by direct calls to the code implementing the method.

Existing class analyses are all whole-program analyses that require the entire program to be present at analysis time. There are several reasons for why it is desirable to improve this situation. The size of the object-oriented code bases to be analysed means that a whole-program analysis is lengthy. Having to re-analyse all the program every time a modification is made means that the analysis is of little use during a development phase. Furthermore, dealing with languages that allow *dynamic class loading* means that not all code is available at analysis time. These shortcomings must be resolved by developing more incremental and modular analyses, that can deal with fragments of programs.

Modular program analysis has been the object of several recent studies. Cousot and Cousot [10] examine the various approaches to modular program analysis and recast these in a uniform abstract interpretation framework. The essence of their analysis is a characterisation of modular program analysis as the problem of calculating approximations to a higher-order fixpoint. In this paper

---
* This work was partially funded by the IST FET/Open project "Secsafe".

we demonstrate how this fixpoint characterisation can be instantiated to the case of class analyses expressed using DATALOG clauses. In this case, the result of the class analysis is defined as the least solution of the set of clauses generated from the program in a syntax-directed manner. A modular analysis is a procedure that transforms a partial set of constraint into an equivalent "more resolved" set, where "more resolved" means that the number of iterations required to reach the least solution has been reduced.

The class analysis will be expressed as a translation from a simple object-oriented programming language into constraints specified using the DATALOG language. DATALOG is a simple relational query language yet rich enough to give a uniform description of a number of control flow analyses of object-oriented languages, including the set-based analysis of Palsberg and Schwartzbach. It has an efficient bottom-up evaluator that provides an implementation of the analysis of closed programs for free. The analysis of program fragments gives rise to *open* sets of DATALOG clauses, for which a number of powerful *normalisation* operators exist. Finally, the semantic theory of open logic programs provides a basis for defining abstract union operators on constraint systems corresponding to the union of two program fragments.

The contributions of the paper can be summarised as follows.

- We show how DATALOG can be used for specifying class analyses in a uniform manner. We notably show how a number of existing analyses can be expressed naturally in this framework.
- We extend this to a theory of modular class analysis in which the analysis of program fragments are modelled using *open* DATALOG programs.
- We define a number of partial resolution techniques for reducing an open DATALOG program to a solved form.

Section 2 defines a simple object-oriented programming language. Section 3 recalls basic notions of DATALOG, which is then used to define a number of class analyses in Section 4. Open DATALOG programs arising from analysis of program fragments are introduced in Section 5.1. In Section 5.2, we give a characterisation of correct modular resolution methods. We then show, in Section 6, how several modular resolution techniques fit into this framework.

2 An Object-Oriented Language

Our analysis is defined with respect to an untyped imperative class-based object-oriented language. To focus on the class analysis principles, language constructs are kept to a minimum. The precise syntax is defined in Figure 1.

A program P is made of a set of class declarations. Each class C is identified by a unique name c and define a set of methods. It may extend an existing class c'. Within a class, each method M is uniquely identified by its signature m/i where m is the method name and i the number of arguments. The method body is a sequence of instructions. The instruction $x:=$ new c creates an object of class c. Instruction $x.fd:=y$ assigns the value of variable y to the field fd of the object

$$P ::= \{C_1, \ldots, C_n\}$$
$$C ::= \text{class } c\{M_1, \ldots, M_n\} \mid$$
$$\quad\quad \text{class } c \text{ extends } c'\{M_1, \ldots, M_n\}$$
$$M ::= m(x_1, \ldots, x_n) \quad IL$$
$$IL ::= [I_1, \ldots, I_n]$$
$$I ::= x := \text{new } c \mid x.fd := y \mid x := y.fd \mid$$
$$\quad\quad x := x_0.f(x_1, \ldots, x_n) \mid \text{ret } x$$

Fig. 1. A minimalist object-oriented language

referenced by x. Similarly, $x:=y.fd$ transfers the content of field fd of y to variable x. The instruction $x:=x_0.f(x_1, \ldots, x_n)$ invokes the method f on the object stored in x_0 with $x_1, \ldots, x_n$ as arguments and stores the result in x. Finally, ret x ends the execution of an invoked method by returning the value of x. Except the last instruction that models method return, all the other instructions are different kinds of assignments: object creation, field update, field access and dynamic method invocation. Following the object-oriented conventions, in a method body, the current active object is referenced as *self*.

Execution of a program starts at the first instruction of the method main of class main. The inheritance relation between the classes of a program is acyclic. Because our language does not provide multiple inheritance, the class hierarchy is a forest (of trees). Virtual method resolution is defined by a method lookup algorithm that given a class name c and a method signature m returns the class c' that implements m for the class c. In order to take inheritance into account, the method lookup algorithm walks up the class hierarchy from class c and eventually returns the first class c' that defines a matching method m.

3 DATALOG

We recall some basic facts about DATALOG [29] that will serve as language for specifying the class analyses. Syntactically, DATALOG can be defined as PROLOG with only nullary functions symbols *i.e.*, constants. Hence, most of the definitions and properties of DATALOG programs are inherited from PROLOG. It can also be presented as a relational query language extended with recursion.

The denotation of a DATALOG program is the least set of atoms that satisfy the clauses of the program. The fundamental difference with respect to Prolog is that the least Herbrand model is computable.

Definition 1. *Let Π be a (finite) set of predicate symbols and V (resp. C) a set of variables (resp. constant symbols).*

- *An atom is a term $p(x_1, \ldots, x_n)$ where $p \in \Pi$ is a predicate symbol of arity n and each x_i ($i \in [1, \ldots, n]$) is either a variable or a constant ($x_i \in V \uplus C$).*

- A *clause* is a formula $H \leftarrow B$ where H (the head) is an atom while the body B is a finite set of atoms.
- A *program* P is a set of clauses.

For atom A, $Var(A)$ is the set of variables occurring in A and $Pred(A)$ is the predicate symbol of A. Var and $Pred$ are extended the obvious way to clauses and programs. An atom A is said *ground* if its set of variables is empty. A substitution $\sigma : V \to V \uplus C$ is a mapping from variables to variables or constants. A *ground* substitution maps variables to constants. We note $A\sigma$ the application of a substitution σ to an atom A.

A Herbrand interpretation I is a set of ground atoms. Given a set of predicate symbols Π and a set of constant C, the Herbrand base $HB(\Pi, C)$ is the (greatest) set of ground atoms that can be built from the predicate symbols in Π and constants in C. The least Herbrand model of a program P is a Herbrand interpretation defined as the least fixed point of a monotonic, continuous operator T_P known as the *immediate consequence operator* [2].

Definition 2. *For a program P and a Herbrand interpretation I, the operator T_P is defined by:*

$$T_P(I) = \{A \mid \exists (H \leftarrow B \in P, \sigma : V \to C). \forall (b \in B). b\sigma \in I, A = H\sigma\}$$

In the following, the fixed point operator is noted *lfp*. Hence, the least Herbrand model of a program P is $lfp(T_P)$.

4 Class Analysis in DATALOG

In this section we describe a class analysis in the form of a syntax-directed translation that maps a term L of the object-oriented language defined in Section 2 to a set of DATALOG clauses. The result of the analysis is the least fixpoint of these clauses. The analysis presented in this section deals with complete programs; the following sections will be concerned with showing how to combine separate analyses of individual classes to eventually recover the result of the analysis of the complete program.

One of the advantages of DATALOG is that it allows to specify a collection of class analyses in a common framework, thus allowing to relate a number of known analyses. To make this point clear, we first give an intuitive description of the basic analysis and then explain how it can be varied to obtain analyses of different degree of precision. Intuitively, the basic analysis works as follows. For each variable x defined in method m of class c in the program we introduce a unary predicate named $c.m.x$ that characterises the set of objects being stored in that variable. Each assignment to a variable will result in a clause defining the corresponding predicate. The heap of allocated objects is represented by a collection of binary predicates $fd(\_, \_)$, one for each field name fd used in the program. If an object o_1 of class c_1 references an object o_2 of class c_2 via field fd then $fd(c_1, c_2)$ holds. To deal with method calls, each method signature m gives rise to a pair of predicates $m.call$ and $m.ret$ such that $m.call$ collects the arguments of all calls to methods named m while $m.ret$ collects the return values from the different calls to m.

A number of syntactic properties of a program are represented by the predicates *class*, *subclass*, *sig* and *define*. Given an object-oriented program P, we have: $class(c)$ if c is a class of P; $subclass(c, c')$ if c is a direct subclass of c' in P; $sig(m)$ if m is a method signature of P and $define(c, m)$ if class c of P defines a method of signature m. The dynamic method lookup is encoded by the predicate lk such that $lk(o, f, c)$ if a call to method f on an object of class o is resolved to the definition of f found in class c.

$$lk(c, m, c) \leftarrow \{define(c, m)\}$$
$$lk(c, m, c') \leftarrow \{notDefine(c, m), subclass(c, c''), lk(c'', m, c')\}$$
$$notDefine(c, m) \leftarrow \{class(c), sig(m), \neg define(c, m)\}$$

A technical note: because of the use of negation ($\neg$), the clause defining the predicate *notDefine* does not strictly comply with our definition of clauses. However, as long as negations are stratified – recursion cycles are negation free – the least Herbrand model exists.

4.1 Context-Sensitive Analyses

There are a number of places in which the precision of the basic class analysis can be fine-tuned:

- Modelling of the heap of objects. In the basic analysis, objects in the heap are simply abstracted by their class identifier, hence the abstract domain of objects is defined by $Object = Class$. Other ways of abstracting objects take into account the *creation context*. For instance, objects can be distinguished by their program point of creation, in which case we get $Objet = Class \times PP$ where $PP = Class \times Meth \times PC$ is the set of program points.
- Distinguishing different calls to the same method. The precision of an analysis can be improved by keeping track of the program point at which a method was invoked $Context = PP$. Other ways of separating the method calls is by distinguishing them according to the class of their arguments (see the Cartesian Product abstraction below).
- Distinguishing different occurrences of the same variable. The basic analysis keeps one set for each variable. All assignments to that variable will contribute to this set. Introducing one set for each occurrence of a variable can lead to more precise analysis results, see *e.g.,* [18] for the benefits obtained in the case of binding-time analysis for imperative languages.

The last type of context sensitivity is relatively straightforward to obtain by syntactic transformations so here we focus on the first two items: creation- and call-context sensitive analyses.

Context sensitivity is expressed separately by means of the predicates *object*, *objCtx*, *methCtx/n* and *classOf*. The predicate *object* is used to define the abstract domain of objects. The predicate *objCtx* models a function that given

Program

$$[\![\{C_1, \ldots C_n\}]\!] = \bigcup_{i \in [1, \ldots, n]} [\![C_i]\!] \cup \left\{ \begin{array}{l} main.call(o, ctx) \leftarrow \\ \quad \left\{ \begin{array}{l} objCtx(\underline{0}, \underline{0}, \underline{0}, \underline{main}, \underline{0}, \underline{0}, o), \\ methCtx/n(\underline{0}, \underline{0}, \underline{0}, o, \underline{0}, ctx) \end{array} \right\} \end{array} \right\}$$

Class

$$[\![\ \texttt{class}\ c\ \ Meths\ ]\!] = [\![Meths]\!]_c \cup \{class(\underline{c}) \leftarrow \{\}\}$$
$$[\![\ \texttt{class}\ c\ \texttt{extends}\ c'\ \ Meths\ ]\!] = [\![Meths]\!]_c \cup \left\{ \begin{array}{l} subclass(\underline{c}, \underline{c'}) \leftarrow \{\} \\ class(\underline{c}) \quad\quad\quad\ \leftarrow \{\} \end{array} \right\}$$

Methods

$$[\![\{M_1, \ldots, M_n\}]\!]_c = \bigcup_{i \in [1, \ldots, n]} [\![M_i]\!]_c$$

$$[\![m(x_1, \ldots, x_n)IL]\!]_c = [\![m(x_1, \ldots, x_n)]\!]_c \cup [\![IL]\!]_{c,m}$$

$$[\![m(x_1, \ldots, x_n)]\!]_c = \left\{ \begin{array}{ll} define(\underline{c}, \underline{m/n}) & \leftarrow \{\} \\ sig(\underline{m/n}) & \leftarrow \{\} \\ c.m.ctx(ctx) & \leftarrow \left\{ \begin{array}{l} m.call(o, o_1, \ldots, o_n, ctx), \\ classOf(o, c'), lk(c', \underline{m/n}, \underline{c}) \end{array} \right\} \\ c.m.self(o, ctx) \leftarrow \{m.call(o, o_1, \ldots, o_n, ctx), c.m.ctx(ctx)\} \\ c.m.x_1(o_1, ctx) \leftarrow \{m.call(o, o_1, \ldots, o_n, ctx), c.m.ctx(ctx)\} \\ \ldots \\ c.m.x_n(o_n) \quad\ \leftarrow \{m.call(o, o_1, \ldots, o_n, ctx), c.m.ctx(ctx)\} \end{array} \right\}$$

Instructions

$$[\![[I_1, \ldots, I_n]]\!]_{c,m} = \bigcup_{i \in [1, \ldots, n]} [\![I_i]\!]_{c,m,i}$$

$$[\![x := \texttt{new}\ c']\!]_{c,m,i} = \left\{ c.m.x(o, ctx) \leftarrow \left\{ \begin{array}{l} c.m.self(o', ctx), \\ objCtx(\underline{c}, \underline{m}, \underline{i}, \underline{c'}, ctx, o', o) \end{array} \right\} \right\}$$

$$[\![x.fd := y]\!]_{c,m} = \{fd(o, o') \leftarrow c.m.x(o, ctx), c.m.y(o', ctx)\}$$

$$[\![x := x_0.f(x_1, \ldots, x_n)]\!]_{c,m,i} = \left\{ \begin{array}{l} c.m.i.call(o_0, \ldots, o_n, ctx, ctx') \leftarrow \\ \quad \left\{ \begin{array}{l} x_0(o_0, ctx), \ldots, x_n(o_n, ctx), \\ methCtx/n(\underline{c}, \underline{m}, \underline{i}, o_0, \ldots, o_n, ctx, ctx') \end{array} \right\} \\ f.call(o_0, \ldots, o_n, ctx') \leftarrow \\ \quad \{c.m.i.call(o_0, \ldots, o_n, ctx, ctx')\} \\ c.m.x(o, ctx) \leftarrow \\ \quad \{f.ret(o, ctx'), c.m.i.call(o_0, \ldots, o_n, ctx, ctx')\} \end{array} \right\}$$

$$[\![\texttt{ret}\ x]\!]_{c,m,i} = \{m.ret(o, ctx) \leftarrow c.m.x(o, ctx)\}$$

Fig. 2. Generation algorithm for class analysis

a syntactic program point (class, method, program counter), a class to instantiate and an analysis context yields a new object. If

$$objCtx(c, m, i, c', ctx, self, newObj)$$

holds then $newObj$ is a novel object of class c' built from the program point (c, m, i), for the call context ctx and the current object $self$.

The predicate family $methCtx/n$ models a function that given a syntactic program point (class, method, program point), the n arguments of the call and the current call context yields a novel call context. If

$$methCtx/n(c, m, i, self, o_1, \ldots, o_n, ctx, newCtx)$$

holds then $newCtx$ is a novel call context built from the program point (c, m, i), for the call context ctx and the argument objects of the call $self, o_1, \ldots, o_n$. Finally, the predicate $classOf(o, c)$ permits to obtain the class c of the object o. The predicates $objCtx$ and $classOf(o, c)$ must satisfy the following coherence constraint: $objCtx(c, m, i, c', ctx, o) \Rightarrow classOf(o, c')$.

4.2 Example Analyses

In the following we specify a number of known analyses as variations of the analysis in Figure 2. We do this by specifying the abstract domains of objects and contexts, and by defining the instantiation of the predicates $objCtx$, $methCtx$ and $classOf$. For certain analyses, we make use of a tuple notation which is not part of DATALOG. However, this extension is not a theoretical problem: such finite depth terms can be flattened and encoded by adding extra arguments to predicate symbols. To give a more uniform presentation, we keep a tuple notation.

0-CFA. 0-CFA is a degenerated context sensitive analysis in which objects are abstracted by their class and where there exists a single call context identified by the constant $\underline{ctx}$. Hence, we have $Object = Class$ and $Context = \{\underline{ctx}\}$.

$$\begin{array}{ll} objCtx(c, m, i, c', ctx, c') & \leftarrow \{\} \\ methCtx/n(c, m, i, o_0, \ldots, o_n, ctx, \underline{ctx}) & \leftarrow \{\} \\ classOf(c, c) & \leftarrow \{\} \end{array}$$

1/2-CFA. Some analyses of object-oriented programs deal with inheritance by copying the inherited methods into the inheriting class [23]. This syntactic unfolding adds a certain degree of call context sensitivity to an analysis because it distinguishes between a method according to which class of object it is called on. To model this effect of unfolding the inheritance mechanism, we keep as call context the class of the receiver of the current call. This is expressed by the repeated occurrence of $self$ in the definition of $methCtx$. We have $Object = Class$ and $Context = Object$.

$$\begin{array}{ll} objCtx(c, m, i, c', ctx, c') & \leftarrow \{\} \\ methCtx/n(c, m, i, self, o_1, \ldots, o_n, ctx, self) & \leftarrow \{\} \\ classOf(c, c) & \leftarrow \{\} \end{array}$$

k-l-CFA. The principle of the k-l-CFA hierarchy of analysis is to keep a call string of length k and a creation string of length l. As a result, the call context is a tuple of the k call instructions that lead to the call. Similarly, an object o_1 now contains information about the object o_2 that created it, and the object o_3 that created o_2, and ... the object o_l that created the object o_{l-1}. We have $Object = Class \times PP^l$ and $Context = PP^k$.

$$objCtx(c, m, i, c', ctx, o, o') \leftarrow \left\{ \begin{array}{l} o = (c'', (p_1, \ldots, p_l)), \\ o' = (c', ((c, m, i), p_1, \ldots, p_{l-1})) \end{array} \right\}$$

$$methCtx/n(c, m, i, o_0, \ldots, o_n, ctx, ctx') \leftarrow \left\{ \begin{array}{l} ctx = (p_1, \ldots, p_k), \\ ctx' = ((c, m, i), p_1, \ldots, p_{k-1}), \end{array} \right\}$$

$$classOf((c, l), c) \leftarrow \{object((c, l))\}$$

Cartesian Product Algorithm. This kind of context sensitivity for class analysis was first discussed by Agesen [1]. A call context is built from the arguments of the call. Calls to the same method are distinguished as soon as the arguments are different. The set of call contexts of a method with n arguments is then $Context_n = Object^n$. Thus, the precision of the overall analysis depends on the object abstraction. Here, we show an instantiation where the object creation context is the program point of creation ($Object = Class \times PP$).

$$objCtx(c, m, i, c', ctx, o, o') \leftarrow \{ o' = (c', (c, m, i)), \}$$
$$methCtx/n(c, m, i, o_0, \ldots, o_n, ctx, ctx') \leftarrow \{ ctx' = (o_0, \ldots, o_n), \}$$
$$classOf((c, l), c) \leftarrow \{object(c, l)\}$$

Example 1. Consider the following contrived program

$$P = \{ \text{ class } main\{main()[self := self.fd; \text{ ret } self]\}$$

For the 0-CFA analysis, here are the generated constraints.

$$main/0.call(\underline{main}) \leftarrow \{\}$$
$$define(\underline{main}, main/0) \leftarrow \{\}$$
$$main.main/0.\overline{self}(o) \leftarrow \{main/0.call(o), lk(o, main/0, \underline{main})\}$$
$$main.main/0.self(o) \leftarrow \{main.main/0.\overline{self}(o'), fd(o', o)\}$$
$$main/0.ret(o) \leftarrow \{main.main/0.self(o)\}$$

Next section, we detail how the clauses defining *self* can be reduced using a combination of modular resolution techniques.

5 Modular Resolution

The results in this section form the theoretical basis for analysing a class hierarchy in a compositional fashion. In this approach, each class is first analysed separately and the resulting DATALOG programs reduced towards a solved form. Then, the reduced programs are joined together and further reductions can take place.

For a class, the generation algorithm yields a set of DATALOG clauses. However, because a class is not a stand-alone program, code in one class may invoke methods defined in another class. This means that some predicate symbols appearing in the clauses modelling a single class may be either partially or totally undefined. For those predicates, other classes may enrich their definition. To make this explicit, we introduce the term *open* predicates. Being *open* is a property that depends on the scoping rules of the analysed language. For our class analysis, *open* predicate symbols arise from the analysis of method calls, method declaration, method returns and field updates. For instance, the return instruction of a method of signature m defined by a class c contributes to the definition of the $m.ret$ predicate. Because any class implementing a method m also contributes to the definition of the predicate symbol $m.ret$, its definition is kept *open* until all the program is analysed.

5.1 Open DATALOG Programs

Bossi *et al.* [4] define a compositional semantics for open logic programs. We use their definition of open programs.

Definition 3 (Bossi *et al.* [4]). *An open DATALOG program P^Ω is a (DATALOG) program P together with a subset Ω of its predicate symbols ($\Omega \subseteq Pred(P)$). A predicate symbol in Ω is considered to be only partially defined in P.*

The immediate consequence operator T is extended to open programs by ignoring the set of open predicates: $T_{P^\Omega} = T_P$.

Open clauses generated from individual classes are joined to model the analysis of the whole program. Such union of open programs requires common predicate symbols to be open. Otherwise, union is undefined. While analysing a class in isolation, it is then mandatory to declare open any predicate symbol that may be referenced elsewhere.

Definition 4. *Let $P_1^{\Omega_1}$ and $P_2^{\Omega_2}$ be open programs. Under the condition that $Pred(P_1) \cap Pred(P_2) \subseteq \Omega_1 \cap \Omega_2$, $P_1^{\Omega_1} \cup P_2^{\Omega_2}$ is defined by*

$$P_1^{\Omega_1} \cup P_2^{\Omega_2} = (P_1 \cup P_2)^{\Omega_1 \cup \Omega_2}$$

Property 1. Union of open programs is associative.

This property is essential for our purpose: the order in which analyses of classes are joined does not matter.

At this point, we are (only) able to map classes to open DATALOG clauses and join them incrementally to get the clauses modelling the whole program being analysed. Since these operations are strictly syntactic, no resolution occurs. Next sections will characterise and provide modular resolution methods.

5.2 Approximation of Open Programs

A modular resolution method maps open programs to open programs while preserving the overall correctness of the whole analysis. We formalise the notion of approximation by means of a pre-order relation $\sqsubseteq$ over open programs. This generalises the usual containment relation over DATALOG programs [28].

Definition 5. *Let $P_1^{\Omega_1}$ and $P_2^{\Omega_2}$ be DATALOG open programs. $P_2^{\Omega_2}$ is an over-approximation of $P_1^{\Omega_1}$ ($P_1^{\Omega_1} \sqsubseteq P_2^{\Omega_2}$) if and only if:*

- $\Omega_1 = \Omega_2$ and $Pred(P_1) = Pred(P_2)$
- *for all Q^Ω such that $P_1^{\Omega_1} \cup Q^\Omega$ and $P_2^{\Omega_1} \cup Q^\Omega$ are defined, we have*

$$lfp(T_{P_1 \cup Q}) \subseteq lfp(T_{P_2 \cup Q})$$

Property 2. The relation $\sqsubseteq$ is reflexive and transitive.

The relation $\sqsubseteq$ gives rise to an equivalence relation between open programs.

Definition 6. *Let P_1^Ω, P_2^Ω be open programs. P_1^Ω is equivalent to P_2^Ω ($P_1^\Omega \equiv P_2^\Omega$) if and only if $P_1^\Omega \sqsubseteq P_2^\Omega$ and $P_2^\Omega \sqsubseteq P_1^\Omega$.*

The relevance of $\sqsubseteq$ for modular resolution lies in the following fundamental lemma. It shows that open programs remain in relation by $\sqsubseteq$ when an arbitrary open program is adjoined to them. This is the key property of modular resolution methods: whatever the unknown clauses that could be added later, the transformation preserves the correctness of the analysis.

Lemma 1. *Let $P_1^{\Omega_1}$, $P_2^{\Omega_2}$ and Q^Ω be open programs. If $P_1^{\Omega_1} \sqsubseteq P_2^{\Omega_2}$ and $P_1^{\Omega_1} \cup Q^\Omega$ is defined, then we have*

$$P_1^{\Omega_1} \cup Q^\Omega \sqsubseteq P_2^{\Omega_2} \cup Q^\Omega$$

Proof. To begin with, we observe that $P_2^{\Omega_2} \cup Q^\Omega$ is defined. This follows trivially from the definition of $\sqsubseteq$ ($P_1^{\Omega_1} \sqsubseteq P_2^{\Omega_2}$).

Now, consider an arbitrary open program $Q'^{\Omega'}$. To prove the lemma, we show that if $(P_1^{\Omega_1} \cup Q^\Omega) \cup Q'^{\Omega'}$ and $(P_1^{\Omega_1} \cup Q^\Omega) \cup Q'^{\Omega'}$ are defined then the fixpoints are ordered by set inclusion: $lfp(T_{(P_1 \cup Q) \cup Q'}) \subseteq lfp(T_{(P_1 \cup Q) \cup Q'})$. Because union of open programs is associative (Prop 1), we have $(P_1^{\Omega_1} \cup Q^\Omega) \cup Q'^{\Omega'} = P_1^{\Omega_1} \cup (Q \cup Q')^{\Omega \cup \Omega'}$ and $(P_2^{\Omega_2} \cup Q^\Omega) \cup Q'^{\Omega'} = P_2^{\Omega_2} \cup (Q \cup Q')^{\Omega \cup \Omega'}$. Exploiting that $P_1^{\Omega_1} \sqsubseteq P_2^{\Omega_2}$, we conclude that $lfp(T_{P_1 \cup (Q \cup Q')}) \subseteq lfp(T_{P_1 \cup (Q \cup Q')})$. As a result, by associativity of union of sets, the lemma holds.

Based on the relation $\sqsubseteq$ on open programs, we define the notion of correct and exact resolution methods.

Definition 7. *A correct (resp. exact) resolution method $\mathcal{R}^\subseteq$ (resp. $\mathcal{R}^=$) is such that for all open program P^Ω, we have*

$$P^\Omega \sqsubseteq \mathcal{R}^\subseteq(P^\Omega) \qquad P^\Omega \equiv \mathcal{R}^=(P^\Omega)$$

It should be noted that equivalence of DATALOG programs is undecidable [28]. This is of little concern to us because we are only interested in *transformations* that are guaranteed either to preserve equivalence or to yield a safe approximation.

Finally, theorem 1 formally states that correct resolution methods as defined above are indeed correct for the global analysis.

Theorem 1. *Let* $P = \bigcup_{i \in [1,\ldots,n]} P_i^{\Omega_i}$ *a union of open programs. For any collection of correct resolution methods* $\mathcal{R}_1^{\subseteq}, \ldots, \mathcal{R}_n^{\subseteq}$ *the following holds :*

$$lfp(T_{\bigcup_i P_i^{\Omega_i}}) \subseteq lfp(T_{\bigcup_i \mathcal{R}_i^{\subseteq}(P_i^{\Omega_i})})$$

Proof. Because $\mathcal{R}_i^{\subseteq}$ are correct resolution methods (Def 7), we have for any $i \in [1,\ldots,n]$ that $P_i^{\Omega_i} \sqsubseteq \mathcal{R}_i^{\subseteq}(P_i^{\Omega_i})$. Because unions are defined, by recursively applying Lemma 1, we obtain that $\bigcup_i P_i^{\Omega_i} \sqsubseteq \bigcup_i \mathcal{R}_i^{\subseteq}(P_i^{\Omega_i})$. By definition of $\sqsubseteq$, since $T_{P^{\Omega}} = T_P$, the theorem holds: $lfp(T_{\bigcup_i P_i^{\Omega_i}}) \subseteq lfp(T_{\bigcup_i \mathcal{R}_i^{\subseteq}(P_i^{\Omega_i})})$.

6 Modular Resolution Methods

The previous section showed that resolution methods can be applied locally to parts of a DATALOG program. Here, we exhibit a number of resolution methods and relate them to some of the traditional techniques for modular analysis listed by Cousot and Cousot in [10].

6.1 Fixpoint Based Methods

One type of resolution techniques rely on the fixpoint computation of the least Herbrand model of DATALOG programs. These techniques require the ability to re-construct a DATALOG program from a Herbrand interpretation.

Definition 8. *The* extensional database *built from a Herbrand interpretation I is the program $edb(I)$ defined by $edb(I) = \{e \leftarrow \{\} \mid e \in I\}$.*

Worst Case. Worst case analysis is a usual modular resolution method in which the worst assumption is made for the unknowns: they are assigned the top element of the lattice. The worst case consists in computing the fixpoint of this enriched system. For an open program P^{Ω}, we add an empty clause per open predicate symbol.

$$W_{\Omega} = \{p(x_1,\ldots,x_n) \leftarrow \{\} \mid p \in \Omega, x_i \text{ are distinct variables}\}$$

Property 3. For any Herbrand interpretation I, we have $T_{W_{\Omega}}(I) = HB(\Omega, C)$

Because a modular resolution method must yield a program, the least Herbrand model of $P \cup W_{\Omega}$ is computed and translated back to a program. Theorem 2 states the correctness of this approximate resolution method.

Theorem 2. *The worst case resolution of an open program P^Ω is defined by $WC = edb(lfp(T_{P \cup W_\Omega}))$. It is a correct resolution method.*

$$P^\Omega \sqsubseteq WC^\Omega$$

Proof. Consider an arbitrary open program $Q^{\Omega'}$ and suppose that $P^\Omega \cup Q^{\Omega'}$ and $WC^\Omega \cup Q^{\Omega'}$ are defined. We show that $lfp(T_{P \cup Q}) \subseteq lfp(T_{WC \cup Q})$. To begin with, we prove the equality

$$lfp(T_{P \cup W_\Omega \cup Q}) = lfp(T_{WC \cup Q})$$

To do this, we apply several rewriting steps. First, we exploit the distributivity of T and the property 3 to rewrite the left-hand side to $lfp(\lambda I.T_P(I) \cup H \cup T_Q(I))$ where H denotes the Herbrand base generated from the predicate symbols in Ω ($H = HB(\Omega, C)$). In general, the fixpoint operator does not distribute with respect to $\cup$. However, in our case, at each iteration step the computation of $T_P(I) \cup H$ does not depend on Q. Intuitively, potential interactions are captured by H. As a result, we have $lfp(\lambda I.T_P(I) \cup H \cup T_Q(I)) = lfp(\lambda I.lfp(\lambda I.T_P(I) \cup H) \cup T_Q(I))$. We rewrite now the right-hand side of the equality ($lfp(T_{WC \cup Q})$). By definition of WC and distributivity of T, we have $lfp(T_{WC \cup Q}) = lfp(\lambda I.T_{edb(lfp(T_{P \cup W_\Omega}))}(I) \cup T_Q(I))$. Since we have $T_{edb(I_1)}(I_2) = I_1$, we obtain $lfp(\lambda I.T_{edb(lfp(T_{P \cup W_\Omega}))}(I) \cup T_Q(I)) = lfp(\lambda I.lfp(T_{P \cup W_\Omega}) \cup T_Q(I))$. The proof of the equality follows because $lfp(T_{P \cup W_\Omega}) = lfp(\lambda I.T_P(I) \cup H)$.

Given this equality, it remains to show that $lfp(T_{P \cup Q}) \subseteq lfp(T_{P \cup W_\Omega \cup Q})$. It is a direct consequence of the monotonicity of lfp and T. Hence, the theorem holds.

In practice, the worst case may lead to a very imprecise global analysis. However, if the original clauses are kept, some precision can be recovered *a posteriori* by techniques such as restarting the iteration [5] or iterating separate worst case analyses ([10] Sect. 8.2).

Partial Fixpoint. Rather than a worst case assumption, we can make the assumption that free predicate symbols will never be given a definition and open predicate symbols will never be enriched by additional clauses. The minimal fixpoint of the program can be computed but will only constitute a correct resolution as long as the assumption is valid *i.e.*, nothing is added to the program. However, we obtain an exact resolution method if we *enrich* an open program with this least fixpoint.

Theorem 3. *Let P be an Ω-open program, $P^\Omega \equiv (P \cup edb(lfp(T_P)))^\Omega$.*

The practical interest of this method highly depends on the clauses in P. Indeed, if the partial fixpoint is empty, nothing is gained. Otherwise, the pre-computed partial fixpoint will speed-up the convergence of future fixpoint iterations.

6.2 Unfolding and Minimisation

Unfolding is a standard transformation of logic programs. Here we present exact resolution methods based on unfolding. Definition 9 recalls the unfolding operator *unf* as present in the literature, see *e.g.*, Levi [20].

Definition 9. *Let P and Q be* DATALOG *programs that do not share variable names*[1]. *The unfolding of P with respect to Q is a program defined by*

$$unf(P,Q) = \{H\sigma \leftarrow \bigcup_{i \in [1,\ldots,n]} D'_i\sigma \mid \exists (H \leftarrow \{B_1,\ldots,B_n\} \in P).$$
$$\exists B'_1 \leftarrow D'_1 \in Q, \ldots, B'_n \leftarrow D'_n \in Q.$$
$$\sigma = mgu((B_1,\ldots,B_n),(B'_1,\ldots,B'_n))\}$$

where mgu is the most general unifier operator.

Simple Unfolding. In the context of logic programs, unfolding has been studied extensively (see *e.g.*, [20,11]). A well-known result is that a DATALOG program and its unfolding by itself have the same least Herbrand model.

$$lfp(T_P) = lfp(T_P^2) = lfp(T_{unf(P,P)})$$

To cope with open DATALOG programs, following Bossi *et al.* [4], we model incomplete knowledge by adjoining *tautologic* clauses.

Definition 10. *The tautological clauses Id of a set S of predicate symbols is defined by $Id_S = \{p(x_1,\ldots,x_n) \leftarrow p(x_1,\ldots,x_n) \mid p \in S\}$ where $x_1, \ldots, x_n$ are distinct variables.*

To get an exact resolution method, we unfold a DATALOG program with respect to itself enriched with *tautological* clauses for open predicates symbols.

Theorem 4. *Let P^Ω be an open program. $P^\Omega \equiv unf(P, P \cup Id_\Omega)$*

Minimisation. Syntactically distinct DATALOG programs may denote the same T operator. Obviously, such programs are equivalent.

$$T_{P_1} = T_{P_2} \Rightarrow P_1 \equiv P_2$$

For DATALOG programs, there exists a minimisation procedure *Min* that computes a normal form such that $T_P = T_{Min(P)}$. Such minimisation was first proposed by Chandra and Merlin [6] for conjunctive queries and then extended by Sagiv and Yannakakis [27] to sets of clauses. The minimisation yields a reduced clause for which redundant atoms have been eliminated. The idea of the algorithm is to merge variables names to obtain a subset of the initial body. As an example (due to Chandra and Merlin and rephrased in DATALOG terms), the clause $H(x) \leftarrow \{R(x,v,w), R(x,z,w), S(u,w), S(u,v), S(y,w), S(y,v), S(y,z)\}$ is minimised to $H(x) \leftarrow \{R(x,v,w), S(u,w), S(u,v)\}$ by the substitution $[y \mapsto u, z \mapsto v]$. The immediate consequence operator T is stable with respect to such transformations. Hence, minimisation is an exact modular resolution method.

---

[1] To lift this restriction, a renaming is needed.

Iterative Unfolding. The two previous transformations are complementary. Minimisation procedure gives a normal form to non-recursive programs but ignore recursive dependencies while unfolding is one step unrolling of recursions. Iterating these transformations until fixpoint yields an exact modular resolution method.

Theorem 5. *Let P^Ω be an open-program, $P^\Omega \equiv lfp(\lambda q.Min(unf(P, q \cup Id_\Omega)))^\Omega$*

If unfolding were considered without minimisation, the iteration would diverge for all recursive program. To improve convergence, it is desirable to normalise programs at each iteration step. If the open predicates are exactly the free variables (*i.e.*, there are no partially defined predicates) the fixpoint program is non-recursive (at each iteration step, it is only expressed in terms of the free variables). Naugthon [21] proved that there exists a non-recursive equivalent program if and only if the iteration converges. Such programs are said to be *bounded*. Unfortunately, boundedness is not decidable [14] even for programs with a single recursive predicate.

If necessary, termination can be enforced by means of a widening operator [9]. Divergence comes from the fact that, in a clause body, the length of atoms/variables dependencies cannot be bounded. Typically, we have sets of atoms like $\{x(o_1, o_2), x(o_2, o_3), \ldots, x(o_{n-1}, o_n)\}$. The idea of the widening proposed by Codish *et al.* [8,7] is to limit the length of such dependencies. They choose to trigger widening as soon as a dependency chain goes twice through the same predicate symbol at the same argument position. Each occurrence of the variable responsible for this (potential) cyclic dependency is then renamed to a fresh variable. This is a conservative transformation that ensure convergence.

Example 2. To illustrate unfolding, normalisation and widening transformations, we extract an open set of clauses from Example 1.

$$P = \left\{ \begin{array}{l} self(o) \leftarrow \{main.call(o), lk(o, \underline{main}, \underline{main})\} \\ self(o) \leftarrow \{self(o'), fd(o', o)\} \end{array} \right\}$$

The set of open predicate symbols is $\{main.call, lk, fd\}$. By iterative unfolding (no minimisation applies), an infinite ascending chain of programs is computed.

$$\begin{array}{ll} P_0 & = \{\} \\ P_1 & = \{self(o) \leftarrow \{main.call(o), lk(o, \underline{main}, \underline{main})\}\} \\ P_2 & = \left\{ \begin{array}{l} self(o) \leftarrow \{main.call(o), lk(o, \underline{main}, \underline{main})\} \\ self(o_2) \leftarrow \{main.call(o_1), lk(o_1, \underline{main}, \underline{main}), fd(o_1, o_2)\} \end{array} \right\} \end{array}$$

$$\ldots$$

$$P_{n+1} = P_n \cup \left\{ self(o_n) \leftarrow \left\{ \begin{array}{l} main.call(o_1), lk(o_1, \underline{main}, \underline{main}), \\ fd(o_1, o_2), \ldots fd(o_{n-1}, o_n) \end{array} \right\} \right\}$$

P_3 is widened by renaming the first occurrence of o_2 by α and the second by β.

$$\Delta(P_2) = \left\{ \begin{array}{l} self(o) \leftarrow \{main.call(o), lk(o, \underline{main}, \underline{main})\} \\ self(o_2) \leftarrow \{main.call(o_1), lk(o_1, \underline{main}, \underline{main}), fd(o_1, \alpha), fd(\beta, o_2)\} \end{array} \right\}$$

At the next iteration step, widening is also triggered and we obtain.

$$\Delta(P_3) = \begin{cases} self(o) \leftarrow \{main.call(o), lk(o, \underline{main}, \underline{main})\} \\ self(o_2) \leftarrow \{main.call(o_1), lk(o_1, \underline{main}, \underline{main}), fd(o_1, \alpha), fd(\beta, o_2)\} \\ self(o) \leftarrow \begin{cases} main.call(o_2), lk(o_1, \underline{main}, \underline{main}), \\ fd(o_1, \alpha), fd(\beta, \gamma), fd(\delta, o_2) \end{cases} \end{cases}$$

The last clause is minimised by renaming $[\beta \mapsto \delta, \gamma \mapsto o_2]$ and we obtain the following program

$$\begin{cases} self(o) \leftarrow \{main.call(o), lk(o, \underline{main}, \underline{main})\} \\ self(o_2) \leftarrow \{main.call(o_1), lk(o_1, \underline{main}, \underline{main}), fd(o_1, \alpha), fd(\beta, o_2)\} \end{cases}$$

which is stable by the iteration step. While the first clause is directly inherited from the initial clauses, the second is computed by the resolution process. Widening is responsible for the introduction of the fresh variables α and β. Without widening, there would be a path via fd fields between α and β objects.

7 Related Work

The use of logic languages such as DATALOG to specify static analyses is not new but seems to have stayed within the imperative and logic programming realm. The approach called *abstract compilation* evolves around the idea of translating a program into a set of Horn clauses that can then combined with particular queries to obtain information about the program being analysed. Reps proposed to use logic databases in order to have a demand-driven dataflow-analysis for free [25]. Hill and Spoto studied the use of logic programs to compactly model abstract denotations of programs [17]. They cite an experiment with class analysis but do not provide details.

Nielson and Seidl have proposed to use Alternation-Free Least Fixed Point Logic (ALFP) as a general formalism for expressing static analyses (in particular 0-CFA control-flow analysis [22]) in the Flow Logic framework. Hansen [16] shows how to encode a flow logic for an idealised version of Java Card. The ALFP logic is more expressive than DATALOG but as shown here, this added expressiveness does not seem required in the particular case of class analysis. It is unknown to us how our resolution techniques for open programs carry over to this more powerful logic.

The notion of context-sensitive analyses has been around for a long time. The article by Hornof and Noyé [18] describes various types of context-sensitivity for static analysis of imperative languages. For object-oriented languages, DeFouw et al. [15] describe a parameterised framework to define context-sensitive class analyses, but in a somewhat more operational setting than here. Jensen and Spoto [19] classify a number of low-cost, context-insensitive class analyses such as Rapid Type Analysis and 0-CFA in a language-independent abstract interpretation framework.

In their survey of modular analysis methods, Cousot and Cousot [10] write that modular analysis consists in computing a parameterised fixpoint

$$\lambda(p_1,\ldots,p_n).\mathit{lfp}(\lambda p'.f(p')(p_1,\ldots,p_n))$$

but note that a direct approach is not in general feasible. By restricting attention to a particular type of analysis that can be expressed in the simple specification language DATALOG we have been able to re-express this fixpoint computation as the solution of a set of open DATALOG clauses and to propose a number of resolution techniques that can help in this resolution.

Flanagan and Felleisen [13] developed a *componential set based analysis* for Scheme. Each module gives rise to a constraint set separately minimized under a notion of observational equivalence. For this particular constraint language, equivalence under observational equivalence is decidable (though computationally expensive). It means that a normal form for constraints exists. This is not the case for DATALOG, and hence the resolution techniques are not in general guaranteed to yield a normal form.

Rountev *et al.* [26] define a framework to refine the result of a whole program analysis by applying a more precise analysis on program fragments. Basically, whole program information is used to abstract the behaviour at the boundaries of the fragment. The pros of this technique is that the fragment is only analysed in contexts relevant for the whole program being analysed. The cons is that the fragment is to be re-analysed as other parts of the program change.

Bossi *et al.* [4] defined a compositional semantics for (open) logic programs for which the semantics domain is defined by *syntactic* objects: sets of clauses. Based on this semantics, Codish *et al.* [7] proposed a framework for the modular analysis of logic programs. Alike this line of work, our modular analysis does not require to give a semantics to open object-oriented programs. Our presentation does not even explicit a semantics for open DATALOG programs but formalises what safe approximations are through the $\sqsubseteq$ relation. Anyway, at the end, our approaches converge since iterative unfolding of clauses (Section 6.2) is the semantics of open programs proposed by Bossi *et al.*

8 Conclusions

We have demonstrated the use of DATALOG as a specification language for class analysis of object-oriented languages, by showing how a variety of context-sensitive analyses can be expressed as instances of a common framework. For closed programs, this provides a straightforward implementation of the analysis through a bottom-up evaluator for DATALOG. We have also shown its use for developing modular program analyses. Analysis of program fragments gives rise to DATALOG programs with partially or undefined predicates. Such programs can be reduced using a number of iteration and normalisation operators, all expressible in the DATALOG framework.

As noted in the section on resolution by unfolding and minimisation (Section 6.2), the resolution might in certain cases need a widening operator to enforce convergence. The next step in our work is to design suitable widenings in order to be able to experiment with the analysis of realistic code fragments. Another issue that needs to be treated formally is how to take into account the structuring mechanisms and scoping rules of the programming language (such as the visibility modifiers and package structure in Java) when determining what predicates can be considered closed and what must be kept open. A precise modelling of this is important since the more predicates can be considered closed, the more resolution can take place.

References

1. O. Agesen. Constraint-Based Type Inference and Parametric Polymorphism. In B. Le Charlier, editor, *Proc. of the 1st International Static Analysis Symposium*, volume 864 of *LNCS*, pages 78–100. Springer-Verlag, 1994.
2. K. R. Apt. Introduction to logic programming. In J. van Leeuwen, editor, *Handbook of Theoretical Computer Science: Volume B: Formal Models and Semantics*, pages 493–574. Elsevier, Amsterdam, 1990.
3. D. F. Bacon and P. F. Sweeney. Fast Static Analysis of C++ Virtual Function Calls. In *Proc. of OOPSLA'96*, volume 31(10) of *ACM SIGPLAN Notices*, pages 324–341, New York, 1996. ACM Press.
4. A. Bossi, M. Gabbrielli, G. Levi, and M. C. Meo. A Compositional Semantics for Logic Programs. *Theoretical Computer Science*, 122(1-2):3–47, 1994.
5. M. G. Burke and B. G. Ryder. A critical analysis of incremental iterative data flow analysis algorithms. *IEEE Transactions on Software Engineering*, 16(7):723–728, 1990.
6. A. K. Chandra and P. M. Merlin. Optimal implementation of conjunctive queries in relational data bases. In *Proc. of the 9th ACM symposium on Theory of computing*, pages 77–90, 1977.
7. M. Codish, S. K. Debray, and R. Giacobazzi. Compositional analysis of modular logic programs. In *Proc. of the 20th ACM symposium on Principles of programming languages*, pages 451–464. ACM Press, 1993.
8. M. Codish, M. Falaschi, and K. Marriott. Suspension analysis for concurrent logic programs. *ACM Transactions on Programming Languages and Systems*, 16(3):649–686, 1994.
9. P. Cousot and R. Cousot. Comparing the Galois connection and widening/narrowing approaches to abstract interpretation, invited paper. In M. Bruynooghe and M. Wirsing, editors, *Proc. of the International Workshop Programming Language Implementation and Logic Programming,*, volume 631 of *LNCS*, pages 269–295. Springer, 1992.
10. P. Cousot and R.Cousot. Modular static program analysis, invited paper. In R.N. Horspool, editor, *Proc. of the 11th International Conference on Compiler Construction*, volume 2304 of *LNCS*, pages 159–178, Grenoble, France, April 2002. Springer.
11. F. Denis and J-P Delahaye. Unfolding, procedural and fixpoint semantics of logic programs. In *Proc. of the 8th Annual Symposium on Theoretical Aspects of Computer Science*, volume 480 of *LNCS*, pages 511–522, Hamburg, Germany, February 1991. Springer.
12. A. Diwan, J. E. B. Moss, and K. S. McKinley. Simple and Effective Analysis of Statically Typed Object-Oriented Programs. In *Proc. of OOPSLA'96*, volume 31(10) of *ACM SIGPLAN Notices*, pages 292–305, New York, 1996. ACM Press.

13. C. Flanagan and M. Felleisen. Componential set-based analysis. *ACM Transactions on Programming Languages and Systems*, 21(2):370–416, 1999.
14. H. Gaifman, H. Mairson, Y. Sagiv, and M. Y. Vardi. Undecidable optimization problems for database logic programs. In *Proc. Symposium on Logic in Computer Science*, pages 106–115, Ithaca, New York, jun 1987. IEEE Computer Society.
15. D. Grove and C. Chambers. A framework for call graph construction algorithms. *ACM Transactions on Programming Languages and Systems*, 23(6):685–746, 2001.
16. R. R. Hansen. Flow logic for carmel. Technical Report Secsafe-IMM-001, IMM, Technical U. of Denamrk, 2002.
17. P. M. Hill and F. Spoto. Logic Programs as Compact Denotations. Proc. of the Fifth International Symposium on Practical Aspects of Declarative Languages, PADL '03, 2003.
18. L. Hornof and J. Noyé. Accurate binding-time analysis for imperative languages: flow, context, and return sensitivity. *Theoretical Computer Science*, 248(1–2):3–27, 2000.
19. T. Jensen and F. Spoto. Class analysis of object-oriented programs through abstract interpretation. In F. Honsell and M. Miculan, editors, *Proc. of Foundations of Software Science and Computation Structures (FoSSaCS'01)*, pages 261–275. Springer LNCS vol .2030, 2001.
20. G. Levi. Models, unfolding rules and fixpoint semantics. In Robert A. Kowalski and Kenneth A. Bowen, editors, *Proc. of the 5th International Conference and Symposium on Logic Programming*, pages 1649–1665, Seatle, 1988. ALP, IEEE, The MIT Press.
21. J. F. Naughton. Data independent recursion in deductive databases. *Journal of Computer and System Sciences*, 38(2):259–289, April 1989.
22. F. Nielson and H. Seidl. Control-flow analysis in cubic time. In *Proc. of European Symp. on Programming (ESOP'01)*, pages 252–268. Springer LNCS vol. 2028, 2001.
23. J. Palsberg and M. I. Schwartzbach. *Object-Oriented Type-Systems*. John Wiley & Sons, 1994.
24. J. Plevyak and A. Chien. Precise Concrete Type Inference for Object-Oriented Languages. In *Proc. of OOPSLA '94*, volume 29(10) of *ACM SIGPLAN Notices*, pages 324–340. ACM Press, October 1994.
25. T. Reps. Demand interprocedural program analysis using logic databases. In *Applications of Logic Databases*, pages 163–196, Boston, MA, 1994. Kluwer.
26. A. Rountev, B. G. Ryder, and W. Landi. Data-flow analysis of program fragments. In *Proc. of the 7th international symposium on Foundations of software engineering*, pages 235–252. Springer-Verlag, 1999.
27. Y. Sagiv and M. Yannakakis. Equivalences among relational expressions with the union and difference operators. *Journal of the ACM*, 27(4):633–655, 1980.
28. O. Shmueli. Decidability and expressiveness aspects of logic queries. In *Proc. of the 6th ACM symposium on Principles of database systems*, pages 237–249. ACM Press, 1987.
29. J. D. Ullman. *Principles of database and knowledge-base systems, volume 2*, volume 14 of *Principles of Computer Science*. Computer Science Press, 1988.

Class-Level Modular Analysis for Object Oriented Languages

Francesco Logozzo

STIX - École Polytechnique
F-91128 Palaiseau, France
Francesco.Logozzo@polytechnique.fr

Abstract. In this paper we address the problem of performing a class static analysis in a modular fashion, i.e. by just analyzing the class code and not the full program. In particular we show two things: the first one is how starting from a class C we can derive an approximation C^a to be used either as a class documentation or as a tester for a client using C; the second one is how to discover, in a fully automatic way, a class invariant. Two methods for class invariant computation are presented, proved correct and their usage is discussed.

1 Introduction

The object oriented paradigm is a widespread methodology for structuring and thinking about large systems that widely influenced the development of computer science in the last years. Objects deeply influenced fields as software engineering [28], database management [3] and programming languages both in theory [1] and implementation [20]. In all these fields the new paradigm caused the introduction of new tools and techniques. For example in languages such as C++ or Java the problem of efficiently resolving the dynamic methods dispatching originated in the introduction of virtual call tables at implementation, or in type theory the researches about co-variance/contra-variance led to a deep understandings of the subtype/inheritance concepts. In the field of static analysis the state seems to be slightly different. In fact despite the large number of analyses presented for object oriented languages (e.g. [31, 24, 18, 25, 27, 4]) just few of them takes into account some peculiarities of OO languages, as for example the organization of code in classes, the state encapsulation and more in general the modular features of the object oriented programming. In particular, existing analyses are not able to discover class-level properties as class invariants as most of the times they assume the full program being available in memory. When this is not the case then they rely either on heavy human annotations or on smart strategies for fixpoint computation.

1.1 Our Contribution

In this work we will present a class-level modular analysis for object oriented languages. An analysis is said to be modular when it is performed on a code fragment, i.e. when the whole program source does not need to reside in memory. In an object oriented language it is natural to assume that the fragment is a class definition. In this paper we show how to perform such an analysis starting from a basic idea: given a class method its input/output behavior can be approximated by a set of constraints *symbolically* relating input values (instance fields and formal parameters) with outputs (updated instance fields and return value). Therefore, given a class C each one of its methods m_i is approximated by a set of constraints $c_{m_i}[x_{in}, x_F, x_{out}, x_{F'}]$ where x_{in} and x_F are respectively the method formal parameters and the class fields at m_i's entry-point, x_{out} is the return value (if any) and $x_{F'}$ symbolically represent the values of class fields at the exit-point.

An immediate application is the generation of automatic documentation: since the constraints describe the methods' behavior, they can be shipped as class documentation. The main advantage is that they are directly generated from the source and no human intervention is required when the code changes: it is sufficient to (re-)run the analysis on the modified methods. Another application is the derivation of an abstract[1] class C^a to be used in full program analysis: the methods of C are replaced by their abstract counterparts c_{m_i}. In whole-program analysis the use of an (already computed) abstraction of m_i brings to a global analysis speedup.

A main result of the paper is the automatic derivation of a class invariant. Informally, a class invariant [19] is a property that is true for each possible instantiation of the class, before and after any method execution. In our framework, it can be derived by *collecting* together all the method approximations and abstracting away from all but the class fields variables. This automatically gives out a class invariant. The result can be improved by performing a fixpoint computation: the so-obtained invariant is pushed at methods entry points, new constraints are computed, they are collected together and then the non-field variables are abstracted, etc. till a fixpoint is reached (or convergence is forced by means of a widening operator [8]). An example of the results obtained in this way is given in the next section.

Comparison with Existing Work. Several works have been done on the semantics, the analysis and the verification of object oriented programming languages.

As far as the semantics of inheritance is concerned, [5] is probably the first to introduce the model of objects as records used in the present paper. A consequence of such a view is that two objects are considered the same if they have the same fields and the same values so that object aliasing is not considered.

Several static analyses have been developed for object oriented languages as e.g. [31, 24, 18, 4] and some of them have modular features as [6, 25] in that they analyze a program fragment without requiring the full program to stay in

---

[1] In this paper context we employ the term *abstract* in the sense of abstract interpretation theory and not of OOP: hence by an abstract class C^a we mean a *semantic object* that approximates the semantics of C, and not a class that is higher in the class hierarchy.

memory. Nevertheless the cited analyses are different from our in that both are not able to discover class invariants, essentially because they exploit modularity at method, and not class, level. This is not the case of the analysis presented in [2]. In that work the authors presented an analysis capable to infer class invariants in the form of a $==$ null $\vee$ $0 \leq$ b $\leq$ a.*Length*, where a is an array and b an integer. However, our work handles more generic properties, presents two different form of class invariant computation and their soundness is proved.

The work that probably is the closest to ours is [26]. It addresses the problem of verifying whether the client of a class uses it in a *correct* way. To do it, the paper essentially derives a symbolic class invariant and checks that a given client does not violate it. However, our work is different since we do not require any human interaction for deriving the methods' approximations and our analysis does not necessarily need a client in order to derive class integrity properties.

The concept of class invariant is widely used in semi-automatic verification of object oriented programs. In that case the idea is to hand-annotate a class with an invariant and its methods with pre- and post-conditions. Therefore a theorem prover is used to check that everything is fine [29, 17, 14]. These works are different from ours in that we do not require any human interaction: the class invariant is automatically inferred and not just checked. Another approach to (likely) class invariant discovery is presented in [15]. In that case the idea is to run the program on a test suite and to try to infer likely-invariants from the so-obtained execution traces. Indeed this approach is not sound, unlike ours.

Outline. The rest of the paper is organized as follows. Section 2 introduces the paper running example, a Java class implementing a stack. In Section 3 we define the syntax and the semantics for classes and methods. Section 4 explains the technique for approximating a method semantics with a set of constraints. Sections 5 and 6 introduce the two main results of this paper: respectively how to generate a class approximation C^a and how to automatically discover a class invariant. Eventually Section 7 presents conclusions and future work.

2 A Stack Example

The paper running example is the code of Fig.1, taken from [19]. It describes a class Stack which implements a stack parameterized by its dimension, specified at object creation time. The annotations on the right have been automatically derived by instantiating the results of this paper. The comments at lines 6 to 8 specify the class invariant, i.e. a property that, for each possible instantiation of the class Stack, is valid before and after the execution of each method in the class. In particular, it states that the size of the stack is always greater than zero and it does not change during the execution. Moreover the stack pointer pos is always positive and smaller or equal to the array size. It is worth noting that the result is obtained without any hypothesis on the class instantiation context so that the analysis is carried on in a fully *context*-modular fashion.

```
1   class StackError extends Exception {
2   }
3
4   public class Stack {
5
6     private int size;                    // 1 <= size
7     private int pos;                     // 0 <= pos <= size
8     private Object[] stack;              // size = stack.Length
9
10    Stack(int size) {
11      this.size = Math.max(size,1);
12      this.pos  = 0;
13      this.stack = new Object[size];
14    }
15    boolean isEmpty() {
16      return (pos <= 0);
17    }
18    boolean isFull() {
19      return (pos >= size);
20    }
21    Object top() {
22      return stack[pos-1];               // -1 <= pos-1 < stack.Length
23    }
24    void push(Object o) throws StackError {
25      if(!isFull()) {
26        stack[pos] = o;                  // 0 <= pos < size
27        pos++;
28      } else
29        throw new StackError();
30    }
31    void pop() throws StackError {
32      if(!isEmpty())
33        pos--;
34      else
35        throw new StackError();
36    }
37  }
```

Fig. 1. Java source code and annotations for the Stack class

The class invariant can be used either to automatically produce the code documentation or to point out possible runtime errors as for example at line 22 where a negative array access may be performed if the stack is empty. Moreover the same property can be used to optimize the generated bytecode: in fact for each possible instantiation of the Stack and for each possible calling context it is sure that the array upper bound is never accessed or overcome so that this check can be avoided in the compiled code. Analogously at line 26 at bytecode level the array checks can be omitted as it is proved that pos is *always* in the array boundaries.

3 Syntax and Semantics

There are several possible definitions for objects. In this paper we will use the *"objects as records"* paradigm of [5]: intuitively an object is made up of an internal state (fields in OOP terminology) and some functions (methods) that can be accessed through a label. The set of labels of an object is called the *interface*.

A class is a description for a set of objects that have the same interface. Each class has a particular function, called the *constructor* that is invoked to set up the internal state of a newly created object. Formally:

Definition 1 (Class). *A class* C *is a triple* $\langle \{f_j\}, \texttt{init}, \{m_i\} \rangle$ *where* $\{f_j\}$ *is a set of distinct variables,* init *is the constructor and* $\{m_i\}$ *is a set of functions.*

Without any loss of generality, in the following we will suppose that the object fields are all private, that is they are directly accessible only by objects belonging to the same class. This hypothesis not only simplifies the following technical exposition but it seems to be a realistic feature in last generation OO languages, e.g. the *properties* of C# [22].

3.1 Partial Trace Semantics of Methods

Methods semantics is expressed by means of partial execution traces. A trace is a sequence of states. A state is a couple $\langle \texttt{pp}, \varrho \rangle$, where pp is a program point and ϱ is an environment, i.e. a mapping from variable names to values.

Given a method m_i and a set of initial environments, the computation begins at method entry point and it goes on by successive applications of a transition relation $\rightarrow$ till blocked. The collecting semantics is then the set of traces of all the states reached in a computation. This can be formalized as follows:

Definition 2 (Method Semantics). *Let Σ be a set of states,* $\rightarrow \in \wp(\Sigma \times \Sigma)$ *a transition relation,* $\text{Tr}(\Sigma)$ *the set of finite and infinite traces over Σ, and* $F \in [\text{Tr}(\Sigma) \rightarrow \text{Tr}(\Sigma)]$ *the function defined as*

$$F(X) = \{\sigma_0 \sigma_1 \ldots \sigma_n \sigma' \mid \sigma_0 \sigma_1 \ldots \sigma_n \in X \text{ and } \sigma_n \rightarrow \sigma'\}.$$

Then the trace semantics of m_i *with input environments* R_0 *is*

$$\mathcal{S}[\![m_i]\!](R_0) = \text{lfp}^{\subseteq}(\lambda X. \{\langle \texttt{entryPoint}(m_i), \varrho \rangle \mid \varrho \in R_0\} \cup F(X)) \qquad (1)$$

where entryPoint(m_i) *returns the entry-point of the method* m_i *and* $\text{lfp}^{\subseteq}$ *denotes the least fixpoint of the function w.r.t. the subset inclusion order.*

In particular (1) can be applied when R_0 is the set of all possible input environments $R_\top$. Therefore $\mathcal{S}[\![m_i]\!](R_\top)$ is the set of traces that represents all the possible executions, for all the possible input values of m_i. In the next section we show how this set can be approximated by a (finite) set of constraints between the input and output states. This will be the base for constructing a class-level semantic-sound modular analysis.

4 Approximating Method Semantics by Constraints

A natural way to approximate a method semantics is by keeping relations between the input and output values. For example [9] has shown how linear inequalities can be used to approximate the input/output behavior of a function.

More generally there is a whole class of modular static analyses (e.g. [9, 6, 21]) called symbolic relational [11], based on the idea of approximating a program part P by giving symbolic names to all the entities used or modified by P. Our goal is to exploit these analyses for class invariant derivation. Therefore in this section we give a formalization of their common points: we present a generic abstract domain parameterized by a set of relations, we show how it relates to the concrete domain and we give the axioms for a constraint simplification, or dropping operator.

4.1 Constraints

The idea of the abstract domain is that constraints describe the interdependencies between variable values at different program points and that a function/method modular analysis can be obtained by keeping the relations involving variables at entry and exit points. Informally, we can say that the semantics $S[\![m_i]\!]$ of a method can be approximated by a set of constraints $c_{m_i}[x_{in}, x_F, x_{out}, x_{F'}]$, where x_{in} are the method formal parameters, x_F and $x_{F'}$ symbolically represents the fields values for this at respectively method invocation and method return, and x_{out} is the return value, if any.

Example 1 (Stack Constructor). With reference to Fig. 1 we can abstract the semantics of the object constructor Stack(int size) with the following set of linear inequalities [13]:

$$c_{\text{Stack(int)}}[\text{size}_{in}, \text{size}_F, \text{pos}_F, \text{stack}_F, x_{out}, \text{size}_{F'}, \text{pos}_{F'}, \text{stack}_{F'}] =$$
$$\{\text{size}_{in} \leq \text{size}_{F'}, 1 \leq \text{size}_{F'},$$
$$\text{stack}_{F'}.Length = \text{size}_{F'}, \text{pos}_{F'} = 0\}.$$

It is worth noting that since the constructor is not supposed to return a value x_{out} is not tied by any constraint. □

Formally we assume that we have a (possibly infinite) set of constraints

$$\text{Rel} = \{\rho(x_1, \ldots x_n) \mid \rho \text{ is a relation constructor and } x_i \in \text{Vars}\},$$

where Vars is the set of annotated program variables, i.e. variables endowed with a subscript specifying the program point they refer to. Examples of annotated program variables are size_{in} and $\text{size}_{F'}$ where the two subscripts in and F' specify that in the first case we consider the variable size at the method entry point (hence it is the actual parameter) and in the latter is the value of the object field size at exit's. The formal meaning is given by:

Definition 3 (Annotated Variables Interpretation (Γ)). *Let* Vars *be a set of annotated variables in the form* x_{pp} *where* pp *is an encoding of the program point the variable* x *refers to, and* $\text{Dom}(x)$ *is the domain over which the values of* x *range. Then:* $\Gamma(x_{pp}) = \{\sigma \in \Sigma \mid \sigma = \langle pp, \varrho \rangle \text{ and } \varrho(x) \in \text{Dom}(x)\}.$

In addition we need a function that given a set of constraints returns the set of constrained variables, e.g. tiedVars($\{$PointsTo$(y_3, $null$)\}) = \{y_3\}$. So it is immediate to define the function tiedVars$\in [\wp_{\text{fin}}(\text{Rel}) \to \wp(\text{Vars})]$ as tiedVars(c) = $\bigcup_{\rho(x_1...x_n) \in c} \{x_1, \ldots x_n\}$.

In general $\mathcal{S}[\![m_i]\!]$ may be approximated by several constraints (e.g. in Ex.1), so it is natural to take subsets of Rel as elements of our domain. Moreover, since we want an effective analysis we require these subsets to be computer-representable, hence finite. Nevertheless, it is worth noting that this does not imply the finiteness of the space-state they describe (cf. Ex.1).

How is the set of constraints related to the semantics? First, suppose we have an interpretation for a constraint, i.e. a boolean function $\mathcal{R}[\![\cdot]\!]$ that given an n-tuple of values says if they satisfy or not the relation. Then the concretization of a constraint is the set of all the traces verifying it, i.e. all the traces whose states are compatible with the interpretation $\mathcal{R}[\![\cdot]\!]$. Finally, the concretization of a set of constraints is simply the intersection of the concretizations of its elements. Therefore we can state the:

Definition 4 (Meaning Function (γ_c)). *Let* $\Gamma \in [\text{Vars} \to \wp(\Sigma)]$ *be the interpretation for symbolic values,* D_i *the range domain of the i-th variable and* $\mathcal{R}[\![\cdot]\!] \in [\text{Rel} \times D_1 \times \cdots \times D_{|\text{Vars}|} \to \text{Bool}]$ *the interpretation for constraints. Then the concretization of a single constraint* $\gamma_\rho \in [\wp_{\text{fin}}(\text{Rel}) \to \text{Tr}(\Sigma)]$ *is defined as:*

$$\gamma_\rho(\rho(x_1, \ldots x_n)) = \{\tau \in \text{Tr}(\Sigma) \mid \forall \sigma_1 \ldots \sigma_n \in \tau.$$
$$\sigma_1 \in \Gamma(x_1), \sigma_1 = \langle pp_1, \varrho_1 \rangle, \varrho_1(x_1) = v_{x_1},$$
$$\ldots$$
$$\sigma_n \in \Gamma(x_n), \sigma_n = \langle pp_n, \varrho_n \rangle, \varrho_n(x_n) = v_{x_n}$$
$$\Rightarrow \mathcal{R}[\![\rho(x_1, \ldots x_n)]\!](v_{x_1}, \ldots v_{x_n})\}.$$

The concretization of a set of constraints $\gamma_c \in [\wp_{\text{fin}}(\text{Rel}) \to \text{Tr}(\Sigma)]$ *is* $\gamma_c(c) = \bigcap_{\rho(x_1,\ldots x_n) \in c} \gamma_\rho(\rho(x_1, \ldots x_n))$.

By means of this last definition we can say that a set of constraints c_{m_i} approximates the semantics of a method m_i iff $\mathcal{S}[\![m_i]\!](R_T) \subseteq \gamma_c(c_{m_i})$. In general, given a set of relations as e.g. linear equalities or inequalities, types or parameterized aliasing analysis [6], c_{m_i} is given by an abstract semantic function $\mathcal{S}[\![\cdot]\!]^a \in [\text{Methods} \to \wp_{\text{fin}}(\text{Rel})]$ such that $\mathcal{S}[\![m_i]\!]^a = c_{m_i}$.

The $\sqsubseteq^c$-order arises in a natural way: it states that the more the constraints and the more the information, the less the traces:

Lemma 1 (Order on $\wp_{\text{fin}}(\text{Rel})$ ($\sqsubseteq^c$)). $\sqsubseteq^c$ *defined as* $\forall c_1, c_2 \in \wp_{\text{fin}}(\text{Rel}). c_1 \sqsubseteq^c c_2 \Leftrightarrow \gamma_c(c_1) \subseteq \gamma_c(c_2)$ *is a preorder. Moreover, the largest element* $\top^c$ *is* $\emptyset$.

In addition we require an operator $\sqcup^c$ such that $\forall c_1, c_2 \in \wp_{\text{fin}}(\text{Rel}). c_1 \sqsubseteq^c c_1 \sqcup^c c_2$ and $c_2 \sqsubseteq^c c_1 \sqcup^c c_2$. The underlying intuition is that $\sqcup^c$ is the abstract counterpart of the logical "or". An example is the convex-hull operation on linear inequalities [2].

---

[2] Note that we do not require $\sqcup^c$ to be the least upper bound, since in general it may not exist [10].

4.2 Variable Dropping

We have seen that constraints relate together different variables. But what about the inverse operation, i.e. the variable elimination? In this section we introduce an axiomatic characterization of an operator δ whose goal is to eliminate a given variable from a set of constraints: for example $\delta_x(\{x^2+y^2+z^2 \leq 1\}) = \{y^2+z^2 \leq 1\}$. Intuitively a drop operator δ is required to preserve the logical implication *(monotonicity)* and to lose all the information about a variable at once *(variable elimination)*. Moreover, dropping a variable causes a loss of information *(extensivity)*, the application order does not matter *(commutativity)* and dropping a variable that is not restrained has no effect *(unit)*. This is formalized by the next definition:

Definition 5 (Dropping Operator Axioms). *A dropping operator on* $\wp_{\text{fin}}(\text{Rel})$ *is a function* $\delta \in [\text{Vars} \to \langle \wp_{\text{fin}}(\text{Rel}), \sqsubseteq^c \rangle \to \langle \wp_{\text{fin}}(\text{Rel}), \sqsubseteq^c \rangle]$ *such that* $\forall x, y \in \text{Vars}$ *and* $\forall c_1, c_2 \in \wp_{\text{fin}}(\text{Rel})$:

- $c_1 \sqsubseteq^c c_2 \Rightarrow \delta_x(c_1) \sqsubseteq^c \delta_x(c_2)$ *(monotonicity)*
- $x \notin \text{tiedVars}(\delta_x(c_1))$ *(variable elimination)*
- $c_1 \sqsubseteq^c \delta_x(c_1)$ *(extensivity)*
- $\delta_x \circ \delta_y(c_1) = \delta_y \circ \delta_x(c_1)$ *(commutativity)*
- $\delta_x(c_1) = c_1$, *if* $x \notin \text{tiedVars}(c_1)$ *(unit)*.

It is immediate to see that δ is idempotent, e.g. $\delta_x \circ \delta_x(c) = \delta_x(c)$ so that it is an upper closure operator. Because of the commutativity property of δ we write $\delta_{x_1,x_2,\ldots}$ for $\delta_{x_1} \circ \delta_{x_2} \circ \ldots$. In addition, the dual of δ, i.e. the function that drops all the variables but the specified ones will be denoted as $\overline{\delta}_{x_1,x_2,\ldots}(c) \triangleq \delta_{\text{Vars}-\{x_1,x_2,\ldots\}}(c)$.

5 First Abstraction: Approximating Classes

In this section we show how to build a class approximation on the top of methods abstraction. The idea is quite simple: given a class C, we replace each field f_j of type C_j with a field f_j^a of type C_j^a and we replace each one of its methods m_i with the corresponding abstraction c_{m_i} obtaining an approximated class C^a.

5.1 Applications

The approximation C^a can be used in two ways. The <u>first</u> one is as C documentation. In fact, constraints describe the methods' behavior, so that they can be used as a description of the compiled code. The main advantage of this way of doing is that the documentation is obtained automatically from the source code and not from user annotations [30], saving programmer time and being less error-prone.

The <u>second</u> one is for class client abstract debugging. In fact suppose to have a program P using the class C. In a static analysis of P we can employ C^a either to save time by avoiding the analysis of C's methods at each (abstract) invocation or to test that P uses the class in a correct way, e.g. in the Stack example it never pops an element from an empty stack.

5.2 Abstract Class Definition

The definition of the abstract class follows:

Definition 6 (Abstract Class (C^a)). *Let* $C = \langle \{f_j\}, \text{init}, \{m_i\} \rangle$ *be a class. For each field* f_j *of type* C_j *let* f_j^a *of type* C_j^a *the corresponding abstract field and for each method* m_i *let* c_{m_i} *be a correct approximation of its semantics, i.e.* $\mathcal{S}[\![m_i]\!](R_\top) \subseteq \gamma_c(c_{m_i})$. *In addition, let* $\mathcal{S}[\![\text{init}]\!](R_\top) \subseteq \gamma_c(c_{\text{init}})$. *Then the abstract class is defined as* $C^a = \langle \{f_j^a\}, c_{\text{init}}, \{c_{m_i}\} \rangle$.

*Example 2 (Abstract Stack (*Stack^a*)).* Still referring to our running example, methods in Stack can be (automatically) approximated by set of linear inequalities in order to obtain the abstract class Stack^a of Fig. 2.

More in detail, the approximation of a method is obtained by giving formal names (e.g. pos$_F$) to the values of the actual parameters and instance fields corresponding to the initial values at method entry-point and by establishing a relation with the final value (e.g. pos$_{F'}$) of these variables. In our case this relation can be established by abstractly executing the methods on the polyhedra abstract domain[3].

Some further comments:

- F and F' are the fields values before and after the execution on a method;
- F_p and F'_p are as above except that they do not contain (respectively) the variables pos$_F$ and pos$_{F'}$;
- The internal representation of the stack, i.e. the array Object[] stack is abstracted with the integer variable stacklen representing its dimension (stacklen = stack.*Length*);
- $\Omega(\text{Exc})$ denotes that the exception Exc is thrown;
- The return value of method top is abstracted to be everything. □

Remark 1. From the last example it follows that if a class A uses[4] a class B then either the abstract class B^a must be available before the derivation of the abstract class A^a or, if the two are mutually dependents, the derivation of A^a and B^a must be performed at the same time. □

An interesting use of Stack^a is to check for client well-behavior, i.e. to check that a client which uses this class does not cause an exception raised by pushing an object on a full stack, or calling top() on the empty stack. Therefore we can say that Stack^a abstracts away from Stack the effective values of the array but it behaves in the same way with respect to the *exceptional* behavior.

In Fig. 3 it is given a general schema for performing a client debugging: at first the client instantiates a new object o of the abstract class C^a. This gives out an approximation of the internal object fields $o.x_{F'}$. In our running example it

---

[3] Actually it is not totally exact to say that we use the polyhedra domain. In fact the example is obtained by refining the polyhedra domain with trace partitioning [16].
[4] For example it has a field of type B.

```
Stackᵃ {
   int size;
   int pos;
   int stacklen;

   Stack(int size) ↦ {size_in ≤ size_F', 1 ≤ size_F',
                      stacklen_F' = size_F', pos_F' = 0}
   boolean isEmpty() ↦ {x_out = (pos_F ≤ 0)} ∪ {F = F'}
   boolean isFull()  ↦ {x_out = (pos_F ≥ size_F)} ∪ {F = F'}
   Object top() ↦ {if(pos_F > size_F or pos_F ≤ 0) then
                         x_out = Ω(ArrayIndexOutOfBoundsException)
                   else {F = F'}}
   void push(Object o) ↦ {if pos_F < size_F then
                              if pos_F ≥ 0 then
                                 pos_F' = pos_F + 1, pos_F' > 0, pos_F' ≤ size_F
                              else x_out = Ω(ArrayIndexOutOfBoundsException)
                           else x_out = Ω(StackError)} ∪{F_p = F'_p}
   void pop() ↦ {if pos_F > 0 then
                     pos_F' = pos_F - 1, pos_F' ≥ 0
                 else x_out = Ω(StackError)} ∪{F_p = F'_p}
}
```

Fig. 2. Abstraction of Stack

essentially reduces to give the stack size. Then, whenever the client calls a method m_i with an input value v, the corresponding approximation $c_{m_i}[x_{in}, x_F, x_{out}, x_{F'}]$ is fetched and instantiated with $x_{in} \mapsto v$ and $x_F \mapsto o.x_{F'}$ resulting in a new set of constraints $c'[x_{out}, x_{F'}]$. Eventually the return value for the client is obtained by keeping the value of x_{out}, hence $\overline{\delta}_{x_{out}}(c'[x_{out}, x_{F'}])$. Analogously the new o internal state is $o.x_{F'} = \overline{\delta}_{x_{F'}}(c'[x_{out}, x_{F'}])$.

Example 3 (Stack Overflow). Suppose that for a given instantiated stack s, $s.\text{size}_{F'} = 10$ and $s.\text{pos}_{F'} = 0$. Then the result of the method invocation $s.\text{push}(o)$ is $\overline{\delta}_{x_{F'}}(c_{push}[o, 10, 0, x_{out}, \text{size}_{F'}, \text{pos}_{F'}]) = \{\text{size}_{F'} = 10, \text{pos}_{F'} = 1\}$ and that of $s.\text{top}()$ is $\overline{\delta}_{x_{out}}(c_{top}[10, 0, x_{out}, \dots]) = \Omega(\text{ArrayIndexOutOfBounds-Exception})$, i.e. it raises an exception. □

5.3 Soundness

The soundness comes out from the following observation: the construction proposed in Def. 6 is essentially a program transformation, i.e. a meaning-preserving mapping defined on the program syntax [12]. In fact given a semantics for classes[5]

---

[5] Informally a class semantics is the set of all the possible instances of C. The semantics of an instance is the tree of all its possible method invocations. See also the proof sketch of Th. 2.

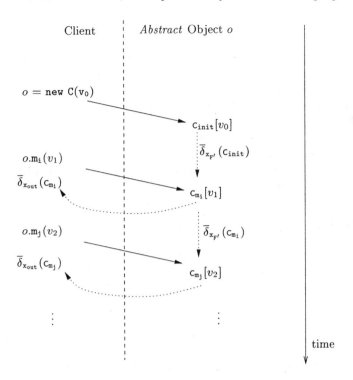

Fig. 3. A schema of a client using an instance of an abstract class C^a

$\mathcal{C}[\![\cdot]\!]$, the above definition is equivalent to saying that we have a program transformer t on the syntax and a concretization function γ such that the following diagram commutes:

$$\begin{array}{ccc} C^a & \xrightarrow{\text{Semantics}} & \mathcal{C}[\![C^a]\!] \\ t \uparrow & & \downarrow \gamma \\ C & \xrightarrow{\text{Semantics}} & \mathcal{C}\overset{\supseteq}{[\![}C]\!] \end{array}.$$

Differently stated, if we transform the class source and we take its semantics then we obtain an upper approximation of the original class semantics.

6 Second Abstraction: Automatic Discovery of Class Invariants

On the base of the abstract classes previously introduced, in this section we show how to automatically derive a class invariant. Intuitively a class invariant is a property that is true for each class instantiation, before and after each method invocation.

6.1 Applications

The use of a class invariant is twofold. The <u>first</u> one is for code generation: a compiler can produce an optimized code where some redundant checks are omitted preserving the semantics of the original. For example at line 26 the analysis proves that there is no need to check that pos is inside the array boundaries since it always is.

The <u>second</u> one is for verification. For example the running example code is not correct since in method top the programmer forgot to check if the stack is empty. This situation is pointed out by our analysis so that it can help to find out bugs in programs.

6.2 History-Insensitive Class Invariant

On the theoretical path of last sections, it is natural to think that if C has, for example, just two methods m_1 and m_2 and they are approximated by c_{m_1} and c_{m_2} then the property "c_{m_1} or c_{m_2}" is always true for each instance of C and for each calling context. Thus it is a class invariant. In this paper setting, it is formally expressed as: $I_C = \bar{\delta}_{x_{F'}}(c_{m_1}) \sqcup^c \bar{\delta}_{x_{F'}}(c_{m_2})$.

In general a class invariant can be obtained by gathering together all the method approximations of the object local environment. This is sound since the object fields can be accessed and modified only by class methods, so that we can state the:

Theorem 1 (History-Insensitive Class Invariant). *Let* $C = \langle \{f_j\}, \text{init}, \{m_i\} \rangle$ *be a class and* $C^a = \langle \{f_j^a\}, c_{\text{init}}, \{c_{m_i}\} \rangle$ *the corresponding abstract class. Then*

$$I_C = \bigsqcup_{m_i \in C}^{c} \bar{\delta}_{x_{F'}}(c_{m_i}) \tag{2}$$

is a class invariant for C. *Moreover each* I'_C *such that* $I_C \sqsubseteq^c I'_C$ *is a class invariant.*

Proof (Sketch). The proof relies on the definition of C semantics as the forest built in the following way:

- Each tree in the forest is a possible instantiation of class C;
- Each tree is built in the following way:
  - The root is the semantics of $\text{init}(v_0)$, i.e. $\mathcal{S}[\![\text{init}]\!](\{\langle x_{\text{in}} \mapsto v_0 \rangle\})$;
  - At depth $k+1$ for each method m_i in C and each possible actual parameter v_{k+1} there is a node $\mathcal{S}[\![m_i]\!](\{\langle x_{\text{in}} \mapsto v_{k+1}, x_F \mapsto x_{F'(k)} \rangle\})$ with $x_{F'(k)}$ being the values of object fields at parent node.

Theorem hypotheses guarantee that for each tree in the forest and for each level in the tree we have a correct approximation of its nodes. Therefore I_C soundness comes out from join ($\sqcup^c$) definition and property *(extensivity)* of $\bar{\delta}$. Nevertheless, the full proof takes into account the fact that the tree height in general is transfinite. □

We called (2) a history-insensitive class invariant since the method invocation history is not considered in method's analyses, as can be seen in the next example:

Example 4 (I-Class Invariant for Stack*).* If we apply (2) to the Stack example, we obtain:

$$I_{\texttt{Stack}} \sqsubseteq^c \{\texttt{pos}_{F'} = 0\} \sqcup^c \{0 < \texttt{pos}_{F'} \leq \texttt{size}_{F'}\} \sqcup^c \{0 \leq \texttt{pos}_{F'}\}$$
$$= \{0 \leq \texttt{pos}_{F'}\}$$

since isEmpty(), isFull() and top() do not modify the object fields. The $\sqsubseteq^c$ comes out from the fact that, for example purposes, we do not consider the value of stack.*Length* and that size is not modified after constructor invocation. The intuitive meaning of $I_{\texttt{Stack}}$ is that whatever method is invoked the field variable pos is positive. □

The invariant discovered in the last example immediately allows us to point out that at line 22 of Fig.1 there is a possible out of the bounds array access. The programmer did not provide any check for it, so that if the stack is empty (i.e. pos = 0) a runtime exception is thrown. However $I_{\texttt{Stack}}$ does not give any upper bound for the stack pointer value. Hence the code generated for lines 22 and 26 cannot be optimized by removing the check pos < stack.Length. In the next section we show how to obtain a more precise (but more expensive to compute) class invariant.

6.3 History-Sensitive Class Invariant

When carefully looking at (2) it is possible to realize that the result can be improved by exploiting the inter-relations between the different methods. Differently stated, if we proceed as in last section, we completely abstract away from the method invocation history. In particular (2) does not consider the fact that the first called method is the class constructor, that intuitively sets up the object local environment. So, in order to avoid this problem we propose an iterative algorithm to compute a class invariant.

The first step performs an approximation of the object internal state after the invocation of its constructor, i.e. $J^0 = \overline{\delta}_{x_{F'}}(\mathcal{S}[\![\texttt{init}]\!]^a(R_\top))$. After that (an approximation of) the method's semantics is computed with the input partially[6] specified by J^0, obtaining for each method a $J_i^1 = \mathcal{S}[\![\texttt{m}_i]\!]^a(J^0)$. Intuitively this can be justified as follows: after the object creation, the client invokes the method $\texttt{m}_j$. Thus, when the method returns it has changed the object internal state, that is now $\overline{\delta}_{x_{F'}}(J_i^1)$. Now, since we are performing a modular analysis, i.e. without considering the client context, we do not know which method is called. Equivalently, we can say that the invoked method is either the first one, or the second one, or the third, etc. In our framework this writes down as: $\bigsqcup^c_{\texttt{m}_i \in C} \overline{\delta}_{x_{F'}}(J_i^1)$.

---

[6] "Partially" since we make no hypotheses on the methods actual parameters: these will be captured by some constraint.

Eventually since we are interested in the class invariant, we must collect the effects (on the internal fields) of the first and the second step, obtaining:

$$J^1 = J^0 \sqcup^c \left(\bigsqcup_{m_i \in C}^c \overline{\delta}_{x_{F'}}(J_i^1) \right).$$

Then we can iterate, obtaining $J^2, J^3, \ldots$. It is immediate to see that this sequence is an increasing chain: $J^0 \sqsubseteq^c J^1 \sqsubseteq^c J^2 \ldots \sqsubseteq^c J^k \sqsubseteq^c J^{k+1} \ldots$. Moreover, in general it is possible that it is infinite, i.e. the analysis does not terminate. So, as usual in abstract interpretation, in order to force the convergence of the sequence (and hence of the analysis) we use a widening operator [8]. Informally a widening ∇^c is a kind of join for which every increasing sequence is stationary after a finite number of steps and that somehow *extrapolates* the sequence limit. Different widening designs are possible. Nevertheless, in this paper we adopt a strategy that consists in limiting the sequence of *exact* iterations to a given step n and then to replace the $\sqcup^c$ with ∇^c.

Theorem 2 (History-Sensitive Class Invariant). *Let* $C = \langle \{f_j\}, \text{init}, \{m_i\} \rangle$ *be a class,* $\gamma \in [\wp_{\text{fin}}(\text{Rel}) \to \wp(\text{Env})]$ *the concretization function that maps constraints to environments (and not traces as* γ_c*),* $S[\![\cdot]\!]^a \in [\text{Methods} \times \wp_{\text{fin}}(\text{Rel}) \to \wp_{\text{fin}}(\text{Rel})]$ *a semantic function satisfying:*

$$R_{\text{in}} \subseteq \gamma(c_{\text{in}}) \Rightarrow S[\![m_i]\!](R_{\text{in}}) \subseteq \gamma_c(S[\![m_i]\!]^a(c_{\text{in}}))$$

and n *a positive integer. Then the limit* J_C *of the sequence constructed as follows:*

$$\begin{aligned}
J^0 &= \overline{\delta}_{x_{F'}}(S[\![\text{init}]\!]^a(\top^c)) \\
J^{k+1} &= J^k \sqcup^c \bigsqcup_{m_i \in C}^c \overline{\delta}_{x_{F'}}(S[\![m_i]\!]^a(J^k)) &\quad \text{if } 0 \leq k < n \\
J^{k+1} &= J^k \nabla^c \bigsqcup_{m_i \in C}^c \overline{\delta}_{x_{F'}}(S[\![m_i]\!]^a(J^k)) &\quad \text{if } k \geq n
\end{aligned} \qquad (3)$$

exists and it is a class invariant.

Proof (Sketch). The convergence comes out from ∇^c definition. The invariant proof relies on the definitions of a class C semantics as in the proof sketch of Th. 2 and of the class invariant as the solution of the equation $J = \overline{\delta}_{x_{F'}}(S[\![\text{init}]\!](R_\top)) \sqcup \bigsqcup_{m_i \in C} \overline{\delta}_{x_{F'}}(S[\![m_i]\!](J))$. Then it is sufficient to show that J_C is an upper (hence safe) approximation of J: this is a consequence of $\gamma_c, \overline{\delta}, \sqcup^c$ and ∇^c properties. □

The presented method is more precise but also more expensive as a further fixpoint computation is introduced: in addition to the local fixpoint computations (the ones for the $S[\![m_i]\!]^a$) there is the big, external one of (3). Nevertheless the results are very good. In fact in the next example, 6 iterations are sufficient to compute J_{Stack}, the stack invariant.

Example 5 (J-Class Invariant for Stack*).* Applying the iteration strategy of (3) with $n = 4$, it is possible to discover the following class invariant for the Stack:

$$J_{\texttt{Stack}} = \{1 \leq \texttt{size}_{F'}, 0 \leq \texttt{pos}_{F'} \leq \texttt{size}_{F'}\}.$$

It is worth noting as by this second method we are able to discover the class invariant pos $\leq$ size and to produce the code annotations of Fig. 1. □

6.4 On Comparing the I_C and J_C Invariants

We have pointed out, and we illustrated with an example, that the history-sensitive class invariant is more precise than the history insensitive one. So why not always use the second one? The reason is the cost, both in time and memory.

In fact it is clear that in general, in order to compute J_C we need more iterations than for I_C and in certain cases this computation may be so expensive to make the analysis in practice infeasible. So, in our opinion, the choice between the two must be made by carefully looking at the precision/cost trade-off. We consider some heuristics for two typical scenarios:

The first scenario is during code development. At this stage a tool that helps the programmer to quickly find source(s) of (potential) bugs is welcome. However such a tool is required to run in a reasonable amount of time. Thus the use of an invariant computation based on the history-insensitive method makes sense. For example, a tool adopting such a strategy can indicate at early stages of program developing the missing check at line 22.

The second scenario is at code shipping time. Suppose that the code exiting from the development cycle is ready to be shipped. At this stage the cost of a long but precise analysis can be afforded. This because a precise analysis is useful

- to prove that the code is correct, e.g. it contains no run-time errors, all the exception raised are caught, etc. and
- to optimize the compiled code, e.g. removing superfluous checks, statically resolving the virtual methods calls, etc.

Therefore in this second scenario it is reasonable to think of a tool computing a J_C-style class invariant.

7 Conclusions and Future Work

In this paper we showed how to perform a class-level modular analysis for object oriented languages. We presented two successive abstractions:

- The first one is a program transformation that given a class C, allows the construction of a transformed version C^a to be used for client conformance testing or for class documentation;
- The second one is the automatic discovery of class invariant to be used either for verification or as support for an optimizing compiler.

It is worth noting that the two techniques are fully automatic: they do not require any code-annotation [29] or any interaction with a theorem prover, e.g. in [17]. Moreover the results are sound, i.e. if the analysis reports no errors then the program is correct (unlike [14, 15]).

For the future we plan to extend this work to inheritance. It is easy to see that with a naive understanding of inheritance as a *cut-and-paste* in which the source code from the super-class is carefully[7] copied into the subclass the paper results immediately apply. However this approach is unsatisfactory because for real-world size class hierarchies the *expanded* class can be really huge, causing a big impact on the analysis performances. Therefore, having a class C, its invariant Y_C and a subclass D our goal will be to derive an invariant Y_D for D without seeing the code for C, i.e. by just using the pre-computed invariant and the D code. The the first step toward our goal is to use a more *semantic* characterization of inheritance in the style of [7, 5].

Another direction for further development is on the analyzed properties: in this work we have only considered sets of relations between the method inputs/outputs. But what happens if we consider non-relational properties? The paper results still apply provided that the method actual parameters are given the value ⊤, i.e. "absence of information".

Acknowledgments

We wish to thank Patrick and Radhia Cousot, Jérôme Feret, Charles Hymans and Xavier Rival for their comments on an early draft of this paper.

References

1. M. Abadi and L. Cardelli. *A Theory of Objects*. Springer-Verlag, New York, 1996.
2. A. Aggarwal and K.H. Randall. Related field analysis. In *ACM SIGPLAN Conference on Programming Language Design and Implementation (PLDI'01)*. ACM, June 2001.
3. M. Atkinson, F. Bancilhon, D. DeWitt, K. Dittrich, D. Maier, and S. Zdonik. The object-oriented database system manifesto. In *Proceedings of the First International Conference on Deductive and Object-Oriented Databases (DOOD '89)*, pages 223–240, Kyoto, Japan, 1989.
4. B. Blanchet. Escape analysis for object oriented languages. Application to Java. In *14th ACM Conference on Object-Oriented Programming, Systems, Languages and Applications (OOPSLA'99)*, pages 20–34, Denver, Colorado, November 1999.
5. L. Cardelli. A semantics of multiple inheritance. In G. Kahn, D. MacQueen, and G. Plotkin, editors, *Semantics of Data Types*, volume 173 of *Lecture Notes in Computer Science*, pages 51–67. Springer-Verlag, 1984. Full version in *Information and Computation*, 76(2/3): 138–164, 1988.
6. R. Chatterjee, B.G. Ryder, and W.A. Landi. Relevant context inference. In *26th ACM Symposium on Principles of Programming Languages (POPL'99)*, ACM SIGPLAN Notices, pages 133–146, New York, NY, USA, 1999. ACM Press.

---

[7] "Carefully" since the redefined methods are renamed, the occurrences of **super** are replaced by **this**, etc. More details can be found in Sect. 6.4 of [23].

7. W. Cook and J. Palsberg. A denotational semantics of inheritance and its correctness. *Information and Computation*, 114(2): 329–350, 1 November 1994.
8. P. Cousot and R. Cousot. Abstract interpretation: a unified lattice model for static analysis of programs by construction or approximation of fixpoints. In *4th ACM SIGPLAN-SIGACT Symposium on Principles of Programming Languages (POPL'77)*, pages 238–252, Los Angeles, California, 1977. ACM Press, New York, NY.
9. P. Cousot and R. Cousot. Relational abstract interpretation of higher-order functional programs. JTASPEFL'91, Bordeaux. *BIGRE*, 74:33–36, October 1991.
10. P. Cousot and R. Cousot. Abstract interpretation frameworks. *Journal of Logic and Computation*, 2(4):511–547, 1992.
11. P. Cousot and R. Cousot. Modular static program analysis, invited paper. In R.N. Horspool, editor, *Proceedings of the Eleventh International Conference on Compiler Construction (CC 2002)*, pages 159–178, Grenoble, France, April 6—14 2002. LNCS 2304, Springer, Berlin.
12. P. Cousot and R. Cousot. Systematic design of program transformation frameworks by abstract interpretation. In *29th ACM SIGPLAN-SIGACT Symposium on Principles of Programming Languages (POPL 2002)*, pages 178–190, Portland, Oregon, January 2002. ACM Press, New York, NY.
13. P. Cousot and N. Halbwachs. Automatic discovery of linear restraints among variables of a program. In *5th ACM SIGPLAN-SIGACT Symposium on Principles of Programming Languages (POPL'78)*, pages 84–97, Tucson, Arizona, 1978. ACM Press, New York, NY.
14. D.L. Detlefs, K. Rustan, M. Leino, G. Nelson, and Saxe J.B. Extended static checking. Research Report #159, Compaq Systems Research Center, Palo Alto, USA, December 1998.
15. M. Ernst. *Dynamically Discovering Likely Program Invariants*. PhD thesis, University of Washington Department of Computer Science and Engineering, 2002.
16. M. Handjieva and S. Tzolovski. Refining static analyses by trace-based partitioning using control flow. In *Proceedings of the Static Analysis Symposium (SAS'98)*, volume 1503 of *Lectures Notes in Computer Science*, pages 200–215, 1998.
17. M. Huisman, B. Jacobs, and J. van den Berg. A case study in class library verification: Java's vector class. In A. Moreira and D. Demeyer, editors, *Object-Oriented Technology: ECOOP'99 Workshop Reader*, volume 1743 of *Lecture Notes in Computer Science*, pages 109–110, Lisbon, Portugal, June 1999. Springer-Verlag.
18. T. Jensen and F. Spoto. Class analysis of object-oriented programs through abstract interpretation. In F. Honsell and M. Miculan, editors, *Proceedings of the FOSSACS 2001 Conference*, volume 2030 of *Lecture Notes in Computer Science*, pages 261–275, Genova, Italy, April 2001. Springer-Verlag.
19. G.T. Leavens, A.L. Baker, and C. Ruby. *Preliminary Design of JML: A Behavioral Interface Specification Language for Java*, October 2002. www.cs.iastate.edu/~leavens/JML/prelimdesign/prelimdesign_toc.html.
20. T. Lindholm and F. Yellin. *The Java Virtual Machine Specification*. The Java Series. Addison Wesley Longman, Inc., 2nd edition, April 1999.
21. L. Mauborgne. Abstract interpretation using typed decision graphs. *Science of Computer Programming*, 31(1):91–112, May 1998.
22. Microsoft. *Microsoft C# Language Specifications*. Microsoft Press, 2001.
23. J. Palsberg and M.I. Schwartzbach. *Object-Oriented Type Systems*. John Wiley & Sons, Chichester, 1994.

24. I. Pollet, B. Le Charlier, and A. Cortesi. Distinctness and sharing domains for static analysis of Java programs. In *Proceedings of ECOOP '01*, volume 2072 of *Lectures Notes in Computer Science*, pages 77–98. Springer-Verlag, 2001.
25. C. Probst. Modular control flow analysis for libraries. In *Proceedings of the Static Analysys Symposium (SAS 2002)*, volume 2477, pages 165–179. Springer-Verlag, 2002.
26. G. Ramalingam, A. Warshavsky, J. Field, D. Goyal, and M. Sagiv. Deriving specialized program analyses for certifying component-client conformance. In *ACM SIGPLAN 2002 Conference on Programming Language Design and Implementation (PLDI 2002)*, volume 37, 5 of *ACM SIGPLAN Notices*, pages 83–94, New York, June 17–19 2002. ACM Press.
27. A. Rountev, A. Milanova, and B.G. Ryder. Points-to analysis for Java using annotated constraints. In *16th ACM Conference on Object Oriented Programming, Systems, Languages and Applications (OOPSLA'01)*, pages 43–55. ACM, November 2001.
28. J. Rumbaugh, I. Jacobson, and G. Booch. *The Unified Modeling Language Reference Manual*. Addison-Wesley, Reading, Massachusetts, USA, 1st edition, 1999.
29. S. Khurshid, D. Marinov, and D. Jackson. An analyzable annotation language. In *17th ACM Conference on Object-Oriented Programming, Systems, Languages, and Applications (OOPSLA 2002)*, November 2002.
30. Sun Microsystem, Inc. *javadoc Tool Home Page*, 2002. http://java.sun.com/j2se/javadoc/.
31. K. Zee and M. Rinard. Write barrier removal by static analysis. In *17th Annual ACM Conference on Object-Oriented Programming, Systems, Languages and Applications (OOPSLA 2002)*. ACM, 2002.

Checking Interference with Fractional Permissions[*]

John Boyland[**]

University of Wisconsin-Milwaukee, USA
boyland@cs.uwm.edu

Abstract. We describe a type system for checking interference using the concept of linear capabilities (which we call "permissions"). Our innovations include the concept of "fractional" permissions: reads can be permitted with fractional permissions whereas writes require complete permissions. This distinction expresses the fact that reads on the same state do not conflict with each other. One may give shared read access at one point while still retaining write permission afterwards. We give an operational semantics of a simple imperative language with structured parallelism and prove that the permission system enables parallelism to proceed with deterministic results.

1 Introduction

In this paper we describe a new way to check effects on mutable state (reads and writes) in imperative code for the purpose of determining when two segments of code are non-interfering. This information can be used by a compiler for scheduling purposes, or by a refactoring tool when reordering code. Analysis is made modular by having an effects specification for each procedure. Thus two tasks must be performed: checking that a procedure meets its effect specification; and the original task—checking interference for two statements.

Previous work suggests two different models:

Effect-Based. In this model, one infers effects for statements. Effects inference has been studied extensively for functional languages [1, 2]. For a modular analysis, inferred effects for a procedure body are then checked against the declared effects. Interference is checked by comparing inferred effects. Each statement is type-checked in context Γ and produces a set of effects φ. For interference checking, a side condition $\varphi_1 \# \varphi_2$ is used to check that if there is a write in one set of effects, the other set includes no reads or writes on the same state:

$$\frac{\Gamma \vdash s_1 \,!\, \varphi_1 \quad \Gamma \vdash s_2 \,!\, \varphi_2 \quad \varphi_1 \# \varphi_2}{\Gamma \vdash s_1 \text{ does not interfere with } s_2}$$

---

[*] This material is based upon work supported by the National Science Foundation under Grant No. 9984681
[**] The author wishes to acknowledge support through the High Dependability Computing Program from NASA Ames cooperative agreement NCC-2-1298.

See for example Reynolds syntactic control of interference [3], our earlier work [4] or Clarke and Drossopoulou's JOE [5].

Permission-Based. In this model, one checks a statement to see if it can be executed under a given set of permissions. (For example, consider the lock checking of Flanagan and Abadi [6], or Boyapati et al [7, 8].) A procedure is checked by determining whether the body can be typed using the declared effects (viewed as permissions). To determine if two statements can be executed in interleaved fashion, we see if the set of permissions can be partitioned into two sets, one for each statement:

$$\frac{\Pi_1 \vdash s_1 \qquad \Pi_2 \vdash s_2}{\Pi_1, \Pi_2 \vdash s_1 \text{ does not interfere with } s_2}$$

The permissions are treated as *linear* keys: they cannot be duplicated, or discarded. See for example Walker, Crary and Morrisett's capability system [9], Ishtiaq and O'Hearn's use of "bunched implication" (BI) logic [10], or Reynolds' "separation logic" [11, 12].

These two models are almost duals of each other (especially when the typing rules given above are seen simply as relations) but the practical difference between checking effect conflict $\varphi_1 \# \varphi_2$ and splitting of permissions Π_1, Π_2 causes the two approaches to be incomparable.

1.1 Problems with Effects and Permissions

Our earlier work [4] used an effect-based system: effects inferred for a method body were checked against the method's declared effects and two statement effects were compared to see if they conflict or not. When effects were compared, we needed the answer to an aliasing question to determine if there was overlap and hence conflict. Consider the following two compound statements:

```
{ ...; *x = 10; ... }      { ...; *y = 42; ... }
```

In order to determine whether these statements interfere, we need to know whether x could be the same as y. More precisely, we need to know if the set of cells that x could point to at the point that the assignment *x = 10 occurs, could overlap the set of cells that y could point to at the second assignment. We call this kind of question a "MayEqual" question [13]. One simple way to answer the question conservatively is to use the fact that objects of different type cannot be aliases of each other. This approach is used by Clarke and Drossopoulou where the addition of ownership parameterization allows for fine type distinctions. But any less conservative analysis, such as a Steensgaard's "Points-To" analysis [14], will need to examine the code. In fact, to do a good job at MayEqual, one needs to know about data dependencies, in particular, about effects. Thus we are left with the unsatisfying result that the inferred effects do not in themselves include enough information to perform the interference checking; we must combine the effects analysis with an alias analysis.

An alternate technique is to use permissions. Each individual permission applies to a single part of the store and thus the mere existence of two separate (write) permissions ensures that they do not refer to the same area of storage. In order to handle allocation and deallocation which manufacture and consume permissions respectively, we check statements with an input and output set of permissions: $\Pi \vdash s \Rightarrow \Pi'$ means that s can be executed given permissions Π after which permissions Π' are available.

A problem that arises is how to distinguish reads (which do not conflict with each other) from writes (which conflict with each other and with reads). For example, Reynolds' separation logic [12] (unlike his earlier work [3]) does not permit one to separate two side-effecting computations that read the same state. Two different solutions have been used in previous work:

- Permit a linear key (giving write permission) to be coerced into a nonlinear key, which then permits only reads from this point forward. (This approach is possible using subtyping in the calculus of capabilities [9].)
- Permit a linear key to be treated non-linearly in a bounded context. Wadler's **let!** construct [15] permits a linear variable to be used nonlinearly by code that only needs read access. SCIR [16] permits a linear key to be moved into a non-linear section while type checking a statement that only needs read permission. The calculus of capabilities uses bounded quantification to pass a unique region to a function that can use any kind of region.

In the first case, we irrevocably lose the permission to write. In the second case, it is restored after the section needing read-only access is done. This "amplification" is sound as long as the context needing read permissions is not able to retain this permission for later use. For instance **let!** forbids the code using the variable nonlinearly from (among other things) returning a function, since a reference could be hidden in the closure. The calculus of capabilities does not permit a closure to hold capabilities at all. Neither does it permit a capability variable to be used wherever its bound can be used. Assuming r^+ is a duplicable capability, the calculus permits the contraction rule on the left, but not the right:

$$\frac{r^+, r^+, \Pi \vdash s \Rightarrow \Pi'}{r^+, \Pi \vdash s \Rightarrow \Pi'} \text{ OK} \qquad \frac{\epsilon \leq r^+ \quad \epsilon, r^+, \Pi \vdash s \Rightarrow \Pi'}{\epsilon, \Pi \vdash s \Rightarrow \Pi'} \text{ NotOk}$$

A system that permits a linear capability to be treated non-linearly will need to use some rules that are at the surface-level, unmotivated. The problem is (speaking roughly) that if a permission is arbitrarily duplicable, then there is no way to determine if one has all the copies.

One is left with the unpalatable choice between conservatively surrendering write permission irrevocably, and conservatively restricting the type system.

1.2 Fractional Permissions

Our solution to this dilemma is to avoid non-linearity: read permissions are not duplicable. The major innovation of this paper is to show how one can manufacture arbitrarily many read permissions without copying a permission: we *split* permissions. Each piece has a definite fraction and thus we can determine if all the pieces have been recovered and reconstruct the whole permission. This property is enabled by adding a single substructural rule:

$$\pi \equiv \varepsilon\pi, (1-\varepsilon)\pi$$

where ε is some fraction between zero and one (exclusive) and π is a permission.[1]

This solution gives a simple explanation of why writes conflict with reads and writes, but that reads do not conflict with each other: two pieces can co-exist but one cannot have the whole thing at the same time as another piece of it.

Consider a procedure requiring read permission to a cell and returning this read permission as well as read permission to some unknown cell. We don't have a "contraction" rule in this system and thus cannot take a read permission and convert it into two read permissions that are identical to the first. Instead if one wants to get two read permissions from one, one needs to split it into smaller permissions. Thus if the second result returned by the procedure is an alias of the parameter, it will be unable to return the entire read permission of the parameter; it will have to return a smaller fraction (which will at least appear as a *different* fraction than was delivered to the procedure). Even if the caller had write permission to the parameter before the call, afterwards, it will not be possible to reassemble an (unsafe) write permission.

On the other hand, if the second returned permission is *not* an alias of the parameter, it will be possible to return the same read permission that was passed, and the caller will be able to reassemble a write permission.

1.3 Contributions

The contribution of this work are as follows:

- We provide a way to check read-write effects with permissions—there is no need for a MayEqual analysis.
- We provide a new substructural rule for permissions-like systems to enable sharing of read-only state without needing to include non-linear permissions.
- We provide a way for a writable key to be temporarily made read-only while still being able to track all the copies, thus preventing unsoundness if a read permission is retained in some way.
- We present the idea in a simple language with aliasing, procedures and parallel computations. We give an operational semantics and define a permission type system (including simple existential return values) and prove soundness.
- We prove that checkable parallel constructs do not interfere: execution leads to deterministic results.

---

[1] In this paper, we define a fraction to be a real number. The proofs would also all work with rational fractions, or fractions with powers of two as denominators. Other non-numeric encodings are possible, with suitable changes to definitions and proofs.

Section 2 describes the simple language, gives an operational semantics and a permission type system. Then we prove the main result: that the type system ensures non-interference. The following section describes a variety of extensions made possible using fractional permissions. Section 4 reviews related work.

2 Types and Permissions

This section first describes the operational semantics of a simple language with pointers to cells containing integers. Then it describes the permission type system that can be used to check non-interference. We prove that this check of non-interference permits the execution of two pieces of code to be interleaved.[2]

2.1 Operational Semantics

The language used to demonstrate the permissions system is a simple language where source level global variables may point to allocated cells which hold integers. We have a (finite) set of variables V, an infinite set of (cell) locations[3] L and a set of memories (stores) M which map variables to locations and some (finite subset of) locations to integers ($\mathbb{Z}$):

source vars $\qquad v \in V$
locations $\qquad\quad l \in L$
memory $\qquad (\mu_V, \mu_L) = \mu \in M = (V \to L) \times (L \rightharpoonup \mathbb{Z})$ where $\mathrm{Dom}\,\mu_L \supseteq \mu_V(V)$

where $\rightharpoonup$ denotes a partial finite function. The side condition ensures that a memory does not have dangling pointers (here $\mu_V(V) = \{\mu_V\, v \mid v \in V\}$). We permit μ to apply directly to variables and locations. Thus if $\mu = (\mu_V, \mu_L)$ then $\mu(\mu\, v)$ is short for $\mu_L(\mu_V\, v)$. The notation $\mu[v \mapsto l]$ updates the pointer stored in a variable and $\mu[l \mapsto i]$ updates the integer stored in a cell. We write $\mu_1 \sim \mu_2$ to mean that two memories are isomorphic.

A program consists of a (finite) set of procedures. Each procedure has a statement for its body, and thus a program is represented by a map from each procedure to a statement. (For simplicity, there are no local variables.)

procedures $p \in P$
programs $\;\; g \in G = P \to S$

One can allocate a cell, copy pointers or update cell contents. We have sequential (;) and parallel (||) composition, as well as conditionals and procedure calls:

statements $S \ni s ::= v\!:=\!\mathtt{new} \mid v\!:=\!v' \mid *v\!:=\!e \mid \mathtt{skip}$
$\qquad\qquad\qquad\;\; \mid\; s\,;\,s' \mid s \mid\mid s' \mid \mathtt{if}\,b\,\mathtt{then}\,s\,\mathtt{else}\,s' \mid \mathtt{call}\,p$

---

[2] This paper has a separate appendix which contains the lemmas and proofs. URL: http://www.cs.uwm.edu/faculty/boyland/papers/permissions-appendix.ps
[3] In this paper, we do not model the possibility of running out of heap storage.

Integer expressions include literals, additions and dereferencing of variables. Boolean expressions permit pointer comparison or comparison with zero.

$$\text{integer expressions } e ::= n \mid e\texttt{+}e \mid \texttt{*}v$$
$$\text{boolean expressions } b ::= \texttt{true} \mid \texttt{false} \mid v\texttt{==}v' \mid e\texttt{!=0}$$

Figure 1 gives a small-step semantics for statements and expressions. A pair $\langle \mu, x \rangle$ where μ is a memory and x is a statement, an integer expression or a boolean expression is rewritten as a new pair for one step of evaluation. The rewriting for statements is subscripted with a program g because statements may include procedure calls and a program maps procedure names to bodies.

The evaluation of new statements stores 0 into the cell to prevent a dangling pointer. None of the other rules can introduce dangling pointers either. The evaluation of parallel compositions is nondeterministic: either branch may be evaluated one step further. The parallel composition can be eliminated once both branches are done. The lack of dangling pointers means that evaluation cannot get stuck.

Example. Two different runs of the same parallel composition may yield different results. Consider the example in Fig. 2. If we evaluate it in a memory where v4 points to the same cell as v1 or v2, nondeterminism could lead to different results. For example, consider $\mu(\texttt{v1}) = \mu(\texttt{v4}) = l_1$, $\mu(\texttt{v2}) = \mu(\texttt{v3}) = l_2$, $\mu(l_1) = \mu(l_2) = 1$. If the left part is fully evaluated before the right, then at the end *v1 will be 4. If the right part is fully evaluated before the left, the end result of *v1 will be 1. However, in other memories, nondeterminism in execution leads to the same result. For instance, if all of the variables point to different cells, then the execution of the two parts can be interleaved arbitrarily without affecting the final result.

If we use an effect system to check interference, it first notices that neither part writes a variable the other reads (a simple matter of matching names), and thus the two parts only interfere if MayEqual($\texttt{v1}_1, \texttt{v3}_2$) ∨ MayEqual($\texttt{v1}_1, \texttt{v2}_2$) ∨ MayEqual($\texttt{v2}_1, \texttt{v3}_2$) where the subscripts refer to the occurrences of the variables. A precise answer will require an alias analysis smart enough to determine that $\texttt{v3}_2 = \texttt{v4}_1$ and such. An effect system simply does not provide sufficient information on its own to determine interference. Reynolds' original syntactic control of interference has the same difficulty with this example.

On the other hand, BI-logic or separation logic will fail to determine noninterference since both parts need to access the cell pointed to by v2. These logics do not distinguish shared reading from shared writing, and thus cannot determine that the sharing in this case is safe. (The sharing of v4 is non-problematic since only the heap is partitioned.)

O'Hearn et al's SCIR *can* handle this example by temporarily making v4 and *v2 read-only, but this solution is not sound in the presense of existentials as seen in the discussion of Fig. 5.

If one were to define noninterference using the Walker et al's capability system (not its intended purpose), one encounters a problem with *v2. If the permission

$$\frac{l \notin \mathrm{Dom}\,\mu_L}{\langle \mu, v\mathtt{:=new} \rangle \to_g \langle \mu[v \mapsto l, l \mapsto 0], \mathtt{skip} \rangle} \qquad \langle \mu, v\mathtt{:=}v' \rangle \to_g \langle \mu[v \mapsto \mu\,v'], \mathtt{skip} \rangle$$

$$\frac{\langle \mu, e \rangle \to \langle \mu, e' \rangle}{\langle \mu, \mathtt{*}v\mathtt{:=}e \rangle \to_g \langle \mu, \mathtt{*}v\mathtt{:=}e' \rangle} \qquad \langle \mu, \mathtt{*}v\mathtt{:=}i \rangle \to_g \langle \mu[\mu\,v \mapsto i], \mathtt{skip} \rangle$$

$$\frac{\langle \mu, s_1 \rangle \to_g \langle \mu', s_1' \rangle}{\langle \mu, s_1; s_2 \rangle \to_g \langle \mu', s_1'; s_2 \rangle} \qquad \langle \mu, \mathtt{skip}; s \rangle \to_g \langle \mu, s \rangle \qquad \frac{\langle \mu, s_1 \rangle \to_g \langle \mu', s_1' \rangle}{\langle \mu, s_1 || s_2 \rangle \to_g \langle \mu', s_1' || s_2 \rangle}$$

$$\frac{\langle \mu, s_2 \rangle \to_g \langle \mu', s_2' \rangle}{\langle \mu, s_1 || s_2 \rangle \to_g \langle \mu', s_1 || s_2' \rangle} \qquad \langle \mu, \mathtt{skip} || \mathtt{skip} \rangle \to_g \langle \mu, \mathtt{skip} \rangle$$

$$\langle \mu, \mathtt{if\ true\ then}\ s_1\ \mathtt{else}\ s_2 \rangle \to_g \langle \mu, s_1 \rangle$$

$$\langle \mu, \mathtt{if\ false\ then}\ s_1\ \mathtt{else}\ s_2 \rangle \to_g \langle \mu, s_2 \rangle$$

$$\frac{\langle \mu, b \rangle \to \langle \mu, b' \rangle}{\langle \mu, \mathtt{if}\ b\ \mathtt{then}\ s_1\ \mathtt{else}\ s_2 \rangle \to_g \langle \mu, \mathtt{if}\ b'\ \mathtt{then}\ s_1\ \mathtt{else}\ s_2 \rangle}$$

$$\langle \mu, \mathtt{call}\ p \rangle \to_g \langle \mu, g\,p \rangle \qquad \frac{\langle \mu, e_1 \rangle \to \langle \mu, e_1' \rangle}{\langle \mu, e_1\mathtt{+}e_2 \rangle \to \langle \mu, e_1'\mathtt{+}e_2 \rangle} \qquad \frac{\langle \mu, e_2 \rangle \to \langle \mu, e_2' \rangle}{\langle \mu, n_1\mathtt{+}e_2 \rangle \to \langle \mu, n_1\mathtt{+}e_2' \rangle}$$

$$\langle \mu, n_1\mathtt{+}n_2 \rangle \to \langle \mu, n_1 + n_2 \rangle \qquad \langle \mu, \mathtt{*}v \rangle \to \langle \mu, \mu(\mu\,v) \rangle \qquad \langle \mu, v\mathtt{==}v' \rangle \to \langle \mu, \mu\,v = \mu\,v' \rangle$$

$$\frac{\langle \mu, e \rangle \to \langle \mu, e' \rangle}{\langle \mu, e\mathtt{!=0} \rangle \to \langle \mu, e'\mathtt{!=0} \rangle} \qquad \langle \mu, i\mathtt{!=0} \rangle \to \langle \mu, i \neq 0 \rangle$$

Fig. 1. Evaluation

```
(*v1 := *v2; v1 := v4)  ||  (v3 := v4; *v3 := 3+*v2)
```

Fig. 2. Example program

to read this value is represented by a duplicable capability r^+, then there is no difficulty, but then write permission to *v2 can never be recovered. On the other hand, if we have write permission in the form of a unique capability r^1, it does not seem to be possible to check noninterference in the example here without irreversibly downgrading this permission. One can prove $r^1 < \{r^+, r^+\}$ and use this with bounded quantification, but a capability such as ϵ cannot be split into two pieces, even if we know $\epsilon < \{r^+, r^+\}$, without destroying it. A split (similar to what occurs in SCIR) would result in unsoundness because the capability system has existential return types (in the guise of polymorphic continuations).

In the following section, we define a permission type system that can handle such examples. Well-typed statements always have deterministic results.

2.2 Permission Types

We follow Smith, Walker and Morrisett [17] in using a singleton type ptr(ρ) to type pointer variables containing the pointer to location ρ. (The permission type system uses location variables in all places rather than actual locations.)

$$\text{location var } \rho \in R$$

We have two kinds of base permissions: one to permit reading/writing of a source-level variable v (and also to give its type) and one to permit reading/writing the integer in a cell:

$$\text{base permission } \beta ::= v : \text{ptr}(\rho) \mid \rho$$

We do not use fraction constants, but make use of fraction variables which represent some fraction between zero and one, exclusive:

$$\text{fraction var } z \in Z$$

Base permissions can be "multiplied" by fractions. Syntactically we distinguish between fractions that may be complete (ξ) from ones that are strictly between zero and one (ε).

$$\begin{array}{lll} \text{permission} & \pi & ::= \xi\beta \\ \text{fraction} & \xi & ::= 1 \mid \varepsilon \\ \text{partial fraction } \mathcal{E} \ni \varepsilon & ::= z \mid 1 - \varepsilon \mid \varepsilon\varepsilon \end{array}$$

A complete fraction permits writing (as well as reading), but a partial fraction permits only reading.

A statement is permission-checked in an environment E consisting of a set Δ of free location and fraction variables, and a "set" of permissions Π:

$$\begin{array}{ll} \text{environment } E ::= \Delta; \Pi \\ \text{context} & \Delta \subseteq R \cup Z \\ \text{permissions } \Pi ::= \cdot \mid \pi \mid \Pi, \Pi \end{array}$$

We have three simple sub-structural rules on permission "sets":

$$\cdot, \Pi \equiv \Pi$$
$$\Pi_1, \Pi_2 \equiv \Pi_2, \Pi_1$$
$$\Pi_1, (\Pi_2, \Pi_3) \equiv (\Pi_1, \Pi_2), \Pi_3$$

We have the permission splitting operation on a complete environment only to ensure we don't split a permission using an unbound variable:

$$\frac{\Delta \vdash \varepsilon \text{ frac}}{\Delta; \varepsilon\pi, (1-\varepsilon)\pi, \Pi \equiv \Delta; \pi, \Pi}$$

where we define $\varepsilon(\xi\beta) = (\varepsilon\xi)\beta$ with $\varepsilon 1 = \varepsilon$. We also have rules for fractions:

$$\varepsilon\varepsilon' \equiv \varepsilon'\varepsilon$$
$$\varepsilon(\varepsilon'\varepsilon'') \equiv (\varepsilon\varepsilon')\varepsilon''$$
$$(1 - (1 - \varepsilon)) \equiv \varepsilon$$

A procedure accepts a "set" of permissions and returns a "set" of permissions. It is polymorphic in a type context (the $\forall$ scopes over the whole type) and returns existentially bound permissions. The program type maps procedures to types:

$$\text{procedure type } A \ni \alpha ::= \forall \Delta.\Pi \to \exists \Delta.\Pi$$
$$\text{program type } \omega \in \Omega = P \to A$$

When we perform a call, we need to substitute actual partial fractions for fraction variables and actual location variables for location variables:

$$\text{substitution } \sigma \in \Sigma = (R \to R) \times (Z \to \mathcal{E})$$

As with μ, we permit the pair to apply to either kind of variable, and we say $\text{Dom}(\sigma_R, \sigma_Z) = \text{Dom}\,\sigma_R \cup \text{Dom}\,\sigma_Z$. Application is extended to permissions and fractions, and to variables not in the domain:

$$\sigma\rho = \rho \text{ if } \rho \notin \text{Dom}\,\sigma_R \qquad \sigma z = z \text{ if } z \notin \text{Dom}\,\sigma_Z \qquad \sigma 1 = 1$$

$$\sigma(1 - \varepsilon) = 1 - \sigma\varepsilon \qquad \sigma(\varepsilon\varepsilon') = (\sigma\varepsilon)(\sigma\varepsilon') \qquad \sigma \cdot = \cdot$$

$$\sigma(v : \text{ptr}(\rho)) = v : \text{ptr}(\sigma\rho) \qquad \sigma\,\xi\beta = (\sigma\,\xi)(\sigma\,\beta) \qquad \sigma(\Pi,\Pi') = \sigma\Pi,\sigma\Pi'$$

Fig. 3 gives the rules for well-formedness of the various syntactic entities with respect to a set of location and fraction variables. Essentially well-formedness merely checks whether all variables are bound. Well-formedness of a substitution checks that the variables in the domain context are mapped to well-formed entities in the range context. Using this definition we extend substitution to complete environments: if $\vdash \sigma : \Delta \to \Delta'$ then $\sigma(\Delta''; \Pi'') = (\Delta' \cup (\Delta'' - \Delta); \sigma\Pi'')$.

Figure 4 gives the rules for permission-checking a program. Allocating a cell (NEW) requires write permission on the variable and gets write permission on the new cell. The singleton types for variables permit the system to keep track of aliasing in the COPY rule. The permissions are "threaded" through both parts of a sequential composition but are split into two for a parallel composition and then recombined.

For if statements, the environment is sent to both branches and the resulting permissions may be different. Linearity prevents discarding permissions and thus there must exist two substitutions σ_1 and σ_2 that can be used to represent each branch's result as an instance of the unified result. At a call, we need two substitutions: one to determine what the actual locations and fractions will be and another to rename the existentially bound resulting variables. Permissions that are not needed in a procedure around the call are preserved. The corresponding rule PROC checks that it is possible to witness the existential variables.

$$\frac{\rho \in \Delta}{\Delta \vdash \rho \text{ loc-var}} \quad \frac{v \in V \quad \Delta \vdash \rho \text{ loc-var}}{\Delta \vdash v : \text{ptr}(\rho) \text{ base-perm}} \quad \frac{\Delta \vdash \rho \text{ loc-var}}{\Delta \vdash \rho \text{ base-perm}} \quad \frac{z \in \Delta}{\Delta \vdash z \text{ frac}}$$

$$\frac{}{\Delta \vdash 1 \text{ frac}} \quad \frac{\Delta \vdash \varepsilon \text{ frac} \quad \Delta \vdash \varepsilon' \text{ frac}}{\Delta \vdash \varepsilon\varepsilon' \text{ frac}} \quad \frac{\Delta \vdash \varepsilon \text{ frac}}{\Delta \vdash 1 - \varepsilon \text{ frac}}$$

$$\frac{\Delta \vdash e \text{ frac} \quad \Delta \vdash \beta \text{ base-perm}}{\Delta \vdash e\beta \text{ perms}} \quad \frac{}{\Delta \vdash \cdot \text{ perms}}$$

$$\frac{\Delta \vdash \Pi_1 \text{ perms} \quad \Delta \vdash \Pi_2 \text{ perms}}{\Delta \vdash \Pi_1, \Pi_2 \text{ perms}}$$

$$\frac{\Delta \vdash \Pi \text{ perms} \quad \Delta \cap \Delta' = \emptyset \quad \Delta, \Delta' \vdash \Pi' \text{ perms}}{\vdash \forall \Delta.\Pi \rightarrow \exists \Delta'.\Pi' \text{ proc-type}} \quad \frac{\text{For all } p \in P, \vdash \omega\, p \text{ proc-type}}{\vdash \omega \text{ prog-type}}$$

$$\frac{\text{Dom}\, \sigma = \Delta \quad \text{For all } \rho \in \Delta, \Delta' \vdash \sigma_R\, \rho \text{ loc-var} \quad \text{For all } z \in \Delta, \Delta' \vdash \sigma_Z\, z \text{ frac}}{\vdash \sigma : \Delta \rightarrow \Delta'}$$

Fig. 3. Well-formedness rules

Examples. The example code previously shown in Fig. 2 can be permission-checked using

$$\Pi = 1\text{v1} : \text{ptr}(\rho), z\text{v2} : \text{ptr}(\rho'), 1\text{v3} : \text{ptr}(\rho'), z'\text{v4} : \text{ptr}(\rho''), 1\rho, 1\rho', 1\rho''$$

(here the key ρ' needs to be divided between the two parallel parts because each needs read access) but not using

$$\Pi' = 1\text{v1} : \text{ptr}(\rho), z\text{v2} : \text{ptr}(\rho'), 1\text{v3} : \text{ptr}(\rho''), z'\text{v4} : \text{ptr}(\rho'), 1\rho, 1\rho', 1\rho''$$

because the left part needs some fraction of ρ' but the right needs the whole key. This shows that the permissions system can check noninterference more precisely than BI-logic or separation logic, at least for examples such as this.

The next example, Fig. 5, gives the code for two procedures: one that returns (v2) an alias of its parameter (v1); and one that returns a new cell. The procedure alias has the first type α_1, but the second procedure noalias has both types α_1 and α_2. Both procedure types α_1 and α_2 require permission to read v1 and write v2 and to read the cell that v1 points to. Both procedure types also say that the read permission for v1 and the write permission for v2 are returned to the caller as is read permission for the cell pointed to by (the presumably changed) pointer in v2.[4] The two procedure types differ only in what fraction is returned

---

[4] The reason why the procedures need to return two permissions to ρ'' is because a fraction variable can never refer to 1. If fraction variables could be one, then a fraction $1 - z$ could be zero and render the permission type system unsound.

$$\frac{\rho \text{ fresh}}{\Delta; 1v : \text{ptr}(\rho'), \Pi \vdash_\omega v\mathtt{:=new} \Rightarrow \{\rho\} \cup \Delta; 1\rho, 1v : \text{ptr}(\rho), \Pi} \text{ New}$$

$$\frac{}{\Delta; 1v : \text{ptr}(\rho), \xi v' : \text{ptr}(\rho'), \Pi \vdash_\omega v\mathtt{:=}v' \Rightarrow \Delta; 1v : \text{ptr}(\rho'), \xi v' : \text{ptr}(\rho'), \Pi} \text{ Copy}$$

$$\frac{E = (\Delta; \xi v : \text{ptr}(\rho), 1\rho, \Pi') \quad E \vdash e : \text{Int}}{E \vdash_\omega \mathtt{*}v\mathtt{:=}e \Rightarrow E} \text{ Update} \quad \frac{}{E \vdash_\omega \mathtt{skip} \Rightarrow E} \text{ Skip}$$

$$\frac{E \vdash_\omega s_1 \Rightarrow E' \quad E' \vdash_\omega s_2 \Rightarrow E''}{E \vdash_\omega s_1\mathtt{;}\ s_2 \Rightarrow E''} \text{ Seq}$$

$$\frac{\Delta; \Pi_1 \vdash_\omega s_1 \Rightarrow \Delta'_1; \Pi'_1 \quad \Delta; \Pi_2 \vdash_\omega s_2 \Rightarrow \Delta'_2; \Pi'_2}{\Delta; \Pi_1, \Pi_2 \vdash_\omega s_1\mathtt{||}s_2 \Rightarrow \Delta'_1 \cup \Delta'_2; \Pi'_1, \Pi'_2} \text{ Par}$$

$$\frac{\Delta; \Pi \vdash b : \text{Bool} \quad \Delta; \Pi \vdash_\omega s_1 \Rightarrow \Delta_1; \sigma_1 \Pi_3 \quad \Delta; \Pi \vdash_\omega s_2 \Rightarrow \Delta_2; \sigma_2 \Pi_3 \quad \Delta_3 \text{ fresh} \quad \Delta \cup \Delta_3 \vdash \Pi_3 \text{ perms} \quad \vdash \sigma_1 : \Delta_3 \to \Delta_1 \quad \vdash \sigma_2 : \Delta_3 \to \Delta_2}{\Delta; \Pi \vdash_\omega \mathtt{if}\ b\ \mathtt{then}\ s_1\ \mathtt{else}\ s_2 \Rightarrow \Delta \cup \Delta_3; \Pi_3} \text{ If}$$

$$\frac{\omega\, p = \forall \Delta_1.\Pi_1 \to \exists \Delta_2.\sigma_2\, \Pi_3 \quad \Delta_3 \text{ fresh} \quad \vdash \sigma_1 : \Delta_1 \to \Delta \quad \vdash \sigma_2 : \Delta_3 \to \Delta_2}{\Delta; \sigma_1 \Pi_1, \Pi \vdash_\omega \mathtt{call}\ p \Rightarrow \Delta \cup \Delta_3; \sigma_1 \Pi_3, \Pi} \text{ Call}$$

$$\frac{\Pi = \xi_1 v_1 : \text{ptr}(\rho_1), \xi_2 v_2 : \text{ptr}(\rho_2), \Pi'}{\Delta; \Pi \vdash v_1 \mathtt{==} v_2 : \text{Bool}} \text{ Eq} \quad \frac{E \vdash e : \text{Int}}{E \vdash e\mathtt{!=0} : \text{Bool}} \text{ NotEq} \quad \frac{b \in \{\mathtt{true}, \mathtt{false}\}}{E \vdash b : \text{Bool}} \text{ Bool}$$

$$\frac{E \vdash e_1 : \text{Int} \quad E \vdash e_2 : \text{Int}}{E \vdash e_1\mathtt{+}e_2 : \text{Int}} \text{ Plus} \quad \frac{\Pi = \xi v : \text{ptr}(\rho), \xi' \rho, \Pi'}{\Delta; \Pi \vdash \mathtt{*}v : \text{Int}} \text{ Deref} \quad \frac{n \in \mathbb{Z}}{E \vdash n : \text{Int}} \text{ Int}$$

$$\frac{\Delta_1; \Pi_1 \vdash_\omega s \Rightarrow \Delta'_1; \sigma \Pi_2 \quad \Delta'_1 \cap \Delta_2 = \emptyset \quad \vdash \sigma : \Delta_2 \to \Delta'_1}{\vdash_\omega s : \forall \Delta_1.\Pi_1 \to \exists \Delta_2.\Pi_2} \text{ Proc}$$

$$\frac{\text{For all } p \in P,\ \vdash_\omega g\, p : \omega\, p}{\vdash g : \omega} \text{ Prog}$$

Fig. 4. Permission-checking a program

of the read permission for the cell pointed to by v1. The first procedure type does not specify how "much" is returned; the new fraction is bound existentially. The second procedure type specifies that the same fraction coming in is returned. If one has write permission to the cell pointed to by v1 and calls a procedure with type α_2, one can recover write permission after the procedure is complete, but if the callee has type α_1, one cannot.

In Walker et al's capability system, one can formulate corresponding procedure types that either permit or forbid aliasing in the result value. Polymorphic continuations gives roughly the same power as existential return types.

$$g \text{ alias} = \texttt{v2} := \texttt{v1}$$
$$g \text{ noalias} = \texttt{v2} := \texttt{new}$$

$$\alpha_1 = \forall \{\rho, \rho', z, z'\}.z\texttt{v1} : \text{ptr}(\rho), 1\texttt{v2} : \text{ptr}(\rho'), z'\rho$$
$$\rightarrow \exists \{\rho'', y, y', y''\}.z\texttt{v1} : \text{ptr}(\rho), 1\texttt{v2} : \text{ptr}(\rho''), y\rho, y'\rho'', y''\rho''$$
$$\alpha_2 = \forall \{\rho, \rho', z, z'\}.z\texttt{v1} : \text{ptr}(\rho), 1\texttt{v2} : \text{ptr}(\rho'), z'\rho$$
$$\rightarrow \exists \{\rho'', y, y', y''\}.z\texttt{v1} : \text{ptr}(\rho), 1\texttt{v2} : \text{ptr}(\rho''), z'\rho, y'\rho'', y''\rho''$$

Fig. 5. Two simple procedures and their types

In an effects system, the procedures would not need to have read permission on the cell pointed to by v1 because it is not accessed; the types would be much simpler, but then this information must be recovered by the alias analysis used to answer MayEqual questions. A similar situation occurs with separation logic or BI-logic: information about the heap is not needed to type either procedure but any potential aliasing after the procedure is finished is not described.

Recall that in SCIR, a writeable variable may be given a read-only type temporarily. This rule is not sound if we add the ability to pack a copy of a read-only permission in an existential (as in procedure type α_1), and to unpack it later. After the write permission is recovered, the read-only permission could be mistakenly seen as not interfered with. In our system, in contrast, even read-only permissions cannot be duplicated; if read-only permission is retained, the procedure is unable to return as "much" of the permission as it received from the caller, making it impossible to recover the write permission.

2.3 Consistency

In order to prove correctness of the type system we need to use a typing invariant with regard to a memory. A memory μ includes the values of pointer variables, but the type system introduces new variables: key variables and fraction variables. Let Ψ be mappings (partial function) from location and fraction variables to locations and numbers between zero and 1, respectively:

$$\text{type variable map } \psi \in \Psi = (R \rightharpoonup L) \times (Z \rightharpoonup (0, 1))$$

As with memories, we treat the pair of mappings as a single mapping with both types. We extend a mapping ψ to run on fraction expressions ($\psi \xi \in (0, 1]$):

$$\psi 1 = 1$$
$$\psi(\varepsilon\varepsilon') = (\psi\varepsilon)(\psi\varepsilon')$$
$$\psi(1 - \varepsilon) = 1 - \psi\varepsilon$$

These rules ensure that ψ works the same on equivalent fractions: $\xi \equiv \xi' \Rightarrow \psi(\xi) = \psi(\xi')$. We further extend a mapping to apply to permissions. Now instead of getting a single value, we get a value for each variable or cell. Thus the result is a function from variables and locations to real numbers: $\psi\, \Pi : ((V \cup L) \to \mathbb{R})$. The function is made total by mapping all other $x \in V \cup L$ to zero:

$$\psi\, . = []$$
$$\psi(\xi v : \mathrm{ptr}(\rho)) = [v \mapsto \psi\, \xi]$$
$$\psi(\xi \rho) = [\psi\, \rho \mapsto \psi\, \xi]$$
$$\psi(\Pi_1, \Pi_2) = (\psi\, \Pi_1) + (\psi\, \Pi_2)$$
where
$$(\psi\, \Pi_1 + \psi\, \Pi_2)\, x = (\psi\, \Pi_1)\, x + (\psi\, \Pi_2)\, x$$

The range of the result is syntactically only guaranteed to be nonnegative. A memory is not considered consistent with the environment unless the range includes only numbers between zero and one, inclusive. The ψ is also used to check that variables indeed have the location represented in their type, and that there are no dangling pointers.

$$\frac{\mathrm{Dom}\, \psi = \Delta \quad \mathrm{Rng}\, (\psi\, \Pi) \subseteq [0,1] \quad \psi; \mu \vdash \Pi \text{ consistent}}{\Delta; \Pi \vdash \mu \text{ ok}}$$

$$\psi; \mu \vdash \cdot \text{ consistent} \qquad \frac{\psi; \mu \vdash \Pi_1 \text{ consistent} \quad \psi; \mu \vdash \Pi_2 \text{ consistent}}{\psi; \mu \vdash \Pi_1, \Pi_2 \text{ consistent}}$$

$$\frac{\psi(\rho) = \mu(v)}{\psi; \mu \vdash \xi v : \mathrm{ptr}(\rho) \text{ consistent}} \qquad \frac{\psi\, \rho \in \mathrm{Dom}\, \mu}{\psi; \mu \vdash \xi \rho \text{ consistent}}$$

2.4 Non-interference

Non-interference in the checking of parallel composition permits us to prove a strong result: terminating evaluation always leads to an isomorphic store. In other words, the nondeterminism cannot affect the final result.

Theorem 1. *If we have a well-typed program g ($\vdash g : \omega$) and a statement s that permission-checks in an environment E ($E \vdash_\omega s \Rightarrow E'$) and a memory μ_1 that is consistent with the environment ($E \vdash \mu_1$ ok), and s can be fully evaluated in this memory in k steps ($\langle \mu_1, s \rangle \xrightarrow{k}_g \langle \mu_1^*, \mathtt{skip} \rangle$) then for any isomorphic memory $\mu_2 \sim \mu_1$, any other evaluation sequence $\langle \mu_2, s \rangle \to_g \langle \mu_2', s' \rangle \to_g \ldots$ terminates in exactly k steps and has an isomorphic result $\mu_2^* \sim \mu_1^*$.*

2.5 Summary

We have taken a simple language with aliasing and explicit parallelism and have shown that fractional permissions give us a way to ensure determinism of execution through non-interference. The following section considers how this basic system can be lifted to more complex situations.

3 Extensions

This section explores further work made possible with fractional permissions.

Algorithmic Checking. The permission checking system described in this paper is not algorithmic since the splitting required for a parallel composition is not deterministic. The solution is to permission-check the first branch with all the permissions, but keep track of which ones are actually needed. When only a fraction of a permission is needed, split it before recording the use of the fraction. After checking the first branch, check the second branch using the permissions that were not needed during the first branch.

Aliasing Information. The system here does not make use of pointer equality checking in `if` conditions. Equality is useful in order to connect a variable with an unknown pointer with a permission on an unknown cell. Inequality is useful in asserting uniqueness. To handle both situations, one can add a separate aliasing context that expresses known equalities and inequalities between location variables, and even logical connectives between these facts. For example if one knows that a variable z is equal to one of x and y, then if we have write permission for the cells pointed to by both x and y, then we also implicitly have permission for the cell pointed to by z. In general, one can use any three-valued logic [18] to hold this information. This information represents "facts" and not permissions and thus can be copied to both sides of a parallel composition.

Memory Management. Adding garbage collection could be accomplished using a formulation similar to that of Morrisett, Felleisen and Harper [19]. Instead of the isomorphicity constraint, one would ensure that a final integer expression would have a value unchanged by garbage collection. We would also need a way to remove permissions to unreachable cells.

Adding explicit memory management (`dispose`) can be handled. Deallocation removes a key just as allocation introduces it. The usual semantics of `dispose` leaves dangling pointers in place, and the proof of determinism fails when dangling pointers exist: the sequence `v1 := v2; dispose v2; new v2` may reallocate the same memory location for `v1` or not, leading to non-isomorphic memories. There are at least two possible ways around this difficulty: (1) relax isomorphicity and then prevent dangling pointers from being compared to other pointers; or (2) change the semantics of dispose to work only in ways that do not leave dangling pointers. In the first solution, one needs permission to compare pointers, which corresponds to the **I** access right of BNR capabilities [20].

The permission system described here cannot check recursive procedures that allocate cells on their recursive path, since each allocation produces a new key which cannot be forgotten. This brings us to the next extension topic.

Records and Recursive Data Types. When we have singleton types for pointers, then record types and especially recursive data types require the use of existentials [21]. The existentials include not just bindings, but also permissions. This permits us to represent an unknown unique pointer: the complete permission stored with the pointer. Immutable pointers are represented by storing an existential fraction of the permission with the pointer.

Since the packed existential includes (linear) witness permissions, a variable with existential type cannot be read or written (that is, copying or destroying the value) until the existential is unpacked. Therefore a permission system needs to distinguish "open variables" (variables with singleton type) from "closed variables" (variables with existential type). Closed variables can be fractionally opened in which case only a fraction of the witness permissions are usable.

Adoption and Ownership. Adoption involves logically storing a key inside another one. Adoption cannot be undone. In this way, it is similar to ownership. In adoption and focus, the adoptee can only be made accessible by temporarily making the adopter inaccessible. With fractions, one could access a fraction of the adoptee (and thus have read-only access) given only a fraction of the adopter.

A shared variable is modeled by adopting its complete permission into a globally accessible key. "Fractional adoption" permits the modeling of unique-write variables, variables that are globally read-only with write access at a single point. For such a variable, a known fraction is adopted by a globally accessible key and the remainder is kept at the write-access point. The two fractions can be put together to gain write access.

4 Related Work

Reynolds' "syntactic control of interference" [3] checked that call-by-name would not cause "covert interference" where a parameter and a procedure each observe the same changing state. This work was revisited by O'Hearn and others [16] (SCIR). SCIR split the context into two parts: an active part (writable); and a passive part (read only). The passive part can be duplicated in two branches of the proof (unlike the active part) enabling the sharing of read-only state. An interesting rule called "passification" enabled a write of a variable to be ignored if the result was a passive type. A monadic-like structure ensures that (visible) state mutations cannot be hidden in a passively-type result.

Reynolds and O'Hearn have continued analysis of mutable data structures using the logic of "bunched implications" [10] and "separation logic" [12]. A spatial conjunction operator in the logics allows parts of the heap to be analyzed separately. Allocation and deallocation add and remove spatial conjuncts. However, the spatial conjunction operator strictly separates heap access: it does not distinguish reads from writes. It appears that fractions could be applied, so that one could have $P \models \varepsilon P * (1 - \varepsilon)P$ and get the ability to share read-only heaps.

Walker, Crary and Morrisett's static capability system [9] inspired DeLine and Fähndrich's alias typing system for Vault [22], from which adoption and focus [23] grew. The capabilities or guards can be seen as permissions. With the "focus" operation, one temporarily gives up a guard in order to get unrestricted access to a unique variable. Once uniqueness is re-established the guard can be returned. This process is handled with a linear implication $h \multimap g$.

Effects systems have been used to check non-interference [4, 5] but need to be augmented with MayEqual information to check for conflict. One simple (but conservative) analysis is to assume any two references with the same type (or compatible types) may be aliased.

In the area of compilers, non-interference is traditionally checked through using a data-flow graph (or some superset thereof). From early on, the interdependence between aliasing and data dependencies has been recognized. Traditionally, the alias information is presented in terms of may-alias (and must-alias) facts, pairs of aliases at program points. MayEqual, on the other hand, compares pointer expressions at disparate program points [13]. Ross and Sagiv [24] have show how data dependencies can be recovered from may-alias information by instrumenting the program (in a global transformation).

Rugina and Rinard give an algorithm for doing flow-sensitive pointer analysis in programs with structured parallelism [25]. It models interference by assuming that any mutation performed in one parallel branch may be visible at any time in other parallel branches. The analysis described here is simpler since interference between parallel branches is forbidden.

5 Conclusions

We define a permission type system which enables us to solve the interdependent problems of uniqueness and effects in a single formalism. We extend earlier work on permissions to distinguish reads from writes using fractional permissions, rather than non-linearity. We define a simple language with aliasing and parallelism and show that well-typed programs have deterministic results.

Acknowledgments

I thank Dave Clarke, Manuel Fähndrich and Bill Retert for helping me frame this idea and reading innumerable drafts. All remaining errors are strictly my own.

References

1. Jouvelot, P., Gifford, D.K.: Algebraic reconstruction of types and effects. In: Conference Record of the Eighteenth Annual ACM SIGACT/SIGPLAN Symposium on Principles of Programming Languages. ACM Press, New York (1991) 303–310
2. Talpin, J.P., Jouvelot, P.: Polymorphic type, region and effect inference. Journal of Functional Programming **2** (1992) 245–271
3. Reynolds, J.C.: Syntactic control of interference. In: Conference Record of the Fifth ACM Symposium on Principles of Programming Languages, New York, ACM Press (1978) 39–46

4. Greenhouse, A., Boyland, J.: An object-oriented effects system. In Guerraoui, R., ed.: ECOOP'99 — Object-Oriented Programming, 13th European Conference. Volume 1628 of Lecture Notes in Computer Science., Berlin, Heidelberg, New York, Springer (1999) 205–229
5. Clarke, D., Drossopoulou, S.: Ownership, encapsulation and the disjointness of type and effect. In: OOPSLA'02 Conference Proceedings—Object-Oriented Programming Systems, Languages and Applications. Volume 37., New York, ACM Press (2002) 292–310
6. Flanagan, C., Abadi, M.: Types for safe locking. In Swierstra, S.D., ed.: ESOP'99 — Programming Languages and Systems, 8th European Symposium on Programming. Volume 1576 of Lecture Notes in Computer Science., Berlin, Heidelberg, New York, Springer (1999) 91–108
7. Boyapati, C., Rinard, M.: A parameterized type system for race-free Java programs. In: OOPSLA'01 Conference Proceedings—Object-Oriented Programming Systems, Languages and Applications. Volume 36., New York, ACM Press (2001) 56–69
8. Boyapati, C., Lee, R., Rinard, M.: Ownership types for safe programming: Preventing data races and deadlocks. In: OOPSLA'02 Conference Proceedings—Object-Oriented Programming Systems, Languages and Applications. Volume 37., New York, ACM Press (2002) 211–230
9. Walker, D., Crary, K., Morrisett, G.: Typed memory management via static capabilities. ACM Transactions on Programming Languages and Systems **22** (2000) 701–771
10. Ishtiaq, S.S., O'Hearn, P.W.: BI as an assertion language for mutable data structures. In: Conference Record of the Twenty-eighth Annual ACM SIGACT/SIGPLAN Symposium on Principles of Programming Languages, New York, ACM Press (2001) 14–26
11. Reynolds, J.C.: Intuitionistic reasoning about shared mutable data structure. In: Millenial Perspectives in Computer Science, Palgrave (to appear) Draft dated July 28, 2000.
12. Reynolds, J.: Separation logic: A logic for shared mutable data structures. In: Logic in Computer Science, Los Alamitos, California, IEEE Computer Society (2002) 55–74
13. Boyland, J., Greenhouse, A.: MayEqual: A new alias question. Presented at IWAOOS '99: Intercontinental Workshop on Aliasing in Object-Oriented Systems. http://cuiwww.unige.ch/~ecoopws/iwaoos/papers/papers/greenhouse.ps.gz (1999)
14. Steensgaard, B.: Points-to analysis in almost linear time. In: Conference Record of the Twenty-third Annual ACM SIGACT/SIGPLAN Symposium on Principles of Programming Languages, New York, ACM Press (1996) 32–41
15. Wadler, P.: Linear types can change the world! In Broy, M., Jones, C.B., eds.: Programming Concepts and Methods. Elsevier, North-Holland (1990)
16. O'Hearn, P.W., Takeyama, M., Power, A.J., Tennent, R.D.: Syntactic control of interference revisited. In: MFPS XI, conference on Mathematical Foundations of Program Semantics. Volume 1., Elsevier (1995)
17. Smith, F., Walker, D., Morrisett, J.G.: Alias types. In Smolka, G., ed.: ESOP'00 — Programming Languages and Systems, 9th European Symposium on Programming. Volume 1782 of Lecture Notes in Computer Science., Berlin, Heidelberg, New York, Springer (2000) 366–381

18. Sagiv, M., Reps, T., Wilhelm, R.: Parametric shape analysis via 3-valued logic. In: Conference Record of the Twenty-sixth Annual ACM SIGACT/SIGPLAN Symposium on Principles of Programming Languages, New York, ACM Press (1999) 105–118
19. Morrisett, G., Felleisen, M., Harper, R..: Abstract models of memory management. In: Proceedings of the Seventh International Conference on Functional Programming Languages and Computer Architecture (FPCA'95), New York, ACM Press (1995) 66–77
20. Boyland, J., Noble, J., Retert, W.: Capabilities for sharing: A generalization of uniqueness and read-only. In Knudsen, J.L., ed.: ECOOP'01 — Object-Oriented Programming, 15th European Conference. Volume 2072 of Lecture Notes in Computer Science., Berlin, Heidelberg, New York, Springer (2001) 2–27
21. Walker, D., Morrisett, G.: Alias types for recursive data structures. In: Types in Compilation: Third International Workshop, TIC 2000. Volume 2071 of Lecture Notes in Computer Science., Berlin, Heidelberg, New York, Springer (2001) 177–206
22. DeLine, R., Fähndrich, M.: Enforcing high-level protocols in low-level software. In: Proceedings of the ACM SIGPLAN '01 Conference on Programming Language Design and Implementation. Volume 36., New York, ACM Press (2001) 59–69
23. Fähndrich, M., DeLine, R.: Adoption and focus: Practial linear types for imperative programming. In: Proceedings of the ACM SIGPLAN '02 Conference on Programming Language Design and Implementation. Volume 37., New York, ACM Press (2002) 13–24
24. Ross, J.L., Sagiv, M.: Building a birdge between pointer aliases and program dependencies. In Hankin, C., ed.: ESOP'98 — Programming Languages and Systems, 7th European Symposium on Programming. Volume 1381 of Lecture Notes in Computer Science., Berlin, Heidelberg, New York, Springer (1998) 221–235
25. Rugina, R., Rinard, M.C.: Pointer analysis for structured parallel programs. ACM Transactions on Programming Languages and Systems **25** (2003) 70–116

Message Analysis for Concurrent Languages*

Richard Carlsson, Konstantinos Sagonas, and Jesper Wilhelmsson

Computing Science Department, Uppsala University, Sweden
{richardc,kostis,jesperw}@csd.uu.se

Abstract. We describe an analysis-driven storage allocation scheme for concurrent languages that use message passing with copying semantics. The basic principle is that in such a language, data which is not part of any message does not need to be allocated in a shared data area. This allows for deallocation of thread-specific data without requiring global synchronization and often without even triggering garbage collection. On the other hand, data that is part of a message should preferably be allocated on a shared area, which allows for fast ($O(1)$) interprocess communication that does not require actual copying. In the context of a dynamically typed, higher-order, concurrent functional language, we present a static message analysis which guides the allocation. As shown by our performance evaluation, conducted using an industrial-strength language implementation, the analysis is effective enough to discover most data which is to be used as a message, and to allow the allocation scheme to combine the best performance characteristics of both a process-centric and a shared-heap memory architecture.

1 Introduction

Many programming languages nowadays come with some form of built-in support for concurrent processes (or threads). Depending on the concurrency model of the language, interprocess communication takes place either through synchronized shared structures (as e.g. in Java), using synchronous message passing on typed channels (as e.g. in Concurrent ML), or using asynchronous message passing (as e.g. in ERLANG). Most of these languages typically also require support for automatic memory management, usually implemented using a garbage collector. So far, research has largely focused on the memory reclamation aspects of these concurrent systems. As a result, by now, many different garbage collection techniques have been proposed and their characteristics are well-known; see e.g. [15].

A less treated, albeit key issue in the design of a concurrent language implementation is that of memory allocation. It is clear that, regardless of the concurrency model of the language, there exist several different ways of structuring the memory architecture, each having its pros and cons. Perhaps surprisingly, till recently, there has not been any in-depth investigation of the performance tradeoffs that are involved in the choice between these alternative architectures. In [14], we provided the first detailed characterization of the advantages and disadvantages of different memory architectures in a language where communication occurs through message passing.

---

* Research supported in part by the ASTEC (Advanced Software Technology) competence center with matching funds by Ericsson Development.

The reasons for focusing on this type of languages are both principled and pragmatic. Pragmatic because we are involved in the development of a production-quality system of this type, the Erlang/OTP system, which is heavily used as a platform for the development of highly concurrent (thousands of processes) commercial applications. Principled because, despite current common practice, we hold that concurrency through (asynchronous) message passing with copying semantics is fundamentally superior to concurrency through shared data structures. Considerably less locking is required, and consequently the method has better performance and scales better. Furthermore, the copying semantics makes distribution transparent.

Our Contributions. Our first contribution, which motivates our analysis, is in the area of runtime system organization. Based on the pros and cons of different memory architectures described in [14], we describe two different variants of a runtime system architecture that has process-specific areas for allocation of local data, and a common area for data that is shared between communicating processes (i.e., is part of some message). In doing so, it allows interprocess communication to occur without actual copying, uses less overall space due to avoiding data replication, and allows for the frequent process-local heap collections to take place without a need for global synchronization of processes, reducing the level of system irresponsiveness due to garbage collection.

Our second and main contribution is to present in detail a static analysis, called *message analysis*, whose aim is to discover which data is to be used as message, and which can guide the allocation in such a runtime system architecture. Novel characteristics of the analysis are that it does not rely on the presence of type information and does not sacrifice precision when handling list types.

Finally, we have implemented these schemes in the context of an industrial-strength implementation used for highly concurrent time-critical applications, and report on the effectiveness of the analysis, the overhead it incurs on compilation times, and the performance of the resulting system.

Summary of Contents. We begin by introducing ERLANG and reviewing our prior work on heap architectures for concurrent languages. Section 3 goes into more detail about implementation choices in the hybrid architecture. Section 4 describes the escape analysis and message analysis, and Sect. 5 explains how the information is used to rewrite the program. Section 6 contains experimental results measuring both the effectiveness of the analysis and the effect that the use of the analysis has on improving execution performance. Finally, Sect. 7 discusses related work and Sect. 8 concludes.

2 Preliminaries and Prior Work

2.1 Erlang and Core Erlang

ERLANG [1] is a strict, dynamically typed functional programming language with support for concurrency, distribution, communication, fault-tolerance, on-the-fly code replacement, and automatic memory management. ERLANG was designed to ease the programming of large soft real-time control systems like those commonly developed in the telecommunications industry. It has so far been used quite successfully both by

Ericsson and other companies around the world to construct large (several hundred thousand lines of code) commercial applications.

ERLANG's basic data types are atoms (symbols), numbers (floats and arbitrary precision integers), and process identifiers; compound data types are lists and tuples. Programs consist of function definitions organized in *modules*. There is no destructive assignment of variables or data. Because recursion is the only means to express iteration in ERLANG, tail call optimization is a required feature of ERLANG implementations.

Processes in ERLANG are extremely light-weight (lighter than OS threads), their number in typical applications can be large (in some cases up to 50,000 processes on a single node), and their memory requirements vary dynamically. ERLANG's concurrency primitives – spawn, "!" (send), and receive – allow a process to spawn new processes and communicate with other processes through asynchronous message passing. Any value can be sent as a message and processes may be located on any machine. Each process has a *mailbox*, essentially a message queue, where all messages sent to the process will arrive. Message selection from the mailbox is done by pattern matching. In send operations, the receiver is specified by its process identifier, regardless of where it is located, making distribution all but invisible. To support robust systems, a process can register to receive a message if some other process terminates. ERLANG provides mechanisms for allowing a process to timeout while waiting for messages and a catch/throw-style exception mechanism for error handling.

ERLANG is often used in "five nines" high-availability (i.e., 99.999% of the time available) systems, where down-time is required to be less than five minutes per year. Such systems cannot be taken down, upgraded, and restarted when software patches and upgrades arrive, since that would not respect the availability requirement. Consequently, ERLANG systems support upgrading code while the system is running, a mechanism known as *dynamic code replacement*.

Core Erlang [7, 6] is the official core language for ERLANG, developed to facilitate compilation, analysis, verification and semantics-preserving transformations of ERLANG programs. When compiling a module, the compiler reduces the ERLANG code to Core Erlang as an intermediate form on which static analyzes and optimizations may be performed before low level code is produced. While ERLANG has unusual and complicated variable scoping rules, fixed-order evaluation, and only allows top-level function definitions, Core Erlang is similar to the untyped lambda calculus with let- and letrec-bindings, and imposes no restrictions on the evaluation order of arguments.

2.2 Heap Architectures for Concurrent Languages Using Message Passing

In [14] we examined three different runtime system architectures for concurrent language implementations: One *process-centric* where each process allocates and manages its private memory area and all messages have to be copied between processes, one which is *communal* and all processes get to share the same heap, and finally we proposed a *hybrid* runtime system architecture where each process has a private heap for local data but where a shared heap is used for data sent as messages. Figure 1 depicts memory areas of these architectures when three processes are currently in the system; shaded areas show currently unused memory; the filled shapes and arrows in Fig. 1(c) represent messages and pointers.

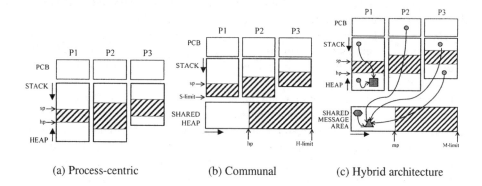

Fig. 1. Different runtime system architectures for concurrent languages

For each architecture, we discussed its pros and cons focusing on the architectural impact on the speed of interprocess communication and garbage collection (GC). We briefly review them below:

Process-centric. This is currently the default configuration of Erlang/OTP. Interprocess communication requires copying of messages, thus is an $O(n)$ operation where n is the message size. Also, memory fragmentation is high. Pros are that the garbage collection times and pauses are expected to be small (as the root set need only consist of the stack of the process requiring collection), and upon termination of a process, its allocated memory area can be reclaimed without GC. This property in turn encourages the use of processes as a form of *programmer-controlled regions*: a computation that requires a lot of auxiliary space can be performed in a separate process that sends its result as a message to its consumer and then dies. This memory architecture has recently also been exploited in the context of Java; see [11].

Communal (shared heap). The biggest advantage is very fast ($O(1)$) interprocess communication, simply consisting of passing a pointer to the receiving process, and low memory requirements due to message sharing. Disadvantages include having to consider the stacks of all processes as root set (expected higher GC latency) and possibly poor cache performance due to processes' data being interleaved on the shared heap.

Hybrid. Tries to combine the advantages of the above two architectures: interprocess communication is fast and GC latency for the frequent collections of the per-process heaps is expected to be small. Also, this architecture allows for reclamation of data of short-lived, memory-intensive processes to happen without GC, but simply by attaching the process-local heap to a free list. However, to take advantage of this architecture, the system should be able to distinguish between data that is process-local and data which is to be shared and used as messages. This can be achieved by user annotations on the source code, by dynamically monitoring the creation of data as recently proposed in [11], or by a static analysis as we describe in Sect. 4.

Note that these runtime system architectures are applicable to all message-passing concurrent languages. They are *generic*: their advantages and disadvantages in no way depend on characteristics of the ERLANG language or the current ERLANG implementation.

3 The Hybrid Architecture

A key point in the hybrid architecture is to be able to garbage collect the process-local heaps individually and without looking at the shared heap. In a multi-threaded system this allows collection of process-local heaps without any locking or synchronization. If, on the other hand, pointers from the shared area to the local heaps are allowed, these must then be traced so that what they point to is regarded as live during a local collection. This could be achieved by a read or write barrier, which typically incurs a relatively large overhead on the overall runtime. The alternative, which is our choice, is to maintain as an invariant that there are no pointers from the shared area to the local heaps, nor from one process-local heap to another; cf. Fig. 1(c).

There are two possible strategies for the implementation of allocation and message passing in the hybrid architecture:

Local allocation of non-messages. Here, only data that is known to *not* be part of a message may be allocated on the process-local heap, while all other data is allocated on the shared heap. This gives $O(1)$ process communication for processes residing on the same node, since all possible messages are guaranteed to already be in the shared area, but utilization of the local heaps depends on the ability to decide through program analysis which data is definitely not shared. This approach is used by [19]. Because it is not possible in general to determine what will become part of a message, underapproximation is necessary. In the worst case, nothing is allocated in the process-local heaps, and the behavior of the hybrid architecture with this allocation strategy reduces to that of the shared heap architecture.

Shared allocation of possible messages. In this case, data that is likely to be part of a message is allocated speculatively on the shared heap, and all other data on the process-local heaps. This requires that the message operands of all send-operations are wrapped with a copy-on-demand operation, which verifies that the message resides in the shared area, and otherwise copies the locally allocated parts to the shared heap. If program analysis can determine that a message operand must already be on the shared heap, the copy operation can be statically eliminated. Without such analysis, the behavior will be similar to the process-centric architecture, except that data which is repeatedly passed as message from one process to another will only be copied once. If the analysis overapproximates too much, most of the data will be allocated on the shared heap, and we will not benefit from the process-local heaps; on the contrary, we may introduce unnecessary copying.

Copying of Messages. If the second strategy is used, as is the case in our implementation of the hybrid system, we must be prepared to copy (parts of) messages as necessary to ensure the pointer directionality invariant. Since we do not know how much of a message needs to be copied and how much already resides in the shared area, we can not ensure that the space available on the shared heap will be sufficient before we begin to copy data.

At the start of the copying, we only know the size of the topmost constructor of the message. We allocate space in the message area for this constructor. Non pointer data are simply copied to the allocated space, and all pointer fields are initialized to Nil. This is necessary because the object might be scanned as part of a garbage collection before all its children have been copied. The copying routine is then executed again for each child. When space for a child has been allocated and initialized, the child will update the corresponding pointer field of the parent, before proceeding to copy its own children.

If there is not enough memory on the shared heap for a constructor at some point, the garbage collector is called on-the-fly to make room. If a copying garbage collector is used, as is the case in our system, it will move those parts of the message that have already been copied, including the parent constructor. Furthermore, in a global collection, both source and destination will be moved. Since garbage collection might occur at any time, all local pointer variables have to be updated after a child has been copied. To keep the pointers up to date, two stacks are used during message copying: one for storing all destination pointers, and one for the source pointers. The source stack is updated when the sending process is garbage collected (in a global collection), and the destination stack is used as a root set (and is thus updated) in the collection of the shared heap.

4 Message Analysis

To use the hybrid architecture without user annotations on what is to be allocated on the local and shared heap respectively, program analysis is necessary. If data is allocated on the shared heap by default, we need to single out the data which is guaranteed to not be included in any message, so it can be allocated on the per-process heap. This amounts to escape analysis of process-local data [4, 5, 8].

If data is by default allocated on the local heaps, we instead want to identify data that is sure to be part of a message, so it can be directly allocated in the shared area in order to avoid the copying operation when the message is eventually passed. We will refer to this special case of escape analysis as *message analysis*. Note that since copying will be performed if necessary whenever some part of a message could be residing on a process-local heap, both under- and overapproximation of the set of run-time message constructors is safe.

4.1 The Analyzed Language

Although our analyzes have been implemented for the complete Core Erlang language, for the purposes of this paper, the details of Core Erlang are unimportant. To keep the exposition simple, we instead define a sufficiently powerful language of A-normal forms [12], shown in Fig. 2, with the relevant semantics of the core language (strict, higher-order, dynamically typed and without destructive updates), and with operators for asynchronous send, blocking receive, and process spawning. We also make the simplifying assumption that all primitive operations return atomic values and do not cause escapement; however, our actual implementation does not rely on that assumption.

$c \in Const$ Constants (atoms, integers, pids and *nil*)
$x \in Var$ Variables
$e \in Expr$ Expressions
$l \in Label$ Labels, including *xcall* and *xlambda*
$o \in Primops$ Primitive operations (==, >, is_nil, is_cons, is_tuple, ...)

$$v ::= c \mid x$$
$$e ::= v \mid (v_1\ v_2)^l \mid \text{if } v \text{ then } e_1 \text{ else } e_2 \mid \text{let } x = b \text{ in } e$$
$$b ::= v \mid (v_1\ v_2)^l \mid (\lambda x'.e')^l \mid \text{fix } (\lambda x'.e')^l \mid v_1 :^l v_2 \mid \{v_1, \ldots, v_n\}^l \mid \text{hd } v \mid \text{tl } v \mid$$
$$\text{element}_k\ v \mid v_1 !\ v_2 \mid \text{receive} \mid \text{spawn } (v_1\ v_2)^l \mid \text{primop } o(v_1, ..., v_n)$$

Fig. 2. A mini-Erlang language

Since the language is dynamically typed, the second argument of a list constructor $v_1 : v_2$ might not always be a list, but in typical ERLANG programs all lists are proper. Tuple constructors are written $\{v_1, \ldots, v_n\}$, for all $n \geq 1$. Each constructor expression in the program, as well as each call site and lambda expression, is given a unique label l. All variables in the program are assumed to be uniquely named.

Recursion is introduced with the explicit fixpoint operator fix $(\lambda x'.e')^l$. Operators hd and tl select the first (head) and second (tail) element, respectively, of a list constructor. The operator element$_k$ selects the k:th element of a tuple, if the tuple has at least k elements.

The spawn operator starts evaluation of the application $(v_1\ v_2)$ as a separate process, then immediately continues returning a new unique process identifier ("pid"). When evaluation of a process terminates, the final result is discarded. The send operator $v_1 !\ v_2$ sends message v_2 asynchronously to the process identified by pid v_1, yielding v_2 as result. Each process is assumed to have an unbounded queue where incoming messages are stored until extracted. The receive operator extracts the oldest message from the queue, or blocks if the queue is empty. This is a simple model of the concurrent semantics of ERLANG.

4.2 General Framework

The analyzes we have this far implemented are first-order dataflow analyzes, and are best understood as extensions of Shivers' closure analysis [18]. Indeed, we assume that closure analysis has been done, so that:

– The label *xcall* represents all call sites external to the program, and the label *xlambda* represents all possible external lambdas.
– There is a mapping *calls*: *Label* → $\mathcal{P}(Label)$ from each call site label (including *xcall*) to the corresponding set of possible lambda expression labels (which may include *xlambda*).

The domain V is defined as follows:

$$V_0 = \mathcal{P}(\textit{Label}) \times \{\langle\rangle, \top\}$$
$$V_i = V_{i-1} \cup \mathcal{P}(\textit{Label}) \times \bigcup_{n \geq 0} \{\langle v_1, \ldots, v_n\rangle \mid v_1, \ldots, v_n \in V_{i-1}\} \quad \text{for all } i > 0$$
$$V = \bigcup_{i \geq 0} V_i$$

Let R^* denote the reflexive and transitive closure of a relation R, and define $\sqsubseteq$ to be the smallest relation on V such that:

$$(s_1, w) \sqsubseteq_i (s_2, \top) \text{ if } s_1 \subseteq s_2, \text{ for all } i \geq 0$$
$$(s_1, \langle u_1, \ldots, u_n\rangle) \sqsubseteq_i (s_2, \langle v_1, \ldots, v_m\rangle)$$
$$\quad \text{if } s_1 \subseteq s_2 \wedge n \leq m \wedge \forall j \in [1, n] : u_j \sqsubseteq_{i-1} v_j, \text{ for all } i \geq 0$$
$$v_1 \sqsubseteq_i v_2 \text{ if } v_1 \sqsubseteq_{i-1} v_2, \text{ for all } i > 0$$

$$\sqsubseteq \; = \bigcup_{i \geq 0} \sqsubseteq_i^*$$

It is then easy to see that $\langle V, \sqsubseteq \rangle$ is a complete lattice.

Intuitively, our abstract values represent sets of constructor trees, where each node in a tree is annotated with the set of source code labels that could possibly be the origin of an actual constructor at that point. A node $(S, \top)$ represents the set of all possible subtrees where each node is annotated with set S. We identify $\bot$ with the pair $(\emptyset, \langle\rangle)$.

We define the expression analysis function $\mathcal{V}_e[\![e]\!]$ as:

$$\mathcal{V}_v[\![c]\!] = \bot$$
$$\mathcal{V}_v[\![x]\!] = \textit{Val}(x)$$

$$\mathcal{V}_e[\![v]\!] = \mathcal{V}_v[\![v]\!]$$
$$\mathcal{V}_e[\![(v_1\ v_2)^l]\!] = \textit{In}(l)$$
$$\mathcal{V}_e[\![\text{if } v \text{ then } e_1 \text{ else } e_2]\!] = \mathcal{V}_e[\![e_1]\!] \sqcup \mathcal{V}_e[\![e_2]\!]$$
$$\mathcal{V}_e[\![\text{let } x = b \text{ in } e]\!] = \mathcal{V}_e[\![e]\!]$$

and the bound-value analysis function $\mathcal{V}_b[\![b]\!]$ as:

$$\mathcal{V}_b[\![v]\!] = \mathcal{V}_v[\![v]\!]$$
$$\mathcal{V}_b[\![(v_1\ v_2)^l]\!] = \textit{In}(l)$$
$$\mathcal{V}_b[\![(\lambda x'.e')^l]\!] = (\{l\}, \langle\rangle)$$
$$\mathcal{V}_b[\![\text{fix }(\lambda x'.e')^l]\!] = (\{l\}, \langle\rangle)$$
$$\mathcal{V}_b[\![v_1 :^l v_2]\!] = \textit{cons } l\ \mathcal{V}_v[\![v_1]\!]\ \mathcal{V}_v[\![v_2]\!]$$
$$\mathcal{V}_b[\![\{v_1, \ldots, v_n\}^l]\!] = \textit{tuple } l\ \langle \mathcal{V}_v[\![v_1]\!], \ldots, \mathcal{V}_v[\![v_n]\!]\rangle$$
$$\mathcal{V}_b[\![\text{hd } v]\!] = \textit{head}(\mathcal{V}_v[\![v]\!])$$
$$\mathcal{V}_b[\![\text{tl } v]\!] = \textit{tail}(\mathcal{V}_v[\![v]\!])$$
$$\mathcal{V}_b[\![\text{element}_k\ v]\!] = \textit{elem } k\ \mathcal{V}_v[\![v]\!]$$
$$\mathcal{V}_b[\![v_1 !\ v_2]\!] = \mathcal{V}_v[\![v_2]\!]$$
$$\mathcal{V}_b[\![\text{receive}]\!] = \bot$$

$$\mathcal{V}_b[\![\texttt{spawn } (v_1 \, v_2)^l]\!] = \bot$$
$$\mathcal{V}_b[\![\texttt{primop } o(v_1, ..., v_n)]\!] = \bot$$

where

$$cons \; l \; x \; y = (\{l\}, \langle x \rangle) \sqcup y$$
$$tuple \; l \; \langle x_1, \ldots, x_n \rangle = (\{l\}, \langle x_1, \ldots, x_n \rangle)$$

and

$$head \, (s, w) = \begin{cases} (s, \top) & \text{if } w = \top \\ v_1 & \text{if } w = \langle v_1, \ldots v_n \rangle, n \geq 1 \\ \bot & \text{otherwise} \end{cases}$$

$$tail \, (s, w) = \begin{cases} (s, \top) & \text{if } w = \top \\ (s, w) & \text{if } w = \langle v_1, \ldots v_n \rangle, n \geq 1 \\ \bot & \text{otherwise} \end{cases}$$

$$elem \, k \, (s, w) = \begin{cases} (s, \top) & \text{if } w = \top \\ v_k & \text{if } w = \langle v_1, \ldots v_n \rangle, k \in [1, n] \\ \bot & \text{otherwise} \end{cases}$$

Because lists are typically much more common than other recursive data structures, we give them a nonstandard treatment in order to achieve decent precision by simple means. We make the assumption that in all or most programs, cons cells are used exclusively for constructing proper lists, so the loss of precision for non-proper lists is not an issue.

Suppose $z = cons \; l \; x \; y$. If y is $(s, \langle v, \ldots \rangle)$, then the set of top-level constructors of z is $s \cup \{l\}$. Furthermore, $head \; z$ will yield $x \sqcup v$, and $tail \; z$ yields z itself. Thus even if a list is of constant length, such as [A, B, C], we will not be able to make distinctions between individual elements. The approximation is safe; in the above example, $x \sqsubseteq head \; z$ and $y \sqsubseteq tail \; z$.

For each label l of a lambda expression $(\lambda x.e)^l$ in the program, define $Out(l) = \mathcal{V}_e[\![e]\!]$. Then for all call sites $(v_1 \, v_2)^l$ in the program, including spawns and the dummy external call labeled xcall, we have $\forall l' \in calls(l) : Out(l') \sqsubseteq In(l)$, and also $\forall l' \in calls(l) : \mathcal{V}_v[\![v_2]\!] \sqsubseteq Val(x')$, when l' is the label of $(\lambda x'.e')$. Furthermore, for each expression let $x = b$ in e' we have $\mathcal{V}_b[\![b]\!] \sqsubseteq Val(x)$.

4.3 Termination

Finding the least solution for *Val*, *In*, and *Out* to the above constraint system for some program by fixpoint iteration will however not terminate, because of infinite chains such as $(\{l\}, \langle \rangle) \sqsubseteq (\{l\}, \langle (\{l\}, \langle \rangle) \rangle) \sqsubseteq \ldots$ To ensure termination, we use a variant of depth-k limiting.

We define the limiting operator θ_k as:

$$\theta_k \, (s, \top) = (s, \top)$$
$$\theta_k \, (s, \langle \rangle) = (s, \langle \rangle)$$
$$\theta_k \, (s, \langle v_1, \ldots, v_n \rangle) = (s, \langle \theta_{k-1} v_1, \ldots, \theta_{k-1} v_n \rangle), \text{if } k > 0$$
$$\theta_k \, (s, w) = (labels \, (s, w), \top), \text{if } k \leq 0$$

where

$$labels\,(s, \top) = s$$
$$labels\,(s, \langle\rangle) = s$$
$$labels\,(s, \langle v_1, \ldots, v_n\rangle) = \bigcup_{i=1}^{n} labels\,v_i \cup s$$

The rules given in Sect. 4.2 are modified as follows: For all call sites $(v_1\ v_2)^l$, $\forall l' \in calls(l): \theta_k Out(l') \sqsubseteq In(l)$, and $\forall l' \in calls(l): \theta_k \mathcal{V}_v[\![v_2]\!] \sqsubseteq Val(x')$, when l' is the label of $(\lambda x'.e')^l$.

Note that without the special treatment of list constructors, this form of approximation would generally lose too much information; in particular, recursion over a list would confuse the spine constructors with the elements of the same list. In essence, we have a "poor man's escape analysis on lists" [16] for a dynamically typed language.

4.4 Escape Analysis

As mentioned, in the scheme where data is allocated on the shared heap by default, the analysis needs to determine which heap-allocated data cannot escape the creating process, or reversely, which data can possibly escape. Following [18], we let *Escaped* represent the set of all escaping values, and add the following straightforward rules:

1. $In(xcall) \sqsubseteq Escaped$
2. $\mathcal{V}_v[\![v_2]\!] \sqsubseteq Escaped$ for all call sites $(v_1\ v_2)^l$ such that $xlambda \in calls(l)$
3. $\mathcal{V}_v[\![v_2]\!] \sqsubseteq Escaped$ for all send operators $v_1\ !\ v_2$
4. $\mathcal{V}_v[\![v_1]\!] \sqsubseteq Escaped$ and $\mathcal{V}_v[\![v_2]\!] \sqsubseteq Escaped$ for every spawn $(v_1\ v_2)$ in the program

After the fixpoint iteration converges, if the label of a data constructor operation (including lambdas) in the program is not in *labels(Escaped)*, the result produced by that operation does not escape the process.

It is easy to extend this escape analysis to simultaneously perform a more precise closure analysis than [18], which only uses sets, but doing so here would cloud the issues of this paper. Also, ERLANG programs tend to use fewer higher-order functions, in comparison with typical programs in e.g. Scheme or ML, so we expect that the improvements to the determined call graphs would not be significant in practice. Note that although our analysis is not in itself higher-order, we are able to handle the full higher-order language with generally sufficient precision.

4.5 Message Analysis

If we instead choose to allocate data on the local heap by default, we want the analysis to tell us which data could be part of a message, or reversely, which data cannot (or is not likely to). Furthermore, we need to be able to see whether or not a value could be a data constructor passed from outside the program.

For this purpose, we let the label *unknown* denote any such external constructor, and let *Message* represent the set of all possible messages.

We have the following rules:
1. $(\{unknown\}, \top) \sqsubseteq In(l)$ for all call sites $(v_1\ v_2)^l$ such that $xlambda \in calls(l)$
2. $\mathcal{V}_v[\![v_2]\!] \sqsubseteq Message$ for every $v_1\ !\ v_2$ in the program
3. $\mathcal{V}_v[\![v_1]\!] \sqsubseteq Message$ and $\mathcal{V}_v[\![v_2]\!] \sqsubseteq Message$ for every spawn $(v_1\ v_2)$ in the program

The main difference from the escape analysis, apart from also tracking unknown inputs, is that in this case we do not care about values that leave the current process except through explicit message passing. (The closure and argument used in a spawn can be viewed as being "sent" to the new process.) Indeed, we want to find only those values that may be passed from the constructor point to a send operation without leaving the current process.

Upon reaching a fixpoint, if the label of a data constructor is not in $labels(Message)$, the value constructed at that point is not part of any message. Furthermore, for each argument v_i to any constructor, if $unknown \notin labels(\mathcal{V}_v[\![v_i]\!])$, the argument value cannot be the result of a constructor outside the analyzed program. Note that since the result of a receive is necessarily a message, we know that it already is located in the shared area, and therefore not "unknown".

5 Using the Analysis Information

Depending on the selected scheme for allocation and message passing, the gathered escape information is used as follows in the compiler for the hybrid architecture:

5.1 Local Allocation of Non-messages

In this case, each data constructor in the program such that a value constructed at that point is known to *not* be part of any message, is rewritten so that the allocation will be performed on the local heap. No other modifications are needed. Note that with this scheme, unless the analysis is able to report some constructors as non-escaping, the process-local heaps will not be used at all.

5.2 Shared Allocation of Possible Messages

This requires two things:
1. Each data constructor in the program such that a value constructed at that point is likely to be a part of a message, is rewritten so that the allocation will be done on the shared heap.
2. For each argument of those message constructors, and for the message argument of each send-operation, if the passed value is not guaranteed to already be allocated on the shared heap, the argument is wrapped in a call to copy, in order to maintain the pointer directionality requirement.

In effect, with this scheme, we attempt to push the run-time copying operations backwards past as many allocation points as possible or suitable. It may then occur that because of over-approximation, some constructors will be made globally allocated although they will in fact not be part of any message. It follows that if an argument to such a constructor might be of unknown origin, it could be unnecessarily copied from the private heap to the shared area at runtime.

```
1   -module(test).
2   -export([main/3]).
3
4   main(Xs, Ys, Zs) ->
5       P = spawn(fun receiver/0),
6       mapsend(P, fun (X) -> element(2, X) end,
7               filter(fun (X) -> mod:test(X) end,
8                      zipwith3(fun (X, Y, Z) -> {X, {Y, Z}} end,
9                              Xs, Ys, Zs))),
10      P ! stop.
11
12  zipwith3(F, [X | Xs], [Y | Ys], [Z | Zs]) ->
13      [F(X, Y, Z) | zipwith3(F, Xs, Ys, Zs)];
14  zipwith3(F, [], [], []) -> [].
15
16  filter(F, [X | Xs]) ->
17      case F(X) of
18          true -> [X | filter(F, Xs)];
19          false -> filter(F, Xs)
20      end;
21  filter(F, []) -> [].
22
23  mapsend(P, F, [X | Xs]) ->
24      P ! F(X), mapsend(P, F, Xs);
26  mapsend(P, F, []) -> ok.
27
28  receiver() ->
29      receive
30          stop -> ok;
31          {X, Y} -> io:fwrite("~w: ~w.\n", [X, Y]), receiver()
33      end.
```

Fig. 3. ERLANG program example

5.3 Example

In Fig. 3, we show an example of an ERLANG program using two processes. The `main` function takes three equal-length lists, combines them into a single list of nested tuples, filters that list using a boolean function `test` defined in some other module `mod`, and sends the second component of each element in the resulting list to the spawned child process, which echoes the received values to the standard output.

The corresponding Core Erlang code looks rather similar. Translation to the language of this paper is straightforward, and mainly consists of expanding pattern matching, currying functions and identifying applications of primitives such as `hd`, `tl`, `!`, $element_k$, `receive`, etc., and primitive operations like `>`, `is_nil` and `is_cons`. Because of separate compilation, functions residing in other modules, as in the calls to `mod:test(X)` and `io:fwrite(...)`, are treated as unknown program parameters.

For this example, our escape analysis determines that only the list constructors in the functions zipwith3 and filter (lines 13 and 18, respectively) are guaranteed to not escape the executing process, and can be locally allocated. Since the actual elements of the list, created by the lambda passed to zipwith3 (line 8), are being passed to an unknown function via filter, they must be conservatively viewed as escaping.

On the other hand, the message analysis recognizes that only the innermost tuple constructor in the lambda body in line 8, plus the closure fun receiver/0 (line 5), can possibly be messages. If the strategy is to allocate locally by default, then placing that tuple constructor directly on the shared heap could reduce copying. However, the arguments Y and Z could both be created externally, and could thus need to be copied to maintain the pointer directionality invariant. The lambda body then becomes

$$\{X, \text{shared\_2\_tuple}(\text{copy}(Y), \text{copy}(Z))\}$$

where the outer tuple is locally allocated. (Note that the copy wrappers will not copy data that already resides on the shared heap; cf. Sect. 3.)

6 Performance Evaluation

The default runtime system architecture of Erlang/OTP R9 (Release 9)[1] is the process-centric one. Based on R9, we have also implemented the modifications needed for the hybrid architecture using the local-by-default allocation strategy, and included the above analyzes and transformations as a final stage on the Core Erlang representation in the Erlang/OTP compiler. By default, the compiler generates byte code from which, on SPARC or x86-based machines, native code can also be generated. We expect that the hybrid architecture will be included as an option in Erlang/OTP R10.

6.1 The Benchmarks

The performance evaluation was based on the following benchmarks:

life. Conway's game of life on a 10 by 10 board where each square is implemented as a process.
eddie. A medium-sized ERLANG application implementing an HTTP parser which handles http-get requests. This benchmark consists of a number of ERLANG modules and tests the effectiveness of our analyzes under separate (i.e., modular) compilation.
nag. A synthetic benchmark which creates a ring of processes. Each process creates one message which will be passed on 100 steps in the ring. **nag** is designed to test the behavior of the memory architectures under different program characteristics. The arguments are the number of processes to create and the size of the data passed in each message. It comes in two flavors: **same** and **keep**. The **same** variant creates one *single* message which is wrapped in a tuple together with a counter and is then continously forwarded. The **keep** variant creates a new message at every step, but keeps received messages live by storing them in a list.

---

[1] Available commercially from www.erlang.com and as open-source from www.erlang.org.

6.2 Effectiveness of the Message Analysis

Table 1 shows numbers of messages and words copied between the process-local heaps and the message area in the hybrid system, both when the message analysis is not used[2] and when it is.

Table 1. Numbers of messages sent and (partially) copied in the hybrid system

Benchmark	Messages sent	Messages copied No analysis	Messages copied Analysis	Words sent	Words copied No analysis	Words copied Analysis
life	8,000,404	100%	0.0%	32,002,806	100%	0.0%
eddie	20,050	100%	0.3%	211,700	81%	34%
nag - same 1000x250	103,006	100%	1.0%	50,829,185	1.6%	< 0.02%
nag - keep 1000x250	103,006	100%	1.0%	50,329,185	100%	< 0.02%

In the **life** benchmark, we see that while there is hardly any reuse of message data, so that the plain hybrid system cannot avoid copying data from the local heaps to the shared area, when the analysis is used the amount of copying shrinks to zero. This is expected, since the messages are simple and are typically built just before the send operations. The **eddie** benchmark, which is a real-world concurrent program, reuses about one fifth of the message data, but with the analysis enabled, the amount of copying shrinks from 81% to 34%. That this figure is not even lower is likely due to the separate compilation of its component modules, which limits the effectiveness of the analysis. In the **same** benchmark, we see that the hybrid system can be effective even without analysis when message data is heavily reused (only the top level message wrapper is copied at each send), but the analysis still offers an improvement. The **keep** version, on the other hand, creates new message data each time, and needs the analysis to avoid copying. It is clear from the table that, especially when large amounts of data are being sent, using message analysis can avoid much of the copying by identifying data that can be preallocated on the shared heap.

6.3 Compilation Overhead Due to the Analysis

In the byte code compiler, the analysis takes on average 19% of the compilation time, with a minimum of 3%. However, the byte code compiler is fast and relatively simplistic; for example, it does not in itself perform any global data flow analyzes. Including the message analysis as a stage in the more advanced HiPE native code compiler [13], its portion of the compilation time is below 10% in all benchmarks. ERLANG modules are separately compiled, and most source code files are small (less than 1000 lines). The numbers for **eddie** show the total code size and compilation times for all its modules. We have included the non-concurrent programs **prettyprint**, **pseudoknot**, and **inline** to show the overhead of the analysis on the compilation of larger single-module applications.

---

[2] The number of messages partially copied when no analysis is used can in principle be less than 100%, but only if messages are being forwarded exactly as is, which is rare.

Table 2. Compilation and analysis times

Benchmark	Lines	Byte code compilation			Native code compilation	
		Size (bytes)	Time (s)	Analysis part	Time (s)	Analysis part
life	201	2,744	0.7	6%	2.3	2%
eddie	2500	86,184	10.5	9%	76.4	1%
nag	149	2,764	0.7	5%	2.2	1%
prettyprint	1081	10,892	0.9	30%	13.1	2%
pseudoknot	3310	83,092	4.2	30%	12.7	9%
inline	2700	36,412	4.0	49%	19.3	7%

6.4 Runtime Performance

All benchmarks were ran on a dual processor Intel Xeon 2.4 GHz machine with 1 GB of RAM and 512 KB of cache per processor, running Linux. Times reported are the minimum of three runs and are presented excluding garbage collection times and normalized w.r.t. the process-centric memory architecture. Execution is divided into four parts: calculating message size (only in the process-centric architecture), copying of messages, bookkeeping overhead for sending messages, and mutator time (this includes normal process execution and scheduling, data allocation and initialization, and time spent in built-in functions).

In the figures, the columns marked P represent the process-centric (private heap) system, which is the current baseline implementation of ERLANG/OTP. Those marked H represent the hybrid system *without* any analysis to guide it (i.e., all data is originally allocated on the process-local heaps), and the columns marked A are those representing the hybrid system *with* the message analysis enabled.

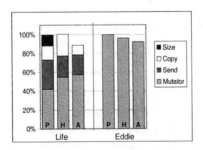

Fig. 4. Performance of non-synthetic programs

In Fig. 4, the **life** benchmark shows the behavior when a large number of small messages are being passed. The hybrid system with analysis is about 10% faster than the process-centric system, but we can see that although enabling the analysis removes the need for actual copying of message data (cf. Table 1), we still have a small overhead for the runtime safety check performed at each send operation (this could in principle be removed), which is comparable to the total copying time in the process-centric system when messages are very small. We can also see how the slightly more complicated bookkeeping for sending messages is noticeable in the process-centric system, and how on the other hand the mutator time can be larger in the hybrid system. (One reason is that allocation on the shared heap is more expensive.) In **eddie**, the message passing time is just a small fraction of the total runtime, and we suspect that the slightly better performance of the hybrid system is due to better locality because of message sharing (cf. Table 1).

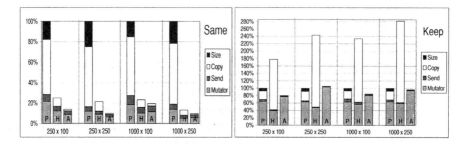

Fig. 5. Performance of the **same** and **keep** variants of the **nag** benchmark

Figure 5 shows the performance of the **nag** benchmark. Here, the hybrid system shows its advantages compared to the process-centric system when messages are larger, especially in the **same** program where most of the message data is reused. (Naturally, the speedup can be made arbitrarily large by increasing the message size, but we think that we have used reasonable sizes in our benchmarks, and that forwarding of data is not an atypical task in concurrent applications.) In the **keep** case, we see that the hybrid system with message analysis enabled is usually faster than the process-centric system also when there is no reuse. The excessive copying times in the hybrid system without the analysis show a weakness of the current copying routine, which uses the C call stack for recursion (the messages in this benchmark are lists).

7 Related Work

Our message analysis is in many respects similar to escape analysis. Escape analysis was introduced by Park and Goldberg [16], and further refined by Deutsch [9] and Blanchet [3]. So far, its main application has been to permit stack allocation of data in functional languages. In [4], Blanchet extended his analysis to handle assignments and applied it to the Java language, allocating objects on the stack and also eliminating synchronization on objects that do not escape their creating thread. Concurrently with Blanchet's work, Bogda and Hölzle [5] used a variant of escape analysis to similarly remove unnecessary synchronization in Java programs by finding objects that are reachable only by a single thread and Choi et al. [8] used a reachability graph based escape analysis for the same purposes. Ruf [17] focuses on synchronization removal by regarding only properties over the whole lifetimes of objects, tracking the flow of values through global state but sacrificing precision within methods and especially in the presence of recursion. It should be noted that with the exception of [8], all these escape analyzes rely heavily on static type information, and in general sacrifice precision in the presence of recursive data structures. Recursive data structures are extremely common in ERLANG and type information is not available in our context.

Our hybrid memory model is inspired in part by a runtime system architecture described by Doligez and Leroy in [10] that uses thread-specific areas for young generations and a shared data area for the old generation. It also shares characteristics with the architecture of KaffeOS [2], an operating system for executing Java programs. Using escape analysis to guide a memory management system with thread-specific heaps was described by Steensgaard [19].

Notice that it is also possible to view the hybrid model as a runtime system architecture with a shared heap and separate *regions* for each process. Region-based memory management, introduced by Tofte and Talpin [20], typically allocates objects in separate areas according to their lifetimes. The compiler, guided by a static analysis called *region inference*, is responsible to generate code that deallocates these areas. The simplest form of region inference places objects in areas whose lifetimes coincide with that of their creating functions. In this respect, one can view the process-specific heaps of the hybrid model as regions whose lifetime coincides with that of the top-level function invocation of each process, and see our message analysis as a simple region inference algorithm for discovering data which outlives their creating processes.

8 Concluding Remarks

Aiming to employ a runtime system architecture which is tailored to the intended use of data in high-level concurrent languages, we have devised a powerful and practical static analysis, called *message analysis*, that can be used to guide the allocation process. Notable characteristics of our analysis are that it is tailored to its context, a dynamically typed, higher-order, concurrent language employing asynchronous message passing, and the fact that it does not sacrifice precision in the presence of recursion over lists. As shown in our performance evaluation, the analysis is in practice fast, effective enough to discover most data which is to be used as a message, and allows the resulting system to combine the best performance characteristics of both a process-centric and a shared-heap architecture and achieve (often significantly) better performance.

References

1. J. Armstrong, R. Virding, C. Wikström, and M. Williams. *Concurrent Programming in Erlang*. Prentice-Hall, second edition, 1996.
2. G. Back, W. C. Hsieh, and J. Lepreau. Processes in KaffeOS: Isolation, resource management, and sharing in Java. In *Proceedings of the 4th USENIX Symposium on Operating Systems Design and Implementation*, Oct. 2000. http://www.cs.utah.edu/flux/papers/.
3. B. Blanchet. Escape analysis: Correctness proof, implementation and experimental results. In *Conference Record of the 25th ACM SIGACT-SIGPLAN Symposium on Principles of Programming Languages (POPL'98)*, pages 25–37. ACM Press, Jan. 1998.
4. B. Blanchet. Escape analysis for object oriented languages. Application to Java^{TM}. In *Proceedings of the 14th Conference on Object-Oriented Programming Systems, Languages and Applications (OOPSLA'99)*, pages 20–34. ACM Press, Nov. 1999.

5. J. Bogda and U. Hölzle. Removing unnecessary synchronization in Java. In *Proceedings of the 14th Conference on Object-Oriented Programming Systems, Languages and Applications (OOPSLA'99)*, Nov. 1999.
6. R. Carlsson. An introduction to Core Erlang. In *Proceedings of the PLI'01 Erlang Workshop*, Sept. 2001.
7. R. Carlsson, B. Gustavsson, E. Johansson, T. Lindgren, S.-O. Nyström, M. Pettersson, and R. Virding. Core Erlang 1.0 language specification. Technical Report 030, Information Technology Department, Uppsala University, Nov. 2000.
8. J.-D. Choi, M. Gupta, M. Serrano, V. C. Shreedhar, and S. Midkiff. Escape analysis for Java. In *Proceedings of the 14th Conference on Object-Oriented Programming Systems, Languages and Applications (OOPSLA'99)*, pages 1–19. ACM Press, Nov. 1999.
9. A. Deutsch. On the complexity of escape analysis. In *Conference Record of the 24th Annual ACM SIGACT-SIGPLAN Symposium on Principles of Programming Languages*, pages 358–371, Jan. 1997.
10. D. Doligez and X. Leroy. A concurrent, generational garbage collector for a multithreaded implementation of ML. In *Conference Record of the ACM SIGPLAN-SIGACT Symposium on Principles of Programming Languages*, pages 113–123. ACM Press, Jan. 1993.
11. T. Domani, G. Goldshtein, E. Kolodner, E. Lewis, E. Petrank, and D. Sheinwald. Thread-local heaps for Java. In *Proceedings of ISMM'2002: ACM SIGPLAN International Symposium on Memory Management*, pages 76–87. ACM Press, June 2002.
12. C. Flanagan, A. Sabry, B. F. Duba, and M. Felleisen. The essence of compiling with continuations. In *Proceedings of the ACM SIGPLAN Conference on Programming Language Design and Implementation*. ACM Press, June 1993.
13. E. Johansson, M. Pettersson, and K. Sagonas. HiPE: A High Performance Erlang system. In *Proceedings of the ACM SIGPLAN Conference on Principles and Practice of Declarative Programming*, pages 32–43. ACM Press, Sept. 2000.
14. E. Johansson, K. Sagonas, and J. Wilhelmsson. Heap architectures for concurrent languages using message passing. In *Proceedings of ISMM 2002: ACM SIGPLAN International Symposium on Memory Management*, pages 88–99. ACM Press, June 2002.
15. R. E. Jones and R. Lins. *Garbage Collection: Algorithms for automatic memory management*. John Wiley & Sons, 1996.
16. Y. G. Park and B. Goldberg. Escape analysis on lists. In *Proceedings of the ACM SIGPLAN Conference on Programming Language Design and Implementation*, pages 116–127. ACM Press, July 1992.
17. E. Ruf. Effective synchronization removal for Java. In *Proceedings of the SIGPLAN Conference on Programming Language Design and Implementation*, pages 208–218. ACM Press, June 2000.
18. O. Shivers. Control flow analysis in Scheme. In *Proceedings of the ACM SIGPLAN Conference on Programming Language Design and Implementation*, pages 164–174. ACM Press, June 1988.
19. B. Steensgaard. Thread-specific heaps for multi-threaded programs. In *Proceedings of the ACM SIGPLAN International Symposium on Memory Management*, pages 18–24. ACM Press, Oct. 2000.
20. M. Tofte and J.-P. Talpin. Region-based memory management. *Information and Computation*, 132(2):109–176, Feb. 1997.

Instantaneous Termination in Pure Esterel

Olivier Tardieu and Robert de Simone

INRIA, Sophia Antipolis, France

Abstract. Esterel is a design language for the representation of embedded systems. Based on the synchronous reactive paradigm, its execution relies on a clear distinction of instants of computation. As a consequence, deciding whether a piece of a program may or may not run instantaneously is central to any compilation scheme, both for correctness and efficiency. In general, this information can be obtained by an exhaustive exploration of all possible execution paths, which is expensive. Most compilers approximate it through algorithmic methods amenable to static analysis. In our contribution, we first formalize the analysis involved in detecting statements that may run instantaneously. Then, we identify statements that may terminate and be instantaneously reentered. This allows us to model precisely these compilers front-end activities with a clear mathematical specification and led us to uncover inefficiencies in the Esterel v5 academic compiler from *Ecole des Mines* and *INRIA*.

1 Introduction

We shall introduce a number of static analysis techniques specific to the synchronous reactive language Esterel [6–9]. Interestingly, Esterel both allows and requires these static analyses. It allows them because of its structural "process calculus"-flavored syntax, because of its formal operational semantics, and because of its finite-state interpretation, all which Cavour easy application of static analysis methods. It requires them mainly because the synchronous paradigm promotes a crisp division of reactive behaviors between *discrete instants*, and that the definition of instantaneous reactions has to be *well-founded*. Compilers for Esterel not only benefit from static analysis techniques in optimization passes, but they heavily rely on them just to achieve correct compilation!

We give two examples of typical phenomena involved with the notion of discrete reactions, which will be at the heart of our studies:

Instantaneous loops stand for diverging behaviors, which never reach completion inside a reaction, so that the end of the instant never comes. They can be branded as *non-convergent* or *non-Zeno* behaviors. Example 1 of Figure 1 is pattern of program that may exhibit such diverging behavior. If the dots are traversed instantaneously and if the signal I is present then the loop is restarted infinitely many times within an instant. An extra difficulty in the case of Esterel comes from the presence of *parallel* statements as well as fancy *exception* raising/trapping mechanisms, so that a proper static notion of *instantaneous termination* is not all that obvious;

```
           loop                                loop
             trap T in                           signal S in
               ...;                                present S then ... end;
    (1)        present I then exit T end;   (2)    pause;
             pause                                 emit S
           end                                   end
         end                                   end
```

Fig. 1. Potentially incorrect (1) or schizophrenic (2) loop bodies

Schizophrenic (sub)programs are those compound statements which can be run and exited or terminated *and* reentered *inside* the same reaction [3, 5, 18]. Such statements can be problematic because the local variables and signals involved may end up having two distinct occurrences in the same reaction, with differing values. In Example 2, the signal S is defined inside the loop. Each iteration refers to a fresh signal S. In a given instant two instances of S cohabit: the first being emitted at the end of the loop, and the second being tested as the loop is reentered. As in general (not here) the multiple values of such a signal have to be computed *simultaneously*, more than one object has to be allocated for this signal. Due to the kind of embedded application code targeted by Esterel this has to be done statically at compile time.

These analyses will serve to formally define and justify front-end parts of the previously developed compiler, which were implemented without such formal information. In some places we even spotted several minor problems in the existing code when (and because of) formalizing these issues.

After a brief presentation of the core Esterel language and its semantic features relevant to our study (Section 2), we turn to the issue of *instantaneous termination* detection by dedicated static analysis computation (Section 3). Then we face the *schizophrenia* problem with similar aims (Section 4). In all cases we provide formal definitions by structural recursion along the syntax for our techniques, and then we informally discuss their correctness and complexity. We conclude with comments on how and where our modelization as static analysis techniques of these specific front-end compiling activities helped gain better insights of them (Section 5).

2 The Pure Esterel Kernel Language

Esterel [6–9] is an imperative synchronous parallel programming language dedicated to reactive systems [14, 17]. Pure Esterel is the fragment of the full Esterel language where data variables and data-handling primitives are discarded. Thus, the information carried by a signal is limited to a *presence/absence* status. While this paper concentrates on Pure Esterel, extending the results to the full Esterel language is straightforward. Moreover, without loss of generality, we focus on the Pure Esterel kernel language as defined by Berry in [5], which retains just enough of the Pure Esterel language syntax to attain its full expressive power.

nothing	do nothing (terminate instantaneously)
pause	freeze until next instant
signal S in p end	declare signal S in p
emit S	emit signal S (i.e. S is present)
present S then p else q end	if S is present then do p else do q
suspend p when S	suspend execution of p if S is present
loop p end	repeat p forever
$p; q$	do q in sequence with p
[$p \parallel q$]	do p in parallel with q
trap T in p end	declare and catch exception T in p
exit T	throw exception T

Fig. 2. Statements of pure Esterel

2.1 Syntax and Intuitive Semantics

The Pure Esterel kernel language defines three kinds of objects: *statements*, *signals* and *exceptions*. Signals and exceptions are identifiers. Statements are recursively defined as shown by Figure 2. The non-terminals p and q denote statements, S signals and T exceptions. Signals and exceptions are lexically scoped and respectively declared inside statements by the instructions "signal *signal* in *statement* end" and "trap *exception* in *statement* end".

We say a statement is closed with respect to exceptions iff any exception T is bounded by a declaration of T, in other words iff any "exit T" occurs inside a "trap T in ... end" statement. We call these statements *programs*.

We consider free signals in programs as *interface signals*. We call *input signals* the interface signals that are never emitted inside the program. We call *output signals* the rest of them. Moreover, bounded signals are said to be *local signals*.

The disambiguation of the scopes of nested sequential and parallel compositions is obtained by enclosing parallel statements into brackets. Then or else branches of present statements may be omitted. Finally, note that the suspend statement will not be discussed as it introduces no technical difficulty on its own.

2.2 The Synchronous Reactive Paradigm

An Esterel program runs in steps called reactions. Each reaction takes one instant. When the clock first ticks, the execution starts. It may either terminate instantaneously or freeze until next instant (next clock cycle), through *pause* instructions, from where the execution is resumed when the clock ticks again. If so, it may then terminate or freeze again. And so on...

"emit A; pause; emit B; emit C; pause; emit D" emits the signal A in the first instant of its execution, then emits B and C in the second instant, then emits D and terminates in the third instant. It takes three instants to complete, or in other words, proceeds by three reactions.

Reactions take no logical time. All statements executed during a reaction are considered to be simultaneous. In this first example, there is no notion of B being emitted before C.

Parallelism in Esterel is very different from the asynchronous composition of many concurrent languages or formalisms such as ADA or OCCAM [2, 19]: execution propagates in parallel branches in a deterministic synchronous way.

"[pause; emit A; pause; emit B || emit C; pause; emit D]" emits the signal C in the first instant of its chain reaction, then emits A and D in the second instant, then emits B and terminates. By definition, "[p || q]" terminates when the last of p and q terminates (in the absence of exceptions).

2.3 Loops and Non-Zenoness Condition

"loop emit S; pause end" emits S at each instant and never terminates. This compound statement is the kernel expansion of the instruction "sustain S". Note that using exceptions, it will be possible to escape from loops.

Remark the "pause" inside the loop. In Esterel, the body of a loop is not allowed to terminate instantaneously when started. It must execute either a pause or an exit statement. This constraint ensures *non-Zenoness* of Esterel programs: as each loop body is traversed at most once at a given instant, the computation of one reaction of a correct program always ends. This is of course expected from a reactive language, which claims to proceed by instantaneous reactions! Section 3 will be devoted to methods that ensure this requirement holds for a given program.

2.4 Exceptions

Exceptions in sequential code behave as structural gotos to the end of the trap. "trap T in emit A; pause; emit B; exit T; emit C end; emit D" emits A first, then B and D and terminates. In this case, the statement "emit C" is unreachable. Exceptions may also occur in parallel constructions as in:

```
trap T in
  [emit A; pause; emit B; pause; emit C || emit D; pause; exit T]
end;
emit E
```

A and D are emitted in the first instant, then B and E in the second instant. As expected, "emit C" is never reached. The second "pause" of the left branch of the parallel is *reached* but not *executed* because it is *preempted* by the simultaneously occurring exception. However, since "exit T" does not prevent B to be emitted, we say that exceptions implement *weak* preemption.

Exceptions may also be nested. In such a case, the outermost exception has priority. In the following program, A is not emitted since T has priority on U: "trap T in trap U in [exit T || exit U] end; emit A end".

If we consider not only programs but statements in general, we may encounter undeclared exceptions, as in "trap T in [exit T || exit U] end; exit T". The left "exit T" raises an exception matched within the statement by the enclosing "trap T in ... end", while both "exit U" and the second "exit T" refer to undeclared/unmatched exceptions. We say that by raising such an exception a statement *exits*.

2.5 Signals

In an instant, a signal S is either present or absent. If S is present all executed "present S" statements execute their then branch in this instant; if S is absent, they all execute their else branch. A local or output signal S is present iff it is explicitly emitted, absent otherwise. The input signals are provided by the *environment*. Each execution cycle involves the following steps:

- The environment provides the *valuation*[1] of the input signals. The *set of inputs* of a reaction is the set of input signals set present by the environment.
- The reaction occurs.
- The environment observes the resulting valuation of the output signals.

2.6 Logical Correctness and Behavioral Semantics

Since signal emissions can occur inside present statements, it is possible to write incorrect programs such as:

- "signal S in present S else emit S end end"
  If S is present it cannot be emitted. On the other hand, if S is not present it is emitted. Both cases are contradictory.
- "signal S in present S then emit S end end"
  S may either be present or absent. This program is not deterministic.

A program is said to be *logically correct* iff there exists exactly one possible valuation of its signals for any set of inputs at any stage of the execution. In addition, a valuation of the free signals of a given statement is said to be *admissible* for this statement if it can be extended into a unique valuation of all its signals coherent with the statement semantics. This is formalized by the *logical behavioral semantics* of Esterel, which we briefly sketch in Appendix A.

2.7 Constructive Semantics

There is no efficient algorithm to compute these valuations in general. The program "signal S in present S then emit S else emit S end end" is logically correct since S can only be present. Nevertheless, its execution relies on a guess. The signal S has first to be guessed present before it can be emitted.

The *constructive semantics* of Esterel precisely avoid such guesses by restricting the set of correct programs to the so called *constructive programs*. The execution of a "present S" statement is blocked until S is known to be present or absent. The signal S is present as soon as one "emit S" is certainly executed in the current reaction. It is absent as soon as all "emit S" statements are proved to be unreachable in the current reaction, due to effective choices taken so far.

We strongly encourage the reader to refer to [4, 5] for further information about these issues and more generally about Esterel formal semantics. In the sequel, we focus on logically correct programs and behavioral semantics as the refinement provided by the constructive semantics is orthogonal to our concerns.

---

[1] In Pure Esterel, *valuation* is just a shortcut for "present/absent statuses".

3 Instantaneous Termination

The first reaction of a program may either terminate its execution or lead to (at least) one more reaction. Thus, for a given set of inputs, the execution of a program may either be *instantaneous* if it completes in a single reaction or *non-instantaneous* it if does not, that is to say if it lasts for at least two instants. We say that a program *cannot be instantaneous* iff its execution is never instantaneous i.e. is non-instantaneous for any inputs.

We want to extend this definition to statements. For a given admissible valuation of its free signals, the behavior of a statement is deterministic. Its first reaction may either (i) lead to one more reaction or (ii) exit or (iii) terminate its execution (without exiting). Thus, the execution of a statement either:

lasts by taking at least two reactions to complete
exits instantaneously by raising a free exception
terminates instantaneously otherwise

We says that a statement *cannot be instantaneous* iff, for any admissible valuation of its free signals, it does not terminate instantaneously i.e. it either lasts or exits instantaneously. As a consequence, if a statement cannot be instantaneous, its execution cannot start and terminate within a unique reaction of the program it is part of. If a statement p cannot be instantaneous, then q is never reached in the first instant of the execution of "p; q". Let's consider a few examples:

- "`exit T`" cannot be instantaneous (as it always exits)
- "`present I then exit T end`" may be instantaneous
- "`present I then exit T else pause end`" cannot be instantaneous
- "`trap T in exit T end`" may be instantaneous (is always instantaneous)

The definition of Esterel specifies that the body of a loop cannot be instantaneous (cf. Section 2.3). In the rest of this section, we discuss methods to ensure that a given statement cannot be instantaneous. First we consider exact analysis in Section 3.1, then we formalize efficient static analyses. Because of exceptions, this is not straightforward. Thus, we start by restricting ourselves to exception-free statements in Section 3.2. We further introduce exceptions in two steps in Sections 3.3 and 3.4. We discuss the current implementation in Section 3.5.

3.1 Exact Analysis

The exact decision procedure is obvious. For a given statement, it consists in computing its first reaction for all possible valuations of its free signals and checking that the execution does not terminate instantaneously in each admissible case.

The number of valuations is finite but exponential in the number of free signals, which can be linear in the size of the statement. In fact, as illustrated by Figure 3, SAT (the problem of boolean satisfiability in propositional logic) can be expressed in terms of instantaneous termination of Pure Esterel programs (by a polynomial reduction). A valuation satisfies the boolean formula iff it makes the

$(A \lor \neg B \lor C) \land (\neg A \lor C \lor \neg D) \land (\neg B \lor \neg C \lor D)$ is satisfiable

$\Updownarrow$

```
present A else present B then present C else pause end end end;
present A then present C else present D then pause end end end;
present B then present C then present D else pause end end end
```
may be instantaneous

Fig. 3. Reducing SAT to instantaneous termination

execution of the corresponding program terminate instantaneously. Reciprocally, there exists no such valuation iff the program cannot be instantaneous.

To the best of our knowledge, this procedure has never been experimented with. Whether it is tractable in practice or not remains an open question. Nevertheless, NP complexity is a strong argument in favor of approximate analysis.

3.2 Static Analysis for Exception-Free Statements

Since we are now interested in conservative analysis, a statement labeled with "may be instantaneous" could well be a statement that "cannot be instantaneous", which we missed because of approximations. On the other hand, a statement labeled with "cannot be instantaneous" truly cannot be.

Figure 4 gives a first set of rules applicable to exception-free statements. For example, in order for the execution of "p; q" to terminate instantaneously it has to be true that p is executed instantaneously, instantaneously transferring control to q, which itself has to terminate instantaneously. By quantifying on all admissible valuation, we extract the rule: "p; q" cannot be instantaneous as soon as p or q cannot be instantaneous.

`nothing`	may be instantaneous
`pause`	cannot be instantaneous
`signal S in p end`	cannot be instantaneous if p cannot
`emit S`	may be instantaneous
`present S then p else q end`	cannot be instantaneous if both p and q cannot
`suspend p when S`	cannot be instantaneous if p cannot
`loop p end`	cannot be instantaneous, p *has to be* non-instantaneous
p; q	cannot be instantaneous if p or q cannot
$[p \;||\; q]$	cannot be instantaneous if p or q cannot

Fig. 4. Non-instantaneous exception-free statements

These rules can provably be shown to match formally an abstraction [11] of Pure Esterel semantics. The proof of the last analysis of this section (the more complex) is detailed in Appendix B.

Deriving from the rules a compositional algorithm that proceeds by structural recursion along the syntax of a statement is straightforward: the entries of

Figure 4 are the facts and predicates of a logic program, which can be run by a Prolog like depth-first search algorithm.

This analysis is compositional, in the sense that the denotation of a compound statement is a function of the denotations of its subterms. More precisely in this first framework, the denotation of a statement p is the boolean value $\mathcal{D}_p$ of the predicate "(we know that) p cannot be instantaneous" and the composition functions are boolean conjunctions or disjunctions. In particular, $\mathcal{D}_{p;\ q}$ is equal to $\mathcal{D}_p \vee \mathcal{D}_q$.

However, even if p and q may be instantaneous, this does not imply in general that "$p;\ q$" may also be. The analysis fails to prove this program cannot be instantaneous: "present S then pause end; present S else pause end". As the rules for "$p;\ q$" and "$[p\ ||\ q]$" do not take into account synchronization between p and q, the results may be imprecise (but correct). There is a trade-off between efficiency and precision. The analysis only requires a linear number of constant-time computations, so its complexity is linear in the size of the statement. Dealing with correlated signal statuses and potential synchronization configurations would very quickly reintroduce the complexity of exact analysis.

3.3 Static Analysis for All Statements

In order to extend this analysis to handle exceptions, the calculus detailed in Figure 5 has also to decide whether the body p of a "trap T in p end" statement may instantaneously raise T or not, since this would lead the statement to terminate instantaneously.

p	$\mathcal{D}_p$	$\mathcal{X}_p$
nothing	$false$	$\emptyset$
pause	$true$	$\emptyset$
signal S in p end	$\mathcal{D}_p$	$\mathcal{X}_p$
emit S	$false$	$\emptyset$
present S then p else q end	$\mathcal{D}_p \wedge \mathcal{D}_q$	$\mathcal{X}_p \cup \mathcal{X}_q$
suspend p when S	$\mathcal{D}_p$	$\mathcal{X}_p$
loop p end	$true$	$\mathcal{X}_p$
$p;\ q$	$\mathcal{D}_p \vee \mathcal{D}_q$	$\mathcal{X}_p \cup [\neg \mathcal{D}_p \to \mathcal{X}_q]$
$[p\ ||\ q]$	$\mathcal{D}_p \vee \mathcal{D}_q$	$\mathcal{X}_p \cup \mathcal{X}_q$
trap T in p end	$\mathcal{D}_p \wedge (T \notin \mathcal{X}_p)$	$\mathcal{X}_p \backslash \{T\}$
exit T	$true$	$\{T\}$

Fig. 5. Non-instantaneous statements

The denotation of a statement p becomes a pair $(\mathcal{D}_p, \mathcal{X}_p)$ where:

- $\mathcal{D}_p$ remains the predicate "p cannot be instantaneous";
- $\mathcal{X}_p$ is the set of exceptions that p may raise instantaneously.

It is now possible to define $\mathcal{D}_{\text{trap } T \text{ in } p \text{ end}}$ as $\mathcal{D}_p \wedge (T \notin \mathcal{X}_p)$. In Figure 5 and thereafter, we use the notation $[\mathcal{P} \to \mathcal{S}]$ as a shortcut for "if $\mathcal{P}$ then $\mathcal{S}$ else

$\emptyset$". The set of exceptions that "$p; q$" may raise instantaneously is $\mathcal{X}_p \cup \mathcal{X}_q$ if p may be instantaneous or $\mathcal{X}_p$ only if p cannot be instantaneous, that is to say $\mathcal{X}_p \cup [\neg \mathcal{D}_p \to \mathcal{X}_q]$.

This new analysis remains linear in the size of the code, if we suppose that the number of levels of nested trap statements never exceeds a fixed bound. We remark that the Esterel v5 compiler has a hard 32 limit.

3.4 Static Analysis Using Completion Codes

In the previous section, we have described a procedure to ensure that a statement cannot be instantaneous. It is approximate but conservative: it may be unable to prove that a statement cannot be instantaneous even if it cannot be, but it never concludes that a statement cannot be instantaneous if it can be.

We achieved linear complexity by (i) providing a compositional algorithm which proceeds by structural recursion along the syntax of the statement and (ii) abstracting away signal statuses so that the denotation of a statement remains a simple object (a boolean plus a set of bounded size).

These two constraints leave hardly any room for improvement. But we can still do better, as we have not yet taken into account trap priorities. Let's consider the following statement:

```
trap T in
    trap U in
        trap V in [exit U || exit V] end; exit T
    end;
    pause
end
```

As we have defined $\mathcal{X}_{[p \,||\, q]}$ as $\mathcal{X}_p \cup \mathcal{X}_q$, the computation proceeds as follows:

$\mathcal{X}_{[\text{exit U } ||\text{ exit V}]} = \{\text{U, V}\}$
$\mathcal{D}_{\text{trap V in [exit U || exit V] end}} = \mathit{false}$
$\mathcal{X}_{\text{trap V in [exit U || exit V] end; exit T}} = \{\text{T, U}\}$
$\mathcal{X}_{\text{trap U in trap V in [exit U || exit V] end; exit T end; pause}} = \{\text{T}\}$
$\mathcal{D}_{\text{trap T in trap U in trap V in [exit U || exit V] end; exit T end; pause end}} = \mathit{false}$

It concludes that the statement may be instantaneous. However, since U has priority on V, a more precise analysis seems feasible, something like:

$\mathcal{X}_{[\text{exit U } ||\text{ exit V}]} = \{\text{U}\}$
$\mathcal{D}_{\text{trap V in [exit U || exit V] end}} = \mathit{true}$
$\mathcal{X}_{\text{trap V in [exit U || exit V] end; exit T}} = \{\text{U}\}$
$\mathcal{X}_{\text{trap U in trap V in [exit U || exit V] end; exit T end; pause}} = \emptyset$
$\mathcal{D}_{\text{trap T in trap U in trap V in [exit U || exit V] end; exit T end; pause end}} = \mathit{true}$

In other words, as the analyzer decomposes a compound statement into its parts, it should keep track of the relative priorities of exceptions. Then, this order would be taken into account in the rule for "[p || q]".

Such a calculus is possible. It relies on the idea of completion codes[2] introduced in Esterel by Gonthier [15]. Let's consider a statement s such that no two exceptions of s share the same name (applying alpha-conversion to these names if necessary). There exists a function that associates with each exception T occurring in s a completion code $k_T \in \mathbb{N} \cup \{+\infty\}$ such that:

- $\forall T, k_T \geq 2$
- $\forall T, k_T = +\infty$ if T is unmatched in s, $k_T \in \mathbb{N}$ otherwise
- $\forall U, \forall V, U \neq V \Rightarrow k_U \neq k_V$
- $\forall U, \forall V, scope(V) \subset scope(U)$ (i.e. U has priority over V) $\Rightarrow k_U > k_V$

For example, the set $\{k_T = 8, k_U = 3, k_V = +\infty\}$ is admissible for the statement "trap T in trap U in [exit T || exit U] end end; exit V".

Using these completion codes, it is now possible to compute potential instantaneous behaviors of a subterm p of s with respect to termination as described by Figure 6. The denotation of a statement p is the set $\mathcal{K}_p$ of its potential completion codes, that is to say a set that contains:

- 0 if p may instantaneously terminate
- 1 if p may instantaneously execute a "pause" statement
- k_T if p may instantaneously raise the exception T local to s
- $+\infty$ if p may instantaneously raise an exception not caught in s

p	$\mathcal{K}_p$
nothing	$\{0\}$
pause	$\{1\}$
signal S in p end	$\mathcal{K}_p$
emit S	$\{0\}$
present S then p else q end	$\mathcal{K}_p \cup \mathcal{K}_q$
suspend p when S	$\mathcal{K}_p$
loop p end	$\mathcal{K}_p$ (by hypothesis $0 \notin \mathcal{K}_p$)
$p; q$	$(\mathcal{K}_p \backslash \{0\}) \cup [(0 \in \mathcal{K}_p) \to \mathcal{K}_q]$
[p || q]	$\{\max(k,l) | \forall k \in \mathcal{K}_p, \forall l \in \mathcal{K}_q\}$
trap T in p end	$(\mathcal{K}_p \backslash \{k_T\}) \cup [(k_T \in \mathcal{K}_p) \to \{0\}]$
exit T	$\{k_T\}$

Fig. 6. Potential completion codes

This analysis is essentially equivalent to the previous one. As expected, the rule for "exit T" encodes the level of priority of T. Remark the rule associated with "[p || q]". If p may have completion code k and q may have completion code l then "[p || q]" may admit completion code $\max(k,l)$ as illustrated by Figure 7. With completion codes, we have not only encoded trap priorities

---

[2] For the sake of simplicity, we refrain from introducing here the classical de Bruijn encoding [12] of completion codes and describe a similar but less efficient encoding.

[p || q]	k	l	max(k,l)
[nothing || nothing]	0	0	0
[nothing || pause]	0	1	1
[pause || pause]	1	1	1
[nothing || exit T]	0	k_T	k_T
[pause || exit T]	1	k_T	k_T
[exit T || exit U]	k_T	k_U	$\max(k_T, k_U)$

Fig. 7. The Max formula

making the last line of this table possible, but also precedence relations between nothing, pause and exit statements, so that the "max" formula always works.

The analysis is conservative. Its complexity is linear in the size of the statement under the hypotheses of (i) bounded depth of nested traps and (ii) usage of de Bruijn [12, 15] completion codes. The subset $\mathcal{K}_s$ of $\{0, 1, +\infty\}$ computed for the statement s itself contains the set of completion codes that may be observed while running s. Going back to the initial problem, we conclude:

- s cannot be instantaneous if $0 \notin \mathcal{K}_s$;
- s must be instantaneous if $\mathcal{K}_s = \{0\}$.

3.5 Comparison with Current Implementation

In the Esterel v5 compiler, the analysis of instantaneous termination occurs twice, applied first to an internal representation of the kernel language structure, then to the circuit representation (as part of the cyclicity analysis). While the initial rejection of potentially instantaneous loop bodies relies on the formalism of the last section, the second analysis (more precisely the current combination of the translation into circuits with the cyclicity analysis) is less precise. For example, "loop [... || pause]; emit S; pause; present S then ... end end" passes the first analysis but not the second one!

We characterized the patterns of programs that expose this behavior of the compiler and identified the changes required in the translation into circuits to avoid it.

4 Schizophrenia

In Section 3, we have formalized an algorithm to check if a Pure Esterel statement cannot be instantaneous. In this section, we shall consider a second, rather similar problem. Given a statement q in a program p, is it possible for the statement q to terminate or exit and be restarted within the same reaction? For example, if p is "loop q end", when q terminates (if it eventually does), then q is instantaneously restarted by the enclosing loop. On the other hand, if p is "loop pause; q end" then q cannot terminate or exit and be restarted instantaneously, thanks to the "pause" statement.

As usual in the Esterel terminology, we say that q is *schizophrenic* if the answer is yes [3, 5, 18]. The point is: we do not like signal and parallel statements to be schizophrenic! A schizophrenic signal may carry two different values within a single reaction (cf. Section 1). Similarly, a schizophrenic parallel requires two synchronizations. Obviously, without some kind of unfolding, both are incompatible with single-static-assignment frameworks such as Digital Sequential Circuits[3].

Having introduced the notion of schizophrenic contexts in Section 4.1, we discuss static analyses again in two steps: first considering exception-free contexts in Section 4.2, then getting rid of the restriction in Section 4.3. We relate our formalization to the current implementation in Section 4.4.

4.1 Contexts

From now on, if q is a statement of the program p, we call *context of q in p* and note $C[\ ]$ the rest of p, that is to say, p where q has been replaced by a hole [ ]. In the last example, the context of q in p is $C[\ ] \equiv$ "loop pause; [ ] end".

Contexts are recursively defined:

- [ ] is the empty context;
- if $C[\ ]$ is a context then $C[\text{present } S \text{ then } [\ ] \text{ else } q \text{ end}]$ is a context...

As usual [1], $C[x]$ denotes the statement (respectively context) obtained by substituting the hole [ ] of $C[\ ]$ by the statement (respectively context) x. We say that $C[\ ]$ is a *valid* context for the statement p, if $C[p]$ is not only a statement but also a correct program. In the sequel, we shall consider only such compositions.

The fact that p is schizophrenic in $C[\ ]$ depends on both p and $C[\ ]$. If $C[\ ]$ is "signal S in loop [ ]; present S then pause end end end" and p is "pause" then p is schizophrenic in this context. On the other hand, if p is "pause; emit S" then p is not schizophrenic since the then branch of the present statement is taken. We say that $C[\ ]$ is *schizophrenic* if and only if there exists a p such that p is schizophrenic in $C[\ ]$.

4.2 Static Analysis for Exception-Free Contexts

This first case is quite simple. Obviously in order for a statement to be instantaneously restarted, it has to appear enclosed in a loop. It may be enclosed in many nested loops, however since loops are infinite only the innermost loop has to be taken into account. Then, if in the body of this loop, this statement is in sequence somehow with a statement which cannot be instantaneous, it is not schizophrenic. Otherwise, it probably is.

This is exactly the reasoning steps we implement in Figure 8. In a manner similar to Figure 4, we describe sufficient conditions for a context to be non-schizophrenic. These conditions provide the rules of a conservative static analysis of contexts.

---

[3] In fact, unfolding in time (i.e. using a memory cell twice within a reaction) is not correct in general. Thus, the same result holds even in the absence of the single-static-assignment constraint, as in C code generation for example.

[ ]	is not schizophrenic
$\mathcal{C}[\text{signal } S \text{ in } [\ ] \text{ end}]$	is not schizophrenic if $\mathcal{C}[\ ]$ is not
$\mathcal{C}[\text{present } S \text{ then } [\ ] \text{ else } q \text{ end}]$	is not schizophrenic if $\mathcal{C}[\ ]$ is not
$\mathcal{C}[\text{present } S \text{ then } p \text{ else } [\ ] \text{ end}]$	is not schizophrenic if $\mathcal{C}[\ ]$ is not
$\mathcal{C}[\text{suspend } [\ ] \text{ when } S]$	is not schizophrenic if $\mathcal{C}[\ ]$ is not
$\mathcal{C}[\text{loop } [\ ] \text{ end}]$	is schizophrenic
$\mathcal{C}[[\ ]; q]$	is not schizo. if $\mathcal{C}[\ ]$ is not or q cannot be inst.
$\mathcal{C}[p; [\ ]]$	is not schizo. if $\mathcal{C}[\ ]$ is not or p cannot be inst.
$\mathcal{C}[[\ ] \parallel q]$	is not schizophrenic if $\mathcal{C}[\ ]$ is not
$\mathcal{C}[p \parallel [\ ]]$	is not schizophrenic if $\mathcal{C}[\ ]$ is not

Fig. 8. Non-schizophrenic exception-free contexts

4.3 Static Analysis for All Contexts

In order to handle all contexts, we associate with a context $\mathcal{C}[\ ]$ a set of completion codes $\mathcal{S}_{\mathcal{C}[\ ]}$ such that: for all p, if p does not admit any completion code in $\mathcal{S}_{\mathcal{C}[\ ]}$ then p is not schizophrenic in $\mathcal{C}[\ ]$. For example, if $\mathcal{C}[\ ]$ is the context "loop trap T in loop trap U in [ ]; pause end end end; pause end", p is schizophrenic in $\mathcal{C}[\ ]$ iff if it may raise exception U. Thus $\{k_U\}$ is an admissible value for $\mathcal{S}_{\mathcal{C}[\ ]}$. Note that a larger set (less precise), such as $\{0, k_U\}$, would also be.

Figure 9 describes the computation of $\mathcal{S}_{\mathcal{C}[\ ]}$ we propose[4]. In summary:

- $\mathcal{C}[\ ]$ is proven to be non-schizophrenic iff $\mathcal{S}_{\mathcal{C}[\ ]}$ is empty;
- p is proven to be non-schizophrenic in $\mathcal{C}[\ ]$ iff p does not admit a completion code in $\mathcal{S}_{\mathcal{C}[\ ]}$.

$$
\begin{aligned}
\mathcal{S}_{[\ ]} &\equiv \emptyset \\
\mathcal{S}_{\mathcal{C}[\text{signal } S \text{ in } [\ ] \text{ end}]} &\equiv \mathcal{S}_{\mathcal{C}[\ ]} \\
\mathcal{S}_{\mathcal{C}[\text{present } S \text{ then } [\ ] \text{ else } q \text{ end}]} &\equiv \mathcal{S}_{\mathcal{C}[\ ]} \\
\mathcal{S}_{\mathcal{C}[\text{present } S \text{ then } p \text{ else } [\ ] \text{ end}]} &\equiv \mathcal{S}_{\mathcal{C}[\ ]} \\
\mathcal{S}_{\mathcal{C}[\text{suspend } [\ ] \text{ when } S]} &\equiv \mathcal{S}_{\mathcal{C}[\ ]} \\
\mathcal{S}_{\mathcal{C}[\text{loop } [\ ] \text{ end}]} &\equiv \{0\} \cup \mathcal{S}_{\mathcal{C}[\ ]} \\
\mathcal{S}_{\mathcal{C}[[\ ]; q]} &\equiv (\mathcal{S}_{\mathcal{C}[\ ]} \setminus \{0\}) \cup [(\mathcal{K}_q \cap \mathcal{S}_{\mathcal{C}[\ ]} \neq \emptyset) \to \{0\}] \\
\mathcal{S}_{\mathcal{C}[p; [\ ]]} &\equiv [(0 \in \mathcal{K}_p) \to \mathcal{S}_{\mathcal{C}[\ ]}] \\
\mathcal{S}_{\mathcal{C}[\text{trap } T \text{ in } [\ ] \text{ end}]} &\equiv \mathcal{S}_{\mathcal{C}[\ ]} \cup [(0 \in \mathcal{S}_{\mathcal{C}[\ ]}) \to \{k_T\}]
\end{aligned}
$$

Fig. 9. Potentially schizophrenic completion codes

Let's focus on the last four rules:

- If p terminates in $\mathcal{C}[\text{loop } p \text{ end}]$ then it is instantaneously restarted by the inner loop. Consequently, $\{0\} \in \mathcal{S}_{\mathcal{C}[\text{loop } [\ ] \text{ end}]}$. Moreover, if p raises exception T, it traverses "loop p end" and reaches the context $\mathcal{C}[\ ]$. Thus, $(\mathcal{S}_{\mathcal{C}[\ ]} \setminus \{0\}) \subset \mathcal{S}_{\mathcal{C}[\text{loop } [\ ] \text{ end}]}$. As a consequence, $\mathcal{S}_{\mathcal{C}[\text{loop } [\ ] \text{ end}]} \equiv \{0\} \cup \mathcal{S}_{\mathcal{C}[\ ]}$.

---

[4] We omitted the entries corresponding to parallel contexts. In practice, there is no need for such rules. A correct but weak extension of this formalism to parallel contexts may be obtained via the rules: $\mathcal{S}_{\mathcal{C}[[\ ] \parallel q]} \equiv \mathcal{S}_{\mathcal{C}[p \parallel [\ ]]} \equiv [(\mathcal{S}_{\mathcal{C}[\ ]} \neq \emptyset) \to \mathbb{N}]$.

- As in the previous case, if p may raise exception T, it may traverse "$[p;\ q]$" and reach the context $\mathcal{C}[\ ]$. Thus, $(\mathcal{S}_{\mathcal{C}[\ ]}\backslash\{0\}) \subset \mathcal{S}_{\mathcal{C}[[\ ];\ q]}$. In addition, if q may instantaneously produce a completion code in $\mathcal{S}_{\mathcal{C}[\ ]}$ i.e. if $\mathcal{K}_q \cap \mathcal{S}_{\mathcal{C}[\ ]} \neq \emptyset$ then, if p eventually terminates, "$[p;\ q]$" may be instantaneously restarted. Thus, in this case $\{0\} \in \mathcal{S}_{\mathcal{C}[[\ ];\ q]}$.
- If p cannot be instantaneous then q in $\mathcal{C}[p;\ q]$ cannot be instantaneously restarted. On the other hand, if p may, then $\mathcal{S}_{\mathcal{C}[p;\ [\ ]]}$ is equal to $\mathcal{S}_{\mathcal{C}[\ ]}$.
- If p raises exception U ($U \neq T$) or terminates, then "trap T in p end" does the same, so $\mathcal{S}_{\mathcal{C}[\ ]} \subset \mathcal{S}_{\mathcal{C}[\text{trap } T \text{ in } [\ ] \text{ end}]}$. Note that $k_T \notin \mathcal{S}_{\mathcal{C}[\ ]}$ since we have supposed that no two exceptions share the same name. Moreover, if $0 \in \mathcal{S}_{\mathcal{C}[\ ]}$ then $k_T \in \mathcal{S}_{\mathcal{C}[\text{trap } T \text{ in } [\ ] \text{ end}]}$, since by raising exception T, p makes "trap T in p end" terminate.

4.4 Comparison with Current Implementation

The Esterel v5 implementation of the detection of schizophrenic contexts cannot be directly compared with this last analysis. It is in some cases more precise, less in others. Nevertheless, the analysis implemented and the one we presented have common weaknesses, that our formalization helped to identify.

For example, in "loop signal S in pause; ... end end", the declaration of the signal S occurs in a schizophrenic context, thus it triggers unfolding routines. However, because of the pause statement, the status of S is not used when entering the loop. As a consequence, unfolding is not necessary.

We remarked that both analyses could be refined to embody a static liveness analysis of signals. This has been implemented into the Esterel v5 compiler.

5 Conclusion and Future Work

We have formalized several important property checks on Esterel in the form of static analysis methods. Namely, analyses are used to establish when:

- a statement cannot terminate instantaneously,
- a statement cannot terminate or exit and be instantaneously reentered.

The correctness of these analyses is induced by the fact that they can be shown to be abstractions of the "official" Pure Esterel *logical behavioral* semantics. Their complexity is quasi-linear in practice in the program size.

This work was mostly motivated by a revisitation of the Esterel v5 academic compiler, from *Ecole des Mines* and *INRIA*. Front-end processors are heavily relying on algorithms implementing those property checks, but so far without a formal specification. These checks are needed to enforce programs to be free of instantaneous loops, and to contain no schizophrenic subcomponents (in the first case faulty programs are discarded as incorrect, in the second case they are unfolded to secure proper separation).

Static analysis cannot be deactivated: it is required to generate correct code. Thus, the need for precise formalization and correctness proof is far greater, in

```
loop                                            
[                                               
   present S then pause; ... end;      loop
   present S else pause; ... end   →     present S then pause; ... end;
   ||                                     present S else pause; ... end
   pause                                 end
]
end
```

Fig. 10. A simple program transformation

our view, than in the case of "-O3" kind of static analysis. We see our work as a form of formal compiler specification, which can be referred to as a guideline for correctness.

As the Esterel v5 algorithmic approach was only informally specified, we were able to spot several minor mistakes in the actual implementation, as well as to introduce more aggressive optimization techniques for specific program patterns, saving unnecessary unfolding.

Since the methods we described and more generally the techniques in use only provide approximate (but conservative) results, some Esterel programs are rejected by current compilers [10, 13, 21] while they are provably correct. This is rather unusual! Of course, this is well known and comes from other sources as well, mainly an incomplete causality analysis [21]. But as a consequence these compilers have a weak support for program transformation. Even the simple rewriting illustrated by Figure 10 produces a program that is rejected by compilers, as the static analysis of the rewritten loop body fails.

According to the authors of the Esterel v5 compiler, the semantic program equivalence relation is not sufficient when it comes to compiling programs. Because of the static analyses involved, the behavior of the compiler (both rejection and optimization) is sometimes unstable and may change a lot from one program to an equivalent program. In particular, and in opposition to what suggests the documentation of the language, the expansion of high-level constructs into low-level primitives has to be done very carefully to avoid unexpected issues related to those techniques.

In the future we plan to investigate the feasibility of more powerful analyses, hopefully having a more intuitive and stable behavior, starting from the exact analysis of Section 3.1. In addition, we would like to consider the more generic problem of distance analysis in Esterel. In this paper we considered the question: "will there be a pause executed between these two points of the program?" Now, we would like to know how many pause statements there are. Combined with classical delay analysis (i.e. analysis of counters) [16], we believe this would lead to powerful verification tools.

References

1. H. P. Barendregt. *The Lambda Calculus. Its Syntax and Semantics*, volume 103 of *Studies in Logic and the Foundations of Mathematics*. North-Holland, 1984.
2. G. Berry. Real-time programming: General purpose or special-purpose languages. In G. Ritter, editor, *Information Processing 89*, pages 11–17. Elsevier Science Publishers B.V. (North Holland), 1989.
3. G. Berry. Esterel on hardware. *Philosophical Transactions of the Royal Society of London, Series A*, 19(2):87–152, 1992.
4. G. Berry. The semantics of pure Esterel. In M. Broy, editor, *Program Design Calculi*, volume 118 of *Series F: Computer and System Sciences*, pages 361–409. NATO ASI Series, 1993.
5. G. Berry. The constructive semantics of pure Esterel. Draft version 3. http://www-sop.inria.fr/meije/, July 1999.
6. G. Berry. The Esterel v5 language primer. http://www-sop.inria.fr/meije/, July 2000.
7. G. Berry. The foundations of Esterel. In *Proof, Language and Interaction: Essays in Honour of Robin Milner*. MIT Press, 2000.
8. G. Berry and G. Gonthier. The Esterel synchronous programming language: Design, semantics, implementation. *Science of Computer Programming*, 19(2):87–152, 1992.
9. F. Boussinot and R. de Simone. The Esterel language. *Another Look at Real Time Programming, Proceedings of the IEEE*, 79:1293–1304, 1991.
10. E. Closse, M. Poize, J. Pulou, P. Vernier, and D. Weil. Saxo-rt: Interpreting Esterel semantic on a sequential execution structure. *Electronic Notes in Theoretical Computer Science*, 65, 2002.
11. P. Cousot and R. Cousot. Abstract interpretation: a unified lattice model for static analysis of programs by construction or approximation of fixpoints. In *Principles of Programming Languages*, pages 238–252, 1977.
12. N. G. de Bruijn. Lambda calculus notation with nameless dummies. a tool for automatic formula manipulation with application to the church-rosser theorem. *Indagationes Mathematicae*, 34:381–392, 1972.
13. S.A. Edwards. Compiling Esterel into sequential code. In *Proceedings CODES'99*, Rome, Italy, May 1999.
14. S.A. Edwards. *Languages for Digital Embedded Systems*. Kluwer, 2000.
15. G. Gonthier. *Sémantique et modèles d'exécution des langages réactifs synchrones: application à Esterel*. Thèse d'informatique, Université d'Orsay, Paris, France, March 1988.
16. N. Halbwachs. Delay analysis in synchronous programs. In *Computer Aided Verification*, pages 333–346, 1993.
17. N. Halbwachs. *Synchronous Programming of Reactive Systems*. Kluwer, 1993.
18. F. Mignard. *Compilation du langage Esterel en systèmes d'équations booléennes*. Thèse d'informatique, Ecole des Mines de Paris, October 1994.
19. R. Milner. *Communication and Concurrency*. Series in Computer Science. Prentice Hall, 1989.
20. G. Plotkin. A structural approach to operational semantics. Report DAIMI FN-19, Aahrus University, 1981.
21. H. Toma. *Analyse constructive et optimisation séquentielle des circuits générés à partir du langage synchrone réactif Esterel*. Thèse d'informatique, Ecole des Mines de Paris, September 1997.

A Logical Behavioral Semantics of Esterel

Reactions are defined in a structural operational style [20] by a statement transition relation of the form:

$$p \xrightarrow[E]{E', k} p'$$

Here, E' lists the free signals of p emitted by p under the hypothesis that E is the set of present signals, because of (i) the statement p itself and (ii) its context/environment. The rules of the semantics enforce E' to be a subset of E. k is the completion code of the reaction in the sense of Section 3.4. If $k \neq 0$ then p' represents the new state reached by p after the reaction, that is to say the residual statement that has to be executed in the next reaction.

(1) $\text{nothing} \xrightarrow[E]{\emptyset, 0} \text{nothing}$

(2) $\text{pause} \xrightarrow[E]{\emptyset, 1} \text{nothing}$

(3) $\text{exit } T \xrightarrow[E]{\emptyset, k_T} \text{nothing}$

(4) $\dfrac{S \in E}{\text{emit } S \xrightarrow[E]{\{S\}, 0} \text{nothing}}$

(5) $\dfrac{p \xrightarrow[E]{E', k} p' \quad k \neq 0}{p;\, q \xrightarrow[E]{E', k} p';\, q}$

(6) $\dfrac{p \xrightarrow[E]{E', 0} p' \quad q \xrightarrow[E]{F', l} q'}{p;\, q \xrightarrow[E]{E' \cup F', l} q'}$

(7) $\dfrac{S \in E \quad p \xrightarrow[E]{E', k} p'}{\text{present } S \text{ then } p \text{ else } q \text{ end} \xrightarrow[E]{E', k} p'}$

(8) $\dfrac{S \notin E \quad q \xrightarrow[E]{F', l} q'}{\text{present } S \text{ then } p \text{ else } q \text{ end} \xrightarrow[E]{F', l} q'}$

(9) $\dfrac{p \xrightarrow[E]{E', k} p' \quad k = 0 \text{ or } k = k_T}{\text{trap } T \text{ in } p \text{ end} \xrightarrow[E]{E', 0} \text{nothing}}$

(10) $\dfrac{p \xrightarrow[E]{E', k} p' \quad k > 0 \text{ and } k \neq k_T}{\text{trap } T \text{ in } p \text{ end} \xrightarrow[E]{E', k} \text{trap } T \text{ in } p' \text{ end}}$

(11) $\dfrac{p \xrightarrow[E]{E', k} p' \quad q \xrightarrow[E]{F', l} q}{[p\|q] \xrightarrow[E]{E' \cup F',\, \max(k,l)} [p'\|q']}$

(12) $\dfrac{p \xrightarrow[E]{E', k} p' \quad k \neq 0}{\text{loop } p \text{ end} \xrightarrow[E]{E', k} p';\, \text{loop } p \text{ end}}$

(13) $\dfrac{p \xrightarrow[E \cup \{S\}]{E', k} p' \quad S \in E'}{\text{signal } S \text{ in } p \text{ end} \xrightarrow[E]{E' \setminus \{S\}, k} \text{signal } S \text{ in } p' \text{ end}}$

(14) $\dfrac{p \xrightarrow[E \setminus \{S\}]{E', k} p' \quad S \notin E'}{\text{signal } S \text{ in } p \text{ end} \xrightarrow[E]{E', k} \text{signal } S \text{ in } p' \text{ end}}$

Fig. 11. Behavioral semantics

Figure 11 sketches the semantics as a set of deduction rules. For simplicity, we omit the rules defining the suspend statement.

A valuation E is *admissible* for the statement p iff there exists a unique proof tree that establishes a fact of the form $p \xrightarrow[E]{E',k} p'$.

The rules 13 and 14 introduce potential non-determinism in the system. As announced in Section 2.7, in order to avoid *guesses*, more powerful semantic tools are required, that is to say the *constructive semantics of Esterel*.

Remark the side condition $k \neq 0$ in the rule 12. It corresponds to rejecting instantaneous loop bodies. Note the systematic unrolling. It takes care of schizophrenia.

For detailed explanations of these rules please refer to [5].

B Proof of the Analysis of Section 3.4

The rules of Figure 6 are derived from the rules of Figure 11 via the abstraction:

$p \xrightarrow[E]{E',k} p'$ is abstracted into $p \xrightarrow{\cdot,k} \cdot$ (that we note $p \hookrightarrow k$ in the sequel).

It consists in forgetting E, E' and p' in the rules. The set $\mathcal{K}_p$ introduced in Section 3.4 precisely gathers all completion codes that can be derived for the statement p in the abstract proof domain. Figure 12 lists the abstract deduction rules corresponding to the concrete rules of Appendix A. The rules of Figure 6 are obtained by regrouping the abstract rules corresponding to the same statement (i.e. rules 5 and 6, rules 7 and 8, rules 9 and 10, rules 13 and 14).

$$(1) \quad \texttt{nothing} \hookrightarrow 0$$

$$(2) \quad \texttt{pause} \hookrightarrow 1$$

$$(3) \quad \texttt{exit } T \hookrightarrow k_T$$

$$(4) \quad \texttt{emit } S \hookrightarrow 0$$

$$(5) \quad \frac{p \hookrightarrow k \quad k \neq 0}{p;\, q \hookrightarrow k}$$

$$(6) \quad \frac{p \hookrightarrow 0 \quad q \hookrightarrow l}{p;\, q \hookrightarrow l}$$

$$(13) \quad \frac{p \hookrightarrow k}{\texttt{signal } S \texttt{ in } p \texttt{ end} \hookrightarrow k}$$

$$(7) \quad \frac{p \hookrightarrow k}{\texttt{present } S \texttt{ then } p \texttt{ else } q \texttt{ end} \hookrightarrow k}$$

$$(8) \quad \frac{q \hookrightarrow l}{\texttt{present } S \texttt{ then } p \texttt{ else } q \texttt{ end} \hookrightarrow l}$$

$$(9) \quad \frac{p \hookrightarrow k \quad k = 0 \text{ or } k = k_T}{\texttt{trap } T \texttt{ in } p \texttt{ end} \hookrightarrow 0}$$

$$(10) \quad \frac{p \hookrightarrow k \quad k > 0 \text{ and } k \neq k_T}{\texttt{trap } T \texttt{ in } p \texttt{ end} \hookrightarrow k}$$

$$(11) \quad \frac{p \hookrightarrow k \quad q \hookrightarrow l}{[p||q] \hookrightarrow \max(k,l)}$$

$$(12) \quad \frac{p \hookrightarrow k \quad k \neq 0}{\texttt{loop } p \texttt{ end} \hookrightarrow k}$$

$$(14) \quad \frac{p \hookrightarrow k}{\texttt{signal } S \texttt{ in } p \texttt{ end} \hookrightarrow k}$$

Fig. 12. Abstract deduction rules

Stack Size Analysis
for Interrupt-Driven Programs[*]

Krishnendu Chatterjee[1], Di Ma[2], Rupak Majumdar[1],
Tian Zhao[3], Thomas A. Henzinger[1], and Jens Palsberg[2]

[1] University of California, Berkeley
{c_krish,rupak,tah}@cs.berkeley.edu
[2] Purdue University
{madi,palsberg}@cs.purdue.edu
[3] University of Wisconsin, Milwaukee
tzhao@cs.uwm.edu

Abstract. We study the problem of determining stack boundedness and the exact maximum stack size for three classes of interrupt-driven programs. Interrupt-driven programs are used in many real-time applications that require responsive interrupt handling. In order to ensure responsiveness, programmers often enable interrupt processing in the body of lower-priority interrupt handlers. In such programs a programming error can allow interrupt handlers to be interrupted in cyclic fashion to lead to an unbounded stack, causing the system to crash. For a restricted class of interrupt-driven programs, we show that there is a polynomial-time procedure to check stack boundedness, while determining the exact maximum stack size is PSPACE-complete. For a larger class of programs, the two problems are both PSPACE-complete, and for the largest class of programs we consider, the two problems are PSPACE-hard and can be solved in exponential time.

1 Introduction

Most embedded software runs on resource-constrained processors, often for economic reasons. Once the processor, RAM, etc. have been chosen for an embedded system, the programmers has to fit everything into the available space. For example, on a Z86 processor, the stack exists in the 256 bytes of register space, and it is crucial that the program does not overflow the stack, corrupting other data. Estimating the stack size used by a program is therefore of paramount interest to the correct operation of these systems. A tight upper bound is necessary to check if the program fits into the available memory, and to prevent precious system resources (e.g., registers) from being allocated unnecessarily.

---

[*] Jens Palsberg, Di Ma, and Tian Zhao were supported by the NSF ITR award 0112628. Thomas A. Henzinger, Krishnendu Chatterjee, and Rupak Majumdar were supported by the AFOSR grant F49620-00-1-0327, the DARPA grants F33615-C-98-3614 and F33615-00-C-1693, the MARCO grant 98-DT-660, and the NSF grants CCR-0208875 and CCR-0085949.

Stack size analysis is particularly challenging for *interrupt-driven software*. Interrupt-driven software is often used in embedded real-time applications that require fast response to external events. Such programs usually have a fixed number of external interrupt sources, and for each interrupt source, a handler that services the interrupt. When an external interrupt occurs, control is transferred automatically to the corresponding handler if interrupt processing is enabled. To maintain fast response, interrupts should be enabled most of the time, in particular, higher-priority interrupts are enabled in lower-priority handlers. Interrupt handling uses stack space: when a handler is called, a return address is placed on the stack, and if the handler itself gets interrupted, then another return address is placed on the stack, and so on. A programming error occurs when the interrupt handlers can interrupt each other indefinitely, leading to an unbounded stack. Moreover, since stack boundedness violations may occur only for particular interrupt sequences, these errors are difficult to replicate and debug, and standard testing is often inadequate. Therefore, algorithms that statically check for stack boundedness and automatically provide precise bounds on the maximum stack size will be important development tools for interrupt-driven systems.

In this paper, we provide algorithms for the following two problems (defined formally in Section 2.3) for a large class of interrupt-driven programs:

- **Stack boundedness problem.** Given an interrupt-driven program, the stack boundedness problem asks if the stack size is bounded by a finite constant. More precisely, given a program p, the stack boundedness problem returns "yes" if there exists a finite integer K such that on all executions of the program p, the stack size never grows beyond K, and "no" if no such K exists.
- **Exact maximum stack size problem.** Given an interrupt-driven program, the exact maximum stack size problem asks for the maximum possible stack size. More precisely, given a program p, the exact maximum stack size problem returns an integer K such that for all executions of the program p, the stack size never grows beyond K, and such that there is a possible schedule of interrupts and an execution of the program p such that the stack size becomes K; the problem returns ∞ if there is an execution where the stack can grow unbounded.

We model interrupt-driven programs in the untyped *interrupt calculus* of Palsberg and Ma [3]. The interrupt calculus contains essential constructs for programming interrupt-driven systems. For example, we have found that the calculus can express the core aspects of seven commercial micro-controllers from Greenhill Manufacturing Ltd. A program in the calculus consists of a main part and some interrupt handlers. In the spirit of such processors as the Intel MCS-51 family (8051, etc.), Motorola Dragonball (68000 family), and Zilog Z86, the interrupt calculus supports an interrupt mask register (imr). An imr value consists of a master bit and one bit for each interrupt source. For example, the Motorola Dragonball processor can handle 22 interrupt sources. An interrupt handler is enabled, if *both* the master bit and the bit for that interrupt handler is set. When an interrupt handler is called, a return address is stored on the stack, and the master bit is automatically turned off. At the time of return, the master bit is turned back on (however, the handler can turn the master bit on at any point). A program execution has access to:

- the interrupt mask register, which can be updated during computation,
- a stack for storing return addresses, and
- a memory of integer variables; output is done via memory-mapped I/O.

Each element on the stack is a return address. When we measure the size of the stack, we simply count the number of elements on the stack. Our analysis is approximate: when doing the analysis, we ignore the memory of integer variables and the program statements that manipulate this memory. In particular, we assume that both branches of a conditional depending on the memory state can be taken. Of course, all the problems analyzed in this paper become undecidable if integer variables are considered in the analysis.

We consider three versions of Palsberg and Ma's interrupt calculus, here presented in increasing order of generality:

- **Monotonic programs.** These are interrupt calculus programs that satisfy the following monotonicity restriction: when a handler is called with an imr value imr_b, then it returns with an imr value imr_r such that $imr_r \leq imr_b$, where $\leq$ is the logical bitwise implication ordering. In other words, every interrupt that is enabled upon return of a handler must have been enabled when the handler was called (but could have possibly been disabled during the execution of the handler).
- **Monotonic enriched programs.** This calculus enriches Palsberg and Ma's calculus with conditionals on the interrupt mask register. The monotonicity restriction from above is retained.
- **Enriched programs.** These are programs in the enriched calculus, without the monotonicity restriction.

We summarize our results in Table 1. We have determined the complexity of stack boundedness and exact maximum stack size both for monotonic programs and for monotonic programs enriched with tests. For general programs enriched with tests, we have a PSPACE lower bound and an EXPTIME upper bound for both problems; tightening this gap remains an open problem. While the complexities are high, our algorithms are *polynomial* (linear or cubic) in the size of the program, and exponential only in the number of interrupts. In other words, our algorithms are polynomial if the number of interrupts is fixed. Since most real systems have a fixed small number of interrupts (for example Motorola Dragonball processor handles 22 interrupt sources), and the size of programs is the limiting factor, we believe the algorithms should be tractable in practice. Experiments are needed to settle this.

We reduce the stack boundedness and exact stack size problems to state space exploration problems over certain graphs constructed from the interrupt-driven program. We then use the structure of the graph to provide algorithms for the two problems. Our first insight is that for monotonic programs, the maximum stack

Table 1. Complexity results

Calculus	Problem	Complexity	Reference
Monotonic	Stack boundedness	NLOGSPACE-complete	Theorem 1
	Exact maximum stack size	PSPACE-complete	Theorems 2,4
Monotonic enriched	Stack boundedness	PSPACE-complete	Theorems 3,4
	Exact maximum stack size	PSPACE-complete	Theorems 2,4
Enriched	Stack boundedness	PSPACE-hard, EXPTIME	Theorems 3,6
	Exact maximum stack size	PSPACE-hard, EXPTIME	Theorems 2,6

bounds are attained without any intermediate handler return. The polynomial-time algorithm for monotonic programs is reduced to searching for cycles in a graph; the polynomial-space algorithm for determining the exact maximum stack size of monotonic enriched programs is based on finding the longest path in a (possibly exponential) acyclic graph. Finally, we can reduce the stack boundedness problem and exact maximum stack size problem for enriched programs to finding context-free cycles and context-free longest paths in graphs. Our EXPTIME algorithm for enriched programs is based on a novel technique to find the longest context-free path in a DAG. Our lower bounds are obtained by reductions from reachability in a DAG (which is NLOGSPACE-complete), satisfiability of quantified boolean formulas (which is PSPACE-complete), and reachability for polynomial-space Turing Machines (which is PSPACE-complete). We also provide algorithms that determine, given an interrupt-driven program, whether it is monotonic. In the nonenriched case, monotonicity can be checked in polynomial time (NLOGSPACE); in the enriched case, in co-NP. In Section 2, we recall the interrupt calculus of Palsberg and Ma [3]. In Section 3, we consider monotonic programs, in Section 4, we consider monotonic enriched programs, and in Section 5, we consider enriched programs without the monotonicity restriction.

Related Work. Palsberg and Ma [3] present a type system and a type checking algorithm for the interrupt calculus that guarantees stack boundedness and certifies that the stack size is within a given bound. Each type contains information about the stack size and serves as documentation of the program. However, this requires extensive annotations from the programmer (especially since the types can be exponential in the size of the program), and the type information is absent in legacy programs. Our work can be seen as related to *type inference* for the interrupt calculus. In particular, we check stack properties of programs without annotations. Thus, our algorithms work for existing, untyped programs. Moreover, from our algorithms, we can infer the types of [3].

Brylow, Damgaard, and Palsberg [1] do stack size analysis by running a context-free reachability algorithm for model checking. They use, essentially, the same abstraction that our EXPTIME algorithm uses for enriched programs. Our paper gives more algorithmic details and clarifies that the complexity is exponential in the number of handlers.

Hughes, Pareto, and Sabry [2,5] use *sized types* to reason about liveness, termination, and space boundedness of reactive systems. However, they require types with explicit space information, and do not address interrupt handling.

Wan, Taha, and Hudak [7] present event-driven Functional Reactive Programming (FRP), which is designed such that the time and space behavior of a program are necessarily bounded. However, the event-driven FRP programs are written in continuation-style, and therefore do not need a stack. Hence stack boundedness is not among the resource issues considered by Wan et al.

2 The Interrupt Calculus

2.1 Syntax

We recall the (abstract) syntax of the interrupt calculus of [3]. We use x to range over a set of program variables, we use *imr* to range over bit strings, and we use c to range over integer constants.

$$
\begin{array}{lll}
\text{(program)} & p & ::= (m, \bar{h}) \\
\text{(main)} & m & ::= \text{loop } s \mid s \, ; \, m \\
\text{(handler)} & h & ::= \text{iret} \mid s \, ; \, h \\
\text{(statement)} & s & ::= x = e \mid \text{imr} = \text{imr} \land \textit{imr} \mid \text{imr} = \text{imr} \lor \textit{imr} \mid \\
& & \quad \text{if0 } (x) \, s_1 \text{ else } s_2 \mid s_1 \, ; \, s_2 \mid \text{skip} \\
\text{(expression)} & e & ::= c \mid x \mid x + c \mid x_1 + x_2
\end{array}
$$

The pair $p = (m, \bar{h})$ is an *interrupt program* with main program m and interrupt handlers $\bar{h}$. The over-bar notation $\bar{h}$ denotes a sequence $h_1 \ldots h_n$ of handlers. We use the notation $\bar{h}(i) = h_i$. We use a to range over m and h.

2.2 Semantics

We use R to denote a *store*, that is, a partial function mapping program variables to integers. We use σ to denote a *stack* generated by the grammar $\sigma ::= \text{nil} \mid a :: \sigma$. We define the size of a stack as $|\text{nil}| = 0$ and $|a :: \sigma| = 1 + |\sigma|$.

We represent the imr as a bit sequence $imr = b_0 b_1 \ldots b_n$, where $b_i \in \{0, 1\}$. The 0th bit b_0 is the master bit, and for $i > 0$, the ith bit b_i is the bit for interrupts from source i, which are handled by handler i. Notice that the master bit is the most significant bit, the bit for handler 1 is the second-most significant bit, and so on. This layout is different from some processors, but it simplifies the notation used later. For example, the imr value 101b means that the master bit is set, the bit for handler 1 is not set, and the bit for handler 2 is set. We use the notation $imr(i)$ for bit b_i. The predicate *enabled* is defined as

$$enabled(imr, i) = (imr(0) = 1) \land (imr(i) = 1), \quad i \in 1..n.$$

We use 0 to denote the imr value where all bits are 0. We use t_i to denote the imr value where all bits are 0's except that the ith bit is set to 1. We will use $\land$

to denote bitwise logical conjunction, ∨ to denote bitwise logical disjunction, ≤ to denote bitwise logical implication, and ¬ to denote bitwise logical negation. Notice that $enabled(t_0 \vee t_i, j)$ is true if $i = j$, and false otherwise. The imr values, ordered by ≤, form a lattice with bottom element 0.

A *program state* is a tuple $\langle \bar{h}, R, imr, \sigma, a \rangle$ consisting of interrupt handlers $\bar{h}$, a store R, an interrupt mask register imr, a stack σ of return addresses, and a program counter a. We refer to a as *the current statement*; it models the instruction pointer of a CPU. We use P to range over program states. If $P = \langle \bar{h}, R, imr, \sigma, a \rangle$, then we use the notation $P.stk = \sigma$. For $p = (m, \bar{h})$, the initial program state for executing p is $P_p = \langle \bar{h}, \lambda x.0, 0, \text{nil}, m \rangle$, where the function $\lambda x.0$ is defined on the variables that are used in the program p.

A small-step operational semantics for the language is given by the reflexive, transitive closure of the relation $\rightarrow$ on program states:

$$\langle \bar{h}, R, imr, \sigma, a \rangle \rightarrow \langle \bar{h}, R, imr \wedge \neg t_0, a :: \sigma, \bar{h}(i) \rangle \quad (1)$$
$$\text{if } enabled(imr, i)$$

$$\langle \bar{h}, R, imr, \sigma, \text{iret} \rangle \rightarrow \langle \bar{h}, R, imr \vee t_0, \sigma', a \rangle \quad \text{if } \sigma = a :: \sigma' \quad (2)$$

$$\langle \bar{h}, R, imr, \sigma, \text{loop } s \rangle \rightarrow \langle \bar{h}, R, imr, \sigma, s; \text{loop } s \rangle \quad (3)$$

$$\langle \bar{h}, R, imr, \sigma, x = e; a \rangle \rightarrow \langle \bar{h}, R\{x \mapsto eval_R(e)\}, imr, \sigma, a \rangle \quad (4)$$

$$\langle \bar{h}, R, imr, \sigma, \text{imr} = \text{imr} \wedge imr'; a \rangle \rightarrow \langle \bar{h}, R, imr \wedge imr', \sigma, a \rangle \quad (5)$$

$$\langle \bar{h}, R, imr, \sigma, \text{imr} = \text{imr} \vee imr'; a \rangle \rightarrow \langle \bar{h}, R, imr \vee imr', \sigma, a \rangle \quad (6)$$

$$\langle \bar{h}, R, imr, \sigma, (\text{if0 }(x) \ s_1 \text{ else } s_2); a \rangle \rightarrow \langle \bar{h}, R, imr, \sigma, s_1; a \rangle \quad \text{if } R(x) = 0 \quad (7)$$

$$\langle \bar{h}, R, imr, \sigma, (\text{if0 }(x) \ s_1 \text{ else } s_2); a \rangle \rightarrow \langle \bar{h}, R, imr, \sigma, s_2; a \rangle \quad \text{if } R(x) \neq 0 \quad (8)$$

$$\langle \bar{h}, R, imr, \sigma, \text{skip}; a \rangle \rightarrow \langle \bar{h}, R, imr, \sigma, a \rangle \quad (9)$$

where the function $eval_R(e)$ is defined as:

$$eval_R(c) = c \qquad eval_R(x + c) = R(x) + c$$
$$eval_R(x) = R(x) \qquad eval_R(x_1 + x_2) = R(x_1) + R(x_2).$$

Rule (1) models that if an interrupt is enabled, then it may occur. The rule says that if $enabled(imr, i)$, then it is a possible transition to push the current statement on the stack, make $\bar{h}(i)$ the current statement, and turn off the master bit in the imr. Notice that we make no assumptions about the interrupt arrivals; any enabled interrupt can occur at any time, and conversely, no interrupt has to occur. Rule (2) models interrupt return. The rule says that to return from an interrupt, remove the top element of the stack, make the removed top element the current statement, and turn on the master bit. Rule (3) is an unfolding rule for loops, and Rules (4)–(9) are standard rules for statements. Let $\rightarrow^*$ denote the reflexive transitive closure of $\rightarrow$.

A *program execution* is a sequence $P_p \rightarrow P_1 \rightarrow P_2 \rightarrow \cdots \rightarrow P_k$ of program states. Consider a program execution γ of the form $P_p \rightarrow^* P_i \rightarrow P_{i+1} \rightarrow^* P_j \rightarrow P_{j+1}$ with $P_i = \langle \bar{h}, R, imr_b, \sigma, a \rangle$ and $P_j = \langle \bar{h}, R', imr', \sigma', a' \rangle$. The handler $\bar{h}(i)$ is *called in γ with imr_b* from state P_i and *returns with imr_r* from state P_j if

$$P_i \rightarrow P_{i+1} = \langle \bar{h}, R, imr_b \wedge \neg t_0, a :: \sigma, \bar{h}(i) \rangle \quad \text{and } enabled(imr_b, i),$$
$$P_j \rightarrow P_{j+1} = \langle \bar{h}, R', imr_r, \sigma, a \rangle \quad \text{and } \sigma' = a :: \sigma,$$

```
imr = imr or 111b                  handler 2 {
loop { imr = imr or 111b }            imr = imr and 110b
handler 1 {                           imr = imr or  010b
   imr = imr and 101b                 imr = imr or  100b
   imr = imr or  100b                 imr = imr and 101b
   iret                               iret
}                                  }
```

Fig. 1. A program in the interrupt calculus

and $P_k.stk \neq \sigma$ for all $i < k \leq j$. We say that there is no handler call in γ between P_i and P_j if for all $i \leq k < j$, the transition $P_k \to P_{k+1}$ is not a transition of the form (1). Similarly, given an execution $P_p \to^* P_i \to^* P_j$, there is no handler return between P_i and P_j if for all $i \leq k < j$, the transition $P_k \to P_{k+1}$ is not a transition of the form (2).

2.3 Stack Size Analysis

We consider the following problems of stack size analysis.

- **Stack boundedness problem** Given an interrupt program p, the stack boundedness problem returns "yes" if there exists a finite integer K such that for all program states P', if $P_p \to^* P'$, then $|P'.stk| \leq K$; and returns "no" if there is no such K.

- **Exact maximum stack size problem** For a program state P we define $maxStackSize(P)$ as the least $K \geq 0$ such that for all P', if $P \to^* P'$, then $|P'.stk| \leq K$; and "infinite" in case no such K exists. The exact maximum stack size problem is given an interrupt program p and returns $maxStackSize(P_p)$.

Figure 1 shows an example of a program in the interrupt calculus. The bit sequences such as 111b are imr values. Notice that each of the two handlers can be called from different program points with different imr values. The bodies of the two handlers manipulate the imr, and both are at some point during the execution open to the possibility of being interrupted by the other handler. However, the maximum stack size is 3. This stack size happens if handler 1 is called first, then handler 2, and then handler 1 again, at which time there are three return addresses on the stack.

We shall analyze interrupt programs under the usual program analysis assumption that all paths in the program are executable. More precisely, our analysis assumes that each data assignment statement $x = e$ in the program has been replaced by skip, and each conditional if0 (x) s_1 else s_2 has been replaced by if0 $(*)$ s_1 else s_2, where $*$ denotes nondeterministic choice. While this is an overapproximation of the actual set of executable paths, we avoid trivial undecidability results for deciding if a program path is actually executable. Since the data manipulation in interrupt programs is usually independent of the manipulation of the imr, this is a valid assumption.

3 Monotonic Interrupt Programs

We first define monotonic interrupt programs and then analyze the stack boundedness and exact maximum stack size problems for such programs. A handler h_i of program p is *monotonic* if for every execution γ of p, if h_i is called in γ with an imr value imr_b and returns with an imr value imr_r, then $imr_r \leq imr_b$. The program p is *monotonic* if all handlers $h_1 \ldots h_n$ of p are monotonic. The handler h_i of p is *monotonic in isolation* if for every execution γ of p, if h_i is called in γ with an imr value imr_b from a state P_i and returns with an imr value imr_r from a state P_j such that there is no handler call between P_i and P_j, then $imr_r \leq imr_b$.

We first show that a program $p = (m, \bar{h})$ is monotonic iff every handler $h_i \in \bar{h}$ is monotonic in isolation. Moreover, a handler h_i is monotonic in isolation iff, whenever h_i is called with imr value $t_0 \vee t_i$ from state P_i and returns with imr_r from state P_j, with no handler calls between P_i and P_j, then $imr_r \leq t_0 \vee t_i$. These observations can be used to efficiently check if an interrupt program is monotonic: for each handler, we check that the return value imr_r of the imr when called with $t_0 \vee t_i$ satisfies $imr_r \leq t_0 \vee t_i$.

Proposition 1. *It can be checked in linear time (NLOGSPACE) if an interrupt program is monotonic.*

3.1 Stack Boundedness

We now analyze the complexity of stack boundedness of monotonic programs. Our main insight is that the maximum stack size is achieved without any intermediate handler returns. First observe that if handler h is enabled when the imr is imr_1, then it is enabled for all imr $imr_2 \geq imr_1$. We argue the case where the maximum stack size is finite, the same argument can be formalized in case the maximum stack size is infinite. Fix an execution sequence that achieves the maximum stack size. Let h be the last handler that returned in this sequence (if there is no such h then we are done). Let the sequence of statements executed be $s_0, s_1, \ldots s_{i-1}, s_i, \ldots s_j, s_{j+1}, \ldots$ where s_i was the starting statement of h and s_j the iret statement of h. Suppose h was called with imr_b and returned with imr_r such that $imr_r \leq imr_b$. Consider the execution sequence of statements $s_0, s_1, \ldots s_{i-1}, s_{j+1}, \ldots$ with the execution of handler h being omitted. In the first execution sequence the imr value while executing statement s_{j+1} is imr_r and in the second sequence the imr value is imr_b. Since $imr_r \leq imr_b$ then repeating the same sequence of statements and same sequence of calls to handlers with h omitted gives the same stack size. Following a similar argument, we can show that all handlers that return intermediately can be omitted without changing the maximum stack size attained.

Lemma 1. *For a monotonic program p, let $P_{\max}$ be a program state such that $P_p \to^* P_{\max}$ and for any state P', if $P_p \to^* P'$ then $|P_{\max}.stk| \geq |P'.stk|$. Then there is a program state P'' such that $P_p \to^* P''$, $|P''.stk| = |P_{\max}.stk|$, and there is no handler return between P_p and P''.*

We now give a polynomial-time algorithm for the stack boundedness problem for monotonic programs. The algorithm reduces the stack boundedness question to the presence of cycles in the *enabled graph* of a program. Let $h_1 \ldots h_n$ be the n handlers of the program. Given the code of the handlers we build the enabled graph $G = \langle V, E \rangle$ as follows:

- There is a node for each handler, i.e., $V = \{h_1, h_2, \ldots h_n\}$.
- Let the instructions of h_i be $C_i = i_1, i_2, \ldots i_m$. There is an edge between (h_i, h_j) if any of the following condition holds
  1. There is l, k such that $l \leq k$, the instruction at i_l is imr = imr ∨ imr with $t_0 \leq imr$, the instruction at i_k is imr = imr ∨ imr with $t_j \leq imr$ and for all statement i_m between i_l and i_k if i_m is imr = imr ∧ imr then $t_0 \leq imr$.
  2. There is l, k such that $l \leq k$, the instruction at i_l is imr = imr ∨ imr with $t_j \leq imr$, the instruction at i_k is imr = imr ∨ imr with $t_0 \leq imr$ and for all statement i_m between i_l and i_k if i_m is imr = imr ∧ imr then $t_j \leq imr$.
  3. There is l such that the instruction at i_l is imr = imr ∨ imr with $t_0 \leq imr$ and for all statement i_m between i_1 and i_l if i_m is imr = imr ∧ imr then $t_i \leq imr$.

Since we do not model the program variables, we can analyze the code of h_i and detect all outgoing edges (h_i, h_j) in time linear in the length of h_i. We only need to check that there is an ∨ statement with an imr constant with jth bit 1 and then the master bit is turned on with no intermediate disabling of the jth bit or vice versa. Hence the enabled graph for program p can be constructed in time $n^2 \times |p|$ (where $|p|$ denotes the length of p).

Let G_p be the enabled graph for a monotonic interrupt program p. If G_p has a cycle, then the stack is unbounded, that is, for all positive integer K there is a program state P' such that $P_p \to^* P'$ and $|P'.stk| > K$. Since cycles in the enabled graph can be found in NLOGSPACE, the stack boundedness problem for monotonic programs is in NLOGSPACE; note that the enabled graph of a program can be generated on the fly in logarithmic space. Hardness for NLOGSPACE follows from the hardness of DAG reachability.

Theorem 1. *Stack boundedness for monotonic interrupt programs can be checked in time linear in the size of the program and quadratic in the number of handlers. The complexity of stack boundedness for monotonic interrupt programs is NLOGSPACE-complete.*

In case the stack is bounded, we can get a simple upper bound on the stack size as follows. Let G_p be the enabled graph for a monotonic interrupt program p. If G_p is a DAG, and the node h_i of G_p has order k in topological sorting order, then we can prove by induction that the corresponding handler h_i of p can occur at most $2^{(k-1)}$ times in the stack. Hence for any program state P' such that $P_p \to^* P'$, we have $|P'.stk| \leq 2^n - 1$. In fact, this bound is tight: there is a program with n handlers that achieves a maximum stack size of $2^n - 1$. We show that starting with an imr value of all 1's one can achieve the maximum stack length of $2^n - 1$ and the stack remain bounded. We give an inductive strategy to achieve this. With one handler which does not turn itself on we can have a stack length 1 starting with imr value 11. By induction hypothesis, using $n-1$ handlers starting with imr value all 1's we can achieve a stack length of $2^{n-1} - 1$. Now we add the nth handler and modify the previous $n-1$ handlers such that they do not change the bit for the nth handler. The n-th handler turns on every bit except itself, and then turns on the master bit. The following sequence achieves a stack size of $2^n - 1$. First, the first $n-1$ handlers achieve a stack size of $2^{n-1} - 1$ using the inductive strategy. After this, the nth handler is called. It enables the $n-1$ handlers but disables itself. Hence the sequence of stack of $2^{n-1} - 1$ can be repeated twice and the n the handler can occur once in the stack in between. The total length of stack is thus $1 + (2^{n-1} - 1) + (2^{n-1} - 1) = 2^n - 1$. Since none of the other handlers can turn the nth handler on, the stack size is in fact bounded. However, the exact maximum stack size problem can be solved only in PSPACE. We defer the algorithm to the next section, where we solve the problem for a more general class of programs.

3.2 Maximum Stack Size

We now prove that the exact maximum stack size problem is PSPACE-hard. We define a subclass of monotonic interrupt calculus which we call simple interrupt calculus and show the exact maximum stack size problem is already PSPACE-hard for this class.

For imr', imr'' where $imr'(0) = 0$ and $imr''(0) = 0$, define $\mathcal{H}(imr'; imr'')$ to be the interrupt handler

$$\mathsf{imr} = \mathsf{imr} \wedge \neg imr';$$
$$\mathsf{imr} = \mathsf{imr} \vee (t_0 \vee imr'');$$
$$\mathsf{imr} = \mathsf{imr} \wedge \neg(t_0 \vee imr'');$$
$$\mathsf{iret}.$$

A program $p = (m, \bar{h})$ is *simple* if the main program h has the form

$$\mathsf{imr} = \mathsf{imr} \vee (imr_S \vee t_0); \; \mathsf{loop\ skip}$$

where $imr_S(0) = 0$, and every interrupt handler in $\bar{h}$ has the form $\mathcal{H}(imr'; imr'')$. Intuitively, a handler of a simple interrupt program first disables some handlers, then enables other handlers and enables interrupt handling. This opens the door to the handler being interrupted by other handlers. After that, it disables interrupt handling, and makes sure that the handlers that are enabled on exit are a subset of those that were enabled on entry to the handler.

For a handler $h(i)$ of the form $\mathcal{H}(imr';\ imr'')$, we define function $f_i(imr) = imr \wedge (\neg imr') \vee imr''$. Given a simple interrupt program p, we define a directed graph $G(p) = (V, E)$ where $V = \{imr \mid imr(0) = 0\}$ and $E = \{(imr, f_i(imr)) \mid t_i \leq imr\}$.

The edge $(imr, f_i(imr))$ in $G(p)$ represents the call to the interrupt handler $h(i)$ when imr value is imr. We define imr_S as the start node of $G(p)$ and we define $\mathcal{M}(imr)$ as the longest path in $G(p)$ from node imr. The notation $\mathcal{M}(imr)$ is ambiguous because it leaves the graph unspecified; however, in all cases below, the graph in question can be inferred from the context.

Lemma 2. *For a simple program p, we have $maxStackSize(P_p) = |\mathcal{M}(imr_S)|$.*

We now show PSPACE-hardness for simple interrupt calculus. Our proof is based on a polynomial-time reduction from the *quantified boolean satisfiability* (QSAT) problem [4]. The proof is technical, and given in the full paper.

We illustrate the reduction by a small example. Suppose we are given a QSAT instance $S = \exists x_2 \forall x_1\ \phi$ with $\phi = (l_{11} \vee l_{12}) \wedge (l_{21} \vee l_{22}) = (x_2 \vee \neg x_1) \wedge (x_2 \vee x_1)$, We construct a simple interrupt program $p = (m, \bar{h})$ with an imr register, where $\bar{h} = \{h(x_i), h(\bar{x}_i), h(w_i), h(\bar{w}_i), h(l_{ij}) \mid i,j = 1, 2\}$ are 12 handlers. The imr contains 13 bits: a master bit, and each remaining bit 1-1 maps to each handler in $\bar{h}$. Let $\mathcal{D} = \{x_i, \bar{x}_i, w_i, \bar{w}_i, l_{ij} \mid i,j = 1,2\}$. We use t_x, where $x \in \mathcal{D}$, to denote the imr value where all bits are 0's except the bit corresponding to handler $h(x)$ is set to 1. The initial imr value imr_S is set to $imr_S = t_{x_2} \vee t_{\bar{x}_2}$.

We now construct $\bar{h}$. Let $E(h(x))$, $x \in \mathcal{D}$, be the set of handlers that $h(x)$ enables. This *enable* relation between the handlers of our example is illustrated in Figure 2, where there is an edge from $h(x_i)$ to $h(x_j)$ iff $h(x_i)$ enables $h(x_j)$. Let $D(h(x))$, $x \in \mathcal{D}$, be the set of handlers that $h(x)$ disables. Let $L = \{h(l_{ij}) \mid i,j = 1,2\}$. The $D(h(x)), x \in \mathcal{D}$, are defined as follows:

$$D(h(x_2)) = D(h(\bar{x}_2)) = \{h(x_2), h(\bar{x}_2)\}, \tag{10}$$

$$D(h(x_1)) = \{h(x_1)\},\quad D(h(\bar{x}_1)) = \{h(\bar{x}_1)\}, \tag{11}$$

$$D(h(w_2)) = D(h(\bar{w}_2)) = \{h(x_1), h(\bar{x}_1)\} \cup \{h(w_i), h(\bar{w}_i) \mid i = 1,2\} \cup L, \tag{12}$$

$$D(h(w_1)) = D(h(\bar{w}_1)) = \{h(w_1), h(\bar{w}_1)\} \cup L, \tag{13}$$

$$D(h(l_{ij})) = \{h(l_{i1}), h(l_{i2})\} \cup \{h(w_k) \mid \text{if } l_{ij} = \neg x_k\} \cup \{h(\bar{w}_k) \mid \text{if } l_{ij} = x_k\} \tag{14}$$

If $h(x) = \mathcal{H}(imr'; imr'')$, then $imr' = \bigvee_{h(y) \in E(h(x))} t_y$ and $imr'' = \bigvee_{h(z) \in D(h(x))} t_z$, where $x, y, z \in \mathcal{D}$.

We claim that the QSAT instance S is satisfiable iff $|\mathcal{M}(imr_S)| = 10$, where $imr_S = t_{x_2} \vee t_{\bar{x}_2}$. We sketch the proof as follows.

Let $imr_L = \bigvee_{h(l) \in L} t_l$, where $l \in \mathcal{D}$. From (14) and Figure 2, it can be shown that $|\mathcal{M}(imr_L)| = 2$. From Figure 2, we have $E(h(x_1)) = \{h(w_1)\} \cup L$; and together with (13), and (14), it can be shown that

$$|\mathcal{M}(t_{x_1})| = 1 + |\mathcal{M}(t_{w_1} \vee imr_L)| \leq 2 + |\mathcal{M}(imr_L)| = 4$$

and the equality holds iff $\exists j_1, j_2 \in 1, 2$, such that $l_{1j_1}, l_{2j_2} \neq \neg x_1$, because otherwise handler $h(w_1)$ would be surely disabled. Similarly, it can be shown that

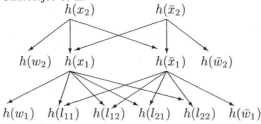

Fig. 2. Enable relation of interrupt handlers

$|\mathcal{M}(t_{\bar{x}_1})| \leq 4$, and that

$$|\mathcal{M}(t_{x_1} \vee t_{\bar{x}_1})| \leq |\mathcal{M}(t_{x_1})| + |\mathcal{M}(t_{\bar{x}_1})| \leq 8,$$

where the equality holds iff $\exists j_1, j_2$, such that $l_{1j_1}, l_{2j_2} \neq \neg x_1$ and $\exists j'_1, j'_2$, such that $l_{1j'_1}, l_{2j'_2} \neq x_1$. From Figure 2, we have $E(h(x_2)) = \{h(w_2), h(x_1), h(\bar{x}_1)\}$. Thus,

$$|\mathcal{M}(t_{x_2})| = 1 + |\mathcal{M}(t_{w_2} \vee t_{x_1} \vee t_{\bar{x}_1})| \leq 2 + |\mathcal{M}(t_{x_1} \vee t_{\bar{x}_1})| = 10,$$

and it can be shown from (12) and (14), that the equality holds iff $\exists j_1, j_2$ such that $l_{ij_1}, l_{ij_2} \neq \neg x_2, \neg x_1$ and $\exists j'_1, j'_2$ such that $l_{ij'_1}, l_{ij'_2} \neq \neg x_2, x_1$, which implies that both $x_2 = \mathsf{true}, x_1 = \mathsf{true}$ and $x_2 = \mathsf{true}, x_1 = \mathsf{false}$ are satisfiable truth assignments to ϕ. Similarly, it can be shown that $|\mathcal{M}(t_{\bar{x}_2})| = 10$ iff both $x_2 = \mathsf{false}, x_1 = \mathsf{true}$ and $x_2 = \mathsf{false}, x_1 = \mathsf{false}$ are satisfiable truth assignments to ϕ.

From (10), we have $|\mathcal{M}(t_{x_2} \vee t_{\bar{x}_2})| = \max(|\mathcal{M}(t_{x_2})|, |\mathcal{M}(t_{\bar{x}_2})|)$. Therefore, $|\mathcal{M}(imr_S)| = 10$ iff there exists x_2 such that for all x_1, ϕ is satisfiable, or equivalently iff S is satisfiable. For our example, S is satisfiable since $\exists x_2 = \mathsf{true}$ such that $\forall x_1$, ϕ is satisfiable. Correspondingly, $|\mathcal{M}(imr_S)| = |\mathcal{M}(x_2)| = 10$.

Theorem 2. *The exact maximum stack size problem for monotonic interrupt programs is PSPACE-hard.*

4 Monotonic Enriched Interrupt Programs

We now introduce an enriched version of the interrupt calculus, where we allow conditionals on the interrupt mask register. The conditional can test if some bit of the imr is on, and then take the bitwise or of the imr with a constant bit sequence; or it can test if some bit of the imr is off, and then take the bitwise and of the imr with a constant. The syntax for *enriched interrupt programs* is given by the syntax from Section 2 together with the following clauses:

(statement) $s ::= \cdots$ | if(bit i on)imr = imr $\vee$ imr | if(bit i off) imr = imr $\wedge$ imr

The small-step operational semantics is given below:

$\langle \bar{h}, R, imr, \sigma, \mathsf{if}(\mathsf{bit}\ i\ \mathsf{on})\mathsf{imr} = \mathsf{imr} \vee imr'; a \rangle \to \langle \bar{h}, R, imr \vee imr', \sigma, a \rangle$ if $imr(i) = 1$
$\langle \bar{h}, R, imr, \sigma, \mathsf{if}(\mathsf{bit}\ i\ \mathsf{on})\mathsf{imr} = \mathsf{imr} \vee imr'; a \rangle \to \langle \bar{h}, R, imr, \sigma, a \rangle$ if $imr(i) = 0$
$\langle \bar{h}, R, imr, \sigma, \mathsf{if}(\mathsf{bit}\ i\ \mathsf{off})\mathsf{imr} = \mathsf{imr} \wedge imr'; a \rangle \to \langle \bar{h}, R, imr \wedge imr', \sigma, a \rangle$ if $imr(i) = 0$
$\langle \bar{h}, R, imr, \sigma, \mathsf{if}(\mathsf{bit}\ i\ \mathsf{off})\mathsf{imr} = \mathsf{imr} \vee imr'; a \rangle \to \langle \bar{h}, R, imr, \sigma, a \rangle$ if $imr(i) = 1$

Unlike the conditional statement if0 (x) s_1 else s_2 on data that has been overapproximated, our analysis will be path sensitive in the imr-conditional.

Proposition 2. *Monotonicity of enriched interrupt programs can be checked in time exponential in the number of handlers (in co-NP).*

For monotonic enriched interrupt programs, both the stack boundedness problem and the exact maximum stack size problem are PSPACE-complete. To show this, we first show that the stack boundedness problem is PSPACE-hard by a generic reduction from polynomial-space Turing machines. We fix a PSPACE-complete Turing machine M. Given input x, we construct in polynomial time a program p such that M accepts x iff p has an unbounded stack. We have two handlers for each tape cell (one representing zero, and the other representing one), and a handler for each triple (i, q, b) of head position i, control state q, and bit b. The handlers encode the working of the Turing machine in a standard way. The main program sets the bits corresponding to the initial state of the Turing machine, with x written on the tape. Finally, we have an extra handler that enables itself (and so can cause an unbounded stack) which is set only when the machine reaches an accepting state.

Theorem 3. *The stack boundedness problem for monotonic enriched interrupt programs is PSPACE-hard.*

We now give a PSPACE algorithm to check the exact maximum stack size. Since we restrict our programs to be monotonic it follows from Lemma 1 that the maximum length of the stack can be achieved with no handler returning in between. Given a program p with m statements and n handlers, we label the statements as $pc_1, \ldots pc_m$. Let PC denote the set of all statements, i.e., $PC = \{pc_1, \ldots pc_m\}$. Consider the graph G_p where there is a node v for every statement with all possible imr values (i.e., $v = \langle pc, imr \rangle$ for some value among PC and some imr value). Let $v = \langle pc, imr \rangle$ and $v' = \langle pc', imr' \rangle$ be two nodes in the graph. There is an edge between v, v' in G if any of the following two conditions hold:

- on executing the statement at pc with imr value imr the control goes to pc' and the value of imr is imr'. The weight of this edge is 0.
- pc' is a starting address of a handler h_i and $enabled(imr, i)$ and $imr' = imr \wedge \neg t_0$. The weight of this edge is 1.

We also have a special node in the graph called *target* and add edges to *target* of weight 0 from all those nodes which correspond to a $pc \in PC$ which is a *iret* statement. This graph is exponential in the size of the input as there are $O(|PC| \times 2^n)$ nodes in the graph. The starting node of the graph is the node with pc_1 and $imr = 0$. If there is a node in the graph which is the starting address of a handler h and which is reachable from the start node and also self-reachable then the stack length would be infinite. This is because the sequence of calls from the starting statement to the handler h is first executed and then the cycle of handler calls is repeated infinitely many times. As the handler h is in stack when it is called again the stack would grow infinite. Since there is a sequence of interrupts which achieves the maximum stack length without any handler returning in between (follows from Lemma 1) if there is no cycle in G_p we need to find the longest path in the DAG G_p.

Theorem 4. *The exact maximum stack size for monotonic enriched interrupt programs can be found in time linear in the size of the program and exponential in the number of handlers. The complexity of exact maximum stack size for monotonic enriched interrupt programs is PSPACE.*

In polynomial space one can generate in lexicographic order all the nodes that have a *pc* value of the starting statement of a handler. If such a node is reachable from the start node, and also self-reachable, then the stack size is infinite. Since the graph is exponential, this can be checked in PSPACE. If no node has such a cycle, we find the longest path from the start node to the target. Again, since longest path in a DAG is in NLOGSPACE, this can be achieved in PSPACE. It follows that both the stack boundedness and exact maximum stack size problems for monotonic enriched interrupt programs are PSPACE-complete.

5 Nonmonotonic Enriched Interrupt Programs

In this section we consider interrupt programs with tests, but do not restrict handlers to be monotonic. We give an EXPTIME algorithm to check stack boundedness and find the exact maximum stack size for this class of programs. The algorithm involves computing longest context-free paths in context-free DAGs, a technique that may be of independent interest.

5.1 Longest Paths in Acyclic Context-Free Graphs

We define a context-free graph as in [6]. Let Σ be a collection of k opening and closing parentheses, i.e., $\Sigma = \{(^1, (^2, \ldots, (^k,)^1,)^2, \ldots,)^k\}$. A *context-free graph* is a tuple $G = (V, E, \Sigma)$ where V is a set of nodes and $E \subseteq (V \times V \times (\Sigma \cup \{\tau\}))$ is a set of labeled edges (and τ is a special symbol not in Σ). We associate with each edge a *weight function* $wt : E \to \{0, +1, -1\}$ defined as follows:

- $wt(e) = 0$ if e is of the form (v, v', τ),
- $wt(e) = -1$ if e is of the form $(v, v',)^i)$ for some i,
- $wt(e) = 1$ if e is of the form $(v, v', (^i)$ for some i.

Let $\Sigma = \{(^1, (^2, \ldots, (^k,)^1,)^2, \ldots,)^k\}$ be an alphabet of matched parentheses. Let $\mathcal{L}$ be the language generated by the context-free grammar

$$M \to M(^i S \quad \text{for } 1 \le i \le k$$
$$S \to \epsilon \mid (^i S)^i S \text{ for } 1 \le i \le k$$

from the starting symbol M. Thus $\mathcal{L}$ defines words of matched parentheses with possibly some opening parentheses mismatched. A *context-free path* π in

Algorithm 1 Function LongestContextFreePath

Input: A context-free DAG G, a vertex v_1 of G
Output: For each vertex v of G, return the length of the longest context-free path from v to v_1, and 0 if there is no context-free path from v to v_1
1. For each vertex $v_j \in V$: $val[v_j] = 0$
2. Construct the transitive closure matrix T such that
   $T[i, j] = 1$ iff there is a context-free path from i to j
3. For $j = 1$ to n:
   3.1 For each immediate successor v_i of v_j such that
   the edge e_{v_j,v_i} from v_j to v_i satisfies $wt(e_{v_j,v_i}) \geq 0$:
   $val[v_j] = \max\{val[v_j], val[v_i] + wt(e_{v_j,v_i})\}$
   3.2 For each vertex $v_i \in V$:
   3.2.1 if($T[i,j]$) (v_j is context-free reachable from v_i)
   $val[v_i] = \max\{val[v_i], val[v_j]\}$

---

a context-free graph G is a sequence of vertices $v_1, v_2, \ldots v_k$ such that for all $i = 1 \ldots k - 1$, there is an edge between v_i and v_{i+1}, i.e., there is a letter $\sigma \in \Sigma \cup \{\tau\}$ such that $(v_i, v_{i+1}, \sigma) \in E$ and the projection of the labels along the edges of the path on to Σ is a word in $\mathcal{L}$. Given a context-free path π with edges $e_1, e_2, \ldots e_k$ the *cost* of the path $Cost(\pi)$ is defined as $\sum_i wt(e_i)$. Note that $Cost(\pi) \geq 0$ for any context-free path π. A context-free graph G is a *context-free DAG* iff there is no cycle C of G such that $\sum_{e \in C} wt(e) > 0$. Given a context-free DAG $G = (V, E, \Sigma)$ we define an ordering $order : V \to \mathbb{N}$ of the vertices satisfying the following condition: if there is a path π in G from vertex v_i to v_j and $Cost(\pi) > 0$ then $order(v_j) < order(v_i)$. This ordering is well defined for context-free DAGs. Let G be a context-free DAG G, and let $V = \{v_1, v_2, \ldots v_n\}$ be the ordering of the vertex set consistent with $order$ (i.e., $order(v_i) = i$). We give a polynomial-time procedure to find the longest context-free path from any node v_i to v_1 in G.

The correctness proof of our algorithm uses a function Num from paths to $\mathbb{N}$. Given a path π we define $Num(\pi)$ as $\max\{order(v) \mid v \text{ occurs in } \pi\}$. Given a node v let $L_v = \{L_1, L_2, \ldots L_k\}$ be the set of longest paths from v to v_1. Then we define $Num_{v_1}(v) = \min\{Num(L_i) \mid L_i \in L_v\}$. The correctness of the algorithm follows from the following set of observations. First, if there is a longest path L from a node v to v_1 such that L starts with an opening parenthesis (^{i} that is not matched along the path L then $order(v) = Num_{v_1}(v)$. A node v in the DAG G satisfies the following conditions.

- If $Num_{v_1}(v) = order(v) = j$ then within the execution of Statement 3.1 of the j-th iteration of Loop 3 of function LongestContextFreePath, $val[v]$ is equal to the cost of a longest path from v to v_1.
- If $order(v) < Num(v) = j$ then by the j-th iteration of Loop 3 of function LongestContextFreePath $val[v]$ is equal to the cost of a longest path from v to v_1.

Finally, notice that at the end of function LongestContextFreePath(G, v_1), for each vertex v, the value of $val[v]$ is equal to the longest context-free path to v_1, and equal to zero if there is no context-free path to v_1. In the Function LongestContextFreePath the statement 3.2.1 gets executed at most n^2 times since the loop 3 gets executed n times at most and the nested loop 3.2 also gets executed n times at most. The context-free transitive closure can be constructed in $O(n^3)$ time [8]. Hence the complexity of our algorithm is polynomial and it runs in time $O(n^2 + n^3) = O(n^3)$.

Theorem 5. *The longest context-free path of a context-free DAG can be found in time cubic in the size of the graph.*

To complete our description of the algorithm, we must check if a given context-free graph is a context-free DAG, and generate the topological ordering *order* for a context-free DAG. We give a polynomial-time procedure to check given a context-free graph whether it is a DAG. Given a context-free graph $G = (V, E, \Sigma)$ let its vertex set be $V = \{1, 2, \ldots n\}$. For every node $k \in V$ the graph G can be unrolled as a DAG for depth $|V|$ and it can be checked if there is a path π from k to k such that $Cost(\pi) > 0$. Given the graph G and a node k we create a context-free DAG $G_k = (V_k, E_k, \Sigma)$ as follows:

1. $V_k = \{k_0\} \cup \{(i, j) \mid 1 \leq i \leq n - 2, 1 \leq j \leq n\} \cup \{k_{n-1}\}$
2. $E_k = \{\langle k_0, (1, j) \rangle, * \rangle \mid \langle k, j, * \rangle \in E\} \cup \{\langle (i, j), (i + 1, j'), * \rangle \mid \langle j, j', * \rangle \in E\}$
   $\cup \{\langle (n - 2, j), k_{n-1}, * \rangle \mid \langle j, k, * \rangle \in E\} \cup \{\langle k_0, (1, k) \rangle\} \cup \{\langle (i, k), (i + 1, k) \rangle\}$

where $*$ can represent a opening parenthesis, closing parenthesis or can be τ. Notice that the edges in the last line ensure that if there is a cycle of positive cost from k to itself with length $t < n$ then it is possible to go from k_0 to $(n - t - 1, k)$ and then to reach k_{n-1} by a path of positive cost.

We can find the longest context-free path from k_0 to k_n in G_n (by the function LongestContextFreePath). If the length is positive, then there is a positive cycle in G from k to k. If for all nodes the length of the longest path in G_n is 0, then G is a context-free DAG and the longest context-free path can be computed in G. Given a context-free DAG G we can define $order(v)$ in polynomial time. If a vertex v can reach v' and v' can reach v put them in the same group of vertices. Both the path from v to v' and v' to v must be cost 0 since there is no cycle of positive cost. Hence the ordering of vertices within a group can be arbitrary. We can topologically order the graph induced by the groups and then assign an order to the vertices where vertices in the same group are ordered arbitrarily.

5.2 Stack Size Analysis

We present an algorithm to check for stack boundedness and exact maximum stack size. The idea is to perform context-free longest path analysis on the state space of the program. Given a program p with m statements and n handlers, we label the statements as $pc_1, pc_2, \ldots pc_m$. Let $PC = \{pc_1, \ldots pc_m\}$ as before. We construct a context-free graph $G_p = \langle V, E, \Sigma \rangle$, called the *state graph of p*, where $\Sigma = \{(^1, (^2, \ldots, (^m,)^1,)^2, \ldots)^m\}$ as follows:

Algorithm 2 Function StackSizeGeneral

Input: Enriched interrupt program p
Output: $maxStackSize(P_p)$
1. Build the state graph $G_p = \langle V, E, \Sigma \rangle$ from the program p
2. Let $V' = \{v' \mid$ there is a context-free path from the starting vertex to $v'\}$
3. Let G'_p be the subgraph of G_p induced by the vertex set V'
4. If G'_p is not a context-free DAG then return "infinite"
5. Else create $G''_p = (V'', E'', \Sigma)$ as follows :
   5.1 $V'' = V' \cup \{target\}$ and $E'' = E' \cup \{(v, target) \mid v \in V'\}$
6. Return the value of the longest context-free path from the starting vertex to $target$

- $V = PC \times IMR$, where IMR is the set of all 2^n possible imr values.
- $E \subseteq (V \times V \times \Sigma) \cup (V \times V)$
  1. Handler call: $(v, v', (_i)) \in E$ iff $v = (pc_i, imr_1)$ and $v' = (pc_j, imr_2)$ and pc_j is the starting address of some handler h_j such that $enabled(imr_1, j)$ and $imr_2 = imr_1 \wedge \neg t_0$.
  2. Handler return: $(v, v',)_i) \in E$ iff $v = (pc_i, imr_1)$ and $v' = (pc_j, imr_2)$ and pc_j is the iret statement of some handler and $imr_1 = imr_2 \vee t_0$.
  3. Statement execution: $(v, v') \in E$ iff $v = (pc_i, imr_1)$ and $v' = (pc_j, imr_2)$ and executing the statement at pc_i with imr value imr_1 the control goes to pc_j and the imr value is imr_2.

The vertex $(pc_1, 0)$ is the starting vertex of G_p. Let G'_p be the induced subgraph of G_p containing only nodes that are context-free reachable from the start node. If G'_p is not a context-free DAG then we report that stack is unbounded, else we create a new DAG G'''_p by adding a new vertex $target$ and adding edges to $target$ from all nodes of G'_p of weight 0 and find the value of the longest context-free path from the start vertex to $target$ in the DAG G'''_p.

From the construction of the state graph, it follows that there is a context-free path from a vertex $v = (pc, imr)$ to $v' = (pc', imr')$ in the state graph G_p iff there exists stores R, R' and stacks σ, σ' such that $\langle \bar{h}, R, imr, \sigma, pc \rangle \rightarrow^* \langle \bar{h}, R', imr', \sigma' pc' \rangle$. Moreover, if G'_p is the reachable state graph then there exists K such that for all P' such that $P_p \rightarrow^* P'$ we have $|P'.stk| \leq K$ iff G'_p is a context-free DAG. To see this, first notice that if G'_p is not a context-free DAG then there is a cycle of positive cost. Traversing this cycle infinitely many times makes the stack grow unbounded. On the other hand, if the stack is unbounded then there is a program address that is visited infinitely many times with the same imr value and the stack grows between the successive visits. Hence there is a cycle of positive cost in G'_p. These observations, together with Theorem 5 show that function **StackSizeGeneral** correctly computes the exact maximum stack size of an interrupt program p.

Theorem 6. *The exact maximum stack size of nonmonotonic enriched interrupt programs can be found in time cubic in the size of the program and exponential in the number of handlers.*

The number of vertices in G_p is $m \times 2^n$, for m program statements and n interrupt handlers. It follows from Theorem 5 and the earlier discussion that the steps 1, 2, 3, 4, 5, and 6 of StackSizeGeneral can be computed in time polynomial in G_p. Since G_p is exponential in the size of the input program p, we have an EXPTIME procedure for determining the exact maximum stack size of nonmonotonic enriched interrupt programs. Notice also that our syntax ensures that all statements that modify the imr are monotonic: if $imr_1 \leq imr_2$, and for $i = 1, 2$, we have $P(imr_i) \to P'(imr_i')$ for any two program states $P(imr)$ and $P'(imr)$ parameterized by imr, then $imr_1' \leq imr_2'$. In particular, we only allow bitwise or's on the imr if we test if a bit is set, and only allow bitwise and's on the imr if we test if a bit is unset. Indeed, we can extend the syntax of the enriched calculus to allow any imr operations, and the above algorithm still solves the exact maximum stack size problem, with no change in complexity.

We leave open whether the exact maximum stack size problem for nonmonotonic interrupts programs, in the nonenriched and enriched cases, is EXPTIME-hard or PSPACE-complete (PSPACE-hardness follows from Theorem 3).

References

1. D. Brylow, N. Damgaard, and J. Palsberg. Static checking of interrupt-driven software. In *ICSE: International Conference on Software Engineering*, pp. 47–56. ACM/IEEE, 2001.
2. J. Hughes, L. Pareto, and A. Sabry. Proving the correctness of reactive systems using sized types. In *POPL: Principles of Programming Languages*, pp. 410–423. ACM, 1996.
3. J. Palsberg and D. Ma. A typed interrupt calculus. In *FTRTFT: Formal Techniques in Real-Time and Fault-tolerant Systems*, LNCS 2469, pp. 291–310. Springer, 2002.
4. C. Papadimitriou. *Computational Complexity*. Addision-Wesley, 1994.
5. L. Pareto. *Types for Crash Prevention*. PhD thesis, Chalmers University of Technology, 2000.
6. T. Reps, S. Horwitz, and M. Sagiv. Precise interprocedural dataflow analysis via graph reachability. In *POPL: Principles of Programming Languages*, pp. 49–61. ACM, 1995.
7. Z. Wan, W. Taha, and P. Hudak. Event-driven FRP. In *PADL: Practical Aspects of Declarative Languages*, LNCS 2257, pp. 155–172. Springer, 2002.
8. M. Yannakakis. Graph-theoretic methods in database theory. In *PODS: Principles of Database Systems*, pp. 203–242. ACM, 1990.

Program Development Using Abstract Interpretation (And the Ciao System Preprocessor)

Manuel V. Hermenegildo[1,2], Germán Puebla[1],
Francisco Bueno[1], and Pedro López-García[1]

[1] Department of Computer Science, Technical University of Madrid (UPM)
{herme,german,bueno,pedro}@fi.upm.es
WWW home page: http://www.clip.dia.fi.upm.es/
[2] Departments of Computer Science and Electrical and Computer Engineering
University of New Mexico

Abstract. The technique of Abstract Interpretation has allowed the development of very sophisticated global program analyses which are at the same time provably correct and practical. We present in a tutorial fashion a novel program development framework which uses abstract interpretation as a fundamental tool. The framework uses modular, incremental abstract interpretation to obtain information about the program. This information is used to validate programs, to detect bugs with respect to partial specifications written using assertions (in the program itself and/or in system libraries), to generate and simplify run-time tests, and to perform high-level program transformations such as multiple abstract specialization, parallelization, and resource usage control, all in a provably correct way. In the case of validation and debugging, the assertions can refer to a variety of program points such as procedure entry, procedure exit, points within procedures, or global computations. The system can reason with much richer information than, for example, traditional types. This includes data structure shape (including pointer sharing), bounds on data structure sizes, and other operational variable instantiation properties, as well as procedure-level properties such as determinacy, termination, non-failure, and bounds on resource consumption (time or space cost). CiaoPP, the preprocessor of the Ciao multi-paradigm programming system, which implements the described functionality, will be used to illustrate the fundamental ideas.
Keywords: Program Development, Global Analysis, Abstract Interpretation, Debugging, Verification, Partial Evaluation, Program Transformation, Optimization, Parallelization, Resource Control, Programming Environments, Multi-Paradigm Programming, (Constraint) Logic Programming.

1 Introduction

The technique of Abstract Interpretation [12] has allowed the development of sophisticated program analyses which are at the same time provably correct and practical. The semantic approximations produced by such analyses have been traditionally applied to high- and low-level *optimizations* during program compilation, including *program transformation*. More recently, novel and promising applications of semantic approximations have been proposed in the more general context of program development, such as *verification* and *debugging*.

We present a novel programming framework which uses extensively abstract interpretation as a fundamental tool in the program development process. The framework uses modular, incremental abstract interpretation to obtain information about the program, which is then used to validate programs, to detect bugs with respect to partial specifications written using assertions (in the program itself and/or in system libraries), to generate run-time tests for properties which cannot be checked completely at compile-time and simplify them, and to perform high-level program transformations such as multiple abstract specialization, parallelization, and resource usage control, all in a provably correct way.

After introducing some of the basic concepts underlying the approach, the framework is described in a tutorial fashion through the presentation of its implementation in CiaoPP, the preprocessor of the Ciao program development system [2].[3] Ciao is a multi-paradigm programming system, allowing programming in logic, constraint, and functional styles (as well as a particular form of object-oriented programming). At the heart of Ciao is an efficient logic programming-based kernel language. This allows the use of the very large body of approximation domains, inference techniques, and tools for abstract interpretation-based semantic analysis which have been developed to a powerful and mature level in this area (see, e.g., [37, 8, 21, 3, 22, 26] and their references). These techniques and systems can approximate at compile-time, always safely, and with a significant degree of precision, a wide range of properties which is much richer than, for example, traditional types. This includes data structure shape (including pointer sharing), independence, storage reuse, bounds on data structure sizes, and other operational variable instantiation properties, as well as procedure-level properties such as determinacy, termination, non-failure, and bounds on resource consumption (time or space cost).

In the rest of the paper we first discuss briefly the specific role of abstract interpretation in different parts of our program development framework (Section 2) and then illustrate in a tutorial fashion aspects of how the actual process of program development is aided in an implementation of this framework, by showing examples of CiaoPP at work (Section 3).

Space constraints prevent us from providing a complete set of references to related work on the many topics touched upon in the paper. Thus, we only provide the references most directly related to the papers where all the techniques used in CiaoPP are discussed in detail, which are often our own work. We ask the reader to kindly forgive this. The publications referenced do themselves contain much more comprehensive references to the related work.

---

[3] A demonstration of Ciao and CiaoPP at work was performed at the meeting.

2 The Role of Abstract Interpretation

We start by recalling some basic concepts from abstract interpretation. We consider the important class of semantics referred to as *fixpoint semantics*. In this setting, a (monotonic) semantic operator (which we refer to as S_P) is associated with each program P. This S_P function operates on a semantic domain which is generally assumed to be a complete lattice or, more generally, a chain complete partial order. The meaning of the program (which we refer to as $[\![P]\!]$) is defined as the least fixpoint of the S_P operator, i.e., $[\![P]\!] = \text{lfp}(S_P)$. A well-known result is that if S_P is continuous, the least fixpoint is the limit of an iterative process involving at most ω applications of S_P and starting from the bottom element of the lattice.

In the abstract interpretation technique, the program P is interpreted over a non-standard domain called the *abstract* domain D_α which is simpler than the *concrete* domain D. The abstract domain D_α is usually constructed with the objective of computing safe approximations of the semantics of programs, and the semantics w.r.t. this abstract domain, i.e., the *abstract semantics* of the program, is computed (or approximated) by replacing the operators in the program by their abstract counterparts. The abstract domain D_α also has a lattice structure. The concrete and abstract domains are related via a pair of monotonic mappings: *abstraction* $\alpha : D \mapsto D_\alpha$, and *concretization* $\gamma : D_\alpha \mapsto D$, which relate the two domains by a Galois insertion (or a Galois connection) [12].

One of the fundamental results of abstract interpretation is that an abstract semantic operator S_P^α for a program P can be defined which is correct w.r.t. S_P in the sense that $\gamma(\text{lfp}(S_P^\alpha))$ is an approximation of $[\![P]\!]$, and, if certain conditions hold (e.g., ascending chains are finite in the D_α lattice), then the computation of $\text{lfp}(S_P^\alpha)$ terminates in a finite number of steps. We will denote $\text{lfp}(S_P^\alpha)$, i.e., the result of abstract interpretation for a program P, as $[\![P]\!]_\alpha$.

Typically, abstract interpretation guarantees that $[\![P]\!]_\alpha$ is an *over*-approximation of the abstract semantics of the program itself, $\alpha([\![P]\!])$. Thus, we have that $[\![P]\!]_\alpha \supseteq \alpha([\![P]\!])$, which we will denote as $[\![P]\!]_{\alpha+}$. Alternatively, the analysis can be designed to safely *under*-approximate the actual semantics, and then we have that $[\![P]\!]_\alpha \subseteq \alpha([\![P]\!])$, which we denote as $[\![P]\!]_{\alpha-}$.

2.1 Abstract Verification and Debugging

Both program verification and debugging compare the *actual semantics* of the program, i.e., $[\![P]\!]$, with an *intended semantics* for the same program, which we will denote by $\mathcal{I}$. This intended semantics embodies the user's requirements, i.e., it is an expression of the user's expectations. In Table 1 we define classical verification problems in a set-theoretic formulation as simple relations between $[\![P]\!]$ and $\mathcal{I}$.

Using the exact actual or intended semantics for automatic verification and debugging is in general not realistic, since the exact semantics can be typically only partially known, infinite, too expensive to compute, etc. On the other hand the abstract interpretation technique allows computing *safe* approximations of

Table 1. Set theoretic formulation of verification problems

Property	Definition
P is partially correct w.r.t. $\mathcal{I}$	$[\![P]\!] \subseteq \mathcal{I}$
P is complete w.r.t. $\mathcal{I}$	$\mathcal{I} \subseteq [\![P]\!]$
P is incorrect w.r.t. $\mathcal{I}$	$[\![P]\!] \not\subseteq \mathcal{I}$
P is incomplete w.r.t. $\mathcal{I}$	$\mathcal{I} \not\subseteq [\![P]\!]$

the program semantics. The key idea in our approach [5, 27, 40] is to use the abstract approximation $[\![P]\!]_\alpha$ directly in program verification and debugging tasks.

A number of approaches have already been proposed which make use to some extent of abstract interpretation in verification and/or debugging tasks. Abstractions were used in the context of algorithmic debugging in [31]. Abstract interpretation for debugging of imperative programs has been studied by Bourdoncle [1], by Comini et al. for the particular case of algorithmic debugging of logic programs [10] (making use of partial specifications) and [9], and very recently by P. Cousot [11].

Our first objective herein is to present the implications of the use of *approximations* of both the intended and actual semantics in the verification and debugging process. As we will see, the possible loss of accuracy due to approximation prevents full verification in general. However, and interestingly, it turns out that in many cases useful verification and debugging conclusions can still be derived by comparing the approximations of the actual semantics of a program to the (also possibly approximated) intended semantics.

In our approach we actually compute the abstract approximation $[\![P]\!]_\alpha$ of the concrete semantics of the program $[\![P]\!]$ and compare it directly to the (also approximate) intention (which is given in terms of *assertions* [39]), following almost directly the scheme of Table 1. This approach can be very attractive in programming systems where the compiler already performs such program analysis in order to use the resulting information to, e.g., optimize the generated code, since in these cases the compiler will compute $[\![P]\!]_\alpha$ anyway. Alternatively, $[\![P]\!]_\alpha$ can always be computed on demand.

For now, we assume that the program specification is given as a semantic value $\mathcal{I}_\alpha \in D_\alpha$. Comparison between actual and intended semantics of the program is most easily done in the same domain, since then the operators on the abstract lattice, that are typically already defined in the analyzer, can be used to perform this comparison. Thus, it is interesting to study the implications of comparing $\mathcal{I}_\alpha$ and $[\![P]\!]_\alpha$, which is an approximation of $\alpha([\![P]\!])$.

In Table 2 we propose (sufficient) conditions for correctness and completeness w.r.t. $\mathcal{I}_\alpha$, which can be used when $[\![P]\!]$ is approximated. Several instrumental conclusions can be drawn from these relations.

Analyses which over-approximate the actual semantics (i.e., those denoted as $[\![P]\!]_{\alpha+}$), are specially suited for proving partial correctness and incompleteness with respect to the abstract specification $\mathcal{I}_\alpha$. It will also be sometimes possible to prove incorrectness in the extreme case in which the semantics inferred for

Table 2. Validation problems using approximations

Property	Definition	Sufficient condition
P is partially correct w.r.t. $\mathcal{I}_\alpha$	$\alpha(\llbracket P \rrbracket) \subseteq \mathcal{I}_\alpha$	$\llbracket P \rrbracket_{\alpha+} \subseteq \mathcal{I}_\alpha$
P is complete w.r.t. $\mathcal{I}_\alpha$	$\mathcal{I}_\alpha \subseteq \alpha(\llbracket P \rrbracket)$	$\mathcal{I}_\alpha \subseteq \llbracket P \rrbracket_{\alpha-}$
P is incorrect w.r.t. $\mathcal{I}_\alpha$	$\alpha(\llbracket P \rrbracket) \not\subseteq \mathcal{I}_\alpha$	$\llbracket P \rrbracket_{\alpha-} \not\subseteq \mathcal{I}_\alpha$, or $\llbracket P \rrbracket_{\alpha+} \cap \mathcal{I}_\alpha = \emptyset \wedge \llbracket P \rrbracket_\alpha \neq \emptyset$
P is incomplete w.r.t. $\mathcal{I}_\alpha$	$\mathcal{I}_\alpha \not\subseteq \alpha(\llbracket P \rrbracket)$	$\mathcal{I}_\alpha \not\subseteq \llbracket P \rrbracket_{\alpha+}$

the program is incompatible with the abstract specification, i.e., when $\llbracket P \rrbracket_{\alpha+} \cap \mathcal{I}_\alpha = \emptyset$. We also note that it will only be possible to prove completeness if the abstraction is *precise*, i.e., $\llbracket P \rrbracket_\alpha = \alpha(\llbracket P \rrbracket)$. According to Table 2 only $\llbracket P \rrbracket_{\alpha-}$ can be used to this end, and in the case we are discussing $\llbracket P \rrbracket_{\alpha+}$ holds. Thus, the only possibility is that the abstraction is precise.

On the other hand, if analysis under-approximates the actual semantics, i.e., in the case denoted $\llbracket P \rrbracket_{\alpha-}$, it will be possible to prove completeness and incorrectness. In this case, partial correctness and incompleteness can only be proved if the analysis is precise.

If analysis information allows us to conclude that the program is incorrect or incomplete w.r.t. $\mathcal{I}_\alpha$, an (abstract) symptom has been found which ensures that the program does not satisfy the requirement. Thus, debugging should be initiated to locate the program construct responsible for the symptom. Since $\llbracket P \rrbracket_{\alpha+}$ often contains information associated to program points, it is often possible to use the this information directly and/or the analysis graph itself to locate the earliest program point where the symptom occurs (see Section 3.2). Also, note that the whole setting is even more interesting if the $\mathcal{I}_\alpha$ itself is considered an approximation (i.e., we consider $\mathcal{I}_\alpha^+$ and $\mathcal{I}_\alpha^-$), as is the case in the assertions providing upper- and lower-bounds on cost in the examples of Section 3.2.

It is important to point out that the use of safe approximations is what gives the essential power to the approach. As an example, consider that classical examples of assertions are type declarations. However, herein we are interested in supporting a much more powerful setting in which assertions can be of a much more general nature, stating additionally other properties, some of which cannot always be determined statically for all programs. These properties may include properties defined by means of user programs and extend beyond the predefined set which may be natively understandable by the available static analyzers. Also, only a small number of (even zero) assertions may be present in the program, i.e., the assertions are *optional*. In general, we do not wish to limit the programming language or the language of assertions unnecessarily in order to make the validity of the assertions statically decidable (and, consequently, the proposed framework needs to deal throughout with approximations).

Additional discussions and more details about the foundations and implementation issues of our approach can be found in [5, 27, 40, 38].

2.2 Abstract Executability and Program Transformation

In our program development framework, abstract interpretation also plays a fundamental role in the areas of program transformation and program optimization. Optimizations are performed by means of the concept of *abstract executability* [23, 43]. This allows reducing at compile-time certain program fragments to the values *true, false,* or *error,* or to a simpler program fragment, by application of the information obtained via abstract interpretation. This allows optimizing and transforming the program (and also detecting errors at compile-time in the case of *error*).

For simplicity, we will limit herein the discussion to reducing a procedure call or program fragment L (for example, a "literal" in the case of logic programming) to either *true* or *false.* Each run-time invocation of the procedure call L will have a *local environment* which stores the particular values of each variable in L for that invocation. We will use θ to denote this environment (composed of assignments of values to variables, i.e., *substitutions*) and the restriction (projection) of the environment θ to the variables of a procedure call L is denoted $\theta|_L$.

We now introduce some definitions. Given a procedure call L without side-effects in a program P we define the *trivial success set* of L in P as $TS(L,P) = \{\theta|_L : L\theta$ succeeds exactly once in P with empty answer substitution $(\epsilon)\}$. Similarly, given a procedure call L from a program P we define the *finite failure set* of L in P as $FF(L,P) = \{\theta|_L : L\theta$ fails finitely in $P\}$.

Finally, given a procedure call L from a program P we define the *run-time substitution set* of L in P, denoted $RT(L,P)$, as the set of all possible substitutions (run-time environments) in the execution state just prior to executing the procedure call L in any possible execution of program P.

Table 3 shows the conditions under which a procedure call L is abstractly executable to either *true* or *false.* In spite of the simplicity of the concepts, these definitions are not directly applicable in practice since $RT(L,P), TS(L,P),$ and $FF(L,P)$ are generally not known at compile time. However, it is usual to use a *collecting semantics* as concrete semantics for abstract interpretation so that analysis computes for each procedure call L in the program an abstract substitution λ_L which is a safe approximation of $RT(L,P)$, i.e. $\forall L \in P . RT(L,P) \subseteq \gamma(\lambda_L)$.

Also, under certain conditions we can compute either automatically or by hand sets of abstract values $A_{TS}(\overline{L}, D_\alpha)$ and $A_{FF}(\overline{L}, D_\alpha)$ where $\overline{L}$ stands for the *base form* of L, i.e., where all the arguments of L contain distinct free variables.

Table 3. Abstract executability

Property	Definition	Sufficient condition
L is abstractly executable to *true* in P	$RT(L,P) \subseteq TS(L,P)$	$\exists \lambda' \in A_{TS}(\overline{B}, D_\alpha) : \lambda_L \sqsubseteq \lambda'$
L is abstractly executable to *false* in P	$RT(L,P) \subseteq FF(L,P)$	$\exists \lambda' \in A_{FF}(\overline{B}, D_\alpha) : \lambda_L \sqsubseteq \lambda'$

Intuitively they contain abstract values in domain D_α which guarantee that the execution of $\overline{L}$ trivially succeeds (resp. finitely fails). For soundness it is required that $\forall \lambda \in A_{TS}(\overline{L}, D_\alpha)\ \gamma(\lambda) \subseteq TS(\overline{L}, P)$ and $\forall \lambda \in A_{FF}(\overline{L}, D_\alpha)\ \gamma(\lambda) \subseteq FF(\overline{L}, P)$.

Even though the simple optimizations illustrated above may seem of narrow applicability, in fact for many builtin procedures such as those that check basic types or which inspect the structure of data, even these simple optimizations are indeed very relevant. Two non-trivial examples of this are their application to simplifying independence tests in program parallelization [44] (Section 3.3) and the optimization of delay conditions in logic programs with dynamic procedure call scheduling order [41].

These and other more powerful abstract executability rules are embedded in the multivariant abstract interpreter in our program development framework. The resulting system performs essentially all high- and low-level program optimizations and transformations during program development and in compilation. In fact, the combination of the concept of abstract executability and multivariant abstract interpretation has been shown to be a very powerful program transformation and optimization tool, capable of performing essentially all the transformations traditionally done via partial evaluation [44, 46, 13, 30]. Also, the class of optimizations which can be performed can be made to cover traditional lower-level optimizations as well, provided the lower-level code to be optimized is "reflected" at the source level or if the abstract interpretation is performed directly at the object level.

3 Program Development in the Ciao System

In this section we illustrate our program development environment by presenting what is arguably the first and most complete implementation of these ideas: CiaoPP [38, 26], the preprocessor of the Ciao program development system [2].[4] As mentioned before, Ciao is free software distributed under GNU (L)GPL licenses, multi-paradigm programming system. At the heart of Ciao is an efficient logic programming-based kernel language. It then supports, selectively for each module, extensions and restrictions such as, for example, pure logic programming, functions, full ISO-Prolog, constraints, objects, concurrency, or higher-order. Ciao is specifically designed to a) be highly extensible and b) support modular program analysis, debugging, and optimization. The latter tasks are performed in an integrated fashion by CiaoPP.

---

[4] In fact, the implementation of the preprocessor is generic in that it can be easily customized to different programming systems and dialects and in that it is designed to allow the integration of additional analyses in a simple way. As a particularly interesting example, the preprocessor has been adapted for use with the CHIP CLP(FD) system. This has resulted in CHIPRE, a preprocessor for CHIP which has been shown to detect non-trivial programming errors in CHIP programs. More information on the CHIPRE system and an example of a debugging session with it can be found in [38].

In the following, we present an overview of CiaoPP at work. Our aim is to present not the techniques used by CiaoPP, but instead the main functionalities of the system in a tutorial way, by means of examples. However, again we do provide references where the interested reader can find the details on the actual techniques used. Section 3.1 presents CiaoPP at work performing program analysis, while Section 3.2 does the same for program debugging and validation, and Section 3.3 for program transformation and optimization.

3.1 Static Analysis and Program Assertions

The fundamental functionality behind CiaoPP is static global program analysis, based on abstract interpretation. For this task CiaoPP uses the PLAI abstract interpreter [37,4], including extensions for, e.g., incrementality [28,42], modularity [3,45,6], analysis of constraints [15], and analysis of concurrency [34].

The system includes several abstract analysis domains developed by several groups in the LP and CLP communities and can infer information on variable-level properties such as moded types, definiteness, freeness, independence, and grounding dependencies: essentially, precise data structure shape and pointer sharing. It can also infer bounds on data structure sizes, as well as procedure-level properties such as determinacy, termination, non-failure, and bounds on resource consumption (time or space cost). CiaoPP implements several techniques for dealing with "difficult" language features (such as side-effects, meta-programming, higher-order, etc.) and as a result can for example deal safely with arbitrary ISO-Prolog programs [3]. A unified language of assertions [3,39] is used to express the results of analysis, to provide input to the analyzer, and, as we will see later, to provide program specifications for debugging and validation, as well as the results of the comparisons performed against the specifications.

Modular Static Analysis Basics: As mentioned before, CiaoPP takes advantage of modular program structure to perform more precise and efficient, incremental analysis. Consider the program in Figure 1, defining a module which exports the qsort predicate and imports predicates geq and lt from module compare. During the analysis of this program, CiaoPP will take advantage of the fact that the only predicate that can be called from outside is the *exported* predicate qsort. This allows CiaoPP to infer more precise information than if it had to consider that all predicates may be called in any possible way (as would be true had this been a simple "user" file instead of a module). Also, assume that the compare module has already been analyzed. This allows CiaoPP to be more efficient and/or precise, since it will use the information obtained for geq and lt during analysis of compare instead of either (re-)analyzing compare or assuming topmost substitutions for them. Assuming that geq and lt have a similar binding behavior as the standard comparison predicates, a mode and independence analysis ("sharing+freeness" [36]) of the module using CiaoPP yields the following results:[5]

---

[5] In the "sharing+freeness" domain var denotes variables that do not point yet to any data structure, mshare denotes pointer sharing patterns between variables. Derived

```
:- module(qsort, [qsort/2], [assertions]).
:- use_module(compare,[geq/2,lt/2]).

qsort([X|L],R) :-
        partition(L,X,L1,L2),
        qsort(L2,R2), qsort(L1,R1),
        append(R1,[X|R2],R).
qsort([],[]).

partition([],_B,[],[]).
partition([E|R],C,[E|Left1],Right):-
        lt(E,C),  partition(R,C,Left1,Right).
partition([E|R],C,Left,[E|Right1]):-
        geq(E,C), partition(R,C,Left,Right1).

append([],Ys,Ys).
append([X|Xs],Ys,[X|Zs]):- append(Xs,Ys,Zs).
```

Fig. 1. A modular qsort program

```
:- true pred qsort(A,B)
         : mshare([[A],[A,B],[B]])
        => mshare([[A,B]]).
:- true pred partition(A,B,C,D)
         : ( var(C), var(D), mshare([[A],[A,B],[B],[C],[D]]) )
        => ( ground(A), ground(C), ground(D), mshare([[B]]) ).
:- true pred append(A,B,C)
         : ( ground(A), mshare([[B],[B,C],[C]]) )
        => ( ground(A), mshare([[B,C]]) ).
```

These *assertions* express, for example, that the third and fourth arguments of partition have "output mode": when partition is called (:) they are free unaliased variables and they are ground on success (=>). Also, append is used in a mode in which the first argument is input (i.e., ground on call). Also, upon success the arguments of qsort will share all variables (if any).

Assertions and Properties: The above output is given in the form of CiaoPP *assertions*. These assertions are a means of specifying *properties* which are (or should be) true of a given predicate, predicate argument, and/or *program point*. If an assertion has been proved to be true it has a prefix true –like the ones above. Assertions can also be used to provide information to the analyzer in order to increase its precision or to describe predicates which have not been coded yet during program development. These assertions have a trust prefix [3]. For example, if we commented out the use_module/2 declaration in Figure 1,

---

properties ground and indep denote respectively variables which point to data structures which contain no pointers, and pairs of variables which point to data structures which do not share any pointers.

we could describe the mode of the (now missing) geq and lt predicates to the analyzer for example as follows:

```
:- trust pred geq(X,Y) => ( ground(X), ground(Y) ).
:- trust pred lt(X,Y)  => ( ground(X), ground(Y) ).
```

The same approach can be used if the predicates are written in, e.g., an external language. Finally, assertions with a check prefix are the ones used to specify the *intended* semantics of the program, which can then be used in debugging and/or validation, as we will see in Section 3.2. Interestingly, this very general concept of assertions is also particularly useful for generating documentation automatically (see [24] for a description of their use by the Ciao auto-documenter).

Assertions refer to certain program points. The true pred assertions above specify in a combined way properties of both the entry (i.e., upon calling) and exit (i.e., upon success) points of *all calls* to the predicate. It is also possible to express properties which hold at points between clause literals. The following is a fragment of the output produced by CiaoPP for the program in Figure 1 when information is requested at this level:

```
qsort([X|L],R) :-
   true((ground(X),ground(L),var(R),var(L1),var(L2),var(R2), ...
   partition(L,X,L1,L2),
   true((ground(X),ground(L),ground(L1),ground(L2),var(R),var(R2), ...
   qsort(L2,R2), ...
```

In CiaoPP properties are just predicates, which may be builtin or user defined. For example, the property var used in the above examples is the standard builtin predicate to check for a free variable. The same applies to ground and mshare. The properties used by an analysis in its output (such as var, ground, and mshare for the previous mode analysis) are said to be *native* for that particular analysis. The system requires that properties be marked as such with a prop declaration which must be visible to the module in which the property is used. In addition, properties which are to be used in run-time checking (see later) should be defined by a (logic) program or system builtin, and also visible. Properties declared and/or defined in a module can be exported as any other predicate. For example:

```
:- prop list/1.
list([]).
list([_|L]) :- list(L).
```

defines the property "list". A list is an instance of a very useful class of user-defined properties called *regular types* [48, 14, 21, 20, 47], which herein are simply a syntactically restricted class of logic programs. We can mark this fact by stating ":- regtype list/1." instead of ":- prop list/1." (this can be done automatically). The definition above can be included in a user program or, alternatively, it can be imported from a system library, e.g.:

```
:- use_module(library(lists),[list/1]).
```

Type Analysis: CiaoPP can infer (parametric) types for programs both at the predicate level and at the literal level [21, 20, 47]. The output for Figure 1 at the predicate level, assuming that we have imported the lists library, is:

```
:- true pred qsort(A,B)
        : ( term(A), term(B) )
       => ( list(A), list(B) ).
:- true pred partition(A,B,C,D)
        : ( term(A), term(B), term(C), term(D) )
       => ( list(A), term(B), list(C), list(D) ).
:- true pred append(A,B,C)
        : ( list(A), list1(B,term), term(C) )
       => ( list(A), list1(B,term), list1(C,term) ).
```

where term is any term and prop list1 is defined in library(lists) as:

```
:- regtype list1(L,T) # "@var{L} is a list of at least one @var{T}'s."
list1([X|R],T) :- T(X), list(R,T).
:- regtype list(L,T) # "@var{L} is a list of @var{T}'s."
list([],_T).
list([X|L],T) :- T(X), list(L).
```

We can use entry assertions [3] to specify a restricted class of calls to the module entry points as acceptable:

```
:- entry qsort(A,B) : (list(A, num), var(B)).
```

This informs the analyzer that in all external calls to qsort, the first argument will be a list of numbers and the second a free variable. Note the use of builtin properties (i.e., defined in modules which are loaded by default, such as var, num, list, etc.). Note also that properties natively understood by different analysis domains can be combined in the same assertion. This assertion will aid goal-dependent analyses obtain more accurate information. For example, it allows the type analysis to obtain the following, more precise information:

```
:- true pred qsort(A,B)
        : ( list(A,num), term(B) )
       => ( list(A,num), list(B,num) ).
:- true pred partition(A,B,C,D)
        : ( list(A,num), num(B), term(C), term(D) )
       => ( list(A,num), num(B), list(C,num), list(D,num) ).
:- true pred append(A,B,C)
        : ( list(A,num), list1(B,num), term(C) )
       => ( list(A,num), list1(B,num), list1(C,num) ).
```

Non-failure and Determinacy Analysis: CiaoPP includes a non-failure analysis, based on [17], which can detect procedures and goals that can be guaranteed not to fail, i.e., to produce at least one solution or not terminate. It also can detect predicates that are "covered", i.e., such that for any input (included in the calling type of the predicate), there is at least one clause whose "test" (head unification and body builtins) succeeds. CiaoPP also includes a determinacy analysis which can detect predicates which produce at most one solution, or predicates whose clause tests are disjoint, even if they are not fully deterministic (because they call other predicates which are nondeterministic). For example, the result of these analyses for Figure 1 includes the following assertion:

```
:- true pred qsort(A,B)
        : ( list(A,num), var(B) ) => ( list(A,num), list(B,num) )
        + ( not_fails, covered, is_det, mut_exclusive ).
```

(The + field in pred assertions can contain a conjunction of global properties of the *computation* of the predicate.)

Size, Cost, and Termination Analysis: CiaoPP can also infer lower and upper bounds on the sizes of terms and the computational cost of predicates [18, 19]. The cost bounds are expressed as functions on the sizes of the input arguments and yield the number of resolution steps. Various measures are used for the "size" of an input, such as list-length, term-size, term-depth, integer-value, etc. Note that obtaining a non-infinite upper bound on cost also implies proving *termination* of the predicate.

As an example, the following assertion is part of the output of the upper bounds analysis:

```
:- true pred append(A,B,C)
        : ( list(A,num), list1(B,num), var(C) )
        => ( list(A,num), list1(B,num), list1(C,num),
             size_ub(A,length(A)), size_ub(B,length(B)),
             size_ub(C,length(B)+length(A)) )
        + steps_ub(length(A)+1).
```

Note that in this example the size measure used is list length. The assertion size_ub(C,length(B)+length(A)) means that an (upper) bound on the size of the third argument of append/3 is the sum of the sizes of the first and second arguments. The inferred upper bound on computational steps is the length of the first argument of append/3.

The following is the output of the lower-bounds analysis:

```
:- true pred append(A,B,C)
        : ( list(A,num), list1(B,num), var(C) )
        => ( list(A,num), list1(B,num), list1(C,num),
             size_lb(A,length(A)), size_lb(B,length(B)),
             size_lb(C,length(B)+length(A)) )
        + ( not_fails, covered, steps_lb(length(A)+1) ).
```

The lower-bounds analysis uses information from the non-failure analysis, without which a trivial lower bound of 0 would be derived.

Decidability, Approximations, and Safety: As a final note on the analyses, it should be pointed out that since most of the properties being inferred are in general undecidable at compile-time, the inference technique used, abstract interpretation, is necessarily *approximate*, i.e., possibly imprecise. On the other hand, such approximations are also always guaranteed to be safe, in the sense that (modulo bugs, of course) they are never *incorrect*.

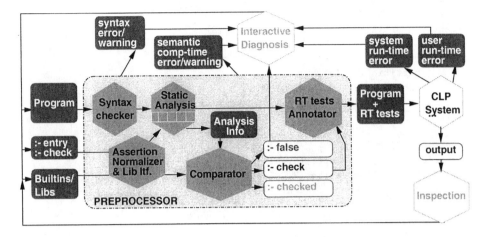

Fig. 2. Architecture of the Preprocessor

3.2 Program Debugging and Assertion Validation

CiaoPP is also capable of combined static and dynamic validation, and debugging using the ideas outlined so far. To this end, it implements the framework described in [27, 38] which involves several of the tools which comprise CiaoPP. Figure 2 depicts the overall architecture. Hexagons represent the different tools involved and arrows indicate the communication paths among them.

Program verification and detection of errors is first performed at compile-time by using the sufficient conditions shown in Table 2, i.e., by inferring properties of the program via abstract interpretation-based static analysis and comparing this information against (partial) specifications I_α written in terms of assertions.

Both the static and the dynamic checking are provably *safe* in the sense that all errors flagged are definite violations of the specifications.

Static Debugging: The idea of using analysis information for debugging comes naturally after observing analysis outputs for erroneous programs. Consider the program in Figure 3. The result of regular type analysis for this program includes the following code:

```
:- true pred qsort(A,B)
       : ( term(A), term(B) )
      => ( list(A,t113), list(B,^x) ).

:- regtype t113/1.
t113(A) :- arithexpression(A).
t113([]).
t113([A|B]) :- arithexpression(A), list(B,t113).
t113(e).
```

where `arithexpression` is a library property which describes arithmetic expressions and `list(B,^x)` means "a list of x's." A new name (`t113`) is given to one

```
:- module(qsort, [qsort/2], [assertions]).
:- entry qsort(A,B) : (list(A, num), var(B)).

qsort([X|L],R) :-
        partition(L,L1,X,L2),
        qsort(L2,R2), qsort(L1,R1),
        append(R2,[x|R1],R).
qsort([],[]).

partition([],_B,[],[]).
partition([e|R],C,[E|Left1],Right):-
        E < C, !, partition(R,C,Left1,Right).
partition([E|R],C,Left,[E|Right1]):-
        E >= C,   partition(R,C,Left,Right1).

append([],X,X).
append([H|X],Y,[H|Z]):- append(X,Y,Z).
```

Fig. 3. A tentative qsort program

of the inferred types, and its definition included, because no definition of this type was found visible to the module. In any case, the information inferred does not seem compatible with a correct definition of qsort, which clearly points to a bug in the program.

Static Checking of System Assertions: In addition to manual inspection of the analyzer output, CiaoPP includes a number of automated facilities to help in the debugging task. For example, CiaoPP can find incompatibilities between the ways in which library predicates are called and their intended mode of use, expressed in the form of assertions in the libraries themselves. Also, the preprocessor can detect inconsistencies in the program and check the assertions present in other modules used by the program.

For example, turning on compile-time error checking and selecting type and mode analysis for our tentative qsort program in Figure 3 we obtain the following messages:

```
WARNING: Literal partition(L,L1,X,L2) at qsort/2/1/1 does not succeed!
ERROR: Predicate E>=C at partition/4/3/1 is not called as expected:
        Called:   num>=var
        Expected: arithexpression>=arithexpression
```

where qsort/2/1/1 stands for the first literal in the first clause of qsort and partition/4/3/1 stands for the first literal in the third clause of partition.[6]

The first message warns that all calls to partition will fail, something normally not intended (e.g., in our case). The second message indicates a wrong

---

[6] In the actual system line numbers and automated location of errors in source files are provided.

call to a builtin predicate, which is an obvious error. This error has been detected by comparing the mode information obtained by global analysis, which at the corresponding program point indicates that E is a free variable, with the assertion:

```
:- check calls A<B (arithexpression(A), arithexpression(B)).
```

which is present in the default builtins module, and which implies that the two arguments to </2 should be ground. The message signals a compile-time, or *abstract*, incorrectness symptom [5], indicating that the program does not satisfy the specification given (that of the builtin predicates, in this case). Checking the indicated call to partition and inspecting its arguments we detect that in the definition of qsort, partition is called with the second and third arguments in reversed order – the correct call is partition(L,X,L1,L2).

After correcting this bug, we proceed to perform another round of compile-time checking, which produces the following message:

```
WARNING: Clause 'partition/4/2' is incompatible with its call type
         Head:      partition([e|R],C,[E|Left1],Right)
         Call Type: partition(list(num),num,var,var)
```

This time the error is in the second clause of partition. Checking this clause we see that in the first argument of the head there is an e which should be E instead. Compile-time checking of the program with this bug corrected does not produce any further warning or error messages.

Static Checking of User Assertions: Though, as seen above, it is often possible to detect error without adding assertions to user programs, if the program is not correct, the more assertions are present in the program the more likely it is for errors to be automatically detected. Thus, for those parts of the program which are potentially buggy or for parts whose correctness is crucial, the programmer may decide to invest more time in writing assertions than for other parts of the program which are more stable. In order to be more confident about our program, we add to it the following check assertions:[7]

```
:- calls qsort(A,B) : list(A, num).                              % A1
:- success qsort(A,B)   => (ground(B), sorted_num_list(B)).      % A2
:- calls partition(A,B,C,D) : (ground(A), ground(B)).            % A3
:- success partition(A,B,C,D) => (list(C, num),ground(D)).       % A4
:- calls append(A,B,C) : (list(A,num),list(B,num)).              % A5
:- comp partition/4 + not_fails.                                 % A6
:- comp partition/4 + is_det.                                    % A7
:- comp partition(A,B,C,D) + terminates.                         % A8

:- prop sorted_num_list/1.
sorted_num_list([]).
sorted_num_list([X]):- number(X).
sorted_num_list([X,Y|Z]):-
        number(X), number(Y), X=<Y, sorted_num_list([Y|Z]).
```

---

[7] The check prefix is assumed when no prefix is given, as in the example shown.

where we also use a new property, sorted_num_list, defined in the module itself. These assertions provide a partial specification of the program. They can be seen as integrity constraints: if their properties do not hold, the program is incorrect. Calls assertions specify properties of all calls to a predicate, while success assertions specify properties of exit points for all calls to a predicate. Properties of successes can be restricted to apply only to calls satisfying certain properties upon entry by adding a ":" field to success assertions. Finally, Comp assertions specify *global* properties of the execution of a predicate. These include complex properties such as determinacy or termination and are in general not amenable to run-time checking. They can also be restricted to a subset of the calls using ":". More details on the assertion language can be found in [39].

CiaoPP can perform compile-time checking of the assertions above, by comparing them with the assertions inferred by analysis (see Table 2 and [5,40] for details), producing:

```
:- checked calls qsort(A,B) : list(A,num).                              % A1
:- check success qsort(A,B) => sorted_num_list(B).                      % A2
:- checked calls partition(A,B,C,D) : (ground(A),ground(B)).            % A3
:- checked success partition(A,B,C,D) => (list(C,num),ground(D) ).      % A4
:- false calls append(A,B,C) : ( list(A,num), list(B,num) ).            % A5
:- checked comp partition/4 + not_fails.                                % A6
:- checked comp partition/4 + is_det.                                   % A7
:- checked comp partition/4 + terminates.                               % A8
```

Assertion A5 has been detected to be false. This indicates a violation of the specification given, which is also flagged by CiaoPP as follows:

```
ERROR: (lns 22-23) false calls assertion:
  :- calls append(A,B,C) : list(A,num),list(B,num)
     Called append(list(^x),[^x|list(^x)],var)
```

The error is now in the call append(R2,[x|R1],R) in qsort (x instead of X). Assertions A1, A3, A4, A6, A7, and A8 have been detected to hold, but it was not possible to prove statically assertion A2, which has remained with check status. Note that though the predicate partition may fail in general, in the context of the current program it can be proved not to fail. Note also that A2 has been simplified, and this is because the mode analysis has determined that on success the second argument of qsort is ground, and thus this does not have to be checked at run-time. On the other hand the analyses used in our session (types, modes, non-failure, determinism, and upper-bound cost analysis) do not provide enough information to prove that the output of qsort is a *sorted* list of numbers, since this is not a native property of the analyses being used. While this property could be captured by including a more refined domain (such as constrained types), it is interesting to see what happens with the analyses selected for the example.[8]

---

[8] Not that while property sorted_num_list cannot be proved with only (over approximations) of mode and regular type information, it may be possible to prove that it does *not* hold (an example of how properties which are not natively understood

Dynamic Debugging with Run-time Checks: Assuming that we stay with the analyses selected previously, the following step in the development process is to compile the program obtained above with the "generate run-time checks" option. CiaoPP will then introduce run-time tests in the program for those calls and success assertions which have not been proved nor disproved during compile-time checking. In our case, the program with run-time checks will call the definition of sorted_num_list at the appropriate times. In the current implementation of CiaoPP we obtain the following code for predicate qsort (the code for partition and append remain the same as there is no other assertion left to check):

```
qsort(A,B) :-
      new_qsort(A,B),
      postc([ qsort(C,D) : true => sorted(D) ], qsort(A,B)).

new_qsort([X|L],R) :-
      partition(L,X,L1,L2),
      qsort(L2,R2), qsort(L1,R1),
      append(R2,[X|R1],R).
new_qsort([],[]).
```

where postc is the library predicate in charge of checking postconditions of predicates. If we now run the program with run-time checks in order to sort, say, the list [1,2], the Ciao system generates the following error message:

```
?- qsort([1,2],L).
ERROR: for Goal qsort([1,2],[2,1])
Precondition: true  holds, but
Postcondition: sorted_num_list([2,1]) does not.

L = [2,1] ?
```

Clearly, there is a problem with qsort, since [2,1] is not the result of ordering [1,2] in ascending order. This is a (now, run-time, or *concrete*) incorrectness symptom, which can be used as the starting point of diagnosis. The result of such diagnosis should indicate that the call to append (where R1 and R2 have been swapped) is the cause of the error and that the right definition of predicate qsort is the one in Figure 1.

Performance Debugging and Validation: Another very interesting feature of CiaoPP is the possibility of stating assertions about the efficiency of the program which the system will try to verify or falsify. This is done by stating lower and/or upper bounds on the computational cost of predicates (given in number of execution steps). Consider for example the naive reverse program in Figure 4. Assume also that the predicate append is defined as in Figure 1.

---

by the analysis can also be useful for detecting bugs at compile-time): while the regular type analysis cannot capture perfectly the property sorted_num_list, it can still approximate it (by analyzing the definition) as list(B, num). If type analysis for the program were to generate a type for B not compatible with list(B, num), then a definite error symptom would be detected.

```
:- module(reverse, [nrev/2], [assertions]).
:- use_module(library('assertions/native_props')).
:- entry nrev(A,B) : (ground(A), list(A, term), var(B)).

nrev([],[]).
nrev([H|L],R) :-
        nrev(L,R1),
        append(R1,[H],R).
```

Fig. 4. The naive reverse program.

Suppose that the programmer thinks that the cost of nrev is given by a linear function on the size (list-length) of its first argument, maybe because he has not taken into account the cost of the append call). Since append is linear, it causes nrev to be quadratic. We will show that CiaoPP can be used to inform the programmer about this false idea about the cost of nrev. For example, suppose that the programmer adds the following "check" assertion:

```
:- check comp nrev(A,B) + steps_ub(length(A)+1).
```

With compile-time error checking turned on, and mode, type, non-failure and lower-bound cost analysis selected, we get the following error message:

```
ERROR: false comp assertion:
        :- comp nrev(A,B) : true => steps_ub(length(A)+1)
     because in the computation the following holds:
        steps_lb(0.5*exp(length(A),2)+1.5*length(A)+1)
```

This message states that nrev will take at least $0.5\ (length(A))^2 + 1.5\ length(A) + 1$ resolution steps (which is the cost analysis output), while the assertion requires that it take at most $length(A) + 1$ resolution steps. The cost function in the user-provided assertion is compared with the lower-bound cost assertion inferred by analysis. This allows detecting the inconsistency and proving that the program does not satisfy the efficiency requirements imposed. Upper-bound cost assertions can also be proved to hold, i.e., can be *checked*, by using upper-bound cost analysis rather than lower-bound cost analysis. In such case, if the upper-bound computed by analysis is lower or equal than the upper-bound stated by the user in the assertion. The converse holds for lower-bound cost assertions.

3.3 Source Program Optimization

We now turn our attention to the program optimizations that are available in CiaoPP. These include abstract specialization, parallelization (including granularity control), multiple program specialization, and integration of abstract interpretation and partial evaluation. All of them are performed as source to source transformations of the program. In most of them static analysis is instrumental, or, at least, beneficial.

Abstract Specialization: Program specialization optimizes programs for known values (substitutions) of the input. It is often the case that the set of possible input values is unknown, or this set is infinite. However, a form of specialization can still be performed in such cases by means of abstract interpretation, specialization then being with respect to abstract values, rather than concrete ones. Such abstract values represent a (possibly infinite) set of concrete values. For example, consider the definition of the property sorted_num_list/1, and assume that regular type analysis has produced:

```
:- true pred sorted_num_list(A) : list(A,num) => list(A,num).
```

Abstract specialization can use this information to optimize the code into:

```
sorted_num_list([]).
sorted_num_list([_]).
sorted_num_list([X,Y|Z]):- X=<Y, sorted_num_list([Y|Z]).
```

which is clearly more efficient because no number tests are executed. The optimization above is based on abstractly executing the number literals to the value true, as discussed in Section 2.2.

CiaoPP can also apply abstract specialization to the optimization of programs with dynamic scheduling (e.g., using delay declarations) [41]. The transformations simplify the conditions on the *delay declarations* and also move delayed literals later in the rule body, leading to substantial performance improvement. This is used by CiaoPP, for example, when supporting complex computation models, such as Andorra-style execution [25].

Parallelization: An example of a non-trivial program optimization performed using abstract interpretation in CiaoPP is program parallelization [4]. It is also performed as a source-to-source transformation, in which the input program is *annotated* with parallel expressions. The parallelization algorithms, or annotators [35], exploit parallelism under certain *independence* conditions, which allow guaranteeing interesting correctness and no-slowdown properties for the parallelized programs [29, 16]. This process is complicated by the presence of shared variables and pointers among data structures at run-time.

We consider again the program of Figure 1. A possible parallelization (obtained in this case with the "MEL" annotator) is:

```
qsort([X|L],R) :-
        partition(L,X,L1,L2),
        ( indep([[L1,L2]]) -> qsort(L2,R2) & qsort(L1,R1)
                            ; qsort(L2,R2), qsort(L1,R1) ),
        append(R1,[X|R2],R).
```

which indicates that, provided that L1 and L2 do not have variables in common (at execution time), then the recursive calls to qsort can be run in parallel. Given the information inferred by the abstract interpreter using, e.g., the mode and independence analysis (see Section 3.1), which determines that L1 and L2 are ground after partition (and therefore do not share variables), the independence test and the conditional can be simplified via abstract executability and the annotator yields instead:

```
qsort([X|L],R) :-
      partition(L,X,L1,L2),
      qsort(L2,R2) & qsort(L1,R1),
      append(R1,[X|R2],R).
```

which is much more efficient since it has no run-time test. This test simplification process is described in detail in [4] where the impact of abstract interpretation in the effectiveness of the resulting parallel expressions is also studied.

The tests in the above example aim at *strict* independent and-parallelism. However, the annotators are parameterized on the notion of independence. Different tests can be used for different independence notions: non-strict independence [7], constraint-based independence [16], etc. Moreover, all forms of and-parallelism in logic programs can be seen as independent and-parallelism, provided the definition of independence is applied at the appropriate granularity level.[9]

Resource and Granularity Control: Another application of the information produced by the CiaoPP analyzers, in this case cost analysis, is to perform combined compile–time/run–time resource control. An example of this is task granularity control [33] of parallelized code. Such parallel code can be the output of the process mentioned above or code parallelized manually.

In general, this run-time granularity control process involves computing sizes of terms involved in granularity control, evaluating cost functions, and comparing the result with a threshold[10] to decide for parallel or sequential execution. Optimizations to this general process include cost function simplification and improved term size computation, both of which are illustrated in the following example.

Consider again the qsort program in Figure 1. We use CiaoPP to perform a transformation for granularity control, using the analysis information of type, sharing+freeness, and upper bound cost analysis, and taking as input the parallelized code obtained in the previous section. CiaoPP adds a clause: "qsort(_1,_2) :- g_qsort(_1,_2)." (to preserve the original entry point) and produces g_qsort/2, the version of qsort/2 that performs granularity control (s_qsort/2 is the sequential version):

```
g_qsort([X|L],R) :-
      partition_o3_4(L,X,L1,L2,_2,_1),
      ( _1>7 -> (_2>7 -> g_qsort(L2,R2) & g_qsort(L1,R1)
                       ; g_qsort(L2,R2), s_qsort(L1,R1))
              ; (_2>7 -> s_qsort(L2,R2), g_qsort(L1,R1)
                       ; s_qsort(L2,R2), s_qsort(L1,R1))),
      append(R1,[X|R2],R).
g_qsort([],[]).
```

---

[9] For example, stream and-parallelism can be seen as independent and-parallelism if the independence of "bindings" rather than goals is considered.

[10] This threshold can be determined experimentally for each parallel system, by taking the average value resulting from several runs.

Note that if the lengths of the two input lists to the qsort program are greater than a threshold (a list length of 7 in this case) then versions which continue performing granularity control are executed in parallel. Otherwise, the two recursive calls are executed sequentially. The executed version of each of such calls depends on its grain size: if the length of its input list is not greater than the threshold then a sequential version which does not perform granularity control is executed. This is based on the detection of a recursive invariant: in subsequent recursions this goal will not produce tasks with input sizes greater than the threshold, and thus, for all of them, execution should be performed sequentially and, obviously, no granularity control is needed.

In general, the evaluation of the condition to decide which predicate versions are executed will require the computation of cost functions and a comparison with a cost threshold (measured in units of computation). However, in this example a test simplification has been performed, so that the input size is simply compared against a size threshold, and thus the cost function for qsort does not need to be evaluated.[11] Predicate partition_o3_4/6:

```
partition_o3_4([],_B,[],[],0,0).
partition_o3_4([E|R],C,[E|Left1],Right,_1,_2) :-
      E<C, partition_o3_4(R,C,Left1,Right,_3,_2), _1 is _3+1.
partition_o3_4([E|R],C,Left,[E|Right1],_1,_2) :-
      E>=C, partition_o3_4(R,C,Left,Right1,_1,_3), _2 is _3+1.
```

is the transformed version of partition/4, which "on the fly" computes the sizes of its third and fourth arguments (the automatically generated variables _1 and _2 represent these sizes respectively) [32].

Multiple Specialization: Sometimes a procedure has different uses within a program, i.e. it is called from different places in the program with different (abstract) input values. In principle, (abstract) program specialization is then allowable only if the optimization is applicable to all uses of the predicate. However, it is possible that in several different uses the input values allow different and incompatible optimizations and then none of them can take place. In CiaoPP this problem is overcome by means of "multiple program specialization" where different versions of the predicate are generated for each use. Each version is then optimized for the particular subset of input values with which it is to be used. The abstract multiple specialization technique used in CiaoPP [44] has the advantage that it can be incorporated with little or no modification of some existing abstract interpreters, provided they are *multivariant* (PLAI and similar frameworks have this property).

This specialization can be used for example to improve automatic parallelization in those cases where run-time tests are included in the resulting program. In such cases, a good number of run-time tests may be eliminated and invariants extracted automatically from loops, resulting generally in lower overheads and in several cases in increased speedups. We consider automatic parallelization of a program for matrix multiplication using the same analysis and parallelization

---

[11] This size threshold will obviously be different if the cost function is.

algorithms as the qsort example used before. This program is automatically parallelized without tests if we provide the analyzer (by means of an entry declaration) with accurate information on the expected modes of use of the program. However, in the interesting case in which the user does not provide such declaration, the code generated contains a large number of run-time tests. We include below the code for predicate multiply which multiplies a matrix by a vector:

```
multiply([],_,[]).
multiply([V0|Rest],V1,[Result|Others]) :-
   (ground(V1),
    indep([[V0,Rest],[V0,Others],[Rest,Result],[Result,Others]]) ->
      vmul(V0,V1,Result) & multiply(Rest,V1,Others)
   ;  vmul(V0,V1,Result), multiply(Rest,V1,Others)).
```

Four independence tests and one groundness test have to be executed prior to executing in parallel the calls in the body of the recursive clause of multiply. However, abstract multiple specialization generates four versions of the predicate multiply which correspond to the different ways this predicate may be called (basically, depending on whether the tests succeed or not). Of these four variants, the most optimized one is:

```
multiply3([],_,[]).
multiply3([V0|Rest],V1,[Result|Others]) :-
   (indep([[Result,Others]]) ->
      vmul(V0,V1,Result) & multiply3(Rest,V1,Others)
   ;  vmul(V0,V1,Result), multiply3(Rest,V1,Others)).
```

where the groundness test and three out of the four independence tests have been eliminated. Note also that the recursive calls to multiply use the optimized version multiply3. Thus, execution of matrix multiplication with the expected mode (the only one which will succeed in Prolog) will be quickly directed to the optimized versions of the predicates and iterate on them. This is because the specializer has been able to detect this optimization as an invariant of the loop. The complete code for this example can be found in [44]. The multiple specialization implemented incorporates a minimization algorithm which keeps in the final program as few versions as possible while not losing opportunities for optimization. For example, eight versions of predicate vmul (for vector multiplication) would be generated if no minimizations were performed. However, as multiple versions do not allow further optimization, only one version is present in the final program.

Integration of Abstract Interpretation and Partial Evaluation: In the context of CiaoPP we have also studied the relationship between abstract multiple specialization, abstract interpretation, and partial evaluation. Abstract specialization exploits the information obtained by multivariant abstract interpretation where information about values of variables is propagated by simulating program execution and performing fixpoint computations for recursive calls. In contrast, traditional partial evaluators (mainly) use unfolding for both propagating values of variables and transforming the program. It is known that abstract interpretation is a better technique for propagating success values than unfolding. However, the program transformations induced by unfolding may lead to important optimizations which are not directly achievable in the existing frameworks for multiple specialization based on abstract interpretation. In [46] we present a specialization framework which integrates the better information propagation of abstract interpretation with the powerful program transformations performed by partial evaluation.

We are currently investigating the use of abstract domains based on improvements of regular types [47] for their use for partial evaluation.

More Info: For more information, full versions of papers and technical reports, and/or to download Ciao and other related systems please access: http://www.clip.dia.fi.upm.es/.

Acknowledgments

This work has been funded in part by MCyT projects CUBICO (TIC02-0055), EDIPIA (TIC99-1151) and ADELA (HI2000-0043), and by EU IST FET project ASAP (IST-2001-38059). The Ciao system is a collaborative effort of members of several institutions, including UPM, UNM, U.Melbourne, Monash U., U.Arizona, Linköping U., NMSU, K.U.Leuven, Bristol U., Ben-Gurion U, and INRIA. The system documentation and related publications contain more specific credits.

References

1. F. Bourdoncle. Abstract debugging of higher-order imperative languages. In *Programming Languages Design and Implementation'93*, pages 46–55, 1993.
2. F. Bueno, D. Cabeza, M. Carro, M. Hermenegildo, P. López-García, and G. Puebla. The Ciao Prolog System. Reference Manual. The Ciao System Documentation Series–TR CLIP3/97.1, School of Computer Science, Technical University of Madrid (UPM), August 1997. System and on-line version of the manual available at http://clip.dia.fi.upm.es/Software/Ciao/.
3. F. Bueno, D. Cabeza, M. Hermenegildo, and G. Puebla. Global Analysis of Standard Prolog Programs. In *European Symposium on Programming*, number 1058 in LNCS, pages 108–124, Sweden, April 1996. Springer-Verlag.
4. F. Bueno, M. García de la Banda, and M. Hermenegildo. Effectiveness of Abstract Interpretation in Automatic Parallelization: A Case Study in Logic Programming. *ACM Transactions on Programming Languages and Systems*, 21(2):189–238, March 1999.
5. F. Bueno, P. Deransart, W. Drabent, G. Ferrand, M. Hermenegildo, J. Maluszynski, and G. Puebla. On the Role of Semantic Approximations in Validation and Diagnosis of Constraint Logic Programs. In *Proc. of the 3rd. Int'l Workshop on Automated Debugging–AADEBUG'97*, pages 155–170, Linköping, Sweden, May 1997. U. of Linköping Press.
6. F. Bueno, M. García de la Banda, M. Hermenegildo, K. Marriott, G. Puebla, and P. Stuckey. A Model for Inter-module Analysis and Optimizing Compilation. In *Logic-based Program Synthesis and Transformation*, number 2042 in LNCS, pages 86–102. Springer-Verlag, 2001.

7. D. Cabeza and M. Hermenegildo. Extracting Non-strict Independent And-parallelism Using Sharing and Freeness Information. In *1994 International Static Analysis Symposium*, number 864 in LNCS, pages 297–313, Namur, Belgium, September 1994. Springer-Verlag.
8. B. Le Charlier and P. Van Hentenryck. Experimental Evaluation of a Generic Abstract Interpretation Algorithm for Prolog. *ACM Transactions on Programming Languages and Systems*, 16(1):35–101, 1994.
9. M. Comini, G. Levi, M. C. Meo, and G. Vitiello. Abstract diagnosis. *Journal of Logic Programming*, 39(1–3):43–93, 1999.
10. M. Comini, G. Levi, and G. Vitiello. Declarative diagnosis revisited. In *1995 International Logic Programming Symposium*, pages 275–287, Portland, Oregon, December 1995. MIT Press, Cambridge, MA.
11. P. Cousot. Automatic Verification by Abstract Interpretation, Invited Tutorial. In *Fourth International Conference on Verification, Model Checking and Abstract Interpretation (VMCAI)*, number 2575 in LNCS, pages 20–24. Springer, January 2003.
12. P. Cousot and R. Cousot. Abstract Interpretation: a Unified Lattice Model for Static Analysis of Programs by Construction or Approximation of Fixpoints. In *Fourth ACM Symposium on Principles of Programming Languages*, pages 238–252, 1977.
13. P. Cousot and R. Cousot. Systematic Design of Program Transformation Frameworks by Abstract Interpretation. In *POPL'02: 29ST ACM SIGPLAN-SIGACT Symposium on Principles of Programming Languages*, pages 178–190, Portland, Oregon, January 2002. ACM.
14. P.W. Dart and J. Zobel. A Regular Type Language for Logic Programs. In F. Pfenning, editor, *Types in Logic Programming*, pages 157–187. MIT Press, 1992.
15. M. García de la Banda, M. Hermenegildo, M. Bruynooghe, V. Dumortier, G. Janssens, and W. Simoens. Global Analysis of Constraint Logic Programs. *ACM Trans. on Programming Languages and Systems*, 18(5):564–615, 1996.
16. M. García de la Banda, M. Hermenegildo, and K. Marriott. Independence in CLP Languages. *ACM Transactions on Programming Languages and Systems*, 22(2):269–339, March 2000.
17. S.K. Debray, P. López-García, and M. Hermenegildo. Non-Failure Analysis for Logic Programs. In *1997 International Conference on Logic Programming*, pages 48–62, Cambridge, MA, June 1997. MIT Press, Cambridge, MA.
18. S.K. Debray, P. López-García, M. Hermenegildo, and N.-W. Lin. Estimating the Computational Cost of Logic Programs. In *Static Analysis Symposium, SAS'94*, number 864 in LNCS, pages 255–265, Namur, Belgium, September 1994. Springer-Verlag.
19. S.K. Debray, P. López-García, M. Hermenegildo, and N.-W. Lin. Lower Bound Cost Estimation for Logic Programs. In *1997 International Logic Programming Symposium*, pages 291–305. MIT Press, Cambridge, MA, October 1997.
20. J. Gallagher and G. Puebla. Abstract Interpretation over Non-Deterministic Finite Tree Automata for Set-Based Analysis of Logic Programs. In *Fourth International Symposium on Practical Aspects of Declarative Languages*, number 2257 in LNCS, pages 243–261. Springer-Verlag, January 2002.
21. J.P. Gallagher and D.A. de Waal. Fast and precise regular approximations of logic programs. In Pascal Van Hentenryck, editor, *Proc. of the 11th International Conference on Logic Programming*, pages 599–613. MIT Press, 1994.

22. M. García de la Banda, M. Hermenegildo, M. Bruynooghe, V. Dumortier, G. Janssens, and W. Simoens. Global Analysis of Constraint Logic Programs. *ACM Transactions on Programming Languages and Systems*, 18(5):564–615, September 1996.
23. F. Giannotti and M. Hermenegildo. A Technique for Recursive Invariance Detection and Selective Program Specialization. In *Proc. 3rd. Int'l Symposium on Programming Language Implementation and Logic Programming*, number 528 in LNCS, pages 323–335. Springer-Verlag, August 1991.
24. M. Hermenegildo. A Documentation Generator for (C)LP Systems. In *International Conference on Computational Logic, CL2000*, number 1861 in LNAI, pages 1345–1361. Springer-Verlag, July 2000.
25. M. Hermenegildo, F. Bueno, D. Cabeza, M. Carro, M. García de la Banda, P. López-García, and G. Puebla. The CIAO Multi-Dialect Compiler and System: An Experimentation Workbench for Future (C)LP Systems. In *Parallelism and Implementation of Logic and Constraint Logic Programming*, pages 65–85. Nova Science, Commack, NY, USA, April 1999.
26. M. Hermenegildo, F. Bueno, G. Puebla, and P. López-García. Program Analysis, Debugging and Optimization Using the Ciao System Preprocessor. In *1999 International Conference on Logic Programming*, pages 52–66, Cambridge, MA, November 1999. MIT Press.
27. M. Hermenegildo, G. Puebla, and F. Bueno. Using Global Analysis, Partial Specifications, and an Extensible Assertion Language for Program Validation and Debugging. In K. R. Apt, V. Marek, M. Truszczynski, and D. S. Warren, editors, *The Logic Programming Paradigm: a 25-Year Perspective*, pages 161–192. Springer-Verlag, July 1999.
28. M. Hermenegildo, G. Puebla, K. Marriott, and P. Stuckey. Incremental Analysis of Constraint Logic Programs. *ACM Transactions on Programming Languages and Systems*, 22(2):187–223, March 2000.
29. M. Hermenegildo and F. Rossi. Strict and Non-Strict Independent And-Parallelism in Logic Programs: Correctness, Efficiency, and Compile-Time Conditions. *Journal of Logic Programming*, 22(1):1–45, 1995.
30. M. Leuschel. Program Specialisation and Abstract Interpretation Reconciled. In *Joint International Conference and Symposium on Logic Programming*, June 1998.
31. Y. Lichtenstein and E. Y. Shapiro. Abstract algorithmic debugging. In R. A. Kowalski and K. A. Bowen, editors, *Fifth International Conference and Symposium on Logic Programming*, pages 512–531, Seattle, Washington, August 1988. MIT.
32. P. López-García and M. Hermenegildo. Efficient Term Size Computation for Granularity Control. In *International Conference on Logic Programming*, pages 647–661, Cambridge, MA, June 1995. MIT Press, Cambridge, MA.
33. P. López-García, M. Hermenegildo, and S.K. Debray. A Methodology for Granularity Based Control of Parallelism in Logic Programs. *J. of Symbolic Computation, Special Issue on Parallel Symbolic Computation*, 22:715–734, 1996.
34. K. Marriott, M. García de la Banda, and M. Hermenegildo. Analyzing Logic Programs with Dynamic Scheduling. In *20th. Annual ACM Conf. on Principles of Programming Languages*, pages 240–254. ACM, January 1994.
35. K. Muthukumar, F. Bueno, M. García de la Banda, and M. Hermenegildo. Automatic Compile-time Parallelization of Logic Programs for Restricted, Goal-level, Independent And-parallelism. *Journal of Logic Programming*, 38(2):165–218, February 1999.

36. K. Muthukumar and M. Hermenegildo. Combined Determination of Sharing and Freeness of Program Variables Through Abstract Interpretation. In *1991 International Conference on Logic Programming*, pages 49–63. MIT Press, June 1991.
37. K. Muthukumar and M. Hermenegildo. Compile-time Derivation of Variable Dependency Using Abstract Interpretation. *Journal of Logic Programming*, 13(2/3):315–347, July 1992.
38. G. Puebla, F. Bueno, and M. Hermenegildo. A Generic Preprocessor for Program Validation and Debugging. In P. Deransart, M. Hermenegildo, and J. Maluszynski, editors, *Analysis and Visualization Tools for Constraint Programming*, number 1870 in LNCS, pages 63–107. Springer-Verlag, September 2000.
39. G. Puebla, F. Bueno, and M. Hermenegildo. An Assertion Language for Constraint Logic Programs. In P. Deransart, M. Hermenegildo, and J. Maluszynski, editors, *Analysis and Visualization Tools for Constraint Programming*, number 1870 in LNCS, pages 23–61. Springer-Verlag, September 2000.
40. G. Puebla, F. Bueno, and M. Hermenegildo. Combined Static and Dynamic Assertion-Based Debugging of Constraint Logic Programs. In *Logic-based Program Synthesis and Transformation (LOPSTR'99)*, number 1817 in LNCS, pages 273–292. Springer-Verlag, 2000.
41. G. Puebla, M. García de la Banda, K. Marriott, and P. Stuckey. Optimization of Logic Programs with Dynamic Scheduling. In *1997 International Conference on Logic Programming*, pages 93–107, Cambridge, MA, June 1997. MIT Press.
42. G. Puebla and M. Hermenegildo. Optimized Algorithms for the Incremental Analysis of Logic Programs. In *International Static Analysis Symposium*, number 1145 in LNCS, pages 270–284. Springer-Verlag, September 1996.
43. G. Puebla and M. Hermenegildo. Abstract Specialization and its Application to Program Parallelization. In J. Gallagher, editor, *Logic Program Synthesis and Transformation*, number 1207 in LNCS, pages 169–186. Springer-Verlag, 1997.
44. G. Puebla and M. Hermenegildo. Abstract Multiple Specialization and its Application to Program Parallelization. *J. of Logic Programming. Special Issue on Synthesis, Transformation and Analysis of Logic Programs*, 41(2&3):279–316, November 1999.
45. G. Puebla and M. Hermenegildo. Some Issues in Analysis and Specialization of Modular Ciao-Prolog Programs. In *Special Issue on Optimization and Implementation of Declarative Programming Languages*, volume 30 of *Electronic Notes in Theoretical Computer Science*. Elsevier - North Holland, March 2000.
46. G. Puebla, M. Hermenegildo, and J. Gallagher. An Integration of Partial Evaluation in a Generic Abstract Interpretation Framework. In O Danvy, editor, *ACM SIGPLAN Workshop on Partial Evaluation and Semantics-Based Program Manipulation (PEPM'99)*, number NS-99-1 in BRISC Series, pages 75–85. University of Aarhus, Denmark, January 1999.
47. C. Vaucheret and F. Bueno. More precise yet efficient type inference for logic programs. In *International Static Analysis Symposium*, number 2477 in LNCS, pages 102–116. Springer-Verlag, September 2002.
48. E. Yardeni and E. Shapiro. A Type System for Logic Programs. *Concurrent Prolog: Collected Papers*, pages 211–244, 1987.

Selective Tail Call Elimination

Yasuhiko Minamide

Institute of Information Sciences and Electronics
University of Tsukuba
and
PRESTO, JST
minamide@is.tsukuba.ac.jp

Abstract. Tail calls are expected not to consume stack space in most functional languages. However, there is no support for tail calls in some environments. Even in such environments, proper tail calls can be implemented with a technique called a trampoline. To reduce the overhead of trampolining while preserving stack space asymptotically we propose selective tail call elimination based on an effect system. The effect system infers the number of successive tail calls generated by the execution of an expression, and trampolines are introduced only when they are necessary.

1 Introduction

Tail calls are expected not to consume stack space in most functional languages. Implementation of proper tail calls requires some support from a target environment, but some environments including C and Java Virtual Machine (JVM) [10] do not provide such support. Even in such environments, proper tail calls can be implemented with a technique called a *trampoline*. However, the trampoline technique is based on a non-standard calling convention and is considered to introduce too much overhead. Thus, most compilers for such environments do not adopt trampolining and abandon proper tail calls [2, 17, 3].

To solve this problem we selectively introduce trampolines based on an effect system. We consider a typed call-by-value language as a source language of selective tail call elimination. Effect systems were originally proposed to infer side-effects of a program by Gifford and Lucassen [8, 11], and an extension was applied to estimate the execution time of a program [6, 15]. Our effect system infers the number of successive tail calls that can be generated by the execution of an expression. Based on effects, functions are divided into two kinds: those that lead to a finite number of successive tail calls and those that may lead to an infinite number of successive tail calls. Then, it is necessary to adopt trampolines only for the latter kind. In this manner we can reduce the overhead of trampolining while preserving stack space asymptotically.

Our effect system includes the rule of subtyping, and some applications may call both kinds of functions. To support subtyping on functions and enable selective elimination of tail calls, we introduce a transformation that translates a function into a record containing two functions supporting different calling conventions. We prove that the increase of stack space usage caused by this transformation is bounded by a factor determined by the effect system.

We have incorporated selective tail call elimination into the MLj compiler [2], which complies Standard ML into Java bytecodes. Results for benchmark programs show that our effect system is strong enough to indicate that most functions are safe without tail call elimination. We show that there is little degradation of performance for most benchmark programs. We also measure impact of tail call elimination on stack space usage. It shows that general tail call elimination sometimes greatly reduces stack space usage.

This paper is organized as follows. In Section 2, we review the trampolining transformation and clarify its problem. In Section 3, we introduce our selective tail call elimination and prove its soundness. In Section 4, the effect system is extended with a wider class of effects. In Section 5 we outline effect inference for our effect system. Section 6 shows some examples where our effect system shows that a function is unsafe without tail call elimination. In Section 7 we describe our implementation and discuss the results of our experiments. Finally, we review related work and present our conclusions.

2 Tail Call Elimination with Trampolines

In functional languages, loops are often expressed with tail calls and thus they are expected not to consume stack space. Let us consider the following program written in Standard ML. The application sum (x-1, a+x) in this program is called a tail call because there is nothing to do in the function sum after the application.

```
let fun sum (x, a) = if x = 0 then a else sum (x-1, a+x)
in
    sum (y, 0)
end
```

If the tail call is properly implemented, the program above requires only constant stack space. On the other hand, if it is not properly implemented, it requires stack space proportional to y. Loops are often expressed in this way in functional languages and thus it is important to implement proper tail calls.

However, it is not straightforward to implement proper tail calls in environments without direct support of tail calls, such as in C and JVM. In such environments it is possible to implement proper tail calls with a non-standard calling convention called a trampoline [1]. We will explain the trampoline technique as a source-to-source transformation. The example above is transformed into the following program.

```
datatype 'a ret = Thunk (unit -> 'a ret) | Val 'a

fun loop (Val x) = x
```

```
  | loop (Thunk f) = loop (f ())

let fun sum (x, a) =
        if x=0 then Val a else Thunk (fn () => sum (x-1, a+x))
in
    loop (sum (y, 0))
end
```

The tail call in the program is translated into the creation of a closure. Then the closure is called from the loop.[1] This technique was used in a Standard ML to C compiler [18] and is also useful to implement various features of programming languages [7]. However, it is clear that this technique introduces a lot of overhead. Thus, most compilers into C and JVM do not adopt trampolining and abandon proper tail calls.

3   Selective Tail Call Elimination

To reduce the overhead introduced by implementation of proper tail calls by techniques such as trampolining, we propose selective elimination of tail calls that preserves the asymptotic complexity of the stack space.

The basic idea is that if the number of successive tail calls generated by a function call is bounded by some constant, it is not necessary to adopt a trampoline for the function. Let us consider the following program.

```
let fun f x = x
    fun g x = f x
in
    g 0
end
```

There are two tail calls in this program: f x and g 0. However, it is not necessary to introduce a trampoline for this program. The execution of the function f leads to no tail call and thus f x generates only one successive tail call. The function g calls f at a tail-call position and thus the function call g 0 generates two successive tail calls. Since the number of successive tail calls is bounded in this program, it is safe to execute this program without tail call elimination.

On the other hand, in the following program the number of successive tail calls that the application h y leads to cannot be bounded. Thus it is necessary to introduce a trampoline for the program.

```
let fun h x = if x > 0 then h (x - 1) else 0
in
    h y
end
```

---
[1] The function loop should be implemented so as not to consume stack space.

If we can statically analyze the number of successive tail calls generated by execution of each function, we can avoid introducing trampolines for functions satisfying some safety condition and selectively eliminate tail calls with trampolines. In the next section we introduce an effect system to eliminate tail calls selectively.

3.1 Effect System

We introduce sized effects to check the number of successive tail calls generated by the execution of an expression. The following are the effects we consider.

$$\rho ::= \omega \mid 0 \mid 1 \mid \ldots$$

We consider an order relation $\rho \leq \rho'$ between effects: the usual order relation between natural numbers and $i \leq \omega$ for any natural number i. For a finite effect i, the effect i^+ is defined as $i^+ = i + 1$. Then we consider the following types where a function type is annotated with an effect.

$$\tau ::= \mathsf{nat} \mid \tau \to^\rho \tau$$

We include nat as a base type for natural numbers and we also use other base types in examples. The functions we discussed above have the following types.

```
f : int →¹ int
g : int →² int
h : int →ω int
```

Application of f at a tail-call position leads to one tail call. Since the application of g leads to a subsequent application of f, the type of g is annotated with 2. On the other hand, the number of successive tail calls generated by h cannot be bounded. Thus its type is annotated with ω.

We consider the subtyping relation defined by the following rules.

$$\tau \leq \tau \qquad \frac{\tau_1 \leq \tau_1' \quad \tau_2' \leq \tau_2 \quad \rho' \leq \rho}{\tau_1' \to^{\rho'} \tau_2' \leq \tau_1 \to^\rho \tau_2}$$

We formalize our effect system for the following language, where abstractions and applications are annotated with effects.

$$V ::= x \mid 0 \mid \mathsf{suc}(V) \mid \mathsf{fix}\, x.\lambda^\rho y.M$$
$$M ::= V \mid @^\rho M M \mid \mathsf{case}\, V \,\mathsf{of}\, 0 \Rightarrow M, \mathsf{suc}(x) \Rightarrow M$$

We will discuss how to annotate the language without effect annotations in Section 5. The values 0 and suc(V) are of natural numbers. Judgments of the effect system have the following forms:

$$E \vdash V : \tau$$
$$E \vdash M : \tau\,!\,\rho$$

$$\frac{x:\tau \in E}{E \vdash x : \tau} \qquad E \vdash 0 : \mathsf{nat} \qquad \frac{E \vdash V : \mathsf{nat}}{E \vdash \mathsf{suc}(V) : \mathsf{nat}} \qquad \frac{E \vdash V : \tau}{E \vdash V : \tau\,!\,0}$$

$$\frac{E, x : \tau_1 \to^{i^+} \tau_2, y : \tau_1 \vdash M : \tau_2\,!\,i}{E \vdash \mathsf{fix}\,x.\lambda^{i^+}y.M : \tau_1 \to^{i^+} \tau_2} \qquad \frac{E, x : \tau_1 \to^{\omega} \tau_2, y : \tau_1 \vdash M : \tau_2\,!\,\omega}{E \vdash \mathsf{fix}\,x.\lambda^{\omega}y.M : \tau_1 \to^{\omega} \tau_2}$$

$$\frac{E \vdash M_1 : \tau_1 \to^{\rho} \tau_2\,!\,\rho_1 \quad E \vdash M_2 : \tau_1\,!\,\rho_2}{E \vdash @^{\rho} M_1 M_2 : \tau_2\,!\,\rho} \qquad \frac{E \vdash M : \tau'\,!\,\rho' \quad \rho' \leq \rho \quad \tau' \leq \tau}{E \vdash M : \tau\,!\,\rho}$$

$$\frac{E \vdash V : \mathsf{nat} \quad E \vdash M_1 : \tau\,!\,\rho \quad E, x : \mathsf{nat} \vdash M_2 : \tau\,!\,\rho}{E \vdash \mathsf{case}\,V\,\mathsf{of}\,0 \Rightarrow M_1,\,\mathsf{suc}(x) \Rightarrow M_2 : \tau\,!\,\rho}$$

Fig. 1. Type system

where ρ represents the maximum number of successive tail calls generated by evaluation of M. The rules of the effect system are defined in Figure 1. The rules of abstraction and application are explained as follows.

- If the body of a function leads to i successive tail calls, application of the function at a tail-call position leads to i^+ successive tail calls.
- If the body of a function has effect ω, the function has effect ω. That means successive tail calls generated by application of the function cannot be bounded.
- The effects of M_1 and M_2 are ignored in the rule of application because they correspond to evaluation at non-tail-call positions. Thus, the effect of the application $@^{\rho}M_1M_2$ is determined only by the effect annotation of the function type.

To discuss the soundness of selective tail elimination we introduce an operational semantics that profiles stack space and models evaluation with proper implementation of tail calls. We define a big-step operational semantics with the following judgments:

$$\vdash_T M \Downarrow^i V$$

$$\vdash_N M \Downarrow^i V$$

with the meanings that M is evaluated to V with i stack frames at a tail-call position or a non-tail-call position, respectively. A whole program is considered to be evaluated at a tail-call position. The rules are given in Figure 2 where $\vdash_\alpha M \Downarrow^n V$ means the rule holds both for $\alpha = N$ and $\alpha = T$. At a tail-call position, the evaluation of the body of a function requires no new stack frame. Thus, the stack space required for evaluation of the application is $\mathsf{max}(l, m, n)$. On the other hand, at a non-tail-call position, it requires a new stack frame: the stack space is $\mathsf{max}(l, m, n + 1)$. This semantics models stack space usage when a program is executed after compilation. Correspondence to a semantics that models execution based on an interpreter is discussed in [12].

$$\vdash_T V \downarrow^0 V \qquad \vdash_N V \downarrow^0 V$$

$$\frac{\vdash_N M_1 \downarrow^l \text{fix}\, x.\lambda^{\rho'} y.M_0 \quad \vdash_N M_2 \downarrow^m V_2 \quad \vdash_T M_0[\text{fix}\, x.\lambda^{\rho'} y.M_0/x][V_2/y] \downarrow^n V}{\vdash_T @^\rho M_1 M_2 \downarrow^{\max(l,m,n)} V}$$

$$\frac{\vdash_N M_1 \downarrow^l \text{fix}\, x.\lambda^{\rho'} y.M_0 \quad \vdash_N M_2 \downarrow^m V_2 \quad \vdash_T M_0[\text{fix}\, x.\lambda^{\rho'} y.M_0/x][V_2/y] \downarrow^n V}{\vdash_N @^\rho M_1 M_2 \downarrow^{\max(l,m,n+1)} V}$$

$$\frac{\vdash_\alpha M_1 \downarrow^n V}{\vdash_\alpha \text{case}\, 0\, \text{of}\, 0 \Rightarrow M_1, \text{suc}(x) \Rightarrow M_2 \downarrow^n V}$$

$$\frac{\vdash_\alpha M_2[V_0/x] \downarrow^n V}{\vdash_\alpha \text{case}\, \text{suc}(V_0)\, \text{of}\, 0 \Rightarrow M_1, \text{suc}(x) \Rightarrow M_2 \downarrow^n V}$$

Fig. 2. Operational semantics

With respect to the operational semantics, the soundness of the type system in the usual sense is proved. However, the following lemma says nothing about effects inferred by the effect system.

Lemma 1 (Soundness).

1. If $\emptyset \vdash M : \tau!\rho$ and $\vdash_N M \downarrow^m V$ then $\emptyset \vdash V : \tau$.
2. If $\emptyset \vdash M : \tau!\rho$ and $\vdash_T M \downarrow^m V$ then $\emptyset \vdash V : \tau$.

3.2 Transformation

We introduce a program transformation that selectively eliminates tail calls based on effect annotations. The idea is to eliminate tail calls of the form $@^\omega MM$ with trampolining and to adopt the standard calling convention for $@^i MM$.[2]

However, implementation based on this idea is not so simple because $\tau_1 \to^i \tau_2$ can be considered as $\tau_1 \to^\omega \tau_2$ by subtyping. Let us consider the following program.

```
let fun f x = x
    fun g x = if ... then x else g (x - 1)
in
    (if ... then f else g) 0
end
```

The functions f and g have types int $\to^1$ int and int $\to^\omega$ int, respectively. It is not possible to determine the kinds of functions that are called by the application in the body of the let-expression. Thus, it is not straightforward to compile the application in the body.

---

[2] We assume that the standard calling convention does not support tail call elimination.

To solve this problem, we represents $\tau_1 \to^i \tau_2$ as a record that contains two functions: one for a trampoline and one for the standard calling convention. Then subtyping on function types is translated into record (object) subtyping.

For the target language of the transformation we consider the following types.

$$\sigma ::= \mathsf{nat} \mid \sigma \to \sigma \mid \sigma \to^t \sigma \mid \{\mathsf{fun} : \sigma, \mathsf{tfun} : \sigma\} \mid \{\mathsf{tfun} : \sigma\}$$

There are two kinds of function types: $\sigma \to \sigma$ uses the standard calling convention without proper tail calls, and $\sigma \to^t \sigma$ uses the non-standard calling convention with tail call elimination. There is no subtyping relation between $\sigma_1 \to \sigma_2$ and $\sigma_1 \to^t \sigma_2$. Two kinds of record types, $\{\mathsf{tfun} : \sigma\}$ and $\{\mathsf{fun} : \sigma, \mathsf{tfun} : \sigma\}$, are included to translate function types and we consider the following subtyping relation between them.

$$\{\mathsf{fun} : \sigma_1, \mathsf{tfun} : \sigma_2\} \leq \{\mathsf{tfun} : \sigma_2\}$$

Then our transformation translates function types into record types so that the subtyping relation is preserved. The translation of types $|\tau|$ is defined as follows:

$$|\tau_1 \to^\omega \tau_2| = \{\mathsf{tfun} : |\tau_1| \to^t |\tau_2|\}$$

$$|\tau_1 \to^i \tau_2| = \{\mathsf{fun} : |\tau_1| \to |\tau_2|, \mathsf{tfun} : |\tau_1| \to^t |\tau_2|\}$$

We therefore have the following translation of subtyping.

$$|\tau_1 \to^i \tau_2| \leq |\tau_1 \to^\omega \tau_2|$$

This translation of subtyping is natural for compilation to Java bytecodes because JVM has subtyping on objects through inheritance of classes.

The syntax of the target language is defined as follows. It includes two kinds of abstraction and application, and syntax for records and field selection.

$$N ::= W \mid @NN \mid @^t NN \mid N.\mathsf{fun} \mid N.\mathsf{tfun} \mid \mathsf{case}\, W\, \mathsf{of}\, 0 \Rightarrow N, \mathsf{suc}(x) \Rightarrow N$$
$$W ::= x \mid 0 \mid \mathsf{suc}(W) \mid \lambda x.N \mid \lambda^t x.N \mid \mathsf{fix}\, x.\{\mathsf{fun} = W, \mathsf{tfun} = W\} \mid$$
$$\mathsf{fix}\, x.\{\mathsf{tfun} = W\}$$

The fields of a record expression are restricted to values: this restriction is sufficient for our transformation. The type system of the target language is standard and does not include effects. The definition of the type system is shown in Appendix A.

We define an operational semantics of the target language in the same manner as that of the source language: we define a big-step operational semantics with following judgments.

$$\vdash_T N \Downarrow^i W$$
$$\vdash_N N \Downarrow^i W$$

The main rules are defined as follows. It should be noted that tail calls are not properly implemented for application $@N_1 N_2$ and thus the evaluation of the body of the function requires a new stack frame: the stack space required is not $\max(l, m, n)$, but $\max(l, m, n + 1)$.

$$\frac{\vdash_N N_1 \downarrow^l \lambda^t x.N \quad \vdash_N N_2 \downarrow^m W_2 \quad \vdash_T N[W_2/x] \downarrow^n W}{\vdash_T @^t N_1 N_2 \downarrow^{\max(l,m,n)} W}$$

$$\frac{\vdash_N N_1 \downarrow^l \lambda x.N \quad \vdash_N N_2 \downarrow^m W_2 \quad \vdash_T N[W_2/x] \downarrow^n W}{\vdash_T @ N_1 N_2 \downarrow^{\max(l,m,n+1)} W}$$

The other rules are shown in Appendix B.

The transformation of selective tail call elimination is defined as follows:

$$[\![x]\!] = x$$
$$[\![0]\!] = 0$$
$$[\![\mathsf{suc}(V)]\!] = \mathsf{suc}([\![V]\!])$$
$$[\![\mathsf{fix}\, x.\lambda^\omega y.M]\!] = \mathsf{fix}\, x.\{\mathsf{tfun} = \lambda^t y.[\![M]\!]\}$$
$$[\![\mathsf{fix}\, x.\lambda^i y.M]\!] = \mathsf{fix}\, x.\{\mathsf{fun} = \lambda y.[\![M]\!], \mathsf{tfun} = \lambda^t y.[\![M]\!]\}$$
$$[\![@^i M_1 M_2]\!] = @([\![M_1]\!].\mathsf{fun})\,[\![M_2]\!]$$
$$[\![@^\omega M_1 M_2]\!] = @^t([\![M_1]\!].\mathsf{tfun})\,[\![M_2]\!]$$
$$[\![\mathsf{case}\, V\, \mathsf{of}\, 0 \Rightarrow M_1, \mathsf{suc}(x) \Rightarrow M_2]\!] = \mathsf{case}\, [\![V]\!]\, \mathsf{of}\, 0 \Rightarrow [\![M_1]\!], \mathsf{suc}(x) \Rightarrow [\![M_2]\!]$$

We extend the translation of types to type environments as $|E|(x) = |E(x)|$. Then the type correctness of this transformation is formulated as the following lemma and proved by induction on the derivation of $E \vdash M : \tau!\rho$.

Lemma 2 (Type Soundness). *If $E \vdash M : \tau!\rho$ then $|E| \vdash [\![M]\!] : |\tau|$.*

To formalize the soundness of the transformation we introduce the following notation: $\vdash_T M \downarrow^{\leq k} V$ if $\vdash_T M \downarrow^{k'} V$ for some $k' \leq k$. The factor of increase of stack space usage by selective tail call elimination is determined by the maximum of the effect annotations in M, denoted by $\max(M)$.

Theorem 1 (Soundness). *Let $C = \max(M) + 1$.*

1. *If $\emptyset \vdash M : \tau!i$ and $\vdash_T M \downarrow^k V$ then $\vdash_T [\![M]\!] \downarrow^{\leq Ck+i} [\![V]\!]$.*
2. *If $\emptyset \vdash M : \tau!\omega$ and $\vdash_T M \downarrow^k V$ then $\vdash_T [\![M]\!] \downarrow^{\leq Ck+C-1} [\![V]\!]$.*
3. *If $\emptyset \vdash M : \tau!\rho$ and $\vdash_N M \downarrow^k V$ then $\vdash_N [\![M]\!] \downarrow^{\leq Ck} [\![V]\!]$.*

This theorem ensures that the stack space usage of a program is preserved asymptotically.

For example, $@^\omega(\mathtt{fix}\, f.\lambda^\omega x.@^1(\mathtt{fix}\, g.\lambda^1 y.y)x)0$ and its translation are evaluated as follows:

$$\vdash_N @^\omega(\mathtt{fix}\, f.\lambda^\omega x.@^1(\mathtt{fix}\, g.\lambda^1 y.y)x)0 \downarrow^1 0$$

$$\vdash_N @^t(\mathtt{fix}\, f.\{\mathsf{tfun} = \lambda^t x.@(\mathtt{fix}\, g.\{\mathsf{fun} = \lambda y.y, \mathsf{tfun} = \lambda^t y.y\}.\mathsf{fun})x\}.\mathsf{tfun})0 \downarrow^2 0$$

This example corresponds to the worst case: $k = 1$ and $C = 2$. The proof of the theorem appears in Appendix C.

4 Extension of the Effect System

Th effect system we have presented has one unnatural limitation: ω must always be assigned to a function which calls a function with effect ω at tail call position, even if the function is safe without tail call elimination. In this section, we extend our effect system to overcome this limitation by considering a wider class of effects.

We first show an example where the limitation of our effect system appears. Let us consider the following program.

```
fun f x = f x
fun g x = f x
fun h (0,x) = g x
  | h (n,x) = h (n-1,x)
```

The function g is safe without tail call elimination: the stack space usage is increased by 1 even if it is implemented with the standard calling convention. However, in our effect system the function is assigned the effect ω to because it calls the function f of the effect ω at a tail call position.

We solve this limitation by extending the effects in our type system into the following form.

$$\rho ::= \omega \cdot i + j$$

where i and j are natural numbers. The intuition is that the function with effect $\omega \cdot i + j$ such that $j > 0$ is safe without tail call elimination. We identifies $\omega \cdot i + 0$ and $\omega \cdot 0 + j$ with $\omega \cdot i$ and j, respectively. The effect ρ^+ and the subeffect relation $\rho \leq \rho'$ are defined as follows:

$$(\omega \cdot i + j)^+ = \omega \cdot i + (j+1)$$

$$\omega \cdot i + j \leq \omega \cdot i' + j' \quad \text{iff} \quad i < i', \text{ or } i = i' \text{ and } j \leq j'$$

The typing rules of abstraction in the effect system are extended as follows:

$$\frac{E, x : \tau_1 \to^{\rho^+} \tau_2, y : \tau_1 \vdash M : \tau_2 \,!\, \rho}{E \vdash \text{fix}\, x.\lambda^{\rho^+} y.M : \tau_1 \to^{\rho^+} \tau_2} \qquad \frac{E, x : \tau_1 \to^{\omega \cdot i} \tau_2, y : \tau_1 \vdash M : \tau_2 \,!\, \omega \cdot i}{E \vdash \text{fix}\, x.\lambda^{\omega \cdot i} y.M : \tau_1 \to^{\omega \cdot i} \tau_2}$$

Then we can assign the following types and thus g can be safely implemented with the standard calling convention.

```
f : int →^ω int
g : int →^{ω+1} int
h : int × int →^{ω·2} int
```

We also need to modify the transformation to implement selective tail call elimination. Since a function with effect $\omega \cdot i$ can be considered to have effect

$\omega \cdot i + 1$ in this system, a function with effect $\omega \cdot i$ must support both calling conventions. The transformation is modified as follows:

$$[\![\texttt{fix}\, x.\lambda^\rho y.M]\!] = \texttt{fix}\, x.\{\mathsf{fun} = \lambda y.[\![M]\!], \mathsf{tfun} = \lambda^t y.[\![M]\!]\}$$
$$[\![@^{\omega\cdot i+j} M_1 M_2]\!] = @([\![M_1]\!].\mathsf{fun})\,[\![M_2]\!]$$
$$[\![@^{\omega\cdot i} M_1 M_2]\!] = @^t([\![M_1]\!].\mathsf{tfun})\,[\![M_2]\!]$$

where $j > 0$. The intuitive meaning of extended effects can be explained with this transformation.

- A tail call with effect ω generates successive tail calls of $@^t$ and then successive tail calls of $@$. The successive tail calls of $@$ may be generated by subeffect relation $i \leq \omega$.
- A tail call with effect $\omega \cdot i$ may repeat i times the pattern of tail calls for ω
- A tail call with effect $\omega \cdot i + j$ may generate j successive tail calls of $@$ and then generates tail calls of the pattern for $\omega \cdot i$.

The soundness theorem is extended in the following form. We write $\mathsf{max}^i(M)$ for the maximum j of $\omega \cdot i + j$ appearing in M.

Theorem 2 (Soundness).
Let $C = \sum_{i=0}^{\infty} \mathsf{max}^i(M) + 1$ and $D(j) = \sum_{i=0}^{j-1} \mathsf{max}^i(M)$.

1. If $\emptyset \vdash M : \tau\,!\,(\omega \cdot i + j)$ and $\vdash_T M \downarrow^k V$ then $\vdash_T [\![M]\!] \downarrow^{\leq Ck + D(i) + j} [\![V]\!]$.
2. If $\emptyset \vdash M : \tau\,!\,\rho$ and $\vdash_N M \downarrow^k V$ then $\vdash_N [\![M]\!] \downarrow^{\leq Ck} [\![V]\!]$.

5 Effect Inference

We show how to infer effects in this section. Th effect inference can be formalized as a type system with constraints, where a constraint generated by the type system is solved with a simple graph-based algorithm. We assume that types are already inferred with the standard type inference and consider the following explicitly-typed language for effect inference.

$$\tau ::= \mathsf{nat} \mid \tau \to^\alpha \tau$$
$$V ::= 0 \mid \mathsf{suc}(V) \mid x \mid \texttt{fix}\, x : \tau.\lambda y.M$$
$$M ::= V \mid @^\alpha M M \mid \mathsf{case}\, V\, \mathsf{of}\, 0 \Rightarrow M,\, \mathsf{suc}(x) \Rightarrow M$$

where α denotes an effect variable. The effect annotation of a lambda abstraction can be determined from the type annotation of the `fix`-expression. We assume effect variables appearing in a program are distinct.

Judgments of the effect system have the following forms: $E; C \vdash V : \tau$ and $E; C \vdash M : \tau\,!\,\alpha$ where C is a set of subeffect relations: $\alpha < \alpha'$ and $\alpha \leq \alpha'$. A constraint $\alpha < \alpha'$ holds if $\alpha \leq \alpha'$ and $\alpha \neq \alpha'$, or $\alpha = \alpha' = \omega \cdot i$ for some i. The main rules of the effect system are given as follows:

$$\frac{E; C \vdash V : \tau \quad \alpha\ \text{is fresh}}{E; C \vdash V : \tau\,!\,\alpha} \qquad \frac{E, x : \tau_1 \to^\alpha \tau_2, y : \tau_1; C \vdash M : \tau_2\,!\,\alpha'}{E; C \cup \{\alpha' < \alpha\} \vdash \texttt{fix}\, x : \tau_1 \to^\alpha \tau_2.\lambda y.M : \tau_1 \to^\alpha \tau_2}$$

$$\frac{E; C_1 \vdash M_1 : \tau_1 \to^{\alpha'} \tau_2 \,!\, \alpha_1 \quad E; C_2 \vdash M_2 : \tau_1' \,!\, \alpha_2}{E; C_1 \cup C_2 \cup \{\alpha' \leq \alpha\} \cup C_\leq(\tau_1', \tau_1) \vdash @^\alpha M_1 M_2 : \tau_2 \,!\, \alpha}$$

where $C_\leq(\tau_1', \tau_1)$ is the constraint to obtain the subtyping $\tau_1' \leq \tau_1$.

$$C_\leq(\mathsf{nat}, \mathsf{nat}) = \emptyset$$
$$C_\leq(\tau_1 \to^\alpha \tau_2, \tau_1' \to^{\alpha'} \tau_2') = C_\leq(\tau_1', \tau_1) \cup C_\leq(\tau_2, \tau_2') \cup \{\alpha \leq \alpha'\}$$

The constraint obtained by the rules above can be solved in the following manner. We consider the graph of the relations $\alpha < \alpha'$ and $\alpha \leq \alpha'$, and compute the strongly connected components of the graph. If a strongly connected component contains a relation of the form $\alpha < \alpha'$, the effect of the form $\omega \cdot i$ must be assigned to the effect variables appearing in the component. It is clear that an effect $\omega \cdot i + j$ ($j > 0$) can be assigned to an effect variable not belonging to such components.

6 Examples

There are several situations where an effect of the form $\omega \cdot i$ is assigned to a function. Although some of them are actually unsafe without tail call elimination, our effect system sometimes assigns $\omega \cdot i$ to functions safe without tail call elimination. In this section we show some examples of both the situations.

In our effect system, $\omega \cdot i$ must be assigned to tail recursive functions in general. However, tail recursive calls in a single recursive function can be implemented as a loop and thus trampolining can be avoided for such tail calls. Our effect system can be extended to be consistent with this implementation and then such functions are not assigned $\omega \cdot i$ to. Then there are two common examples where recursive functions are unsafe without tail call elimination: mutually tail recursive functions and higher order recursive functions.

In the following example, the functions f and g contains mutually recursive tail calls and thus must be assigned ω to.

```
fun f 0 = 0
  | f n = g (n-1)
and g n = f (n-1)
```

However, it is possible to implement the tail calls as a loop if only one of f and g are used from the other part of a program or the functions are copied into two definitions.

The following is an example with a higher order function.

```
fun h 0 y = y
  | h x y = h (x-1) (x+y)
```

The function h has type int $\to$ int $\to$ int. The tail recursive call of h (x-1) (x+y) cannot be implemented as a loop. However, if the function is uncurried, the tail call in the function can be implemented as a loop and thus the function can be safely implemented without tail call elimination.

As the third example, we show a program that is safe without tail call elimination, but is assigned ω to with our effect system.

```
let fun f (g:int -> int) = g 0
in
    f (fn x => f (fn y => y))
end
```

You can check this program is safe without tail call elimination. Let us infer the type of f. By assuming that f has type $(\text{int} \to^{\alpha_1} \text{int}) \to^{\alpha_2} \text{int}$, the constraints $\alpha_1 < \alpha_2$ and $\alpha_2 < \alpha_1$ must be satisfied where the first constraint is obtained from the definition of f and the second constraint is obtained from the body of the let-expression. Then the effects α_1 and α_2 must be $\omega \cdot i$ for some i. This weakness of our effect system appears in the benchmark "logic" we will discuss in the next section: many functions similar to the function above appear in the program.

7 Implementation and Measurements

We have incorporated our selective tail call elimination into the MLj compiler [2], which translates Standard ML into Java bytecodes. In MLj, tail calls are compiled into Java method invocations except recursive calls which are implemented as loops. MLj uses an intermediate language based on monads to represent effects such as IO operations, exception, and non-termination. We extended the effects of the intermediate language with our effect. The effects for selective tail call elimination are inferred in a late stage of compilation and the transformation is merged into the code generation phase of the compiler.

The translation of a function presented in Section 3.2 and 4 has one problem: the body of $\lambda^i x.M$ is copied into two functions and thus the translation may increase the code size. This problem can be solved by the following translation.

$$\lambda^i y.M = \texttt{let } y = \lambda x.[\![M]\!] \texttt{ in } \{\text{fun} = y, \text{tfun} = \lambda^t x.@yx\}$$

However, we do not adopt this translation because it makes it difficult to compare stack space usage. The worst case increase of code size observed for the benchmark programs we will discuss later is about 35 %.[3]

We measured the effectiveness of our selective tail call elimination for the most benchmark programs obtained from the following URL.[4]
ftp://ftp.research.bell-labs.com/dist/smlnj/benchmarks/

---

[3] The pair representation is not used for the known function that are safe without tail call elimination.

[4] We excluded two programs count-graphs and mlyacc that are difficult to compile with MLj because of the limitation of MLj.

Table 1. Maximum stack size: (in number of frames)

	total	(A)	(B)	(C)	(D)		total	(A)	(B)	(C)	(D)
barnes-hut	25	0	0	0	2	mandelbrot	6	0	0	0	1
boyer	24	0	0	0	2	nucleic	38	0	0	0	3
fft	28	0	0	0	3	ratio-regions	51	0	0	0	2
knuth-bendix	83	5	5	5	3	ray	82	2	2	0	3
lexgen	110	13	11	2	3	simple	175	0	0	0	4
life	30	1	1	0	2	tsp	20	0	0	0	2
logic	58	51	36	36	2	vliw	463	19	18	16	4

Table 2. Results of effect inference

	MLj	TCE	STCE
knuth-bendix	3895	3373	3485
lexgen	1259	94	94
life	298	49	49
logic	3814	236	260

Table 2 summarizes the results of our effect analysis. The column total shows the number of the functions generated for each benchmark program. The columns (A), (B) and (C) are the numbers of functions the analysis assigns an effect of the form $\omega \cdot i$: (A), (B) and (C) are the numbers for selective tail call elimination without extension, with extension and with extension and an extra phase of optimization, respectively. The column (D) shows $\sum_{i=0}^{\infty} \mathsf{max}(P)$ for each program P, which determines the theoretical upper bound of increase of stack space usage.

- Eight programs out of 13 are shown safe without tail call elimination. Even for the other programs except for the program logic, the ratio of the function of effect $\omega \cdot i$ is small.
- The most functions of the program logic have effect $\omega \cdot i$ by the reason we described in Section 6. The extension reduces the number, but more than half of the functions still have $\omega \cdot i$.
- Since the maximum of the numbers in column (D) is 4, the theoretical upper bound of stack space increase for selective tail call elimination compared to tail call elimination is 5.
- The effectiveness of our selective tail call elimination depends on other phases of compilation. An extra phase of optimization including uncurrying decreased the number of functions of effect $\omega \cdot i$ for three programs.

Table 1 shows the maximum stack size during execution measured by the number of frames. The table shows the results for the benchmark programs where

Table 3. Execution time (in seconds)

	Interpreted-mode			HotSpot Client VM		
	MLj	TCE	STCE	MLj	TCE	STCE
barnes-hut	5.77	6.30(109.2)	5.83(101.0)	1.22	1.21(99.2)	1.23(100.8)
boyer	1.41	1.65(117.0)	1.41(100.0)	0.81	0.58(71.6)	0.82(101.2)
fft	1.71	2.12(124.0)	1.71(100.0)	0.57	0.60(105.3)	0.64(112.3)
knuth-bendix	11.09	10.80(97.4)	8.19(73.9)	2.00	2.12(106.0)	1.61(80.5)
lexgen	3.50	3.40(97.1)	3.49(99.7)	0.61	0.75(123.0)	0.63(103.3)
life	1.24	1.24(100.0)	1.15(92.7)	0.36	0.37(102.8)	0.35(97.2)
logic	17.40	18.90(108.6)	16.49(94.8)	4.51	2.79(61.9)	2.70(59.9)
mandelbrot	4.18	6.45(154.3)	4.22(101.0)	0.52	1.49(286.5)	0.55(105.8)
nucleic	0.68	0.73(107.4)	0.67(98.5)	0.34	0.44(129.4)	0.34(100.0)
ratio-regions	212.93	216.38(101.6)	209.11(98.2)	33.62	42.34(125.9)	33.67(100.1)
ray	5.77	6.20(107.5)	5.68(98.4)	1.88	1.13(60.1)	2.12(112.8)
simple	6.61	7.35(111.2)	6.38(96.5)	1.49	1.63(109.4)	1.54(103.4)
tsp	4.78	5.13(107.3)	4.75(99.4)	0.88	0.96(109.1)	0.84(95.5)
vliw	6.26	7.32(116.9)	6.42(102.6)	1.34	2.37(176.9)	1.46(109.0)

tail call elimination has some impact on the results. For all the other program, the numbers are between 33 and 103. The results supports that tail call elimination is desirable: stack sizes are greatly reduced for several programs. Selective tail call elimination may increase stack size compared to tail call elimination. However, the increase is relatively small, compared to the theoretical upper bound.

Table 3 shows execution times. The columns TCE and STCE are the results for tail call elimination and selective tail call elimination, respectively. The numbers in the parenthesis are the ratios to those of MLj. Even for TCE, all the non-tail-calls are implemented with the standard calling convention based on the pair representation of functions. Measurements were done using Sun JDK 1.4.0, Java HotSpot Client VM on a Linux PC. We measured execution time on the interpreted-mode with the -Xint option, and on the mode where HotSpot compilation is enabled because it is sometimes difficult to interpret results on the HotSpot VM. Each benchmark was run five times and we chose the fastest run.

- TCE sometimes degrades the performance a lot. The worst case overhead is 54.3 % and 186.5 % for the interpreted-mode and the HotSpot VM, respectively. Compared to TCE, STCE causes little overhead: the worst case overhead is 2.6 % and 12.8 %, respectively.
- For benchmark programs where stack size is reduced by tail call elimination, execution times are sometimes reduced for both TCE and STCE: knuth-bendix and logic. This can be explained as a reduction of garbage collection

(GC) time. For example, the GC times for logic are 2.43, 0.49 and 0.49 for MLj, TCE, and STCE, respectively. The same phenomenon was observed by Schinz and Odersky in their tail call elimination for JVM [16].
- There are unexpected results on boyer and ray: the big improvement of execution time over MLj and STCE is observed for TCE. We checked the profiling data of executions and found that better decisions on compilation are made by the HotSpot VM for TCE and the programs compiled by MLj and STCE spent more time on interpreted methods.

8 Related Work

Dornic, Jouvelot, and Gifford proposed an effect system to estimate execution time of a program [6], and their work was extended by Reistad and Gifford [15] with sized types [9]. By adapting the effect system extended with sized types we may obtain more information about the stack usage of a program. However, our simple effect system gives enough information for selective tail call elimination.

Implementation of proper tail calls and space safety are discussed by Clinger [5]. He considered that an implementation is safe with respect to space if it does not increase the asymptotic space complexity of programs. Our selective tail call elimination satisfies the criterion on stack space, but the factor of increase of stack space depends on the program and is determined by the effect system.

Schinz and Odersky proposed tail call elimination for the Java virtual machine [16] that preserves complexity on stack space. Their method is dynamic: it keeps track of the number of successive tail calls and execution is returned to a trampoline if some predefined limit is exceeded. We think that it is possible to reduce the overhead of their method with selective elimination of tail calls.

We have translated a function in the source language into a record with two functions supporting different calling conventions. Similar translation was used to support multiple calling conventions in type-directed unboxing by Minamide and Garrigue [14], and the vectorized functions of Chakravarty and Keller [4].

9 Conclusion and Future Work

We have presented an effect system and a program transformation to eliminate tail calls selectively. The transformation translates a function into a record with two functions supporting different calling conventions. The transformation preserves stack space asymptotically.

Our effect system will be useful even for target environments that directly supports tail calls. Various program transformations sometimes translate tail calls into non-tail calls. With our effect system, it is possible to check if such translation is safe for each tail call.

We incorporated our effect system into the MLj compiler and measured the proportion of functions that are unsafe without tail call elimination. The results indicated that selective tail call elimination is very effective for most programs and most functions can be implemented with the standard calling convention.

However, there is a limitation that our effect system is monovariant. This limitation may be solved if we extend our effect system with effect polymorphism or intersection types.

By selective tail call elimination, the asymptotic complexity of stack space is preserved. The factor of the increase is determined by effect analysis and depends on a program. However, it is also possible to guarantee the factor of stack space increase by translating applications with annotations greater than the predefined factor as applications with annotation ω.

Acknowledgments

This work is partially supported by Grant-in-Aid for Encouragement of Young Scientists, No. 13780193.

References

1. H. Baker. Cons should not cons its arguments, part II: Cheney on the M.T.A. *SIGPLAN Notices*, 30(9):17–20, 1995.
2. N. Benton, A. Kennedy, and G. Russell. Compiling Standard ML to Java bytecodes. In *Proceedings of the Third ACM SIGPLAN International Conference on Functional Programming (ICFP '98)*, pages 129–140, 1998.
3. P. Bothner. Kawa - Compiling dynamic languages to the Java VM. In *Proceedings of the USENIX 1998 Technical Conference*, 1998.
4. M. M. T. Chakravarty and G. Keller. More types for nested data parallel programming. In *Proceedings of the Fifth ACM SIGPLAN International Conference on Functional Programming*, pages 94–105, 1999.
5. W. D. Clinger. Proper tail recursion and space efficiency. In *Proceedings of the ACM SIGPLAN'98 Conference on Programming Language Design and Implementation*, pages 174–185. ACM Press, 1998.
6. V. Dornic, P. Jouvelot, and D. K. Gifford. Polymorphic time systems for estimating program complexity. *ACM Letters on Programming Languages and Systems (LOPLAS)*, 1(1):33–45, 1992.
7. S. D. Ganz, D. P. Friedman, and M. Wand. Trampolined style. In *Proceedings of the 4th ACM SIGPLAN International Conference on Functional Programming (ICFP '99)*, pages 18–22, 1999.
8. D. K. Gifford and J. M. Lucassen. Integrating functional and imperative programming. In *Proceedings of the ACM Conference on Lisp and Functional Programming*, pages 28–38, 1986.
9. J. Hughes, L. Pareto, and A. Sabry. Proving the correctness of reactive systems. In *Proceedings of the 23rd ACM SIGPLAN-SIGACT Symposium on Principles of Programming Languages*, pages 410–423, 1996.
10. T. Lindholm and F. Yellin. *The Java Virtual Machine Specification*. Addison Wesley, 1999.
11. J. M. Lucassen and D. K. Gifford. Polymorphic effect systems. In *Proceedings of the Fifteenth ACM SIGACT-SIGPLAN Symposium on Principles of Programming Languages*, pages 47–57, 1988.
12. Y. Minamide. A new criterion for safe program transformations. In *Proceedings of the Forth International Workshop on Higher Order Operational Techniques in Semantics (HOOTS)*, volume 41(3) of *ENTCS*, Montreal, 2000.

13. Y. Minamide. Selective tail call elimination. Technical Report ISE-TR-03-192, Institute of Information Sciences and Electronics, University of Tsukuba, 2003.
14. Y. Minamide and J. Garrigue. On the runtime complexity of type-directed unboxing. In *Proceedings of the Third ACM SIGPLAN International conference on Functional Programming*, pages 1–12, 1998.
15. B. Reistad and D. K. Gifford. Static dependent costs for estimating execution time. In *Proceedings of the 1994 ACM Conference on LISP and Functional Programming*, pages 65–78, 1994.
16. M. Schinz and M. Odersky. Tail call elimination on the Java virtual machine. In *Proceedings of the First International Workshop on Multi-Language Infrastructure and Interoperability (BABEL)*, volume 59(1) of *ENTCS*, 2001.
17. B. Serpette and M. Serrano. Compiling Scheme to JVM bytecode: a performance study. In *Proceedings of the Seventh ACM SIGPLAN International Conference on Functional Programming*, pages 259–270, 2002.
18. D. Tarditi, A. Acharya, and P. Lee. No assembly required: Compiling standard ML to C. *ACM Letters on Programming Languages and Systems (LOPLAS)*, 1(2):161–177, 1992.

A Type System of the Target Language

The type system of the target language is defined as a deductive system with judgments of the form $E \vdash N : \sigma$. We do not show the rules for 0, suc(W), and case-expressions that are the same as those for the source language.

$$\frac{x : \sigma \in E}{E \vdash x : \sigma} \qquad \frac{E \vdash N : \sigma' \quad \sigma' \leq \sigma}{E \vdash N : \sigma}$$

$$\frac{E, x : \sigma_1 \vdash N : \sigma_2}{E \vdash \lambda x.N : \sigma_1 \to \sigma_2} \qquad \frac{E, x : \sigma_1 \vdash N : \sigma_2}{E \vdash \lambda^t x.N : \sigma_1 \to^t \sigma_2}$$

$$\frac{E \vdash N_1 : \sigma_1 \to \sigma_2 \quad E \vdash N_2 : \sigma_1}{E \vdash @N_1 N_2 : \sigma_2} \qquad \frac{E \vdash N_1 : \sigma_1 \to^t \sigma_2 \quad E \vdash N_2 : \sigma_1}{E \vdash @^t N_1 N_2 : \sigma_2}$$

$$\frac{E, x : \{\mathsf{fun} : \sigma_1, \mathsf{tfun} : \sigma_2\} \vdash W_1 : \sigma_1 \quad E, x : \{\mathsf{fun} : \sigma_1, \mathsf{tfun} : \sigma_2\} \vdash W_2 : \sigma_2}{E \vdash \mathsf{fix}\, x.\{\mathsf{fun} = W_1, \mathsf{tfun} = W_2\} : \{\mathsf{fun} : \sigma_1, \mathsf{tfun} : \sigma_2\}}$$

$$\frac{E, x : \{\mathsf{tfun} : \sigma\} \vdash W : \sigma}{E \vdash \mathsf{fix}\, x.\{\mathsf{tfun} = W\} : \{\mathsf{tfun} : \sigma\}}$$

$$\frac{E \vdash N : \{\mathsf{fun} : \sigma_1, \mathsf{tfun} : \sigma_2\}}{E \vdash N.\mathsf{fun} : \sigma_1} \qquad \frac{E \vdash N : \{\mathsf{tfun} : \sigma\}}{E \vdash N.\mathsf{tfun} : \sigma}$$

B Operational Semantics of the Target Language

The following are the rules of the operational semantics of the target language. We write $\vdash_\alpha N \Downarrow^n W$ if the rule holds for both $\vdash_N N \Downarrow^n W$ and $\vdash_T N \Downarrow^n W$.

$$\frac{\vdash_N N_1 \Downarrow^l \lambda x.N \quad \vdash_N N_2 \Downarrow^m W_2 \quad \vdash_\alpha N[W_2/x] \Downarrow^n W}{\vdash_\alpha @N_1 N_2 \Downarrow^{\max(l,m,n+1)} W}$$

$$\dfrac{\vdash_\alpha W \downarrow^0 W \quad \vdash_N N \downarrow^n \mathsf{fix}\, x.\{\mathsf{tfun} = W\}}{\vdash_\alpha N.\mathsf{tfun} \downarrow^n W[\mathsf{fix}\, x.\{\mathsf{tfun} = W\}/x]}$$

$$\dfrac{\vdash_N N \downarrow^n \mathsf{fix}\, x.\{\mathsf{fun} = W_1, \mathsf{tfun} = W_2\}}{\vdash_\alpha N.\mathsf{tfun} \downarrow^n W_2[\mathsf{fix}\, x.\{\mathsf{fun} = W_1, \mathsf{tfun} = W_2\}/x]}$$

$$\dfrac{\vdash_N N \downarrow^n \mathsf{fix}\, x.\{\mathsf{fun} = W_1, \mathsf{tfun} = W_2\}}{\vdash_\alpha N.\mathsf{fun} \downarrow^n W_1[\mathsf{fix}\, x.\{\mathsf{fun} = W_1, \mathsf{tfun} = W_2\}/x]}$$

C Proof of Soundness

The following lemma is crucial to establish soundness of transformation.

Lemma 3. $[\![M[V/x]]\!] \equiv [\![M]\!][[\![V]\!]/x]$.

We prove the main theorem in the following form to simplify case-analysis.

Lemma 4. *Let* $C = \max(M) + 1$.

1. *If* $\emptyset \vdash M : \tau!\rho$ *and* $\vdash_T M \downarrow^k V$ *then* $\vdash_T [\![M]\!] \downarrow^{\leq Ck + D(\rho)} [\![V]\!]$.
2. *If* $\emptyset \vdash M : \tau!\rho$ *and* $\vdash_N M \downarrow^k V$ *then* $\vdash_N [\![M]\!] \downarrow^{\leq Ck} [\![V]\!]$.

where $D(\rho)$ *is a function such that* $D(i) = i$ *and* $D(\omega) = \max(M)$.

Proof. By mutual induction on the derivations of $\vdash_T M \downarrow^k V$ and $\vdash_N M \downarrow^k V$. Due to lack of space, we show only one case of application for the property 1. The details of the proof can be found in the technical report [13].

Case: $\vdash_T @^i M_1 M_2 \downarrow^k V$ is derived from $\vdash_N M_1 \downarrow^l V_1$ and $\vdash_N M_2 \downarrow^m V_2$ and $\vdash_T M[V_1/x][V_2/y] \downarrow^n V$ where $V_1 \equiv \mathtt{fix}\, x.\lambda^{j^+} y.M$ and $k = \max(l, m, n)$. From the definition of the type system, $j < i$. From $\emptyset \vdash @^i M_1 M_2 : \tau!\rho$, $i \leq \rho$. We also have $x : \tau' \to^{j^+} \tau, y : \tau' \vdash M : \tau!j$.
By the induction hypothesis, $\vdash_N [\![M_1]\!] \downarrow^{\leq Cl} [\![V_1]\!]$ and $\vdash_N [\![M_2]\!] \downarrow^{\leq Cm} [\![V_2]\!]$.
From $\emptyset \vdash M[V_1/x][V_2/y] : \tau!j$, by the induction hypothesis,

$$\vdash_T [\![M]\!][[\![V_1]\!]/x][[\![V_2]\!]/y] \downarrow^{\leq Cn+j} [\![V]\!]$$

This case is proved by the following derivation.

$$\dfrac{\vdash_N [\![M_1]\!].\mathsf{fun} \downarrow^{\leq Cl} \lambda y.[\![M]\!][[\![V_1]\!]/x] \quad \vdash_N [\![M_2]\!] \downarrow^{\leq Cm} [\![V_2]\!] \quad \vdash_T [\![M]\!][[\![V_1]\!]/x][[\![V_2]\!]/y] \downarrow^{\leq Cn+j} [\![V]\!]}{\vdash_T @([\![M_1]\!].\mathsf{fun})[\![M_2]\!] \downarrow^{\leq \max(Cl,Cm,Cn+j+1)} [\![V]\!]}$$

where $\max(Cl, Cm, Cn + j + 1) \leq Ck + D(\rho)$.

Inserting Safe Memory Reuse Commands into ML-Like Programs*

Oukseh Lee, Hongseok Yang, and Kwangkeun Yi

Dept. of Computer Science/ Research On Program Analysis System
http://ropas.kaist.ac.kr
Korea Advanced Institute of Science and Technology
{cookcu,hyang,kwang}@ropas.kaist.ac.kr

Abstract. We present a static analysis that estimates reusable memory cells and a source-level transformation that adds explicit memory-reuse commands into the program text. For benchmark ML programs, our analysis and transformation achieves the memory reuse ratio from 5.2% to 91.3%. The small-ratio cases are for programs that have too prevalent sharings among memory cells. For other cases, our experimental results are encouraging in terms of accuracy and cost. Major features of our analysis are: (1) poly-variant analysis of functions by parameterization for the argument heap cells; (2) use of multiset formulas in expressing the sharings and partitionings of heap cells; (3) deallocations conditioned by dynamic flags that are passed as extra arguments to functions; (4) individual heap cell as the granularity of explicit memory-free. Our analysis and transformation is fully automatic.

1 Overview

Our goal is to automatically insert explicit memory-reuse commands into ML-like programs so that they should not blindly request memory when constructing data.

We present a static analysis and a source-level transformation that adds explicit memory-reuse commands into the program text. The explicit memory-reuse is by inserting explicit memory-free commands right before data-construction expressions. Because the unit of both memory-free and allocation is an individual cell, such memory-free and allocation sequences can be implemented as memory reuses.[1]

Example 1. Function call "insert i l" returns a new list where integer i is inserted into its position in the sorted list l.

```
fun insert i l = case l of []    => i::[]           (1)
                        | h::t => if i<h then i::l  (2)
                                  else h::(insert i t) (3)
```

---

* This work is supported by Creative Research Initiatives of the Korean Ministry of Science and Technology.
[1] This approach's drawback might be that the memory reuse "bandwidth" is limited by the data-construction expressions in the program text. But our experimental results show that such a drawback is imaginary.

Let's assume that the argument list l is not used after a call to insert. If we program in C, we can destructively add one node for i into l so that the insert procedure should consume only one cons-cell. Meanwhile, the ML program's line (3) will allocate as many new cons-cells as that of the recursive calls. Knowing that list l is not used anymore, we can reuse the cons-cells from l:

```
fun insert i l = case l of []    => i::[]
                         | h::t => if i<h then i::l
                                   else let z = insert i t
                                        in  (free l; h::z)         (4)
```

In line (4), "free l" will deallocate the single cons-cell pointed to by l. The very next expression's data construction "::" will reuse the freed cons-cell. □

1.1 Related Works

The type systems [25, 24, 2] based on linear logic fail to achieve Example 1 case because variable l is used twice. Kobayashi [10], and Aspinall and Hofmann [1] overcome this shortcoming by using more fine-grained usage aspects, but their systems still reject Example 1 because variable l and t are aliased at line (2)–(3). They cannot properly handle aliasing: for "let x=y in e" where y points to a list, this list cannot in general be reused at e in their systems. Moreover, Aspinall and Hofmann did not consider an automatic transformation for reuse. Kobayashi provides an automatic transformation, but he requires the memory system to bookkeep a reference counter for every heap cell.

Deductive systems like the separation logic [9, 16, 17] and the alias-type system [18, 26] are powerful enough to reason about shared mutable data structures, but they cannot be used for our goal; they are not automatic. They need the programmer's help about memory invariants for loops or recursive functions.

The region-based memory managements [22, 23, 4, 5, 7] use a fixed partitioning strategy for recursive data structures, which is either implied by the programmer's region declarations or hard-wired inside the region-inference engine [20, 21]. Since every heap cell in a single region has the same lifetime, this "predetermined" partitioning can be too coarse; for example, transformations like the one in Example 1 are impossible.

Blanchet's escape analysis [3] and ours are both relational, covering the same class of relations (inclusion and sharing) among memory objects. The difference is the relation's targets and deallocation's granularity. His relation is between memory objects linked from program variables and their binding expression's results. Ours is between memory objects linked from any two program variables. His deallocation is at the end of a let or function body. Transformations like the one in Example 1 are impossible in his system. Harrison's [8] and Mohnen's [14] escape analyses have similar limitation: the deallocations is at the end of function body.

1.2 Our Solution

The features of our analysis and transformation are:

- In analyzing functions, parameterized abstract sharing-information between heap cells is maintained. The parameter in a function's analysis result is for the function's argument heap cells. A function's analysis result consists of terms called "*multiset formula*." A multiset formula symbolically manifests an abstract sharing relation between heap cells.
- The parameterized multiset formula is instantiated at each function call, in order to finalize the sharing and/or disjointness properties for the function's input and output. This polyvariant analysis is not done by re-analyzing a function body multiple times.
- Partitioning of heap cells in a multiset formula is pivoted by two axes: one by structures (e.g. heads and tails for lists, roots and subtrees for trees, etc.) and the other by set exclusions (e.g. cells A excluding B). This double-axed partitioning is expressive enough to isolate proper reusable cells from others.
- Individual heap cell for each data constructor is the granularity of inserted memory-free commands.
- Dynamic flags are inserted to functions in order to condition their free commands on their call sites. Dynamic flags are simple boolean expressions composed of $\wedge, \vee,$ and $\neg$.

Our contribution is a cost-effective automatic analysis and transformation for fine-grained memory reuses for recursive/algebraic data structures in ML-like programs. Our experimental results show that for small to large ML benchmark programs the memory reuse ratio ranges from 5.2% to 91.3%. The small-ratio cases expose that our analysis and transformation is weak for programs that have too prevalent sharings among memory cells. Other than those "torturing" cases, our experimental results are encouraging in terms of accuracy and cost. The analysis cost ranges from about 400 to 4500 lines per second. The limitation is that we only consider ML-like immutable recursive data.

Section 1.3 intuitively presents the features of our method for an example program. Section 2 defines the core of the target language, which consists of the source language plus explicit memory reuse commands. Section 3 presents the key abstract domain (memory-types) for our analysis. Section 4 shows, for the same example as in Section 1.3, a more detailed explanation on how our analysis and transformation works. Section 5 shows our experimental results and concludes.

1.3 Exclusion Among Heap Cells and Dynamic Flags

The accuracy of our algorithm depends on how precisely we can separate the two sets of heap cells: cells that are safe to deallocate and others that are not. If the separation is blurred, we hardly find deallocation opportunities.

For a precise separation of such two groups of heap cells, we have found that the standard partitioning by structures (e.g. heads and tails for lists, roots and subtrees for trees, etc.) is not enough. We need to refine the partitions by the notion of exclusion. Consider a function that builds a tree from an input tree. Let's assume that the input tree is not used after the call. In building the result tree, we want to reuse the nodes of the input tree. Can we free every node of the input? No, if the output tree shares some of its parts with the input tree. In that case, we can free only those nodes of the input that are *not* parts of the output. A concrete example is the following `copyleft` function. Both of its input and output are trees. The output tree's nodes along its left-most path are separate copies from the input tree and the rest are shared with the input tree.

```
fun copyleft t = case t of Leaf        => Leaf
                         | Node (t1,t2) => Node (copyleft t1, t2)
```

The Leaf and Node are the binary tree constructors. Node needs a heap cell that contains two fields to store the locations for the left and right subtrees. The opportunity of memory reuse is in the case-expression's second branch. When we construct the node after the recursive call, we can reuse the pattern-matched node of the input tree, but only when the node is *not* included in the output tree. Our analysis maintains such notion of exclusion.

Our transformation inserts `free` commands that are conditioned on dynamic flags passed as extra arguments to functions. These dynamic flags make different call sites to the same function have different deallocation behavior. By our free-commands insertion, above `copyleft` function is transformed to:

```
fun copyleft [β, βns] t =
    case t of Leaf        => Leaf
            | Node (t1,t2) => let p = copyleft [β ∧ βns, βns] t1
                              in  (free t when β; Node (p,t2))
```

Flag β is true when the argument t to `copyleft` can be freed inside the function. Hence the free command is conditioned on it: "free t when β." By the recursive calls, all the nodes along the left-most path of the input will be freed. The analysis with the notion of exclusion informs us that, in order for the free to be safe, the nodes must be excluded from the output. They are excluded if they are not reachable from the output. They are not reachable from the output if the input tree has no sharing between its nodes, because some parts (e.g. t2) of the input are included in the output. Hence the recursive call's actual flag for β is $\beta \wedge \beta_{ns}$, where flag β_{ns} is true when there is no sharing inside the input tree.

1.4 Correctness Proof

The correctness of our analysis and transformation has been proved via a type system for safe memory deallocations [11]. We first proved our memory-type system sound: every well-typed program in the system does not access any deallocated heap cells. Then we proved that programs resulting from our analysis and transformation are always well-typed in the memory-type system. Since our transformation only inserts `free` commands, a transformed program's computational behavior modulo the memory-free operations remains intact.

Because of space limitation, we focus on our analysis and transformation in this paper. The details of our correctness proof are in [11].

2 Language

Figure 1 shows the syntax and semantics of the source language: a typed call-by-value language with first-order recursive functions, data constructions (memory

SYNTAX

$$\begin{aligned}
\textit{Type } \tau &::= \text{tree} \mid \text{tree} \to \text{tree} \\
\textit{Boolean Expression } b &::= \beta \mid \text{true} \mid \text{false} \mid b \vee b \mid b \wedge b \mid \neg b \\
\textit{Storable Value } a &::= \text{Leaf} \mid l \\
\textit{Value } v &::= a \mid x \mid \text{fix } x \, [\beta_1, \beta_2] \, \lambda x.e \\
\textit{Expression } e &::= v & \text{value} \\
&\mid \text{Node}\,(v, v) & \text{allocation} \\
&\mid \text{free } v \text{ when } b & \text{deallocation} \\
&\mid \text{case } v \, (\text{Node}\,(x, y) \Rightarrow e_1) \, (\text{Leaf} \Rightarrow e_2) & \text{match} \\
&\mid v \, [b_1, b_2] \, v & \text{application} \\
&\mid \text{let } x = e \text{ in } e & \text{binding}
\end{aligned}$$

OPERATIONAL SEMANTICS

$$h \in \text{Heaps} \stackrel{\Delta}{=} \text{Locations} \stackrel{\text{fin}}{\to} \{(a_1, a_2) \mid a_i \text{ is a storable value}\}$$
$$f \in \text{FreedLocations} \stackrel{\Delta}{=} \wp(\text{Locations})$$
$$k \in \text{Continuations} \stackrel{\Delta}{=} \{(x_1, e_1) \ldots (x_n, e_n) \mid x_i \text{ is a variable and } e_i \text{ an expression}\}$$

$(\text{Node}\,(a_1, a_2), h, f, k) \leadsto (l, h \cup \{l \mapsto (a_1, a_2)\}, f, k)$
    where l does not occur in $(\text{Node}\,(a_1, a_2), h, f, k)$
$(\text{free } l \text{ when } b, h, f, k) \leadsto (\text{Leaf}, h, f \cup \{l\}, k)$ if $b \Leftrightarrow \text{true}$, $l \notin f$, and $l \in \text{dom}(h)$
$(\text{free } l \text{ when } b, h, f, k) \leadsto (\text{Leaf}, h, f, k)$ if $b \not\Leftrightarrow \text{true}$
$(\text{case } l \, (\text{Node}(x_1, x_2) \Rightarrow e_1) \, (\text{Leaf} \Rightarrow e_2), h, f, k) \leadsto (e_1[a_1/x_1, a_2/x_2], h, f, k)$
    where $h(l) = (a_1, a_2)$ and $l \notin f$
$(\text{case Leaf } (\text{Node}(x_1, x_2) \Rightarrow e_1) \, (\text{Leaf} \Rightarrow e_2), h, f, k) \leadsto (e_2, h, f, k)$
$((\text{fix } y \, [\beta_1, \beta_2] \, \lambda x.e) \, [b_1, b_2] \, v, h, f, k) \leadsto$
    $(e[(\text{fix } y \, [\beta_1, \beta_2] \, \lambda x.e)/y, b_1/\beta_1, b_2/\beta_2, v/x], h, f, k)$
$(\text{let } x = e_1 \text{ in } e_2, h, f, k) \leadsto (e_1, h, f, (x, e_2) \cdot k)$
$(v, h, f, (x, e) \cdot k) \leadsto (e[v/x], h, f, k)$

Fig. 1. The syntax and the semantics

allocations), de-constructions (case matches), and memory deallocations. All expressions are in the K-normal form [20,10]: every non-value expression is bound to a variable by let. Each expression's value is either a tree or a function. A tree is implemented as linked cells in the heap memory. The heap consists of binary cells whose fields can store locations or a Leaf value. For instance, a tree Node(Leaf, Node(Leaf, Leaf)) is implemented in the heap by two binary cells l and l' such that l contains Leaf and l', and l' contains Leaf and Leaf.

The language has three constructs for the heap: Node(v_1, v_2) allocates a node cell in the heap, and sets its contents by v_1 and v_2; a case-expression reads the contents of a cell; and free v when b deallocates a cell v if b holds. A function has two kinds of parameters: one for boolean values and the other for an input tree. The boolean parameters are only used for the guards for free commands inside the function.

Throughout the paper, to simplify the presentation, we assume that all functions are closed, and we consider only well-typed programs in the usual monomorphic type system, with types being tree or tree→tree. In our implementation, we handle higher-order functions, and arbitrary algebraic data types, not just binary trees. We explain more on this in Section 5.

The algorithm in this paper takes a program that does not have locations, free commands, or boolean expressions for the guards. Our analysis analyzes such programs, then automatically inserts the free commands and boolean parameters into the program.

3 Memory-Types: An Abstract Domain for Heap Objects

Our analysis and transformation uses what we call *memory-types* to estimate the heap objects for expressions' values. Memory-types are defined in terms of multiset formulas.

3.1 Multiset Formula

Multiset formulas are terms that allow us to abstractly reason about disjointness and sharing among heap locations. We call "multiset formulas" because formally speaking, their meanings (concretizations) are multisets of locations, where a shared location occurs multiple times.

The multiset formulas L express sharing configuration inside heap objects by the following grammar:

$$L ::= A \mid R \mid X \mid \pi.\text{root} \mid \pi.\text{left} \mid \pi.\text{right} \mid \emptyset \mid L \sqcup L \mid L \oplus L \mid L \setminus L$$

Symbols A's, R's, X's and π's are just names for multisets of locations. A's symbolically denote the heap cells in the input tree of a function, X's the newly allocated heap cells, R's the heap cells in the result tree of a function, and π's for heap objects whose roots and left/right subtrees are respectively $\pi.\text{root}$, $\pi.\text{left}$, and $\pi.\text{right}$. $\emptyset$ means the empty multiset, and symbol $\oplus$ constructs a term for a multiset-union. The "maximum" operator symbol $\sqcup$ constructs a term for the join of two multisets: term $L \sqcup L'$ means to include two occurrences of a location just if L or L' already means to include two occurrences of the same location. Term $L \setminus L'$ means multiset L excluding the locations included in L'.

Figure 2 shows the formal meaning of L in terms of abstract multisets: a function from locations to the lattice $\{0, 1, \infty\}$ ordered by $0 \sqsubseteq 1 \sqsubseteq \infty$. Note that we consider only good instantiations η of name X's, A's, and π's in Figure 2. The pre-order for L is:

$$L_1 \sqsubseteq L_2 \text{ iff } \forall \eta. \text{goodEnv}(\eta) \Longrightarrow [\![L_1]\!]\eta \sqsubseteq [\![L_2]\!]\eta.$$

3.2 Memory-Types

Memory-types are in terms of the multiset formulas. We define memory-types μ_τ for value-type τ using multiset formulas:

$$\begin{aligned} \mu_{\text{tree}} &::= \langle L, \mu_{\text{tree}}, \mu_{\text{tree}} \rangle \mid L \\ \mu_{\text{tree} \to \text{tree}} &::= \forall A. A \to \exists X. (L, L) \end{aligned}$$

SEMANTICS OF MULTISET FORMULAS

lattice Labels $\triangleq \{0, 1, \infty\}$, ordered by $0 \sqsubseteq 1 \sqsubseteq \infty$
lattice MultiSets $\triangleq$ Locations $\to$ Labels, ordered pointwise

For all η mapping X's, A's, R's, π.root's, π.left's, and π.right's to MultiSets,

$$[\![\emptyset]\!]\eta \triangleq \bot$$
$$[\![V]\!]\eta \triangleq \eta(V) \qquad (V \text{ is } X, A, R, \pi.\text{root}, \pi.\text{left}, \text{ or } \pi.\text{right})$$
$$[\![L_1 \sqcup L_2]\!]\eta \triangleq [\![L_1]\!]\eta \sqcup [\![L_2]\!]\eta$$
$$[\![L_1 \oplus L_2]\!]\eta \triangleq [\![L_1]\!]\eta \oplus [\![L_2]\!]\eta$$
$$[\![L_1 \setminus L_2]\!]\eta \triangleq [\![L_1]\!]\eta \setminus [\![L_2]\!]\eta$$

where

$\oplus$ and $\setminus$: MultiSets $\times$ MultiSets $\to$ MultiSets
$S_1 \oplus S_2 \triangleq \lambda l.$ if $S_1(l) = S_2(l) = 1$ then ∞ else $S_1(l) \sqcup S_2(l)$
$S_1 \setminus S_2 \triangleq \lambda l.$ if $S_2(l) = 0$ then $S_1(l)$ else 0

REQUIREMENTS ON GOOD ENVIRONMENTS

goodEnv$(\eta) \triangleq$ for all different names X and X' and all A,
  $\eta(X)$ is a *set* disjoint from both $\eta(X')$ and $\eta(A)$; and
  for all π,
  $\eta(\pi.\text{root})$ is a *set* disjoint from both $\eta(\pi.\text{left})$ and $\eta(\pi.\text{right})$

SEMANTICS OF MEMORY-TYPES FOR TREES

$[\![\langle L, \mu_1, \mu_2 \rangle]\!]_{\text{tree}}\, \eta \triangleq \{\langle l, h\rangle \mid h(l) = (a_1, a_2) \land [\![L]\!]\eta\, l \sqsupseteq 1 \land \langle a_i, h\rangle \in [\![\mu_i]\!]_{\text{tree}}\, \eta\}$

$[\![L]\!]_{\text{tree}}\, \eta \triangleq \left\{\langle l, h\rangle \,\middle|\, \begin{array}{l} l \in \text{dom}(h) \\ \land\, \forall l'.\text{ let } n = \text{number of different paths from } l \text{ to } l' \text{ in } h \\ \quad \text{in } (n \geq 1 \Rightarrow [\![L]\!]\eta\, l' \sqsupseteq 1) \land (n \geq 2 \Rightarrow [\![L]\!]\eta\, l' = \infty) \end{array}\right\}$
$\cup\, \{\langle \text{Leaf}, h\rangle \mid h \text{ is a heap}\}$

Fig. 2. The semantics of multiset formulas and memory-types for trees

A memory-type μ_{tree} for a **tree**-typed value abstracts a set of heap objects. A heap object is a pair $\langle a, h\rangle$ of a storable value a and a heap h that contains all the reachable cells from a. Intuitively, it represents a tree reachable from a in h when a is a location; otherwise, it represents Leaf. A memory-type is either in a *structured* or *collapsed* form. A structured memory-type is a triple $\langle L, \mu_1, \mu_2\rangle$, and its meaning (concretization) is a set of heap objects $\langle l, h\rangle$ such that L, μ_1, and μ_2 abstract the location l and the left and right subtrees of $\langle l, h\rangle$, respectively. A collapsed memory-type is more abstract than a structured one. It is simply a multiset formula L, and its meaning (concretization) is a set of heap objects $\langle a, h\rangle$ such that L abstracts every reachable location and its sharing in $\langle a, h\rangle$. The formal meaning of memory-types is in Figure 2. The pre-order $\sqsubseteq_{\text{tree}}$ for memory-types for trees is:

$$\mu_1 \sqsubseteq_{\text{tree}} \mu_2 \quad \text{iff} \quad \forall \eta.\text{goodEnv}(\eta) \implies [\![\mu_1]\!]_{\text{tree}}\, \eta \subseteq [\![\mu_2]\!]_{\text{tree}}\, \eta.$$

During our analysis, we switch between a structured memory-type and a collapsed memory-type. We can collapse a structured one by the collapse function:

$$\mathsf{collapse}(\langle L, \mu_1, \mu_2 \rangle) \triangleq L \sqcup (\mathsf{collapse}(\mu_1) \dot{\oplus} \mathsf{collapse}(\mu_2))$$
$$\mathsf{collapse}(\mu) \triangleq \mu \qquad \text{(for collapsed } \mu\text{)}$$

Note that when combining L and $\mathsf{collapse}(\mu_1) \dot{\oplus} \mathsf{collapse}(\mu_2)$, we use $\sqcup$ instead of $\dot{\oplus}$: it is because a root cell abstracted by L cannot be in the left or right subtree. We can also reconstruct a structured memory-type from a collapsed one when given splitting name π:

$$\mathsf{reconstruct}(L, \pi) \triangleq (\{\pi \mapsto L\}, \langle \pi.\mathsf{root}, \pi.\mathsf{left}, \pi.\mathsf{right} \rangle)$$
$$\mathsf{reconstruct}(\mu, \pi) \triangleq (\emptyset, \mu) \qquad \text{(for structured } \mu\text{)}$$

The second component of the result of reconstruct is a resulting structured memory-type and the first one is a record that L is a collection of $\pi.\mathsf{root}$, $\pi.\mathsf{left}$, and $\pi.\mathsf{right}$. The join of two memory-types is done by operator $\uplus$ that returns an upper-bound[2] of two memory-types. The operator $\uplus$ is defined using function collapse:

$$L_1 \uplus L_2 \triangleq L_1 \sqcup L_2$$
$$\langle L, \mu_1, \mu_2 \rangle \uplus \langle L', \mu'_1, \mu'_2 \rangle \triangleq \langle L \sqcup L', \mu_1 \uplus \mu'_1, \mu_2 \uplus \mu'_2 \rangle$$
$$L \uplus \langle L', \mu_1, \mu_2 \rangle \triangleq L \sqcup \mathsf{collapse}(\langle L', \mu_1, \mu_2 \rangle)$$

For a function type tree → tree, a memory-type describes the behavior of functions. It has the form of $\forall A.A \to \exists X.(L_1, L_2)$, which intuitively says that when the input tree has the memory type A, the function can only access locations in L_2 and its result must have a memory-type L_1. Note that the memory-type does not keep track of deallocated locations because the input programs for our analysis are assumed to have no `free` commands. The name A denotes all the heap cells reachable from an argument location, and X denotes all the heap cells newly allocated in a function. Since we assume every function is closed, the memory-type for functions is always closed. The pre-order for memory-types for functions is the pointwise order of its result part L_1 and L_2.

4 The free-Insertion Algorithm

We explain our analysis and transformation using the `copyleft` example in Section 1.3:

```
fun copyleft t = case t of Leaf        => Leaf                  (1)
                         | Node (t1,t2) => let p = copyleft t1  (2)
                                           in Node (p,t2)       (3)
```

We first analyze the memory-usage of all expressions in the `copyleft` program; then, using the analysis result, we insert safe `free` commands to the program.

---

[2] The domain of memory-types for trees is not a lattice: the least upper-bound of two memory-types does not exist in general.

$$\begin{array}{rl}
Environment & \Delta \in \{x \mid x \text{ is a variable}\} \xrightarrow{\text{fin}} \{\mu \mid \mu \text{ is a memory-type}\} \\
Bound & \mathcal{B} \in \{V \mid V \text{ is } R \text{ or } \pi\} \xrightarrow{\text{fin}} \{L \mid L \text{ is a multiset formula}\} \\
Substitution & \mathcal{S} \in \{L/V \mid V \text{ is } X \text{ or } A, \text{ and } L \text{ is a multiset formula}\}
\end{array}$$

$\boxed{\Delta \triangleright e : \mathcal{B}, \mu, L}$ Given environment Δ and expression e, we compute e's memory-type μ and usage L with a bound $\mathcal{B}$ for newly introduced R's and π's.

$$\frac{\Delta \triangleright v_1 : \mu_1 \quad \Delta \triangleright v_2 : \mu_2 \quad (\text{fresh } X)}{\Delta \triangleright \texttt{Node}\,(v_1, v_2) : \emptyset, \langle X, \mu_1, \mu_2 \rangle, \emptyset} \text{ U-NODE}$$

$$\frac{\Delta \triangleright v : \mu}{\Delta \triangleright v : \emptyset, \mu, \emptyset} \text{ U-VALUE} \qquad \frac{\Delta \triangleright e_1 : \mathcal{B}_1, \mu_1, L_1 \quad \Delta \cup \{x \mapsto \mu_1\} \triangleright e_2 : \mathcal{B}_2, \mu_2, L_2}{\Delta \triangleright \texttt{let } x = e_1 \texttt{ in } e_2 : \mathcal{B}_1 \cup \mathcal{B}_2, \mu_2, L_1 \sqcup L_2} \text{ U-LET}$$

$$\frac{\begin{array}{c}(\mathcal{B}, \langle L, \mu'_1, \mu'_2 \rangle) \stackrel{\Delta}{=} \text{reconstruct}(\mu, \pi) \quad (\text{fresh } \pi) \\ \Delta \cup \{x \mapsto \langle L, \mu'_1, \mu'_2 \rangle, x_1 \mapsto \mu'_1, x_2 \mapsto \mu'_2\} \triangleright e_1 : \mathcal{B}_1, \mu_1, L_1 \\ \Delta \cup \{x \mapsto \emptyset\} \triangleright e_2 : \mathcal{B}_2, \mu_2, L_2 \end{array}}{\begin{array}{c}\Delta \cup \{x \mapsto \mu\} \triangleright \texttt{case } x\,(\texttt{Node}\,(x_1, x_2) \texttt{ => } e_1)\,(\texttt{Leaf => } e_2) : \\ \mathcal{B}_1 \cup \mathcal{B}_2 \cup \mathcal{B},\ \mu_1 \uplus \mu_2,\ L_1 \sqcup L_2 \sqcup L \end{array}} \text{ U-CASE}$$

$$\frac{\Delta \triangleright v_1 : \forall A.A \to \exists X.(L_1, L_2) \quad \Delta \triangleright v_2 : \mu_2 \quad \mathcal{S} \stackrel{\Delta}{=} [\text{collapse}(\mu_2)/A, X'/X] \quad (\text{fresh } X', R)}{\Delta \triangleright v_1\,v_2 : \{R \mapsto \mathcal{S}L_1\}, R, \mathcal{S}L_2} \text{ U-APP}$$

$\boxed{\Delta \triangleright v : \mu}$ Given environment Δ and value v, we compute v's memory-type μ.

$$\frac{x \in \text{dom}(\Delta)}{\Delta \triangleright x : \Delta(x)} \text{ U-VAR} \qquad \frac{}{\Delta \triangleright \texttt{Leaf} : \emptyset} \text{ U-LEAF}$$

$$\frac{\mu_{\text{lfp}} \stackrel{\Delta}{=} \text{fix}\left(\begin{array}{c}\lambda\mu.\ \forall A.A \to \exists X.(\text{widen}_{\mathcal{B}}(\text{collapse}(\mu')), \text{widen}_{\mathcal{B}}(L)) \\ \text{where } \{f \mapsto \mu, x \mapsto A\} \triangleright e : \mathcal{B}, \mu', L\end{array}\right)}{\Delta \triangleright \texttt{fix } f\ \lambda x.e : \mu_{\text{lfp}}} \text{ U-FUN}$$

Fig. 3. Step one: The memory-Usage analysis

4.1 Step One: The Memory-Usage Analysis

Our memory-usage analysis (shown in Figure 3) computes memory-types for all expressions in `copyleft`. In particular, it gives the memory-type $\forall A.A \to \exists X.(A \sqcup X, A)$ to `copyleft` itself. Intuitively, this memory-type says that when A denotes all the cells in the argument tree `t`, the application "`copyleft t`" may create new cells, named X in the memory-type, and returns a tree consisting of cells in A or X; but it uses only the cells in A.

This memory-type is obtained by a fixpoint iteration (U-FUN). We start from the least memory-type $\forall A.A \to \exists X.(\emptyset, \emptyset)$ for a function. Each iteration assumes that the recursive function itself has the memory-type obtained in the previous step, and the argument to the function has the (fixed) memory-type A. Under this assumption, we calculate the memory-type and the used cells for the function body. To guarantee the termination, the resulting memory-type and the used cells are approximated by "widening" after each iteration.

We focus on the last iteration step. This analysis step proceeds with five parameters A, X_2, X_3, X, and R, and with a splitting name π: A denotes the cells in the input tree t, X_2 and X_3 the newly allocated cells at lines (2) and (3), respectively, X the set of all the newly allocated cells in copyleft, and R the cells in the returned tree from the recursive call "copyleft t1" at line (2); the splitting name π is used for partitioning the input tree t to its root, left subtree, and right subtree. With these parameters, we analyze the copyleft function once more, and its result becomes stable, equal to the previous result $\forall A. A \to \exists X.(A \sqcup X, A)$:

- **Line (1)**: The memory-type for Leaf is $\emptyset$, which says that the result tree is empty. (U-LEAF)
- **Line (2)**: The Node-branch is executed only when t is a non-empty tree. We exploit this fact to refine the memory-type A of t. We partition A into three parts: the root cell named π.root, the left subtree named π.left, and the right subtree named π.right, and record that their collection is A: $\pi.\text{root} \sqcup (\pi.\text{left} \dot{\oplus} \pi.\text{right}) = A$. Then t1 and t2 have π.left and π.right, respectively. (U-CASE)

  The next step is to compute a memory-type of the recursive call "copyleft t1." In the previous iteration's memory-type $\forall A. A \to \exists X.(A \sqcup X, A)$ of copyleft, we instantiate A by the memory-type π.left of the argument t1, and X by the name X_2 for the newly allocated cells at line (2). The instantiated memory-type $\pi.\text{left} \to (\pi.\text{left} \sqcup X_2, \pi.\text{left})$ says that when applied to the left subtree t1 of t, the function returns a tree consisting of new cells or the cells already in the left subtree t1, but uses only the cells in the left subtree t1. So, the function call's result has the memory-type $\pi.\text{left} \sqcup X_2$, and uses the cells in π.left. However, we use name R for the result of the function call, and record that R is included in $\pi.\text{left} \sqcup X_2$. (U-APP)
- **Line (3)**: While analyzing line (2), we have computed the memory-types of p and t2, that is, R and π.right, respectively. Therefore, "Node (p,t2)" has the memory-type $\langle X_3, R, \pi.\text{right} \rangle$ where X_3 is a name for the newly allocated root cell at line (3), R for the left subtree, and π.right for the right subtree. (U-NODE)

After analyzing the branches separately, we join the results from the branches. The memory-type for the Leaf-branch is $\emptyset$, and the memory-type for the Node-branch is $\langle X_3, R, \pi.\text{right} \rangle$. We join these two memory-types by first collapsing $\langle X_3, R, \pi.\text{right} \rangle$ to get $X_3 \sqcup (R \dot{\oplus} \pi.\text{right})$, and then joining the two collapsed memory-types $X_3 \sqcup (R \dot{\oplus} \pi.\text{right})$ and $\emptyset$. So, the function body has the memory-type $X_3 \sqcup (R \dot{\oplus} \pi.\text{right})$.

How about the cells used by copyleft? In the Node-branch of the case-expression, the root cell π.root of the tree t is pattern-matched, and at the function call in line (2), the left subtree cells π.left are used. Therefore, we conclude that copyleft uses the cells in $\pi.\text{root} \sqcup \pi.\text{left}$.

The last step of each fixpoint iteration is widening: reducing all the multiset formulas into simpler yet more approximated ones. We widen the result memory-type $X_3 \sqcup (R \dot{\oplus} \pi.\text{right})$ and the used cells $\pi.\text{root} \sqcup \pi.\text{left}$ with the records $\mathcal{B}(R) =$

$Reduced\ Form\quad L_R ::= V \mid V \dot{\oplus} V \mid \emptyset \mid L_R \sqcup L_R \quad (V\ \text{is}\ A\ \text{or}\ X)$

$\boxed{\text{widen}_\mathcal{B}(L)}$ gives a formula in a reduced form such that the formula only has free names A and X and is greater than or equal to L when $\mathcal{B}$ holds.

$\text{widen}_\mathcal{B}(L) \triangleq \mathcal{S}(\text{reduce}_\mathcal{B}(L))$ \hfill (w1)
$\quad (\mathcal{S} = \{X/X' \mid X'\ \text{appears in reduce}_\mathcal{B}(L)\}\ \text{for the fixed}\ X)$

where $\text{reduce}_\mathcal{B}(L)$ uses the first available rule in the following:

$\text{reduce}_\mathcal{B}(R) \triangleq \text{reduce}_\mathcal{B}(\mathcal{B}(R))$ \hfill (w2)
$\text{reduce}_\mathcal{B}(\pi.o) \triangleq \text{reduce}_\mathcal{B}(\mathcal{B}(\pi))$ \hfill (w3)
$\text{reduce}_\mathcal{B}(L_1 \sqcup L_2) \triangleq \text{reduce}_\mathcal{B}(L_1) \sqcup \text{reduce}_\mathcal{B}(L_2)$ \hfill (w4)
$\text{reduce}_\mathcal{B}(L_1 \dot{\oplus} L_2) \triangleq \text{reduce}_\mathcal{B}(L_1) \sqcup \text{reduce}_\mathcal{B}(L_2)$ (if $\text{disjoint}_\mathcal{B}(L_1, L_2) \Leftrightarrow \text{true}$) \hfill (w5)
$\qquad\qquad$ (disjoint is defined in Figure 6)
$\text{reduce}_\mathcal{B}(R \dot{\oplus} L) \triangleq \text{reduce}_\mathcal{B}(\mathcal{B}(R) \dot{\oplus} L)$ \hfill (w6)
$\text{reduce}_\mathcal{B}(\pi.o_1 \dot{\oplus} \pi.o_2) \triangleq \begin{cases} \text{reduce}_\mathcal{B}(\mathcal{B}(\pi) \dot{\oplus} \mathcal{B}(\pi)), & \text{if}\ o_1 = o_2 \\ \text{reduce}_\mathcal{B}(\mathcal{B}(\pi)), & \text{otherwise} \end{cases}$ \hfill (w7)
$\text{reduce}_\mathcal{B}(\pi.o \dot{\oplus} L) \triangleq \text{reduce}_\mathcal{B}(\mathcal{B}(\pi) \dot{\oplus} L)$ \hfill (w8)
$\text{reduce}_\mathcal{B}((L_1 \sqcup L_2) \dot{\oplus} L_3) \triangleq \text{reduce}_\mathcal{B}(L_1 \dot{\oplus} L_3) \sqcup \text{reduce}_\mathcal{B}(L_2 \dot{\oplus} L_3)$ \hfill (w9)
$\text{reduce}_\mathcal{B}((L_1 \dot{\oplus} L_2) \dot{\oplus} L_3) \triangleq$
$\qquad\qquad \text{reduce}_\mathcal{B}(L_1 \dot{\oplus} L_2) \sqcup \text{reduce}_\mathcal{B}(L_2 \dot{\oplus} L_3) \sqcup \text{reduce}_\mathcal{B}(L_3 \dot{\oplus} L_1)$ (w10)
$\text{reduce}_\mathcal{B}(L) \triangleq L$ \hfill (for all other L) (w11)

Fig. 4. The widening process

$\pi.\text{left} \sqcup X_2$ and $\mathcal{B}(\pi) = A$. In the following, each widening step is annotated by the rule names of Figure 4:

$X_3 \sqcup (R \dot{\oplus} \pi.\text{right})$
$\sqsubseteq X_3 \sqcup ((\pi.\text{left} \sqcup X_2) \dot{\oplus} \pi.\text{right})$ $\quad (\mathcal{B}(R) = \pi.\text{left} \sqcup X_2)$ \hfill (w6)
$= X_3 \sqcup (\pi.\text{left} \dot{\oplus} \pi.\text{right}) \sqcup (X_2 \dot{\oplus} \pi.\text{right})$ $\quad (\dot{\oplus}\ \text{distributes over}\ \sqcup)$ \hfill (w9)
$\sqsubseteq X_3 \sqcup A \sqcup (X_2 \dot{\oplus} \pi.\text{right})$ $\quad (\mathcal{B}(\pi) = A\ \text{thus}\ \pi.\text{left} \dot{\oplus} \pi.\text{right} \sqsubseteq A)$ \hfill (w7)
$\sqsubseteq X_3 \sqcup A \sqcup (X_2 \dot{\oplus} A)$ $\quad (\mathcal{B}(\pi) = A\ \text{thus}\ \pi.\text{right} \sqsubseteq A)$ \hfill (w8)
$= X_3 \sqcup A \sqcup X_2 \sqcup A$ $\quad (A\ \text{and}\ X_2\ \text{are disjoint})$ \hfill (w5)

Finally, by replacing all the newly introduced X_i's by a fixed name X (w1) and by removing redundant A and X, we obtain $A \sqcup X$. By rules (w4&w3) in Figure 4, $\pi.\text{root} \sqcup \pi.\text{left}$ for the used cells is reduced to A.

The widening step ensures the termination of fixpoint iterations. It produces a memory-type all of whose multiset formulas are in a reduced form and can only have free names A and X. Note that there are only finitely many such multiset formulas that do not have a redundant sub-formula, such as A in $A \sqcup A$. Consequently, after the widening step, only finitely many memory-types can be given to a function.

Although information is lost during the widening step, important properties of a function still remain. Suppose that the result of a function is given a multiset formula L after the widening step. If L does not contain the name A for the input tree, the result tree of the function cannot overlap with the input.[3] The presence of $\dot{\oplus}$ and A in L indicates whether the result tree has a shared sub-part. If neither $\dot{\oplus}$ nor A is present in L, the result tree can not have shared sub-parts, and if A is present but $\dot{\oplus}$ is not, the result tree can have a shared sub-part only when the input has.[4]

4.2 Step Two: free Commands Insertion

Using the result from the memory-usage analysis, our transformation algorithm (shown in Figure 5) inserts free commands, and adds boolean parameters β and β_{ns} (called *dynamic flags*) to each function. The dynamic flag β says that a cell in the argument tree can be safely deallocated, and β_{ns} that no sub-parts of the argument tree are shared. We have designed the transformation algorithm based on the following principles:

1. We insert free commands right before allocations because we intend to deallocate a heap cell only if it can be reused immediately after the deallocation.
2. We do not deallocate the cells in the result.

Our algorithm transforms the copyleft function as follows:

```
fun copyleft [β, βns] t =
    case t of Leaf         => Leaf                                    (1)
            | Node (t1,t2) => let p = copyleft [β ∧ βns, βns] t1      (2)
                              in  (free t when β; Node (p,t2))        (3)
```

Note that "$e_1; e_2$" is an abbreviation of "let $x = e_1$ in e_2" when x does not appear in e_2.

The algorithm decides to pass $\beta \wedge \beta_{ns}$ and β_{ns} in the recursive call (2). To find the first parameter, we collect constraints about conditions for which heap cells we should not free. Then, the candidate heap cells to deallocate must be disjoint with the cells to preserve. We derive such disjointness condition, expressed by a simple boolean expression. A preservation constraint has the conditional form $b \Rightarrow L$: when b holds, we should not free the cells in multiset L because, for instance, they have already been freed, or will be used later. For the first parameter, we get two constraints "$\neg \beta \Rightarrow A$" and "true $\Rightarrow X_3 \sqcup (R \dot{\oplus} \pi.\text{right})$" from the algorithm in Figure 5 (rules I-FUN and I-LET). The first constraint means that we should not free the cells in the argument tree t if β is false, and the second that we should not free the cells in the result tree of the copyleft function. Now the candidate heap cells to deallocate inside the recursive call's body are $\pi.\text{left} \setminus R$ (the heap cells for t1 excluding those in the result of the recursive call). For each constraint $b \Rightarrow L$, the algorithm finds a boolean expression which guarantees that L and $\pi.\text{left} \setminus R$ are disjoint if b is true; then, it takes the conjunction of all the found boolean expressions.

---

[3] This disjointness property of the input and the result is related to the usage aspects 2 and 3 of Aspinall and Hofmann [1].
[4] This sharing information is reminiscent of the "polymorphic uniqueness" in the Clean system [2].

Preservation Constraints $\mathcal{C} \subseteq \{b \Rightarrow L \mid b \text{ is a boolean expression}\}$

| $\triangleright v_1^{(\Delta,\mu)} \Rightarrow v_2$ | takes v_1 annotated with the analysis result (Δ, μ), and produces free-inserted v_2. |

$$\frac{}{\triangleright x \Rightarrow x} \text{ I-VAR} \qquad \frac{}{\triangleright \texttt{Leaf} \Rightarrow \texttt{Leaf}} \text{ I-LEAF} \qquad \frac{\mathcal{B}, \{\neg\beta \Rightarrow A\}, \text{true} \triangleright e \Rightarrow e' : \mathcal{C}}{\triangleright \texttt{ fix } f \ \lambda x.(e^{(\cdot,\mathcal{B},\cdot,\cdot)}) \Rightarrow \texttt{fix } f \ [\beta, \beta_{\text{ns}}] : \lambda x.e'} \text{ I-FUN}$$

| $\mathcal{B}, \mathcal{C}_1, b \triangleright e_1^{(\Delta,\mathcal{B}',\mu,L)} \Rightarrow e_2 : \mathcal{C}_2$ | takes an expression e_1 annotated with the analysis result $(\Delta, \mathcal{B}', \mu, L)$, a bound $\mathcal{B}$ for free names, and b and $\mathcal{C}_1$ that prohibit certain cells from being freed: b says that the result of e_1 should not be freed, and each $b' \Rightarrow L'$ in $\mathcal{C}_1$ that L' should not be freed when b' holds. The algorithm returns a free-inserted e_2 and $\mathcal{C}_2$ whose $b' \Rightarrow L'$ expresses that L' is freed in e_2 when b' holds. |

$$\frac{\triangleright v \Rightarrow v'}{\mathcal{B}, \mathcal{C}, b \triangleright v \Rightarrow v' : \emptyset} \text{ I-VALUE} \qquad \frac{\neg \exists x. \Delta(x) = \langle L, \mu_1, \mu_2 \rangle \quad \triangleright v_1 \Rightarrow v_1' \quad \triangleright v_2 \Rightarrow v_2'}{\mathcal{B}, \mathcal{C}, b \triangleright (\texttt{Node } (v_1, v_2))^{(\Delta,\cdot,\cdot,\cdot)} \Rightarrow \texttt{Node } (v_1', v_2') : \emptyset} \text{ I-NOF}$$

$$\frac{\exists x. \Delta(x) = \langle L, \mu_1, \mu_2 \rangle \quad \triangleright v_1 \Rightarrow v_1' \quad \triangleright v_2 \Rightarrow v_2' \quad \mathcal{C}' \triangleq \mathcal{C} \cup \{b \Rightarrow \text{collapse}(\mu)\} \quad b' \triangleq \text{free}_{\mathcal{B},\mathcal{C}'}(L)}{\mathcal{B}, \mathcal{C}, b \triangleright (\texttt{Node } (v_1, v_2))^{(\Delta,\cdot,\mu,\cdot)} \Rightarrow (\texttt{free } x \texttt{ when } b'; \texttt{ Node } (v_1', v_2')) : \{b' \Rightarrow L\}} \text{ I-FREE}$$

$$\frac{\mathcal{B}, \mathcal{C}, b \triangleright e_1 \Rightarrow e_1' : \mathcal{C}_1 \quad \mathcal{B}, \mathcal{C}, b \triangleright e_2 \Rightarrow e_2' : \mathcal{C}_2}{\mathcal{B}, \mathcal{C}, b \triangleright \texttt{case } x \ (\texttt{Node } (x_1, x_2) \Rightarrow e_1) \ (\texttt{Leaf} \Rightarrow e_2) \Rightarrow \texttt{case } x \ (\texttt{Node } (x_1, x_2) \Rightarrow e_1') \ (\texttt{Leaf} \Rightarrow e_2') : \mathcal{C}_1 \cup \mathcal{C}_2} \text{ I-CASE}$$

$$\frac{\mathcal{B}, \mathcal{C} \cup \{\text{true} \Rightarrow L, b \Rightarrow \text{collapse}(\mu)\}, \text{false} \triangleright e_1 \Rightarrow e_1' : \mathcal{C}_1 \quad \mathcal{B}, \mathcal{C} \cup \mathcal{C}_1, b \triangleright e_2 \Rightarrow e_2' : \mathcal{C}_2}{\mathcal{B}, \mathcal{C}, b \triangleright \texttt{let } x = e_1 \texttt{ in } (e_2^{(\cdot,\cdot,\mu,L)}) \Rightarrow \texttt{let } x = e_1' \texttt{ in } e_2' : \mathcal{C}_1 \cup \mathcal{C}_2} \text{ I-LET}$$

$$\frac{\triangleright v \Rightarrow v' \quad L \triangleq \text{collapse}(\mu) \quad b \triangleq \text{free}_{\mathcal{B},\mathcal{C}}(L \setminus R) \quad b_{\text{ns}} \triangleq \text{nosharing}_{\mathcal{B}}(L)}{\mathcal{B}, \mathcal{C}, b' \triangleright (x \ (v^{(\Delta,\mu)}))^{(\cdot,\cdot,R,\cdot)} \Rightarrow x \ [b, b_{\text{ns}}] \ v' : \{b' \hookrightarrow L \setminus R\}} \text{ I-APP}$$

| $\text{free}_{\mathcal{B},\mathcal{C}}(L)$ | calculates a safe condition to free L from the bound $\mathcal{B}$ for free names and the constraint $\mathcal{C}$ that says when certain cells should not be freed. |

$$\text{free}_{\mathcal{B},\mathcal{C}}(L) \triangleq \bigwedge \left\{ \neg b \lor \text{disjoint}_{\mathcal{B}}(L, L') \mid (b \Rightarrow L') \in \mathcal{C} \right\}$$

Fig. 5. Step two: The algorithm to insert free commands

- For "$\neg\beta \Rightarrow A$," the algorithm in Figure 6 returns false for the condition that A and $\pi.\text{left} \setminus R$ are disjoint:

$$\begin{aligned}\text{disjoint}_{\mathcal{B}}(A, \pi.\text{left} \setminus R) &= \text{disjoint}_{\mathcal{B}'}(A, \pi.\text{left}) & \text{(excluding } R\text{)} & \quad \text{(D5)} \\ &= \text{disjoint}_{\mathcal{B}'}(A, A) & (\pi.\text{root} \sqcup (\pi.\text{left} \dot{\oplus} \pi.\text{right}) = A) & \quad \text{(D9)} \\ &= \text{false} & (A = A) & \quad \text{(D10)}\end{aligned}$$

where $\mathcal{B} = \{R \mapsto \pi.\text{left} \sqcup X_2, \pi \mapsto A\}$ and $\mathcal{B}' = \{R \mapsto \emptyset, \pi \mapsto A\}$. We take $\neg(\neg\beta) \lor \text{false}$, equivalently, β.

– For "true $\Rightarrow X_3 \sqcup (R \dot\oplus \pi.\text{right})$," the algorithm in Figure 6 finds out that β_{ns} ensures the disjointness requirement:

$\text{disjoint}_{\mathcal{B}}(X_3 \sqcup (R \dot\oplus \pi.\text{right}), \pi.\text{left} \setminus R)$
$= \text{disjoint}_{\mathcal{B}'}(X_3 \sqcup (R \dot\oplus \pi.\text{right}), \pi.\text{left})$ \hfill (D5)
$= \text{disjoint}_{\mathcal{B}'}(X_3, \pi.\text{left}) \wedge \text{disjoint}_{\mathcal{B}'}(R, \pi.\text{left}) \wedge \text{disjoint}_{\mathcal{B}'}(\pi.\text{right}, \pi.\text{left})$ \hfill (D7&D8)
$= \text{disjoint}_{\mathcal{B}'}(X_3, A) \wedge \text{disjoint}_{\mathcal{B}'}(\emptyset, \pi.\text{left}) \wedge \text{nosharing}_{\mathcal{B}'}(A)$ \hfill (D9&D6&D4)
$= \text{true} \wedge \text{true} \wedge \beta_{\text{ns}}$ \hfill (D1&D1&D11)

Thus the conjunction $\beta \wedge \beta_{\text{ns}}$ becomes the condition for the recursive call body to free a cell in its argument t1.

$\boxed{\text{disjoint}_{\mathcal{B}}(L_1, L_2)}$ gives a condition that L_1 and L_2 are disjoint under $\mathcal{B}$. We apply the first available rule in the followings:

$\text{disjoint}_{\mathcal{B}}(A, X) \stackrel{\Delta}{=} \text{true}$, and $\text{disjoint}_{\mathcal{B}}(\emptyset, L) \stackrel{\Delta}{=} \text{true}$ \hfill (D1)
$\text{disjoint}_{\mathcal{B}}(X_1, X_2) \stackrel{\Delta}{=} \text{true}$ \hfill (when $X_1 \neq X_2$) (D2)
$\text{disjoint}_{\mathcal{B}}(\pi.\text{root}, \pi.o) \stackrel{\Delta}{=} \text{true}$ \hfill (when $o = $ left or right) (D3)
$\text{disjoint}_{\mathcal{B}}(\pi.\text{left}, \pi.\text{right}) \stackrel{\Delta}{=} \text{nosharing}_{\mathcal{B}}(\mathcal{B}(\pi))$ \hfill (D4)
$\text{disjoint}_{\mathcal{B} \cup \{R \mapsto L\}}(L_1 \setminus R, L_2) \stackrel{\Delta}{=} \text{disjoint}_{\mathcal{B} \cup \{R \mapsto \emptyset\}}(L_1, L_2)$ \hfill (D5)
$\text{disjoint}_{\mathcal{B}}(R, L) \stackrel{\Delta}{=} \text{disjoint}_{\mathcal{B}}(\mathcal{B}(R), L)$ \hfill (D6)
$\text{disjoint}_{\mathcal{B}}(L_1 \sqcup L_2, L_3) \stackrel{\Delta}{=} \text{disjoint}_{\mathcal{B}}(L_1, L_3) \wedge \text{disjoint}_{\mathcal{B}}(L_2, L_3)$ \hfill (D7)
$\text{disjoint}_{\mathcal{B}}(L_1 \dot\oplus L_2, L_3) \stackrel{\Delta}{=} \text{disjoint}_{\mathcal{B}}(L_1, L_3) \wedge \text{disjoint}_{\mathcal{B}}(L_2, L_3)$ \hfill (D8)
$\text{disjoint}_{\mathcal{B}}(\pi.o, L) \stackrel{\Delta}{=} \text{disjoint}_{\mathcal{B}}(\mathcal{B}(\pi), L)$ \hfill (D9)
$\text{disjoint}_{\mathcal{B}}(L_1, L_2) \stackrel{\Delta}{=} \text{false}$ \hfill (for other L_1 and L_2) (D10)

$\boxed{\text{nosharing}_{\mathcal{B}}(L)}$ gives a condition that L is a *set* under $\mathcal{B}$:

$\text{nosharing}_{\mathcal{B}}(A) \stackrel{\Delta}{=} \beta_{\text{ns}}$ \hfill (D11)
\quad (where β_{ns} is the second dynamic flag of the enclosing function)
$\text{nosharing}_{\mathcal{B}}(L) \stackrel{\Delta}{=} \text{true}$ \hfill (when $L = X$, $\pi.\text{root}$, or $\emptyset$) (D12)
$\text{nosharing}_{\mathcal{B}}(\pi.o) \stackrel{\Delta}{=} \text{nosharing}_{\mathcal{B}}(\mathcal{B}(\pi))$ \hfill (when $o = $ left or right) (D13)
$\text{nosharing}_{\mathcal{B}}(R) \stackrel{\Delta}{=} \text{nosharing}_{\mathcal{B}}(\mathcal{B}(R))$ \hfill (D14)
$\text{nosharing}_{\mathcal{B}}(L_1 \sqcup L_2) \stackrel{\Delta}{=} \text{nosharing}_{\mathcal{B}}(L_1) \wedge \text{nosharing}_{\mathcal{B}}(L_2)$ \hfill (D15)
$\text{nosharing}_{\mathcal{B}}(L_1 \dot\oplus L_2) \stackrel{\Delta}{=} \text{nosharing}_{\mathcal{B}}(L_1) \wedge \text{nosharing}_{\mathcal{B}}(L_2) \wedge \text{disjoint}_{\mathcal{B}}(L_1, L_2)$ \hfill (D16)
$\text{nosharing}_{\mathcal{B}}(L \setminus R) \stackrel{\Delta}{=} \text{nosharing}_{\mathcal{B}}(L)$ \hfill (D17)

Fig. 6. The algorithm to find a condition for the disjointness

---

For the second boolean flag in the recursive call (2), we find a boolean expression that ensures no sharing of a sub-part inside the left subtree t1. We use the memory-type $\pi.\text{left}$ of t1, and find a boolean expression that guarantees no sharing inside the multiset $\pi.\text{left}$; β_{ns} becomes such an expression: $\text{nosharing}_{\mathcal{B}}(\pi.\text{left}) = \text{nosharing}_{\mathcal{B}}(A) = \beta_{\text{ns}}$ (D13 & D11).

The algorithm inserts a `free` command right before "Node (p,t2)" at line (3), which deallocates the root cell of the tree t. But the `free` command is safe only in certain circumstances: the cell should not already have been freed by the

program	lines	(1) total[a]	(2) reuse[a]	(2)/(1)	cost(s[b])
sieve[c]	18	161112	131040	81.3%	0.004
quicksort[d]	24	675925	617412	91.3%	0.007
merge[e]	30	120012	59997	50.0%	0.007
mergesort[d]	61	440433	390429	88.7%	0.019
queens[f]	66	118224	6168	5.2%	0.017
mirage[g]	141	208914	176214	84.4%	0.114
life[h]	169	84483	8961	10.6%	0.113
kb[h]	557	2747397	235596	8.6%	0.850
k-eval[i]	645	271591	161607	59.5%	1.564
nucleic[h]	3230	1616487	294067	18.2%	3.893

analysis cost (logarithmic scale), slope = 1.46

[a] words: the amount of total allocated heap cells and reused heap cells by our transformation
[b] seconds: our analysis and transformation is compiled by the Objective Caml 3.04 native compiler [12], and executed in Sun Sparc 400Mhz, Solaris 2.7
[c] prime number computation by the sieve of Eratosthenes (size = 10000)
[d] quick/merge sort of an integer list (size=10000)
[e] merging two ordered integer lists to an ordered list (size = 10000)
[f] eight queen problem
[g] an interpreter for a tiny non-deterministic programming language
[h] the benchmark programs from SML/NJ [19] benchmark suite (loop=50)
[i] a type-checker and interpreter for a tiny imperative programming language

Fig. 7. Experimental results for inserting safe deallocations

recursive call (2), and the cell is neither freed nor used after the return of the current call. Our algorithm shows that we can meet all these requirements if the dynamic flag β is true; so, the algorithm picks β as a guard for the inserted free command. The process to find β is similar to the one for the first parameter of the call (2). We first collect constraints about conditions for which heap cells we should not free:

- we should not free cells that can be freed before $(\beta \wedge \beta_{ns} \Rightarrow \pi.\text{left} \setminus R)$,
- we should not free the input cells when β is false $(\neg \beta \Rightarrow A)$, and
- we should not free cells that are included in the function's result (true $\Rightarrow X_3 \sqcup (R \dot{\oplus} \pi.\text{right}))$.

These three constraints are generated by rules I-APP, I-FUN and I-FREE in Figure 5, respectively. From these constraints, we find a condition that cell π.root to free is disjoint with those cells we should not free. We use the same process as used for finding the first dynamic flag of the call (2). The result is β.

Theorem 1 (Correctness). *For every well-typed closed expression e, when e is transformed to e' by the memory-usage analysis $(\emptyset \triangleright e : \mathcal{B}, \mu, L)$ and the free-insertion algorithm $(\mathcal{B}, \emptyset, \text{false} \triangleright e^{(\emptyset,\mathcal{B},\mu,L)} \Rightarrow e' : \mathcal{C})$, then expression e' is well-typed in the sound memory-type system in [11].*

The complete proofs are in [11].

5 Experiments

We experimented the insertion algorithm with ML benchmark programs which use various data types such as lists, trees, and abstract syntax trees. We first pre-processed benchmark programs to monomorphic and closure-converted [13] programs, and then applied the algorithm to the pre-processed programs.

We extended the presented algorithm to analyze and transform programs with more features. (1) Our implementation supports more data constructors than just Leaf and Node. It analyzes heap cells with different constructors separately, and it inserts twice as many dynamic flags as the number of constructors for each parameter. (2) For functions with several parameters, we made the dynamic flag β also keep the alias information between function parameters so that if two parameters share some heap cells, both of their dynamic flags β are turned off. (3) For higher-order cases, we simply assumed the worst memory-types for the argument functions. For instance, we just assumed that an argument function, whose type is tree $\to$ tree, has memory-type $\forall A.A \to \exists X.(L,L)$ where $L = (A \dot\oplus A) \sqcup (X \dot\oplus X)$. (4) When we have multiple candidate cells for deallocation, we chose one whose guard is weaker than the others. For incomparable guards, we arbitrarily chose one.

The experimental results are shown in Figure 7. Our analysis and transformation achieves the memory reuse ratio (the fifth column) of 5.2% to 91.3%. For the two cases whose reuse ratio is low (queens and kb), we found that they have too much sharing. The kb program heavily uses a term-substitution function that can return a shared structure, where the number of shares depends on an argument value (e.g. a substitution item e/x has every x in the target term share e). Other than such cases, our experimental results are encouraging in terms of accuracy and cost. The graph in Figure 7 indicates that the analysis and transformation cost can be less than square in the program size in practice although the worst-case complexity is exponential.

6 Conclusion and Future Work

We have presented a static analysis and a source-level transformation that adds explicit memory-reuse commands into the program text, and we have shown that it effectively finds memory-reuse points.

We are currently implementing the analysis and transformation inside our nML compiler [15] to have it used in daily programming. The main issues in the implementation are to reduce the runtime overhead of the dynamic flags and to extend our method to handle polymorphism and mutable data structures. The runtime overhead of dynamic flags can be substantial because, for instance, if a function takes n parameters and each parameter's type has k data constructors, the function has to take $2 \times n \times k$ dynamic flags according to the current scheme. We are considering to reduce this overhead by doing a constant propagation for dynamic flags; omitting some unnecessary flags; associating a single flag with several data constructors of the same size; implementing flags by bit-vectors; and duplicating a function according to the different values of flags.

To extend our method for polymorphism, we need a sophisticated mechanism for dynamic flags. For instance, a polymorphic function of type $\forall \alpha. \alpha \to \alpha$ can take a value with two constructors or one with three constructors. So, this polymorphic input parameter does not fit in the current method because currently we insert twice as many dynamic flags as the number of constructors for each parameter. Our tentative solution is to assign only two flags to the input parameter of type α and to take conjunctions of flags in a call site: when a function is called with an input value with two constructors, instead of passing the four dynamic flags β, β_{ns}, β', and β'_{ns}, we pass $\beta \wedge \beta'$ and $\beta_{ns} \wedge \beta'_{ns}$. For mutable data structures, we plan to take a conservative approach similar to that of Gheorghioiu et al. [6]: heap cells possibly reachable from modifiable cells cannot be reused.

Acknowledgment

We thank Uday Reddy, Peter O'Hearn, Bruno Blanchet, and the anonymous referees for their helpful comments.

References

1. David Aspinall and Martin Hofmann. Another type system for in-place update. In *Proceedings of the European Symposium on Programming*, volume 2305 of *Lecture Notes in Computer Science*, pages 36–52, April 2002.
2. Erik Barendsen and Sjaak Smetsers. Uniqueness typing for functional languages with graph rewriting semantics. *Mathematical Structures in Computer Science*, 6:579–612, 1995.
3. Bruno Blanchet. Escape analysis: Correctness proof, implementation and experimental results. In *Proceedings of The ACM SIGPLAN-SIGACT Symposium on Principles of Programming Languages*, pages 25–37, 1998.
4. Karl Crary, David Walker, and Greg Morrisett. Typed memory management in a calculus of capabilities. In *Proceedings of the ACM Symposium on Principles of Programming Languages*, pages 262–275, January 1999.
5. David Gay and Alex Aiken. Language support for regions. In *Proceedings of the ACM Conference on Programming Language Design and Implementation*, pages 70–80, June 2001.
6. Ovidiu Gheorghioiu, Alexandru Sălcianu, and Martin Rinard. Interprocedural compatibility analysis for static object preallocation. In *Proceedings of the ACM Symposium on Principles of Programming Languages*, pages 273–284, January 2003.
7. Dan Grossman, Greg Morrisett, Trevor Jim, Michael Hicks, Yanling Wang, and James Cheney. Region-based memory management in Cyclone. In *Proceedings of the ACM Conference on Programming Language Design and Implementation*, June 2002.
8. Williams L. Harrison III. The interprocedural analysis and automatic parallelization of scheme programs. *Lisp and Symbolic Computation*, 2(3/4):179–396, 1989.
9. Samin Ishtiaq and Peter O'Hearn. BI as an assertion language for mutable data structures. In *Proceedings of the ACM Symposium on Principles of Programming Languages*, January 2001.

10. Naoki Kobayashi. Quasi-linear types. In *Proceedings of the ACM Symposium on Principles of Programming Languages*, pages 29–42, 1999.
11. Oukseh Lee. A correctness proof on an algorithm to insert safe memory reuse commands. Tech. Memo. ROPAS-2003-19, Research On Program Analysis System, Korea Advanced Institute of Science and Technology, February 2003. http://ropas.kaist.ac.kr/memo.
12. Xavier Leroy, Damien Doligez, Jacques Garrigue, Didier Rémy, and Jérôme Vouillon. The Objective Caml system release 3.04. Institut National de Recherche en Informatique et en Automatique, December 2001. http://caml.inria.fr.
13. Yosuhiko Minamide, Greg Morrisett, and Robert Harper. Typed closure conversion. In *Proceedings of the ACM Symposium on Principles of Programming Languages*, pages 271–283, January 1996.
14. Markus Mohnen. Efficient compile-time garbage collection for arbitrary data structures. In *Proceedings of Programming Languages: Implementations, Logics and Programs*, volume 982 of *Lecture Notes in Computer Science*, pages 241–258. Springer-Verlag, 1995.
15. nML programming language system, version 0.92a. Research On Program Analysis System, Korea Advanced Institute of Science and Technology, March 2002. http://ropas.kaist.ac.kr/n.
16. Peter O'Hearn, John C. Reynolds, and Hongseok Yang. Local reasoning about programs that alter data structures. In *The Proceedings of Computer Science and Logic*, pages 1–19, 2001.
17. John C. Reynolds. Separation logic: A logic for shared mutable data structures. In *Proceedings of the Seventeenth Annual IEEE Symposium on Logic in Computer Science*, July 2002.
18. Frederick Smith, David Walker, and Greg Morrisett. Alias types. In *Proceedings of the European Symposium on Programming*, volume 1782 of *Lecture Notes in Computer Science*, pages 366–382, March/April 2000.
19. The Standard ML of New Jersey, version 110.0.7. Bell Laboratories, Lucent Technologies, October 2000. http://cm.bell-labs.com/cm/cs/what/smlnj.
20. Mads Tofte and Lars Birkedal. A region inference algorithm. *ACM Transactions on Programming Languages and Systems*, 20(4):734–767, July 1998.
21. Mads Tofte, Lars Birkedal, Martin Elsman, Niels Hallenberg, Tommy Højfeld Olesen, and Peter Sestoft. Programming with regions in the ML Kit (for version 4). IT University of Copenhagen, April 2002. http://www.it-c.dk/research/mlkit.
22. Mads Tofte and Jean-Pierre Talpin. Implementation of the typed call-by-value λ-calculus using a stack of regions. In *Proceedings of the ACM Symposium on Principles of Programming Languages*, pages 188–201, 1994.
23. Mads Tofte and Jean-Pierre Talpin. Region-based memory management. *Information and Computation*, 132(2):109–176, 1997.
24. David N. Turner, Philip Wadler, and Christian Mossin. Once upon a type. In *International Conference on Functional Programming and Computer Architecture*, pages 25–28, June 1995.
25. Philip Wadler. Linear types can change the world! In *Programming Concepts and Methods*. North Holland, April 1990.
26. David Walker and Greg Morrisett. Alias types for recursive data structures. In *Workshop on Types in Compilation*, volume 2071 of *Lecture Notes in Computer Science*, pages 177–206, September 2000.

Weighted Pushdown Systems and Their Application to Interprocedural Dataflow Analysis*

Thomas Reps[1], Stefan Schwoon[2], and Somesh Jha[1]

[1] Comp. Sci. Dept., University of Wisconsin
{reps,jha}@cs.wisc.edu
[2] Fakultät Inf., Universität Stuttgart
schwoosn@informatik.uni-stuttgart.de

Abstract. Recently, pushdown systems (PDSs) have been extended to *weighted PDSs*, in which each transition is labeled with a value, and the goal is to determine the meet-over-all-paths value (for paths that meet a certain criterion). This paper shows how weighted PDSs yield new algorithms for certain classes of interprocedural dataflow-analysis problems.

1 Introduction

This paper explores a connection between interprocedural dataflow analysis and model checking of pushdown systems (PDSs). Various connections between dataflow analysis and model checking have been established in past work, e.g., [6, 9, 23, 27, 28]; however, with one exception ([9]), past work has shed light only on the relationship between model checking and *bit-vector* dataflow-analysis problems, such as live-variable analysis and partial-redundancy elimination. In contrast, the results presented in this paper apply to (i) bit-vector problems, (ii) the one non-bit-vector problem addressed in [9], as well as (iii) certain dataflow-analysis problems that cannot be expressed as bit-vector problems, such as linear constant propagation. In general, the approach can be applied to any distributive dataflow-analysis problem for which the domain of transfer functions has no infinite descending chains. (Safe solutions are also obtained for problems that are monotonic but not distributive.)

The paper makes use of a recent result that extends PDSs to *weighted PDSs*, in which each transition is labeled with a value, and the goal is to determine the meet-over-all-paths value (for paths that meet a certain criterion) [25]. The paper shows how weighted PDSs yield new algorithms for certain classes of interprocedural dataflow-analysis problems. These ideas are illustrated by the application of weighted PDSs to linear constant propagation.

---

* Supported by ONR contract N00014-01-1-0708.

The contributions of the paper can be summarized as follows:

- Conventional dataflow-analysis algorithms merge together the values for all states associated with the same program point, regardless of the states' calling context. With the dataflow-analysis algorithm obtained via weighted PDSs, dataflow queries can be posed with respect to a regular language of stack configurations. Conventional merged dataflow information can also be obtained by issuing appropriate queries; thus, the new approach provides a strictly richer framework for interprocedural dataflow analysis than is provided by conventional interprocedural dataflow-analysis algorithms.
- Because the algorithm for solving path problems in weighted PDSs can provide a witness set of paths, it is possible to provide an explanation of why the answer to a dataflow query has the value reported.

The algorithms described in the paper have been implemented in a library that solves reachability problems on weighted PDSs [24]. The library has been used to create prototype implementations of context-sensitive interprocedural dataflow-analysis algorithms for linear constant propagation [22] and the detection of affine relationships [16]. The library is available on the Internet, and may be used by third parties in the creation of dataflow-analysis tools.

The remainder of the paper is organized as follows: Section 2 introduces terminology and notation used in the paper, and defines the generalized-pushdown-reachability (GPR) framework. Section 3 presents the algorithm from [25] for solving GPR problems. Section 4 presents the new contribution of this paper—the application of the GPR framework to interprocedural dataflow analysis. Section 5 discusses related work. Appendix A describes an enhancement to the algorithm from Section 3 to generate a witness set for an answer to a GPR problem.

2 Terminology and Notation

In this section, we introduce terminology and notation used in the paper.

2.1 Pushdown Systems

A pushdown system is a transition system whose states involve a stack of unbounded length.

Definition 1. *A **pushdown system** is a triple $\mathcal{P} = (P, \Gamma, \Delta)$, where P and Γ are finite sets called the **control locations** and the **stack alphabet**, respectively. A **configuration** of $\mathcal{P}$ is a pair $\langle p, w \rangle$, where $p \in P$ and $w \in \Gamma^*$. Δ contains a finite number of **rules** of the form $\langle p, \gamma \rangle \hookrightarrow_{\mathcal{P}} \langle p', w \rangle$, where $p, p' \in P$, $\gamma \in \Gamma$, and $w \in \Gamma^*$, which define a transition relation $\Rightarrow$ between configurations of $\mathcal{P}$ as follows:*

If $r = \langle p, \gamma \rangle \hookrightarrow_{\mathcal{P}} \langle p', w \rangle$, then $\langle p, \gamma w' \rangle \xRightarrow{\langle r \rangle}_{\mathcal{P}} \langle p', w w' \rangle$ for all $w' \in \Gamma^*$.

We write $c \Rightarrow_\mathcal{P} c'$ to express that there exists some rule r such that $c \xrightarrow{\langle r \rangle}_\mathcal{P} c'$; we omit the index $\mathcal{P}$ if $\mathcal{P}$ is understood. The reflexive transitive closure of $\Rightarrow$ is denoted by $\Rightarrow^*$. Given a set of configurations C, we define $pre^*(C) := \{\, c' \mid \exists c \in C\colon c' \Rightarrow^* c\,\}$ and $post^*(C) := \{\, c' \mid \exists c \in C\colon c \Rightarrow^* c'\,\}$ to be the sets of configurations that are reachable—backwards and forwards, respectively—from elements of C via the transition relation.

Without loss of generality, we assume henceforth that for every $\langle p, \gamma \rangle \hookrightarrow \langle p', w \rangle$ we have $|w| \leq 2$; this is not restrictive because every pushdown system can be simulated by another one that obeys this restriction and is larger by only a constant factor; e.g., see [13].

Because pushdown systems have infinitely many configurations, we need some symbolic means to represent sets of configurations. We will use finite automata for this purpose.

Definition 2. *Let $\mathcal{P} = (P, \Gamma, \Delta)$ be a pushdown system. A $\mathcal{P}$-automaton is a quintuple $\mathcal{A} = (Q, \Gamma, \to, P, F)$ where $Q \supseteq P$ is a finite set of* **states**, $\to \subseteq Q \times \Gamma \times Q$ *is the set of* **transitions**, *and $F \subseteq Q$ are the* **final states**. *The* **initial states** *of $\mathcal{A}$ are the control locations P. A configuration $\langle p, w \rangle$ is* **accepted** *by $\mathcal{A}$ if $p \xrightarrow{w}{}^* q$ for some final state q. A set of configurations of $\mathcal{P}$ is* **regular** *if it is recognized by some $\mathcal{P}$-automaton. (We frequently omit the prefix $\mathcal{P}$ and simply refer to "automata" if $\mathcal{P}$ is understood.)*

A convenient property of regular sets of configurations is that they are closed under forwards and backwards reachability. In other words, given an automaton $\mathcal{A}$ that accepts the set C, one can construct automata $\mathcal{A}_{pre^*}$ and $\mathcal{A}_{post^*}$ that accept $pre^*(C)$ and $post^*(C)$, respectively. The general idea behind the algorithm for pre^* [3,8] is as follows:

Let $\mathcal{P} = (P, \Gamma, \Delta)$ be a pushdown system and $\mathcal{A} = (Q, \Gamma, \to_0, P, F)$ be a $\mathcal{P}$-automaton accepting a set of configurations C. Without loss of generality we assume that $\mathcal{A}$ has no transition leading to an initial state. $pre^*(C)$ is obtained as the language of an automaton $\mathcal{A}_{pre^*} = (Q, \Gamma, \to, P, F)$ derived from $\mathcal{A}$ by a saturation procedure. The procedure adds new transitions to $\mathcal{A}$ according to the following rule:

If $\langle p, \gamma \rangle \hookrightarrow \langle p', w \rangle$ and $p' \xrightarrow{w}{}^* q$ in the current automaton, add a transition (p, γ, q).

In [8] an efficient implementation of this procedure is given, which requires $\mathcal{O}(|Q|^2 |\Delta|)$ time and $\mathcal{O}(|Q| |\Delta| + |\to_0|)$ space. Moreover, another procedure (and implementation) are presented for constructing a $\mathcal{P}$-automaton that accepts $post^*(C)$. In Section 3, we develop generalizations of these procedures. (We present these extensions for pre^*; the same basic idea applies to $post^*$, but is omitted for lack of space.)

2.2 Weighted Pushdown Systems

A weighted pushdown system is a pushdown system whose rules are given values from some domain of weights. The weight domains of interest are the bounded idempotent semirings defined in Definition 3.

Definition 3. *A **bounded idempotent semiring** is a quintuple $(D, \oplus, \otimes, 0, 1)$, where D is a set, 0 and 1 are elements of D, and $\oplus$ (the combine operation) and $\otimes$ (the extend operation) are binary operators on D such that*

1. *$(D, \oplus)$ is a commutative monoid with 0 as its neutral element, and where $\oplus$ is idempotent (i.e., for all $a \in D$, $a \oplus a = a$).*
2. *$(D, \otimes)$ is a monoid with the neutral element 1.*
3. *$\otimes$ distributes over $\oplus$, i.e. for all $a, b, c \in D$ we have*

$$a \otimes (b \oplus c) = (a \otimes b) \oplus (a \otimes c) \quad \text{and} \quad (a \oplus b) \otimes c = (a \otimes c) \oplus (b \otimes c).$$

4. *0 is an annihilator with respect to $\otimes$, i.e., for all $a \in D$, $a \otimes 0 = 0 = 0 \otimes a$.*
5. *In the partial order $\sqsubseteq$ defined by: $\forall a, b \in D$, $a \sqsubseteq b$ iff $a \oplus b = a$, there are no infinite descending chains.*

Definition 4. *A **weighted pushdown system** is a triple $\mathcal{W} = (\mathcal{P}, \mathcal{S}, f)$ such that $\mathcal{P} = (P, \Gamma, \Delta)$ is a pushdown system, $\mathcal{S} = (D, \oplus, \otimes, 0, 1)$ is a bounded idempotent semiring, and $f: \Delta \to D$ is a function that assigns a value from D to each rule of $\mathcal{P}$.*

Let $\sigma \in \Delta^*$ be a sequence of rules. Using f, we can associate a value to σ, i.e., if $\sigma = [r_1, \ldots, r_k]$, then we define $v(\sigma) := f(r_1) \otimes \ldots \otimes f(r_k)$. Moreover, for any two configurations c and c' of $\mathcal{P}$, we let $path(c, c')$ denote the set of all rule sequences $[r_1, \ldots, r_k]$ that transform c into c', i.e., $c \xrightarrow{\langle r_1 \rangle} \cdots \xrightarrow{\langle r_k \rangle} c'$.

Definition 5. *Given a weighted pushdown system $\mathcal{W} = (\mathcal{P}, \mathcal{S}, f)$, where $\mathcal{P} = (P, \Gamma, \Delta)$, and a regular set $C \subseteq P \times \Gamma^*$, the **generalized pushdown reachability (GPR) problem** is to find for each $c \in P \times \Gamma^*$:*

- *$\delta(c) := \bigoplus \{ v(\sigma) \mid \sigma \in path(c, c'), c' \in C \}$;*
- *a **witness set** of paths $\omega(c) \subseteq \bigcup_{c' \in C} path(c, c')$ such that $\bigoplus_{\sigma \in \omega(c)} v(\sigma) = \delta(c)$.*

Notice that the extender operation $\otimes$ is used to calculate the value of a path. The value of a set of paths is computed using the combiner operation $\oplus$. In general, it is enough for $\omega(c)$ to contain only a finite set of paths whose values are minimal elements of $\{ v(\sigma) \mid \sigma \in path(c, c'), c' \in C \}$, i.e., minimal with respect to the partial order $\sqsubseteq$ defined in Definition 3(5).

3 Solving the Generalized Pushdown Reachability Problem

This section presents the algorithm from [25] for solving GPR problems.

For the entire section, let $\mathcal{W}$ denote a fixed weighted pushdown system: $\mathcal{W} = (\mathcal{P}, \mathcal{S}, f)$, where $\mathcal{P} = (P, \Gamma, \Delta)$ and $\mathcal{S} = (D, \oplus, \otimes, 0, 1)$; let C denote a fixed regular set of configurations, represented by a $\mathcal{P}$-automaton $\mathcal{A} = (Q, \Gamma, \rightarrow_0, P, F)$ such that $\mathcal{A}$ has no transition leading to an initial state.

The GPR problem is a multi-target meet-over-all-paths problem on a graph. The vertices of the graph are the configurations of $\mathcal{P}$, and the edges are defined by $\mathcal{P}$'s transition relation. The target vertices are the vertices in C. Both the graph and the set of target vertices can be infinite, but have some built-in structure to them; in particular, C is a regular set.

Because the GPR problem concerns infinite graphs, and not just an infinite set of paths, it differs from other work on meet-over-all-paths problems. As in the ordinary pushdown-reachability problem [3, 8], the infinite nature of the (GPR) problem is addressed by reporting the answer in an indirect fashion, namely, in the form of an (annotated) automaton. An answer automaton without its annotations is identical to an $\mathcal{A}_{pre^*}$ automaton created by the algorithm of [8]. For each $c \in pre^*(C)$, the values of $\delta(c)$ and $\omega(c)$ can be read off from the annotations by following all accepting paths for c in the automaton; for $c \notin pre^*(C)$, the values of $\delta(c)$ and $\omega(c)$ are 0 and $\emptyset$, respectively.

The algorithm is presented in several stages:

- We first define a language that characterizes the sequences of transitions that can be made by a pushdown system $\mathcal{P}$ and an automaton $\mathcal{A}$ for C.
- We then turn to weighted pushdown systems and the GPR problem. We use the language characterizations of transition sequences, together with previously known results on a certain kind of grammar problem [15, 17] to obtain a solution to the GPR problem.
- However, the solution based on grammars is somewhat inefficient; to improve the performance, we specialize the computation to our case, ending up with an algorithm for creating an annotated automaton that is quite similar to the pre^* algorithm from [8].

3.1 Languages that Characterize Transition Sequences

In this section, we make some definitions that will aid in reasoning about the set of paths that lead from a configuration c to configurations in a regular set C. We call this set the *reachability witnesses* for $c \in P \times \Gamma^*$ with respect to C: $ReachabilityWitnesses(c, C) = \bigcup_{c' \in C} path(c, c')$.

It is convenient to think of PDS $\mathcal{P}$ and $\mathcal{P}$-automaton $\mathcal{A}$ (for C) as being combined in sequence, to create a combined PDS, which we will call $\mathcal{PA}$. $\mathcal{PA}$'s states are $P \cup Q = Q$, and its rules are those of $\mathcal{P}$, augmented with a rule $\langle q, \gamma \rangle \hookrightarrow \langle q', \epsilon \rangle$ for each transition $q \xrightarrow{\gamma} q'$ in $\mathcal{A}$'s transition set $\rightarrow_0$.

We say that a configuration $c = \langle p, \gamma_1 \gamma_2 \ldots \gamma_n \rangle$ is *accepted* by $\mathcal{PA}$ if there is a path to a configuration $\langle q_f, \epsilon \rangle$ such that $q_f \in F$. Note that because $\mathcal{A}$ has no transitions leading to initial states, $\mathcal{PA}$'s behavior during an accepting run can be divided into two phases—transitions during which $\mathcal{PA}$ mimics $\mathcal{P}$, followed by transitions during which $\mathcal{PA}$ mimics $\mathcal{A}$: once $\mathcal{PA}$ reaches a state in $(Q - P)$, it can only perform a sequence of pops, possibly reaching a state in F. If the run of $\mathcal{PA}$ does reach a state in F, in terms of the features of the original $\mathcal{P}$ and $\mathcal{A}$, the second phase corresponds to automaton $\mathcal{A}$ accepting some configuration c' that has been reached by $\mathcal{P}$, starting in configuration c. In other words, $\mathcal{PA}$ accepts a configuration c iff $c \in pre^*(C)$.

The first language that we define characterizes the *pop sequences* of $\mathcal{PA}$. A pop sequence for $q \in Q$, $\gamma \in \Gamma$, and $q' \in Q$ is a sequence of $\mathcal{PA}$'s transitions that (i) starts in a configuration $\langle q, \gamma w \rangle$, (ii) ends in a configuration $\langle q', w \rangle$, and (iii) throughout the transition sequence the stack is always of the form $w'w$ for some non-empty sequence $w' \in \Gamma^+$, except in the last step, when the stack shrinks to w. Because w remains unchanged throughout a pop sequence, we need only consider pop sequences of a canonical form, i.e., those that (i) start in a configuration $\langle q, \gamma \rangle$, and (ii) end in a configuration $\langle q', \varepsilon \rangle$. The pop sequences for a given q, γ, and q' can be characterized by the complete derivation trees[3] derived from nonterminal $PS_{(q,\gamma,q')}$, using the grammar shown in Figure 1.

Production	for each
(1) $PS_{(q,\gamma,q')} \to \epsilon$	$q \xrightarrow{\gamma} q' \in \to_0$
(2) $PS_{(p,\gamma,p')} \to \epsilon$	$\langle p, \gamma \rangle \hookrightarrow \langle p', \varepsilon \rangle \in \Delta$, $p \in P$
(3) $PS_{(p,\gamma,q)} \to PS_{(p',\gamma',q)}$	$\langle p, \gamma \rangle \hookrightarrow \langle p', \gamma' \rangle \in \Delta$, $p \in P$, $q \in Q$
(4) $PS_{(p,\gamma,q)} \to PS_{(p',\gamma',q')} \; PS_{(q',\gamma'',q)}$	$\langle p, \gamma \rangle \hookrightarrow \langle p', \gamma'\gamma'' \rangle \in \Delta$, $p \in P$, $q, q' \in Q$

Fig. 1. A context-free language for the pop sequences of $\mathcal{PA}$, and the $\mathcal{PA}$ rules that correspond to each production

Theorem 1. *PDS $\mathcal{PA}$ has a pop sequence for q, γ, and q' iff nonterminal $PS_{(q,\gamma,q')}$ of the grammar shown in Figure 1 has a complete derivation tree. Moreover, for each derivation tree with root $PS_{(q,\gamma,q')}$, a preorder listing of the derivation tree's production instances (where Figure 1 defines the correspondence between productions and PDS rules) gives a sequence of rules for a pop sequence for q, γ, and q'; and every such sequence of rules has a derivation tree with root $PS_{(q,\gamma,q')}$.*

Proof (Sketch). To shrink the stack by removing the stack symbol on the left-hand side of each rule of $\mathcal{PA}$, there must be a transition sequence that removes each of the symbols that appear in the stack component of the rule's right-hand side. In other words, a pop sequence for the left-hand-side stack symbol must involve a pop sequence for each right-hand-side stack symbol.

---

[3] A derivation tree is *complete* if it has is a terminal symbol at each leaf.

The left-hand and right-hand sides of the productions in Figure 1 reflect the pop-sequence obligations incurred by the corresponding rule of $\mathcal{PA}$.

To capture the set $ReachabilityWitnesses(\langle p, \gamma_1\gamma_2 \ldots \gamma_n \rangle, C)$, where C is recognized by automaton $\mathcal{A}$, we define a context-free language given by the set of productions

$$Accepting[\gamma_1\gamma_2 \ldots \gamma_n]_{(p,q)} \rightarrow PS_{(p,\gamma_1,q_1)} \; PS_{(q_1,\gamma_2,q_2)} \; \cdots \; PS_{(q_{n-1},\gamma_n,q)}$$
$$\text{for each } q_i \in Q, \text{ for } 1 \leq i \leq n-1; \text{ and } q \in F$$
$$Accepted[\gamma_1\gamma_2 \ldots \gamma_n]_{(p)} \rightarrow Accepting[\gamma_1\gamma_2 \ldots \gamma_n]_{(p,q)} \quad \text{for each } q \in F$$

This language captures all ways in which PDS $\mathcal{PA}$ can accept $\langle p, \gamma_1\gamma_2 \ldots \gamma_n \rangle$: the set of reachability witnesses for $\langle p, \gamma_1\gamma_2 \ldots \gamma_n \rangle$ corresponds to the complete derivation trees derivable from nonterminal $Accepted[\gamma_1\gamma_2 \ldots \gamma_n]_{(p)}$. The subtree rooted at $PS_{(q_{i-1},\gamma_i,q_i)}$ gives the pop sequence that $\mathcal{PA}$ performs to consume symbol γ_i. (If there are no reachability witnesses for $\langle p, \gamma_1\gamma_2 \ldots \gamma_n \rangle$, there are no complete derivation trees with root $Accepted[\gamma_1\gamma_2 \ldots \gamma_n]_{(p)}$.)

3.2 Weighted PDSs and Abstract Grammar Problems

Turning now to weighted PDSs, we will consider the weighted version of $\mathcal{PA}$, denoted by $\mathcal{WA}$, in which weighted PDS W is combined with $\mathcal{A}$, and each rule $\langle q, \gamma \rangle \hookrightarrow \langle q', \epsilon \rangle$ that was added due to transition $q \xrightarrow{\gamma} q'$ in $\mathcal{A}$'s transition set $\rightarrow_0$ is assigned the weight 1.

We are able to reason about semiring sums ($\oplus$) of weights on the paths that are characterized by the context-free grammars defined above using the following concept:

Definition 6. *[15, 17] Let $(S, \sqcap)$ be a semilattice. An* **abstract grammar** *over $(S, \sqcap)$ is a collection of context-free grammar productions, where each production θ has the form*

$$X_0 \rightarrow g_\theta(X_1, \ldots, X_k).$$

Parentheses, commas, and g_θ (where θ is a production) are terminal symbols. Every production θ is associated with a function $g_\theta \colon S^k \rightarrow S$. Thus, every string α of terminal symbols derived in this grammar (i.e., the yield of a complete derivation tree) denotes a composition of functions, and corresponds to a unique value in S, which we call $val_G(\alpha)$ (or simply $val(\alpha)$ when G is understood). Let $L_G(X)$ denote the strings of terminals derivable from a nonterminal X. The **abstract grammar problem** *is to compute, for each nonterminal X, the value*

$$m_G(X) := \sqcap_{\alpha \in L_G(X)} val_G(\alpha).$$

Because the complete derivation trees with root $Accepted[\gamma_1\gamma_2 \ldots \gamma_n]_{(p)}$ encode the transition sequences by which $\mathcal{WA}$ accepts $\langle p, \gamma_1\gamma_2 \ldots \gamma_n \rangle$, to cast the GPR as a grammar problem, we merely have to attach appropriate production functions to the productions so that for each rule sequence σ, and corresponding derivation tree (with yield) α, we have $v(\sigma) = val_G(\alpha)$. This is done in Figure 2: note how functions g_2, g_3, and g_4 place $f(r)$ at the beginning of the semiring-product expression; this corresponds to a preorder listing of a derivation tree's production instances (cf. Theorem 1).

Production	for each
(1) $PS_{(q,\gamma,q')} \to g_1(\epsilon)$ $g_1 = 1$	$(q,\gamma,q') \in \to_0$
(2) $PS_{(p,\gamma,p')} \to g_2(\epsilon)$ $g_2 = f(r)$	$r = \langle p,\gamma \rangle \hookrightarrow \langle p',\epsilon \rangle \in \Delta,\ p \in P$
(3) $PS_{(p,\gamma,q)} \to g_3(PS_{(p',\gamma',q)})$ $g_3 = \lambda a.f(r) \otimes a$	$r = \langle p,\gamma \rangle \hookrightarrow \langle p',\gamma' \rangle \in \Delta,\ p \in P,\ q \in Q$
(4) $PS_{(p,\gamma,q)} \to g_4(PS_{(p',\gamma',q')}, PS_{(q',\gamma'',q)})$ $g_4 = \lambda a.\lambda b.f(r) \otimes a \otimes b$	$r = \langle p,\gamma \rangle \hookrightarrow \langle p',\gamma'\gamma'' \rangle \in \Delta,\ p \in P,\ q,q' \in Q$
(5) $Accepting[\gamma_1\gamma_2\ldots\gamma_n]_{(p,q)} \to g_5(PS_{(p,\gamma_1,q_1)}, PS_{(q_1,\gamma_2,q_2)}, \ldots, PS_{(q_{n-1},\gamma_n,q)})$ $g_5 = \lambda a_1.\lambda a_2 \ldots \lambda a_n.a_1 \otimes a_2 \otimes \ldots \otimes a_n$	$q_i \in Q$, for $1 \le i \le n-1$, and $q \in F$
(6) $Accepted[\gamma_1\gamma_2\ldots\gamma_n]_{(p)} \to g_6(Accepting[\gamma_1\gamma_2\ldots\gamma_n]_{(p,q)})$ $g_6 = \lambda a.a$	$q \in F$

Fig. 2. An abstract grammar problem for the GPR problem

To solve the GPR problem, we appeal to the following theorem:

Theorem 2. *[15, 17] The abstract grammar problem for G and $(S, \sqcap)$ can be solved by an iterative computation that finds the maximum fixed point when the following conditions hold:*

1. *The semilattice $(S, \sqcap)$ has no infinite descending chains.*
2. *Every production function g_θ in G is distributive, i.e.,*

$$g(\sqcap_{i_1 \in I_1}, \ldots, \sqcap_{i_k \in I_k}) = \sqcap_{(i_1,\ldots,i_k) \in I_1 \times \cdots \times I_k} g(x_{i_1}, \ldots, x_{i_k})$$

   for arbitrary, non-empty, finite index sets $I_1, \ldots, I_k$.
3. *Every production function g_θ in G is strict in 0 in each argument.*

The abstract grammar problem given in Figure 2 meets the conditions of Theorem 2 because

1. By Definition 3, the $\oplus$ operator is associative, commutative, and idempotent; hence $(D, \oplus)$ is a semilattice. By Definition 3(5), $(D, \oplus)$ has no infinite descending chains.
2. The distributivity of each of the production functions g_1, ..., g_6 over arbitrary, non-empty, finite index sets follows from repeated application of Definition 3(3).

3. Production functions $g_3, \ldots, g_6$ are strict in 0 in each argument because 0 is an annihilator with respect to $\otimes$ (Definition 3(4)). Production functions g_1 and g_2 are constants (i.e., functions with no arguments), and hence meet the required condition trivially.

Thus, one algorithm for solving the GPR problem for a given weighted PDS $\mathcal{W}$, initial configuration $\langle p, \gamma_1 \gamma_2 \ldots \gamma_n \rangle$, and regular set C (represented by automaton $\mathcal{A}$) is as follows:

- Create the combined weighted PDS $\mathcal{WA}$.
- Define the corresponding abstract grammar problem according to the schema shown in Figure 2.
- Solve this abstract grammar problem by finding the maximum fixed point using chaotic iteration: for each nonterminal X, the fixed-point-finding algorithm maintains a value $l(X)$, which is the current estimate for X's value in the maximum fixed-point solution; initially, all $l(X)$ values are set to 0; $l(X)$ is updated whenever a value $l(Y)$ changes, for any Y used on the right-hand side of a production whose left-hand-side nonterminal is X.

3.3 A More Efficient Algorithm for the GPR Problem

The approach given in the previous section is not very efficient: for a configuration $\langle p, \gamma_1 \gamma_2 \ldots \gamma_n \rangle$, it takes $\Theta(|Q|^{n-1}|F|)$ time and space just to create the grammar productions in Figure 2 with left-hand-side nonterminal $Accepting[\gamma_1 \gamma_2 \ldots \gamma_n]_{(p,q)}$. However, we can improve on the algorithm of the previous section because not all instantiations of the productions listed in Figure 2 are relevant to the final solution; we want to prevent the algorithm from exploring useless nonterminals of the grammar shown in Figure 2.

Moreover, all GPR questions with respect to a given target-configuration set C involve the same subgrammar for the PS nonterminals. As in the (ordinary) pushdown-reachability problem [3, 8], the information about whether a complete derivation tree with root nonterminal $PS_{(q,\gamma,q')}$ exists (i.e., whether $PS_{(q,\gamma,q')}$ is a *productive* nonterminal) can be precomputed and returned in the form of an (annotated) automaton of size $\mathcal{O}(|Q||\Delta|+|\rightarrow_0|)$. Exploring the PS subgrammar lazily saves us from having to construct the entire PS subgrammar. Productive nonterminals represent automaton transitions, and the productions that involve any given transition can be constructed on-the-fly, as is done in Algorithm 1, shown in Figure 3.

It is relatively straightforward to see that Algorithm 1 solves the grammar problem for the PS subgrammar from Figure 2: *workset* contains the set of transitions (PS nonterminals) whose value $l(t)$ has been updated since it was last considered; in line 8 all values are set to 0. A function call $update(t, r, T)$ computes the new value for transition t if t can be created using rule r and the transitions in the ordered list T. Lines 9–10 process the rules of types (1) and (2), respectively. Lines 11–17 represent the fixed-point-finding loop: line 13, 15, and 17 simulate the processing of rules of types (3) and (4) that involve transition t on their

Algorithm 1
Input: a weighted pushdown system $\mathcal{W} = (\mathcal{P}, \mathcal{S}, f)$,
   where $\mathcal{P} = (P, \Gamma, \Delta)$ and $\mathcal{S} = (D, \oplus, \otimes, 0, 1)$;
   a $\mathcal{P}$-automaton $\mathcal{A} = (Q, \Gamma, \to_0, P, F)$ that accepts C,
   such that $\mathcal{A}$ has no transitions into P states.

Output: a $\mathcal{P}$-automaton $\mathcal{A}_{pre^*} = (Q, \Gamma, \to, P, F)$ that accepts $pre^*(C)$;
   a function l that maps every $(q, \gamma, q') \in \to$ to the value of $m_G(PS_{(q,\gamma,q')})$
      in the abstract grammar problem defined in Figure 2.

```
 1  procedure update(t, r, T)
 2  begin
 3     → := → ∪ {t};
 4     l(t) := l(t) ⊕ (f(r) ⊗ l(T(1)) ⊗ ... ⊗ l(T(|T|)));
 5     if l(t) changed value then workset := workset ∪ {t}
 6  end
 7
 8  → := →₀;  l ≡ 0;  workset := →₀;
 9  for all t ∈ →₀ do l(t) := 1;
10  for all r = ⟨p, γ⟩ ↪ ⟨p', ε⟩ ∈ Δ do update((p, γ, p'), r, ());
11  while workset ≠ ∅ do
12     select and remove a transition t = (q, γ, q') from workset;
13     for all r = ⟨p₁, γ₁⟩ ↪ ⟨q, γ⟩ ∈ Δ do update((p₁, γ₁, q'), r, (t));
14     for all r = ⟨p₁, γ₁⟩ ↪ ⟨q, γγ₂⟩ ∈ Δ do
15        for all t' = (q', γ₂, q'') ∈ → do update((p₁, γ₁, q''), r, (t, t'));
16     for all r = ⟨p₁, γ₁⟩ ↪ ⟨p', γ₂γ⟩ ∈ Δ do
17        if t' = (p', γ₂, q) ∈ → then update((p₁, γ₁, q'), r, (t', t));
18  return ((Q, Γ, →, P, F), l)
```

Fig. 3. An on-the-fly algorithm for solving the grammar problem for the *PS* subgrammar from Figure 2

right-hand side; in particular, line 4 corresponds to invocations of production functions g_3 and g_4. Note that line 4 can change $l(t)$ only to a smaller value (w.r.t. $\sqsubseteq$). The iterations continue until the values of all transitions stabilize, i.e., *workset* is empty.

From the fact that Algorithm 1 is simply a different way of expressing the grammar problem for the *PS* subgrammar, we know that the algorithm terminates and computes the desired result. Moreover, apart from operations having to do with l, the algorithm is remarkably similar to the pre^* algorithm from [8]—the only major difference being that transitions are stored in a workset and processed multiple times, whereas in [8] each transition is processed exactly once. Thus, the time complexity increases from the $\mathcal{O}(|Q|^2|\Delta|)$ complexity of the unweighted case [8] by a factor that is no more than the length of the maximal-length descending chain in the semiring.

Given the annotated pre^* automaton, the value of $\delta(c)$ for any configuration c can be read off from the automaton by following all paths by which c is accepted—accumulating a value for each path—and taking the meet of the resulting value set. The value-accumulation step can be performed using a straightforward extension of a standard algorithm for simulating an NFA (cf. [1, Algorithm 3.4]).

Algorithm 1 is a dynamic-programming algorithm for determining $\delta(c)$; Appendix A describes how to extend Algorithm 1 to keep additional annotations on transitions so that the path set $\omega(c)$ can be obtained.

4 Applications to Interprocedural Dataflow Analysis

This section describes the application of weighted PDSs to interprocedural dataflow analysis, and shows that the algorithm from Section 3 provides a way to generalize previously known frameworks for interprocedural dataflow analysis [22, 26]. The running example used in this section illustrates the application of the approach to linear constant propagation [22]. G. Balakrishnan has also used the approach to implement an interprocedural dataflow-analysis algorithm due to M. Müller-Olm and H. Seidl, which determines, for each program point n, the set of all affine relations that hold among program variables whenever n is executed [16].

Interprocedural Dataflow Analysis, Supergraphs, and Exploded Supergraphs

Interprocedural dataflow-analysis problems are often defined in terms of a program's *supergraph*, an example of which is shown in Figure 4. A supergraph consists of a collection of control-flow graphs—one for each procedure—one of which represents the program's main procedure. The flowgraph for a procedure p has a unique *enter* node, denoted by e_p, and a unique *exit* node, denoted by x_p. The other nodes of the flowgraph represent statements and conditions of the program in the usual way,[4] except that each procedure call in the program is represented in the supergraph by two nodes, a *call* node and a *return-site* node (e.g., see the node-pairs (n_2, n_3), (n_6, n_7), (n_{11}, n_{12}) in Figure 4). In addition to the ordinary intraprocedural edges that connect the nodes of the individual control-flow graphs, for each procedure call—represented, say, by call node c and return-site node r—the supergraph contains three edges: an intraprocedural *call-to-return-site* edge from c to r; an interprocedural *call-to-enter* edge from c to the enter node of the called procedure; an interprocedural *exit-to-return-site* edge from the exit node of the called procedure to r.

Definition 7. *A* **path** *of length j from node m to node n is a (possibly empty) sequence of j edges, which will be denoted by $[e_1, e_2, \ldots, e_j]$, such that the source*

---
[4] The nodes of a flowgraph can represent individual statements and conditions; alternatively, they can represent basic blocks.

```
int x;

void main() {
    n1: x = 5;
    n2,n3: p();
         return;
}

void p() {
    n4: if (...) {
        n5: x = x + 1;
        n6,n7: p();
        n8: x = x - 1;
    }
    n9: else if (...) {
        n10: x = x - 1;
        n11,n12: p();
        n13: x = x + 1;
    }
    return;
}
```

Fig. 4. A program fragment and its supergraph. The environment transformer for all unlabeled edges is $\lambda e.e$

of e_1 is m, the target of e_j is n, and for all i, $1 \leq i \leq j-1$, the target of edge e_i is the source of edge e_{i+1}. Path concatenation is denoted by $\|$.

The notion of an *(interprocedurally) valid path* is necessary to capture the idea that not all paths in a supergraph represent potential execution paths. A valid path is one that respects the fact that a procedure always returns to the site of the most recent call. We distinguish further between a *same-level valid path*—a path that starts and ends in the same procedure, and in which every call has a corresponding return (and vice versa)—and a *valid path*—a path that may include one or more unmatched calls:

Definition 8. *The sets of* **same-level valid paths** *and* **valid paths** *in a supergraph are defined inductively as follows:*

- *The empty path is a* **same-level valid path** *(and therefore a* **valid path***).*
- *Path $p \| [e]$ is a* **valid path** *if either (i) e is not an exit-to-return-site edge and p is a valid path, or (ii) e is an exit-to-return-site edge and $p = p_h \| [e_c] \| p_t$, where p_t is a same-level valid path, p_h is a valid path, and the source node of e_c is the call node that matches the return-site node at the target of e. Such a path is a* **same-level valid path** *if p_h is also a same-level valid path.*

Example 1. In the supergraph shown in Figure 4, the path

$$e_{main} \to n_1 \to n_2 \to e_p \to n_4 \to n_9 \to n_{14} \to x_p \to n_3$$

is a (same-level) valid path; the path

$$e_{main} \to n_1 \to n_2 \to e_p \to n_4 \to n_9$$

is a (non-same-level) valid path because the call-to-start edge $n_2 \to e_p$ has no matching exit-to-return-site edge; the path

$$e_{main} \to n_1 \to n_2 \to e_p \to n_4 \to n_9 \to n_{14} \to x_p \to n_7$$

is not a valid path because the exit-to-return-site edge $x_p \to n_7$ does not correspond to the preceding call-to-start edge $n_2 \to e_p$.

A context-sensitive interprocedural dataflow analysis is one in which the analysis of a called procedure is "sensitive" to the context in which it is called. A context-sensitive analysis captures the fact that calls on a procedure that arrive via different calling contexts can cause different sets of execution states to arise on entry to a procedure. More precisely, the goal of a context-sensitive analysis is to find the *meet-over-all-valid-paths* value for nodes of a supergraph [14, 22, 26].

The remainder of this section considers the Interprocedural Distributive Environment (IDE) framework for context-sensitive interprocedural dataflow analysis [22]. It applies to problems in which the dataflow information at a program point is represented by a finite environment (*i.e.*, a mapping from a finite set of *symbols* to a finite-height domain of *values*), and the effect of a program operation is captured by an "environment-transformer function" associated with each supergraph edge. The transformer functions are assumed to distribute over the meet operation on environments.

Two IDE problems are (decidable) variants of the constant-propagation problem: *copy-constant propagation* and *linear-constant propagation*. The former interprets assignment statements of the form $x = 7$ and $y = x$. The latter also interprets statements of the form $y = -2 * x + 5$.

By means of an "explosion transformation", an IDE problem can be transformed from a path problem on a program's supergraph to a path problem on a graph that is *larger*, but in which every edge is labeled with a much *simpler* edge function (a so-called "micro-function") [22]. Each micro-function on an edge $d_1 \to d_2$ captures the effect that the value of symbol d_1 in the argument environment has on the value of symbol d_2 in the result environment. Figure 5 shows the exploded representations of four environment-transformer functions used in linear constant propagation. Figure 5(a) shows how the identity function $\lambda e.e$ is represented. Figure 5(b)–Figure 5(d) show the representations of the functions $\lambda e.e[x \mapsto 7]$, $\lambda e.e[y \mapsto e(x)]$, and $\lambda e.e[y \mapsto -2 * e(x) + 5]$, which are the dataflow functions for the assignment statements $x = 7$, $y = x$, and $y = -2 * x + 5$, respectively. (The Λ vertices are used to represent the effects of a function that

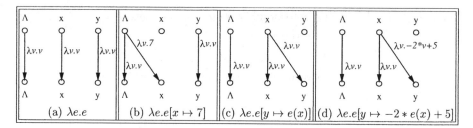

Fig. 5. The exploded representations of four environment-transformer functions used in linear constant propagation

are independent of the argument environment. Each graph includes an edge of the form $\Lambda \to \Lambda$, labeled with $\lambda v.v$; these edges are needed to capture function composition properly [22].)

Figure 6 shows the exploded supergraph that corresponds to the program from Figure 4 for the linear constant-propagation problem.

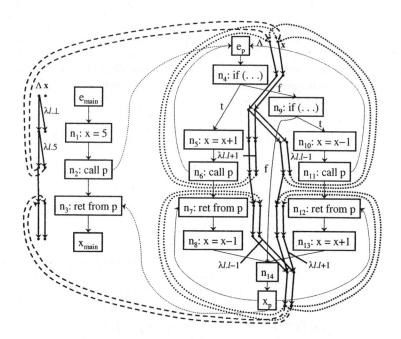

Fig. 6. The exploded supergraph of the program from Figure 4 for the linear constant-propagation problem. The micro-functions are all *id*, except where indicated

From Exploded Supergraphs to Weighted PDSs

We now show how to solve linear constant-propagation problems in a context-sensitive fashion by defining a generalized pushdown reachability problem in which the paths of the (infinite-state) transition system correspond to valid paths in the exploded supergraph from (e_{main}, Λ). To do this, we encode the exploded supergraph as a weighted PDS whose weights are drawn from a semiring whose value set is the set of functions

$$F_{lc} = \{\lambda l.\top\} \cup \{\lambda l.(a * l + b) \sqcap c \mid a \in \mathbb{Z}, b \in \mathbb{Z}, \text{and } c \in \mathbb{Z}_\bot^\top\}.$$

Every function $f \in F_{lc} - \{\lambda l.\top\}$ can be represented by a triple (a, b, c), where $a \in \mathbb{Z}, b \in \mathbb{Z}, c \in \mathbb{Z}_\bot^\top$, and

$$f = \lambda l. \begin{cases} \top & \text{if } l = \top \\ (a * l + b) \sqcap c & \text{otherwise} \end{cases}$$

The third component c is needed so that the meet of two functions can be represented. (See [22] for details.) The semiring value 0 is $\lambda l.\top$; the semiring value 1 is the identity function, whose representation is $(1, 0, \top)$. We also denote the identity function by id. By convention, a constant function $\lambda l.b$ is represented as $(0, b, \top)$.

The operations $\oplus$ and $\otimes$ are defined as follows:

$$(a_2, b_2, c_2) \oplus (a_1, b_1, c_1) = \begin{cases} (a_1, b_1, c_1 \sqcap c_2) & \text{if } a_1 = a_2 \text{ and } b_1 = b_2 \\ (a_1, b_1, c) & \text{where } c = (a_1 * l_0 + b_1) \sqcap c_1 \sqcap c_2, \\ & \text{if } l_0 = (b_1 - b_2)/(a_2 - a_1) \in \mathbb{Z} \\ (1, 0, \bot) & \text{otherwise} \end{cases}$$

$$(a_2, b_2, c_2) \otimes (a_1, b_1, c_1) = ((a_1 * a_2), (a_1 * b_2 + b_1), ((a_1 * c_2 + b_1) \sqcap c_1)).$$

Here it is assumed that $x * \top = \top * x = x + \top = \top + x = \top$ for $x \in \mathbb{Z}_\bot^\top$ and that $x * \bot = \bot * x = x + \bot = \bot + x = \bot$ for $x \in \mathbb{Z}_\bot$. The second case for the combiner operator is obtained by equating the terms $a_1 * y + b_1$ and $a_2 * y + b_2$ and taking the solution for y, provided it is integral.

The control locations correspond to the program's variables (and also to Λ). Stack symbols, such as n_4, n_5 and n_6, correspond to nodes of the supergraph.

With one exception, each edge in the exploded supergraph corresponds to one rule of the weighted PDS. The encoding can be described in terms of the kinds of edges that occur in the supergraph.

A few of the weighted PDS's rules for the (exploded) intraprocedural edges are as follows:

Intraprocedural edges in main	
$\langle \Lambda, n_1 \rangle \hookrightarrow \langle \Lambda, n_2 \rangle$	id
$\langle \Lambda, n_1 \rangle \hookrightarrow \langle x, n_2 \rangle$	$\lambda l.5$
$\langle \Lambda, n_3 \rangle \hookrightarrow \langle \Lambda, x_{main} \rangle$	id
$\langle x, n_3 \rangle \hookrightarrow \langle x, x_{main} \rangle$	id

Intraprocedural edges in p	
$\langle \Lambda, n_4 \rangle \hookrightarrow \langle \Lambda, n_5 \rangle$	id
$\langle x, n_4 \rangle \hookrightarrow \langle x, n_5 \rangle$	id
$\langle \Lambda, n_5 \rangle \hookrightarrow \langle \Lambda, n_6 \rangle$	id
$\langle x, n_5 \rangle \hookrightarrow \langle x, n_6 \rangle$	$\lambda l.l + 1$

In a rule such as

$$\langle x, n_5\rangle \hookrightarrow \langle x, n_6\rangle \qquad \lambda l.l+1 \qquad (1)$$

the second component of each tuple implies that the currently active procedure is p, and the rest of the stack is not changed.

At each call site, each PDS rule that encodes an edge in the exploded representation of a call-to-enter edge has two stack symbols on its right-hand side. The second symbol is the name of the corresponding return-site node, which is pushed on the stack:

Transitions for call site n_2		Transitions for call site n_6		Transitions for call site n_{11}	
$\langle \Lambda, n_2\rangle \hookrightarrow \langle \Lambda, e_p\ n_3\rangle$	id	$\langle \Lambda, n_6\rangle \hookrightarrow \langle \Lambda, e_p\ n_7\rangle$	id	$\langle \Lambda, n_{11}\rangle \hookrightarrow \langle \Lambda, e_p\ n_{12}\rangle$	id
$\langle x, n_2\rangle \hookrightarrow \langle x, e_p\ n_3\rangle$	id	$\langle x, n_6\rangle \hookrightarrow \langle x, e_p\ n_7\rangle$	id	$\langle x, n_{11}\rangle \hookrightarrow \langle x, e_p\ n_{12}\rangle$	id

The process of returning from p is encoded by popping the topmost stack symbols off the stack.

Transitions to return from p	
$\langle \Lambda, x_p\rangle \hookrightarrow \langle \Lambda, \varepsilon\rangle$	id
$\langle x, x_p\rangle \hookrightarrow \langle x, \varepsilon\rangle$	id

Obtaining Dataflow Information from the Exploded Supergraph's Weighted PDS

For linear constant propagation, we are interested in a generalized reachability problem from configuration $\langle \Lambda, e_{main}\rangle$. Thus, to obtain dataflow information from the exploded supergraph's weighted PDS, we perform the following steps:

- Define a regular language R for the configurations of interest. This can be done by creating an automaton for R, and giving each edge of the automaton the weight id.
- Apply Algorithm 1 to create a weighted automaton for $pre^*(R)$.
- Inspect the $pre^*(R)$-automaton to find the transition $\Lambda \xrightarrow{e_{main}}$ $accepting\_state$. Return the weight on this transition as the answer.

In the following, we often write $\langle x, \alpha\rangle$, where α is a regular expression, to mean the set of all configurations $\langle x, w\rangle$ where w is in the language of stack contents defined by α.

Example 2. For the query $pre^*(\langle x, e_p\ (n_{12}\ n_7)^*\ n_3\rangle)$, the semiring value associated with the configuration $\langle \Lambda, e_{main}\rangle$ is $\lambda l.5$, which means that the value of program variable x must be 5 whenever p is entered with a stack of the form "$e_p\ (n_{12}\ n_7)^*\ n_3$"; i.e., main called p, which then called itself recursively an arbitrary number of times, alternating between the two recursive call sites.

A witness-path set for the configuration $\langle A, e_{main} \rangle$ is a singleton set, consisting of the following path:

Semiring value	Configuration	Rule	Rule weight
$\lambda l.5$	$\langle A, e_{main} \rangle$	$\langle A, e_{main} \rangle \hookrightarrow \langle A, n_1 \rangle$	id
$\lambda l.5$	$\langle A, n_1 \rangle$	$\langle A, n_1 \rangle \hookrightarrow \langle x, n_2 \rangle$	$\lambda l.5$
id	$\langle x, n_2 \rangle$	$\langle x, n_2 \rangle \hookrightarrow \langle x, e_p \ n_3 \rangle$	id
id	$\langle x, e_p \ n_3 \rangle$	Configuration accepted by query automaton	

Example 3. One example of a situation in which the stack is of the form $e_p \ (n_{12} \ n_7)^* \ n_3$ is when *main* calls p at n_2 (n_3); p calls p at n_6 (n_7); and finally p calls p at n_{11} (n_{12}). In this case, the stack contains $e_p \ n_{12} \ n_7 \ n_3$. As expected, for the query $pre^*(\langle x, e_p \ n_{12} \ n_7 \ n_3 \rangle)$, the semiring value associated with the configuration $\langle A, e_{main} \rangle$ is $\lambda l.5$.

In this case, a witness-path set for the configuration $\langle A, e_{main} \rangle$ is a singleton set, consisting of the following path:

Semiring value	Configuration	Rule	Rule weight
$\lambda l.5$	$\langle A, e_{main} \rangle$	$\langle A, e_{main} \rangle \hookrightarrow \langle A, n_1 \rangle$	id
$\lambda l.5$	$\langle A, n_1 \rangle$	$\langle A, n_1 \rangle \hookrightarrow \langle x, n_2 \rangle$	$\lambda l.5$
id	$\langle x, n_2 \rangle$	$\langle x, n_2 \rangle \hookrightarrow \langle x, e_p \ n_3 \rangle$	id
id	$\langle x, e_p \ n_3 \rangle$	$\langle x, e_p \rangle \hookrightarrow \langle x, n_4 \rangle$	id
id	$\langle x, n_4 \ n_3 \rangle$	$\langle x, n_4 \rangle \hookrightarrow \langle x, n_5 \rangle$	id
id	$\langle x, n_5 \ n_3 \rangle$	$\langle x, n_5 \rangle \hookrightarrow \langle x, n_6 \rangle$	$\lambda l.l + 1$
$\lambda l.l - 1$	$\langle x, n_6 \ n_3 \rangle$	$\langle x, n_6 \rangle \hookrightarrow \langle x, e_p \ n_7 \rangle$	id
$\lambda l.l - 1$	$\langle x, e_p \ n_7 \ n_3 \rangle$	$\langle x, e_p \rangle \hookrightarrow \langle x, n_4 \rangle$	id
$\lambda l.l - 1$	$\langle x, n_4 \ n_7 \ n_3 \rangle$	$\langle x, n_4 \rangle \hookrightarrow \langle x, n_9 \rangle$	id
$\lambda l.l - 1$	$\langle x, n_9 \ n_7 \ n_3 \rangle$	$\langle x, n_9 \rangle \hookrightarrow \langle x, n_{10} \rangle$	id
$\lambda l.l - 1$	$\langle x, n_{10} \ n_7 \ n_3 \rangle$	$\langle x, n_{10} \rangle \hookrightarrow \langle x, n_{11} \rangle$	$\lambda l.l - 1$
id	$\langle x, n_{11} \ n_7 \ n_3 \rangle$	$\langle x, n_{11} \rangle \hookrightarrow \langle x, e_p \ n_{12} \rangle$	id
id	$\langle x, e_p \ n_{12} \ n_7 \ n_3 \rangle$	Configuration accepted by query automaton	

Notice that the witness-path set for the configuration $\langle A, e_{main} \rangle$ is more complicated in the case of the query $pre^*(\langle x, e_p \ n_{12} \ n_7 \ n_3 \rangle)$ than in the case of the query $pre^*(\langle x, e_p \ (n_{12} \ n_7)^* \ n_3 \rangle)$, even though the latter involves a regular operator.

Example 4. Conventional dataflow-analysis algorithms merge together (via meet, i.e., $\oplus$) the values for each program point, regardless of calling context. The machinery described in this paper provides a strict generalization of conventional dataflow analysis because the merged information can be obtained by issuing an appropriate query.

For instance, the value that the algorithms given in [14, 22, 26] would obtain for the tuple $\langle x, e_p \rangle$ can be obtained via the query $pre^*(\langle x, e_p \ (n_7 + n_{12})^* \ n_3 \rangle)$. When we perform this query, the semiring value associated with the configuration $\langle A, e_{main} \rangle$ is $\lambda l.\bot$. This means that the value of program variable x may not always be the same when p is entered with a stack of the form "$e_p\ (n_7+n_{12})^*\ n_3$". For this situation, a witness-path set for the configuration $\langle \Lambda, e_{main} \rangle$ consists of two paths, which share the first four configurations; the semiring value associated with $\langle x, e_p\ n_3 \rangle$ is $\lambda l.\bot = id \oplus \lambda l.l - 1$:

Semiring value	Configuration	Rule	Rule weight
$\lambda l.\bot$	$\langle \Lambda, e_{main} \rangle$	$\langle \Lambda, e_{main} \rangle \hookrightarrow \langle \Lambda, n_1 \rangle$	id
$\lambda l.\bot$	$\langle \Lambda, n_1 \rangle$	$\langle \Lambda, n_1 \rangle \hookrightarrow \langle x, n_2 \rangle$	$\lambda l.5$
$\lambda l.\bot$	$\langle x, n_2 \rangle$	$\langle x, n_2 \rangle \hookrightarrow \langle x, e_p\ n_3 \rangle$	id
$\lambda l.\bot$	$\langle x, e_p\ n_3 \rangle$		
id	$\langle x, e_p\ n_3 \rangle$	Configuration accepted by query automaton	
$\lambda l.l - 1$	$\langle x, e_p\ n_3 \rangle$	$\langle x, e_p \rangle \hookrightarrow \langle x, n_4 \rangle$	id
$\lambda l.l - 1$	$\langle x, n_4\ n_3 \rangle$	$\langle x, n_4 \rangle \hookrightarrow \langle x, n_9 \rangle$	id
$\lambda l.l - 1$	$\langle x, n_9\ n_3 \rangle$	$\langle x, n_9 \rangle \hookrightarrow \langle x, n_{10} \rangle$	id
$\lambda l.l - 1$	$\langle x, n_{10}\ n_3 \rangle$	$\langle x, n_{10} \rangle \hookrightarrow \langle x, n_{11} \rangle$	$\lambda l.l - 1$
id	$\langle x, n_{11}\ n_3 \rangle$	$\langle x, n_{11} \rangle \hookrightarrow \langle x, e_p\ n_{12} \rangle$	id
id	$\langle x, e_p\ n_{12}\ n_3 \rangle$	Configuration accepted by query automaton	

The Complexity of the Dataflow-Analysis Algorithm

Let E denote the number of edges in the supergraph, and let *Var* denote the number of symbols in the domain of an environment. The encoding of an exploded supergraph as a PDS leads to a PDS with *Var* control locations and $|\Delta| = E \cdot$ *Var* rules. If R is the regular language of configurations of interest, assume that R can be encoded by a weighted automaton with $|Q| = s +$ *Var* states and t transitions. Let l denote the maximal length of a descending chain in the semiring formed by the micro-functions.

The cost of a pre^* query to obtain dataflow information for R is therefore no worse than $\mathcal{O}(s^2 \cdot$ *Var* $\cdot E \cdot l +$ *Var*$^3 \cdot E \cdot l)$ time and $\mathcal{O}(s \cdot$ *Var* $\cdot E +$ *Var*$^2 \cdot E + t)$ space, according to the results of Section 3 and [8].

How Clients of Dataflow Analysis Can Take Advantage of this Machinery

Algorithm 1 and the construction given above provide a new algorithm for interprocedural dataflow analysis. As demonstrated by Examples 2, 3, and 4, with the weighted-PDS machinery, dataflow queries can be posed with respect to a regular language of initial stack configurations, which provides a strict generalization of the kind of queries that can be posed using ordinary interprocedural dataflow-analysis algorithms.

For clients of interprocedural dataflow analysis, such as program optimizers and tools for program understanding, this offers the ability to provide features that were previously unavailable:

– A program optimizer could make a query about dataflow values according to a possible pattern of inline expansions. This would allow the optimizer to determine—*without first performing an explicit expansion*—whether the inline expansion would produce favorable dataflow values that would allow the code to be optimized.
– A tool for program understanding could let users pose queries about dataflow information with respect to a regular language of initial stack configurations.

The first of these possibilities is illustrated by Figure 7, which shows a transformed version of the program from Figure 4. The transformed program takes advantage of the information obtained from Example 2, namely, that in Figure 4 the value of x is 5 whenever p is entered with a stack of the form "$e_p\,(n_{12}\,n_7)^*\,n_3$". In the transformed program, all calls to p that mimic the calling pattern "$(n_{12}\,n_7)^*\,n_3$" (from the original program) are replaced by calls to p'. In p', a copy of p has been inlined (and simplified) at the first recursive call site. Whenever the calling pattern fails to mimic "$(n_{12}\,n_7)^*\,n_3$", the original procedure p is called instead.

```
int x;

void main() {
    x = 5;
    p'();
    return;
}

void p() {
    if (...) {
        x = x + 1;
        p();
        x = x - 1;
    }
    else if (...) {
        x = x - 1;
        p();
        x = x + 1;
    }
    return;
}
```

```
void p'() {
    if (...) {
        if (...) {   // Inlined call n6,n7
            x = 7;
            p();     // n6,n7; n6,n7
        }
        else if (...) {
            p'();    // n6,n7; n11,n12
        } // End inlined call n6,n7
    }
    else if (...) {
        x = 4;
        p();
    }
    x = 5;
    return;
}
```

Fig. 7. A transformed version of the program from Figure 4 that takes advantage of the fact that in Figure 4 the value of x is 5 whenever p is entered with a stack of the form "$e_p\,(n_{12}\,n_7)^*\,n_3$"

5 Related Work

Several connections between dataflow analysis and model checking have been established in past work [27, 28, 23, 6]. The present paper continues this line of inquiry, but makes two contributions:

- Previous work addressed the relationship between model checking and *bit-vector* dataflow-analysis problems, such as live-variable analysis and partial-redundancy elimination. In this paper, we show how a technique inspired by one developed in the model-checking community [3, 8]—but generalized from its original form [25]—can be applied to certain dataflow-analysis problems that cannot be expressed as bit-vector problems.
- Previous work has used temporal-logic expressions to specify dataflow-analysis problems. This paper's results are based on a more basic model-checking primitive, namely pre^*. (The approach also extends to $post^*$.)

These ideas have been illustrated by applying them to linear constant propagation, which is not expressible as a bit-vector problem.

Bouajjani, Esparza, and Toulli [4] independently developed a similar framework, in which pre^* and $post^*$ queries on pushdown systems with weights drawn from a semiring are used to solve (overapproximations of) reachability questions on concurrent communicating pushdown systems. Their method of obtaining weights on automaton transitions significantly differs from ours. Instead of deriving the weights directly, they are obtained using a fixpoint computation on a matrix whose entries are the transitions of the pre^* automaton. This allows them to obtain weights even when the semiring does have infinite descending chains (provided the extender operator is commutative), but leads to a less efficient solution for the finite-chain case. In the latter case, in the terms of Section 4, their algorithm has time complexity $\mathcal{O}(((s+Var) \cdot E \cdot Var + t)^2 \cdot E \cdot Var \cdot (s+Var) \cdot l)$, i.e., proportional to Var^6 and E^3. All but one of the semirings used in [4] have only finite descending chains, so Algorithm 1 applies to those cases and provides a more efficient solution.

The most closely related papers in the dataflow-analysis literature are those that address demand-driven interprocedural dataflow analysis.

- Reps [19, 18] presented a way in which algorithms that solve demand versions of interprocedural analysis problems can be obtained automatically from their exhaustive counterparts (expressed as logic programs) by making use of the "magic-sets transformation" [2], which is a general transformation developed in the logic-programming and deductive-database communities for creating efficient demand versions of (bottom-up) logic programs, and/or tabulation [29], which is another method for efficiently evaluating recursive queries in deductive databases. This approach was used to obtain demand algorithms for interprocedural bit-vector problems.

- Subsequent work by Reps, Horwitz, and Sagiv extended the logic-prgramming approach to the class of IFDS problems [20].[5] They also gave an explicit demand algorithm for IFDS problems that does not rely on the magic-sets transformation [11].
- Both exhaustive and demand algorithms for solving a certain class of IDE problems are presented in [22]. The relationship between the two algorithms given in that paper is similar to the relationship between the exhaustive [20] and demand [11] algorithms for IFDS problems.
- A fourth approach to obtaining demand versions of interprocedural dataflow-analysis algorithms was investigated by Duesterwald, Gupta, and Soffa [7]. In their approach, for each query a collection of dataflow equations is set up on the flow graph (but as if all edges were reversed). The flow functions on the reverse graph are the (approximate) inverses of the forward flow functions. These equations are then solved using a demand-driven fixed-point-finding procedure.

None of the demand algorithms described above support the ability to answer a query with respect to a user-supplied language of stack configurations. As with previous work on dataflow analysis, those algorithms merge together (via meet, i.e., $\oplus$) the values for each program point, regardless of calling context. In addition, past work on demand-driven dataflow analysis has not examined the issue of providing a witness set of paths to show why the answer to a dataflow query for a particular configuration has the value reported.

The IFDS framework can be extended with the ability to answer a query with respect to a language of stack configurations by applying the reachability algorithms for (unweighted) PDSs [3, 8] on the graphs used in [20, 11]; however, that approach does not work for the more general IDE framework. This paper has shown how to extend the IDE framework to answer a query with respect to a language of stack configurations, using our recent generalization of PDS reachability algorithms to weighted PDSs [25].

It should be noted that, like the algorithms from [22], the algorithm for solving GPR problems given in Section 3 is not guaranteed to terminate for all IDE problems; however, like the algorithms from [22], it does terminate for all copy-constant-propagation problems, all linear-constant-propagation problems, and, in general, all problems for which the set of micro-functions contains no infinite descending chains. The asymptotic cost of the algorithm in this paper is the same as the cost of the demand algorithm for solving IDE problems from [22]; however, that algorithm is strictly less general than the algorithm presented here (cf. Example 4).

An application of the theory of PDSs to interprocedural dataflow analysis has been proposed by Esparza and Knoop [9], who considered several bit-vector problems, as well as the faint-variables problem, which is an IFDS problem [21, Appendix A]. These problems are solved using certain *pre** and *post** queries.

---

[5] Logic-programming terminology is not used in [20]; however, the exhaustive algorithm described there has a straightforward implementation as a logic program. A demand algorithm can then be obtained by applying the magic-sets transformation.

With respect to that work, the extension of PDSs to weighted PDSs allows our approach to solve a more general class of dataflow-analysis problems than Esparza and Knoop's techniques can handle; the witness-set generation algorithm can also be used to extend their algorithms. (Esparza and Knoop also consider bit-vector problems for flow-graph systems with parallelism, which we have not addressed.)

Müller-Olm and Seidl have given an interprocedural dataflow-analysis algorithm that determines, for each program point n, the set of all affine relations that hold among program variables whenever n is executed [16]. This method can be re-cast as solving a GPR problem (with the same asymptotic complexity). G. Balakrishnan has created a prototype implementation of this method using the WPDS library [24].

Model checking of PDSs has previously been used for verifying security properties of programs [10, 12, 5]. The methods described in this paper should permit more powerful security-verification algorithms to be developed that use weighted PDSs to obtain a broader class of interprocedural dataflow information for use in the verification process.

Acknowledgments

We thank H. Seidl for making available reference [16].

References

1. A.V. Aho, R. Sethi, and J.D. Ullman. *Compilers: Principles, Techniques and Tools*. Addison-Wesley, 1985.
2. F. Bancilhon, D. Maier, Y. Sagiv, and J. Ullman. Magic sets and other strange ways to implement logic programs. In *Proceedings of the Fifth ACM Symposium on Principles of Database Systems*, New York, NY, 1986. ACM Press.
3. A. Bouajjani, J. Esparza, and O. Maler. Reachability analysis of pushdown automata: Application to model checking. In *Proc. CONCUR*, volume 1243 of *Lec. Notes in Comp. Sci.*, pages 135–150. Springer-Verlag, 1997.
4. A. Bouajjani, J. Esparza, and T. Touili. A generic approach to the static analysis of concurrent programs with procedures. In *Proc. Symp. on Princ. of Prog. Lang.*, pages 62–73, 2003.
5. H. Chen and D. Wagner. MOPS: An infrastructure for examining security properties of software. In *Conf. on Comp. and Commun. Sec.*, November 2002.
6. P. Cousot and R. Cousot. Temporal abstract interpretation. In *Symp. on Princ. of Prog. Lang.*, pages 12–25, 2000.
7. E. Duesterwald, R. Gupta, and M.L. Soffa. Demand-driven computation of interprocedural data flow. In *Symp. on Princ. of Prog. Lang.*, pages 37–48, New York, NY, 1995. ACM Press.
8. J. Esparza, D. Hansel, P. Rossmanith, and S. Schwoon. Efficient algorithms for model checking pushdown systems. In *Proc. Computer-Aided Verif.*, volume 1855 of *Lec. Notes in Comp. Sci.*, pages 232–247, July 2000.
9. J. Esparza and J. Knoop. An automata-theoretic approach to interprocedural data-flow analysis. In *Proceedings of FoSSaCS'99*, volume 1578 of *LNCS*, pages 14–30. Springer, 1999.

10. J. Esparza, A. Kučera, and S. Schwoon. Model-checking LTL with regular valuations for pushdown systems. In *Proceedings of TACAS'01*, volume 2031 of *LNCS*, pages 306–339. Springer, 2001.
11. S. Horwitz, T. Reps, and M. Sagiv. Demand interprocedural dataflow analysis. In *Proceedings of the Third ACM SIGSOFT Symposium on the Foundations of Software Engineering*, pages 104–115, New York, NY, October 1995. ACM Press.
12. T. Jensen, D. Le Metayer, and T. Thorn. Verification of control flow based security properties. In *1999 IEEE Symposium on Security and Privacy*, May 1999.
13. S. Jha and T. Reps. Analysis of SPKI/SDSI certificates using model checking. In *IEEE Comp. Sec. Found. Workshop (CSFW)*. IEEE Computer Society Press, 2002.
14. J. Knoop and B. Steffen. The interprocedural coincidence theorem. In *Int. Conf. on Comp. Construct.*, pages 125–140, 1992.
15. U. Moencke and R. Wilhelm. Grammar flow analysis. In H. Alblas and B. Melichar, editors, *Attribute Grammars, Applications and Systems*, volume 545 of *Lec. Notes in Comp. Sci.*, pages 151–186, Prague, Czechoslovakia, June 1991. Springer-Verlag.
16. M. Müller-Olm and H. Seidl. Computing interprocedurally valid relations in affine programs. Tech. rep., Comp. Sci. Dept., Univ. of Trier, Trier, Ger., January 2003.
17. G. Ramalingam. *Bounded Incremental Computation*, volume 1089 of *Lec. Notes in Comp. Sci.* Springer-Verlag, 1996.
18. T. Reps. Demand interprocedural program analysis using logic databases. In R. Ramakrishnan, editor, *Applications of Logic Databases*. Kluwer Academic Publishers, 1994.
19. T. Reps. Solving demand versions of interprocedural analysis problems. In P. Fritzson, editor, *Proceedings of the Fifth International Conference on Compiler Construction*, volume 786 of *Lec. Notes in Comp. Sci.*, pages 389–403, Edinburgh, Scotland, April 1994. Springer-Verlag.
20. T. Reps, S. Horwitz, and M. Sagiv. Precise interprocedural dataflow analysis via graph reachability. In *Symp. on Princ. of Prog. Lang.*, pages 49–61, New York, NY, 1995. ACM Press.
21. T. Reps, M. Sagiv, and S. Horwitz. Interprocedural dataflow analysis via graph reachability. Tech. Rep. TR 94-14, Datalogisk Institut, Univ. of Copenhagen, 1994. Available at http://www.cs.wisc.edu/wpis/papers/diku-tr94-14.ps.
22. M. Sagiv, T. Reps, and S. Horwitz. Precise interprocedural dataflow analysis with applications to constant propagation. *Theor. Comp. Sci.*, 167:131–170, 1996.
23. D. Schmidt. Data-flow analysis is model checking of abstract interpretations. In *Symp. on Princ. of Prog. Lang.*, pages 38–48, New York, NY, January 1998. ACM Press.
24. S. Schwoon. WPDS – a library for Weighted Pushdown Systems, 2003. Available from http://www7.in.tum.de/~schwoon/moped/#wpds.
25. S. Schwoon, S. Jha, T. Reps, and S. Stubblebine. On generalized authorization problems. In *Comp. Sec. Found. Workshop*, Wash., DC, 2003. IEEE Comp. Soc.
26. M. Sharir and A. Pnueli. Two approaches to interprocedural data flow analysis. In S.S. Muchnick and N.D. Jones, editors, *Program Flow Analysis: Theory and Applications*, chapter 7, pages 189–234. Prentice-Hall, Englewood Cliffs, NJ, 1981.
27. B. Steffen. Data flow analysis as model checking. In *Int. Conf. on Theor. Aspects of Comp. Softw.*, volume 526 of *Lec. Notes in Comp. Sci.*, pages 346–365. Springer-Verlag, 1991.
28. B. Steffen. Generating data flow analysis algorithms from modal specifications. *Sci. of Comp. Prog.*, 21(2):115–139, 1993.
29. D.S. Warren. Memoing for logic programs. *Communications of the ACM*, 35(3):93–111, March 1992.

A Generation of Witness Sets

Section 3.3 gives an efficient algorithm for determining $\delta(c)$; this section addresses the question of how to obtain $\omega(c)$. It may help to think of this problem as that of examining an infinite graph $\mathcal{G}$ whose nodes are pairs (c, d), where c is a configuration and d a value from D, and in which there is an edge from (c_1, d_1) to (c_2, d_2) labeled with $r \in \Delta$ if and only if $c_1 \stackrel{\langle r \rangle}{\Longrightarrow} c_2$ and $f(r) \otimes d_2 = d_1$. For a given configuration c, finding $\omega(c)$ means identifying a set of paths $\sigma_1, \ldots, \sigma_k$ such that path σ_i, $1 \leq i \leq k$, leads from some (c, d_i) to some $(c_i, 1)$, where $c_i \in C$, and $\bigoplus_{i=1}^{k} d_i = \delta(c)$. In other words, $\omega(c) = \{\sigma_1, \ldots, \sigma_k\}$ proves that $\delta(c)$ really has the value computed by Algorithm 1. We note the following properties:

- In general, k may be larger than 1, e.g., we might have a situation where $\delta(c) = d_1 \oplus d_2$ because of two paths with values d_1 and d_2, but there may be no single path with value $d_1 \oplus d_2$.
- We want to keep $\omega(c)$ as small as possible. If a witness set contains two paths σ_1 and σ_2, where $v(\sigma_1) \sqsubseteq v(\sigma_2)$, then the same set without σ_2 is still a witness set.

Like $\delta(c)$, $\omega(c)$ will be given indirectly in the form of another annotation (called n) on the transitions of $\mathcal{A}_{pre^*}$. We use two data structures for this, called *wnode* and *wstruc*. If t is a transition, then $n(t)$ holds a reference to a *wnode*. (We shall denote a reference to some entity e by $[e]$.) A *wnode* is a set of *wstruc* items. A *wstruc* item is of the form $(d, [t], [r], N)$ where $d \in D$, $[t]$ is a reference back to t, $r \in \Delta$ is a rule, and N contains a sequence of references to *wnodes*. References may be *nil*, indicating a missing reference.

We can now extend Algorithm 1. The idea is that during execution, if $n(t) = [S]$, then $l(t) = \bigoplus_{(d,[t],[r],N) \in S} d$. An item $(d, [t], [r], N)$ in S denotes the following: Suppose that $\mathcal{A}_{pre^*}$ has an accepting path starting with t, and c is the configuration accepted by this path. Then, in the pushdown system, there is a path (or rather, a family of paths) with value d from c to some $c' \in C$, and this path starts with r. An accepting path (in $\mathcal{A}_{pre^*}$) for a successor configuration can be constructed by replacing t with the transitions associated with the *wnodes* in N.

The concrete modifications to Algorithm 1 are as follows: In line 8, set $n \equiv nil$. In line 9, create a *wnode* $n := \{(1, [t], nil, ())\}$ for every $t \in \to_0$ and set $n(t) := [n]$.

Figure 8 shows a revised *update* procedure. Line 4 of Figure 8 computes the newly discovered value for transition t, and line 5 records how the new path was discovered. In line 6, if $l(t) \sqsubseteq d$, the update will not change $l(t)$ and nothing further needs to be done. If $d \sqsubset l(t)$ (see line 8), the new addition is strictly smaller than any path to t so far, and $n(t)$ only has to reference the new path. If d and $l(t)$ are incomparable, line 10 creates a new set consisting of the previous paths *and* the new path. Even though d is incomparable to $l(t)$, d might approximate ($\sqsubseteq$) one or more elements of S. The procedure *minimize* (not shown) removes these.

Algorithm 2
1 **procedure** $update(t, r, T)$
2 **begin**
3     $\to := \to \cup \{t\}$;
4     $d := f(r) \otimes l(T(1)) \otimes \ldots \otimes l(T(|T|))$;
5     $s := (d, [t], [r], (n(t') \mid t' \in T))$;
6   **if** $l(t) \sqsubseteq d$ **then return**;
7   **if** $n(t) = nil$ **or** $d \sqsubset l(t)$ **then**
8   create $n := \{s\}$;
9   **else**
10   create $n := minimize(S \cup \{s\})$, where $n(t) = [S]$;
11    $n(t) := [n]$;
12    $l(t) := l(t) \oplus d$;
13    $workset := workset \cup \{t\}$
14 **end**

Fig. 8. Modified *update* procedure

It is fairly straightforward to see that the information contained in S allows the reconstruction of a witness set involving t (see above). Moreover, every *wnode* created during execution contains references only to *wnode*s created earlier. Therefore, the process of reconstructing the witness set by decoding *wnode*/*wstruc* information must eventually terminate in a configuration from C.

During execution of the modified algorithm, several *wnode*s for the same transition t can be created; only one of them is referenced by t at any moment, although the other *wnode*s may still be referenced by other transitions. A garbage collector can be used to keep track of the references and remove those nodes to which there is no longer any chain of references from any transition.

Client-Driven Pointer Analysis

Samuel Z. Guyer and Calvin Lin

Department of Computer Sciences
The University of Texas at Austin, Austin, TX 78712, USA
{sammy,lin}@cs.utexas.edu

Abstract. This paper presents a new *client-driven* pointer analysis algorithm that automatically adjusts its precision in response to the needs of client analyses. We evaluate our algorithm on 18 real C programs, using five significant error detection problems as clients. We compare the accuracy and performance of our algorithm against several commonly-used fixed-precision algorithms. We find that the client-driven approach effectively balances cost and precision, often producing results as accurate as fixed-precision algorithms that are many times more costly. Our algorithm works because many client problems only need a small amount of extra precision applied to the right places in each input program.

1 Introduction

Pointer analysis is critical for effectively analyzing programs written in languages like C, C++, and Java, which make heavy use of pointers and pointer-based data structures. Pointer analysis attempts to disambiguate indirect memory references, so that subsequent compiler passes have a more accurate view of program behavior. In this sense, pointer analysis is not a stand-alone task: its purpose is to provide pointer information to other *client* analyses.

Existing pointer analysis algorithms differ considerably in their precision. Previous research has generally agreed that more precise algorithms are often significantly more costly to compute, but has disagreed on whether more precise algorithms yield more accurate results, and whether these results are worth the additional cost [19, 18, 13, 7, 16]. Despite these differences, a recent survey claims that the choice of pointer analysis algorithm should be dictated by the needs of the client analyses [12].

```
p = safe_string_copy("Good");        char*safe_string_copy(char*s)
q = safe_string_copy("Bad");         {
r = safe_string_copy("Ugly");            if (s!= 0) return strdup(s);
                                         else return 0;
                                     }
```

Fig. 1. Context-insensitive pointer analysis hurts accuracy, but whether or not that matters depends on the client analysis

In this paper we present a new *client-driven* pointer analysis algorithm that addresses this viewpoint directly: it automatically adjusts its precision to match the needs of the client. The key idea is to discover where precision is needed by running a fast initial pass of the client. The pointer and client analyses run together in an integrated framework, allowing the client to provide feedback about the quality of the pointer information it receives. Using these initial results, our algorithm constructs a precision policy customized to the needs of the client and input program. This approach is related to demand-driven analysis [14, 11], but solves a different problem: while demand-driven algorithms determine which parts of the analysis need to be computed, client-driven analysis determines which parts need to be computed using more precision.

For example, consider how context-insensitive analysis treats the string copying routine in Figure 1: the pointer parameter s merges information from all the possible input strings and transfers it to the output string. For a client that associates dataflow facts with string buffers, this could severely hurt accuracy—the appropriate action is to treat the routine context-sensitively. However, for a client that is not concerned with strings, the imprecision is irrelevant.

We evaluate our algorithm using five security and error detection problems as clients. These clients are demanding analysis problems that stress the capabilities of the pointer analyzer, but with adequate support they can detect significant and complex program defects. We compare our algorithm against five fixed-precision algorithms on a suite of 18 real C programs. We measure the cost in terms of time and space, and we measure the accuracy simply as the number of errors reported: the analysis is conservative, so fewer error reports always indicates fewer false positives.

This paper makes the following contributions. (1) We present a client-driven pointer analysis algorithm that adapts its precision policy to the needs of client analyses. For our error detection clients, this algorithm effectively discovers where to apply more analysis effort to reduce the number of false positives. (2) We present empirical evidence that different analysis clients benefit from different kinds of precision—flow-sensitivity, context-sensitivity, or both. In most cases only a small part of each input program needs such precision. Our algorithm works because it automatically identifies these parts. (3) Our results show that whole-program dataflow analysis is an accurate and efficient tool for error detection when it has adequate pointer information.

The rest of this paper is organized as follows. Section 2 reviews related work. Section 3 describes the implementation of our framework, and Section 4 presents our client-driven algorithm. Section 5 describes our experimental methodology. Section 6 presents our results, and we conclude in Section 7.

2 Related Work

Previous work in various kinds of program analysis, including pointer analysis, has explored ways to reduce the cost of analysis while still producing an accurate result. Our client-driven algorithm addresses this problem specifically for the precision of pointer analysis. It is closely related to demand-driven algorithms and mixed-precision analyses. We also describe recent related work in error detection, focusing on the role of pointer analysis.

2.1 Precision versus Cost of Analysis

Iterative flow analysis [15] is the only other algorithm that we are aware of that adjusts its precision automatically in response to the quality of the results. Plevyak and Chien use this algorithm to determine the concrete types of objects in programs written using the Concurrent Aggregates object-oriented language. When imprecision in the analysis causes a type conflict, the algorithm can perform *function splitting*, which provides context-sensitivity, or *data splitting*, which divides object creation sites so that a single site can generate objects of different types. The basic mechanism is similar to ours, but it differs in important ways. First, since the type of an object cannot change, iterative flow analysis does not include flow-sensitivity. By contrast, our approach supports a larger class of client analyses, known as *typestate* problems [20], which include flow-sensitive problems. More significantly, our algorithm manages the precision of both the client and the pointer analysis, allowing it to detect when pointer aliasing is the cause of information loss.

Demand-driven pointer analysis [11] addresses the cost of pointer analysis by computing just enough information to determine the points-to sets for a specific subset of the program variables. Client-driven pointer analysis is similar in the sense that it is driven by a specific query into the results. However, the two algorithms use this information to manage different aspects of the algorithm. Client-driven analysis dynamically varies precision, but still computes an exhaustive solution. Demand-driven pointer analysis is a fixed-precision analysis that computes only the necessary part of the solution. The two ideas are complementary and could be combined to obtain the benefits of both.

Demand interprocedural dataflow analysis [14] also avoids the cost of exhaustive program analysis by focusing on computing specific dataflow facts. This algorithm produces precise results in polynomial time for a class of dataflow analyses problems called IFDS—interprocedural, finite, distributive, subset problems. However, this class does not include pointer analysis, particularly when it supports strong updates (which removes the distributive property).

Combined pointer analysis [23] uses different pointer algorithms on different parts of the program. This technique divides the assignments in a program into classes and uses a heuristic to choose different pointer analysis algorithms for the different classes. Zhang et al. evaluate this algorithm by measuring the number of possible objects accessed or modified at pointer dereferences. Client-driven pointer analysis is more feedback directed: instead of using a heuristic, it determines the need for precision dynamically by monitoring the analysis.

2.2 Pointer Analysis for Error Detection

Automatic error checking of C programs is a particularly compelling application for pointer analysis. One of the major challenges in analyzing C programs is constructing a precise enough model of the store to support accurate error detection. Previous work has generally settled for a low-cost fixed-policy pointer analysis, which computes minimal store information without overwhelming the cost of error detection analysis [17, 2, 8]. Unfortunately, this store information often proves inadequate. Experiences with the ESP system [5] illustrate this problem: while its dataflow analysis engine is more powerful and more efficient than ours, the imprecision of its underlying pointer analysis can block program verification. The authors solve this problem by manually cloning three procedures in the application in order to mimic context-sensitivity. In this paper, our goal is not to propose an alternative technique for detecting errors, but rather to present a pointer analysis algorithm that supports these clients more effectively. Our algorithm detects when imprecision in the store model hampers the client and automatically increases precision in the parts of the program where it's needed.

3 Framework

Our analysis framework is part of the Broadway compiler system, which supports high-level analysis and optimization for C programs [10]. In this section we describe the details of this framework, including the overall architecture, the representation of pointer information, and the implementation of the different precision policies.

We use a lightweight annotation language to specify the client analysis problems [9]. The language is designed to extend compiler support to software libraries; it is not used to describe the application programs. The language allows us to concisely summarize the pointer behavior of library routines, and it provides a way to define new library-specific dataflow analysis problems. The dataflow analysis framework manages both the pointer analysis and the client analyses, which run concurrently. Analysis is whole-program, interprocedural, and uses an iterative worklist algorithm.

3.1 Pointer Representation

Our base pointer analysis can be roughly categorized as an interprocedural "Andersen-style" analysis [1]: it is flow-insensitive, context-insensitive, and inclusion-based. We represent the program store using an enhanced implementation of the storage shape graph [3]. Each memory location—local variable, global variable, or heap-allocated memory—is a node in the graph, with directed *points-to* edges from pointers to their targets. Our algorithm is a "may" analysis: a points-to edge in the graph represents a possible pointer relationship in the actual execution of the program. Conservative approximation of program behavior often leads to multiple outgoing points-to edges. However, when a node has exactly one target it is a "must" pointer, and assignments through it admit strong updates.

3.2 Configurable Precision

We can add precision, at a fine grain, to the base pointer analysis: individual memory locations in the store can be either flow-sensitive or flow-insensitive, and individual procedures can be either context-sensitive or context-insensitive. For a flow-sensitive location, we record separate points-to sets and client dataflow facts for each assignment to the location. We maintain this information using interprocedural factored def-use chains, which are similar to SSA form [4] except that we store the phi functions in a separate data structure. For a flow-insensitive location, we accumulate the information from all of its assignments. Our algorithm still visits assignments in order, however, so our flow-insensitive analysis often yields slightly more precise information than a traditional algorithm.

To analyze a context-sensitive procedure, we treat each call site as a completely separate instantiation, which keeps information from different call sites separate. More efficient methods of implementing context-sensitivity exist [22], but we show in Section 6 that we can often avoid it altogether. To analyze a context-insensitive procedure, we create a single instantiation and merge the information from all of its call sites. Since our analysis is interprocedural, we still visit all of the calling contexts. However, the analyzer can often skip over a context-insensitive procedure call when no changes occur to the input values, which helps the analysis converge quickly. The main drawback of this mode is that it suffers from the unrealizable paths problem [22], in which information from one call site is returned to a different call site.

3.3 Heap Objects

For many C programs, manipulation of heap allocated objects accounts for much of the pointer behavior. Our pointer analyzer contains two features that help improve analysis of these objects. First, the analyzer generates one heap object for each allocation site in each calling context. This feature can dramatically improve accuracy for programs that allocate memory through a wrapper function around malloc(). It also helps distinguish data structure elements that are allocated by a single constructor-like function. By making these functions context-sensitive, we produce a separate object for each invocation of the function.

Second, heap objects in the store model can represent multiple memory blocks at runtime. For example, a program may contain a loop that repeatedly calls malloc()—our analyzer generates one heap object to represent all of the instances. We adopt the multiple instance analysis from Chase et al. [3] to determine when an allocation truly generates only one object. Previous work has also referred to this flow-sensitive property as *linearity* [8].

4 Client-Driven Algorithm

Our client-driven pointer analysis is a two-pass algorithm. The key idea is to use a fast, low-precision pointer analysis in the first pass to discover which parts of the program need more precision. The algorithm uses this information to construct a fine-grained, customized precision policy for the second pass. This approach requires a tighter coupling between the pointer analyzer and the client analyses: in addition to providing memory access information to the client, the pointer analyzer receives feedback from the client about the accuracy of the client flow values. For example, the client analysis can report when a confluence point, such as a control-flow merge or context-insensitive procedure call, adversely affects the accuracy of its analysis. The interface between the pointer analyzer and the client is simple, but it is the core mechanism that allows the framework to tailor its precision for the particular client and target program.

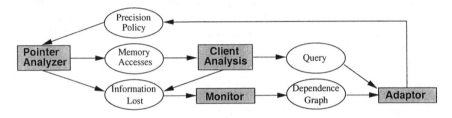

Fig. 2. Our analysis framework allows client analyses to provide feedback, which drives corrective adjustments to the precision

The implementation of this algorithm adds two components to our analysis framework: a *monitor* that detects and tracks loss of information during program analysis, and an *adaptor* that uses the output of the monitor to determine corrective adjustments to the precision. During program analysis, the monitor identifies the places where information is lost, and it uses a dependence graph to track the memory locations that are subsequently affected. When analysis is complete the client takes over and performs its tasks—afterword it reports back to the adaptor with a set of memory locations that are not sufficiently accurate for its purposes. Borrowing terminology from demand-driven analysis, we refer to this set as the *query*. The adaptor starts with the locations in the query and tracks their values back through the dependence graph. The nodes and edges that make up this back-trace indicate which variables and procedures need more precision. The framework reruns the analysis with the customized precision policy. Figure 2 shows a diagram of the system.

Even though the algorithm detects information loss during analysis, it waits until the analysis is complete to change precision. One reason for this is pragmatic: our framework cannot change precision during analysis and recompute the results incrementally. There is a more fundamental reason, however: during analysis it is not readily apparent that imprecision detected in a particular pointer value will adversely affect the client later in the program. For example, a program may contain a pointer variable with numerous assignments, causing the points-to set to grow large. However, if the client analysis never needs the value of the pointer then it is not worth expending extra effort to disambiguate it. By waiting to see its impact, we significantly reduce the amount of precision added by the algorithm.

4.1 Polluting Assignments

The monitor runs along side the main pointer analysis and client analysis, detecting information loss and recording its effects. Loss of information occurs when conservative assumptions about program behavior force the analyzer to merge flow values. In particular, we are interested in the cases where accurate, but conflicting, information is merged, resulting in an inaccurate value—we refer to this as a *polluting assignment*.

For "may" pointer analysis smaller points-to sets indicate more accurate information—a points-to set of size one is the most accurate. In this case the pointer relationship is unambiguous, and assignments through the pointer allow strong updates [3]. Therefore, a pointer assignment is polluting if it combines one or more unambiguous pointers and produces an ambiguous pointer.

For the client analysis information loss is problem-specific, but we can define it generally in terms of dataflow lattice values. We take the compiler community's view of lattices: higher lattice values represent better analysis information. Lower lattice values are more conservative, with lattice bottom denoting the worst case. Therefore, a client update is polluting if it combines a set of lattice values to produces a lattice value that is lower than any of the individual members.

We classify polluting assignments according to their cause. In our framework there are three ways that conservative analysis can directly cause the loss of information [6]. We will refer to them as *directly polluting assignments*, and they can occur in both the pointer analysis and the client analysis:

- Context-insensitive procedure call: the parameter assignment merged conflicting information from different call sites.
- Flow-insensitive assignment: multiple assignments to a single memory location merge conflicting information.
- Control-flow merge: the SSA phi function merges conflicting information from different control-flow paths.

The current implementation of the algorithm is only concerned with the first two classes. It can detect loss of information at control-flow merges, but it currently has no corrective mechanism, such as node splitting or path sensitivity, to remedy it.

In addition to these classes, there are two kinds of polluting assignments that are caused specifically by ambiguous pointers. These assignments are critical to the client-driven algorithm because they capture the relationship between accuracy in the pointer analysis and accuracy in the client. We refer to them as *indirectly polluting assignments,* and they always refer to the offending pointer:

- Weak access: the right-hand side of the assignment dereferences an ambiguous pointer, which merges conflicting information from the pointer targets.
 - Weak update: the left-hand side assigns through an ambiguous pointer, forcing a weak update that loses information.

4.2 Monitoring Analysis

During analysis, the monitor detects the five kinds of polluting assignments described above, both for the client analysis and the pointer analysis, and it records this information in a directed dependence graph. The goal of the dependence graph is to capture the effects of polluting assignments on subsequent parts of the program.

Each node in the graph represents a memory location whose analysis information, either points-to set or client flow value, is polluted. The graph contains a node for each location that is modified by a directly polluting assignment, and each node has a label that lists of all the directly polluting assignments to that memory location—for our experiments we only record the parameter passing or flow-insensitive assignment cases. The monitor builds this graph online by adding nodes to the graph and adding assignments to the labels as they are discovered during analysis. These nodes represent the sources of polluted information, and the labels indicate how to fix the imprecision.

The graph contains two types of directed edges. The first type of edge represents an assignment that passes polluted information from one location to another. We refer to this as a *complicit assignment*, and it occurs whenever the memory locations on the right-hand side are already represented in the dependence graph. The monitor creates nodes for the affected left-hand side locations, if necessary, and adds edges from those nodes back to the right-hand side nodes. Note that the direction of the edge is opposite the direction of assignment so that we can trace dependences backward in the program. The second type of edge represents indirectly polluting assignments. The monitor adds nodes for the left-hand side locations and it adds a directed edge from each of these nodes back to the offending pointer variable. This kind of edge is unique to our analysis because it allows our algorithm to distinguish between the following two situations: (1) an unambiguous pointer whose target is polluted, and (2) an ambiguous pointer whose targets have precise information.

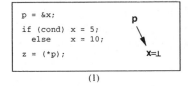
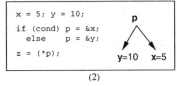

Fig. 3. Both code fragments assign bottom to z: in (1) x is responsible, in (2) p is responsible

Figure 3 illustrates this distinction using constant propagation as an example client. Both code fragments assign lattice bottom to z, but for different reasons. Case (1) is caused by the polluted value of x, so the monitor adds an edge in dependence graph from z back to x. Case (2), however, is caused by the polluted value of the pointer p, so the monitor adds an edge from z to p.

We store the program locations of all assignments, but for performance reasons the monitor dependence graph is fundamentally a flow-insensitive data structure. As a result, the algorithm cannot tell which specific assignments to an memory location affect other location. For example, a location might have multiple polluting assignments, some of which occur later in the program than complicit assignments that read its value. In most cases, this simplification does not noticeably hurt the algorithm, but occasionally it leads to overly aggressive precision, particularly when it involves global variables that are used in many different places and for different purposes.

4.3 Diagnosing Information Loss

When analysis is complete, the client has an opportunity to use the results for its purposes, such as checking for error states or applying an optimization. The client provides feedback to the adaptor, in the form of a query, indicating where it needs more accuracy. The adaptor uses the dependence graph to construct a precision policy specifically tailored to obtain the desired accuracy. The output of the adaptor is a set of memory locations that need flow-sensitivity and a set of procedures that need context-sensitivity. The new precision policy applies to both the pointer analysis and the client analysis.

The client query consists of a set of memory locations that have "unsatisfactory" flow values. For example, if the client tests a variable for a particular flow value, but finds lattice bottom, it could add that variable to the query. The goal of the adaptor is to improve the accuracy of the memory locations in the query. The corresponding nodes in the dependence graph serve as a starting point, and the set of nodes reachable from those nodes represents all the memory locations whose inaccuracy directly or indirectly affects the flow values of the query. The key to our algorithm is that this subgraph is typically much smaller than the whole graph—we rarely to need to fix *all* of the polluting assignments.

The adaptor starts at the query nodes in the graph and visits all of the reachable nodes in the graph. It inspects the list of directly polluting assignments labeling each node (if there are any) and determines the appropriate corrective measures: for polluting parameter assignments it adds the corresponding procedure to the set of procedures that need context-sensitivity; for flow-insensitive assignments it adds the corresponding memory location to the set of locations that need flow-sensitivity.

4.4 Chaining Precision

In addition to addressing each polluting assignment, the adaptor increases precision along the whole path from each polluting assignment back to the original query nodes. When it finds a node that needs flow-sensitivity, it also applies this additional precision to all the nodes back along the path. When it makes a procedure context-sensitive, it also determines the set of procedures that contain all the complicit assignments back along the path, and it adds that set to the context-sensitive set. The motivation for this chaining is to ensure that intermediate locations preserve the additional accuracy provided by fixing polluting assignments.

By aggressively chaining the precision, we also avoid the need for additional analysis passes. The initial pass computes the least precise analysis information and therefore covers all the regions of the program for which more precision might be beneficial. Any polluting assignments detected in later passes would necessarily occur within these regions and thus would already be addressed in the customized precision policy. We validated this design decision empirically: subsequent passes typically discover only spurious instances of imprecision and do not improve the quality of the client analysis.

5 Experiments

In this section we describe our experiments, including our methodology, the five error detection clients, and the input programs. The query that these clients provide to the adaptor consists of the set of memory locations that trigger errors. We compare both the cost and the accuracy of our algorithm against four fixed-precision algorithms. In Section 6 we present the empirical results.

We run all experiments on a Dell OptiPlex GX-400, with a Pentium 4 processor running at 1.7 GHz and 2 GB of main memory. The machine runs Linux with the 2.4.18 kernel. Our system is implemented entirely in C++ and compiled using the GNU g++ compiler version 3.0.3.

5.1 Methodology

Our suite of experiments consists of 18 C programs, five error detection problems, and five pointer analysis algorithms—four fixed-precision pointer algorithms and our client-driven algorithm. The fixed-precision algorithms consist of the four possible combinations of flow-sensitivity and context-sensitivity—we refer to them in the results as *CIFI*, *CIFS*, *CSFI*, and *CSFS*. For each combination of program, error problem, and pointer analysis algorithm, we run the analyzer and collect a variety of measurements, including analysis time, memory consumption, and number of errors reported.

The number of errors reported is the most important of these metrics. The more false positives that an algorithm produces, the more time a programmer must spend sorting through them to find the real errors. Our experience is that this is an extremely tedious and time consuming task. Using a fast inaccurate error detection algorithm is false economy: it trades computer time, which is cheap and plentiful, for programmer time, which is valuable and limited. Our view is that it is preferable to use a more expensive algorithm that can reduce the number of false positives, even if it has to run overnight or over the weekend. When two algorithms report the same number of errors, we compare them in terms of analysis time and memory consumption.

In some cases, we know the actual number of errors present in the programs. This information comes from security advisories published by organizations such as CERT and SecurityFocus. We have also manually inspected some of the programs to validate the errors. For the client-driven algorithm we also record the number of procedures that it makes context-sensitive and the number of memory locations that it makes flow-sensitive. Unlike previous research on pointer analysis, we do not present data on the points-to set sizes because this metric is not relevant to our algorithm.

5.2 Error Detection Clients

We define the five error detection client analyses using our annotation language. This language allows us to define simple dataflow analysis problems that are associated with a library interface: for each library routine, we specify how it affects the flow values of the problem. The language also provides a way to test the results of the analysis and generate reports. For each analysis problem we show some representative examples of the annotations, but due to space limitations we cannot present the full problem specification.

These error detection problems represent realistic errors that actually occur in practice and can cause serious damage. Like many error detection problems, they involve data structures, such as buffers and file handles, that are allocated on the heap and manipulated through pointers. The lifetimes of these data structures often cross many procedures, requiring interprocedural analysis to properly model. Thus, they present a considerable challenge for the pointer analyzer.

File Access Errors. Library interfaces often contain implicit constraints on the order in which their routines may be called. File access rules are one example of this kind of usage constraint. A program can only access a file in between the proper open and close calls. The purpose of this analysis client is to detect possible violations of this usage rule. The first line in Figure 4 defines the flow value for this analysis, which consists of the two possible states, "Open" and "Closed".

To track this state, we annotate the various library functions that open and close files. Figure 4 shows the annotations for the fopen() function. The on_entry and on_exit annotations describe the pointer behavior of the routine: it returns a pointer to a new file stream, which points to a new file handle. The analyze annotation sets the state of the newly created file handle to open. At each use of a file stream or file descriptor, we check to make sure the state is open. Figure 4 shows an annotation for the fgets() function, which emits an error if the file could be closed.

```
property FileState : { Open, Closed }   initially Closed

procedure fopen(path, mode)
{
  on_exit { return --> new file_stream --> new file_handle }
  analyze FileState {  file_handle <- Open  }
}

procedure fgets(s, size, f)
{
  on_entry { f --> file_stream --> handle }
  error if (FileState : handle could-be Closed)
                        "Error: file might be closed";
}
```

Fig. 4. Annotations for tracking file state: to properly model files and files descriptors, we associate the state with an abstract "handle"

Format String Vulnerability (FSV). A number of output functions in the Standard C Library, such as printf() and syslog(), take a format string argument that controls output formatting. A format string vulnerability (FSV) occurs when untrusted data ends up as part of the format string. A hacker can exploit this vulnerability by sending the program a carefully crafted input string that causes part of the code to be overwritten with new instructions. These vulnerabilities are a serious security problem that have been the subject of many CERT advisories.

To detect format string vulnerabilities we define an analysis that determines when data from an untrusted source can become part of a format string. We consider data to be *tainted* [21, 17] when it comes from an untrusted source. We track this data through the program to make sure that all format string arguments are *untainted*.

Our formulation of the Taint analysis starts with a definition of the Taint property, shown at the top of Figure 5, which consists of two possible values, Tainted and Untainted. We then annotate the Standard C Library functions that produce tainted data. These include such obvious sources of untrusted data as scanf() and read(), and less obvious ones such as readdir() and getenv(). Figure 5 shows the annotations for the read() routine. Notice that the annotations assign the Tainted property to the contents of the buffer rather than to the buffer pointer. We then annotate string manipulation functions to reflect how taintedness can propagate from one string to another. The example in Figure 5 annotates the strdup() function: the string copy has the same Taint value as the input string.

Finally, we annotate all the library functions that accept format strings (including sprintf()) to report when the format string is tainted. Figure 5 shows the annotation for the syslog() function, which is often the culprit.

```
property Taint : { Tainted, Untainted }  initially Untainted

procedure read(fd, buffer_ptr, size)
{
  on_entry { buffer_ptr --> buffer }
  analyze Taint { buffer <- Tainted }
}

procedure strdup(s)
{
  on_entry { s --> string }
  on_exit { return --> string_copy }
  analyze Taint { string_copy <- string }
}

procedure syslog(prio, fmt, args)
{
  on_entry { fmt --> fmt_string }
  error if (Taint : fmt_string could-be Tainted)
                    "Error: tainted format string.";
}
```

Fig. 5. Annotations defining the Taint analysis: taintedness is associated with strings and buffers, and can be transferred between them

Remote Access Vulnerability. Hostile clients can only manipulate programs through the various program inputs. We can approximate the extent of this control by tracking the input data and observing how it is used. We label input sources, such as file handles and sockets, according to the level that they are trusted. All data read from these sources is labeled likewise. The first line of Figure 6 defines the three levels of trust in our analysis—internal (trusted), locally trusted (for example, local files), and remote (untrusted).

We start by annotating functions that return fundamentally untrusted data sources, such as Internet sockets. Figure 6 shows the annotations for the socket() function. The level of trust depends on the kind of socket being created. When the program reads data from these sources, the buffers are marked with the Trust level of the source.

The Trust analysis has two distinguishing features. First, data is only as trustworthy as its least trustworthy source. For example, if the program reads both trusted and untrusted data into a single buffer, then we consider the whole buffer to be untrusted. The nested structure of the lattice definition captures this fact. Second, untrusted data has a domino effect on other data sources and sinks. For example, if the file name argument to open() is untrusted, then we treat all data read from that file descriptor as untrusted. The annotations in Figure 6 implement this policy.

```
property Trust : { Remote { External { Internal }}}

procedure socket(domain, type, protocol}
{
  on_exit { return --> new file_handle }
  analyze Trust {
    if (domain == AF_UNIX)   file_handle <- External
    if (domain == AF_INET)   file_handle <- Remote
  }
}

procedure open(path, flags)
{
  on_entry { path --> path_string }
  on_exit { return --> new file_handle }
  analyze Trust { file_handle <- path_string }
}
```

Fig. 6. Annotations defining the Trust analysis. Note the cascading effect: we only trust data from a file handle if we trust the file name used to open it

As with the Taint analysis above, we annotate string manipulation functions to propagate the Trust values from one buffer to another. We generate an error message when untrusted data reaches certain sensitive routines, including any file system manipulation or program execution routines, such as exec().

Remote FSV. The Taint analysis defined above tends to find many format string vulnerabilities that are not exploitable security holes. For example, consider a program that uses a data from a file as part of a format string. If a hacker can dictate the name of the file or can control the contents of the file, then the program contains a remotely exploitable vulnerability. If a hacker cannot control the file, however, then the program still contains a bug, but the bug does not have security implications.

To identify exploitable format string vulnerabilities more precisely, we can combine the Taint analysis with the Trust analysis, which specifically tracks data from remote sources. We revise the error test so that it only emits an error message when the format string is tainted and it comes from a remote source.

FTP Behavior. The most complex of our client analyses checks to see if a program can behave like an FTP (file transfer protocol) server. Specifically, we want to determine if it is possible for the program to send the contents of a file to a remote client, where the name of the file read is determined, at least in part, by the remote client itself. This behavior is not necessarily incorrect: it is the normal operation of the two FTP daemons that we present in our results. We can use this error checker to make sure the behavior is not unintended (for example, in a finger daemon) or to validate the expected behavior of the FTP programs.

We use the Trust analysis defined above to determine when untrusted data is read from one stream to another. However, we need to know that one stream is associated with a file and the other with a remote socket. Figure 7 defines the flow value to track different kinds of sources and sinks of data. We can distinguish between different kinds of sockets, such as "Server" sockets, which have bound addresses for listening, and "Client" sockets, which are the result of accepting a connection.

```
property FDKind : { File, Client, Server, Pipe, Command, StdIO}
procedure write(fd, buffer_ptr, size)
{
  on_entry { buffer_ptr --> buffer
             fd --> file_handle }
  error if ((FDKind : buffer could-be File) &&
            (Trust  : buffer could-be Remote) &&
            (FDKind : file_handle could-be Client) &&
            (Trust  : file_handle could-be Remote))
    "Error :_possible_FTP_behavior";
}
```

Fig. 7. Annotations to track kinds of data sources and sinks. In combination with Trust analysis, we can check whether a call to write() behaves like FTP

Whenever a new file descriptor is opened, we mark it according to the kind. In addition, like the other analyses, we associate this kind with any data read from it. We check for FTP behavior in the write() family of routines, shown in Figure 7, by testing both the buffer and the file descriptor.

5.3 Programs

Table 1 describes our input programs. We use these particular programs for our experiments for a number of reasons. First, they are all real programs, taken from open-source projects, with all of the nuances and complexities of production software. Second, many of them are system tools or daemons that have significant security implications because they interact with remote clients and provide privileged services. Finally, several of them are specific versions of programs that are identified by security advisories as containing format string vulnerabilities. In addition, we also obtain subsequent versions in which the bugs are fixed, so that we can confirm their absence.

We present several measures of program size, including number of lines of source code, number of lines of preprocessed code, and number of procedures. The table is sorted by the number of CFG nodes, and we use this ordering in all subsequent tables.

Table 1. Properties of the input programs. Many of the programs run in privileged mode, making their security critical. Lines of code (LOC) is given both before and after preprocessing. CFG nodes measures the size of the program in the compiler internal representation—the table is sorted on this column

Program	Description	Priv	LOC	CFG nodes	Procedures
stunnel 3.8	Secure TCP wrapper	yes	2K / 13K	2264	42
pfingerd 0.7.8	Finger daemon	yes	5K / 30K	3638	47
muh 2.05c	IRC proxy	yes	5K / 25K	5191	84
muh 2.05d	IRC propy	yes	5K / 25K	5390	84
pure-ftpd 1.0.15	FTP server	yes	13K / 45K	11,239	116
crond (fcron-2.9.3)	cron daemon	yes	9K / 40K	11,310	100
apache 1.3.12 (core only)	Web server	yes	30K / 67K	16,755	313
make 3.75	make		21K / 50K	18,581	167
BlackHole 1.0.9	E-mail filter		12K / 244K	21,370	71
wu-ftpd 2.6.0	FTP server	yes	21K / 64K	22,196	183
openssh client 3.5p1	Secure shell client		38K / 210K	22,411	441
privoxy 3.0.0	Web server proxy	yes	27K / 48K	22,608	223
wu-ftpd 2.6.2	FTP server	yes	22K / 66K	23,107	205
named (BIND 4.9.4)	DNS server	yes	26K / 84K	25,452	210
openssh daemon 3.5p1	Secure shell server	yes	50K / 299K	29,799	601
cfengine 1.5.4	System admin tool	yes	34K / 350K	36,573	421
sqlite 2.7.6	SQL database		36K / 67K	43,333	387
nn 6.5.6	News reader		36K / 116K	46,336	494

6 Results

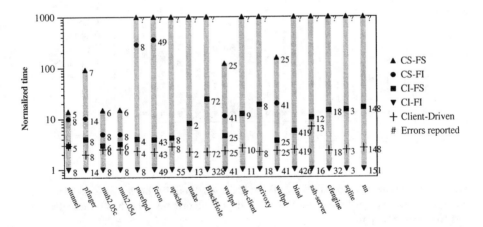

Fig. 8. Checking file access requires flow-sensitivity, but not context-sensitivity. The client-driven algorithm beats the other algorithms because it makes only the file-related objects flow-sensitive

We measure the results for all combinations of pointer analysis algorithms, error detection clients, and input programs—a total of over 400 experiments. We present the results in five graphs, one for each error detection client. Each bar on the graph shows the performance of the different analysis algorithms on the given program. To more easily compare different programs we normalize all

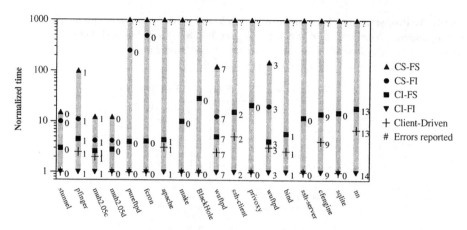

Fig. 9. Detecting format string vulnerabilities rarely benefits from either flow-sensitivity or context-sensitivity—the client-driven algorithm is only slower because it is a two-pass algorithm

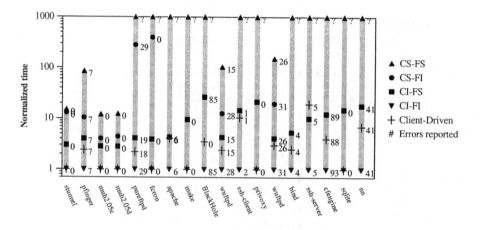

Fig. 10. Detecting remote access vulnerabilities can require both flow-sensitivity and context-sensitivity. In these cases the client-driven algorithm is both the most accurate and the most efficient

execution times to the time of the fastest algorithm on that program, which in all cases is the context-insensitive, flow-insensitive algorithm. Each point on these graphs represents a single combination of error detection client, input program, and analysis algorithm. We label each point with the number of errors reported in that combination. In addition, Figure 13 shows the actual analysis times, averaged over all five clients.

For the 90 combinations of error detection clients and input programs, we find:

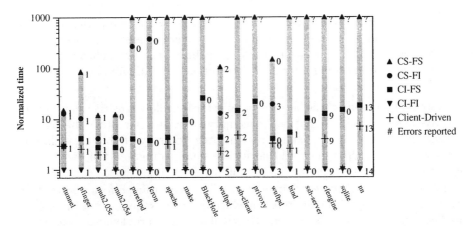

Fig. 11. Determining when a format string vulnerability is remotely exploitable is a more difficult, and often fruitless, analysis. The client-driven algorithm is still competitive with the fastest fixed-precision algorithm, and it even beats the other algorithms in three of the cases

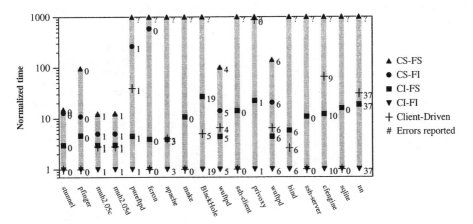

Fig. 12. Detecting FTP-like behavior is the most challenging analysis. In three cases (WU-FTP, privoxy, and CFEngine) the client-driven algorithm achieves accuracy that we believe only the full-precision algorithm can match—if it were able to run to completion

- In 87 out of 90 cases the client-driven algorithm equals or beats the **accuracy** of the best fixed-precision policy. The other three cases appear to be anomalies, and we believe we can address them.
- In 64 of those 87 cases the client-driven algorithm also equals or beats the **performance** of the comparably accurate fixed-precision algorithm. In 29 of these cases the client-driven algorithm is both the fastest *and* the most accurate.

- In 19 of the remaining 23 cases the client-driven algorithm performs within a factor of two or three of the best fixed-precision algorithm. In many of these cases the best fixed-precision algorithm is the fastest fixed-precision algorithm, so in absolute terms the execution times are all low.

Note that for many of the larger programs the fully flow-sensitive and context-sensitive algorithm either runs out of memory or requires an intolerable amount of time. In these cases we cannot measure the accuracy of this algorithm for comparison. However, we do find that for the smaller programs the client-driven algorithm matches the accuracy of the full-precision algorithm.

In general, the only cases where a fixed-policy algorithm performs better than the client-driven algorithm are those in which the client requires little or no extra precision. In particular, the format string vulnerability problem rarely seems to benefit from higher levels of precision. In these cases, though, the analysis is usually so fast that the performance difference is practically irrelevant.

Table 2. The precision policies created by the client-driven algorithm. Different clients have different precision requirements, but the amount of extra precision needed is typically very small

Added Precision:	# of Procedures set C-S					% of Memory Locations set F-S				
Client Program:	File Access	FSV	Remote Access	Remote FSV	FTP Behavior	File Access	FSV	Remote Access	Remote FSV	FTP Behavior
stunnel-3.8	-	-	-	-	-	0.20	-	-	-	0.19
pfinger-0.7.8	-	-	1	-	-	-	0.53	0.20	0.53	0.61
muh2.05c	-	-	-	-	6	0.10	-	-	0.07	0.31
muh2.05d	-	-	-	-	6	0.10	-	-	-	0.33
pure-ftpd-1.0.15	-	-	2	-	9	0.13	-	0.12	-	0.10
fcron-2.9.3	-	-	-	-	-	-	-	0.03	-	0.26
apache-1.3.12	-	2	8	2	10	0.18	0.91	0.89	1.07	0.83
make-3.75	-	-	-	-	-	0.02	-	-	-	2.19
BlackHole-1.0.9	-	-	2	-	5	0.04	-	0.24	-	0.32
wu-ftpd-2.6.0	-	-	-	-	17	0.09	0.22	0.34	0.24	0.08
openssh-3.5p1-client	1	-	10	-	-	0.06	0.55	0.35	0.56	0.96
privoxy-3.0.0-stable	-	-	-	-	5	0.01	-	-	-	0.10
wu-ftpd-2.6.2	-	4	-	4	17	0.09	0.51	0.63	0.53	0.23
bind-4.9.4-REL	-	2	1	1	4	0.01	0.23	0.14	0.20	0.42
openssh-3.5p1-server	1	-	13	-	-	0.59	-	0.49	-	1.19
cfengine-1.5.4	-	1	4	3	31	0.04	0.46	0.43	0.48	0.03
sqlite-2.7.6	-	-	-	-	-	0.01	-	1.47	-	1.43
nn-6.5.6	-	1	2	1	30	0.17	1.99	1.82	2.03	0.97

For the problems that do require more precision, the client-driven algorithm consistently outperforms the fixed-precision algorithms. Table 2 provides some insight into this result. For each program and each client, we record the number of procedures that the algorithm makes context-sensitive and the percentage of memory locations that it makes flow-sensitive. (In this table, hyphens represent the number 0.) These statistics show that client analyses often need some extra precision, but only a very small amount. In particular, the clients that benefit from context-sensitivity only need a tiny fraction of their procedures analyzed in this way.

6.1 Client-Specific Results

The client-driven algorithm reveals some significant differences between the precision requirements of the five error detection problems.

Figure 8 shows the results for the file access client, which benefits significantly from flow-sensitivity but not from context-sensitivity. This result makes sense because the state of a file handle can change over time, but most procedures only accept open file handles as arguments. We suspect that few of these error reports represent true errors, and we believe that many of the remaining false positives could be eliminated using path-sensitive analysis.

Figure 9 shows the results for detecting format string vulnerabilities. The taintedness analysis that we use to detect format string vulnerabilities generally requires no extra precision. We might expect utility functions, such as string copying, to have unrealizable paths that cause spurious errors, but this does not happen in any of our example programs. The high false positive rates observed in previous work [17] are probably due to the use of equality-based analysis.

Figure 11 shows the results for determining the remote exploitability of format string vulnerabilities. We find that this client is particularly difficult for the client-driven analysis, which tends to add too much precision without lowering the false positive count. Interestingly, many spurious FSV errors are caused by typos in the program: for example, cfengine calls sprintf() in several places without providing the string buffer argument.

For two of the input programs, muh and wu-ftp, we obtained two versions of each program: one version known to contain format string vulnerabilities and a subsequent version with the bugs fixed. Our system accurately detects the known vulnerabilities in the old versions and confirm their absence in the newer versions. Our analysis also found the known vulnerabilities in several other programs, including stunnel, cfengine, sshd, and named. In addition, our system reports a format string vulnerability in the Apache web server. Manual inspection, however, shows that it is unexploitable for algorithmic reasons that are beyond the scope of our analysis.

Figure 10 shows the results for remote access vulnerability detection. Accurate detection of remote access vulnerabilities requires both flow-sensitivity and context-sensitivity because the "domino effect" of the underlying Trust analysis causes information loss to propagate to many parts of the program. For example, all of the false positives in BlackHole are due to unrealizable paths through a single function called my_strlcpy(), which implements string copying. The client-driven algorithm detects the problem and makes the routine context-sensitive, which eliminates all the false positives.

Figure 12 shows the results for detecting FTP-like behavior, which is the most challenging problem because it depends on the states of multiple memory locations and multiple client analyses. However, our analysis does properly detect exactly those program points in the two FTP daemons that perform the "get" or "put" file transfer functions. Context-sensitivity helps eliminate a false positive in one interesting case: in wu-ftp, a data transfer function appears to contain an error because the source and target could either be files or sockets. However, when the calling contexts are separated, the combinations that actually occur are file-to-file and socket-to-socket.

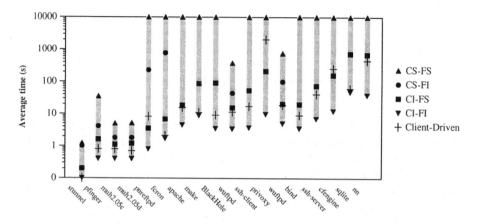

Fig. 13. The client-driven algorithm performs competitively with the fastest fixed-precision algorithm

7 Conclusions

This paper presents a new client-driven approach to managing the tradeoff between cost and precision in pointer analysis. We show that such an approach is needed: no single fixed-precision analysis is appropriate for all client problems and programs. The low-precision algorithms do not provide sufficient accuracy for the more challenging client analysis problems, while the high-precision algorithms waste time over-analyzing the easy problems. Rather than choose any of these fixed-precision policies, we exploit the fact that many client analyses require only a small amount of extra precision applied to specific places in each input program. Our client-driven algorithm can effectively detect these places and automatically apply the necessary additional precision.

Acknowledgments

We would like to thank Kathryn S. McKinley, Michael Hind, and the anonymous reviewers for their valuable and insightful comments.

References

1. L. Andersen. *Program Analysis and Specialization for the C Programming Language.* PhD thesis, University of Copenhagen, DIKU, DIKU report 94/19, 1994.
2. T. Ball and S. K. Rajamani. Automatically validating temporal safety properties of interfaces. In *International SPIN Workshop on Model Checking of Software*, May 2001.
3. D. R. Chase, M. Wegman, and F. K. Zadeck. Analysis of pointers and structures. *ACM SIGPLAN Notices*, 25(6):296–310, June 1990.
4. R. Cytron, J. Ferrante, B. K. Rosen, M. K. Wegman, and F. K. Zadeck. An efficient method of computing static single assignment form. In *16th Annual ACM Symposium on Principles of Programming Languages*, pages 25–35, 1989.
5. M. Das, S. Lerner, and M. Seigle. ESP: path-sensitive program verification in polynomial time. In *ACM SIGPLAN Conference on Programming Language Design and Implementation*, volume 37, 5, pages 57–68, 2002.
6. A. Diwan, K. S. McKinley, and J. E. B. Moss. Using types to analyze and optimize object-oriented programs. *ACM Transactions on Programming Languages and Systems*, 23, 2001.
7. J. S. Foster, M. Fahndrich, and A. Aiken. Polymorphic versus monomorphic flow-insensitive points-to analysis for C. In *Static Analysis Symposium*, pages 175–198, 2000.
8. J. S. Foster, T. Terauchi, and A. Aiken. Flow-sensitive type qualifiers. In *Proceedings of the ACM SIGPLAN 2002 Conference on Programming Language Design and Implementation*, volume 37 (5) of *ACM SIGPLAN Notices*, pages 1–12, 2002.
9. S. Z. Guyer and C. Lin. An annotation language for optimizing software libraries. In *Second Conference on Domain Specific Languages*, pages 39–52, October 1999.
10. S. Z. Guyer and C. Lin. Optimizing the use of high performance software libraries. In *Languages and Compilers for Parallel Computing*, pages 221–238, August 2000.
11. N. Heintze and O. Tardieu. Demand-driven pointer analysis. In *ACM SIGPLAN Conference on Programming Language Design and Implementation*, pages 24–34, 2001.
12. M. Hind. Pointer analysis: Haven't we solved this problem yet? In *Proceedings of the 2001 ACM SIGPLAN - SIGSOFT Workshop on Program Analysis for Software Tools and Engeneering (PASTE-01)*, pages 54–61, 2001.
13. M. Hind and A. Pioli. Evaluating the effectiveness of pointer alias analyses. *Science of Computer Programming*, 39(1):31–55, January 2001.
14. S. Horwitz, T. Reps, and M. Sagiv. Demand Interprocedural Dataflow Analysis. In *Proceedings of SIGSOFT'95 Third ACM SIGSOFT Symposium on the Foundations of Software Engineering*, pages 104–115, October 1995.
15. J. Plevyak and A. A. Chien. Precise concrete type inference for object-oriented languages. *ACM SIGPLAN Notices*, 29(10):324–324, October 1994.
16. E. Ruf. Context-insensitive alias analysis reconsidered. In *SIGPLAN Conference on Programming Language Design and Implementation*, pages 13–22, 1995.
17. U. Shankar, K. Talwar, J. S. Foster, and D. Wagner. Detecting format string vulnerabilities with type qualifiers. In *Proceedings of the 10th USENIX Security Symposium*, 2001.
18. M. Shapiro and S. Horwitz. The effects of the precision of pointer analysis. *Lecture Notes in Computer Science*, 1302, 1997.
19. P. Stocks, B. G. Ryder, W. Landi, and S. Zhang. Comparing flow and context sensitivity on the modification-side-effects problem. In *International Symposium on Software Testing and Analysis*, pages 21–31, 1998.

20. R. Strom and S. Yemini. Typestate: A programming language concept for enhancing software reliabiity. *IEEE Transactions on Software Engineering*, 12(1):157–171, 1986.
21. L. Wall, T. Christiansen, and J. Orwant. *Programming Perl, 3rd Edition*. O'Reilly, July 2000.
22. R. P. Wilson and M. S. Lam. Efficient context-sensitive pointer analysis for C programs. In *Proceedings of the ACM SIGPLAN'95 Conference on Programming Language Design and Implementation*, pages 1–12, 1995.
23. S. Zhang, B. G. Ryder, and W. A. Landi. Experiments with combined analysis for pointer aliasing. *ACM SIGPLAN Notices*, 33(7):11–18, July 1998.

Abstract Interpretation of Programs as Markov Decision Processes

David Monniaux

École Normale Supérieure
Département d'Informatique, 45, rue d'Ulm
75230 Paris cedex 5, France
http://www.di.ens.fr/~monniaux

Abstract. We propose a formal language for the specification of trace properties of probabilistic, nondeterministic transition systems, encompassing the properties expressible in Linear Time Logic. Those formulas are in general undecidable on infinite deterministic transition systems and thus on infinite Markov decision processes. This language has both a semantics in terms of sets of traces, as well as another semantics in terms of measurable functions; we give and prove theorems linking the two semantics. We then apply abstract interpretation-based techniques to give upper bounds on the worst-case probability of the studied property. We propose an enhancement of this technique when the state space is partitioned — for instance along the program points —, allowing the use of faster iteration methods.

1 Introduction

The study of probabilistic programs is of considerable interest for the validation of networking protocols, embedded systems, or simply for compiling optimizations. It is also a difficult matter, due to the undecidability of properties on infinite-state deterministic programs, as well as the difficulties arising from probabilities. In this paper, we provide methods for the analysis of programs represented as infinite-state Markov decision processes.

The analysis of *finite-state* Markov decision processes was originally conducted in the fields of operational research and finance mathematics [23]. More recently, they have been studied from the angle of probabilistic computing systems [1–4,15,24]. Effective resolution techniques include linear programming [23, §7.2.7] [7] and newer data structures such as MTBDDs [2]. However, the problem of large- or infinite-state systems has not been so well studied.

In the case of deterministic or nondeterministic systems without a notion of probability, various analysis techniques have been proposed in the last twenty years. Since the problem is undecidable, those techniques are either partially manual (i.e. require the input of *invariants* or similar), either *approximate* (i.e., the analysis takes a pessimistic point of view when it cannot solve the problem exactly). In this paper, we take the latter approach and build our analysis methods upon the existing framework of *abstract interpretation* [9], a general theory of approximation between semantics.

We have earlier proposed two classes of automatic methods to analyze such system: some *forward* [16,17], some *backward* [19,20]. In this paper, we focus on the backward approach and extend it to a larger class of properties (including those specified by LTL formulas). We also prove that chaotic iterations strategies [8, ß2.9] apply to our case, which allows parallel implementations.

In section 2, we give an introduction to probabilistic transition systems, which we extend in section 3 to nondeterministic and probabilistic systems. In section 4, we give a formal language for the specification of trace properties, including those formulated using Büchi or Rabin automata. In section 5, we explain how to analyze those properties backward and in section 6.1 how to apply abstract analyses.

2 Probabilistic Transition Systems

The natural extension of transition systems to the probabilistic case is *probabilistic transition systems*, also known as *Markov chains* or *discrete-time Markov process*.

2.1 Probabilistic Transitions

We assume that the set of states is *finite* or *countable* so as to avoid technicalities. The natural extension of the notion of deterministic state is the notion of probability distribution on the set of states.

Definition 1. *Let Ω be a finite or countable set of states. A function $f : \Omega \to [0,1]$ is called a* probability distribution *if $\sum_{\omega \in \Omega} f(\omega) = 1$. We shall note $D(\Omega)$ the set of probabilistic distributions on Ω.*

Now that we have the probabilistic counterpart of the notion of state, we need to have the counterpart of the notion of transition.

Definition 2. *Let Ω be a finite or countable set of states. Let us consider a function $T : \Omega \times \Omega \to [0,1]$ such that for all $\omega_1 \in \Omega$, $\sum_{\omega_2 \in \Omega} T(\omega_1; \omega_2) = 1$. (Ω, T) is called a* probabilistic transition system.

If Ω is finite, the relation relation can be given by a *probabilistic transition matrix*. Let us assimilate Ω to $\{1, \ldots, N\}$. Then, the transition matrix M is defined by $m_{i,j} = T(i,j)$ if $i \to j$, 0 otherwise.

The intuitive notion of a probabilistic transition is that it maps an *input distribution* to an *output distribution*. It is the probabilistic counterpart of the notion of a successor state.

Definition 3. *Let T be a transition probability between Ω_1 and Ω_2. Let us define $\vec{T} : D(\Omega_1) \to D(\Omega_2)$ as follows: $\vec{T}(d)(\omega_2) = \sum_{\omega_1 \in \Omega_1} T(\omega_1, \omega_2) d(\omega_1)$.*

Let us now describe the probabilistic counterpart of the notion of predecessor state. Given a transition probability T between Ω_1 and Ω_2 and a boolean property $\pi : \Omega_2 \to \{0,1\}$, the expectation of a state $\omega_1 \in \Omega_1$ to reach π in one step is then $\sum_{\omega_2 \in \Omega_2} T(\omega_1, \omega_2) \pi(\omega_2)$. We have thus defined a function $\Omega_1 \to [0,1]$ mapping each state to its corresponding expectation.

A natural extension of this construction is to consider any function $f \in P(\Omega_2) = \Omega_2 \to [0,1]$. We call such functions *condition functions*.[1]

Definition 4. *Let T be a transition probability between Ω_1 and Ω_2. Let us define $\overleftarrow{T} : P(\Omega_2) \to P(\Omega_1)$ as follows: $\overleftarrow{T}(f)(\omega_1) = \sum_{\omega_2 \in \Omega_2} T(\omega_1, \omega_2) f(\omega_2)$.*

Lemma 1. *For all transition probability T, $\overleftarrow{T}$ is ω-continuous.*

Those functions are linked by the following *adjunction relation*: if T is a transition probability relative to Ω_1 and Ω_2, noting $\langle f, \mu \rangle = \sum_\omega f(\omega) \mu(\omega)$, then

$$\forall f \in P(\Omega_2) \; \forall \mu \in D(\Omega_1) \; \langle f, \overrightarrow{T}.\mu \rangle = \langle \overleftarrow{T}.f, \mu \rangle. \tag{1}$$

2.2 Probability Measures on Traces

We shall also use probability measures on *sets of traces* arising from probabilistic transition systems. Let us start with a simple example — consider sequences of tosses of a fair coin: the coin has probability 0.5 of giving 0 and 0.5 of giving 1. A trace is then an infinite sequence of zeroes and ones. Let us consider the (regular) set $0^n(0|1)^*$ of sequences starting by at least n zeroes. It is obvious that the probability of falling into that set is 2^{-n}. The probability of the singleton containing the sequence of only zeroes is 0.

We use the theorem of Ionescu Tulcea (Appendix B) to construct the probability measure μ_ω on the set of traces according to the probability distribution μ on the initial states and the transition probability T.

The probability of a property $P : \Omega^I N \to \{0,1\}$ on the traces is then $\int P d\mu_\omega$.

3 Nondeterministic and Probabilistic Transition Systems

We shall see how to combine the notions of *nondeterministic choice* (sets of possible choices for which we know no probabilistic properties) and *probabilistic choice* (sets of possible choices for which we know probabilistic properties), obtaining *discrete-time Markov decision processes* [23], which has been studied more particularly in the field of operational research and finance mathematics, as well as machine learning.

Let us now consider the case where the system must be able to do both nondeterministic and probabilistic transitions (example in Fig. 1). The system then has the choice between different transition probabilities.

---

[1] Please note that while those functions look similar to distributions, they are quite different in their meaning and are different mathematical objects when treated in the general, non discrete, case.

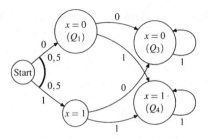

Fig. 1. A probabilistic-nondeterministic transition system

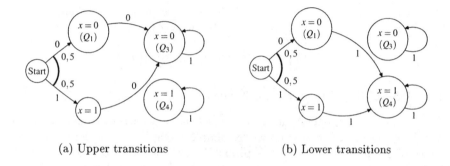

(a) Upper transitions

(b) Lower transitions

Fig. 2. Two purely probabilistic transition systems that define, when composed together nondeterministically, the same probabilistic-nondeterministic transition system as in Fig. 1

For instance, on Fig. 1, in state Q_1, the system has the choice between two partial transition probabilities: the first goes to Q_3 with probability 1, the second goes to Q_4 with probability 1. For an easier intuition, one may think about this choice as if it were made by an adversary willing to induce certain behaviors. The adversary is supposed to follow a strategy or *policy* [23, §2.1.5].

In this paper, we shall assume that the adversary may see the present and past states of the execution. This is realistic if the adversary models a human evildoer as well as the physical environment of an embedded system.

Let us note that other choices can give very different results. For instance, let us consider a program that chooses a Boolean variable x nondeterministically, then chooses a Boolean variable y with uniform probability, then replaces x with the exclusive or of x and y (Fig. 1). Clearly, if the nondeterminism is allowed to "look at the future" and predict the outcome of the random generator, it can always arrange for z to be true. If it can only look at the past, it cannot and z is uniformly distributed.

Let us suppose that our system is defined by a transition probability T from $\Omega \times Y$ to Ω, where Y is the *domain of nondeterministic choices*. For instance, for the system given in Fig. 1, Y is $\{0,1\}$ (choice between the upper and lower arrows, as seen in Fig. 2). The operation of the adversary for the transition between states n and $n+1$ is modeled using an unknown transition probability U_n from Ω^n to Y. The whole transition that is executed by the system is then the composition $T_n = T \circ \begin{bmatrix} Id \\ U_n \end{bmatrix}$, which is a transition probability between Ω^n and Ω. By this notation, we mean that, using the notation of Def. 2,

$$T_n(x_0, \ldots, x_{n-1}; x_n) = T(x_{n-1}, U_n(x_0, \ldots, x_{n-1}); x_n). \tag{2}$$

Ionescu Tulcea's theorem (Appendix B) then constructs from the (T_n) a transition probability $G(T, (U_n)_{n \in IN})$ from Ω (the initial state space) to Ω^{IN}. We note

$$S_T(f, (U_n)_{n \in IN}) = t_0 \mapsto \langle t \mapsto f(t_0, t), G(T, (U_n)_{n \in IN})(t_0) \rangle \tag{3}$$

(S short for S_T if there is no ambiguity about T) and $R(f)$ the set of all functions $S(T, (U_n)_{n \in IN})$ when $(U_n)_{n \in IN}$ is a sequence of transition probabilities, U_n being a transition probability from Ω^n to Y. The λ is here a functional notation.

Let E_+^T or, if there is no confusion possible, $E_+(f) = \sup R(f)$ be the *worst-case semantics* and $E_-(f) = \inf R(f)$ be the *best-case semantics* (those designations assume that f indicates some kind of failure condition). Intuitively, if f is the characteristic function of a set of "faulty" traces, E_+ expresses a "worst case" analysis, modeling an adversary willing to make the system err and E_- a "best case" analysis, modeling an adversary willing to prevent the system from erring. $E_+(f)$ is often called the *value* of the Markov decision process with respect to the reward function f (even though we use a slightly different framework as the one given in [23]).

Lemma 5. $E_+(1) = 1$ and $E_+(0) = 0$. E_+ is monotone and upper-continuous.

4 The Properties to Analyze

We consider a property to analyze on the traces. To each initial state we attach its *expectation*, that is, the integral of the property to analyze over the traces starting from this state (or the set of integrals, if considering nondeterminism). The properties to analyze are expressed as measurable functions from the set of (possible) traces of execution; we call these functions *trace valuators*. We shall actually consider a class of trace valuators defined syntactically by certain formulas.

4.1 Expectation Functions

Let $I = [0,1]$ or $[0,+\infty]$, depending on the kind of properties to analyze. Let Ω be a finite or countable set of states — we impose this cardinality constraint so as to avoid theoretical complexities. $\mathcal{P}\Omega$ is the set of subsets of Ω. Let $\Omega \to I$ be the set of functions from Ω to I, the *expectation functions* of our system; this set, ordered by $\leq$ point-wise, is a complete lattice.

4.2 Trace Valuators

Let $\Omega^I N \to I$ be the set of measurable functions from $\Omega^I N$ to I, ordered point-wise. We shall call such functions "valuators".

Boolean Trace Valuators. We take $I = [0,1]$ or even $I = \{0,1\}$.

We shall consider formulas written in the following language:

$$
\begin{aligned}
\textit{formula1} ::=\ &\textit{name} \\
|\ &\textit{constant} \\
|\ &\textit{name} +_{\textit{set}} \textit{formula1} \text{ where } \textit{set} \subseteq \Omega \\
|\ &\textit{constant} +_{\textit{set}} \textit{formula1} \\
|\ &\text{lfp}(\textit{name} \mapsto \textit{formula1}) \\
|\ &\text{gfp}(\textit{name} \mapsto \textit{formula1}) \\
|\ &\text{shift}(\textit{formula1}) \\
|\ &\text{let } \textit{name} = \textit{formula1} \text{ in } \textit{formula2}
\end{aligned}
$$

Let shift : $\Omega^I N \to \Omega^I N$: $(\text{shift}.t)_k = t_{k+1}$.

Let env_t be the set of environments of valuators, mapping each *name* to a valuator, ordered point-wise.

$[\![\textit{formula}]\!]_t : env_t \to (\Omega^I N \to I)$ is defined inductively as follows:

$$[\![name]\!]_t . env = env(name) \tag{4}$$

$$[\![constant]\!]_t . env = constant \tag{5}$$

$$[\![f_1 +_S f_2]\!]_t . env = \lambda t \chi_S(t_0).([\![f_1]\!]_t\, env) + \chi_{S^C}(t_0).([\![f_2]\!]_t\, env) \tag{6}$$

$$[\![\text{lfp}(name \mapsto f)]\!]_t . env = \text{lfp}(\lambda \phi [\![f]\!]_t . env[name \mapsto \phi]) \tag{7}$$

$$[\![\text{gfp}(name \mapsto f)]\!]_t . env = \text{gfp}(\lambda \phi [\![f]\!]_t . env[name \mapsto \phi]) \tag{8}$$

$$[\![\text{shift}(f)]\!]_t . env = ([\![f]\!]_t . env) \circ \text{shift} \tag{9}$$

$$[\![\text{let } name = f_1 \text{ in } f_2]\!]_t . env = [\![f_2]\!]_t . env[name \mapsto [\![f_1]\!]_t . env] \tag{10}$$

χ_S is the characteristic function of S and S^C the complement of S. $t_0 \in \Omega$ is the first state of the sequence of states $t \in \Omega^I N$.

Let us note that we could introduce a negation operator $\neg$ ($[\![\neg f]\!]_t = 1 - [\![f]\!]_t$) as syntactic sugar — any formula with negations can be transformed into one without by pushing the negations to the leaves.

Lemma 6. *For all formula f, $[\![f]\!]_t$ is monotone. For all formula f without lfp or gfp, $[\![f]\!]_t$ is continuous.*

Some Particularly Interesting Boolean Valuators. We shall consider in this section four very important classes of properties, all of which can be shown to be measurable.

- Let A be a set of states. The *reachability* property associated with A defines the set of traces that pass through A at some point. It corresponds to the formula:
$$\mathrm{lfp}(f \mapsto 1 +_A \mathrm{shift}\, f) \qquad (11)$$

- Let A be a set of states. The *liveness* property associated with A defines the set of traces that always remain in A. It corresponds to the formula:
$$\mathrm{gfp}(f \mapsto \mathrm{shift}\, f +_A 0) \qquad (12)$$

- Let A be a (measurable) set of states. The *Büchi acceptance* property associated with A defines the set of traces that pass through A infinitely often; it is written as:
$$\mathrm{gfp}(C \mapsto \mathrm{lfp}(R \mapsto \mathrm{shift}(C) +_A \mathrm{shift}(R))) \qquad (13)$$

The *co-Büchi* property is just the negation of this formula.

- Given a sequence $\emptyset \subseteq U_{2k} \subseteq \cdots \subseteq U_0 = \Omega$, the *Rabin acceptance property* associated with (U_n) is the set of traces defined by the following temporal property [10, sect. 5]:
$$\mathcal{R} = \bigvee_{i=0}^{k-1} (\Box \diamond U_{2i} \wedge \neg \Box \diamond U_{2i+1}) \qquad (14)$$

It corresponds to the following formula:
$$\mathrm{gfp}(x_{2k-1} \mapsto \mathrm{lfp}(x_{2k} \mapsto \cdots \mathrm{gfp}(x_1 \mapsto \mathrm{lfp}(x_0 \mapsto$$
$$((\cdots (x_{2k-1} + U_{2k-1} x_{2k-2}) \cdots +_{U_1} x_0) +_{U_0} 0) \qquad (15)$$

Summation Valuator. A related family of trace valuators are the *summing valuators*. The summation valuator associated with a (measurable) function $f : \Omega \mapsto [0, +\infty]$ is the function
$$[\![\Sigma A]\!]_t] : \begin{vmatrix} \Omega^{I\!N} & \to [0, +\infty] \\ (x_n)_{n \in I\!N} & \mapsto \sum_{k=0}^{\infty} f(x_k) \end{vmatrix} \qquad (16)$$

Obviously, this function can be formulated as a least fixpoint:
$$[\![\Sigma f]\!]_t = \mathrm{lfp}(\phi \to f + \phi \circ \mathrm{shift}) \qquad (17)$$

This construct has two obvious applications:

- counting the average number of times the program goes through a certain set of states A; here, f is the characteristic function of A;
- counting the average time spent in the process; here f maps each state to the amount of time spent in that state (0 for states meaning "termination").

4.3 Temporal Logics

Temporal logics [5, chapter 3] are expressive means of specifying properties of transition systems.

Linear Time Logic (LTL) and ω-Regular Conditions. A formula F in LTL defines an ω-regular set of traces $[\![F]\!]_t$, that is, a set of traces recognizable by a (nondeterministic) Büchi automaton B [5, §3.2], or, equivalently, by a deterministic Rabin automaton R [25, §4].

Let us consider a (nondeterministic) probabilistic transition system T, and the according definition of E_+^T. Let us consider the synchronous product $T \times R$, and C the associated Rabin acceptance condition. $E_+^T([\![F]\!]_t)$ is then equal to $E_+^{S \times R}([\![C]\!]_t)$ [10, §5].

If B is deterministic, we can similarly consider the synchronous product $T \times B$, and C the associated Büchi condition. $E_+^T([\![F]\!]_t)$ is then equal to $E_+^{S \times B}([\![C]\!]_t)$ [10, §4].[2]

Branching-Time Logic: pCTL and pCTL*. The branching-time logics CTL and CTL* [5, §3.2] have had much success in the analysis of nondeterministic (albeit non probabilistic) systems. It was therefore quite natural to extend this notion to probabilistic systems. Proposed extensions to the probabilistic case include pCTL [11] and pCTL*. We shall see here briefly how we deal with some pCTL* formulas.

CTL* formulas define sets of states as the starting states of sets of traces defined by LTL path formulas (in which state formulas are CTL* state formulas).

The operation that makes a CTL* state formula out of a LTL path formula is the taking of the initial states: if $[\![f]\!]_s$ denotes the semantics of f as a state formula and $[\![f]\!]_p$ its semantics as a path formula, then

$$[\![f]\!]_s = \{x_0 \in \Omega \mid \exists x_1, \ldots \langle x_0, x_1, \ldots \rangle \in [\![f]\!]_p\}. \tag{18}$$

In the case of probabilistic systems, we do not have sets of starting states but expectation functions; such expectation functions are then compared to a threshold value, which gives sets of states. State formulas noted as $f_{\bowtie \alpha}$ are thus obtained, where f is a trace valuator and $\bowtie$ is $\leq, <, =, >$ or $\geq$. The semantics of this construct is as follow:

$$[\![f_{\bowtie \alpha}]\!] = \{x_0 \in \Omega \mid \forall (U_n)_{n \in I\!N} S([\![f]\!]_t, (U_n)_{n \in I\!N})(x_0) \bowtie \alpha\} \tag{19}$$

In the case of $<$ and $\leq$, giving an upper bound on those sets is easy provided we have an upper bound $[\![f]\!]_{e+}^{\#}$ of $E_+([\![t]\!]_t)$ (see §5):

$$\forall x_0 [\![f]\!]_{e+}^{\#}(x_0) \bowtie \alpha \implies x_0 \notin [\![f_{\bowtie \alpha}]\!]. \tag{20}$$

---

[2] Note that this does not hold for nondeterministic Büchi automata, since the automaton is allowed to take its nondeterministic choices with the knowledge of the full sequence of states, not only the past and present states.

5 Backwards Worst Case Analysis

In section 4.2, we gave the syntax and semantics of a logic describing sets of traces, or, more generally, measurable functions over the traces. Given a formula f, one may want to compute its worst-case probability $E_+(\llbracket f \rrbracket_t)$, or at least get an upper bound for it. Unfortunately, the definitions of both $\llbracket f \rrbracket_t$ and E_+ do not yield effective means to do so.

In 5.1 we shall attach to each formula f another semantics $\llbracket f \rrbracket_{e+}$, which we shall show how to abstract in §6. We shall see the abstraction relationship between $E_+(\llbracket f \rrbracket_t)$ and $\llbracket f \rrbracket_{e+}$ in §5.2.

5.1 Backwards Worst Case Semantics on Expectation Functions

A well-known solution to the problem of the optimal value of a Markov decision process is *value iteration* [23, §7.2.4]. This method is mainly of theoretical interest for the analysis of finite state Markov decision processes, since there is little control as to its rate of convergence and much better algorithms are available [23, §7.2.4]. On the other hand, since it is actually a kind of generalization to Markov decision processes of the backwards reachability analysis for nondeterministic systems, we can apply abstract interpretation techniques so as to provide an effective mean to compute upper bounds on the probability of the properties to analyze.

Let env_e be the set of environments of expectation functions (an environment of expectation functions maps each *name* to a expectation function), ordered point-wise.

$\llbracket formula \rrbracket_{e+} : (\Omega \to I) \to (\Omega \to I)$ is defined inductively as follows:

$$\llbracket name \rrbracket_{e+}.env = env(name) \qquad (21)$$

$$\llbracket constant \rrbracket_{e+}.env = \lambda x\, constant \qquad (22)$$

$$\llbracket f_1 +_S f_2 \rrbracket_{e+}.env = \chi_S.(\llbracket f_1 \rrbracket_{e+}\, env) + \chi_{S^c}.(\llbracket f_2 \rrbracket_{e+}\, env) \qquad (23)$$

$$\llbracket \mathrm{lfp}(name \mapsto f) \rrbracket_{e+}.env = \mathrm{lfp}(\lambda \phi \llbracket f \rrbracket_{e+}.env[name \mapsto \phi]) \qquad (24)$$

$$\llbracket \mathrm{gfp}(name \mapsto f) \rrbracket_{e+}.env = \mathrm{gfp}(\lambda \phi \llbracket f \rrbracket_{e+}.env[name \mapsto \phi]) \qquad (25)$$

$$\llbracket \mathrm{shift}(f) \rrbracket_{e+}.env = \sup_{T \in \mathcal{T}}(\overleftarrow{T}(\llbracket f \rrbracket_{e+}.env)) \qquad (26)$$

$$\llbracket \mathrm{let}\ name = f_1\ \mathrm{in}\ f_2 \rrbracket_{e+}.env = \llbracket f_2 \rrbracket_{e+}.env[name \mapsto \llbracket f_1 \rrbracket_{e+}.env] \qquad (27)$$

This semantics is thus some form of μ-calculus, except that "lfp" replaces the μ binder and "gfp" ν; but since we also use μ to note measures, it would have been confusing to also use it in the syntax of the formulas.

$\llbracket formula \rrbracket_{e+}$ is monotone.

Lemma 7. *Let f be a formula not containing* gfp. $\llbracket f \rrbracket_{e+}$ *is ω-upper-continuous.*

As for the summation valuator,

$$\llbracket \Sigma f \rrbracket_{e+} = \mathrm{lfp}\left(\phi \mapsto f + \sup_{T \in \mathcal{T}}(\overleftarrow{T}.\phi)\right) \qquad (28)$$

5.2 The Abstraction Relation between the Semantics

Theorem 8. *Let f be a formula not containing* gfp. *Let env be an environment of valuators. Noting $E_+(env)$ the point-wise application of E_+ to env,*

$$[\![f]\!]_{e+} . (E_+(env)) = E_+([\![f]\!]_t . env) \tag{29}$$

Proof. Proof by induction on the structure of f.

- The cases for "let", *name* and *constant* are trivial.
- For $f_1 +_S f_2$: Let $t_0 \in X$.

$$
\begin{aligned}
& [\![f_1 +_S f_2]\!]_{e+} . (E_+(env)).t_0 \\
&= \chi_S(t_0).([\![f_1]\!]_{e+} . E_+(env).t_0) + \chi_{S^c}(t_0).([\![f_2]\!]_{e+} . E_+(env).t_0) \\
&= \chi_S(t_0).(E_+([\![f_1]\!]_t . env).t_0) + \chi_{S^c}(t_0).(E_+([\![f_2]\!]_t . env).t_0) \quad \text{(induction)} \\
&= E_+(\lambda t \chi_S(t_0).([\![f_1]\!]_t\, envt) + \chi_{S^c}(t_0).([\![f_2]\!]_t\, envt)).t_0 \quad \text{(lemma 2)} \\
&= E_+([\![f_1 +_S f_2]\!]_t).t_0.
\end{aligned}
$$

- For shift: Let us first fix U_1. Let us note $T_1 = T \circ \begin{bmatrix} \text{Id} \\ U_1 \end{bmatrix}$ and consider $\overleftarrow{T_1}.E_+([\![f]\!]_t)$. From lemma 1, $\overleftarrow{T_1}$ is a monotonic, ω-continuous, operator; from lemma 3, $R([\![f]\!]_t)$ is directed; from lemma 4,

$$\bigsqcup_{f \in R([\![f]\!]_t . env)} (\overleftarrow{T_1} f) = \overleftarrow{T_1}(\bigsqcup_{f \in R([\![f]\!]_t . env)} f).$$

It follows that (using the λ-notation for functions),

$$
\overleftarrow{T_1}.E_+([\![f]\!]_t).t_0 = \sup_{\substack{(U_n)_{n \geq 2} \\ U_n \text{ not depending on } t_0}} \times \int \int \lambda \langle t_2, \ldots \rangle ([\![f]\!]_t . env)(\langle t_1, \ldots \rangle)\, \mathrm{d}[G(T, (U_n)_{n \geq 2}).t_1]\, T_1(t_0, \mathrm{d}t_1)
$$

$$
= \sup_{\substack{(U_n)_{n \geq 2} \\ U_n \text{ not depending on } t_0}} \times \int \lambda \langle t_2, \ldots \rangle ([\![f]\!]_t . env)(\langle t_1, \ldots \rangle)\, \mathrm{d}[G(T, (U_n)_{n \geq 1}).t_0]
$$

Let us apply lemma 11 to that last expression. We obtain

$$\overleftarrow{T_1}.E_+([\![f]\!]_t).t_0 = \sup_{(U_n)_{n \geq 2}} \int \lambda \langle t_2, \ldots \rangle ([\![f]\!]_t . env)(\langle t_1, \ldots \rangle)\, \mathrm{d}[G(T, (U_n)_{n \geq 1}).t_0] \tag{30}$$

Let $t_0 \in X$. Let us now consider all U_1's.

$E_+(\llbracket \mathrm{shift}(f) \rrbracket_t . env).t_0$

$= \sup_{(U_n)_{n \geq 1}} \int \lambda \langle t_1, \ldots \rangle (\llbracket f \rrbracket_t . env) \circ \mathrm{shift}(\langle t_0, t_1, \ldots \rangle) \, \mathrm{d}[G(T, (U_n)_{n \geq 1}).t_0]$

$= \sup_{U_1} \sup_{(U_n)_{n \geq 2}} \int \lambda \langle t_1, \ldots \rangle (\llbracket f \rrbracket_t . env)(\langle t_1, \ldots \rangle) \, \mathrm{d}[G(T, (U_n)_{n \geq 1}).t_0]$

$= \left(\sup_{U_1} \overleftarrow{\left(T \circ \left[\mathrm{Id}_{U_1} \right] \right)}.E_+(\llbracket f \rrbracket_t) \right).t_0$ (using Equ. 30)

$= \llbracket \mathrm{shift}(f) \rrbracket_{e+} . E_+(env)$

- $\llbracket \mathrm{lfp}(name \mapsto f) \rrbracket_{e+} . env = \mathrm{lfp}(\lambda \phi \llbracket f \rrbracket_{e+} . env[name \mapsto \phi])$.
  From lemma 7, $\lambda \phi \llbracket f \rrbracket_{e+} . env[name \mapsto \phi]$ is ω-upper-continuous.
  $\llbracket \mathrm{lfp}(name \mapsto f) \rrbracket_t . env = \mathrm{lfp}(\lambda \phi \llbracket f \rrbracket_t . env[name \mapsto \phi])$.
  From lemma 6, $\lambda \phi \llbracket f \rrbracket_t . env[name \mapsto \phi]$ is ω-upper-continuous.
  From the induction hypothesis,

$$E_+ \circ (\lambda \phi \llbracket f \rrbracket_t . env[name \mapsto \phi]) = (\lambda \phi \llbracket f \rrbracket_{e+} . E_+(env)[name \mapsto \phi])).$$

From lemma 5, E_+ is ω-upper-continuous. The conclusion then follows from lemma 5.

The following theorem guarantees the soundness of the abstract analysis for all formulas.

Theorem 9. *Let f be a formula. Let env be an environment of valuators. Let us suppose that $H \geq E_+(env)$ pointwise. Then*

$$\llbracket f \rrbracket_{e+} . (H) \geq E_+(\llbracket f \rrbracket_t . env). \tag{31}$$

Proof by induction similar to that of Th. 8. Also similarly we can guarantee the soundness of the analysis of summations:

Theorem 10. *The semantics of the summing operator satisfies:*

$$E_+(\llbracket \Sigma f \rrbracket_t) = \llbracket \Sigma f \rrbracket_{e+}. \tag{32}$$

6 Abstract Analysis

We shall see here more precisely how to apply abstract interpretation to that backwards semantics.

6.1 General Case

We compute safe approximations of $[\![f]\!]_{e+}$ by abstract interpretation. We introduce an abstract semantics $[\![f]\!]_{e+}^{\#}$ which is an upper approximation of f:

$$\forall env \; \forall env^{\#} \; env^{\#} \geq env \Longrightarrow [\![f]\!]_{e+}^{\#}.env^{\#} \geq [\![f]\!]_{e+}.env. \qquad (33)$$

The computations for $[\![f]\!]_{e+}^{\#}$ will be done symbolically in an *abstract domain* such as the ones described in [19, 20].

- We shall assume that we have an abstract operation for "shift". That is, we have a monotone operation $\text{pre}^{\#}$ such that

$$\forall f, \; \forall T \in \mathcal{T}, \; \text{pre}^{\#}.f \geq T^{*}.f^{\#}. \qquad (34)$$

  This operation will be supplied by the abstract domain that we use. Then

$$\forall env, \; \forall env^{\#}, \; env^{\#} \geq env \Longrightarrow [\![\text{shift}(f)]\!]_{e+}^{\#}.env^{\#} \geq [\![\text{shift}(f)]\!]_{e+}.env. \qquad (35)$$

  provided that

$$\forall env, \; \forall env^{\#}, \; env^{\#} \geq env \Longrightarrow [\![f]\!]_{e+}^{\#}.env^{\#} \geq [\![f]\!]_{e+}.env.$$

- We shall approximate least fixpoints using a *widening operator* [9, §4.3]. A widening operator ∇ is a kind of abstraction of the least upper bound that enforces convergence:
  - $f \nabla g \geq \sup(f, g)$ (pointwise);
  - For any ascending sequence $(v_n)_{n \in \mathbb{N}}$, the sequence $(u_n)_{n \in \mathbb{N}}$ defined inductively by $u_{n+1} = u_n \nabla v_n$ is to be ultimately stationary.

  Then the limit $L^{\#}$ of the sequence defined by $u_0 = 0$ and $u_{n+1} = u_n \nabla f^{\#}(u_n)$, where $f^{\#}$ is an upper approximation of f, is an upper approximation to the least fixpoint of f. More precise upper approximations of the least fixpoint of f can then be reached by iterating f over $L^{\#}$ using a so-called *narrowing operators* [9, §4.3].

- We shall approximate greatest fixpoints using a limited iteration approach: if f is an upper approximation of f, then for any $n \in \mathbb{N}$, $f^{\#^n}(\top) \geq \text{gfp} f$.

6.2 Partitioning in Programs

In the case of programs, the state space is generally $P \times M$, where P is the (finite) set of program points and M the set of possible memory configurations. More generally, P may be a kind of *partitioning* of the program. Non-probabilistic analysis generally operates on abstractions of $\mathcal{P}P \times M \simeq P \times M \to \{0,1\} \simeq P \to \mathcal{P}M$. Given an abstraction of $\mathcal{P}M$ by a lattice $L^{\#}$, one obtains a pointwise abstraction of $P \to \mathcal{P}M$ by $P \to L^{\#}$. Elements of $P \to L^{\#}$ are just vectors of $|P|$ elements of $L^{\#}$.

This approach can be directly extended to our measurable functions: we shall abstract $P \times M \to I$ (where $I = [0, 1]$ or $I = [0, +\infty]$) by $P \to L^\#$ if $L^\#$ is an abstract domain for $M \to I$.

The first problem is to get an abstraction of the operation used in the "shift" construct:

$$F : \begin{vmatrix} (P \times M \to I) \to (P \times M \to I) \\ h \qquad \mapsto (l, m) \mapsto \sup_{y \in Y} \sum_{(l', m') \in P \times M} T((l, m), y; (l', m')) . h(l', m') \end{vmatrix} \quad (36)$$

Let us take the following form for the program instructions: at program point l, the executed instruction represented by T is the sequence:

1. a nondeterministic choice y is taken in the set Y_l;
2. a random choice r is taken in set R_l according to distribution $\mathcal{R}_p$;
3. the memory state is combined deterministically with the two choices to form the new memory state using a function $F_l : (M \times Y) \times R_l \to M$;
4. depending on the memory state m, the program takes a deterministic jump to program point $J(l, m)$.

Let us note $\tau_l(l') = \{m \mid J(l, m) = l'\}$ (the set of memory values m that lead to program point l' from program point l; $\tau_l(l')$ is then essentially the condition for a conditional jump). Then we can rewrite the transition equation as follows

$$(F.h)(l) = \text{choice}^*_{Y_l} \circ \text{random}^*_{R_l} \circ (F_l)_p{}^* \left(\sum_{l' \in P} \phi^*_{\tau_l l'} \left(h(l', \bullet) \right) \right) \quad (37)$$

using the following building blocks:

$$\text{choice}^*_{Y_l}(h) = m \mapsto \sup_{y \in Y_l} h(m, y) \quad (38)$$

$$\text{random}^*_{R_l}(h) = m \mapsto \int h(m, r) \mathrm{d}\mu_{R_l}(r) \quad (39)$$

$$(F_l)_p{}^*(h) = h \circ F_l \quad (40)$$

$$\phi^*_A(h) = h.\chi_A \quad (41)$$

The reasons for those notations are explained in earlier works on the linear adjoint of Kozen's denotational semantics for probabilistic programs [19].

We shall abstract F as the composition of abstractions for:

- $\text{choice}^*_{Y_l}$, nondeterministic choice;
- $\text{random}^*_{R_l}$, probabilistic choice;
- $F_{l_p}{}^*$, deterministic run (arithmetic operations and the like);
- ϕ^*_A, test.

Since the function F is ω-upper-continuous, the least fixpoint of F is obtained as the limit of $F^n(0)$ (let us recall that this is the point-wise limit of a sequence of functions from Ω to I). The expression of the iterates using a partition with respect to P is as follows:

$$f_1^{(n+1)} = F_1(f_1^{(n)}, \ldots, f_{|P|}^{(n)}) \qquad (42)$$

$$\vdots \qquad \vdots \qquad (43)$$

$$f_{|P|}^{(n+1)} = F_{|P|}(f_1^{(n)}, \ldots, f_{|P|}^{(n)}) \qquad (44)$$

In terms of implementation, this means that we update in parallel the $|P|$ elements of the vector representing the iterate. As noted by Cousot [8, ß2.9], this parallel update may be replaced by *chaotic iterations* or *asynchronous iterations*. Chaotic iterations allow us to compute the iterations by taking into account the recently updated elements. All these iteration strategies lead to the same limit (the least fixpoint of F).

Let us consider for instance the following strategy:

$$\begin{array}{l} f_1^{(n+1)} = F_1(f_1^{(n)}, \ldots, f_{|P|}^{(n)}) \\ f_2^{(n+1)} = F_2(f_1^{(n+1)}, \ldots, f_{|P|}^{(n)}) \\ \vdots \qquad \vdots \\ f_{|P|}^{(n+1)} = F_{|P|}(f_1^{(n+1)}, \ldots, f_{|P|}^{(n)}) \end{array} \qquad (45)$$

This strategy is itself a monotone operator whose least fixpoint is to be determined. It has an obvious abstract counterpart leading to an approximate fixpoint in the usual way (ß6.1).

7 Conclusion, Related Works, and Discussion

We showed how to apply abstract interpretation techniques to check various temporal properties of (nondeterministic) probabilistic programs, considered as Markov decision processes (small-step semantics).

The most natural point of view on those processes is that the nondeterministic decisions are taken as the program proceeds, taking into account the current state as well as the previous ones. This how Markov decision processes are usually studied [23] and this is the approach we took here.

It can be argued that this model is excessively pessimistic. Indeed, if nondeterminism is used to model the environment of an embedded system, then it is excessive to assume that the behavior of this environment depends on the history of the *internal state* of the system; only the part of this history observable from the environment should be taken into account. This leads to the study of *partially observable Markov decision processes* (POMDP); however, their effective analysis is much more complex than that of fully observable processes [14].

Cleaveland's work [6] focuses on the model where the nondeterministic choices are taken *after* the probabilistic ones. This simplifies the theory to some extent, since taking the product of the analyzed process with an nondeterministic "observation" process, such as a nondeterministic Büchi automaton, is then easy. We have already proposed a Monte-Carlo method for such semantics [18].

The backwards analysis method we described is a generalization of the value iteration method used in operational research to compute the value of Markov decision processes. Our reachability analysis is related to the study of *positive bounded models* [23, ß7.2], where the reward 1 is granted the first time the process runs through the set of states to consider. The liveness analysis is related to the study of *negative models* [23, ß7.3], where the reward −1 is granted the first time the process leaves the set of states to consider.

Formal languages similar to the one we consider have been introduced by other authors, such as *quantitative game μ-calculus* [10]. The differences between our approach and this game calculus approach are threefold:

- We give a semantics in terms of traces, then prove its link with a semantics in terms of expectation functions; quantitative μ-calculus only gives the interpretation as expectation functions.
- While we prove a generic link between the semantics as an inequality valid for any formula (or an equation for some class), de Alfaro proves an interpretation for some specific formulas (reachability, liveness, deterministic Büchi and Rabin trace properties). We conjecture that we can extend the equality cases of this link.
- De Alfaro considers random two-player games while we consider random single-player games. We mentioned briefly (ß5.2) the differences between Markov decision processes and two-player games. Such problems can model questions such as the choice of an optimal strategy by the program so as to minimize the probability of a problem for all possible environments.

A possible extension of these properties is *discounted models* [23, Ch. 6]. In these, the importance of the future decreases exponentially; for instance, λ-discounted reachability would count passing through A for the first time at step n as λ^n instead of 1 (of course, $0 < \lambda < 1$). The theoretical study of those models is considerably easier than that of non-discounted models, since the fixpoints to study are the fixed points of contraction mappings in Banach spaces. While the extension of the techniques exposed in this paper to discounted models is easy (it suffices to add a multiplication by λ in the semantics of the "shift" operation), the practical interest of such models in the checking of computer programs remains to be seen.

Another possible extension is the computation of averages not only on the space of the program, but also on the time: computing the average value of a certain function as long as the program is running. Since this property is the quotient of two summing properties, there is no obvious method to evaluate it iteratively.

Another possible direction is the study of continuous time probabilistic systems. As usual with continuous-time systems, some kind of reduction to discrete time processes is to be done [12, 13].

References

1. Luca de Alfaro. *Formal Verification of Probabilistic Systems*. PhD thesis, Stanford University, Department of Computer Science, June 1998. CS-TR-98-1601.
2. Christel Baier, Edmund M. Clarke, Vasiliki Hartonas-Garmhausen, and Marta Kwiatkowska. Symbolic model checking for probabilistic processes. In P. Degano, R. Gorrieri, and A. Marchetti-Spaccamela, editors, *Automata, Languages and Programming (ICALP'97)*, volume 1256 of *LNCS*. Springer, 1997.
3. A. Bianco and L. de Alfaro. Model checking of probabilistic and nondeterministic systems. In *FST TCS'95: Foundations of Software Technology and Theoretical Computer Science*, volume 1026 of *Lecture Notes in Computer Science*, pages 499–513. Springer-Verlag, 1995.
4. C.Baier, M.Kwiatkowska, and G.Norman. Computing probability bounds for linear time formulas over concurrent probabilistic systems. *Electronic Notes in Theoretical Computer Science*, 21, 1999.
5. Edmund M. Clarke, Jr., Orna Grumberg, and Doron A. Peled. *Model Checking*. MIT Press, 1999.
6. Rance Cleaveland, Scott A. Smolka, and Amy E. Zwarico. Testing preorders for probabilistic processes. In Werner Kuich, editor, *Automata, Languages and Programming, 19th International Colloquium*, volume 623 of *Lecture Notes in Computer Science*, pages 708–719, Vienna, Austria, 13–17 July 1992. Springer-Verlag.
7. C. Courcoubetis and M. Yannakakis. Markov decision processes and regular events. In *Proc. ICALP'90*, volume 443 of *LNCS*, pages 336–349. Springer, 1990.
8. Patrick Cousot. *Méthodes itératives de construction et d'approximation de points fixes d'opérateurs monotones sur un treillis, analyse sémantique de programmes*. ThÈse d'état Ès sciences mathématiques, Université scientifique et médicale de Grenoble, Grenoble, France, 21 mars 1978.
9. Patrick Cousot and Radhia Cousot. Abstract interpretation and application to logic programs. *J. Logic Prog.*, 2-3(13):103–179, 1992.
10. L. de Alfaro and R. Majumdar. Quantitative solution of omega-regular games. In *STOC'01, 33rd Annual ACM Symposium on Theory of Computing*. ACM, 2001.
11. Hans Hansson and Bengt Jonsson. A logic for reasoning about time and reability. Technical Report R90-13, Swedish Institute of Computer Science, December 1990.
12. Marta Z. Kwiatkowska, Gethin Norman, Roberto Segala, and Jeremy Sproston. Verifying quantitative properties of continuous probabilistic timed automata. Technical Report CSR-00-6, University of Birmingham, School of Computer Science, March 2000.
13. Marta Z. Kwiatkowska, Gethin Norman, Roberto Segala, and Jeremy Sproston. Verifying quantitative properties of continuous probabilistic timed automata. In C. Palamidessi, editor, *CONCUR 2000 - Concurrency Theory 11th International Conference*, number 1877 in LNCS. Springer, 2000.
14. Michael L. Littman, Anthony R. Cassandra, and Leslie Pack Kaelbling. Efficient dynamic-programming updates in partially observable markov decision processes. Technical Report CS-95-19, Brown University, 1995.
15. A. McIver. Reasoning about efficiency within a probabilistic μ-calculus. In *Proc. of PROBMIV*, pages 45–58, 1998. Technical Report CSR-98-4, University of Birmingham, School of Computer Science.
16. David Monniaux. Abstract interpretation of probabilistic semantics. In *Seventh International Static Analysis Symposium (SAS'00)*, number 1824 in Lecture Notes in Computer Science, pages 322–339. Springer Verlag, 2000. Extended version on the author's web site.

17. David Monniaux. An abstract analysis of the probabilistic termination of programs. In *8th International Static Analysis Symposium (SAS'01)*, number 2126 in Lecture Notes in Computer Science, pages 111–126. Springer Verlag, 2001.
18. David Monniaux. An abstract Monte-Carlo method for the analysis of probabilistic programs (extended abstract). In *28th Symposium on Principles of Programming Languages (POPL'01)*, pages 93–101. Association for Computer Machinery, 2001.
19. David Monniaux. Backwards abstract interpretation of probabilistic programs. In *European Symposium on Programming Languages and Systems (ESOP'01)*, number 2028 in Lecture Notes in Computer Science, pages 367–382. Springer Verlag, 2001.
20. David Monniaux. Abstraction of expectation functions using gaussian distributions. In Lenore D. Zuck, Paul C. Attie, Agostino Cortesi, and Supratik Mukhopadhyay, editors, *Verification, Model Checking, and Abstract Interpretation: VMCAI'03*, number 2575 in Lecture Notes in Computer Science, pages 161–173. Springer Verlag, 2003.
21. Jacques Neveu. *Mathematical Foundations of the Calculus of Probabilities.* Holden-Day, 1965.
22. Jacques Neveu. *Bases mathématiques du calcul des probabilités.* Masson et Cie, Éditeurs, Paris, 1970. Préface de R. Fortet. Deuxième édition, revue et corrigée.
23. Martin L. Puterman. *Markov decision processes: Discrete stochastic dynamic programming.* Wiley series in probability and mathematical statistics. John Wiley & Sons, 1994.
24. Roberto Segala. *Modeling and Verification of Randomized Distributed Real-Time Systems.* PhD thesis, Massachusetts Institute of Technology, 1995. Technical report MIT/LCS/TR-676.
25. W. Thomas. Automata on infinite objects. In J. van Leeuwen, editor, *Handbook of Theoretical Computer Science, vol. B*, pages 135–191. Elsevier, 1990.

A Technical Lemmas

Lemma 11. *For all f, t_0 and U_1,*

$$\sup_{(U_n)_{n \geq 2}} \int \lambda \langle t_1, \ldots \rangle f(\langle t_1, \ldots \rangle) \, \mathrm{d}[G(T, (U_n)_{n \in I\!N}).t_0]$$

$$= \sup_{(U_n)_{n \geq 2} \ U_n \ \text{does not depend on } t_0} \int \lambda \langle t_1, \ldots \rangle f(\langle t_1, \ldots \rangle) \, \mathrm{d}[G(T, (U_n)_{n \in I\!N}).t_0]$$

Lemma 2. *For all t_0 in X,*

$$E_+(\lambda t \chi_S(t_0).V_1(t) + \chi_{S^C}(t_0).V_2(t)).t_0 = \chi_S(t_0).(E_+(V_1).t_0) + \chi_{S^C}(t_0).(E_+(V_2).t_0).$$

Lemma 3. *For any trace valuator f, for any g_1 and g_2 in $R(f)$, for any $A \subseteq \Omega$, the function g_3 defined by $g_3(t) = g_1(t)$ if $t_0 \in A$, $g_3(t) = g_2(t)$ otherwise, belongs to $R(f)$.*

Lemma 4. *Let Y be an ordered set. Let $\phi : (X \to I) \to Y$ be a monotonic, ω-upper-continuous function. Let K be a directed subset of $X \to I$. Then $\phi(\sqcup K) = \bigsqcup_{f \in K} \phi(f)$.*

Lemma 5. *Let T_1 and T_2 be two complete lattices. Let $\alpha : T_1 \to T_2$ be an ω-upper-continuous operator such that $\alpha(\bot) = \bot$. Let $\psi_1 : T_1 \to T_1$ and $\psi_2 : T_2 \to T_2$ be two ω-upper-continuous operators such that $\psi_2 \circ \alpha = \alpha \circ \psi_1$. Then $\alpha(\text{lfp}\,\psi_1) = \text{lfp}\,\psi_2$.*

B Ionescu Tulcea's Theorem

The intuitive meaning of this theorem [21, 22, proposition V-I-1] is as follows: if $(E_t)_{t \in \mathrm{IN}}$ is a sequence of measurable spaces and the $(P_{t+1}^{0,\ldots,t})_{t \in \mathrm{IN}}$ is a sequence of transition probabilities, respectively from $E_0 \times E_t$ to E_{t+1}, then we can construct a transition probability P from E_0 to $E_1 \times E_2 \times \cdots$ such that for each $x_0 \in E_0$, $P(x_0, \cdot)$ is the probability distribution on traces starting from x_0 and following the transition probabilities $(E_t)_{t \in \mathrm{IN}}$.

In an even more intuitive fashion: "knowing the starting probability measure, and the transition probabilities to the next states, we can construct the corresponding probability measure on infinite traces".

Theorem 12 (Ionescu Tulcea). *Let $(E_t, \mathcal{F}_t)_{t \in \mathrm{IN}}$ be an infinite sequence of measurable spaces and, for any $t \in \mathrm{IN}$, let $P_{t+1}^{0,\ldots,t}$ be a transition probability relative to the spaces $\left(\prod_{s=0}^{t} E_s, \bigotimes_{s=0}^{t} \mathcal{F}_s \right)$ and $(E_{t+1}, \mathcal{F}_{t+1})$. Then there exists for any $x_0 \in E_0$ a unique probability P_{x_0} on*

$$(\Omega, \mathcal{A}) = \prod_t (E_t, \mathcal{F}_t)$$

whose value for all measurable Cartesian product $\prod_t F_t$ is given by:

$$P_{x_0}\left[\prod_t F_t\right] = \chi_{A_0}(x_0) \int_{x_1 \in F_1} P_1^0(x_0; dx_1) \int_{x_2 \in F_2} P_2^{0,1}(x_0, x_1; dx_2)$$
$$\cdots \int_{x_T \in F_T} P_T^{0,\ldots,T-1}(x_0, \ldots, x_{T-1}; dx_T) \qquad (46)$$

as long as T is sufficiently great such that $F_t = E_t$ if $t > T$ (the second member is then independent of the chosen T). For any positive random variable Y on $(\Omega, \mathcal{A})$ only depending on the coordinates up to T, we have:

$$\int_\Omega Y(\omega') P_{x_0}(d\omega') = \int_{F_1} P_1^0(x_0; dx_1) \int_{F_2} P_2^{0,1}(x_0, x_1; dx_2)$$
$$\cdot \int_{x_T \in F_T} Y(x_0, \ldots, x_T) P_T^{0,\ldots,T-1}(x_0, \ldots, x_{T-1}; dx_T) \qquad (47)$$

Furthermore, for any positive random variable Y on $(\Omega, \mathcal{A})$,

$$x_0 \mapsto \int Y(\omega') P_{x_0}(d\omega') \qquad (48)$$

is a positive random variable on $(E_0, \mathcal{F}_0)$.

A Logic for Analyzing Abstractions of Graph Transformation Systems*

Paolo Baldan[1], Barbara König[2], and Bernhard König[3]

[1] Dipartimento di Informatica, Università Ca' Foscari di Venezia, Italy
[2] Institut für Informatik, Technische Universität München, Germany
[3] Department of Mathematics, University of California, Irvine, USA
baldan@dsi.unive.it, koenigb@in.tum.de, bkoenig@math.uci.edu

Abstract. A technique for approximating the behaviour of graph transformation systems (GTSs) by means of Petri net-like structures has been recently defined in the literature. In this paper we introduce a monadic second-order logic over graphs expressive enough to characterise typical graph properties, and we show how its formulae can be effectively verified. More specifically, we provide an encoding of such graph formulae into quantifier-free formulae over Petri net markings and we characterise, via a type assignment system, a subclass of formulae F such that the validity of F over a GTS $\mathcal{G}$ is implied by the validity of the encoding of F over the Petri net approximation of $\mathcal{G}$. This allows us to reuse existing verification techniques, originally developed for Petri nets, to model-check the logic, suitably enriched with temporal operators.

1 Introduction

Distributed and mobile systems can often be specified by graph transformation systems (GTSs) in a very natural way. However, work on static analysis and verification of GTSs is scarce. The fact that GTSs can be seen as a proper extension of Petri nets suggests the possibility of relying on techniques already developed in the literature for this related formalism. However, unlike Petri nets, graph transformation systems are usually Turing-complete so that many problems decidable for general P/T-nets become undecidable for GTSs.

A technique proposed in [1,2] is based on the approximation of GTSs by means of Petri net-like structures in the spirit of abstract interpretation of reactive systems [10]. More precisely, an approximated unfolding construction maps any given GTS $\mathcal{G}$ to a finite structure $\mathcal{U}(\mathcal{G})$, called *covering* (or approximated unfolding) of $\mathcal{G}$. The covering $\mathcal{U}(\mathcal{G})$ is a so-called *Petri graph*, i.e. a structure consisting of a Petri net with a graphical structure over places. It provides an *over-approximation* of the behaviour of $\mathcal{G}$, in the sense that any graph reachable in $\mathcal{G}$ can be mapped homomorphically to the graph underlying $\mathcal{U}(\mathcal{G})$ and its image is a reachable marking of $\mathcal{U}(\mathcal{G})$. (Note that, since $\mathcal{G}$ is possibly infinite-state,

---

* Research supported by the MIUR Project COFIN 2001013518 COMETA, the FET-GC Project IST-2001-32747 AGILE and the EC RTN 2-2001-00346 SEGRAVIS.

while $\mathcal{U}(\mathcal{G})$ is finite, it would not be possible to have in $\mathcal{U}(\mathcal{G})$ isomorphic images of all graphs reachable in $\mathcal{G}$.) Therefore, given a property over graphs reflected by graph morphisms, if it holds for all states reachable in the abstraction $\mathcal{U}(\mathcal{G})$ then it also holds for all reachable graphs in $\mathcal{G}$. In other words, if T is a temporal logic formula containing only universal quantifiers (e.g. a formula in ACTL* or in a suitable fragment of the modal μ-calculus) and where state predicates are reflected by graph morphisms, then the validity of T over the covering $\mathcal{U}(\mathcal{G})$ allows us to infer the validity of T for the original system [3].

However, several relevant questions remain to be answered. First of all, which logic should we use to specify state predicates (i.e., graph properties)? How can we identify a subclass of such predicates which is reflected by graph morphisms and which can thus be safely checked over the approximation? And finally, given the approximation $\mathcal{U}(\mathcal{G})$, is there a way of encoding formulae expressing graph properties into "equivalent" formulae over Petri net markings?

As for the first point, we propose to describe state predicates, i.e., the graph properties of interest, by means of a monadic second-order logic $\mathcal{L}2$ on graphs, where quantification is allowed over (sets of) edges. (Similar logics are considered in [4].) Relevant graph properties can be expressed in $\mathcal{L}2$, e.g., the non-existence and non-adjacency of edges with specific labels, the absence of certain paths (related to security properties) or cycles (related to deadlock-freedom).

Regarding the second question, we introduce a type inference system characterising a subclass of formulae in the logic $\mathcal{L}2$ which are reflected by graph morphisms. Hence, given any formula F in such a class, if F can be proved for any reachable state of the approximation $\mathcal{U}(\mathcal{G})$ then we can deduce that F holds for any reachable graph of the original GTS $\mathcal{G}$.

Finally, given the approximation $\mathcal{U}(\mathcal{G})$, we define a constructive translation of graph formulae in $\mathcal{L}2$ into formulae over markings of the Petri net underlying the abstraction $\mathcal{U}(\mathcal{G})$. More precisely, any graph formula F is mapped to a formula $\hat{F}$ over markings such that a marking satisfies $\hat{F}$ if and only if the graph it represents satisfies F. Since the graph underlying $\mathcal{U}(\mathcal{G})$ is finite and fixed after computing the abstraction, we can perform quantifier elimination on graph formulae and, surprisingly, encode even monadic second-order logic formulae into propositional formulae on markings, containing only predicates of the form $\#s \leq c$ (the number of tokens in place s is smaller than or equal to c). We remark that the encoding for the first-order fragment of $\mathcal{L}2$ is simpler and can be defined inductively.

Altogether these results allow us to verify behavioural properties of a GTS by reusing existing model-checking techniques for Petri nets. In fact, given a formula T of a suitable temporal logic (e.g. a formula of ACTL* or of a fragment of the modal μ-calculus without $\diamond$ and negation), where state predicates are reflected by graph morphisms, then, by the construction mentioned above and using general results from abstract interpretation [10], T can be translated into a formula which can be checked over the Petri net underlying $\mathcal{U}(\mathcal{G})$. We recall that general temporal state-based logics over Petri nets, i.e., logics where basic predicates have the form $\#s \leq c$, are not decidable in general, but important fragments of such logics are [8, 7, 9].

For the sake of simplicity, although the approximation method of [1, 2] was originally designed for hypergraphs, in this paper we concentrate on directed graphs. The extension to general hypergraphs requires some changes to the graph logic $\mathcal{L}2$. This rises some technical difficulties which are, while not being insurmountable, a hindrance to the clear and easy presentation of our results.

In the rest of the paper we will first summarise the approximation technique for GTSs in [1], shortly mentioning some results from [2]. Then, we will define the monadic second-order logic $\mathcal{L}2$ over graphs and we will introduce the type system characterising a subclass of formulae in $\mathcal{L}2$ which are reflected by graph morphisms, and which can thus be checked on the covering. Finally we will show how to encode these formulae into quantifier-free state-based formulae on the markings of Petri nets, starting from the simpler case of first-order formulae.

2 Approximated Unfolding Construction

In this section we sketch the algorithm, introduced in [1], for the construction of a finite approximation of the unfolding of a graph transformation system. We first define graphs and structure-preserving morphisms on graphs. We will assume that Λ denotes a fixed and finite set of labels. Note that multiple edges between nodes are allowed.

Definition 1 (Graph, Graph Morphism). A *graph* $G = (V_G, E_G, s_G, t_G, l_G)$ consists of a set V_G of nodes, a set E_G of edges, a source and a target function $s_G, t_G : E_G \to V_G$ and a function $l_G : E_G \to \Lambda$ labelling the edges.

A *graph morphism* $\varphi : G_1 \to G_2$ is a pair of mappings $\varphi_V : V_{G_1} \to V_{G_2}$ and $\varphi_E : E_{G_1} \to E_{G_2}$ such that $\varphi_V \circ s_{G_1} = s_{G_2} \circ \varphi_E$, $\varphi_V \circ t_{G_1} = t_{G_2} \circ \varphi_E$ and $l_{G_1} = l_{G_2} \circ \varphi_E$ for each edge $e \in E_{G_1}$. A morphism φ will be called *edge-bijective* if φ_E is a bijection. The subscripts in φ_E and φ_V will be usually omitted.

We next define the notion of a graph transformation system and the corresponding rewriting relation.

Definition 2 (Graph Transformation System). A *graph transformation system (GTS)* $(G_0, \mathcal{R})$ consists of an initial graph G_0 and a set $\mathcal{R}$ of rewriting rules of the form $r = (L, R, \alpha)$, where L, R are graphs, called *left-hand side* and *right-hand side*, respectively, and $\alpha : V_L \to V_R$ is an injective function.

A *match* of a rewriting rule r in a graph G is a morphism $\varphi : L \to G$ which is injective on edges. We can apply r to a match in G obtaining a new graph H, written $G \overset{r}{\Rightarrow} H$. The target graph H is defined as follows

$$V_H = V_G \uplus (V_R - \alpha(V_L)) \qquad E_H = (E_G - \varphi(E_L)) \uplus E_R$$

and, defining $\overline{\varphi} : V_R \to V_H$ by $\overline{\varphi}(\alpha(v)) = \varphi(v)$ if $v \in V_L$ and $\overline{\varphi}(v) = v$ otherwise, the source, target and labelling functions are given by

$$e \in E_G - \varphi(E_L) \;\Rightarrow\; s_H(e) = s_G(e), \quad t_H(e) = t_G(e), \quad l_H(e) = l_G(e)$$
$$e \in E_R \;\Rightarrow\; s_H(e) = \overline{\varphi}(s_R(e)), \quad t_H(e) = \overline{\varphi}(t_R(e)), \quad l_H(e) = l_R(e)$$

Intuitively, the application of r to G at the match φ first removes from G the image of the edges of L. Then the graph G is extended by adding the new nodes in R (i.e., the nodes in $V_R - \alpha(V_L)$) and the edges of R. Observe that the (images of) the nodes in L are preserved, i.e., not affected by the rewriting step.

Example 1. Consider a system where processes compete for resources R_1 and R_2. A process needs both resources in order to perform some task. The system is represented as a GTS Sys as follows. We consider edges labelled by R_1, R_2, R_1^f, R_2^f standing for assigned and free resources, respectively, and P_1, P_2 and P_3 denoting a process waiting for resource R_1, a process waiting for resource R_2 and a process holding both resources, respectively. Furthermore, edges labelled by D_1 and D_2 connect the target node of a process and the source node of a resource when the process is asking for the resource. When the target node of a resource coincides with the source node of a process, this means that the resource is assigned to the process. The initial scenario for Sys is represented in Fig. 1, with a single process P_1 asking for both resources.

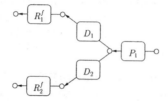

Fig. 1. Start graph of Sys with a process and resources

The rewriting rules of Sys are defined with the aim of avoiding deadlocks in the form of vicious cycles. There are three kind of rules, depicted in Fig. 2: (1) a process P_i can acquire a free resource R_j^f whenever $i = j$ and become P_{i+1}, (2) P_3 can release its resources and (3) processes of the form P_1 can fork creating more processes of the same kind with demand for the same resources. The natural numbers $1, 2, 3, \ldots$ which decorate nodes in the left-hand side and right-hand side of rules implicitly represent the mapping α.

Observe that an additional rule, analogous to rule 1, but with $i = 1$ and $j = 2$, would possibly lead to a vicious cycle with circular demand for resources, in two steps (see Fig. 3).

Some basic notation concerning multisets is needed to deal with Petri nets. Given a set A we will denote by $A^\oplus$ the free commutative monoid over A, whose elements will be called *multisets* over A. In the sequel we will sometime identify $A^\oplus$ with the set of functions $m: A \to \mathbb{N}$ such that the set $\{a \in A \mid m(a) \neq 0\}$ is finite. E.g., in particular, $m(a)$ denotes the multiplicity of an element a in the multiset m. Sometimes a multiset will be also identified with the underlying set, writing, e.g., $a \in m$ for $m(a) \neq 0$. Given a function $f: A \to B$, by $f^\oplus: A^\oplus \to B^\oplus$ we denote its monoidal extension, i.e., $f^\oplus(m)(b) = \sum_{f(a)=b} m(a)$ for every $b \in B$.

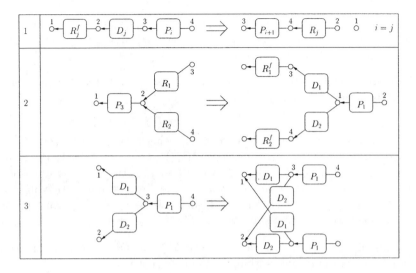

Fig. 2. Rewriting rules of the GTS Sys

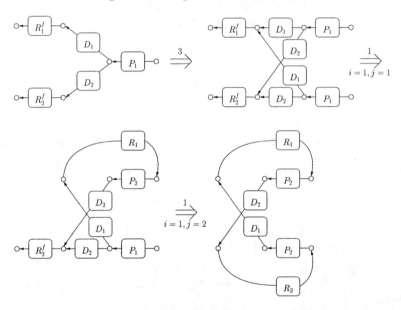

Fig. 3. Vicious cycle representing a deadlock

In order to approximate graph transformation systems we use Petri graphs, introduced in [1], which are basically Petri nets, specifying the operational behaviour, with added graph structure.

Definition 3 (Petri Graphs). Let $\mathcal{G} = (G_0, \mathcal{R})$ be a GTS. A *Petri graph P (over $\mathcal{G}$)* is a tuple (G, N, m_0) where

- G is a graph;
- $N = (E_G, T_N, {}^\bullet(), ()^\bullet, p_N)$ is a Petri net, where the set of places E_G is the edge set, T_N is the set of transitions, ${}^\bullet(), ()^\bullet : T_N \to E_G^\oplus$ specify the post-set and pre-set of each transition and $p_N : T_N \to \mathcal{R}$ is the labelling function;
- $m_0 \in (E_G)^\oplus$ is the *initial marking* of the Petri graph, satisfying $m_0 = \iota^\oplus(E_{G_0})$ for a suitable graph morphism $\iota : G_0 \to G$ (i.e., m_0 must properly correspond to the initial state of the GTS $\mathcal{G}$).

A marking $m \in E_G^\oplus$ will be called *reachable (coverable)* in P if it is reachable (coverable) from the initial marking in the Petri net underlying P.

Remark. The definition of Petri graph is slightly different from the original one in [1], in that we omit some graph morphisms associated to transitions (the μ-component) and to the initial marking, and the so-called irredundancy condition. Both are needed for the actual construction of the Petri graph from a GTS, but they play no role in the results of this paper.

A marking m of a Petri graph can be seen as an abstract representation of a graph in the following sense.

Definition 4. Let (G, N, m_0) be a Petri graph and let $m \in E_G^\oplus$ be a marking of N. The graph *generated* by m, denoted by $graph(m)$, is the graph H defined as follows: $V_H = \{v \in V_G \mid \exists e \in m : (s_G(e) = v \lor t_G(e) = v)\}$, $E_H = \{(e, i) \mid e \in m \land 1 \leq i \leq m(e)\}$, $s_H((e, i)) = s_G(e)$, $t_H((e, i)) = t_G(e)$ and $l_H((e, i)) = l_G(e)$.

Alternatively the graph $graph(m)$ can be defined as the unique graph H, up to isomorphism, such that there exists a morphism $\psi : H \to G$ injective on nodes with $\psi^\oplus(E_H) = m$. An example of a Petri net marking with the corresponding generated graph can be found in Fig. 4.

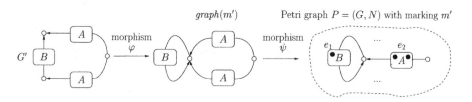

Fig. 4. A pair (G', m') contained in a simulation

Given a GTS $(G_0, \mathcal{R})$, with some minor constraints on the format of rewriting rules (see [1,2]), we can construct a Petri graph approximation of $(G_0, \mathcal{R})$, called *covering* and denoted by $\mathcal{U}(G_0, \mathcal{R})$. The covering is produced by the last step of the following (terminating) algorithm which generates a sequence $P_i = (G_i, N_i, m_i)$ of Petri graphs.

1. $P_0 = (G_0, N_0, m_0)$, where the net N_0 contains no transitions and $m_0 = E_{G_0}$.
2. As long as one of the following steps is applicable, transform P_i into P_{i+1}, giving precedence to folding steps.

   Unfolding. Find a rule $r = (L, R, \alpha) \in \mathcal{R}$ and a match $\varphi \colon L \to G_i$ such that $\varphi(E_L^\oplus)$ is coverable in P_i. Then extend P_i by "attaching" R to G_i according to α and add a transition t, labelled by r, describing the application of rule r.

   Folding. Find a rule $r = (L, R, \alpha) \in \mathcal{R}$ and two matches $\varphi, \varphi' \colon L \to G_i$ such that $\varphi^\oplus(E_L)$ and $\varphi'^\oplus(E_L)$ are coverable in N_i and the second match is causally dependent on the transition unfolding the first match. Then merge the two matches by setting $\varphi(e) \equiv \varphi'(e)$ for each $e \in E_L$ and factoring through the resulting equivalence relation $\equiv$.

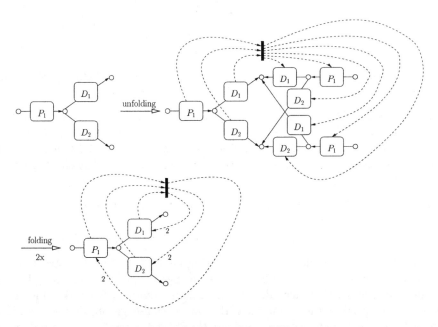

Fig. 5. An unfolding and two folding steps

For instance an unfolding step involving rule 3 is depicted in Fig. 5. Transitions are represented as black rectangles and the Petri net structure is rendered by connecting edges (places) to transitions with dashed lines. The label k for dashed lines represents the weight with which the target/source place occurs in the post-set (pre-set); when the weight is 1, the label is omitted. In the resulting Petri graph we can find three occurrences of the left-hand side of rule 3. The latter two are causally dependent on the first, which means that they can be merged in two folding steps. The algorithm, starting from the start graph in Fig. 1, terminates producing the Petri graph $\mathcal{U}(\mathsf{Sys})$ in Fig. 6, where the initial marking is represented by tokens.

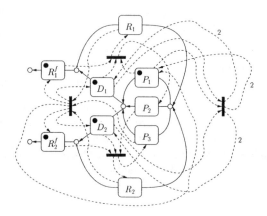

Fig. 6. The Petri graph $\mathcal{U}(\mathsf{Sys})$ computed as covering of Sys

The covering $\mathcal{U}(G_0, \mathcal{R})$ is an abstraction of the original GTS $(G_0, \mathcal{R})$ in the following sense.

Proposition 1 (Abstraction). *Let* $\mathcal{G} = (G_0, \mathcal{R})$ *be a graph transformation system and let* $\mathcal{U}(\mathcal{G}) = (G, N, m_0)$ *be its covering. Furthermore let* **G** *be the set of graphs reachable from* G_0 *in* $\mathcal{G}$ *and let* **M** *be the set of reachable markings in* $\mathcal{U}(\mathcal{G})$. *Then there exists a simulation* $S \subseteq \mathbf{G} \times \mathbf{M}$ *with the following properties:*

- $(G_0, m_0) \in S$;
- *whenever* $(G', m') \in S$ *and* $G' \stackrel{r}{\Rightarrow} G''$, *then there exists a marking* m'' *with* $m' \stackrel{r}{\to} m''$ *and* $(G'', m'') \in S$;
- *for every* $(G', m') \in S$ *there is an edge-bijective morphism* $\varphi \colon G' \to graph(m')$.

The above result will allow us to use existing results concerning abstractions of reactive systems [3, 10]. Consider the system Sys in our running example. We would like to verify that, according to the design intentions, Sys is deadlock-free. This is formalised by the requirement that all reachable graphs do not contain a vicious cycle, i.e., a cycle of edges where P_2-labelled edges (processes holding a resource and waiting for a second resource) occur twice. This graph property is reflected by graph morphisms, hence, by using Proposition 1, if we can prove it on the covering $\mathcal{U}(\mathsf{Sys})$, we could deduce that it holds for the original system Sys as well. Observe that actually, in this case, even the stronger property $\#e \leq 1$, where e is the edge labelled P_2, holds for all reachable markings as it can be easily verified by drawing the coverability graph of the Petri net. This is an ad hoc proof of the property, which instead, by the results in this paper, will follow as an instance of a general theory.

The idea that will be concretized by the results in the paper, is the following. Let $\mathcal{G}$ be a GTS and let $\mathcal{U}(\mathcal{G})$ be its covering. By Proposition 1, $\mathcal{U}(\mathcal{G}) = (G, N, m_0)$ "approximates" $\mathcal{G}$ via a simulation consisting of pairs (G', m') such that G' can be mapped to $graph(m')$ (see, e.g., Fig. 4) via an edge-bijective morphism. Given a formula on graphs F, expressing a state property in $\mathcal{G}$, a corresponding formula $M(F)$ on the markings of $\mathcal{U}(\mathcal{G})$ is constructed such that, for any pair in the simulation,

$$m' \models M(F) \;\Rightarrow\; G' \models F.$$

This will be obtained in two steps. First, we will identify formulae F which are reflected by edge-bijective morphisms, ensuring that $graph(m') \models F$ implies $G' \models F$. Then, we will encode F into a propositional formula $M(F)$ on multisets such that $m' \models M(F) \iff graph(m') \models F$.

Call $\mathcal{F}$ the above mentioned class of graph formulae. Now, one can consider a temporal logic over GTSs, where basic predicates are taken from $\mathcal{F}$. For suitable fragments of such logics, e.g., the modal μ-calculus without negation and the "possibility operator" $\diamond$, by Proposition 1 and exploiting general results in [10], any temporal formula T over graphs can be translated to a formula $M(T)$ over markings (translating the basic predicates as above), such that, if $N \models M(T)$ then $\mathcal{G} \models T$, i.e., T is valid for the original GTS.

3 A Second-Order Monadic Logic for Graphs

We introduce the monadic second-order logic $\mathcal{L}2$ for specifying graph properties. Quantification is allowed over edges, but not over nodes (as, e.g., in [4]).

Definition 5 (Graph Formula). Let $\mathcal{X}_1 = \{x, y, z, \ldots\}$ be a set of (first-order) edge variables and let $\mathcal{X}_2 = \{X, Y, Z, \ldots\}$ be a set of (second-order) variables representing edge sets. The set of *graph formulae* of the logic $\mathcal{L}2$ is defined as follows, where $\ell \in \Lambda$

$$\begin{aligned}
F ::=\;& x = y \;|\; s(x) = s(y) \;|\; s(x) = t(y) \;|\; t(x) = t(y) \;| \\
& lab(x) = \ell \;|\; x \in X && \text{(Predicates)} \\
& F \vee F \;|\; F \wedge F \;|\; F \Rightarrow F \;|\; \neg F && \text{(Connectives)} \\
& \forall x.F \;|\; \exists x.F \;|\; \forall X.F \;|\; \exists X.F && \text{(Quantifiers)}
\end{aligned}$$

We denote by $free(F)$ and $Free(F)$ the sets of first-order and second-order variables, respectively, occurring free in F, defined in the obvious way.

Note that, even if quantification over nodes is disallowed, formulae expressing properties of classes of nodes can be easily stated, e.g., the property "for all non-isolated nodes v it holds that $P(v)$" is formalised as "$\forall x.(P(s(x)) \wedge P(t(x)))$".

Definition 6 (Quantifier Depth). The first-order and second-order *quantifier depth* ($\text{qd}_1(F)$ and $\text{qd}_2(F)$, respectively) of a graph formula F in $\mathcal{L}2$ is inductively defined as follows, where A is a predicate, $op \in \{\wedge, \vee, \Rightarrow\}$ and $i \in \{1, 2\}$.

$$\text{qd}_i(A) = 0 \qquad \text{qd}_i(\neg F_1) = \text{qd}_i(F_1) \qquad \text{qd}_i(F_1 \text{ op } F_2) = \max\{\text{qd}_i(F_1), \text{qd}_i(F_2)\}$$
$$\text{qd}_1(\forall x.F_1) = \text{qd}_1(\exists x.F_1) = \text{qd}_1(F_1) + 1 \qquad \text{qd}_2(\forall x.F_1) = \text{qd}_2(\exists x.F_1) = \text{qd}_2(F_1)$$
$$\text{qd}_1(\forall X.F_1) = \text{qd}_1(\exists X.F_1) = \text{qd}_1(F_1) \qquad \text{qd}_2(\forall X.F_1) = \text{qd}_2(\exists X.F_1) = \text{qd}_2(F_1) + 1$$

The notion of satisfaction is defined in a straightforward way.

Definition 7 (Satisfaction). Let G be a graph, let F be a graph formula in $\mathcal{L}2$, let $\sigma : \textit{free}(F) \to E_G$ and $\Sigma : \textit{Free}(F) \to \mathcal{P}(E_G)$ be valuations for the free first- and second-order variables of F, respectively. The *satisfaction relation* $G \models_{\sigma,\Sigma} F$ is defined inductively, in the usual way; for instance:

$$G \models_{\sigma,\Sigma} x = y \iff \sigma(x) = \sigma(y)$$
$$G \models_{\sigma,\Sigma} s(x) = s(y) \iff s_G(\sigma(x)) = s_G(\sigma(y))$$
$$G \models_{\sigma,\Sigma} lab(x) = \ell \iff l_G(\sigma(x)) = \ell$$
$$G \models_{\sigma,\Sigma} x \in X \iff \sigma(x) \in \Sigma(X)$$

Example 2. The formula NC_ℓ below states that a graph does not contain a cycle including two distinct edges labelled ℓ, a property that will be used to express the absence of vicious cycles in our system Sys. It is based on the formula $NP(x, y)$, which says that there is no path connecting the edges x and y, stating that a set that contains at least all successors of x does not always contain y.

$$NP(x,y) = \neg \forall X.(\forall z.(t(x) = s(z) \vee \exists w.(w \in X \wedge t(w) = s(z))) \Rightarrow z \in X)$$
$$\Rightarrow y \in X)$$

$$NC_\ell = \forall x.\forall y.(lab(x) = \ell \wedge lab(y) = \ell \wedge \neg(x = y) \Rightarrow NP(x,y) \vee NP(y,x))$$

The following standard argument shows that this property can not be stated in first-order logic, a fact which motivates our choice of considering a second-order logic: it is easy to find sentences ψ_n in first-order logic stating that 'there is no cycle of length $\leq n$ through two distinct edges labelled ℓ'. Every finite subset of the theory $T = \{\neg NC_\ell\} \cup \{\psi_n\}_{n \in \mathbb{N}}$ is satisfiable but T itself is not satisfiable. The compactness theorem rules this out for first-order theories, so NC_ℓ cannot be first-order.

4 Preservation and Reflection of Graph Formulae

In this section we introduce a type system over graph formulae in $\mathcal{L}2$ which allows us to single out subclasses of formulae preserved or reflected by edge-bijective morphisms. By Proposition 1, given a GTS $\mathcal{G}$ every graph reachable in $\mathcal{G}$ can be mapped homomorphically via an edge-bijective morphism to the graph generated by a marking reachable in the covering $\mathcal{U}(\mathcal{G})$ of $\mathcal{G}$. Hence a formula reflected by all edge-bijective morphisms can be safely checked over the approximation $\mathcal{U}(\mathcal{G})$, in the sense that if it holds in $\mathcal{U}(\mathcal{G})$, then we can deduce that it holds also in $\mathcal{G}$.

To define the notions of reflection (and preservation) of general graph formulae, possibly with free variables, observe that valuations are naturally "transformed" under graph morphisms. Let F be formula, let $\varphi : G_1 \to G_2$ be a graph morphism, and let $\sigma_1 : \mathit{free}(F) \to E_{G_1}$ and $\Sigma_1 : \mathit{Free}(F) \to \mathcal{P}(E_{G_1})$ be valuations. A valuation for the first-order variables of F in G_2 is naturally given by $\varphi \circ \sigma_1$, while a valuation Σ_2 for second-order variables can be defined by $\Sigma_2(X) = \varphi(\Sigma_1(X))$ for any variable X. Abusing the notation, Σ_2 will be denoted by $\varphi \circ \Sigma_1$.

Definition 8 (Reflection and Preservation). Let F be a formula in $\mathcal{L}2$ and let $\varphi \colon G_1 \to G_2$ be a graph morphism. We say that F is *preserved by* φ if for all valuations $\sigma_1 \colon \mathit{free}(F) \to E_{G_1}$ and $\Sigma_1 \colon \mathit{Free}(F) \to \mathcal{P}(E_{G_1})$

$$G_1 \models_{\sigma_1, \Sigma_1} F \quad \Rightarrow \quad G_2 \models_{\varphi \circ \sigma, \varphi \circ \Sigma_1} F.$$

Symmetrically, F is *reflected* by φ if the above holds where $\Rightarrow$ is replaced by $\Leftarrow$.

Observe that, in particular, a closed formula F is preserved by a graph morphism $\varphi : G_1 \to G_2$ if $G_1 \models_{\emptyset,\emptyset} F$ implies $G_2 \models_{\emptyset,\emptyset} F$.

As mentioned above we are interested in syntactic criteria characterising classes of graph formulae reflected, respectively preserved, by all edge-bijective graph morphisms. For first-order predicate logic, criteria for arbitrary morphisms can be found in [6]. Here we provide a technique which works for general second-order monadic formulae, based on a type system assigning to every formula F either $\to$, meaning that F is preserved, or $\leftarrow$, meaning that F is reflected by edge-bijective morphisms. The type rules are given in Fig. 7 where it is intended that $\to^{-1}=\leftarrow$ and $\leftarrow^{-1}=\to$. Moreover $F :\leftrightarrow$ is a shortcut for $F :\to$ and $F :\leftarrow$, while $F_1, F_2 : d$ stands for $F_1 : d$ and $F_2 : d$.

Typing predicates:

$$s(x) = s(y),\ s(x) = t(y),\ t(x) = t(y) \colon \to \quad x = y,\ \mathit{lab}(x) = \ell,\ x \in X \colon \leftrightarrow$$

Typing connectives and quantifiers:

$$\frac{F:d}{\neg F:d^{-1}} \quad \frac{F_1, F_2:d}{F_1 \vee F_2,\ F_1 \wedge F_2:d} \quad \frac{F_1:d^{-1},\ F_2:d}{F_1 \Rightarrow F_2:d} \quad \frac{F:d}{\forall x.F:d} \quad \frac{F:d}{\exists x.F:d}$$

$$\frac{F:d}{\forall X.F:d} \quad \frac{F:d}{\exists X.F:d}$$

Fig. 7. The type system for preservation and reflection

The type system can be shown to be correct.

Proposition 2 (Correctness). *Let F be a graph formula. If $F \colon \to$ is provable then F is preserved by all edge-bijective morphisms. Similarly, if $F \colon \leftarrow$ is provable then F is reflected by all edge-bijective graph morphisms.*

Example 3. It holds that $NP(x,y)$: ← and NC_ℓ: ←, i.e., absence of paths and of vicious cycles is reflected by edge-bijective morphisms.

Not all formulae that are preserved respectively reflected are recognised by the above type system. The following result shows that this incompleteness is a fundamental problem, due to the undecidability of reflection and preservation.

Proposition 3 (Undecidability of the Reflection (Preservation) Problem for Formulae). *The following two sets are undecidable:*

$$Refl_{FO} = \{F \mid F \text{ closed first-order formula, reflected by edge-bijective graph morphisms}\}$$

$$Pres_{FO} = \{F \mid F \text{ closed first-order formula, preserved by edge-bijective graph morphisms}\}$$

5 A Propositional Logic on Multisets

In order to characterise markings of Petri nets we use the following logic on multisets. We consider a fixed universe A over which all multisets are formed.

Definition 9 (Multiset Formula). *The set of multiset formulae, ranged over by M, is defined as follows, where $a \in A$ and $c \in \mathbb{N}$*

$$M ::= \#a \leq c \mid \neg M \mid M \vee M' \mid M \wedge M'.$$

Let m be a multiset with elements from A. The satisfaction relation $m \models M$ is defined, on basic predicates, as $m \models (\#a \leq c) \iff m(a) \leq c$. Logical connectives are dealt with as usual.

We will consider also derived predicates of the form $\#a \geq c$ and $\#a = c$ where

$$(\#a \geq c) = \begin{cases} \neg(\#e \leq c-1) & \text{if } c > 0 \\ true & \text{otherwise} \end{cases}, \quad (\#e = c) = (\#e \leq c) \wedge (\#e \geq c).$$

6 Encoding First-Order Graph Logic

In this section we show how first-order graph formulae can be encoded into "equivalent" multiset formulae. More precisely, given the fixed Petri graph $P = (G, N, m_0)$ the aim is to find an encoding M_1 of first-order graph formulae into multiset formulae such that $graph(m) \models F \iff m \models M_1(F)$ for every marking m of P and every closed first order graph formula F.

The encoding M_1 is based on the following observation: every graph $graph(m)$ for some marking m of P can be generated from the finite "template graph" G in the following way: some edges of G might be removed and some edges might be multiplied, generating several parallel copies of the same template edge. Whenever a formula has two free variables x, y and $graph(m)$ has n parallel

A Logic for Analyzing Abstractions of Graph Transformation Systems 267

copies $e_1, \ldots, e_n$ of the same edge, it is not necessary to associate x and y with all edges, but it is sufficient to assign e_1 to x and e_2 to y (first alternative) or e_1 to both x and y (second alternative). Thus, whenever we encode a formula F, we have to keep track of the following information: a partition P on the free variables $\mathit{free}(F)$, telling us which variables are mapped to the same edge, and a mapping ρ from $\mathit{free}(F)$ to the edges of G, with $\rho(x) = e$ meaning that x will be instantiated with a copy of the template edge e. Since there might be several different copies of the same template edge, two variables x and y in different sets of P can be mapped by ρ to the same edge of G. Whenever we encode an existential quantifier $\exists x$, we have to form a disjunction over all the possibilities we have in choosing such an x: either x is instantiated with the same edge as another free variable y, in this case x and y should be in the same set of the partition P. Or x is instantiated with a new copy of an edge in G. In this case, a new set $\{x\}$ is added to P and we have to make sure that enough edges are available by adding a suitable predicate.

We need the following notation. We will describe an equivalence relation on a set A by a partition $P \subseteq \mathcal{P}(A)$ of A, where every element of P represents an equivalence class. We will write $x\,P\,y$ whenever x, y are in the same equivalence class. Furthermore we assume that each equivalence P is associated with a function $\mathit{rep} : P \to A$ which assigns a representative to every equivalence class. The encoding given below is independent of any specific choice of representatives.

Given a function $f : A \to B$ such that $f(a) = f(a')$ for all $a, a' \in A$ with aPa' and a fixed $b \in B$ we define $n_{P,f}(b) = |\{k \in P \mid f(\mathit{rep}(k)) = b\}|$, i.e., $n_{P,f}(b)$ is the number of sets in the partition P that are mapped to b.

Definition 10. Let G be a directed graph, let F be graph formula in the first-order fragment of $\mathcal{L}2$, let $\rho : \mathit{free}(F) \to E_G$ and let $P \subseteq \mathcal{P}(\mathit{free}(F))$ be an equivalence relation such that $x\,P\,y$ implies $\rho(x) = \rho(y)$ for all $x, y \in \mathit{free}(F)$. The *encoding* M_1 is defined as follows:

$$M_1[\neg F, \rho, P] = \neg M_1[F, \rho, P]$$
$$M_1[F_1 \vee F_2, \rho, P] = M_1[F_1, \rho, P] \vee M_1[F_1, \rho, P]$$
$$M_1[F_1 \wedge F_2, \rho, P] = M_1[F_1, \rho, P] \wedge M_1[F_1, \rho, P]$$
$$M_1[x = y, \rho, P] = \begin{cases} \mathit{true} & \text{if } x\,P\,y \\ \mathit{false} & \text{otherwise} \end{cases}$$
$$M_1[\mathit{lab}(x) = \ell, \rho, P] = \begin{cases} \mathit{true} & \text{if } l_G(\rho(x)) = \ell \\ \mathit{false} & \text{otherwise} \end{cases}$$
$$M_1[s(x) = s(y), \rho, P] = \begin{cases} \mathit{true} & \text{if } s_G(\rho(x)) = s_G(\rho(y)) \\ \mathit{false} & \text{otherwise} \end{cases}$$

the formulae $t(x) = t(y)$ and $s(x) = t(y)$
are treated analogously

$$M_1[\exists x.F, \rho, P] = \bigvee_{k \in P} (M_1[F, \rho \cup \{x \mapsto \rho(\mathit{rep}(k))\}, P\backslash\{k\} \cup \{k \cup \{x\}\}]) \vee$$
$$\bigvee_{e \in E_G} (M_1[F, \rho \cup \{x \mapsto e\}, P \cup \{\{x\}\}] \wedge (\#e \geq n_{P,\rho}(e) + 1))$$

$$M_1[\forall x.F, \rho, P] = \bigwedge_{k \in P} (M_1[F, \rho \cup \{x \mapsto \rho(rep(k))\}, P\backslash\{k\} \cup \{k \cup \{x\}\}]) \wedge$$
$$\bigwedge_{e \in E_G} ((\#e \geq n_{P,\rho}(e) + 1) \Rightarrow M_1[F, \rho \cup \{x \mapsto e\}, P \cup \{\{x\}\}])$$

If F is closed formula (i.e., without free variables), we define $M_1(F) = M_1[F, \emptyset, \emptyset]$.

It is worth remarking that such an approach is similar to the model-theoretic method of quantifier elimination, defined by Tarski in the 1950's to show decidability and completeness for theories like dense linear orderings or algebraically closed fields (see [14]). We remark that here finiteness of graphs is essential.

We can now show that the encoding is correct in the sense explained above. We will omit the index Σ in $\models_{\sigma,\Sigma}$ when talking about first-order formulae only.

Proposition 4. *Let (G, N, m_0) be a Petri graph, F a first-order formula in $\mathcal{L}2$ and m a marking of N. Then it holds that*

$$graph(m) \models_\sigma F \iff m \models M_1[F, \rho, P],$$

when

- *$\rho : free(F) \to E_G$;*
- *P is an equivalence on $free(F)$ such that $x\,P\,y$ implies $\rho(x) = \rho(y)$ for any $x, y \in free(F)$;*
- *$\sigma : free(F) \to E_{graph(m)}$ satisfies $x\,P\,y \iff \sigma(x) = \sigma(y)$ and $\varphi \circ \sigma = \rho$, where $\varphi: graph(m) \to G$ denotes the projection of $graph(m)$ over G, i.e., a graph morphism such that $\varphi((e, i)) = e \in E_G$.*

Whenever F is closed the proposition above trivially gives us the expected result. i.e., $graph(m) \models F$ iff $m \models M_1(F)$.

Example 4. Consider the formula $F = \exists x.(\underbrace{lab(x) = A \wedge \overbrace{\forall y.\neg(t(x) = s(y))}^{F_2}}_{F_1})$.

The graph under consideration is the graph G on the right in Fig. 4 (containing a looping B-edge e_1 and an A-edge e_2). The encoding goes as follows (with some simplifications of the formula along the way):

$M_1[F, \emptyset, \emptyset]$
$= (M_1[F_1, \{x \mapsto e_1\}, \{\{x\}\}] \wedge (\#e_1 \geq 1)) \vee (M_1[F_1, \{x \mapsto e_2\}, \{\{x\}\}] \wedge (\#e_2 \geq 1))$
$= (\underbrace{M_1[lab(x) = A, \{x \mapsto e_1\}, \{\{x\}\}]}_{=false} \wedge M_1[F_2, \{x \mapsto e_1\}, \{\{x\}\}] \wedge (\#e_1 \geq 1)) \vee$
$(\underbrace{M_1[lab(x) = A, \{x \mapsto e_2\}, \{\{x\}\}]}_{=true} \wedge M_1[F_2, \{x \mapsto e_2\}, \{\{x\}\}] \wedge (\#e_2 \geq 1))$
$\equiv \underbrace{M_1[\neg(t(x) = s(y)), \{x, y \mapsto e_2\}, \{\{x, y\}\}]}_{=true} \wedge$

$(\#e_1 \geq 1 \Rightarrow \underbrace{M_1[\neg(t(x) = s(y)), \{x \mapsto e_2, y \mapsto e_1\}, \{\{x\}, \{y\}\}])}_{=false} \wedge$

$(\#e_2 \geq 2 \Rightarrow \underbrace{M_1[\neg(t(x) = s(y)), \{x, y \mapsto e_2\}, \{\{x\}, \{y\}\}])}_{=true} \wedge (\#e_2 \geq 1)$

$\equiv \neg(\#e_1 \geq 1) \wedge (\#e_2 \geq 1)$

7 Encoding Monadic Second-Order Graph Logic

In this section we show that also general monadic second-order graph formulae in $\mathcal{L}2$ can be encoded into multiset formulae. Differently from the first-order case, the encoding is not defined inductively, but, still, quantifier elimination is possible. We start with an easy but useful lemma.

Lemma 1 (Edge Permutations). *Let σ, Σ be valuations such that $G \models_{\sigma, \Sigma} F$. Furthermore let $\pi : G \to G$ be an automorphism such that $s_G(e) = s_G(\pi(e))$ and $t_G(e) = t_G(\pi(e))$. Then $G \models_{\pi \circ \sigma, \pi \circ \Sigma} F$.*

The encoding uses the fact that multiple copies of an edge are distinguished only by their identity, but have the same source and target nodes and the same label. Hence whenever we want to encode a first-order quantifier, we only have to check all the edges that have already appeared so far and a fresh copy of every edge in G. From this, as we will see, one can infer that for checking the validity of a formula F it is sufficient to consider only up to $\mathrm{qd}_1(F) \cdot 2^{\mathrm{qd}_2(F)}$ copies of every edge in the template graph G.

The following proposition basically states that if there are enough parallel edges which belong to the same sets of the form $\Sigma(X)$, where Σ is a second-order valuation and X a second-order variable, then one of these edges can be removed—provided that it is not in the range of the first-order valuation σ—without changing the validity of a formula F.

Proposition 5. *Let G be a graph, F a graph formula in $\mathcal{L}2$, let σ, Σ be valuations for the free variables in F and let $e \in E_G$ be a fixed edge. Assume that*

(1) the edge e is not in the range of σ and
(2) $|E_\Sigma^G(e)| > (\mathrm{qd}_1(F) + |\mathrm{dom}(\sigma)|) \cdot 2^{\mathrm{qd}_2(F)}$ where

$$E_\Sigma^G(e) = \{e' \in E_G \mid s_G(e) = s_G(e'), t_G(e) = t_G(e'), l_G(e) = l_G(e'),$$
$$\forall X \in \mathrm{dom}(\Sigma).(e \in \Sigma(X) \iff e' \in \Sigma(X))\}$$

Then $G \models_{\sigma, \Sigma} F \iff G \setminus \{e\} \models_{\sigma, \Sigma_e} F$, where $G \setminus \{e\}$ is obtained by removing the edge e from graph G and $\Sigma_e(X) = \Sigma(X) - \{e\}$.

From Proposition 5 we infer the following corollary.

Corollary 1. *Let F be a closed graph formula in $\mathcal{L}2$. Let furthermore G be a graph and $m \in E_G^\oplus$ be a multiset over (the set of edges of) G. Then $\mathrm{graph}(m) \models F$ if and only if $\mathrm{graph}(m') \models F$, where $m' \in E_G^\oplus$ is defined by $m'(e) = \min\{m(e), \mathrm{qd}_1(F) \cdot 2^{\mathrm{qd}_2(F)}\}$.*

Proof. If F has no free variables then $E_\Sigma^{graph(m)}(e) = \{(e,i) \mid 1 \leq i \leq m(e)\}$. Using Proposition 5, we can thus reduce the number of copies for every edge to the number $\mathrm{qd}_1(F) \cdot 2^{\mathrm{qd}_2(F)}$, without changing the truth value of F. □

The following corollary shows that every graph-statement of full monadic second-order logic can be encoded into a multiset formula.

Corollary 2. *Let G be a fixed template graph. A closed graph formula F in $\mathcal{L}2$ can be encoded into a logical formula $M_2(F)$ on multisets as follows. For any multiset $k \in E_G^\oplus$, let C_k be the conjunction over the following formulae:*

- *$\#e = k(e)$ for every $e \in E_G$ satisfying $k(e) < \mathrm{qd}_1(F) \cdot 2^{\mathrm{qd}_2(F)}$ and*
- *$\#e \geq k(e)$ for every $e \in E_G$ satisfying $k(e) = \mathrm{qd}_1(F) \cdot 2^{\mathrm{qd}_2(F)}$.*

Define $M_2(F)$ to be the disjunction of all C_k such that $k \in E_G^\oplus$, $graph(k) \models F$ and $k(e) \leq \mathrm{qd}_1(F) \cdot 2^{\mathrm{qd}_2(F)}$ for every $e \in E_G$.
Then $graph(m) \models F \iff m \models M_2(F)$ for every $m \in E_G^\oplus$.

Proof. Let $m \in E_G^\oplus$ be an arbitrary multiset and let m' be a multiset defined as in Corollary 1, i.e. $m'(e) = \min\{m(e), \mathrm{qd}_1(F) \cdot 2^{\mathrm{qd}_2(F)}\}$. for $e \in E_G$.

If $graph(m) \models F$ then, by Corollary 1, $graph(m') \models F$. Hence, by definition of M_2, $C_{m'}$ appears as a disjunct in $M_2(F)$. Since, clearly, $m \models C_{m'}$, we conclude that $m \models M_2(F)$.

Vice versa, let $m \models M_2(F)$. Then $m \models C_k$ for some $k \in E_G^\oplus$ and $graph(k) \models F$. By the shape of C_k, it is immediate to see that this implies $k = m'$. Therefore $graph(m') \models F$, and thus, by Corollary 1, $graph(m) \models F$. □

To conclude let us show how the general schema outlined at the end of Section 2 applies to our running example. We want to verify that Sys satisfies a safety property, i.e., the absence of vicious cycles, including two distinct P_2 processes, in all reachable graphs. Let $\Box L_\mu$ be a fragment of the μ-calculus without negation and "possibility operator" $\Diamond$ (see [10]), where basic predicates are formulae F taken from our graph logic $\mathcal{L}2$, which can be typed as "reflected by graph morphisms", i.e., such that $F :\leftarrow$ is provable. The property of interest can be expressed in $\Box L_\mu$ as:

$$T_{NC} = \mu\varphi.(NC_{P_2} \wedge \Box\varphi)$$

where NC_ℓ is the formula considered in a previous example. Then T_{NC} can be translated into a formula over markings, by translating its graph formula components according to the techniques described in Sections 6 and 7. This will lead to the formula $M_2(T_{NC}) = \mu\varphi.(M_2(NC_{P_2}) \wedge \Box\varphi)$. By the results in this paper and by the results in [2], for T in $\Box L_\mu$, if $\mathcal{U}(\mathsf{Sys}) \models M_2(T)$ then $\mathsf{Sys} \models T$. Therefore the formula T_{NC} can be checked by verifying $M_2(T_{NC})$ on the Petri net component of the approximated unfolding. In this case it can be easily verified that $M_2(T_{NC})$ actually holds in $\mathcal{U}(\mathsf{Sys})$ and thus we conclude that Sys satisfies the desired property.

8 Conclusion

We have presented a logic for specifying graph properties, useful for the verification of graph transformation systems. A type system allows us to identify formulae of this logic reflected by edge-bijective morphisms, which can therefore be verified on the covering, i.e., on the finite Petri graph approximation of a GTS. Furthermore we have shown how, given a fixed approximation of the original system, we can perform quantifier-elimination and encode these formulae into boolean combination of atomic predicates on multisets. Combined with the approximated unfolding algorithm of [1], this gives a method for the verification and analysis of graph transformation systems. This form of abstraction is different from the usual forms of abstract interpretation since it abstracts the *structure* of a system rather than its *data*. Maybe the closest relation is shape analysis, abstracting the data structures of a program [11, 15].

We would like to add some remarks concerning the practicability of this approach: we are currently developing an implementation of the approximated unfolding algorithm, which inputs and outputs graphs in the Graph Exchange Language (GXL) format, based on XML. It remains to be seen up to which size of a GTS the computation of the approximation is still feasible.

Furthermore encoding a formula into multiset logic may result in a blowup of the size of the formula which is at least exponential. However, provided that formulae are rather small if compared to the size of the system or its approximation, this blowup should be manageable. It is also conceivable to simplify a formula during its encoding (see the example at the end of Section 6). The encoding itself is not yet implemented, but we plan to do so in the future.

Finally the Petri net produced by the approximated unfolding algorithm and the formula itself have to be analysed by a model checker or a similar tool, based on the procedures described in [8, 7, 9]. Note that formulae on multisets can not be combined with the temporal operators of CTL* in an arbitrary way. First, we have to make sure that the resulting formula is still reflected, with respect to the simulation, hence no existential path quantification is allowed. Furthermore, arbitrary combinations of the temporal operators "eventually" and "generally" might make the model-checking problem undecidable. However, important fragments are still decidable, for example a property like "all reachable graphs satisfy F", where F is a multiset formula, can be checked. As far as we know, there is not much tool support for model-checking unbounded Petri nets, but these algorithms usually rely on the computation of the coverability graph of a Petri net, which is a well-studied problem [13].

Currently we are mainly interested in proving safety properties, liveness properties require some more care (see [12]). Another interesting line of future research is to adopt techniques used for the analysis of transition systems specified by integer constraints [5].

Acknowledgements

We are very grateful to Andrea Corradini for his contribution to the development of the approximated unfolding technique on which this paper is based. We would also like to thank Ingo Walther who is currently working on an implementation. We are also grateful to the anonymous referees for their valuable comments.

References

1. Paolo Baldan, Andrea Corradini, and Barbara König. A static analysis technique for graph transformation systems. In *Proc. of CONCUR'01*, pages 381–395. Springer-Verlag, 2001. LNCS 2154.
2. Paolo Baldan and Barbara König. Approximating the behaviour of graph transformation systems. In *Proc. of ICGT'02 (International Conference on Graph Transformation)*, pages 14–29. Springer-Verlag, 2002. LNCS 2505.
3. Edmund M. Clarke, Orna Grumberg, and David E. Long. Model checking and abstraction. *ACM Transactions on Programming Languages and Systems*, 1999.
4. B. Courcelle. The expression of graph properties and graph transformations in monadic second-order logic. In G. Rozenberg, editor, *Handbook of Graph Grammars and Computing by Graph Transformation, Vol.1: Foundations*, chapter 5. World Scientific, 1997.
5. Giorgio Delzanno. Automatic verification of parameterized cache coherence protocols. In *Proc. of CAV'00*, pages 53–68. Springer-Verlag, 2000. LNCS 1855.
6. Wilfrid Hodges. *Model Theory*. Cambridge University Press, 1993.
7. R. Howell and L. Rosier. Problems concerning fairness and temporal logic for conflict-free Petri net. *Theoretical Computer Science*, 64:305–329, 1989.
8. Rodney R. Howell, Louis E. Rosier, and Hsu-Chun Yen. A taxonomy of fairness and temporal logic problems for Petri nets. *Theoretical Computer Science*, 82:341–372, 1991.
9. Petr Jančar. Decidability of a temporal logic problem for Petri nets. *Theoretical Computer Science*, 74:71–93, 1990.
10. Claire Loiseaux, Susanne Graf, Joseph Sifakis, Ahmed Bouajjani, and Saddek Bensalem. Property preserving abstractions for the verification of concurrent systems. *Formal Methods in System Design*, 6:1–35, 1995.
11. Flemming Nielson, Hanne Riis Nielson, and Chris Hankin. *Principles of Program Analysis*. Springer-Verlag, 1999.
12. Amir Pnueli, Jessie Xu, and Lenore Zuck. Liveness with $(0, 1, \infty)$-counter abstraction. In *Proc. of CAV '02*, pages 107–122. Springer-Verlag, 2002. LNCS 2404.
13. W. Reisig. *Petri Nets: An Introduction*. EATCS Monographs on Theoretical Computer Science. Springer-Verlag, Berlin, Germany, 1985.
14. Abraham Robinson. *Introduction to Model Theory and to the Metamathematics of Algebra*. North-Holland, 1963.
15. M. Sagiv, T. Reps, and R. Wilhelm. Solving shape-analysis problems in languages with destructive updating. In *Proc. of POPL '96*, pages 16–31. ACM Press, 1996.

Type Systems for Distributed Data Sharing*

Ben Liblit, Alex Aiken, and Katherine Yelick

University of California, Berkeley
Berkeley, CA 94720-1776

Abstract. Parallel programming languages that let multiple processors access shared data provide a variety of sharing mechanisms and memory models. Understanding a language's support for data sharing behavior is critical to understanding how the language can be used, and is also a component for numerous program analysis, optimization, and runtime clients. Languages that provide the illusion of a global address space, but are intended to work on machines with physically distributed memory, often distinguish between different kinds of pointers or shared data. The result can be subtle rules about what kinds of accesses are allowed in the application programs and implicit constraints on how the language may be implemented. This paper develops a basis for understanding the design space of these sharing formalisms, and codifies that understanding in a suite of type checking/inference systems that illustrate the trade-offs among various models.

1 Introduction

Parallel, distributed, and multithreaded computing environments are becoming increasingly important, but such systems remain difficult to use and reason about. Data sharing (the ability of multiple threads to hold references to the same object) is one source of difficulty. Programming languages such as Java, Titanium, and UPC offer facilities for sharing data that vary in subtle, often implicit, but semantically significant ways.

We take a type-based approach to characterizing data sharing in distributed programming environments. This paper makes four principal contributions:

- We show that there is an essential difference between distributed pointers, which may be either *local* (within one address space) or *global* (across address spaces) and the patterns of access to data, which may be either *private* (used by one processor) or *shared* (used by many processors) [Section 2]. Earlier efforts have not clearly distinguished these two concepts [Section 4].
- We show that there is more than one notion of data sharing, and that various sharing models can be captured in a suite of type systems [Sections 3.1 through 3.3].

---

* This research was supported in part by NASA under NAG2-1210; NSF under EIA-9802069, CCR-0085949, and ACI-9619020; DOE under DE-FC03-01ER25509; and an NDSEG fellowship. The information presented here does not necessarily reflect the position or the policy of the Government and no official endorsement should be inferred.

$$
\begin{array}{lll}
i & ::= & \text{integer literal} \\
x & ::= & \text{program variable} \\
f & ::= & \text{function name}
\end{array}
\qquad
\begin{array}{rl}
e ::= & i \mid x \mid f\,e \mid \uparrow_{\text{shared}} e \mid \uparrow_{\text{private}} e \mid \downarrow e \\
\mid & e\,;\,e \mid e := e \mid \langle e, e \rangle \mid \texttt{@1}\,e \mid \texttt{@2}\,e \\
\mid & \texttt{widen}\,e \mid \texttt{transmit}\,e
\end{array}
$$

Fig. 1. Common grammar for expressions

- We show that type qualifier inference can automatically add detailed sharing information to an otherwise unannotated program, and that such an approach can be used with realistic distributed programming languages [Section 3.4].
- We report on the results of adding sharing inference to a real compiler for a parallel language, which highlights the strengths of our approach. We also present unexpected results on the effect of the underlying memory consistency model on program performance. Our experience in this area may be of independent interest [Section 5].

2 Background

Parallel applications with a distributed address space have two distinct notions of data: whether a pointer is *local* or *global* and whether an object is *private* or *shared*. Previous work has not brought out the distinction between these two ideas (see Section 4). Our primary thesis is that these should be separate concepts. This section explains what these two ideas are and why they are distinct.

Figure 1 introduces a small data manipulation language of pointers and pairs. This language extends one used by Liblit and Aiken [21] with new features to capture data sharing behavior. For the sake of brevity, we omit a detailed formal semantics and soundness proof. The semantics is unchanged from prior work, as our extensions here serve only to restrict which programs are admitted by the type system without changing how accepted programs behave at run time. Soundness is addressed briefly at the close of Section 3.3, and follows as a straightforward adaptation of a more complete proof previously published elsewhere for a related system [22].

A base expression may be an integer literal (i) or a named variable from some predefined environment (x). Function calls ($f\,e$) similarly assume that the function (f) is predefined. A sequencing operator ($e\,;\,e$) provides ordered evaluation. The language has no facilities for defining functions, new types, or recursion. These features are unnecessary to our exposition, though our techniques readily extend to realistic languages.

For our purposes, the essential aspects of the language are data structures (modeled by pairs) and pointers. Data may be combined into pairs ($\langle e, e \rangle$), which are unboxed (held directly as an immediate, flat-structured value, with no intervening levels of indirection). Unboxed pairs and integers may be stored in memory using the allocation operators ($\uparrow_\delta e$), which return boxed values stored in the local processor's memory (i.e., allocation is always on the local processor). The subscript δ states whether a boxed value is to be *shared* or *private*. Informally, a private value can be accessed only by the processor that allocated it. Thus, "$\uparrow_{\texttt{private}} \langle 5, 7 \rangle$" produces a pointer to a private memory cell holding the pair $(5, 7)$. In contrast, shared values can be examined and manipulated by multiple processors across the entire system.

If x holds the value of $\uparrow_{\texttt{private}} \langle 5, 7 \rangle$, then "$\downarrow x$" is the unboxed pair $\langle 5, 7 \rangle$. Each pair selection operator (@1 e or @2 e) accepts a pointer to a boxed pair, and produces an offset pointer to the first or second component of the pair respectively. Thus, if x holds the value of $\uparrow_{\texttt{private}} \langle 5, 7 \rangle$, then "@2 x" yields a pointer to the second component within the boxed pair, and "$\downarrow$ @2 x" yields the unboxed value 7.

The left operand of an assignment $e := e$ must be a pointer; the value given on the right is placed in the memory location named by the pointer given on the left. The explicit treatment of boxing and offset pointers allows us to model the update of components of data structures. For example, the expression

$$(\texttt{@2}\ \uparrow_{\texttt{private}} \langle 5, 7 \rangle) := 9$$

modifies the allocated pair from $\langle 5, 7 \rangle$ to $\langle 5, 9 \rangle$.

The remaining constructs model distributed memory systems. Allocation is local: $\uparrow_\delta e$ always produces a *local* pointer. A local pointer names memory local to a single processor, and corresponds in practice to a simple memory address. It does not make sense to transfer local pointers between processors; for that we need a *global* pointer, which names any location in the entire distributed system. This is akin to a $(processor, address)$ pair, where $processor$ uniquely identifies one processor in the complete distributed system and $address$ is a memory address within that processor's local address space. Local pointers are preferred when data is truly local, as global pointers may be both larger as well as slower to use. The widen operator (widen e) provides coercions from local to global pointers. For clarity we make these coercions explicit. In practice, coercions would be inserted automatically by the compiler.

The transmission operator (transmit e) models sending a value to some other machine. Transmission does not implicitly dereference pointers or serialize interlinked data structures. If e evaluates to an unboxed tuple, then both components of the tuple are sent; if e evaluates to a pointer, then just a single pointer value (not the pointed-to data) is sent. We intentionally leave the communication semantics unspecified; transmit might correspond to a network broadcast, a remote procedure invocation, or any other cross-machine data exchange. The important invariant is that transmit e must produce a representation of e that can be used safely on remote processors. For this reason, it is typical to transmit widened values. Transmitting a local pointer without widening is forbidden, as a local pointer value is meaningless on any but the originating processor.

2.1 Representation Versus Sharing

Consider the expression

$$x := \uparrow_{\texttt{private}} e$$

The referent of x is supposed to be private: no other processor should ever have access to the value of e. Thus, all pointers to e, including x, can use the cheaper local pointer representation. In a single-threaded program, all data is both local and private.

Now consider
$$x := \texttt{transmit}\,(\texttt{widen}\,(\uparrow_{\text{shared}} e))$$
Here the value of e is declared to be shared and a global pointer to this value is transmitted to a remote processor (or processors), where it is stored in a variable x. For example, if transmit broadcasts the value computed on processor 0, then each running processor receives a pointer to processor 0's value of e and stores this in its own instance of the variable x. On each remote processor, then, x is a global pointer to the same piece of shared data.

Finally, consider the following minor variation on the last example:
$$y := \uparrow_{\text{shared}} e;$$
$$x := \texttt{transmit}\,(\texttt{widen}\,(y))$$
As before, x is a global pointer that points to shared data. But what is y? It points to shared data, but y is on the same processor as e. Thus, y should be a local pointer to shared data.

It is this last case that distinguishes local/global from shared/private. The distinction is that local/global determines the representation of pointers, while the shared/private determines how data is used. As illustrated in the examples above, a local pointer may point either to shared or private data. Just having a local pointer does not tell us whether concurrent access from other processors is possible.

While local/global is distinct from shared/private, these two concepts are not quite orthogonal. In particular, global pointers to private data are problematic: What could it mean for a processor to hold a pointer to data that is supposed to be private to another processor? As we show in Section 3, there are multiple possible answers to this question.

2.2 Uses of Sharing Information

In later sections we show how to statically determine which data is private to a single processor versus shared by multiple processors. Such information can support a number of clients. *Autonomous garbage collection* can reclaim private data. as a strictly local operation without coordinating with other processors [33]. *Data location management* can be important when hardware constraints make shared memory a limited resource [26]. *Cache coherence overhead* [1] can be avoided for private data that only one processor ever sees. *Race condition detection* [17, 24, 32] need never consider races on private data. *Program/algorithm documentation* can be augmented by compiler validation of programmers' claims. *Consistency model relaxation* allows more aggressive optimizations on data that other processors cannot see [25]. *Synchronization elimination* boosts performance for private monitors that can never come under contention [3, 7]. *Security* mandates careful treatment of private data in distributed systems without mutual trust.

$$\tau ::= \text{int} \mid \langle \tau, \tau \rangle \mid \text{boxed } \omega \; \delta \; \tau$$
$$\omega ::= \text{local} \mid \text{global}$$
$$\delta ::= \text{shared} \mid \text{mixed} \mid \text{private}$$

shared < mixed   private < mixed

$$\text{boxed } \omega \; \delta \; \tau \leq \text{boxed } \omega \; \delta' \; \tau \iff \delta \leq \delta'$$
$$\langle \tau_1, \tau_2 \rangle \leq \langle \tau_1', \tau_2' \rangle \iff \tau_1 \leq \tau_1' \wedge \tau_2 \leq \tau_2'$$

(a) Grammar for types   (b) Subtyping relations

Fig. 2. Common properties of all type systems

Each of these clients depends upon identifying data accessed by only one processor. Typically, this processor is the one in whose local memory the data lives; the data is accessed by way of local pointers. However, local pointers alone do not suffice, because of the possibility that a global pointer may alias the same location. Furthermore, even if the data itself is only referenced by local pointers, transitive reachability is still a concern: if we have a global pointer to a local pointer to a local pointer to the value 5, the memory cell containing 5 could still be accessed by a remote processor via a sequence of dereference operations that widen the local pointers to global on each dereference. Again, pointer representations are not the same as data sharing patterns, and the latter cannot be trivially deduced from the former.

In Section 3 we show that some clients (in particular, autonomous GC and security) require stronger privacy guarantees than others. This suggests a solution based not on a single definition of privacy, but rather on a family of alternatives from which each client can select according to its needs.

3 Type Systems

Figure 2 presents the types and the subtyping relation used in the following subsections. The basic types are unboxed integers int and unboxed pairs $\langle \tau, \tau \rangle$. Pointers boxed $\omega \; \delta \; \tau$ to values of type τ also carry qualifiers ω and δ, which respectively range over {local, global} and {shared, mixed, private}.

A local pointer may be widened into an equivalent global pointer. However, local and global pointers have distinct physical representations and are manipulated using very different machine-level operations. Therefore, widening is a coercion, not a subtyping relation, which is why widen is included as an explicit operator in the language in Figure 1. On the other hand, sharing qualifiers merely dictate which remote operations are permissible and which are forbidden. In general, shared and private pointers can have identical physical representation and can be manipulated (where allowed at all) by identical machine-level operations.

However, neither coercion nor simplistic subtyping is appropriate between shared and private pointers. Shared pointers have functionality that private pointers do not: they can be widened to global and used at a distance. Private pointers have unique functionality of their own: they admit aggressive optimization that could violate language invariants if observed by remote processors.

Furthermore, any sound type system must ensure that sharing qualifiers are consistent across aliasing: local and global pointers may address the same location simultaneously, but no location may ever be considered to be both shared and private.

There are, however, good reasons to allow code that operates on either shared or private data. For example, consider the type of "this" in the Object() constructor of a Java-like language. As observed earlier, there is no coercion from private to shared or shared to private. If this is shared in the constructor then it can never be called to construct a private object, while if this is private, then no shared object may ever be built. Since every other constructor for every other class ultimately calls Object(), any restrictions introduced here affect the entire system.

Reuse of constructor code, then, requires polymorphism. We find in Section 5.1 that basic utility code is also reused in many contexts and therefore imposes similar requirements on the type system. In this paper we use subtyping polymorphism with a "mixed" sharing qualifier.[1] A mixed datum may be either shared or private; code that manipulates mixed data may do so only in ways sound for both. The subtyping relation is defined in Figure 2(b). Note that subtyping does not cross pointers; this restriction is necessary to avoid the well-known unsoundness problems that would result with subtyping updatable references.

3.1 Late Enforcement

If we define "private" to mean neither read nor written by a remote processor, then global pointers to private data may be freely created, but they cannot be dereferenced. This section presents such a *late enforcement* system.

Typing judgments "$A \vdash e : \tau$" are read "In environment A, it is provable that expression e has type τ." The auxiliary *expand* and *pop* functions defined in Figure 3 describe how types are transformed or constrained by widening and cross-processor communication. Observe that type expansion recursively descends into pairs but never crosses pointers; we expand only the immediate value directly being communicated across processor boundaries. Integers and global pointers are the same everywhere. Local pointers expand to global only at the topmost level of a type (*expand*), but are banned from appearing within expanding pairs (*pop*).

(Global pointers are, in general, larger than local pointers. Therefore, expanding local pointers to global pointers inside a pair would change the size and layout of the pair. This is undesirable in practice for languages where each named structure type (class) must have a single, consistent layout. An alternative would be to allow deep local pointers to remain the same size, but mark them as invalid for use by the remote processor. This possibility is explored in greater detail elsewhere [21], and is omitted here for simplicity.)

---

[1] An alternative is to use parametric polymorphism, which is more expressive, but subtype polymorphism is a little simpler to explain.

$$expand(\texttt{boxed } \omega \ \delta \ \tau) \equiv \texttt{boxed global } \delta \ \tau$$
$$expand(\langle \tau_1, \tau_2 \rangle) \equiv \langle pop(\tau_1), pop(\tau_2) \rangle$$
$$expand(\texttt{int}) \equiv \texttt{int}$$

$$pop(\texttt{boxed global } \delta \ \tau) \equiv \texttt{boxed global } \delta \ \tau$$
$$pop(\langle \tau_1, \tau_2 \rangle) \equiv \langle pop(\tau_1), pop(\tau_2) \rangle$$
$$pop(\texttt{int}) \equiv \texttt{int}$$

Fig. 3. Supporting functions for late enforcement. Notice that *pop* is not defined for local pointers

Types for integers, variables, and function applications are completely standard. Sequencing, pair construction, and subtyping are also given in the typical manner:

$$\frac{}{A \vdash i : \texttt{int}} \qquad \frac{A(x) = \tau}{A \vdash x : \tau} \qquad \frac{A(f) = \tau \to \tau' \quad A \vdash e : \tau}{A \vdash f \, e : \tau'}$$

$$\frac{A \vdash e : \tau \quad A \vdash e' : \tau'}{A \vdash e \, ; e' : \tau'} \qquad \frac{A \vdash e_1 : \tau_1 \quad A \vdash e_2 : \tau_2}{A \vdash \langle e_1, e_2 \rangle : \langle \tau_1, \tau_2 \rangle}$$

$$\frac{A \vdash e : \tau \quad \tau \leq \tau'}{A \vdash e : \tau'}$$

Shared or private allocation creates an appropriately qualified local pointer:

$$\frac{A \vdash e : \tau \quad \delta \in \{\texttt{shared}, \texttt{private}\}}{A \vdash \uparrow_\delta e : \texttt{boxed local } \delta \ \tau}$$

Notice late enforcement places no restrictions on the type of data to be boxed. One may, for example, create a pointer to shared data containing embedded pointers to private data.

Dereferencing of local pointers is standard, and is allowed regardless of the sharing qualifier. For global pointers, we only allow dereferencing if the pointed-to data is known to be shared, and apply pointer widening to the result:

$$\frac{A \vdash e : \texttt{boxed local } \delta \ \tau}{A \vdash \downarrow e : \tau} \qquad \frac{A \vdash e : \texttt{boxed global shared } \tau}{A \vdash \downarrow e : expand(\tau)}$$

This is the first instance in which late enforcement restricts program behavior: private data may not be read across a global pointer. Private data is only visible to the owning processor, by way of local pointers.

Assignment is similar, and represents the second instance in which late enforcement restricts program behavior. A local pointer may be used to modify both shared and private data, while a global pointer may only touch shared data. To enforce that the assigned value embed no local pointers, global assignment carries an additional requirement that the type being assigned be preserved by type expansion:

$$\frac{A \vdash e : \texttt{boxed local } \delta\ \tau \quad A \vdash e' : \tau}{A \vdash e := e' : \tau}$$

$$\frac{A \vdash e : \texttt{boxed global shared } \tau \quad A \vdash e' : \tau \quad expand(\tau) = \tau}{A \vdash e := e' : \tau}$$

Widening directly applies the type expansion function to coerce local pointers into their global equivalents. Transmission across processor boundaries requires that type expansion be the identity, just as for global assignment; typically, one would transmit a value that had just been widened:

$$\frac{A \vdash e : \tau}{A \vdash \texttt{widen } e : expand(\tau)} \qquad \frac{A \vdash e : \tau \quad expand(\tau) = \tau}{A \vdash \texttt{transmit } e : expand(\tau)}$$

Selection propagates the sharing qualifier through pointer displacement in the obvious manner:

$$\frac{A \vdash e : \texttt{boxed } \omega\ \delta\ \langle \tau_1, \tau_2 \rangle \quad n \in \{1,2\}}{A \vdash @n\ e : \texttt{boxed } \omega\ \delta\ \tau_n}$$

Design Implications. In the rules given above, it is only at the point of an actual dereference or assignment that we add restrictions to implement late enforcement. Any program that tries to read or write private or mixed data via a global pointer fails to type check. In conjunction with the *expand* function, these rules implicitly cover the case of global pointers to local pointers as well. Suppose that p is a local pointer to private data, and that q is a global pointer to a shared location containing p. Then:

$p\ \ : \texttt{boxed local private } \tau$

$q\ \ : \texttt{boxed global shared boxed local private } \tau$

$\downarrow q : \texttt{boxed global private } \tau$

Dereferencing q does not yield local pointer p, but rather an equivalent pointer widened to global. Since p points to private data, the widened pointer also points to private data and cannot be dereferenced or assigned through.

In general, the late enforcement system forbids undesirable behavior only if a private value is actually used by a remote processor. A global pointer to private data may be created, copied, sent to other processors, placed into data structures, compared to other pointers, and so on, but the memory location named by the pointer cannot be examined or modified.

We know of two situations in which the type `boxed global private` τ could be desirable. First, this pointer may be embedded in a tuple containing both shared and private components. The shared portions of the data structure may be accessed remotely, while the private portions are not. Type checking such a program requires that we allow global pointers to private data to be formed and manipulated, provided that they are never actually used.

Second, although a global pointer is conservatively assumed to address remote memory, a global pointer may address local memory as well. Real distributed languages typically allow dynamically checked conversion of global pointers back to local. A global pointer to private data, then, might be converted back to a local pointer to private data, whereupon it could be used freely.

Applicability and Limitations. If we intend to use sharing qualifiers to make data location management decisions, the weak guarantees offered by late enforcement are sufficient. When memory is reserved using $\uparrow_{private}$ or $\uparrow_{shared}$, we can use the subscripted qualifier to choose a suitable region of memory. Global pointers may escape to distant processors, but the memory occupied by private data is never examined or modified remotely. Thus, private data can reside in memory that is not network-addressable. Sharable memory, which may be slower or more scarce, is reserved for shared data.

Several other clients can make use of late enforcement guarantees. Distributed cache coherence need not be maintained for data that is never examined remotely. Race condition detection systems need not concern themselves with global pointers to private data, since these can never create races. Similarly, any sequence of operations on private data may be reordered or optimized quite freely even under the strictest of consistency models, because changes to intermediate states are never observable by other processors. Treating lock acquisition as a dereference, private locks can be eliminated at compile time.

However, late enforcement is too late for other applications. Certain languages may be unable to autonomously garbage collect using late enforcement. Security concerns may also be unsatisfied by exposed pointers to private data. Our remaining type systems incrementally impose stricter enforcement policies to accommodate these concerns.

3.2 Export Enforcement

In some languages, late enforcement is too weak to support autonomous garbage collection. As suggested earlier, many distributed programming environments support checked conversion of global pointers back to local. In such a system, the following sequence of actions could take place:

1. Processor A creates private data and sends its address to remote processor B. Processor B now holds a global pointer to this private data.
2. Processor A destroys all of its own references to the private data. The global pointer held by processor B is now the only live reference to this private data.
3. Some time later, the processor B sends the global private pointer back to processor A.
4. Processor A uses a checked conversion to recover a local pointer to its own private data, and subsequently dereferences that pointer.

Autonomous garbage collection requires that any live data have at least one live local reference. If processor A were to autonomously garbage collect between steps 2 and 3, the private data would seem unreachable and the memory it occupies would be reclaimed. Therefore, if a language allows narrowing casts

$$expand(\text{boxed } \omega \text{ shared } \tau) \equiv \text{boxed global shared } \tau$$
$$expand(\langle \tau_1, \tau_2 \rangle) \equiv \langle pop(\tau_1), pop(\tau_2) \rangle$$
$$expand(\text{int}) \equiv \text{int}$$

Fig. 4. Revised type expansion function supporting export enforcement. The subordinate *pop* function is unchanged from Figure 3

from global to local, late enforcement cannot be used to support autonomous garbage collection.

We modify the late enforcement system as follows. One possible source of global pointers to private data is the initial environment (A). We impose a well-formedness requirement on the initial environment, stipulating that boxed global private τ not appear within any part of the type for any variable or function. For compound expressions, the chief source of global pointers is the widen operator, which relies upon *expand* to expand local pointers to global. Figure 4 gives a revised *expand* function that only produces global pointers to shared data. Notice that the new version is not defined for pointers to private or mixed data. Thus, transmit can no longer send pointers to private data across processor boundaries. The widen coercion is similarly restricted, as are global assignment and global dereferencing. Given a well-formed starting environment, the revised *expand* function ensures that no expression has type boxed global private τ.

The new *expand* function guarantees that the only pointers exported are those to shared data. However, observe that when a pointer of type boxed ω shared τ is expanded, there are no restrictions on the type τ of the pointed-to data. In particular, one may freely transmit a pointer to a shared memory cell which, in turn, points to private data: boxed ω shared (boxed ω' private τ') is an identity for *expand*. Thus, this *export enforcement* type system restricts only the actual, immediate values being exported. It does not extend transitively beyond the first level of pointers. This is sufficient to support autonomous garbage collection, as it guarantees that no remote processor can hold the only live reference to any piece of private data.

This approach does not eliminate the need to manage memory used by objects which genuinely are shared. Rather, it complements distributed garbage collection techniques (e.g. stubs and scions [30]) by identifying a private subset of data which can be collected aggressively using simpler, traditional, purely local collection algorithms.

3.3 Early Enforcement

In an untrusted environment, the address at which private data is stored may itself be sensitive information. Security concerns may mandate that no private address ever escape the owning processor. Neither late nor export enforcement can provide that kind of protection. The vulnerability can be seen in the type checking rule for global dereference, which requires that the pointed-to data be shared. In an untrusted environment, a remote processor that willfully disregards this restriction may be able to transitively walk across pointers and ultimately reach private data. Global assignment is similarly vulnerable. Runtime checks could detect such misbehavior, but static (compile-time) assurances may be a more attractive option.

For complete control over private addresses, we refine export enforcement to additionally require that no private data be transitively reachable from shared memory. For variables and functions, we extend the well-formedness requirements on initial environments in the obvious manner. For compound expressions, the only change required is in the type checking rules for allocation. Late and export enforcement allowed either shared or private boxing of any type τ. For early enforcement, we impose an additional restriction on shared allocation:

$$\frac{A \vdash e : \tau}{A \vdash \uparrow_{\text{private}} e : \text{boxed local private } \tau}$$

$$\frac{A \vdash e : \tau \qquad allShared(\tau)}{A \vdash \uparrow_{\text{shared}} e : \text{boxed local shared } \tau}$$

The new *allShared* predicate holds if and only if all pointers directly embedded within a type are shared:

$$allShared(\text{boxed } \omega \; \delta \; \tau) \equiv (\delta = \text{shared})$$
$$allShared(\langle \tau_1, \tau_2 \rangle) \equiv allShared(\tau_1) \wedge allShared(\tau_2)$$
$$allShared(\text{int}) \equiv \text{true}$$

Thus, no pointer to private data may ever be placed in shared memory. If we require that the initial environment (A) obey similar restrictions, then in general no private storage is transitively reachable from shared or global memory. The universe of shared data is transitively closed. A consequence of this is that the sharing constraint in the global dereference and assignment rules is always trivially satisfied: because all data transitively reachable from a global pointer must be shared, it is impossible for a malicious remote processor to disregard the sharing constraint and transitively reach private data.

Applicability and Trade-Offs. Clearly, export enforcement is more restrictive than late enforcement, and early enforcement is more restrictive still. By accepting fewer programs, export and early enforcement allows us to make progressively stronger guarantees about the meaning of "private" in those programs that do type check. Thus, early enforcement can also support all late enforcement clients, such as race detectors or reordering optimizers, as well as autonomous garbage collection. The effectiveness of some clients may be reduced, though, as early enforcement treats some data as shared which late or export enforcement could have taken as private.

The set of programs accepted under each system is a strict subset of those accepted under the one before. We have adapted an earlier proof of local/global soundness [22] to show that the late enforcement system is sound, from which the soundness of the other two systems follows. The additional requirements imposed by each system (e.g. no access to private data by way of a global pointer) are enforced directly by the type checking rules; correctness of these restrictions is verifiable by direct inspection of the type checking rules for the corresponding operations.

3.4 Type Inference

The type systems described above are easily converted from type checking to type inference. We illustrate late enforcement inference here. Inference for export and early enforcement is similar, but has been omitted for the sake of brevity.

We assume that the program is known to type check disregarding sharing qualifiers. The `local/global` qualifiers can also be inferred [21], and one may wish to infer all qualifiers simultaneously. For simplicity we assume here that `local/global` inference has already taken place separately.

Our type inference rules produce a system of constraints that must be solved. Rules are given in Figure 5; additional sharing constraints arise from the *expand* function as defined in Figure 6. For clarity of presentation, the rules use several abbreviations:

1. Constraint sets are not explicitly propagated up from subexpressions; the complete constraint set is the union of all sets of constraints induced by all subexpressions.
2. A nontrivial rule hypothesis such as

$$e : \texttt{boxed global shared } \tau$$

    should be read as an equality constraint

$$e : \tau_0 \qquad \tau_0 = \texttt{boxed global shared } \tau$$

3. All constraint variables are fresh.

Any solution to the constraints induced by these rules gives a valid typing for the program. We note that setting all possible variables to `shared` always produces one legitimate solution. Thus, languages that assume all data to be shared are safe, albeit overly conservative. Because our sharing qualifier lattice has no $\bot$, there is no least solution. Rather, we are interested in the "best" solution, defined as the one having the largest number of `private` qualifiers. This maximally-private solution may be computed efficiently as follows:

1. Assume that initially we have a static typing showing what is a pointer, pair, or integer, as well as which pointers are local or global.
2. Using the equivalences in Figure 2(b), expand type constraints $\tau = \tau'$ and $\tau \leq \tau'$ to obtain the complete set of sharing constraints.
3. Identify the set of qualifier constants that are transitive lower bounds of each qualifier variable. Collect the set $\mathcal{S}$ of all constraint variables that have either `shared` or `mixed` as a transitive lower bound. These variables cannot be `private`.

$$\frac{}{A \vdash i : \mathtt{int}} \qquad \frac{A(x) = \tau}{A \vdash x : \tau}$$

$$\frac{A(f) = \tau \to \tau' \quad A \vdash e : \tau'' \quad \tau'' \leq \tau}{A \vdash f\,e : \tau'} \qquad \frac{A \vdash e : \tau}{A \vdash \uparrow_\delta e : \mathtt{boxed\ local}\ \delta\ \tau}$$

$$\frac{A \vdash e : \mathtt{boxed\ global\ shared}\ \tau \quad expand(\tau,\tau')}{A \vdash \downarrow e : \tau'}$$

$$\frac{A \vdash e : \mathtt{boxed\ local}\ \delta\ \tau}{A \vdash \downarrow e : \tau}$$

$$\frac{A \vdash e : \tau \quad A \vdash e' : \tau'}{A \vdash e\,;\,e' : \tau'} \qquad \frac{A \vdash e : \mathtt{boxed\ local}\ \delta\ \tau \quad A \vdash e' : \tau' \quad \tau' \leq \tau}{A \vdash e := e' : \tau}$$

$$\frac{A \vdash e : \mathtt{boxed\ global\ shared}\ \tau \quad A \vdash e' : \tau' \quad \tau' \leq \tau \quad expand(\tau,\tau)}{A \vdash e := e' : \tau} \qquad \frac{A \vdash e_1 : \tau_1 \quad A \vdash e_2 : \tau_2}{A \vdash \langle e_1, e_2 \rangle : \langle \tau_1, \tau_2 \rangle}$$

$$\frac{A \vdash e : \mathtt{boxed}\ \omega\ \delta\ \langle \tau_1, \tau_2 \rangle \quad n \in \{1,2\}}{A \vdash @n\,e : \mathtt{boxed}\ \omega\ \delta\ \tau_n} \qquad \frac{A \vdash e : \tau \quad expand(\tau,\tau')}{A \vdash \mathtt{widen}\ e : \tau'}$$

$$\frac{A \vdash e : \tau \quad expand(\tau,\tau)}{A \vdash \mathtt{transmit}\ e : \tau}$$

Fig. 5. Type inference rules for late enforcement

4. For each sharing qualifier variable δ not in $\mathcal{S}$, set $\delta = \mathtt{private}$. This may cause private to appear as a transitive lower bound on a variable where it was not present earlier.
5. For each sharing qualifier δ, let d be the least upper bound of its constant transitive lower bounds. Let $\delta = d$ in the final solution.

The meat of this algorithm devolves to graph reachability flowing forward along constraint edges from nodes representing each of the three type qualifiers. The solution, therefore, is computable in time linear with respect to the number of sharing qualifiers in the fully typed program [16, 19]. As local/global inference is also linear, this gives language designers great flexibility. One may expose all of these type choices in the source language, or one may present a

$$expand(\mathtt{boxed}\ \omega\ \delta\ \tau, \mathtt{boxed}\ \omega'\ \delta'\ \tau') \equiv \{\delta = \delta', \tau = \tau'\}$$
$$expand(\langle \tau_1, \tau_2 \rangle, \langle \tau'_1, \tau'_2 \rangle) \equiv expand(\tau_1, \tau'_1) \cup expand(\tau_2, \tau'_2)$$
$$expand(\mathtt{int}, \mathtt{int}) \equiv \emptyset$$

Fig. 6. Additional constraints induced by supporting functions. We assume local/global qualifiers have already been assigned; these functions cover only the additional sharing constraints

Fig. 7. Constraint graph requiring choice between shared and private. An arrow $x \to y$ encodes the constraint $x \leq y$.

simpler source-level model augmented by fast compiler-driven type inference to fill in the details.

The critical feature of this algorithm is that it first identifies all qualifiers that cannot possibly be private, then binds all other variables to private, and lastly chooses between shared and mixed for the variables that could not be made private. This strategy maximizes the number of private qualifiers in exchange for driving some other qualifiers to mixed instead of shared. In the example in Figure 7, our algorithm binds δ to private, which means that δ_1 can be private as well but δ_2 must be mixed. An alternative is to set δ to shared, which would drive δ_1 to mixed but allow δ_2 to be shared. In either case, some δ_n must be mixed. Our algorithm resolves such choices in favor of maximizing the number of variables bound private, as this is most useful to the clients of interest.

4 Related Work

The static type systems of previous proposals have not dealt with local/global and shared/private in a general way. As a result, they are all either less general than is possible, unsafe, or both. Lack of generality prevents programmers from enforcing that data should be private, which makes it more difficult to reason about program correctness and results in missed opportunities for optimization. Lack of safety exhibits itself in unsafe (often implicit) casts among pointer types that impede optimization, or in under-specified semantics where optimization may change program behavior in unexpected ways.

One group of languages guarantees safety but has no facility for declaring private heap data. In these languages the stack is private but the entire heap must be treated as potentially shared. Java, Olden [9], and Titanium (prior to this work) [20] are in this category. For these languages, our techniques provide a basis for automatically inferring private heap data. We also believe it is important for programmers to be able to declare private data explicitly, as knowledge of what data is private is critical in understanding parallel and distributed programs.

Jade is a safe language that distinguishes local from global pointers, and which allows some heap data to be private. This private data can never be transitively reachable from the shared heap [31], which corresponds to our early enforcement system (Section 3.3). Our results show that where security is not a primary concern, significantly more flexible sharing of data is possible, allowing for more data to be statically identified as private and thereby making privacy-dependent analyses more effective.

EARTH-C explicitly offers both local/global and shared/private type qualifiers. Local/global may be inferred [36], but shared/private must be given explicitly [18]. Our approach shows that shared/private is amenable to inference as well, operating either fully automatically or to augment programmer directives. The broader EARTH-C project has also clearly demonstrated the value of identifying local private data to drive analyses such as redundant read/write removal and communication optimization [37].

Among the unsafe (C-derived) languages, AC [10], PCP [8], and UPC [11] offer shared and private data. However, their type systems do not distinguish the addresses of private data from narrowed global pointers to shared data. In effect, these languages offer only **global shared** and **local mixed**. Although private data exists at run time, the static type system cannot identify it in a useful manner, and many of the clients listed in Section 2.2 cannot be deployed.

Also in the C family, CC++ [12] and Split-C [14] do not directly address the notion of private data. This may mean that all data is presumed shared, but it is difficult to know exactly what semantics are required, especially with regard to code reordering and other aggressive optimizations. Cilk explicitly treats all memory as shared, and states that the programmer is responsible for understanding the underlying memory model provided by the host hardware [34]. We believe that sharing inference can support aggressive optimization without the added burden of under-specified semantics.

Our type systems are similar to escape analysis. Previous research has focused on identifying data that does not escape a stack frame or a thread of execution [3, 6, 7, 13, 35]. The early enforcement system may be thought of as identifying data that does not escape a local address space. Considered in this light, the late enforcement system is unusual: escape of addresses is permitted, provided that the data referenced by an escaped address is never actually examined or modified from a distance. This is more permissive than escape analysis, yet it is strong enough to support certain traditional escape analysis clients, such as synchronization removal.

To our knowledge, only one earlier study takes an approach that is similar to late enforcement. The "thread-local analysis" presented by Aldrich et al. [3] defines *multithreaded objects* as objects that escape from one thread and are also written to by a (conservatively defined) distinct thread. An escaped object that is never written to need not be considered multithreaded. This is similar in spirit to late enforcement: a globally reachable piece of data that is not actually accessed remotely need not be considered shared. The question of whether something akin to late enforcement can be applied directly to stack and thread escape analyses warrants further study.

5 Experimental Findings

We have added sharing qualifiers to Titanium, an experimental Java dialect for high performance parallel computing [20]. Unqualified references are assumed to be **shared**; programmers may declare references as **private** or **mixed** subject to validation by the type checker. Stronger (more private) qualifiers are added automatically using type inference. To highlight the bounds of the design space, both late and early enforcement are available. (Export enforcement would yield performance results between these two.) Our inference engine is based on the cqual qualifier inference engine [15].

Our benchmarks are single-program multiple-data (*SPMD*) codes with no explicit sharing qualifiers. All benchmarks are designed for execution on distributed memory multiprocessors, and reflect the scientific focus of SPMD programming. The applications include Monte Carlo integration (pi), sorting (sample-sort), dense linear algebra (lu-fact, cannon), a Fourier transform (3d-fft), particle methods (n-body, particle-mesh, ib [28]), and solvers for computational fluid dynamics (gsrb, pps [4], amr [29], gas [5]).

Whole-program sharing inference including the Java class library (roughly an additional 16,000 lines) takes no more than one second on a 1.3 GHz Pentium 4 Linux workstation. As the inference algorithm itself is linear, it should scale well to much larger code bases.

We studied several of the sharing based analyses and optimizations in Section 2.2. Detailed results appear in a companion report, which also provides additional details on incorporating sharing analysis into a complete programming language [23]. Here we focus on three areas: the static prevalence of various inferred types; dynamic tallies of shared versus private allocation to support data location management; and the performance impact of sharing inference on consistency model relaxation.

5.1 Static Metrics

Table 1 shows the number of static reference declaration sites in each benchmark: places where some sharing qualifier could syntactically appear. The Titanium stack is trivially private, so we exclude local variables and tabulate only heap data. Although whole program inference was used, we include here only those sites appearing in the benchmark application code (not in libraries). For each style of enforcement, we show the fraction of static references inferred as shared, mixed, and private.

In our review of related work, we saw that several distributed languages either have only a private stack or else have no notion of private data at all. We believe that this is an important omission. Regardless of which system is used, we consistently identify large amounts of private heap data in all benchmarks of all sizes. The largest benchmark, gas, has private data at half of all declaration sites. Other benchmarks range from 16% to 75%, and overall 46% of all sites in all benchmarks are inferred private. This is encouraging news for analysis clients which may want to exploit such information. It also reinforces the need for inference: it is unlikely that any human programmer could correctly place all such qualifiers by hand, or maintain such qualifiers over time.

A small number of mixed qualifiers appear in nearly every benchmark. In many cases, mixed is found in utility code shared by distinct parts of the application; parametric polymorphism could certainly be used here instead of subtyping. Elsewhere we find code, not isolated within methods, that performs complex operations on either shared or private data based on complex run time control

Table 1. Benchmark sizes and relative counts of inferred qualifiers

benchmark	lines	sites	late			early		
			shared	mixed	private	shared	mixed	private
pi	56	12	25%	0%	75%	25%	0%	75%
sample-sort	321	73	38%	1%	60%	38%	1%	60%
lu-fact	420	150	54%	3%	43%	54%	3%	43%
cannon	518	162	36%	2%	61%	36%	2%	61%
3d-fft	614	191	37%	1%	63%	37%	1%	63%
n-body	826	113	76%	1%	23%	76%	1%	23%
gsrb	1090	281	48%	1%	51%	48%	1%	51%
particle-grid	1095	201	83%	<1%	16%	84%	0%	16%
pps	3673	551	41%	5%	54%	44%	6%	50%
ib	3777	1094	56%	1%	43%	58%	1%	41%
amr	5206	1353	57%	1%	42%	59%	1%	40%
gas	8841	1699	50%	<1%	50%	51%	<1%	49%

decisions. The mixed qualifier works well here, whereas method-based parametric polymorphism would be difficult to apply without nontrivial code factoring. In both cases, the code is clearly polymorphic with respect to sharing, and without a polymorphic type system significantly more data would be forced to be shared. Polymorphism may be more important to the overall system than the small mixed counts would suggest.

When heap data is shared by several processors, the obvious choice is to address it using global pointers; it is not clear that local pointers to shared data are needed. However, other than pi, all programs show heavy use of local pointers to shared data: 24%–53% of all shared heap data is addressed by local pointers, and these numbers remain high (42% for amr, 32% for gas) even for the largest benchmarks. A local shared pointer often represents the locally allocated portion of some larger, distributed data structure. Each processor retains a local pointer to the data that it created, and may use that pointer for efficient access to the data which it "owns". Earlier work has demonstrated that use of local pointers is critical to performance [21]; if a quarter to half of all statically shared data references were forced to be global, performance can only suffer.

5.2 Data Location Management

Shared memory may be a scarce or costly resource. We have instrumented each benchmark to tally the number of shared and private allocations over the course of an entire run. Table 2 gives these totals, in bytes, for each of late and early enforcement. Observe that we see slight differences between the two enforcement schemes even on small benchmarks which reported identical results in Table 1. This is because that earlier table examined only application code and excluded libraries, whereas these allocation counts apply to the entire program. Slight differences in inference results for library code are visible here as slight differences in allocation counts for late versus early enforcement.

Overall, we see wide variation between benchmarks, ranging from 99% of allocations shared (particle-grid) to nearly 100% of allocations private (n-body).

Table 2. Kilobytes allocated in shared or private memory. We omit `gsrb` and `ib` due to unrelated Titanium bugs which prevent them from running to completion

benchmark	late		early	
	shared	private	shared	private
pi	74 (75%)	25 (25%)	74 (75%)	25 (25%)
sample-sort	3306 (5%)	66453 (95%)	3347 (5%)	67843 (95%)
cannon	8771 (60%)	5768 (40%)	8771 (60%)	5768 (40%)
3d-fft	4755 (52%)	4328 (48%)	4755 (52%)	4328 (48%)
n-body	368 ($<1\%$)	101700 (100%)	368 ($<1\%$)	101700 (100%)
particle-grid	9511 (99%)	123 (1%)	9513 (99%)	123 (1%)
pps	19459 (26%)	55360 (74%)	60518 (81%)	14302 (19%)
amr	36455 (88%)	4841 (12%)	40990 (99%)	306 (1%)
gas	2587611 (55%)	2157523 (45%)	2587866 (55%)	2157267 (45%)

We have examples at both extremes among both the large and small benchmarks. Our largest benchmark, gas, is also the most memory intensive, and we find that 45% of allocated bytes can be placed in private memory.

Most byte counts do not vary appreciably between late and early enforcement, though `amr` sees an 11% shift. The most dramatic shift is found in `pps`: late enforcement allows 74% private allocation, while early enforcement drops that to merely 19%. In Table 1 we observe that `pps` shows a relatively large difference in static private declaration counts as well. Clearly those differences encompass data structures which account for a preponderance of `pps`'s runtime memory consumption. When running on machines with costly shared memory, `pps` stands to benefit greatly from data location management guided by sharing inference.

5.3 Consistency Model Relaxation

Titanium uses a fairly weak consistency model, which allows the compiler or hardware to reorder memory operations [20]. A stronger model would be a more attractive programming target if it did not unacceptably harm performance. As suggested in Section 2.2, we can use sharing inference to allow private data accesses to be reordered while ensuring the stronger semantics at the language level. We have implemented such an optimization for a sequentially consistent variant of Titanium.

Figure 8 presents benchmark running times using each of four configurations. *Naïve* uses no inference: all data is assumed shared, and sequential consistency is enforced everywhere. *Early* and *late* enforce sequential consistency except where private data is inferred using the corresponding type system. *Weak* is the weak consistency model used in Titanium, which is an upper bound on the speedup from allowing reordering.

Because the benchmarks have very different raw performance, we present the running times normalized by the running time of the naïve implementation of sequential consistency. Measurements were taken on an SMP Linux workstation with four Pentium III, 550 MHz CPU's and 4GB of DRAM.

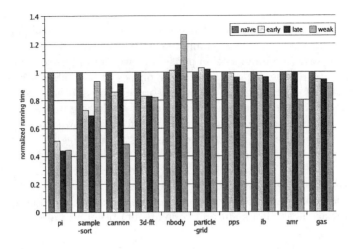

Fig. 8. Performance cost of sequential consistency. We omit `lu-fact` and `gsrb` due to unrelated Titanium bugs which prevent them from running to completion

The large speedup for weak `pi` confirms that sequential consistency is costly if bluntly applied. Sharing inference is able to identify enough private data, though, to erase that penalty in the late and early variants. Hand inspection shows that sharing inference for `pi` is perfect: all data in the main computational loop is inferred `private` and no restrictions are needed on optimizations to enforce sequential consistency. The early, late, and weak versions if `pi` yield identical machine code; apparent performance here are measurement noise.

For most of the other benchmarks, there is only modest improvement between the naïve implementation and the weak consistency model, so the potential speedup from sharing inference is limited. This defies conventional wisdom, which says that sequential consistency is too expensive. There are two potential sources of inefficiency in the sequentially consistent versions: lost optimization opportunities (e.g., loop transformations) and additional memory fences between load and store instructions. Neither of these appear to be significant in our benchmarks. This highlights a limitation of our experimental environment: neither the Titanium compiler nor the Pentium hardware is taking advantage of weak consistency's looser requirements to significantly boost performance over sequential consistency.

Among the larger benchmarks, `cannon`, `3d-fft`, and `amr` show the largest performance gap between the naïve and weak models. These, then, stand to benefit the most from sharing inference. In `3d-fft`, inference (either late or early) is able to nearly match the weak model. Modest benefits are seen in `cannon`, where the larger slowdown is only partly offset by inference. Late and early enforcement yield identical results for `cannon`; the difference between the late and early slowdown factors is measurement noise.

The results for `amr` are interesting. None of the key performance-critical data structures can be inferred private using our current system. Like many

SPMD programs, amr has an alternating-phase structure: all processors exchange boundary information, then each processor updates its own local portion of the shared grid, then all processors communicate again, and so on. Data is shared widely during amr's communication phase, but we would like to treat that same data as private during local computation phases. These phases are delimited by global barrier operations, so no processor looks at another processors' data while the local computations are taking place. For sharing inference to be effective here, it would need to allow for a limited form of flow sensitivity keyed to these phases. Because the structure of barriers is quite regular in practice [2], we believe such an extension of our techniques should be feasible.

Observe that two benchmarks, n-body and particle-grid exhibit unexpected speedups under naïve sequential consistency. Because the direct penalty of sequential consistency here is so small, measurement noise due to secondary effects (such as cache alignment and code layout) becomes more noticeable.

6 Conclusions

We have presented a general approach to describing the data sharing behavior of distributed programming languages, and codified that approach in a suite of type systems. Early enforcement resembles earlier work on escape analysis. Export and late enforcement are unusual in enforcing privacy closer to the point of use, rather than at the point of escape, allowing them to identify more private data in exchange for weaker guarantees as to what "private" actually means. We have considered these type systems in light of the optimizations they would permit, and present experimental data on two such optimizations: data layout management and consistency model relaxation.

The approach is conducive to efficient type qualifier inference, and can be adapted to suit realistic languages. Our survey of related languages suggests that most fall into two categories: those which under-specify the behavior of shared data, and those which equate shared with global and private with local. Our approach points out that other combinations, such as mixed pointers and local shared pointers, have a role to play.

References

1. A. Agarwal, R. Bianchini, D. Chaiken, K. Johnson, D. Kranz, J. Kubiatowicz, B.-H. Lim, K. Mackenzie, and D. Yeung. The MIT Alewife machine: Architecture and performance. In *Proc. of the 22nd Annual Int'l Symp. on Computer Architecture (ISCA '95)*, pages 2–13, June 1995.
2. A. Aiken and D. Gay. Barrier inference. In *Conference Record of POPL'98: The 25th ACM SIGPLAN-SIGACT Symposium on Principles of Programming Languages*, pages 342–354, San Diego, California, January 19–21, 1998.
3. J. Aldrich, E. G. Sirer, C. Chambers, and S. J. Eggers. Comprehensive synchronization elimination for Java. *Science of Computer Programming*, to appear. Also published as University of Washington Technical Report UW-CSE-00-10-01, October 2000.

4. G. T. Balls. *A Finite Difference Domain Decomposition Method Using Local Corrections for the Solution of Poisson's Equation*. PhD thesis, Department of Mechanical Engineering, University of California at Berkeley, 1999.
5. M. Berger and P. Colella. Local adaptive mesh refinement for shock hydrodynamics. *Journal of Computational Physics*, 82(1):64–84, May 1989. Lawrence Livermore Laboratory Report No. UCRL-97196.
6. B. Blanchet. Escape analysis for object oriented languages. Application to Java. In OOPSLA [27], pages 20–34.
7. J. Bogda and U. Hölzle. Removing unnecessary synchronization in Java. In OOPSLA [27], pages 35–46.
8. E. D. Brooks, III. PCP: A parallel extension of C that is 99% fat free. Technical Report UCRL-99673, Lawrence Livermore National Laboratory, Sept. 1988.
9. M. C. Carlisle. *Olden: Parallelizing Programs with Dynamic Data Structures on Distributed-Memory Machines*. PhD thesis, Department of Computer Science, Princeton University, June 1996.
10. W. W. Carlson and J. M. Draper. Distributed data access in AC. In *Proc. 5th ACM SIGPLAN Symposium on Principles and Practice of Parallel Programming, PPoPP'95*, pages 39–47, Santa Barbara, California, July 1995. IDA Supercomputing Research Center.
11. W. W. Carlson, J. M. Draper, D. E. Culler, K. Yelick, E. Brooks, and K. Warren. Introduction to UPC and language specification. Technical Report CCS-TR-99-157, IDA Center for Computing Sciences, May 13 1999.
12. K. M. Chandy and C. Kesselman. Compositional C++: Compositional parallel programming. *Lecture Notes in Computer Science*, 757:124–144, 1993.
13. J.-D. Choi, M. Gupta, M. Serrano, V. C. Sreedhar, and S. Midkiff. Escape analysis for Java. In OOPSLA [27], pages 1–19.
14. D. E. Culler, A. Dusseau, S. C. Goldstein, A. Krishnamurthy, S. Lumetta, T. von Eicken, and K. Yelick. Parallel programming in Split-C. In IEEE, editor, *Proceedings, Supercomputing '93: Portland, Oregon, November 15–19, 1993*, pages 262–273, 1109 Spring Street, Suite 300, Silver Spring, MD 20910, USA, 1993. IEEE Computer Society Press.
15. J. Foster. cqual. Available at http://bane.cs.berkeley.edu/cqual, Nov. 2001.
16. J. S. Foster, M. Fähndrich, and A. Aiken. A theory of type qualifiers. In *Proceedings of the ACM SIGPLAN '99 Conference on Programming Language Design and Implementation*, pages 192–203, Atlanta, Georgia, May 1–4, 1999. *SIGPLAN Notices*, 34(5), May 1999.
17. D. P. Helmbold and C. E. McDowell. Computing reachable states of parallel programs. *ACM SIGPLAN Notices*, 26(12):76–84, Dec. 1991.
18. L. J. Hendren, X. Tang, Y. Zhu, S. Ghobrial, G. R. Gao, X. Xue, H. Cai, and P. Ouellet. Compiling C for the EARTH multithreaded architecture. *International Journal of Parallel Programming*, 25(4):305–338, Aug. 1997.
19. F. Henglein and J. Rehof. The complexity of subtype entailment for simple types. In *Proceedings, Twelth Annual IEEE Symposium on Logic in Computer Science*, pages 352–361, Warsaw, Poland, 29 June–2 July 1997. IEEE Computer Society Press.
20. P. N. Hilfinger, D. Bonachea, D. Gay, S. Graham, B. Liblit, and K. Yelick. Titanium language reference manual. Technical Report CSD-01-1163, University of California, Berkeley, Nov. 2001.
21. B. Liblit and A. Aiken. Type systems for distributed data structures. In *Conference Record of POPL'00: The 27th ACM SIGPLAN-SIGACT Symposium on Principles of Programming Languages*, pages 199–213, Boston, Massachusetts, January 19–21, 2000.

22. B. Liblit and A. Aiken. Type systems for distributed data structures. Technical Report CSD-99-1072, University of California, Berkeley, Jan. 2000. Available at http://sunsite.berkeley.edu/TechRepPages/CSD-99-1072.
23. B. Liblit, A. Aiken, and K. Yelick. Data sharing analysis for Titanium. Technical Report CSD-01-1165, University of California, Berkeley, Nov. 2001. Available at http://sunsite.berkeley.edu/TechRepPages/CSD-01-1165.
24. J. Mellor-Crummey. Compile-time support for efficient data race detection in shared-memory parallel programs. *ACM SIGPLAN Notices*, 28(12):129–139, Dec. 1993.
25. S. P. Midkiff and D. A. Padua. Issues in the optimization of parallel programs. In *Proceedings of the 1990 International Conference on Parallel Processing*, volume II, Software, pages II–105–II–113, University Park, Penn, Aug. 1990. Penn State U. Press. CSRD TR#993, U. Ill.
26. Myricom Inc. *The GM Message Passing System*, July 18 2000. Version 1.1.
27. *OOPSLA'99 ACM Conference on Object-Oriented Systems, Languages and Applications*, volume 34(10) of *ACM SIGPLAN Notices*, Denver, CO, Oct. 1999. ACM Press.
28. C. S. Peskin and D. M. McQueen. A three-dimensional computational method for blood flow in the heart. I. Immersed elastic fibers in a viscous incompressible fluid. *Journal of Computational Physics*, 81(2):372–405, Apr. 1989.
29. G. Pike, L. Semenzato, P. Colella, and P. N. Hilfinger. Parallel 3D adaptive mesh refinement in Titanium. In *Proceedings of the Ninth SIAM Conference on Parallel Processing for Scientific Computing*, San Antonio, Texas, Mar. 1999.
30. D. Plainfossé and M. Shapiro. A survey of distributed garbage collection techniques. In H. Baker, editor, *Proceedings of International Workshop on Memory Management*, volume 986 of *Lecture Notes in Computer Science*, ILOG, Gentilly, France, and INRIA, Le Chesnay, France, Sept. 1995. Springer-Verlag.
31. M. C. Rinard and M. S. Lam. The design, implementation, and evaluation of Jade. *ACM Transactions on Programming Languages and Systems*, 20(3):483–545, May 1998.
32. S. Savage, M. Burrows, G. Nelson, P. Sobalvarro, and T. Anderson. Eraser: A dynamic data race detector for multithreaded programs. *ACM Transactions on Computer Systems*, 15(4):391–411, Nov. 1997.
33. B. Steensgaard. Thread-specific heaps for multi-threaded programs. In T. Hosking, editor, *ISMM 2000 Proceedings of the Second International Symposium on Memory Management*, volume 36(1) of *ACM SIGPLAN Notices*, Minneapolis, MN, Oct. 2000. ACM Press.
34. Supercomputing Technologies Group, MIT Laboratory for Computer Science. *Cilk 5.3.1 Reference Manual*, June 24 2000.
35. J. Whaley and M. Rinard. Compositional pointer and escape analysis for Java programs. In OOPSLA [27], pages 187–206.
36. Y. Zhu and L. Hendren. Locality analysis for parallel C programs. *IEEE Transactions on Parallel and Distributed Systems*, 10(2):99–114, Feb. 1999.
37. Y. Zhu and L. J. Hendren. Communication optimizations for parallel C programs. *ACM SIGPLAN Notices*, 33(5):199–211, May 1998.

Z-Ranking: Using Statistical Analysis to Counter the Impact of Static Analysis Approximations

Ted Kremenek and Dawson Engler

Computer Systems Laboratory, Stanford University
Stanford, CA 94305, U.S.A.
{kremenek,engler}@cs.stanford.edu

Abstract. This paper explores *z-ranking*, a technique to rank error reports emitted by static program checking analysis tools. Such tools often use approximate analysis schemes, leading to false error reports. These reports can easily render the error checker useless by hiding real errors amidst the false, and by potentially causing the tool to be discarded as irrelevant. Empirically, all tools that effectively find errors have false positive rates that can easily reach 30–100%. Z-ranking employs a simple statistical model to rank those error messages most likely to be true errors over those that are least likely. This paper demonstrates that z-ranking applies to a range of program checking problems and that it performs up to an order of magnitude better than randomized ranking. Further, it has transformed previously unusable analysis tools into effective program error finders.

1 Introduction

Most compiler analysis has been built for optimization. In this context, analysis must be conservative in order to preserve program correctness after optimization. If analysis lacks the power to guarantee a decision is correct in a given context, then it is not acted on. Recently there has been a surge of interest in static program checking [2, 4, 6, 7, 1, 13, 8]. Here, the rules are somewhat different. First, sound tools must emit an error unless the tool can guarantee that code cannot violate the check. Insufficiently powerful analyses are no longer silent; instead they fail to suppress erroneous messages. Second, even unsound tools that miss errors make mistakes since practicality limits their (and their sound cousin's) analysis sophistication. These false reports can easily render both types of tools useless by hiding real errors amidst the false, and by potentially causing the tool to be discarded as irrelevant. Empirically, all tools that effectively find errors have false positive rates that can easily reach 30–100% [5, 7, 13, 8].

This paper examines how to use statistical techniques to manage the impact of these (inevitable) analysis mistakes. Program checking takes on different forms, but generally analysis results can be conceived as reports emitted by the analysis tool that take on two forms: (1) locations in the program that satisfied a checked property and (2) locations that violated the checked property. In this paper the former will be referred to as *successful* checks and the latter as *failed* checks (i.e., error reports). The underlying observation of this paper is that the most reliable error reports are based on analysis decisions that (1) flagged few errors (or failed checks) in total and (2) led to many successful checks. There are two reasons for this. First, code has relatively few errors — typical aggregate error rates are less than 5% [3]. We expect valid analysis facts to generate few error reports. Second, in our experience, analysis approximations that interact badly with code will often lead to explosions of (invalid) error reports. In contrast, the code containing a real error tends to have many successful attempts at obeying a checked property and a small number of errors.

This paper develops and evaluates *z-ranking*, a technique to rank errors from most to least probable based on the observations above. It works by (1) counting the number of successful checks versus unsuccessful checks; (2) computing a numeric value based on these frequency counts using the z-test statistic [9]; and (3) sorting error reports based on this number. Z-ranking works well in practice: on our measurements it performed better than randomized ranking 98.5% of the time. Moreover, within the first 10% of reports inspected, z-ranking found 3-7 times more real bugs on average than found by randomized ranking. It has transformed checkers we formerly gave up on into effective error finders. Z-ranking appears to be especially helpful for "safe" software checking analysis, where conservative analysis approximations often interact in unfortunate ways with source code.

In our experience, ranking of error reports is useful in several ways:

1. When a tool is first applied to code, the initial few error reports should be those most likely to be real errors so that the user can easily see if the rest of the errors are worth inspecting. In our experience, and from discussions with other practitioners, users tend to immediately discard a tool if the first two or three error reports are false positives, giving these first few slots an enormous importance. Empirically, z-ranking almost never propagates even a single false positive into these locations.
2. Even if the initial reports are good, in many cases a run of (say) 10-20 invalid errors will cause a user to stop inspecting the tool's output; therefore it is crucial to rank as many true errors at the top.
3. Often rules are only approximately true in that they only apply to certain contexts. For example, shared variables often do not need to be protected by locks in initialization code. Fortunately, when the checker hits a context where the rule does not hold there will be no (or few) successful checks and many error reports, allowing z-ranking to push the invalid errors to the bottom.
4. A tool may deliberately introduce approximations for scalability or speed or to check richer properties than is generally possible. If invalid errors follow the patterns that we hypothesize, then such steps can be taken with some assurance that when the gamble goes bad, the resulting invalid errors can be relegated below true errors.

We provided a cursory sketch of z-ranking in previous work [10], but did not explore it thoroughly and provided no experimental validation; this paper does both. More explicitly, this paper explores the following three hypotheses:

Weak Hypothesis: error reports coupled with many successes are probable errors ("success breeds confidence").

Strong Hypothesis: error reports coupled with many other error reports are improbable errors ("failure begets failure").

No-Success Hypothesis: error reports with no coupled successful checks are exceptionally unlikely errors. This is a useful special case of the strong hypothesis.

In our experiments, the weak hypothesis seems to always hold — its effect is that highly ranked errors tend to be true errors. The strong hypothesis often holds, but can be violated when errors cluster (see Section 6). Its effect is that low ranked error reports tend to be invalid errors.

We measure how well these hold up on data for three program property checkers. Our experimental evaluation uses a mixture of reports from both the Linux operating system and a commercial (anonymous) code base (referred to as "Company X"). Linux is a particularly good test since it is a large, widely-used source code base (we check roughly 2.0 million lines of it). As such, it serves as a known experimental base. Also, because it has been written by so many people, it is representative of many different coding styles and abilities. This helps guard against biasing our conclusions based on the idiosyncrasies of a few programmers. The commercial code base, which also is extensive in size, further facilitates studying the generality of our results.

The paper is organized as follows. Section 2 describes z-ranking. Section 3 describes our experimental setup and Sections 4–6 give the results of three checkers. Section 7 provides a quantitative analysis of z-ranking's performance and how it compares to other schemes. Finally, Section 8 discusses other issues and Section 9 concludes.

2 Z-Ranking

Abstractly, this paper reduces to solving a simple classification problem: given an error report, decide whether it is a true error or a false positive. More formally, let $\mathcal{P}$ be the population of all reports, both successful checks and failed checks, emitted by a program checker analysis tool. $\mathcal{P}$ consists of two subpopulations: $\mathcal{S}$, the subpopulation of successful checks and $\mathcal{E}$, the subpopulation of failed checks (or error reports). The set of error reports $\mathcal{E}$ can be further broken down into two subpopulations: $\mathcal{B}$, the population of true errors or bugs and $\mathcal{F}$, the population of false positives. Our classification problem can then be restated as follows: given an error report $x \in \mathcal{E}$, decide which of the two populations $\mathcal{B}$ and $\mathcal{F}$ it belongs to. The ideal classification system would make this decision perfectly. A realistic classification system will not be perfect, since this would imply the static analysis itself could be perfect, and typically each classification decision will have differing degrees of certainty. Ranking simply sorts error messages based on the confidence in the classification.

In general, classification can use many sources of information that seem relevant — the competence of the programmers involved, historical bug reports, and many others. In this paper, rather than using a priori knowledge of the particular system being inspected, we use the fact that the populations $\mathcal{B}$ and $\mathcal{F}$ have different statistical characteristics. From a statistical point of view, our problem becomes the following. First, determine measurable differences between $\mathcal{B}$ and $\mathcal{F}$. Second, use these measurements to classify error reports and compute the certainty associated with each classification. Third, sort the error reports based on this measurement.

There are many statistical techniques for determining differences between $\mathcal{B}$ and $\mathcal{F}$. In this paper we employ a simple one. Our underlying intuition is that error reports most likely to be bugs are based on analysis decisions that (1) generated few failed checks in total and (2) had many successful checks. Furthermore, error reports based on analysis decisions that (1) generated many failed checks in total and (2) had few successful checks are likely to be false positives. These intuitions rely not only on the fraction of checks that were successes, but also on the number of checks associated with an analysis decision as well. In simple terms, an explosion of failed checks is a likely indicator that something is going wrong with the analysis. Moreover, if we only observe a few failed checks associated with an analysis decision, even if a low number of successful checks occurred as well, we are less inclined to think that the error reports must be false positives.

We pursue these intuitions further for the purpose of ranking error reports first with an explorative example. We then formalize our intuitions using statistical tools and specify the complete z-ranking algorithm.

Lock Example. Consider a simple intraprocedural `lock` program checker that checks that every call to `lock` must be eventually paired with a call to `unlock`. The program checker will likely conduct a flow-sensitive analysis of the procedure's control flow graph, attempting to examine all possible paths of execution. The checker emits a report indicating a *successful check* if an individual call to `lock` was matched by an individual call to `unlock`. If the checker encounters an exit point for the procedure before a matching call to `unlock` is found, however, it emits an error report (i.e., a *failed check*).

For this checker, decision analysis focuses around individual `lock` call sites. Consider three scenarios: (1) one `lock` call site has many failed checks associated with it and no successful ones, (2) a second `lock` call site has many successful checks associated with it and only a few failed ones and finally (3) a third `lock` call site has a few failed checks and a few successful ones (say of roughly equal proportion). The first scenario looks very suspicious; the large number of failed checks and no successful ones indicates the checked rule is violated to an unusual degree for this `lock` call site. The failed checks are likely to be false positives, and we should rank those error reports below those associated with the second and third lock call site. The second case, however, looks promising. The large number of successful checks suggests the analysis can handle the code; consequently the failed checks are likely real errors. Thus, we should rank these error reports high in the inspection ordering. The third population, however, is difficult to conclude anything about. Since it does not have an explosion of failed checks, the analysis tool appears not to be interacting poorly with the code, yet the few number of successes (and the equal proportion of successes and failures) does not imply that the rule definitely holds either. We should thus rank the error reports associated with the third lock call site between the reports for the other two.

2.1 Statistical Formulation

We now proceed to formalize the insights from the above lock checker example into a complete ranking algorithm. First observe that for the lock example we effectively divided the population of checks into three subpopulations, one associated with each lock call site. Although for the lock checker example we grouped messages by the source lock call site, different checkers will have similar notions that sets of successful and failed checks will be associated with a common analysis point. As a useful formalism, denote $\mathcal{G}$ to be the "grouping" operator that groups sets of successful and failed checks related in this manner together and partitions the set of reports $\mathcal{P}$. The precise specification of $\mathcal{G}$ will be tied to a specific checker.

Denote $\{\mathcal{P}_{\mathcal{G}_1}, \ldots, \mathcal{P}_{\mathcal{G}_m}\}$ to be the set of subpopulations of $\mathcal{P}$ created by $\mathcal{G}$. Consider any of the subpopulations $\mathcal{P}_{\mathcal{G}_i}$ of $\mathcal{P}$. Denote the number of successful checks in $\mathcal{P}_{\mathcal{G}_i}$ as $\mathcal{P}_{\mathcal{G}_i}.s$, and the number of failed checks as $\mathcal{P}_{\mathcal{G}_i}.f$. The total number of checks in $\mathcal{P}_{\mathcal{G}_i}$, which is the sum of these two statistics, is denoted $\mathcal{P}_{\mathcal{G}_i}.n$. Clearly the observed proportion of checks in $\mathcal{P}_{\mathcal{G}_i}$ that were successful checks is given by:

$$\mathcal{P}_{\mathcal{G}_i}.\hat{p} = \mathcal{P}_{\mathcal{G}_i}.s / \mathcal{P}_{\mathcal{G}_i}.n . \tag{1}$$

For brevity we will refer to $\mathcal{P}_{\mathcal{G}_i}.\hat{p}$ as $\hat{p}_i$. A naïve scheme would rank the populations $\{\mathcal{P}_{\mathcal{G}_1}, \ldots, \mathcal{P}_{\mathcal{G}_m}\}$ simply by their $\hat{p}_i$ values. However, this ranking ignores population size. For example, assume we have two populations of checks. In the first population, we observe one successful check and two failed checks, thus $\hat{p}_i = \frac{1}{3}$. In the second population, we observe 100 successful checks and 200 failed checks, thus $\hat{p}_i$ is also $\frac{1}{3}$. Clearly, the latter observed proportion is much less likely to be coincidental than the first. We thus wish to rank populations both by their $\hat{p}_i$ values and our degree of confidence in the estimate $\hat{p}_i$.

We do so using *hypothesis testing*, which is a standard statistical technique for comparing population statistics such as frequency counts. To do this, we conceptually treat the checks in $\mathcal{P}_{\mathcal{G}_i}$ as a sequence of "binary trials:" independent and identically distributed events that can take one of two outcomes. This abstraction essentially models the behavior of the program checker for population $\mathcal{P}_{\mathcal{G}_i}$ as a sequence of tosses from a biased coin that has a probability p_i of labeling a check as a "success" and probability $1 - p_i$ as a "failure."[1] Note that we do not know p_i; our estimate $\hat{p}_i$ will converge to it as the population size increases. A standard statistical measure of the confidence of the value of $\hat{p}_i$ as an estimate for p_i is its standard error (SE). If p is the "success" rate, σ^2 the variance, and n the number of observations then the SE for the success rate of a sequence of binary trials is given by [9]:

$$\text{SE} = \sqrt{n} \cdot \sqrt{\sigma^2}/n = \sqrt{p(1-p)/n} \implies \text{SE}_{\hat{p}_i} = \sqrt{p_i(1-p_i)/\mathcal{P}_{\mathcal{G}_i}.n} \ . \quad (2)$$

Notice in Equation 2 that the SE takes into account the sample size $\mathcal{P}_{\mathcal{G}_i}.n$, and higher values for $\mathcal{P}_{\mathcal{G}_i}.n$ lead to lower values for the SE. The SE is often conventionally used to create confidence intervals that specify that the true value of p_i lies within a certain distance of $\hat{p}_i$ with a certain probability. Moreover in the domain of hypothesis testing, the SE can be used to test how likely a given $\hat{p}_i$ could have been observed assuming some value p_0 as the true parameter.[2] A standard hypothesis test for doing this is the *z-test* [9], which measures how many standard errors away an observed $\hat{p}_i$ is from p_0:

$$z = \frac{\text{observed} - \text{expected}}{\text{SE}} = \frac{\hat{p}_i - p_0}{\text{SE}} = \frac{\hat{p}_i - p_0}{\sqrt{p_0(1-p_0)/n}} \ . \quad (3)$$

Equation 3 provides a distance measure between a pre-specified population and an observed one. The SE is calculated assuming that p_0 is the true success rate, and the value computed by Equation 3, called the *z-score*, yields either a positive or negative measure of divergence of $\hat{p}_i$ from p_0. The z-test defines a statistically sound method of measuring the differences between two populations that incorporates both the observed $\hat{p}_i$ values and the population sizes. We can thus construct a p_0 such that populations $\mathcal{P}_{\mathcal{G}_i}$ that follow the weak hypothesis have large positive z-scores and those that follow the strong hypothesis have large negative z-scores. The value of p_0 thus serves as the separation point, or a relative baseline that seeks to differentiate error reports $x \in \mathcal{B}$ from reports $y \in \mathcal{F}$. Using these notions, we can now state the strong and weak hypotheses more formally:

Weak Hypothesis: For a population $\mathcal{P}_{\mathcal{G}_i}$ with high success rate $\hat{p}_i$ and low SE, the error reports $x \in (\mathcal{P}_{\mathcal{G}_i} \cap \mathcal{E})$ will tend to be true errors, and a proper choice of p_0 will cause the population to have a large positive z-score.

Strong Hypothesis: For a population $\mathcal{P}_{\mathcal{G}_i}$ with low success rate $\hat{p}_i$ and low SE, the error reports $x \in (\mathcal{P}_{\mathcal{G}_i} \cap \mathcal{E})$ will tend to be false positives, and a proper choice of p_0 will cause the population to have a large negative z-score.

Notationally we will denote the z-score for population $\mathcal{P}_{\mathcal{G}_i}$ as $\mathcal{P}_{\mathcal{G}_i}.z$. With the above definitions, population ranking using z-scores becomes straightforward.

---

[1] More formally, each check is modeled as a Bernoulli random variable with probability p_i of taking the value 1 (for a success). A sequence of checks is modeled using the Binomial distribution [11].

[2] In hypothesis testing, p_0 is known as the *null hypothesis*.

We choose p_0 so that the conditions of the strong and weak hypotheses generally hold, then compute the z-scores for each population $\mathcal{P}_{\mathcal{G}_i}$ and rank those populations in descending order of their z-scores. The last critical detail is then how to specify p_0. We provide two systematic methods:

Pre-asymptotic Behavior: Consider the case where each subpopulation of checks $\mathcal{P}_{\mathcal{G}_i}$ is "small" (a precise definition of which is given in the next method for estimating p_0), implying a fairly high SE for all $\hat{p}_i$ values. In this case it is not always clear whether a population could be following the strong or weak hypotheses. Despite this problem, the average population success rate is an intuitive baseline that we can measure divergence from for all populations. This value is computed as:

$$\bar{p} = \left(\frac{1}{m}\right) \sum_{i=1}^{m} \hat{p}_i = \left(\frac{1}{m}\right) \sum_{i=1}^{m} \frac{\mathcal{P}_{\mathcal{G}_i}.s}{\mathcal{P}_{\mathcal{G}_i}.n} \; . \tag{4}$$

In Equation 4 the value m is the number of populations created by $\mathcal{G}$. The average success rate as a baseline is useful for the following reason. If we let $p_0 = \bar{p}$, then most populations will have low (in magnitude) z-scores. The populations, however, that have slightly lower SE values than their cousins and slightly lower or higher $\hat{p}_i$ values will have greater (in magnitude) z-scores, and they will be the most promising candidates that exhibit the strong or weak hypotheses because they are departing in the direction of those extremes. Choosing $p_0 = \bar{p}$ institutes ranking based on this divergence, and those populations that have diverged the most from the mean will be ranked the highest/lowest in the ranking.

Asymptotic Behavior: When the size of a population $\mathcal{P}_{\mathcal{G}_i}$ gets large, the SE value for $\hat{p}_i$ becomes reasonably low to believe the general trend we are seeing in that population. In this case, measuring divergences from the average population success rate does not adequately capture our expectations of how many true errors we expect to find, even if a $\hat{p}_i$ value for a population is substantially higher than the mean success rate. The main observation is that populations that are both large and have a fairly high success rate $\hat{p}_i$ but also have a substantial number of failed checks are likely to have a significant portion of those failed checks to be false positives. The basic intuition is that there cannot possibly be that many real errors.

We proceed to formalize these intuitions. For a population of checks, let s be the number of successes, f the number of failures, and b the number of real bugs. We define the error rate of a population of successes and failures as [3]:

$$\text{error rate} = b/(s+f) \; . \tag{5}$$

The error rate corresponds to the ratio of the number of bugs found to the number of times a property was checked. Empirically we know that aggregate error rates are less than 5% [3]. Consider an extreme case of the weak hypothesis

Algorithm 1 Z-Ranking Algorithm

1: APPLY: $\mathcal{G}$ to $\mathcal{P}$ to create subpopulations: $\{\mathcal{P}_{\mathcal{G}_1}, \ldots, \mathcal{P}_{\mathcal{G}_m}\}$
2: **for all** $\mathcal{P}_{\mathcal{G}_i}$ **do**
3: $\quad \mathcal{P}_{\mathcal{G}_i}.\hat{p} \leftarrow \mathcal{P}_{\mathcal{G}_i}.s / \mathcal{P}_{\mathcal{G}_i}.n$
4: **if** $\max\limits_{\mathcal{P}_{\mathcal{G}_i}} \mathcal{P}_{\mathcal{G}_i}.n < 51$ **then**
5: $\quad p_0 \leftarrow \left(\frac{1}{m}\right) \sum\limits_{i=1}^{m} \mathcal{P}_{\mathcal{G}_i}.\hat{p}$
6: **else**
7: $\quad p_0 \leftarrow 0.85$
8: **for all** $\mathcal{P}_{\mathcal{G}_i}$ **do**
9: $\quad$ **if** $\mathcal{P}_{\mathcal{G}_i}.s = 0$ and using *NO-SUCCESS HEURISTIC* **then**
10: $\quad\quad$ Discard $\mathcal{P}_{\mathcal{G}_i}$
11: $\quad$ **else**
12: $\quad\quad \mathcal{P}_{\mathcal{G}_i}.z \leftarrow (\mathcal{P}_{\mathcal{G}_i}.\hat{p} - p_0) / \sqrt{p_0(1-p_0)/\mathcal{P}_{\mathcal{G}_i}.n}$
13: CREATE equivalence classes $\{E_{z_1}, \ldots, E_{z_k}\}$: $E_{z_i} \leftarrow \{\mathcal{P}_{\mathcal{G}_j} \cap \mathcal{E} | \mathcal{P}_{\mathcal{G}_j}.z = z_i\}$
14: SORT $\{E_{z_1}, \ldots, E_{z_k}\}$ by z_i in descending order. Designate that order as $\{E_{z_{(1)}}, \ldots, E_{z_{(k)}}\}$.
15: **for all** $i = 1, \ldots, k$ **do**
16: $\quad$ Inspect error reports in $E_{z_{(i)}}$ using an auxiliary ranking scheme

where all failures are real bugs and we have many successes. Equation 5, along with our knowledge of error rates, then reduces to the following inequality:

$$b/(s+b) \leq 0.5 \implies s/(s+b) \geq 0.95 \implies \hat{p} \geq 0.95 . \tag{6}$$

Equation 6 tells us for the extreme case of the weak hypothesis we generally expect $\hat{p} \geq 0.95$. Furthermore, we desire populations that exhibit this behavior to be ranked as being highly significant. We calibrate the ranking so that populations with this success rate (or greater) and small SE are ranked at least two standard errors away from p_0, providing the following constraint:

$$0.95 - p_0 \geq 2 \text{ SE} . \tag{7}$$

This calibration also causes populations with comparably small SE but smaller $\hat{p}_i$ to have z-scores less than 2, which is essentially the property we originally desired. We also desire that our SE to be adequately small so that our estimate of $\hat{p}_i$ is accurate enough to assume such asymptotic behavior. Thus our second constraint is:

$$\text{SE} = \sqrt{p_0(1-p_0)/n} \leq 0.1 . \tag{8}$$

Putting Equations 7 and 8 together and solving for p_0 and n at the boundary condition of SE $= 0.1$ we have $p_0 = 0.85$ and $n \geq 51$. Thus $n \geq 51$ is our asymptotic threshold and 0.85 is the p_0 we use for ranking.

Refinement: No-Success Heuristic. The no-success heuristic discards error reports in a population that has no successful checks (i.e., $\mathcal{P}_{\mathcal{G}_i}.s = 0$). There are two intuitions for why it works. First, a population with no successes obviously has the lowest possible number of successes (zero), and thus the least likely to have any confidence of all. Second, and more subtly, unlike all other cases of errors, code that has no obeyed example of a checked property is logically consistent in that it always acts as if the checked rule does not apply. A final important observation is that if the code is always incorrect, even a single test case should show it. While programmers rarely test all paths, they often test at least one path, which would cause them to catch the error.

Sections 4-5 illustrate that in practice the no-success heuristic performs well, in one case we observe that employing the heuristic results in only inspecting approximately 25% of the error reports while discovering all true errors.

It is important to note that when the strong hypothesis fails to hold, this heuristic performs poorly. An example of this is given in Section 6 where error reports cluster heavily, causing the strong hypothesis to fail and populations with many true errors and no successes to appear.

Z-Score Ties: Equivalence Classes. If we have two or more populations with the same z-score, we merge all populations $\mathcal{P}_{\mathcal{G}_i}$ with the same z-score value into an equivalence class E_{z_j}. The reason for this is because for ranking purposes populations with the same z-score are indistinguishable, and the reports in those populations should be ranked together.

The complete z-ranking algorithm is specified in Algorithm 1. To apply z-ranking, first we partition the set of reports $\mathcal{P}$ into subpopulations using the grouping operator $\mathcal{G}$ (line 1). Then we compute the $\hat{p}_i$ values for each population (lines 2-3). Next we compute p_0. If we have a population with 51 or more reports in it (our asymptotic behavior threshold), we set $p_0 = 0.85$ (line 7). Otherwise, we set p_0 to the average of the population success rates (line 5). We then iterate through the set of populations, discarding those that have no successful reports in them if we are using the no-success heuristic (line 9), and computing the individual z-scores for the others (line 12). We then merge the remaining populations into equivalence classes, where the equivalence class consists of all populations with the same z-score (line 13). We then order the equivalence classes in decreasing order of their z-scores (line 14) and then inspect the error reports one equivalence class at a time based on that order (lines 15-16). Within an equivalence class, we use an auxiliary ranking scheme to order the error reports, which can be a deterministic method (one candidate being the order the reports were emitted by the analysis tool) or some randomized or partially randomized scheme.

Note that the ranking depends completely on the choice of the grouping operator $\mathcal{G}$. This is the component that maps a particular property checker to the z-ranking algorithm. Sections 4–6 show various ways to map the results of different checkers to the z-ranking algorithm.

3 Experimental Setup

For our experiments, we measure checker results from two systems, both written in the C language. The first is the Linux kernel source tree, release 2.5.8, for which we possess a large collection of inspected results to validate our findings. The second is a large commercial (anonymous) source tree, referred to as "Company X."

The static analysis checker system we used was the *MC* system [5]. The *MC* system is a flexible framework to create a wide range of property checkers. Checkers consist of state machines specified by the checker writer. These state machines consist of patterns to match in the source code and corresponding actions, which can consist of state transitions in the checker. The intraprocedural lock checker from the previous section would use two states to track whether a lock was held and, if held, subsequently released. The state machine enters the initial state when the system recognizes a lock call in the flow graph. The system then traces subsequent possible paths in the flow graph, spawning copies of the state machine at forks in the graph. A call to unlock causes the state machine to transition to a termination state. If no call to unlock is discovered and an exit point in the control flow graph is reached, the state machine transitions to a termination state, but this time emitting an error. To be precise not all possible execution paths are explored because the checker only maintains limited contextual state information, and this allows some paths (and copies of the state machine) to be merged at program points where paths meet (and hence not all paths are fully explored) because they look equivalent from that point on. The analysis the *MC* system performs is approximate because it records only limited state information. This itself can lead to false positives (invalid errors). Furthermore, a rule a property checker inspects for may only hold in certain contexts, also leading to false positives.

We apply z-ranking to the reports of three checkers. The first two were designed around z-ranking: (1) a lock checker that warns when a lock is not paired with an unlock (Section 4) and (2) a free checker that warns about uses of freed memory (Section 5). The remaining checker was not designed to support z-ranking. It provides, however, enough information that we can do a crude application of it, getting a tentative feel for generality. In our experiments z-ranking is compared against three other ranking schemes: (1) optimal ranking, which simply consists of placing all true errors (bugs) at the beginning of the inspection order, (2) a deterministic ranking scheme used by the *MC* system, and (3) random ranking.

The deterministic ranking scheme uses several heuristics to order messages. The most important for our purposes is that it ranks intraprocedural errors over interprocedural, interprocedural errors by the depth of the call chain, and errors that span few lines or conditionals over those that span many. More detail can be found in [10].

Random ranking consists simply of inspecting a report at random, which is equivalent to sampling from a finite set without replacement. Sampling in this manner is modeled using the hypergeometric distribution: if b is the number of bugs and N the total number of reports, then the expected number of bugs found after n inspections is equal to $(b/N) \times n$ [11]. When comparing z-ranking to random ranking, we will plot the expected number of bugs found for random ranking as a function of the number of inspections.

For all checkers, we inspect the majority of all error reports emitted by the checker. We use the MC system to deterministically rank the reports, and we treat the top N messages as our inspection population. Furthermore, when using z-ranking, for inspecting reports *within* populations we employed the MC deterministic ranking scheme.

A key point to note is that the false positive rates for all the checkers are noticeably more pessimistic than what would actually be observed in practice. First, the false positive rates assume almost all messages are inspected. Somewhat surprisingly such diligence is rare: coders often inspect errors until they hit too many false positives and then stop. As a result, good ranking is crucial. Second, in practice putting related error into aggregated equivalence classes makes inspection more efficient since when we hit a false positive, we can suppress the entire class. Finally, many false positives are "historical" in that they were inspected at some point in the past and marked as false positives — the MC system automatically suppresses these in future runs, although in this paper they are counted.

4 Results: Ranking Lock Errors

This section measures the effectiveness of z-ranking on sorting lock errors. The checker takes a list of function pairs $(l_0, u_0), \ldots, (l_n, u_n)$ and, after a call to l_i, traverses all subsequent control flow paths, checking that they contain a call to u_i. As discussed in prior sections, for the purposes of z-ranking, each path where the checker encounters a u_i is considered a success; each path that ends without a u_i generates an error message and is considered a failure. The grouping operator $\mathcal{G}$ groups messages that have a common l_i call site.

The checker suffers from two general approximations. First, its limited intraprocedural world view causes it to falsely flag errors where a required call to u_i is contained in a called function or in the calling function. The second more difficult issue to remedy is the conflated roles of semaphores, which are sometimes used as counters, which need not be paired (and hence should not be checked), and sometimes as locks, which must be paired. Both limits can cause many false positives; both are handled well by statistical ranking.

We checked four pairs of locking functions; while all conceptually must obey the same rule, they form three reasonably distinct populations in Linux.

Population 1: is made of errors from the pair spin_lock-spin_unlock, which are the most widely-used lock functions (roughly 5600 checks in our results). This population has been deformed by many previous bug fixes. In the past, we have reported roughly two hundred errors involving these two functions to Linux maintainers. Most of these errors were fixed. Consequently, the ratio of true errors reported in 2.5.8 to the number of checks is low. Similarly, the

```
// linux/2.5.8/mm/shmem.c:shmem_getpage_locked
repeat:
  spin_lock (&info->lock);  // line 506
  ...
  if (...) {
    // NOTE:517: [SUCCESS=spin_lock:506]
    spin_unlock (&info->lock);
    return page;
  }
  ...
  if (entry->val) {
    ...
    if (...) {
      UnlockPage(page);
      // "ERROR:shmem_getpage_locked:506:554:": Didn't reverse 'spin_lock'
      // [FAIL=spin_lock:506]
      return ERR_PTR(error);
    }
    ...
  }
  ...
wait_retry:
  // NOTE:597: [SUCCESS=spin_lock:506]
  spin_unlock (&info->lock);
...
// 2.5.8/drivers/ieee1394/sbp2.c:sbp2_agent_reset
  if (!(flags & SBP2_SEND_NO_WAIT)) {
  // ERROR: Did not reverse 'down' [FAIL=down:1847]
  down(&pkt->state_change); // signal a state change
```

Fig. 1. Lock check example: in the first function, shmem_getpage_locked, the lock info→lock is acquired at line 506, has five successful releases (two shown, denoted SUCCESS=spin_lock:506) and one error (denoted FAIL=spin_lock:506). The second function sbp2_agent_reset uses the semaphore pkt→state_change to atomically signal a state change rather than as a lock. There were no successes in this function, and the generated error is a false positive.

false positive rate is quite high, since while many errors have been fixed the previous false positives have not been "removed."

The two remaining populations below represent errors for the whole of the kernel's lifetime:

Population 2: is made of two straightforward pairing functions that we did not check previously. They have a higher error rate and a lower false positive rate than spin locks. They come from two pairs. First, lock_kernel-unlock_kernel which control the "the big kernel lock" (or BKL), a coarse-grained lock originally used (as in many initially single-threaded Unix OSes) to make Linux into a large monitor; its use has been gradually phased out in favor of more fine-grained locking. Second, the pair cli-sti and cli-restore_flags, the most widely used way to disable and enable interrupts.

Population 3: down-up semaphore functions, which have a high false positive rate since they have two conflated uses: as atomic counters, which need not be paired, and as locks, which must be paired. Ranking easily distinguishes

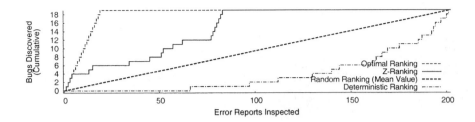

Fig. 2. Results of inspecting Linux spin-lock error reports. Z-ranking uses $p_0 = 0.21$, with 175 populations created by $\mathcal{G}$, and 14 equivalence classes. 202 reports inspected, with 19 real bugs. Within the first 21 ($\sim 10\%$) inspections, z-ranking found 3 times more bugs than the expected number found using random ranking. When using the no-success heuristic, we inspect only the first 83 reports, discovering all real bugs

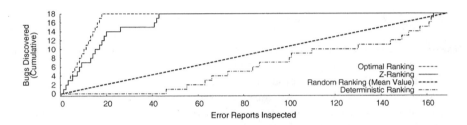

Fig. 3. Results of inspecting Linux down-up (semaphore) pairs. Z-ranking uses $p_0 = 0.15$, with 142 populations created by $\mathcal{G}$, and 11 equivalence classes. 169 reports inspected, with 18 real bugs. Within the first 17 ($\sim 10\%$) inspections, z-ranking found 6.6 times more bugs than the expected number found using random ranking. When using the no-success heuristic, we inspect only the first 43 reports, discovering all real bugs

these two different uses, whereas adding additional traditional analysis will not. (In fact, we had previously given up on checking this rule since the false positive rate was unmanageable.)

Example. Fig. 1 illustrates successes and failures the described checker finds in a section of the Linux 2.5.8 kernel source. An acquisition to spin_lock is made and depicted are two successful releases and one failed one. These checks correspond to the same spin_lock call site, and the grouping operator $\mathcal{G}$ would group these checks into the same population. In addition, an unmatched call to down is shown at the bottom of Fig. 1. This unsuccessful check would be grouped in a different population, since the check corresponds to a different source call site.

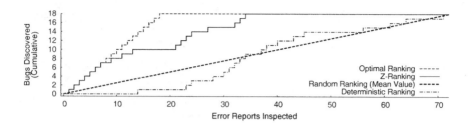

Fig. 4. Results of inspecting Linux BKL calls and interrupt enable/disable calls. Z-ranking uses $p_0 = 0.21$, with 62 populations created by $\mathcal{G}$, and 8 equivalence classes. 72 reports inspected, with 18 real bugs. Within the first 8 ($\sim 10\%$) inspections, z-ranking found 4 times more bugs than the expected number found using random ranking. When using the no-success heuristic, we inspect only the first 34 reports, discovering all real bugs

Results. We compared the use of z-ranking for inspecting error reports to both the deterministic ranking scheme in the MC system and randomized ranking. Depicted in Fig. 2-4 are the comparative z-ranking inspection results. To perform z-ranking, different values for p_0 were automatically estimated according to the procedure in Algorithm 1, and these values are shown in the corresponding figures. In all cases z-ranking performs well.

In the case of the spin_lock errors (Fig. 2), the number of inspections needed to recover all bugs in the report set is very large, but inspection using z-ranking yields numerous bugs in the first few inspections. Moreover, with deterministic ranking over 50 inspections are needed to discover the first bug. Even with random ranking a user would need to inspect on average 10 error reports before discovering a single bug. Furthermore, the no-success heuristic performs very well. After inspecting 83 of the 202 reports (41%) all bugs are discovered.

In the case of the semaphore down data (Fig. 3), z-ranking performs even better. Here the weak hypothesis fervently comes into play as populations where the alternate use of down as atomic counters instead of lock acquisitions will yield very few "successful" pairings with up and these error reports (which are invalid errors) will be pushed towards the end of the inspection ordering. In addition, the no-success heuristic again performs well. After inspecting 43 of 169 reports (25.4%) all the bugs are discovered.

For the remaining population of big kernel lock acquisitions and interrupt enable/disable routines (Fig. 4), z-ranking performs very close to optimal ranking for the first dozen inspections, and performs far better than random ranking and deterministic ranking. Inspection of the reports using z-ranking yields all 18 bugs within the first 38 inspections, while deterministic ranking requires inspecting 77 out of 78 reports to discover all the true errors, which is over twice as many inspections. Moreover, the no-success heuristic remains effective, requiring inspecting roughly half of the error reports to discover all the bugs.

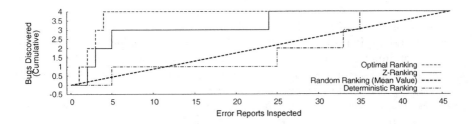

Fig. 5. Results of inspecting lock errors for Company X. Z-ranking uses $p_0 = 0.32$, with 38 populations created by $\mathcal{G}$, and 9 equivalence classes. 46 reports inspected, with 4 real bugs. Within the first 5 ($\sim 10\%$) inspections, z-ranking found 6.9 times more bugs than the expected number found using random ranking. When using the no-success heuristic, we inspect only the first 24 reports, discovering all real bugs

In all cases, the crucial initial few error reports were always true errors. In contrast, random ranking and deterministic ranking both had a very high number of false positives in these slots (often all were false). As noted in the introduction, if these first few reports are false users often immediately give up on the tool.

Company X. The results for Company X came after previous rounds of bug fixes, which deformed the population similarly to the spin_lock population of Linux. As a result there were only four bugs left when the checker ran, making it hard to get a good aggregate picture. The inspection results are shown in Fig. 5. Despite there being only a few remaining bugs, the results seem relatively similar to the Linux results: z-ranking places most bugs at the beginning of the inspection ordering and most false positives are at the end.

5 Results: Ranking Free Errors

The previous section used z-ranking to compensate for intraprocedural analysis approximations. This section uses it to control the impact of inter-procedural analysis approximations for a checker that warns about potential uses of free memory.

The checker is organized as two passes. The first pass uses a flow-insensitive, interprocedural analysis to compute a list of all functions that transitively free their arguments by calling a free function directly (such as kfree, vfree, etc) or by passing an argument to a function that does. The second, flow-sensitive, intraprocedural pass, uses this summary list to find errors. At every function call, it checks if the function is a free function and, if so, marks the pointer passed as the freeing argument as freed. It then emits an error report if any subsequent path uses a freed pointer.

In practice, the checker suffers from two main sources of false positives. First, false paths in the source code can cause it to think that a freed pointer can reach a use when it cannot. Second, and more serious, a small number of functions will free an argument based on the value of another argument. However, the flow-insensitive relaxation is blind to such parameter data dependencies. Thus, it will classify such functions as always freeing their argument. As a result, rather than having an error rate of one error per few hundred call sites, these functions will have rates closer to fifty errors per hundred call sites, giving a flood of false positives. Fortunately, using z-ranking to sort based on these error rates will push real errors to the top of the list and the false positives caused by such functions the analysis could not handle will go to the bottom.

We apply z-ranking to the free errors as follows:

1. We count the number of checks rather than the number of successes. For example, if kfree is a free function, we count a check every time we see a call to kfree.
2. Each error message (where freed memory was used) is a failure.
3. After the source code has been processed, the grouping operator $\mathcal{G}$ groups all checks and failures that correspond to the same free function (the function itself, not a particular call site). We then rank the populations using Algorithm 1.

The end effect is that routines with a high ratio of checks to failures will be ranked at the top and routines with low ratios at the bottom. In the Linux kernel, the routine CardServices is a great example of this. It has a switch statement with over 50 case arms selected by the first parameter. One of these case arms frees the second parameter. Our checker is too weak to detect this data dependency and, since CardServices can free its argument on a single path, the checker assumes it always frees its argument on all paths. Fortunately, the enormous number of (false) error reports push these reports to the lowest of all routines in the ranking, effectively eliminating them.

Interprocedural Results. Our experimental results only consider routines that required interprocedural analysis. Since there were many reports we only inspected errors that involved functions that called free functions with a chain depth of less than four. We expect this result to underestimate the effectiveness of z-ranking since we expect that deeper call chains have even more false positives (since there were more opportunities for mistakes) and hence would benefit more from our technique.

The error report inspection plot for the interprocedural checker is depicted in Fig. 6. The highest ranked population was for function netif_rx which had 180 checks and one failure. The last (worst) ranked population was for the routine CardServices — it had even more false positives than shown, we stopped marking them after a while. Z-ranking does better than random ranking, though not as substantially as with the lock checker. In part this is due to the fact that there are more equivalence classes with a high number of false positives, dragging all ranking methods to the same average.

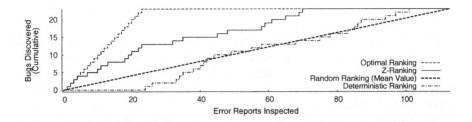

Fig. 6. Results of inspecting interprocedural free calls in Linux. Z-ranking uses $p_0 = 0.85$ (Asymptotic Behavior), with 55 populations created by $\mathcal{G}$, and 21 equivalence classes. 113 reports inspected, with 23 real bugs. Within the first 12 ($\sim 10\%$) inspections, z-ranking found 3.3 times more bugs than the expected number found using random ranking. For this set of reports all populations have at least one failure (the no-success heuristic does not apply)

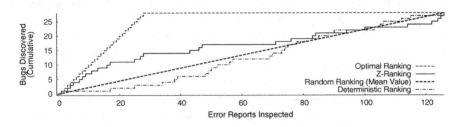

Fig. 7. Unaltered format string checker results for Company X. Z-ranking uses $p_0 = 0.29$, with 108 populations created by $\mathcal{G}$, and 18 equivalence classes. 126 reports inspected, with 28 real bugs. Within the first 13 ($\sim 10\%$) inspections, z-ranking found 3.1 times more bugs than the expected number found using random ranking. When using the no-success heuristic, we inspect only the first 60 reports, discovering 17 real bugs

6 Results: String Format Errors

This section looks at the applicability of z-ranking even for checkers where it would appear not to apply. Although not formally conclusive, these empirical results provide insight on potential "lower-bounds" of how generally applicable z-ranking is for ranking error reports.

We use z-ranking to rank error reports for a checker that looks at security holes caused by format string errors (e.g., `printf`). The results presented were from the application of the security checker to Company X's source code base. The z-ranking results of this checker are pessimistic for three reasons:

1. The checker has not been modified to support z-ranking. For historical reasons it emits a single note for each call site that begins a check rather than emitting a note for each success. Since a single call site can spawn many

errors and only crudely correlate with successful checks, the produced check counts have significant noise.
2. The only report feature available for grouping is the name of the function the report occurred in. Thus, we group all the checks for a function into the same equivalence class. As with the previous approximation, aggregating different checks loses valuable information and can have a marked impact on the checkers from the previous section.
3. The errors are susceptible to "clustering" in that the checkers are for rules that programmers often simply do not understand and thus violate exuberantly. The end results is that in some cases, the presence of one error *increases* the probability of another. This violates our strong hypothesis. However, the weak hypothesis holds in that many checks and one failed check in a population still tends to indicate a likely error.

The inspection results for the security checker are shown in Fig. 7. Even with the above three handicaps the results are extremely encouraging. Within inspecting the first 17 error reports, z-ranking finds 11 of the 28 bugs, while inspection using deterministic ranking only finds 3. Only after around 70 checks does the performance of deterministic ranking overtake z-ranking, although at this point random ranking performs just as well.

It is surprising that despite the presence of errors clustering z-ranking does reasonably well. The weak hypothesis pushes many of the true error reports to the top. We see that after inspecting 10% of the error reports z-ranking still finds 3.1 times more bugs than the expected number found by random ranking. The clustering of errors, however, causes the strong hypothesis not to hold. This appears to have a significant effect on z-ranking's performance, as after inspecting 50% of the reports its performance matches that of random ranking. Fortunately, this performance degradation occurs at the tail of the inspection process and not the beginning. Inspection using the no-success heuristic appears particularly dismal; many real errors are missed on account of the errors clustering. In this case, z-ranking is best applied without the no-success heuristic. Moreover, were the weak hypothesis to also fail z-ranking would likely perform extremely poorly.

7 Quantitative Evaluation

In the previous sections we examined the application of z-ranking to sorting error reports in several checkers. Those results demonstrated that in most cases z-ranking dramatically outperforms randomized rankings. Z-ranking, however, rarely produces an optimal ranking. This section further quantifies the efficacy of z-ranking in the domains we examined.

An analysis tool generates a set of N error reports, where N can be hundreds of error reports. There are $N!$ possible orderings of those reports. For a given p_0, z-ranking chooses a ranking R_Z out of this large space of rankings. One way to quantify how good the choice of R_Z was is by asking how many other rankings

Table 1. Z-Ranking score $S(R_Z)$ compared to the scores of 1.0×10^5 randomly generated rankings. Column 2 lists the number of random rankings whose score $S(R_R)$ was less than or equal to $S(R_Z)$ (lower score is better). Column 3 lists the same quantity as a percentage

Checker	Number of R_R: $S(R_R) \leq S(R_Z)$	Percentage (%)
Linux spin_lock	0	0.0
Linux down-up	0	0.0
Linux BKL, interrupt enable/disable	0	0.0
Company X - lock	825	0.825
Linux Interprocedural Free	0	0.0
Company X - Format String	1518	1.518

R_R could have provided as good or better as an inspection ordering as z-ranking. To pursue this question, we need a quantitative measure to compare rankings. After i inspections, an optimal ranking maximizes the *cumulative number* of true errors discovered. Other ranking schemes should aspire to this goal. Let N be the total number of error reports and b the number of bugs. Let $R(i)$ denote the cumulative number of bugs found by a ranking scheme R on the ith inspection. If R_O is an optimal ranking, note that $R_O(i) = min(b, i)$ (the minimum of b and i). An intuitive scoring for R is the sum of the differences between $R_O(i)$ and $R(i)$ over all inspection steps:

$$S(R) = \sum_{i=1}^{N} [R_O(i) - R(i)] = \sum_{i=1}^{N} [min(i, b) - R(i)] \quad . \tag{9}$$

Note that Equation 9 is simply the *area* between the plots of the cumulative number of bugs found versus the number of inspections for an optimal ranking and a ranking R. Observe that $S(R_O) = 0$, so a lower score is a better score. Using $S(R)$, we can ask the question that out of all the possible $N!$ rankings, what proportion of them perform as good or better than z-ranking? For rankings consisting of greater than 10 error reports it is computationally prohibitive to enumerate all possible rankings. Instead we settle for an approximation. For each of the checkers we applied z-ranking to in this paper, we generated 1.0×10^5 random rankings. The number of random rankings that scored as good or better than R_Z (i.e., $S(R_R) \leq S(R_Z)$) is shown in Table 1. Not surprisingly, the checker with the highest number of random rankings that had a score as good or better than z-ranking was the format string checker. We recall, however, that this checker was not even designed with z-ranking in mind, and the percentage of randomly generated rankings that were better than z-ranking was only 1.518%. Moreover, Table 1 shows that in practice random ranking will rarely perform as well as z-ranking (at least according to Equation 9) for the checkers we analyzed.

8 Discussion: Possible Extensions to Z-Ranking

Z-ranking employs a simple statistical model to rank error reports. Extensions to the simple model may facilitate more sophisticated ranking schemes.

One immediate extension is including prior information into the ranking process about the source code being checked or the checker itself. Such prior knowledge could be specified by hand or possibly be determined using statistical or machine learning techniques. In both cases, one immediate approach would be to encode the prior using a Beta distribution [11], which is conjugate to the Binomial and Bernoulli distributions [12]. In this case, the prior would be represented by "imaginary" success/failure counts. These would then be combined directly with the observed success/failure counts and z-ranking could then be applied as usual on the combined counts. Using the Beta distribution also allows one to specify the "strength" of the prior by varying the number of imaginary counts; this helps facilitate fine tuning of ranking.

Furthermore, besides success/failure counts, populations of error reports (as created by $\mathcal{G}$) may have correlated characteristics that z-ranking will not take into account. One example is the free checker discussed in Section 5. With the free checker, there are some functions associated with a low number of success/failure counts that always free their arguments and do so by passing the freed argument to another function. The called function, however, may correspond to a highly ranked population of reports. The characteristics of the two report populations may be correlated, and the high ranking of one population should boost the ranking of the other. Extensions to the z-ranking methodology may possibly allow the ranking scheme itself to take such correlations into account.

9 Conclusion

This paper has explored and developed the idea of z-ranking, which uses frequency counts of successful and failed checks to rank error messages from most to least probable. We applied it to three different error checkers, two in-depth, and the last briefly. In practice it worked well: (1) true errors generally were pushed to the top of the ranking while (2) false positives were pushed to the bottom. Furthermore, application of the no-success heuristic often reduced the number of reports inspected substantially while still providing for all real bugs to be discovered; in one case roughly only a quarter of all reports were inspected. When compared to 1.0×10^5 randomized error rankings, z-ranking often scored in the top 1%. Moreover, within the first 10% of error report inspections, z-ranking found 3-7 times more bugs than the average number of bugs found by random ranking for the checkers we analyzed.

Furthermore, z-ranking made formerly unusable checkers effective. A good example was that the lock checker could not previously handle semaphores since they had two conflated uses: (1) as paired locks and (2) as unpaired atomic counters (each occurrence of which would generate a false message). Because our checker could not distinguish these cases, previously we had given up. With z-ranking we could easily find such errors.

We believe z-ranking would be useful in many static error checking tools: all tools must make analysis approximations and, as a result, they all have false positives. Z-ranking provides a simple way to control the impact of such approximations.

Acknowledgements

We thank Priyank Garg, Rushabh Doshi, Yichen Xie, Junfeng Yang, Seth Hallem, and Tony Abell for their invaluable comments on clarity and content. This research was supported by DARPA contract MDA904-98-C-A933. Ted Kremenek received additional funding through a National Science Foundation Graduate Fellowship.

References

1. A. Aiken, M. Faehndrich, and Z. Su. Detecting races in relay ladder logic programs. In *Proceedings of the 1st International Conference on Tools and Algorithms for the Construction and Analysis of Systems*, April 1998.
2. T. Ball and S.K. Rajamani. Automatically validating temporal safety properties of interfaces. In *SPIN 2001 Workshop on Model Checking of Software*, May 2001.
3. A. Chou, J. Yang, B. Chelf, S. Hallem, and D. Engler. An empirical study of operating systems errors. In *Proceedings of the Eighteenth ACM Symposium on Operating Systems Principles*, 2001.
4. Manuvir Das, Sorin Lerner, and Mark Seigle. Path-sensitive program verification in polynomial time. In *Proceedings of the ACM SIGPLAN 2002 Conference on Programming Language Design and Implementation*, Berlin, Germany, June 2002.
5. D. Engler, B. Chelf, A. Chou, and S. Hallem. Checking system rules using system-specific, programmer-written compiler extensions. In *Proceedings of Operating Systems Design and Implementation (OSDI)*, September 2000.
6. D. Evans, J. Guttag, J. Horning, and Y.M. Tan. Lclint: A tool for using specifications to check code. In *Proceedings of the ACM SIGSOFT Symposium on the Foundations of Software Engineering*, December 1994.
7. Cormac Flanagan and Stephen N. Freund. Type-based race detection for Java. In *SIGPLAN Conference on Programming Language Design and Implementation*, pages 219–232, 2000.
8. J.S. Foster, T. Terauchi, and Alex Aiken. Flow-sensitive type qualifiers. In *Proceedings of the ACM SIGPLAN 2002 Conference on Programming Language Design and Implementation*, June 2002.
9. D. Freedman, R. Pisani, and R. Purves. *Statistics*. W.W. Norton, third edition, 1998.
10. S. Hallem, B. Chelf, Y. Xie, and D. Engler. A system and language for building system-specific, static analyses. In *SIGPLAN Conference on Programming Language Design and Implementation*, 2002.
11. Sheldon M. Ross. *Probability Models*. Academic Press, London, UK, sixth edition, 1997.
12. Thomas J. Santer and Dianne E. Duffy. *The Statistical Analysis of Discrete Data*. Springer-Verlag, December 1989.
13. D. Wagner, J. Foster, E. Brewer, and A. Aiken. A first step towards automated detection of buffer overrun vulnerabilities. In *2000 NDSSC*, February 2000.

Computer-Assisted Verification of a Protocol for Certified Email

Martín Abadi[1] and Bruno Blanchet[2]

[1] Computer Science Department, University of California, Santa Cruz
abadi@cs.ucsc.edu
[2] Département d'Informatique, École Normale Supérieure, Paris
and Max-Planck-Institut für Informatik, Saarbrücken
Bruno.Blanchet@ens.fr

Abstract. We present the formalization and verification of a recent cryptographic protocol for certified email. Relying on a tool for automatic protocol analysis, we establish the key security properties of the protocol. This case study explores the use of general correspondence assertions in automatic proofs, and aims to demonstrate the considerable power of the tool and its applicability to non-trivial, interesting protocols.

1 Introduction

A great deal of effort has been invested in the development of techniques for specifying and verifying security protocols in recent years. This effort is justified, in particular, by the seriousness of security flaws and the relative simplicity of security protocols. It has produced a number of interesting methods and effective tools. These range from mathematical frameworks for manual proofs to fully automatic model-checkers. The former are fundamentally constrained by the unreliability and time-scarcity of human provers. The latter tend to be limited to basic properties of small systems, such as the secrecy of session keys in finite-state simplifications of protocols; they may be viewed as useful but ultimately limited automatic testers. The development of automatic or semi-automatic tools that overcome these limitations is an important problem and the subject of active research.

In previous work, we have developed a protocol checker [1,6,7] that can establish secrecy and authenticity properties of protocols represented directly as programs in a minimal programming notation (an extension of the pi calculus). The protocols need not be finite-state; the tool can deal with an unbounded number of protocol sessions, even executed in parallel. Nevertheless, the proofs are fully automatic and often fast.

This paper reports on a fairly ambitious application of this tool in the verification of a recently published protocol for certified email [2]. The protocol allows a sender to send an email message to a receiver, in such a way that the receiver gets the message if and only if the sender obtains an unforgeable receipt for the message. The protocol is non-trivial, partly because of a number of real-world constraints. The verification yields assurance about the soundness of the protocol. It also suggests a promising method for reasoning about other, related protocols.

This case study aims to demonstrate the considerable power of the tool and its applicability to interesting protocols. It has also served in guiding certain improvements to the tool. Specifically, formalizing the main properties of the protocol has lead us to a generalization of the tool to handle a large class of correspondence assertions [17]. The bulk of the proofs remains fully automatic; for the code presented in this paper, the automatic proofs take only 80 ms on an Intel Xeon 1.7 GHz processor. Easy manual arguments show that the correspondence assertions capture the expected security guarantees for the protocol. Because the protocol is expressed directly in a programming notation, without limitation to finite-state instances, the need for additional arguments to justify the protocol representation is, if not eliminated, drastically reduced.

Outline. We review the description of the certified email protocol in Section 2. We also review our verification technique, in Section 3, and show how to extend it so as to handle the correspondence assertions on which we rely here. We explain our formal specification of the protocol in Section 4, then prove its security properties in Section 5. We conclude in Section 6, mentioning our work on the analysis of more elaborate variants of the protocol.

Related Work. It is fairly common to reason informally about security protocols, with various degrees of thoroughness and rigor. For instance, Krawczyk gave some informal arguments about the properties of the Skeme protocol (a variant of the core of IPsec) when he introduced Skeme [10]. Similarly, the presentation of the protocol that we treat in this paper included informal proof sketches for some of its central properties [2]. Generally, such proofs are informative, but far from complete and fully reliable.

It has been widely argued that formal proofs are particularly important for security protocols, because of the seriousness of security flaws. Nevertheless, formal proofs for substantial, practical protocols remain relatively rare. Next we mention what seem to be the most relevant results in this area.

The theorem prover Isabelle has been used for verifying (fragments of) several significant protocols with an inductive method, in particular Kerberos [4,5], TLS (a descendant of SSL 3.0) [14], and the e-commerce protocol SET [3]. Following the same general approach, G. Bella and C. Longo are currently working on the verification the certified email protocol that we treat in this paper. It will be interesting to compare definitions and proofs.

Meadows has used the NRL protocol verifier for reasoning about the Internet Key Exchange protocol, a component of proposals for IP security [12]. The reasoning, although enlightening in some respects, was not a full verification.

The finite-state model checker Murphi has served for the verification of SSL 3.0 [13] and of contract-signing protocols [16]. Somewhat similarly, Mocha has been used for the verification of contract-signing protocols within a game model [11]. (Contract-signing protocols have some high-level similarities to protocols for certified email.) Largely because of tool characteristics, the proofs in Murphi and Mocha require non-trivial encodings and simplifications of the protocols under consideration, and of their properties.

Schneider has studied a non-repudiation protocol in a CSP-based model, with manual proofs [15]. That protocol, which is due to Zhou and Gollmann, has commonalities with protocols for certified email.

Gordon and Jeffrey have been developing attractive type-based techniques for proving correspondence assertions of protocols [8,9]. To date, they have had to support only limited forms of correspondence assertions, and they have included a limited repertoire of cryptographic primitives. In these respects, their system is insufficient for the protocol that we treat in this paper, and weaker than the tool that we use. On the other hand, those limitations are probably not intrinsic.

2 The Protocol

This section recalls the description of the protocol for certified email. This section is self-contained, but we refer the reader to the original description [2] for additional details and context.

Protocols for certified email aim to allow a sender, S, to send an email message to a receiver, R, so that R gets the message if and only if S gets a corresponding return receipt. Some protocols additionally aim to ensure the confidentiality of the message.

This protocol, like several others, relies on an on-line trusted third party, TTP. For simplicity, the channels between TTP and the other parties are assumed to guarantee reliable message delivery. Furthermore, the channel between R and TTP should provide secrecy and authentication of TTP to R. (These properties are needed when R gives a password or some other secret to TTP in order to prove its identity.) In practice such a channel might be an SSL connection or, more generally, a channel protected with symmetric keys established via a suitable protocol.

The protocol supports several options for authenticating R. For each email, S picks one of the options; the choice is denoted by authoption. We have done the proofs for all options. For the sake of brevity, however, we only show our results for the mode called BothAuth, in which both TTP and S authenticate R.

– TTP authenticates R using a shared secret RPwd—a password that identifies R to TTP.
– S authenticates R using a query/response mechanism. R is given a query q by the receiver software and r is the response that S expects R to give.

The protocol relies on a number of cryptographic primitives. The corresponding notation is as follows. $E(k, m)$ is an encryption of m using key k under some symmetric encryption algorithm. $H(m)$ is the hash of m in some collision-resistant hashing scheme. $A(k, m)$ is an encryption of m using key k under some public-key encryption algorithm. $S(k, m)$ is a signature of m using key k under a public-key

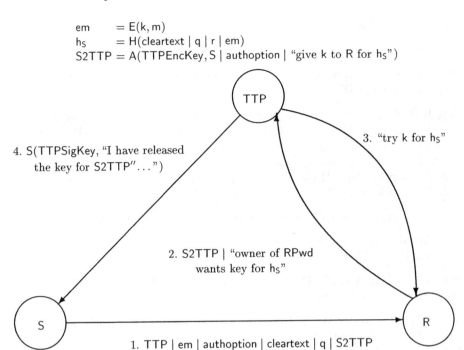

Fig. 1. Protocol sketch

signature algorithm. Finally $m_1 \mid \cdots \mid m_n$ denotes the unambiguous concatenation of the m_is.

TTP has a public key TTPEncKey that S can use for encrypting messages for TTP, and a corresponding secret key TTPDecKey. TTP also has a secret key TTPSigKey that it can use for signing messages and a public key TTPVerKey that S can use for verifying these signatures.

In the first step of the protocol, S encrypts its message under a freshly generated symmetric key, encrypts this key under TTPEncKey, and mails this and the encrypted message to R. Then R forwards the encrypted key to TTP. After authenticating R appropriately, TTP releases the key to R (so R can decrypt and read the message) and sends a receipt to S. In more detail, the exchange of messages goes as follows. (Figure 1, adapted from [2], shows some of this detail.)

Step 1: When S wishes to send a message m to R:

1.1. S generates a key k. S also picks authoption (BothAuth in this paper). S knows or generates a query q to which R should respond r.

1.2. S encrypts m with k, letting em = E(k, m).

1.3. S then computes h_S = H(cleartext | q | r | em). This hash will both identify the message to TTP and serve for authenticating R. The part cleartext is simply a header.

1.4. S computes S2TTP = A(TTPEncKey, S | authoption | "give k to R for h_S").

1.5. S sends Message 1:

MESSAGE 1, S to R: TTP | em | authoption | cleartext | q | S2TTP

Step 2: When R receives a message of the form: TTP | em' | authoption' | cleartext' | q' | S2TTP':

2.1. R reads cleartext', decides whether it wants to read the message with the assistance of TTP, and checks the authentication option (to be BothAuth, in this paper). If R decides to proceed, it constructs a response r' to query q', and recalls its password RPwd for TTP.
2.2. R computes $h_R = H(\text{cleartext}' \mid q' \mid r' \mid \text{em}')$.
2.3. R sends Message 2:

MESSAGE 2, R to TTP: S2TTP' | "owner of RPwd wants key for h_R"

This message and the next one are transmitted on the secure channel that links R and TTP.

Steps 3 and 4: When TTP receives of a message of the form S2TTP'' | "owner of RPwd' wants key for h'_R":

3.1. TTP tries to decrypt S2TTP'' using TTPDecKey. The cleartext should be of the form S | authoption'' | "give k' to R' for h'_S".
3.2. TTP checks that RPwd' is the password for R' and that h'_S equals h'_R. If TTP's checks succeed, it proceeds with Messages 3 and 4.
3.3. TTP sends Message 3:

MESSAGE 3, TTP to R: "try k' for h'_R"

Upon receipt of such a message R uses k' to decrypt em', obtaining m.
4.1. TTP sends Message 4:

MESSAGE 4, TTP to S:
S(TTPSigKey, "I have released the key for S2TTP'' to R'")

4.2. When S receives Message 4, it checks this receipt. Later on, if S ever wants to prove that R has received m to a judge, S can provide this message, em, k, cleartext, q, and r, and the judge should check that these values and TTP's public key match.

3 The Verification Tool

In this section we review the verification tool that we employ for our analysis (see [1, 6, 7] for further information). We also explain how we extend this tool.

The tool requires expressing protocols in a formal language, which we describe below. The semantics of this language is the point of reference for our proofs. The tool is sound, with respect to this semantics. (So proofs with the tool can guarantee the absence of attacks captured in this semantics, but not necessarily of other attacks.) On the other hand, the tool is not complete; however, it is successful in substantial proofs, as we demonstrate.

3.1 The Input Language

The verifier takes as input the description of a protocol in a little programming language, an extension of the pi calculus. This calculus represents messages by terms $M, N, \ldots$, and programs by processes $P, Q, \ldots$. Identifiers are partitioned into names, variables, constructors, and destructors. We often use a, b, and c for names, x for a variable, f for a constructor, and g for a destructor.

Constructors are functions that serve for building terms. Thus, the terms are variables, names, and constructor applications of the form $f(M_1, \ldots, M_n)$. A constructor f of arity n is introduced with the declaration **fun** f/n. On the other hand, destructors do not appear in terms, but only manipulate terms in processes. They are partial functions on terms that processes can apply. The process **let** $x = g(M_1, \ldots, M_n)$ **in** P **else** Q tries to evaluate $g(M_1, \ldots, M_n)$; if this succeeds, then x is bound to the result and P is run, else Q is run. More precisely, a destructor g of arity n is described with a set of reduction rules of the form $g(M_1, \ldots, M_n) \to M$ where $M_1, \ldots, M_n, M$ are terms without free names. These reduction rules are specified in a **reduc** declaration. We extend these rules by $g(M_1', \ldots, M_n') \to M'$ if and only if there exists a substitution σ and a reduction rule $g(M_1, \ldots, M_n) \to M$ in the declaration of g such that $M_i' = \sigma M_i$ for all $i \in \{1, \ldots, n\}$, and $M' = \sigma M$. Pairing and encryption are typical constructors; projections and decryption are typical destructors. More generally, we can represent data structures and cryptographic operations using constructors and destructors, as can be seen below in our coding of the protocol for certified email.

The process calculus includes auxiliary events that are useful in specifying security properties. The process **begin**(M).P executes the event **begin**(M), then P. The process **end**(M).P executes the event **end**(M), then P. We prove security properties of the form "if a certain **end** event has been executed, then certain **begin** events have been executed".

Most other constructs of the language come from the pi calculus. The input process **in**(M, x); P inputs a message on channel M, then runs P with the variable x bound to the input message. The output process **out**(M, N); P outputs the message N on the channel M, then runs P. The nil process **0** does nothing. The process $P \mid Q$ is the parallel composition of P and Q. The replication !P represents an unbounded number of copies of P in parallel. The restriction **new** a; P creates a new name a, then executes P. The let definition **let** $x = M$ **in** P runs P with x bound to M, and **if** $M = N$ **then** P **else** Q runs P when M equals N, otherwise it runs Q. As usual, we may omit an **else** clause when it consists of **0**.

The name a is bound in the process **new** a; P. The variable x is bound in P in the processes **in**(M, x); P, **let** $x = g(M_1, \ldots, M_n)$ **in** P **else** Q, and **let** $x = M$ **in** P. We write $fn(P)$ and $fv(P)$ for the sets of names and variables free in P, respectively. A process is closed if it has no free variables; it may have free names. Processes that represent complete protocols are always closed.

The formal semantics of this language can be defined by a reduction relation on configurations, as explained in the appendix. (This semantics, as well as the proof method, have evolved in minor ways since previous publications [7].) A reduction trace is a finite sequence of reduction steps.

We generally assume that processes execute in the presence of an adversary, which is itself a process in the same calculus. The adversary need not be programmed explicitly; we usually establish results with respect to all adversaries. We need only constrain the initial knowledge of the adversary, which we represent with a set of names *Init*, and restrict the adversary not to use auxiliary events:

Definition 1. *Let Init be a finite set of names. The closed process Q is an Init-adversary if and only if $fn(Q) \subseteq Init$ and Q does not contain* **begin** *or* **end** *events.*

3.2 The Internal Representation and the Proof Engine

Given a protocol expressed as a process in the input language, the verifier first translates it, automatically, into a set of Horn clauses (logic programming rules).

In the rules, messages are represented by patterns, which are expressions similar to terms except that names a are replaced with functions $a[\ldots]$. A free name a is replaced with the function without parameter $a[]$ (or simply a), while a bound name is replaced with a function of inputs above the restriction that creates the name. The rules are written in terms of four kinds of facts:

- $attacker(p)$ means that the adversary may have the message p;
- $mess(p, p')$ means that the message p' may be sent on channel p;
- $begin(p)$ means that the event **begin**(p) may have been executed;
- $end(p)$ means that the event **end**(p) may have been executed.

The verifier uses a resolution-based solving algorithm in order to determine properties of the protocol. Specifically, it implements a function $solve_{P,Init}(F)$ that takes as parameters the protocol P, the initial knowledge of the adversary $Init$, and a fact F, and returns a set of Horn clauses. This function first translates the protocol into a set of Horn clauses $\mathcal{C}$, then saturates this set using a resolution-based algorithm [7, Sections 4.2 and 4.3]. Finally, this function determines what is derivable. More precisely, let F' be an instance of F. Let $\mathcal{C}_b$ be any set of closed facts $begin(p)$. We can show that the fact F' is derivable from $\mathcal{C} \cup \mathcal{C}_b$ if and only if there exist a clause $F_1 \wedge \ldots \wedge F_n \to F_0$ in $solve_{P,Init}(F)$ and a substitution σ such that $F' = \sigma F_0$ and $\sigma F_1, \ldots, \sigma F_n$ are derivable from $\mathcal{C} \cup \mathcal{C}_b$. In particular, when $solve_{P,Init}(F) = \emptyset$, no instance of F is derivable. Other values of $solve_{P,Init}(F)$ give information on which instances of F are derivable, and under which conditions. In particular, the $begin$ facts in the hypotheses of the clauses in $solve_{P,Init}(F)$ indicate which $begin$ facts must be in $\mathcal{C}_b$ in order to prove F', that is, which **begin** events must be executed.

3.3 Secrecy

In the input language, we define secrecy in terms of the communications of a process that executes in parallel with an arbitrary attacker. This treatment of secrecy is a fairly direct adaptation of our earlier one [1], with a generalization from free names to terms.

Definition 2 (Secrecy). *Let P be a closed process and M a term such that $fn(M) \subseteq fn(P)$. The process P preserves the secrecy of all instances of M from Init if and only if for any Init-adversary Q, any $c \in fn(Q)$, and any substitution σ, no reduction trace of $P \mid Q$ executes $\mathbf{out}(c, \sigma M)$.*

The following result provides a method for proving secrecy properties:

Theorem 1 (Secrecy). *Let P be a closed process. Let M be a term such that $fn(M) \subseteq fn(P)$. Let p be the pattern obtained by replacing names a with patterns $a[]$ in the term M. Assume that $solve_{P, Init}(attacker(p)) = \emptyset$. Then P preserves the secrecy of all instances of M from Init.*

Basically, this result says that if the fact $attacker(p)$ is not derivable then the adversary cannot obtain the term M that corresponds to p.

3.4 Correspondence Assertions

As shown in [7], the verifier can serve for establishing correspondence assertions [17] of the restricted form "if $\mathbf{end}(M)$ has been executed, then $\mathbf{begin}(M)$ must have been executed". Here, we extend this technique so as to prove specifications of the more general form "if $\mathbf{end}(N)$ has been executed, then $\mathbf{begin}(M_1)$, ..., $\mathbf{begin}(M_n)$ must have been executed". Deemphasizing technical differences with Woo's and Lam's definitions, we refer to these specifications as correspondence assertions. Below, we use correspondence assertions for establishing that R gets S's message if and only if S gets a corresponding receipt.

We define the meaning of these specifications as follows:

Definition 3 (Correspondence). *Let P be a closed process and $N, M_1, \ldots, M_l$ be terms such that $fn(N) \cup fn(M_1) \cup \ldots \cup fn(M_l) \subseteq fn(P)$. The process P satisfies the correspondence assertion $\mathbf{end}(N) \rightsquigarrow \mathbf{begin}(M_1), \ldots, \mathbf{begin}(M_l)$ with respect to Init-adversaries if and only if, for any Init-adversary Q, for any σ defined on the variables of N, if $\mathbf{end}(\sigma N)$ is executed in some reduction trace of $P \mid Q$, then we can extend σ so that for $k \in \{1, \ldots, l\}$, $\mathbf{begin}(\sigma M_k)$ is executed in this trace as well.*

Analogously to Theorem 1, the next theorem provides a method for proving these correspondence assertions with our verifier.

Theorem 2 (Correspondence). *Let P be a closed process and $N, M_1, \ldots, M_l$ be terms such that $fn(N) \cup fn(M_1) \cup \ldots \cup fn(M_l) \subseteq fn(P)$. Let $p, p_1, \ldots, p_l$ be the patterns obtained by replacing names a with patterns $a[]$ in the terms $N, M_1, \ldots, M_l$, respectively. Assume that, for all rules R in $solve_{P, Init}(end(p))$, there exist σ' and H such that $R = H \wedge begin(\sigma' p_1) \wedge \ldots \wedge begin(\sigma' p_l) \rightarrow end(\sigma' p)$. Then P satisfies the correspondence assertion $\mathbf{end}(N) \rightsquigarrow \mathbf{begin}(M_1), \ldots, \mathbf{begin}(M_l)$ with respect to Init-adversaries.*

Intuitively, the condition on R means that, for the fact $end(\sigma'p)$ to be derivable, $begin(\sigma'p_1), \ldots, begin(\sigma'p_l)$ must be derivable. The conclusion of the theorem is the corresponding statement on events: if **end**(σN) has been executed, then **begin**$(\sigma M_1), \ldots,$ **begin**(σM_l) must have been executed as well.

4 Formalizing the Protocol

In order to analyze the protocol for certified email, we program it in the verifier's input language, following the informal specification rather closely. In the code below, comments such as "Step 1.1" refer to corresponding steps of the informal specification.

The code represents the situation in which all principals proceed honestly. In Section 5, when we consider situations in which S or R are adversarial and may therefore not execute this code, we simplify the specification accordingly. In addition, in order to specify and prove security properties, we add events (at the program points marked *Event* S, *Event* R, and *Event* TTP).

(* Public-key cryptography *)
fun pk/1. **fun** A/2.
reduc decA$(y, A(pk(y), x)) = x$.

(* Signatures *)
fun S/2. **fun** Spk/1.
reduc checkS$(Spk(y), S(y, x)) = x$.
reduc getS$(S(y, x)) = x$.

(* Shared-key cryptography *)
fun E/2.
reduc decE$(y, E(y, x)) = x$.

(* Hash function *)
fun H/1.

(* Constants to identify messages *)
fun Give/0. **fun** Wants/0. **fun** Try/0. **fun** Released/0.
(* Constant authentication modes. We consider only BothAuth here *)
fun BothAuth/0.

(* Function from R's password to R's name *)
fun PasswdTable/1.

(* It is assumed that an attacker cannot relate q and $r =$ Reply(h, q) except for the hosts h it creates itself *)
private fun Reply/2.
reduc ReplyOwnHost$(x, q) = $ Reply(PasswdTable$(x), q)$.

(* Build a message *)
private fun Message/2.

(* Secrecy assumptions *)

not TTPDecKey. **not** TTPSigKey.

(* Free names (public and private constants) *)
free c, cleartext, Sname, TTPname.
private free TTPDecKey, TTPSigKey, RPwd.

let *processS* =
  (* The attacker chooses possible recipients of the message *)
  in(c, *recipient*);

  (* Build the message to send *)
  new *msgid*; **let** *m* = Message(*recipient*, *msgid*) **in**

  (* Step 1 *)
  new *k*; **new** *q*; **let** *r* = Reply(*recipient*, *q*) **in**   *(* Step 1.1 *)*
  let *em* = E(*k*, *m*) **in**   *(* Step 1.2 *)*
  let *hs* = H((cleartext, *q*, *r*, *em*)) **in**   *(* Step 1.3 *)*
                                                                                  (* Step 1.4 *)
  let *S2TTP* = A(TTPEncKey, (Sname, BothAuth, (Give, *k*, *recipient*, *hs*))) **in**
  (* Event S [to be added later] *)
  out(*recipient*, (TTPname, *em*, BothAuth, cleartext, *q*, *S2TTP*)); *(* Step 1.5 *)*

  (* Step 4.2 *)
  !
  in(Sname, *inmess4*);
  let (= Released, = *S2TTP*, = *recipient*) = checkS(TTPVerKey, *inmess4*) **in**
      (* S knows that the recipient has read the message *)
      0
  else out(Sname, *inmess4*).

let *processR* =
  (* Step 2 *)
  in(Rname, (= TTPname, *em2*, = BothAuth, *cleartext2*, *q2*, *S2TTP2*));
  let *r2* = Reply(Rname, *q2*) **in**   *(* Step 2.1 *)*
  let *hr* = H((*cleartext2*, *q2*, *r2*, *em2*)) **in**   *(* Step 2.2 *)*
  (* Establish the secure channel R-TTP *)
  new *secchannel*;
  out(ChannelToTTP, Rname);
  out(ChannelToTTP, *secchannel*);
  let *outchannel* = (TTPname, *secchannel*) **in**
  let *inchannel* = (Rname, *secchannel*) **in**
  (* Event R [to be added later] *)
  out(*outchannel*, (*S2TTP2*, (Wants, RPwd, *hr*)));   *(* Step 2.3 *)*

  (* Step 3.3 *)
  !
  in(*inchannel*, (= Try, *k3*, = *hr*));
  let *m3* = decE(*k3*, *em2*) **in**

(* R has obtained the message m3 = m *)
end(Rreceived(m3)).

let processTTP =
(* Establish the secure channel R-TTP *)
in(ChannelToTTP, receivername);
in(ChannelToTTP, secchannel);
let inchannel = (TTPname, secchannel) in
let outchannel = (receivername, secchannel) in

(* Step 3 *)
in(inchannel, (S2TTP3, (= Wants, RPwd3, hr3)));
let (Sname3, authoption3, (= Give, k3, R3, = hr3)) =   (* Step 3.1 *)
    decA(TTPDecKey, S2TTP3) in
if R3 = PasswdTable(RPwd3) then   (* Step 3.2 *)
if R3 = receivername then
(* Event TTP [to be added later] *)
out(outchannel, (Try, k3, hr3));   (* Step 3.3 *)

(* Step 4.1 *)
out(Sname3, S(TTPSigKey, (Released, S2TTP3, R3))).

process
    let TTPEncKey = pk(TTPDecKey) in out(c, TTPEncKey);
    let TTPVerKey = Spk(TTPSigKey) in out(c, TTPVerKey);
    let Rname = PasswdTable(RPwd) in out(c, Rname);
    new ChannelToTTP;
    ((!processS) | (!processR) | (!processTTP)
       | (!in(c, m); out(ChannelToTTP, m)))

This code first declares cryptographic primitives. For instance, the constructor A is the public-key encryption function, which takes two parameters, a public key and a cleartext, and returns a ciphertext. The constructor pk computes a public key from a secret key. The destructor decA is the corresponding decryption function. From a ciphertext A(pk(y), x) and the corresponding secret key y, it returns the cleartext x. Hence we give the rule decA(y, A(pk(y), x)) = x. We assume perfect cryptography, so the cleartext can be obtained from the ciphertext only when one has the decryption key. We define signatures, shared-key encryption, and a hash function analogously. Note that the constructor Spk that builds a public key for signatures from a secret key is different from the constructor pk that builds a public key for encryptions. The destructor checkS checks the signature, while getS returns the cleartext message without checking the signature. (In particular, the adversary may use getS in order to obtain message contents from signed messages.) Concatenation is represented by tuples, which are pre-declared by default. We also declare a number of constants that appear in messages.

The constructor PasswdTable computes the name of a receiver from its password. This constructor represents the password table (*host name, host password*). Since all host names are public but some passwords are secret, the adversary must not be able to compute the appropriate password from a host name, so we define a function that maps passwords to host names but not the converse: *host name* = PasswdTable(*host password*). One advantage of this encoding is that we can compactly model systems with an unbounded number of hosts.

The challenge-response authentication of R by S goes as follows. S creates an arbitrary query q, and the reply r to this query is computed by the constructor Reply, so $r =$ Reply(h, q) where h is the recipient host name. Both S and R can use the constructor Reply. However, this constructor is declared **private**, that is, the adversary cannot apply it. (Otherwise, it could impersonate R.) The adversary must be able to compute replies for hosts that it creates, that is, when it has the password of the host. Therefore, we define a public destructor ReplyOwnHost that computes a reply from the query and the password of the host.

The constructor Message builds the messages that S sends to R. We assume that these messages are initially secret, so we make the constructor private. We also assume that S sends different messages to different recipients, so let a message be a function of the recipient and of a message identifier.

Secrecy assumptions correspond to an optimization of our verifier. The declaration **not** M indicates to the verifier that M is secret. The verifier can then use this information in order to speed up the solving process. At the end of solving, the verifier checks that the secrecy assumption is actually true, so that a wrong secrecy assumption leads to an error message but not to an incorrect result.

The declaration **free** declares public free names. c is a public channel, cleartext is the header of the messages sent by S, and Sname and TTPname are the names of S and TTP, respectively. R's name is Rname = PasswdTable(RPwd) so it not a free name. (It is declared at the end of the protocol.) The declaration **private free** declares private free names (not known by the adversary); TTPDecKey and TTPSigKey are TTP's secret keys, and RPwd is R's password.

The processes *processS*, *processR*, and *processTTP* represent S, R, and TTP, respectively. These processes are composed in the last part of the protocol specification. This part computes TTP's public encryption key from its secret key by the constructor pk: TTPEncKey = pk(TTPDecKey). The public key TTPEncKey is output on the public channel c so that the adversary can have TTPEncKey. We proceed similarly for the key pair (TTPSigKey, TTPVerKey). At last, we compute R's name from its password: Rname = PasswdTable(RPwd). This name is public, so we send it on channel c, so that the adversary can have it. In the following, we use Rname as an abbreviation for the term PasswdTable(RPwd). The role of ChannelToTTP and of the last element of the parallel composition is explained below in the description of *processR*.

The process *processS* first receives the name of the host to which S is going to send its message, on the public channel c. Thus, the adversary can choose that host. This conservative assumption implies that S can send its message to any host. Then S builds the message: it creates a new message id *msgid*, and builds the message m by calling the constructor Message. Then it executes the steps of the protocol description. For instance, in step 1.1, it creates a new key k by **new** k, a new query q by **new** q, and computes the corresponding reply r. In step 1.4, the sentence "give k to $recipient$ for hs" is represented by a tuple containing the constant Give and the parameters k, $recipient$, and hs. Other sentences are represented analogously. Note that, at step 1.5, we send the message to the recipient on channel $recipient$. In our coding of the protocol, the channel always indicates the destination of the message. This indication makes it easier to define the meaning of "a message reaches its destination", but it is only an indication: when the channel is public, the adversary may still obtain the message or send its own messages on the channel. In the destructor application of step 4.2, we use a pattern-matching construct:

$$\text{let } (= \text{Released}, = S2TTP, = recipient) = \ldots \text{ in } \ldots$$

A pattern $(p_1, \ldots, p_n)$ matches a tuple of arity n, when $p_1, \ldots, p_n$ match the components of the tuple. A pattern x matches any term, and binds x to this term. A pattern $= M$ matches only the term M. So the destructor application of step 4.2 succeeds if and only if $inmess4 = \text{S}(\text{TTPSigKey}, (\text{Released}, S2TTP, recipient))$. The same pattern-matching construct is used for message input. When the check of $inmess4$ fails, the incoming message $inmess4$ is returned on the channel Sname (by the else clause of the destructor application), so that another session of S can get it. We assume that the execution is fair, so that all sessions of S get a chance to have the receipt $inmess4$. Moreover, because of the replication at the beginning of step 4.2, S still waits for a receipt from TTP even after receiving a wrong receipt. In an actual implementation, S would store a set of the messages it has sent recently and for which it has not yet obtained a receipt. When obtaining a receipt, it would look for the corresponding message in this set. Our coding represents this lookup by returning the receipt on Sname until it is consumed by the right session of S.

The process $processR$ first executes steps 2.1 and 2.2, then it establishes a secure connection with TTP. The informal specification does not spell out the details related to this connection, so we need to pick them. Several reasonable choices are available; we explore one here and mention others in Section 6. In order to establish the connection with TTP, R employs an asymmetric channel ChannelToTTP (created at the end of the protocol description) on which anybody can write but only TTP can read. For starting a connection with TTP, one sends its own name $receivername$ (here Rname) and a new name $secchannel$ on ChannelToTTP. Further exchanges between R and TTP are then done on channels (TTPname, $secchannel$) from R to TTP and ($receivername$, $secchannel$) from TTP to R. We use pairs for channels so as to mention explicitly the destination host in the channel name. One might see some similarity with TCP connections, in which packets contain destination addresses. Since the name $secchannel$ created by R is secret, only R and TTP will be able to send or receive messages on (TTPname, $secchannel$) and ($receivername$, $secchannel$), so the channel R-TTP is indeed secure. This channel provides authentication of TTP, since only TTP can read on ChannelToTTP. Any host can send messages on ChannelToTTP, and thus start a connection with TTP. So the authentication of R is not provided by the channel but by the password check that TTP performs (in step 3.2). R writes on that channel, TTP reads on it. In order to allow the adversary to write on that channel, we use a relay process (!in(c, m); out(ChannelToTTP, m)) (last line of the protocol description) that gets a message on c and resends it on ChannelToTTP. Thus, by sending a message on c, the adversary can send it on ChannelToTTP. After establishing the connection with TTP, R continues the execution of steps 2.3 and 3.3. In the end, R emits the event $Rreceived(m3)$, to note that R has correctly received the message $m3$. Below, this event is useful in the security proofs.

The process $processTTP$ first establishes a secure channel with a message recipient, as explained above. Then it executes step 3. Note that, between steps 3.2 and 3.3, it checks that its interlocutor in the connection, $receivername$, actually corresponds to the expected receiver of the message, $R3$. This check ensures that the message on $outchannel$ goes to the expected receiver of the message. Finally, TTP sends the key $k3$ to the receiver of the message (step 3.3) and the receipt to the sender (step 4.1).

5 Results

In this section we present the proofs of the main security properties of the protocol. We heavily rely on the verifier for these proofs.

5.1 Secrecy

Let P_0 be the process that represents the protocol. The verifier can prove automatically that this process preserves the secrecy of the message m sent by S to R.

Proposition 1. *Let* $Init = \{$Sname, TTPname, c, cleartext$\}$. *The process* P_0 *preserves the secrecy of all instances of* Message(Rname, i) *from Init.*

Automatic proof: We give the appropriate query $attacker($Message(Rname, i)$)$. The tool computes $solve_{P_0, Init}(attacker($Message(Rname, i)$)) = \emptyset$. Hence, by Theorem 1, the process P_0 preserves the secrecy of Message(Rname, i) from $Init$.
□

5.2 Receipt

The main correctness property of the protocol is the following: R receives the message m if and only if S gets a proof that R has received the message. This proof should be such that, if S goes to a judge with it, the judge can definitely say that R has received the message.

This property holds only when the delivery of messages is guaranteed on the channels from TTP to R, from TTP to S, and from S to the judge, hence the following definition.

Definition 4. *We say that a message m sent on channel c reaches its destination if and only if it is eventually received by an input on channel c in the initial process P_0 or a process derived from P_0. If the adversary receives the message, it reemits the message on channel c.*

Furthermore, we use the following fairness hypotheses:

- If infinitely often a reduction step can be executed, then it will eventually be executed.
- If a message m is sent on channel c, and some inputs on channel c reemit it, that is, they execute $\mathbf{in}(c, m) \ldots \mathbf{out}(c, m)$, and some do not reemit m on c, then m will eventually be received by an input that does not reemit it.

Although this definition and these hypotheses are stated somewhat informally, they can be made precise in terms of the semantics of the language. Several variants are possible.

The fact that messages reach their destination and the fairness hypotheses cannot be taken into account by our verifier, so it cannot prove the required properties in a fully automatic way. Still, the verifier can prove a correspondence assertion that constitutes the most important part of the proof. Indeed, we have to show properties of the form: if some event e_1 has been executed, then some event e_2 has or will be executed. The verifier shows automatically the correspondence assertion: if e_1 has been executed then some events e_2' have been executed *before* e_1. We show manually that if the events e_2' have been executed, then e_2 will be executed *after* e_2'. Thus the correspondence assertion captures the desired security property. The manual proof just consists in following the execution steps of the process after e_2'. It is much simpler than the first part, which should go backward through all possible execution histories leading to e_1. Fortunately, the first part is fully automatic.

We use the following process to represent the judge to which the informal specification of the protocol alludes:

fun Received/0. **free** Judgename.

let *processJudge* =
  (* S *must send* TTP*'s certificate plus other information* *)
  in(Judgename, $(certif, Sname5, k5, cleartext5, q5, r5, em5)$);
  let (= Released, $S2TTP5, Rname5$) = checkS(TTPVerKey, $certif$) **in**
  let $m5$ = decE($k5, em5$) **in**
  let $hs5$ = H(($cleartext5, q5, r5, em5$)) **in**
  if $S2TTP5$ =
     A(TTPEncKey, ($Sname5$, BothAuth, (Give, $k5, Rname5, hs5$))) **then**
  (* *The judge says that* $Rname5$ *has received* $m5$ *)
  end($JudgeSays$(Received, $Rname5, m5$)).

The judge receives a certificate from S, tries to check it, and if it succeeds, says that the receiver has received the message. This process is executed in parallel with *processR*, *processTTP*, and *processS*. At the end of *processS*, instead of executing **0**, the sender S sends to the judge:

out(Judgename, $(inmess_4,$ Sname, $k,$ cleartext, $q, r, em))$

The result to prove decomposes into two propositions, Propositions 2 and 3.

Proposition 2. *Assume that the messages from* TTP *sent on* Sname3 *and from* S *sent on* Judgename *reach their destinations. If* R *has received* $m,$ *then the judge says that* R *has received* $m.$

In this proof, R is included in the adversary: R tries to get a message without S having the corresponding receipt. So we need not constrain R to follow the protocol. The process for R becomes:

out(c, ChannelToTTP); out(c, RPwd) | in(c, m); end($Rreceived(m)$)

This process reveals all the information that R has. When the adversary obtains some message $m,$ it can send it on c, thus execute the event end($Rreceived(m)$). Since R is included in the adversary, the adversary can compute the constructor Reply, so its declaration becomes: **fun** Reply/2. Writing P_0 for the resulting process that represents the whole system, the proposition becomes, more formally:

Proposition 2'. *Assume that the messages from* TTP *sent on* Sname3 *and from* S *sent on* Judgename *reach their destinations. Let* Init = {Sname, TTPname, Judgename, c, cleartext}. *For any Init-adversary* $Q,$ *if the event* end($Rreceived($Message$(M_x, M_i)))$ *is executed in a reduction trace of* $P_0 \mid Q$ *for some terms* M_x *and* $M_i,$ *then* end($JudgeSays($Received, $M_x,$ Message$(M_x, M_i)))$ *is executed in all continuations of this trace.*

At point *Event* TTP, we introduce the event **begin**($TTP\_send($Sname3, S(TTPSigKey, (Released, $S2TTP3, R3))))$, to note that TTP sends the receipt S(TTPSigKey, (Released, $S2TTP3, R3))$ to S. At point *Event* S, we introduce the event **begin**($S\_has($Sname, $k,$ cleartext, $q, r, m))$, to note that S has all parameters needed to obtain the answer from the judge (except TTP's receipt).

Automatic part of the proof: We invoke our tool with the query $end(Rreceived($Message$(x, i)))$, to determine under which conditions an instance of the corresponding event may be executed. The tool then computes the set of clauses $solve_{P_0, Init}(end(Rreceived($Message$(x, i))))$ and returns a rule of the form:

$begin(TTP\_send($Sname, S(TTPSigKey, (Released, A(TTPEncKey, (Sname,

BothAuth, (Give, $p_k, p_x,$ H((cleartext, $p_q, p_r,$ E($p_k,$ Message$(p_x, p_i)))))))), p_x))))$∧

$begin(S\_has($Sname, $p_k,$ cleartext, $p_q, p_r,$ Message$(p_x, p_i)))$∧

$H \rightarrow end(Rreceived($Message$(p_x, p_i)))$

for some patterns $p_x, p_k, p_q, p_r, p_i,$ and some hypothesis $H.$

So, by Theorem 2, if end($Rreceived($Message$(M_x, M_i)))$ is executed in a trace of $P_0 \mid Q,$ then the events

  begin($TTP\_send($Sname, $certificate))$
  begin($S\_has($Sname, $M_k,$ cleartext, $M_q, M_r,$ Message$(M_x, M_i)))$

are executed in this trace for some terms M_k, M_q, and M_r, with *certificate* = S(TTPSigKey, (Released, A(TTPEncKey, (Sname, BothAuth, (Give, M_k, M_x, H((cleartext, M_q, M_r, E(M_k, Message(M_x, M_i)))))), M_x)).

Manual Part of the Proof: Since TTP executes **begin**(TTP_send(Sname, *certificate*)) as proved above, it is then going to execute **out**(Sname, *certificate*). Since this message reaches its destination, it will then be received by an input on Sname from P_0, that is, by the last input of *processS*. Moreover, the session that has executed **begin**(S_has(Sname, M_k, cleartext, M_q, M_r, Message(M_x, M_i))) does not reemit this message, so by the fairness hypothesis, this message will be received by a session of S that does not reemit it. Such a session successfully checks the certificate and sends it to the judge on the channel Judgename. Since this message reaches its destination, it will be received by the input on Judgename in *processJudge*. Then the judge also checks successfully the certificate (the check always succeeds when S's check succeeds), so the judge executes **end**($JudgeSays$(Received, M_x, Message(M_x, M_i))). □

The verifier proves the required correspondence assertion in a fully automatic way. It is then only a few lines of proof to obtain the desired security property. Moreover, we need not even know in advance the exact correspondence assertion to consider: the verifier tells us which correspondence assertion holds for the given **end** event.

Turning to the guarantees for R, we establish:

Proposition 3. *Assume that the message from* TTP *sent on outchannel reaches its destination. If the judge says that* R *has received* m, *then* R *has received* m.

In this proof, S is included in the adversary: S may try to fool the judge into saying that R has received a message it does not have. Therefore, we need not be specific on how S behaves, so the process for S is simply **0**. The adversary can compute the constructor Reply, so its declaration becomes: **fun** Reply/2. Writing P_0 for the resulting process that represents the whole system, the proposition becomes, more formally:

Proposition 3'. *Assume that the message from* TTP *sent on outchannel reaches its destination. Let Init* = {Sname, TTPname, Judgename, c, cleartext}. *For any Init-adversary Q, if* **end**($JudgeSays$(Received, Rname, M_m)) *is executed in a reduction trace of* P_0 | Q *for some term* M_m, *then the event* **end**($Rreceived(M_m)$) *is executed in all continuations of this trace.*

At point *Event* R, we introduce the event **begin**(R_has(secchannel, em2, hr)), to note that R has received the encrypted message. At point *Event* TTP, we introduce the event **begin**(TTP_send(outchannel, (Try, k3, hr3))) to note that TTP sends the key k3 to R.

Automatic Part: We give our verifier the query $end(JudgeSays$(Received, Rname, m)). The result returned by the verifier shows, using Theorem 2, that, if the event end($JudgeSays$(Received, Rname, M_m)) is executed in a reduction trace of $P_0 \mid Q$ for some term M_m, then the events begin(R_has($M_{secchannel}$, E(M_k, M_m), M_{hr})) and begin(TTP_send((Rname, $M_{secchannel}$), (Try, M_k, M_{hr}))) are executed in this trace for some terms M_k, $M_{secchannel}$, and M_{hr}.

Manual Part: TTP is going to send the Message 3 indicated by the event begin(TTP_send(...)) to R. Since this message reaches its destination, it will be received by the session of R that executes the event begin(R_has(...)) mentioned above (since the value of the channel (Rname, $M_{secchannel}$) must match). This session then executes end($Rreceived(M_m)$). □

6 Conclusion

This paper reports on the formal specification of a non-trivial, practical protocol for certified email, and on the verification of its main security properties. Most of the verification work is done with an automatic protocol verifier, which we adapted for the present purposes. The use of this tool significantly reduces the proof burden. It also reduces the risk of human error in proofs. Although the tool itself has not been verified, we believe that its use is quite advantageous.

We have also specified and verified more elaborate variants of the protocol, through similar methods. (We omit details for lack of space.) In particular, we have treated all four authentication modes. We have also treated three ways of establishing the secure channel between R and TTP: the one explained here, one based on a small public-key protocol, and one based on a simplified version of the SSH protocol with a Diffie–Hellman key agreement (challenging in its own right). For these three versions, the automatic parts of the proofs take 2 min 30 s on an Intel Xeon 1.7 Ghz. The manual parts are as simple as the ones shown above. Writing the specifications was more delicate and interesting than constructing the corresponding proofs.

Acknowledgments

Martín Abadi's research was partly supported by faculty research funds granted by the University of California, Santa Cruz, and by the National Science Foundation under Grants CCR-0204162 and CCR-0208800.

References

1. M. Abadi and B. Blanchet. Analyzing security protocols with secrecy types and logic programs. In *29th Annual ACM SIGPLAN - SIGACT Symposium on Principles of Programming Languages (POPL'02)*, pages 33–44, Portland, OR, Jan. 2002. ACM Press.
2. M. Abadi, N. Glew, B. Horne, and B. Pinkas. Certified email with a light on-line trusted third party: Design and implementation. In *11th International World Wide Web Conference (WWW'02)*, Honolulu, Hawaii, USA, May 2002. ACM Press.

3. G. Bella, F. Massacci, and L. C. Paulson. The verification of an industrial payment protocol: The SET purchase phase. In V. Atluri, editor, *9th ACM Conference on Computer and Communications Security (CCS'02)*, pages 12–20, Washington, DC, Nov. 2002. ACM Press.

4. G. Bella and L. C. Paulson. Using Isabelle to prove properties of the Kerberos authentication system. In *DIMACS Workshop on Design and Formal Verification of Security Protocols*, Piscataway, NJ, Sept. 1997.

5. G. Bella and L. C. Paulson. Kerberos version IV: inductive analysis of the secrecy goals. In J.-J. Quisquater et al., editors, *Computer Security - ESORICS 98*, volume 1485 of *Lecture Notes in Computer Science*, pages 361–375, Louvain-la-Neuve, Belgium, Sept. 1998. Springer Verlag.

6. B. Blanchet. An efficient cryptographic protocol verifier based on Prolog rules. In *14th IEEE Computer Security Foundations Workshop (CSFW-14)*, pages 82–96, Cape Breton, Nova Scotia, Canada, June 2001. IEEE Computer Society.

7. B. Blanchet. From secrecy to authenticity in security protocols. In M. Hermenegildo and G. Puebla, editors, *9th International Static Analysis Symposium (SAS'02)*, volume 2477 of *Lecture Notes in Computer Science*, pages 342–359, Madrid, Spain, Sept. 2002. Springer Verlag.

8. A. Gordon and A. Jeffrey. Authenticity by typing for security protocols. In *14th IEEE Computer Security Foundations Workshop (CSFW-14)*, pages 145–159, Cape Breton, Nova Scotia, Canada, June 2001. IEEE Computer Society.

9. A. Gordon and A. Jeffrey. Types and effects for asymmetric cryptographic protocols. In *15th IEEE Computer Security Foundations Workshop (CSFW-15)*, pages 77–91, Cape Breton, Nova Scotia, Canada, June 2002. IEEE Computer Society.

10. H. Krawczyk. SKEME: A versatile secure key exchange mechanism for internet. In *Proceedings of the Internet Society Symposium on Network and Distributed Systems Security (NDSS'96)*, San Diego, CA, Feb. 1996. Available at http://bilbo.isu.edu/sndss/sndss96.html.

11. S. Kremer and J.-F. Raskin. Game analysis of abuse-free contract signing. In *15th IEEE Computer Security Foundations Workshop (CSFW-15)*, pages 206–222, Cape Breton, Nova Scotia, Canada, June 2002. IEEE Computer Society.

12. C. Meadows. Analysis of the Internet Key Exchange protocol using the NRL protocol analyzer. In *IEEE Symposium on Security and Privacy*, pages 216–231, Oakland, CA, May 1999. IEEE Computer Society.

13. J. C. Mitchell, V. Shmatikov, and U. Stern. Finite-state analysis of SSL 3.0. In *7th USENIX Security Symposium*, pages 201–216, San Antonio, TX, Jan. 1998.

14. L. C. Paulson. Inductive analysis of the Internet protocol TLS. *ACM Transactions on Information and System Security*, 2(3):332–351, Aug. 1999.

15. S. Schneider. Formal analysis of a non-repudiation protocol. In *11th IEEE Computer Security Foundations Workshop (CSFW-11)*, pages 54–65, Rockport, Massachusetts, June 1998. IEEE Computer Society.

16. V. Shmatikov and J. C. Mitchell. Finite-state analysis of two contract signing protocols. *Theoretical Computer Science*, 283(2):419–450, June 2002.

17. T. Y. C. Woo and S. S. Lam. A semantic model for authentication protocols. In *1993 IEEE Symposium on Research on Security and Privacy*, pages 178–194, Oakland, CA, 1993. IEEE Computer Society.

Appendix: Semantics

A semantic configuration is a pair $E, \mathcal{P}$ where the environment E is a finite set of names and $\mathcal{P}$ is a finite multiset of closed processes. The environment E must contain at least all free names of processes in $\mathcal{P}$. The configuration $\{a_1, \ldots, a_n\}, \{P_1, \ldots, P_n\}$ corresponds to the process **new** $a_1; \ldots$ **new** $a_n; (P_1 \mid \ldots \mid P_n)$. The semantics of the calculus is defined by a reduction relation $\rightarrow$ on semantic configurations as follows:

$E, \mathcal{P} \cup \{\, \mathbf{0} \,\} \rightarrow E, \mathcal{P}$ (Red Nil)

$E, \mathcal{P} \cup \{\, !P \,\} \rightarrow E, \mathcal{P} \cup \{\, P, !P \,\}$ (Red Repl)

$E, \mathcal{P} \cup \{\, P \mid Q \,\} \rightarrow E, \mathcal{P} \cup \{\, P, Q \,\}$ (Red Par)

$E, \mathcal{P} \cup \{\, \mathbf{new}\ a; P \,\} \rightarrow E \cup \{a'\}, \mathcal{P} \cup \{\, P\{a'/a\} \,\}$ (Red Res)
  where $a' \notin E$.

$E, \mathcal{P} \cup \{\, \mathbf{out}(N, M).Q, \mathbf{in}(N, x).P \,\} \rightarrow E, \mathcal{P} \cup \{\, Q, P\{M/x\} \,\}$ (Red I/O)

$E, \mathcal{P} \cup \{\, \mathbf{let}\ x = g(M_1, \ldots, M_n)\ \mathbf{in}\ P\ \mathbf{else}\ Q \,\} \rightarrow E, \mathcal{P} \cup \{\, P\{M'/x\} \,\}$
  if $g(M_1, \ldots, M_n) \rightarrow M'$ (Red Destr 1)

$E, \mathcal{P} \cup \{\, \mathbf{let}\ x = g(M_1, \ldots, M_n)\ \mathbf{in}\ P\ \mathbf{else}\ Q \,\} \rightarrow E, \mathcal{P} \cup \{\, Q \,\}$ (Red Destr 2)
  if there exists no M' such that $g(M_1, \ldots, M_n) \rightarrow M'$

$E, \mathcal{P} \cup \{\, \mathbf{let}\ x = M\ \mathbf{in}\ P \,\} \rightarrow E, \mathcal{P} \cup \{\, P\{M/x\} \,\}$ (Red Let)

$E, \mathcal{P} \cup \{\, \mathbf{if}\ M = M\ \mathbf{then}\ P\ \mathbf{else}\ Q \,\} \rightarrow E, \mathcal{P} \cup \{\, P \,\}$ (Red Cond 1)

$E, \mathcal{P} \cup \{\, \mathbf{if}\ M = N\ \mathbf{then}\ P\ \mathbf{else}\ Q \,\} \rightarrow E, \mathcal{P} \cup \{\, Q \,\}$ (Red Cond 2)
  if $M \neq N$

$E, \mathcal{P} \cup \{\, \mathbf{begin}(M).P \,\} \rightarrow E, \mathcal{P} \cup \{\, P \,\}$ (Red Begin)

$E, \mathcal{P} \cup \{\, \mathbf{end}(M).P \,\} \rightarrow E, \mathcal{P} \cup \{\, P \,\}$ (Red End)

A reduction trace $\mathcal{T}$ of a closed process P is a finite sequence of reductions $fn(P), \{P\} \rightarrow \ldots \rightarrow E', \mathcal{P}'$.

The output $\mathbf{out}(M, N)$ *is executed in a trace* $\mathcal{T}$ if and only if this trace contains a reduction $E, \mathcal{P} \cup \{\, \mathbf{out}(N, M).Q, \mathbf{in}(N, x).P \,\} \rightarrow E, \mathcal{P} \cup \{\, Q, P\{M/x\} \,\}$ for some $E, \mathcal{P}, x, P, Q$.

The event $\mathbf{begin}(M)$ *is executed in a trace* $\mathcal{T}$ if and only if this trace contains a reduction $E, \mathcal{P} \cup \{\, \mathbf{begin}(M).P \,\} \rightarrow E, \mathcal{P} \cup \{\, P \,\}$ for some $E, \mathcal{P}, P$.

The event $\mathbf{end}(M)$ *is executed in a trace* $\mathcal{T}$ if and only if this trace contains a reduction $E, \mathcal{P} \cup \{\, \mathbf{end}(M).P \,\} \rightarrow E, \mathcal{P} \cup \{\, P \,\}$ for some $E, \mathcal{P}, P$.

Craig Interpolation and Reachability Analysis

Ken L. McMillan

Cadence Berkeley Labs

Abstract. A Craig interpolant for a mutually inconsistent pair of formulas (A, B) is a formula that is (1) implied by A, (2) inconsistent with B, and (3) expressed over the common variables of A and B. It is known that a Craig interpolant can be efficiently derived from a refutation of $A \wedge B$, for a variety of theories and proof systems. This fact has been used primarily in proving lower bounds for various proof systems.

In this talk, I will discuss a method that uses Craig interpolation to construct abstract image operators relative to a given property to be proved. In essence, the abstract image operator preserves just enough information to prove that the property is not violated within k steps. This provides a sound and complete procedure for reachability in transition systems of finite diameter. For infinite diameter, convergence is not guaranteed. However, the fact that the image operator is abstracted relative to a property may allow convergence in cases where an exact analysis would diverge.

This approach could have applications in software verification, as an alternative or adjunct to predicate abstraction, and to verification of "infinite state" systems in general.

Precise Widening Operators
for Convex Polyhedra*

Roberto Bagnara[1], Patricia M. Hill[2], Elisa Ricci[1], and Enea Zaffanella[1]

[1] Department of Mathematics, University of Parma, Italy
{bagnara,ericci,zaffanella}@cs.unipr.it
[2] School of Computing, University of Leeds, UK
hill@comp.leeds.ac.uk

Abstract. Convex polyhedra constitute the most used abstract domain among those capturing numerical relational information. Since the domain of convex polyhedra admits infinite ascending chains, it has to be used in conjunction with appropriate mechanisms for enforcing and accelerating convergence of the fixpoint computation. Widening operators provide a simple and general characterization for such mechanisms. For the domain of convex polyhedra, the original widening operator proposed by Cousot and Halbwachs amply deserves the name of *standard widening* since most analysis and verification tools that employ convex polyhedra also employ that operator. Nonetheless, there is an unfulfilled demand for more precise widening operators. In this paper, after a formal introduction to the standard widening where we clarify some aspects that are often overlooked, we embark on the challenging task of improving on it. We present a framework for the systematic definition of new and precise widening operators for convex polyhedra. The framework is then instantiated so as to obtain a new widening operator that combines several heuristics and uses the standard widening as a last resort so that it is never less precise. A preliminary experimental evaluation has yielded promising results.

1 Introduction

An ability to reason about numerical quantities is crucial for increasing numbers of applications in the field of automated analysis and verification of complex systems. Of particular interest are representations that capture *relational* information, that is, information relating different quantities such as, for example, the length of a buffer and the contents of a program variable, or the number of agents in different states in the modeling of a distributed protocol.

Convex polyhedra, since the work of Cousot and Halbwachs [19], constitute the most used abstract domain among those capturing numerical, relational information. They have been used to solve, by abstract interpretation [16], several

---

* This work has been partly supported by MURST projects "Aggregate- and number-reasoning for computing: from decision algorithms to constraint programming with multisets, sets, and maps" and "Constraint Based Verification of Reactive Systems".

important data-flow analysis problems such as array bound checking, compile-time overflow detection, loop invariant computations and loop induction variables. Convex polyhedra are also used, among many other applications, for the analysis and verification of synchronous languages [7, 24] and of linear hybrid automata (an extension of finite-state machines that models time requirements) [25, 28], for the computer-aided formal verification of concurrent and reactive systems based on temporal specifications [30], for inferring argument size relationships in logic languages [5, 6], for the automatic parallelization of imperative programs [32], for detecting buffer overflows in C [22], and for the automatic generation of the ranking functions needed to prove progress properties [11].

Since the domain of convex polyhedra admits infinite ascending chains, it has to be used in conjunction with appropriate mechanisms for enforcing and accelerating convergence of the fixpoint computation. *Widening operators* [15–18] provide a simple and general characterization for such mechanisms. In its simplest form, a widening operator on a poset $(L, \sqsubseteq)$ is defined as a partial function $\nabla \colon L \times L \rightarrowtail L$ satisfying:

1. for each $x, y \in L$ such that $x \nabla y$ is defined, we have $x \sqsubseteq x \nabla y$ and $y \sqsubseteq x \nabla y$;
2. for all increasing chains $y_0 \sqsubseteq y_1 \sqsubseteq \cdots$, the increasing chain defined by $x_0 := y_0$ and $x_{i+1} := x_i \nabla y_{i+1}$, for $i \in \mathbb{N}$, is not strictly increasing.

It must be observed that a widening operator may serve different purposes, besides forcing the stabilization of approximated iteration sequences after a finite number of iterations: it may be used to speed up the convergence of iteration sequences and to ensure the existence of the approximations of concrete elements when considering abstract domains that are algebraically weak [17]. Thus a widening does not need to be a total function, the only requirement is that its domain of definition be compatible with the intended application. The application will also affect the required trade-off between precision and efficiency: when speeding up convergence of an (perhaps intrinsically finite) iteration sequence, precision is more willingly given away; in other cases, the objective is to ensure termination without compromising precision too much. As a consequence, it is meaningful to have two or more widening operators, each one tuned with a different compromise between precision and efficiency. The different widenings can be used in different applications or even in the same application, with the system dynamically switching from one to another [13].

For the domain of convex polyhedra, the first widening operator was proposed by Cousot and Halbwachs in [19] and further refined in [23]. It amply deserves the name of *standard widening* since most analysis and verification tools that employ convex polyhedra also employ that operator.

There are a number of applications of convex polyhedra in the field of systems analysis and verification that are particularly sensitive to the precision of the deduced numerical information. The importance of precision in the field of automated verification has led to the use of *extrapolation operators*, that is, binary operators satisfying condition 1 in the definition of widening but not condition 2 (i.e., without convergence guarantees). For instance, in [27], Henzinger and Ho propose a new extrapolation operator for use in the HyTech model checker since "Halbwachs's widening operator [...] is sometimes too coarse for [their] purposes" (symbolic model checking of linear hybrid systems). An even more precise extrapolation operator, also used in the HYTECH system, is presented in [29]: "This operator is tighter than (and therefore less aggressive than) both the widening operator of [24] and the extrapolation operator of [27], which is not monotone in its second argument." Other extrapolation operators based on similar approaches have been sketched in [7]. Still in the field of automatic verification, the need for more precision than warranted by the standard widening is remarked in both [10] and [20]; and a new extrapolation operator on sets of convex polyhedra is defined in each of these papers.

If giving up convergence guarantees is acceptable (though not desirable) for semi-automatic, human-operated verifiers, this is certainly not the case for fully-automatic program analyzers. In this field, the request for more precision has been partly satisfied by delaying the application of the widening operator k times for some fixed parameter $k \in \mathbb{N}$ [13]. A study of the effect of alternative values for k in the automatic determination of linear size relations between the arguments of logic programs has been conducted in [5, 6]. One application of this idea is in termination inference [31]. In order to achieve reasonable precision, the cTI analyzer runs with $k = 3$ as a default, but there are simple programs (such as *mergesort*) whose termination can only be established with $k > 3$. On the other hand, setting $k = 4$ as the default can have a sensible impact on performance of cTI [F. Mesnard, personal communication, 2003]. Another technique to improve upon the results of a widening, while still ensuring termination, is described in [24, 26] and named 'widening up to'. This is meant to recover from those extrapolations that go beyond the limits specified by a *fixed* set of constraints, which are specific of the application domain under consideration or have been obtained by a previous static analysis step.

In this paper, after a formal introduction to the standard widening where we clarify some important aspects that are often overlooked, we embark on the challenging task of improving on it. Elaborating on an idea originally proposed in [7], we present a framework for the systematic definition of new and precise widening operators for convex polyhedra, which is based on the definition of a suitable relation on convex polyhedra satisfying the ascending chain condition. The framework makes it particularly easy to combine several heuristics and prove that the resulting operator is indeed a widening. Here we instantiate it with a selection of extrapolation operators —some of which embody improvements of heuristics already proposed in the literature— and the standard widening so that the new widening operator is always at least as precise as the standard one for a single application. An experimental evaluation of the new widening shows that, for the analysis problem considered, it captures common growth patterns and obtains precision improvements in as many as 33% of the benchmarks.

The paper is structured as follows: Section 2 recalls the required concepts and notations; Section 3 introduces the standard widening, highlighting a few important aspects of its formal definition that are often overlooked; Section 4 presents a framework for the systematic definition of new widening operators improving upon the standard widening; Section 5 instantiates this framework by considering several variants of extrapolations techniques proposed in the literature, as well as one that is new to this paper; Section 6 summarizes the results of our experimental evaluation of the new widening. Section 7 concludes. The proofs of all the stated results can be found in [3].

2 Preliminaries

The cardinality of a set S is denoted by $\#S$. If M and N are finite multisets over $\mathbb{N}$, $\#(n, M)$ denotes the number of occurrences of $n \in \mathbb{N}$ in M and $M \gg N$ means that there exists $j \in \mathbb{N}$ such that $\#(j, M) > \#(j, N)$ and, for each $k \in \mathbb{N}$ with $k > j$, we have $\#(k, M) = \#(k, N)$. The relation $\gg$ satisfies the ascending chain condition [21]. The set of non-negative reals is denoted by $\mathbb{R}_+$.

Any vector $v \in \mathbb{R}^n$ is also regarded as a matrix in $\mathbb{R}^{n \times 1}$ so that it can be manipulated with the usual matrix operations of addition, multiplication (both by a scalar and by another matrix), and transposition, which is denoted by v^T. For each $i = 1, \ldots n$, the i-th component of the vector $v \in \mathbb{R}^n$ is denoted by v_i. The *scalar product* of $v, w \in \mathbb{R}^n$, denoted $\langle v, w \rangle$, is $v^\mathrm{T} w = \sum_{i=1}^n v_i w_i$. The vector of $\mathbb{R}^n$ having all components equal to zero is denoted by $\mathbf{0}$.

Let $V = \{v_1, \ldots, v_k\} \subseteq \mathbb{R}^n$ be a finite set of real vectors. For all scalar constants $\lambda_1, \ldots, \lambda_k \in \mathbb{R}$, the vector $v = \sum_{i=1}^k \lambda_i v_i$ is said to be a *linear combination* of the vectors in V. Such a combination is said to be: (1) *positive* (or *conic*), if $\lambda_i \in \mathbb{R}_+$ for $i = 1, \ldots, k$; (2) *affine*, if $\sum_{i=1}^k \lambda_i = 1$; (3) *convex*, if it is both positive and affine. Let $V \subseteq \mathbb{R}^n$. The subspace of $\mathbb{R}^n$ defined by the set of all affine combinations of finite subsets of V is called the *affine hull* of V and denoted by aff.hull(V); the *orthogonal* of V is $V^\perp := \{ w \in \mathbb{R}^n \mid \forall v \in V : \langle v, w \rangle = 0 \}$; the set $\{ -v \in \mathbb{R}^n \mid v \in V \}$ is denoted by $-V$.

For each vector $a \in \mathbb{R}^n$ and scalar $b \in \mathbb{R}$, where $a \neq \mathbf{0}$, the linear inequality constraint $\langle a, x \rangle \geq b$ defines a topologically closed affine half-space of $\mathbb{R}^n$. We do not distinguish between syntactically different constraints defining the same affine half-space so that, for example, $x \geq 2$ and $2x \geq 4$ are the same constraint. The set $\mathcal{P} \subseteq \mathbb{R}^n$ is a (*closed* and *convex*) *polyhedron* if and only if either $\mathcal{P}$ can be expressed as the intersection of a finite number of closed affine half-spaces of $\mathbb{R}^n$, or $n = 0$ and $\mathcal{P} = \varnothing$. The set of all closed polyhedra on $\mathbb{R}^n$ is denoted by $\mathbb{CP}_n$. In this paper, we only consider polyhedra in $\mathbb{CP}_n$ when $n > 0$. The set $\mathbb{CP}_n$, when partially ordered by subset inclusion, is a lattice where the binary meet operation is set-intersection; the binary join operation, denoted $\uplus$, is called *convex polyhedral hull*, *poly-hull* for short.

We say that $\mathcal{P} \in \mathbb{CP}_n$ has dimension k, and we write $\dim(\mathcal{P}) = k$, if $k \leq n$ is the dimension of the affine subspace aff.hull($\mathcal{P}$). If $\mathcal{P} \neq \varnothing$, the *characteristic cone* of $\mathcal{P}$ is given by the set

$$\mathrm{char.cone}(\mathcal{P}) := \{ w \in \mathbb{R}^n \mid \forall v \in \mathcal{P} : v + w \in \mathcal{P} \}$$

whereas the *lineality space* of $\mathcal{P}$ is $\mathrm{lin.space}(\mathcal{P}) := \mathrm{char.cone}(\mathcal{P}) \cap -\mathrm{char.cone}(\mathcal{P})$.

The linear equality constraint $\langle a, x \rangle = b$ defines an affine hyperplane of $\mathbb{R}^n$ (i.e., the intersection of the affine half-spaces $\langle a, x \rangle \geq b$ and $\langle -a, x \rangle \geq -b$). Each polyhedron $\mathcal{P} \in \mathbb{CP}_n$ can therefore be represented by a finite set of linear equality and inequality constraints $\mathcal{C}$ called a *constraint system*. We write $\mathcal{P} = \text{con}(\mathcal{C})$. The subsets of equality and inequality constraints in system $\mathcal{C}$ are denoted by $\text{eq}(\mathcal{C})$ and $\text{ineq}(\mathcal{C})$, respectively. When $\mathcal{P} = \text{con}(\mathcal{C}) \neq \varnothing$, we say that constraint system $\mathcal{C}$ is in *minimal form* if $\#\,\text{eq}(\mathcal{C}) = n - \dim(\mathcal{P})$ and there does not exist $\mathcal{C}' \subset \mathcal{C}$ such that $\text{con}(\mathcal{C}') = \mathcal{P}$. All the constraint systems in minimal form describing a given polyhedron have the same cardinality.

Let $\mathcal{P} \in \mathbb{CP}_n$. A vector $p \in \mathcal{P}$ is called a *point* of $\mathcal{P}$; a vector $r \in \mathbb{R}^n$, where $r \neq 0$, is called a *ray* of $\mathcal{P}$ if $\mathcal{P} \neq \varnothing$ and $p + \lambda r \in \mathcal{P}$, for all points $p \in \mathcal{P}$ and all $\lambda \in \mathbb{R}_+$; a vector $l \in \mathbb{R}^n$ is called a *line* of $\mathcal{P}$ if both l and $-l$ are rays of $\mathcal{P}$. We do not distinguish between rays (resp., lines) differing by a positive (resp., non-null) factor so that, for example, $(1,3)^\mathsf{T}$ and $(2,6)^\mathsf{T}$ are the same ray.

Given three finite sets of vectors $L, R, P \subseteq \mathbb{R}^n$ such that $L = \{l_1, \ldots, l_\ell\}$, $R = \{r_1, \ldots, r_r\}$, $P = \{p_1, \ldots, p_p\}$ and $0 \notin L \cup R$, then the triple $\mathcal{G} = (L, R, P)$ is called a *generator system* for the polyhedron

$$\text{gen}(\mathcal{G}) := \left\{ \sum_{i=1}^{\ell} \lambda_i l_i + \sum_{i=1}^{r} \rho_i r_i + \sum_{i=1}^{p} \pi_i p_i \;\middle|\; \begin{array}{l} \lambda \in \mathbb{R}^\ell, \rho \in \mathbb{R}^r_+, \pi \in \mathbb{R}^p_+, \\ \sum_{i=1}^{p} \pi_i = 1 \end{array} \right\}.$$

The polyhedron $\text{gen}(\mathcal{G})$ is empty if and only if $P = \varnothing$. If $P \neq \varnothing$, the vectors in L, R and P are lines, rays and points of $\text{gen}(\mathcal{G})$, respectively. We define an ordering '$\preceq$' on generator systems such that, for any generator systems $\mathcal{G}_1 = (L_1, R_1, P_1)$ and $\mathcal{G}_2 = (L_2, R_2, P_2)$, $\mathcal{G}_1 \preceq \mathcal{G}_2$ if and only if $L_1 \subseteq L_2$, $R_1 \subseteq R_2$ and $P_1 \subseteq P_2$; if, in addition, $\mathcal{G}_1 \neq \mathcal{G}_2$, we write $\mathcal{G}_1 \prec \mathcal{G}_2$. When $\text{gen}(\mathcal{G}) \neq \varnothing$, the generator system $\mathcal{G} = (L, R, P)$ is said to be in *minimal form* if $\#L = \dim(\text{lin.space}(\mathcal{P}))$ and there does not exist a generator system $\mathcal{G}' \prec \mathcal{G}$ such that $\text{gen}(\mathcal{G}') = \text{gen}(\mathcal{G})$.

Let $c = (\langle a, x \rangle \bowtie b)$ be a linear constraint, where $\bowtie \in \{\geq, =\}$. We say that a point (resp., a ray or a line) v *saturates* constraint c if and only if $\langle a, v \rangle = b$ (resp., $\langle a, v \rangle = 0$). For each point p and constraint system $\mathcal{C}$, we define the constraint system $\text{sat\_con}(p, \mathcal{C}) := \{ c \in \mathcal{C} \mid p \text{ saturates } c \}$; for each constraint c and generator system $\mathcal{G} = (L, R, P)$, we define the generator system $\text{sat\_gen}(c, \mathcal{G}) := (L', R', P')$, where $L' := \{ l \in L \mid l \text{ saturates } c \}$, $R' := \{ r \in R \mid r \text{ saturates } c \}$ and $P' := \{ p \in P \mid p \text{ saturates } c \}$.

A generator system $\mathcal{G} = (L, R, P)$ is in *orthogonal form* if it is in minimal form and $R \cup P \subseteq L^\perp$. All generator systems in orthogonal form describing a given polyhedron have identical sets of rays and points. A generator system in minimal form can be transformed into an equivalent system in orthogonal form by means of the well-known Gram-Shmidt method. By duality, orthogonal forms can also be defined for constraint systems. For each linear constraint $c = (\langle a, x \rangle \bowtie b)$, let $c_a = a$. A constraint system $\mathcal{C}$ is in orthogonal form if it is in minimal form and $I \subseteq E^\perp$, where $I := \{ c_a \in \mathbb{R}^n \mid c \in \text{ineq}(\mathcal{C}) \}$ and $E := \{ c_a \in \mathbb{R}^n \mid c \in \text{eq}(\mathcal{C}) \}$. All constraint systems in orthogonal form describing a given polyhedron have identical sets of inequality constraints.

3 The Standard Widening

The first widening on polyhedra was introduced in [19]. Intuitively, if $\mathcal{P}_1$ is the polyhedron obtained in the previous step of the upward iteration sequence and the current step yields polyhedron $\mathcal{P}_2$, then the widening of $\mathcal{P}_2$ with respect to $\mathcal{P}_1$ is the polyhedron defined by all the constraints of $\mathcal{P}_1$ that are satisfied by all the points of $\mathcal{P}_2$. An improvement on the above idea was defined in [23]. This operator, termed *standard widening*, has indeed been used almost universally. The specification in [23] requires that each equality constraint is split into the two corresponding inequalities; thus, for each constraint system $\mathcal{C}$, we define

$$\mathrm{repr}_{\geq}(\mathcal{C}) := \Big\{ \langle -a, x \rangle \geq -b \,\Big|\, \big(\langle a, x \rangle = b\big) \in \mathcal{C} \Big\}$$
$$\cup \Big\{ \langle a, x \rangle \geq b \,\Big|\, \big(\langle a, x \rangle \bowtie b\big) \in \mathcal{C}, \bowtie \,\in\, \{\geq, =\} \Big\}.$$

Definition 1. (Standard Widening) [23, Définition 5.3.3, p. 57] *For $i = 1$, 2, let $\mathcal{P}_i \in \mathbb{CP}_n$ be such that $\mathcal{P}_i = \mathrm{con}(\mathcal{C}_i)$ [and let $\mathcal{C}_1$ be either inconsistent or in minimal form]. The polyhedron $\mathcal{P}_1 \triangledown \mathcal{P}_2 \in \mathbb{CP}_n$ is defined by $\mathcal{P}_1 \triangledown \mathcal{P}_2 := \mathcal{P}_2$ if $\mathcal{P}_1 = \varnothing$, and $\mathcal{P}_1 \triangledown \mathcal{P}_2 := \mathrm{con}(\mathcal{C}'_1 \cup \mathcal{C}'_2)$ otherwise, where*

$$\mathcal{C}'_1 := \Big\{ \beta \in \mathrm{repr}_{\geq}(\mathcal{C}_1) \,\Big|\, \mathcal{P}_2 \subseteq \mathrm{con}(\{\beta\}) \Big\},$$
$$\mathcal{C}'_2 := \Big\{ \gamma \in \mathrm{repr}_{\geq}(\mathcal{C}_2) \,\Big|\, \exists \beta \in \mathrm{repr}_{\geq}(\mathcal{C}_1) \,.\, \mathcal{P}_1 = \mathrm{con}\big((\mathrm{repr}_{\geq}(\mathcal{C}_1) \setminus \{\beta\}) \cup \{\gamma\}\big) \Big\}.$$

The constraints in $\mathcal{C}'_1$ are those that would have been selected when using the original proposal of [19], whereas the constraints in $\mathcal{C}'_2$ are added to ensure that this widening is a well-defined operator on the domain of polyhedra (i.e., it does not depend on the particular constraint representations).

The condition in square brackets that $\mathcal{C}_1$, when consistent, should be in minimal form, was implicit from the context of [23, Définition 5.3.3, p. 57], though not explicitly present in the definition itself. Such a requirement has been sometimes neglected in later papers discussing the standard widening (and also in some implementations), but it is actually needed in order to obtain a correct definition. In fact, the following two examples show that if a redundant (i.e., not minimal) constraint description is taken into account, then not only is the widening operator not well defined (see Example 1), but also the chain condition may be violated (see Example 2).

Example 1. For $i = 1, 2$, let $\mathcal{P}_i := \mathrm{con}(\mathcal{C}_i) \in \mathbb{CP}_2$, where

$$\mathcal{C}_1 := \{x \geq 0, y \geq 0, x - y \geq 2\},$$
$$\mathcal{C}_2 := \{x \geq 2, y \geq 0\}.$$

Note that the constraint $x \geq 0$ is redundant in $\mathcal{C}_1$. By applying [23, Définition 5.3.3, p. 57] verbatim, without enforcing minimization, we would obtain the polyhedron $\mathrm{con}(\{x \geq 0, y \geq 0\})$. In contrast, by applying Definition 1, i.e., by enforcing minimization, we obtain the polyhedron $\mathrm{con}(\{y \geq 0\})$.

Example 2. For each $k \in \mathbb{N}$, consider $\mathcal{P}_k := \mathrm{con}(\mathcal{C}_k) \in \mathbb{CP}_1$, where

$$\mathcal{C}_k := \left\{ 0 \leq x, x \leq \frac{k}{k+1} \right\} \cup \{ x \leq 2 \}.$$

Note that no $\mathcal{C}_k$ is in minimal form since the constraint $x \leq 2$ is redundant in all of them. Moreover, the infinite chain constituted by the $\mathcal{P}_k$'s, that is, using an interval notation,

$$\mathcal{P}_0 = [0,0], \ \mathcal{P}_1 = \left[0, \frac{1}{2}\right], \ \mathcal{P}_2 = \left[0, \frac{2}{3}\right], \ \mathcal{P}_3 = \left[0, \frac{3}{4}\right], \ \ldots,$$

is strictly increasing. It is simple to observe that, when computing the standard widening without enforcing minimization, for the infinite chain $\mathcal{Q}_0 := \mathcal{P}_0$, $\ldots, \mathcal{Q}_{k+1} := \mathcal{Q}_k \nabla \mathcal{P}_{k+1}, \ldots$, we have $\mathcal{Q}_n = \mathcal{P}_n$ for each $n \in \mathbb{N}$, so that the chain condition is violated. This is because, by taking $\beta = (x \leq 2) \in \mathcal{C}_k$, any constraint $\gamma \in \mathcal{C}_{k+1}$ can replace β in $\mathcal{C}_k$ still obtaining polyhedron $\mathcal{P}_k$.

3.1 Implementation of the Standard Widening

The proposition below provides an algorithm for computing the standard widening of the pair of polyhedra $\mathcal{P}_1$ and $\mathcal{P}_2$ when $\mathcal{P}_1 \subseteq \mathcal{P}_2$. The idea, which was proposed in [23] and later reported in [26], is to replace the expensive test in the specification of $\mathcal{C}'_2$ in Definition 1 with an appropriate saturation condition to be checked on any generator system for $\mathcal{P}_1$. The algorithm here is an improved version over these proposals since neither the addition of the set of constraints $\mathcal{C}'_1$ as given in Definition 1 nor the splitting of equality constraints into pairs of inequalities is required. A similar result, but without the use of saturation conditions, can be found in [6, Chapter 6].

Proposition 1. *Let $\mathcal{P}_1 = \mathrm{con}(\mathcal{C}_1) = \mathrm{gen}(\mathcal{G}_1) \in \mathbb{CP}_n$ and $\mathcal{P}_2 = \mathrm{con}(\mathcal{C}_2) \in \mathbb{CP}_n$, where $\mathcal{C}_1$ is in minimal form and $\mathcal{P}_1 \subseteq \mathcal{P}_2$. Then $\mathcal{P}_1 \nabla \mathcal{P}_2 = \mathrm{con}(\mathcal{C}_s)$, where*

$$\mathcal{C}_s := \{\, \gamma \in \mathcal{C}_2 \mid \exists \beta \in \mathcal{C}_1 \,.\, \mathrm{sat\_gen}(\gamma, \mathcal{G}_1) = \mathrm{sat\_gen}(\beta, \mathcal{G}_1)\,\}.$$

The next example shows that the inclusion hypothesis $\mathcal{P}_1 \subseteq \mathcal{P}_2$ in Proposition 1, which is only implicitly present in [23,26], is vital in guaranteeing that the algorithm computes an upper approximation of $\mathcal{P}_1$ and $\mathcal{P}_2$. Note that this is independent of the two improvements mentioned above.

Example 3. Let $\mathcal{P}_1 := \mathrm{con}(\mathcal{C}_1) \in \mathbb{CP}_2$ and $\mathcal{P}_2 := \mathrm{con}(\mathcal{C}_2) \in \mathbb{CP}_2$, where

$$\mathcal{C}_1 := \{ x = 0, 0 \leq y \leq 2 \},$$
$$\mathcal{C}_2 := \{ y \geq 2 \}.$$

Then $\mathcal{P}_1 = \mathrm{gen}(\mathcal{G}_1)$, where $\mathcal{G}_1 = (\emptyset, \emptyset, P)$ and $P = \{(0,0)^\mathrm{T}, (2,0)^\mathrm{T}\}$. Note that $\mathcal{P}_1 \not\subseteq \mathcal{P}_2$. By Definition 1, we obtain $\mathcal{C}'_1 = \mathcal{C}'_2 = \emptyset$, so that $\mathcal{P}_1 \nabla \mathcal{P}_2 = \mathbb{R}^2$. Considering the constraints $\beta = (-y \geq -2) \in \mathcal{C}_1$ and $\gamma = (y \geq 2) \in \mathcal{C}_2$, we have

$$\mathrm{sat\_gen}(\beta, \mathcal{G}_1) = \bigl(\emptyset, \emptyset, \{(2,0)^\mathrm{T}\}\bigr) = \mathrm{sat\_gen}(\gamma, \mathcal{G}_1),$$

so that $\gamma \in C_s$. Thus, the result of the algorithm is $\mathcal{P}_2$, which is different from $\mathcal{P}_1 \nabla \mathcal{P}_2$ and it is not an upper approximation of $\mathcal{P}_1$.

To avoid problems such as the one above, in the following we adopt a minor variant of the classical definition of the widening operator given in Section 1 (see the footnote in [18, p. 275]).

Definition 2. *Let $L(\sqsubseteq, \sqcup)$ be a join-semi-lattice (i.e., the least upper bound $x \sqcup y$ exists for all $x, y \in L$). The operator $\nabla \colon L \times L \rightarrowtail L$ is a widening if*

1. *$x \sqsubseteq y$ implies $y \sqsubseteq x \nabla y$ for each $x, y \in L$;*
2. *for all increasing chains $y_0 \sqsubseteq y_1 \sqsubseteq \cdots$, the increasing chain defined by $x_0 := y_0$ and $x_{i+1} := x_i \nabla y_{i+1}$, for $i \in \mathbb{N}$, is not strictly increasing.*

It can be proved that, for any continuous operator $\mathcal{F} \colon L \to L$, the upward iteration sequence with widenings starting at $x_0 \in L$ and defined by

$$x_{i+1} := \begin{cases} x_i, & \text{if } \mathcal{F}(x_i) \sqsubseteq x_i; \\ x_i \nabla \bigl(x_i \sqcup \mathcal{F}(x_i)\bigr), & \text{otherwise;} \end{cases}$$

converges after a finite number of iterations [18]. Note that the widening is always applied to arguments $x = x_i$ and $y = x_i \sqcup \mathcal{F}(x_i)$ satisfying $x \sqsubseteq y$ and $x \neq y$. Thus, without loss of generality, in the following we will assume that the two argument polyhedra satisfy the strict inclusion hypothesis $\mathcal{P}_1 \subset \mathcal{P}_2$.

4 Defining More Precise Widenings

In this section, elaborating on an idea originally proposed in [7], we will present a framework for the systematic definition of new and precise widening operators for polyhedra. In particular, we will state the theoretical result that will be used to ensure that all the instances of the framework are indeed widening operators. In order to do that, we need the following definition.

Definition 3. (Number of Non-null Coordinates of a Vector) *Let $v \in \mathbb{R}^n$. We write $\kappa(v)$ to denote the number of non-null coordinates of v. For each finite set $V \subseteq \mathbb{R}^n$, we define $\kappa(V)$ to be the multiset obtained by applying κ to each of the vectors in V.*

We now define the relation $\curvearrowright \subseteq \mathbb{CP}_n \times \mathbb{CP}_n$ incorporating a notion of, so to speak, "limited growth" or "growth that cannot be indefinite" (graphically, a descending parabola).

Definition 4. *($\curvearrowright \subseteq \mathbb{CP}_n \times \mathbb{CP}_n$) Let $\mathcal{P}_1, \mathcal{P}_2 \in \mathbb{CP}_n$ be two polyhedra. Then $\mathcal{P}_1 \curvearrowright \mathcal{P}_2$ if and only if $\mathcal{P}_1 \subset \mathcal{P}_2$ and either $\mathcal{P}_1 = \varnothing$ or at least one of the following* conditions holds, where, for $i = 1, 2$, $\mathcal{P}_i$ is given by means of a constraint system $\mathcal{C}_i$ in minimal form and a generator system $\mathcal{G}_i = (L_i, R_i, P_i)$ in orthogonal form:

$$\dim(\mathcal{P}_1) < \dim(\mathcal{P}_2); \tag{1}$$
$$\dim(\text{lin.space}(\mathcal{P}_1)) < \dim(\text{lin.space}(\mathcal{P}_2)); \tag{2}$$
$$\#\mathcal{C}_1 > \#\mathcal{C}_2; \tag{3}$$
$$\#\mathcal{C}_1 = \#\mathcal{C}_2 \wedge \#P_1 > \#P_2; \tag{4}$$
$$\#\mathcal{C}_1 = \#\mathcal{C}_2 \wedge \#P_1 = \#P_2 \wedge \kappa(R_1) \gg \kappa(R_2). \tag{5}$$

Note that the '$\curvearrowright$' relation is well defined, since it does not depend on the particular constraint and generator representations chosen; in particular, the requirement that the $\mathcal{G}_i$ are in orthogonal form ensures that the computation of $\kappa(R_i)$ is not ambiguous (see Section 2).

The next result incorporates the basic idea behind the overall approach.

Theorem 1. *Let* $\mathcal{P}_0 \curvearrowright \mathcal{P}_1 \curvearrowright \cdots \curvearrowright \mathcal{P}_i \curvearrowright \cdots$ *be a chain of polyhedra in* $\mathbb{CP}_n$. *Then the chain is finite.*

The '$\curvearrowright$' relation is a variant of a similar notion of limited growth defined in [7, Theorem 3]. These two proposals are not formally comparable since neither relation refines the other. On one hand, in Definition 4, there are convergence criteria that were not considered in [7], namely conditions (3) and (5); on the other hand, to ensure that the relation satisfies the ascending chain condition, condition (4) also requires that the number of constraints is not increasing.

From a more practical point of view, the relation defined in [7] is unsatisfactory, since neither the standard widening ∇, nor the heuristics informally sketched in [7] ensure that consecutive iterates satisfy the given notion of limited growth. In summary, the overall approach does not define a widening operator in the precise sense of Definition 2 [F. Besson, personal communication, 2002]. By contrast, the introduction of condition (3) ensures that applications of ∇ always yield polyhedra that are related to previous iterates by the '$\curvearrowright$' relation.

Theorem 2. *Let* $\mathcal{P}_1 \subset \mathcal{P}_2 \in \mathbb{CP}_n$. *Then* $\mathcal{P}_1 \curvearrowright \mathcal{P}_1 \nabla \mathcal{P}_2$.

This result provides a secure foundation for the definition of new widening operators such as the one proposed here. In fact, the next result, which is an easy consequence of Theorems 1 and 2, shows how any upper bound operator can be used as the basis of a new widening that improves on the standard one.

Theorem 3. *Let* $h: \mathbb{CP}_n^2 \to \mathbb{CP}_n$ *be an upper bound operator and*

$$\mathcal{P}_1 \tilde{\nabla} \mathcal{P}_2 := \begin{cases} h(\mathcal{P}_1, \mathcal{P}_2), & \text{if } \mathcal{P}_1 \curvearrowright h(\mathcal{P}_1, \mathcal{P}_2) \subset \mathcal{P}_1 \nabla \mathcal{P}_2; \\ \mathcal{P}_1 \nabla \mathcal{P}_2, & \text{otherwise.} \end{cases}$$

Then the $\tilde{\nabla}$ *operator is a widening at least as precise as* ∇.

The above scheme is easily extended to any finite set of heuristic techniques that are upper bound operators, still obtaining a widening operator. In the following section we will consider several possible heuristic techniques: the simplest one, also adopted in [7], was actually suggested in [18]; the second one is based on an idea informally sketched in [7]; the third one is a minor variant of the extrapolation operator of [27]; the fourth and last one is new to this paper.

5 Improving the Standard Widening by Heuristics

First Technique: Do Not Widen. The simplest heuristic technique, already suggested in [18], is the one saying 'do not widen': if we are along an iteration chain having finite length, there is no need to provide further approximations, so that we can safely return the most precise upper bound $\mathcal{P}_2$ (remember that we assume $\mathcal{P}_1 \subset \mathcal{P}_2$). In our context, this is the case whenever $\mathcal{P}_1 \curvearrowright \mathcal{P}_2$. Consequently, all other techniques considered here will be applied to polyhedra $\mathcal{P}_1$ and $\mathcal{P}_2$ only if $\mathcal{P}_1 \not\curvearrowright \mathcal{P}_2$ so that, by the inclusion hypothesis, $\dim(\mathcal{P}_1) = \dim(\mathcal{P}_2)$ and $\dim\bigl(\text{lin.space}(\mathcal{P}_1)\bigr) = \dim\bigl(\text{lin.space}(\mathcal{P}_2)\bigr)$.

Second Technique: Combining Constraints. When defining a widening operator on an abstract domain, a common tactic is to split the current abstract description into several components and look at each one in isolation so as to identify what has changed with respect to the previous iteration. Intuitively, the information provided by stable components should be propagated to the next iteration, whereas the information of components that have changed should be extrapolated according to a hypothetical "change pattern". For instance, in the case of the widening in [19], each element of a constraint system is regarded as a separate component and the extrapolation just forgets about the constraints that have changed. The second heuristics, which is a variant of a similar one sketched in [7], can be seen as an application of the above approach, where instead of the constraints we consider the points in the generator system describing the polyhedron of the previous iteration. When using the standard widening it may happen that points that are common to the boundaries[3] of $\mathcal{P}_1$ and $\mathcal{P}_2$ (and, hence, likely to be an invariant feature along the chain of polyhedra) will not lie on the boundary of the widened polyhedron. This is the case, for instance, for the two points p and q in Figure 1. For each such point, the technique forces the presence of an inequality constraint that is saturated by the point, so that it lies on the boundary of the result.

Definition 5. **(Combining Constraints)** *Let $\mathcal{P}_1, \mathcal{P}_2 \in \mathbb{CP}_n$ be two polyhedra such that $\mathcal{P}_1 \subset \mathcal{P}_2$, aff.hull$(\mathcal{P}_1)$ = aff.hull$(\mathcal{P}_2)$ and lin.space$(\mathcal{P}_1)$ = lin.space$(\mathcal{P}_2)$. Let $\mathcal{P}_1 = \text{gen}(\mathcal{G}_1)$, $\mathcal{P}_2 = \text{con}(\mathcal{C}_2)$ and $\mathcal{P}_1 \nabla \mathcal{P}_2 = \text{con}(\mathcal{C}_\nabla)$, where the constraint*

---

[3] In this context, a "boundary point" is any point of $\mathcal{P} \cap \text{lin.space}(\mathcal{P})^\perp$ which is not a relatively interior point for $\mathcal{P}$. Namely, we abstract from both the affine hull and the lineality space of the polyhedron.

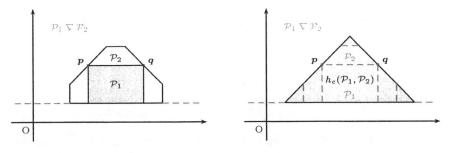

Fig. 1. The heuristics h_c improving on the standard widening

systems $\mathcal{C}_2$ and $\mathcal{C}_\nabla$ and the generator system $\mathcal{G}_1 = (L_1, R_1, P_1)$ are in orthogonal form. Let also

$$\mathcal{C}_\oplus := \left\{ \oplus(\mathcal{C}_p) \;\middle|\; \begin{array}{l} p \in P_1, \mathrm{sat\_con}(p, \mathrm{ineq}(\mathcal{C}_\nabla)) = \varnothing, \\ \mathcal{C}_p = \mathrm{sat\_con}(p, \mathrm{ineq}(\mathcal{C}_2)) \neq \varnothing \end{array} \right\},$$

where the operator $\oplus$ computes a convex combination of a non-empty set of linear inequality constraints (i.e., of the corresponding coefficients), returning another linear inequality constraint. Then $h_c(\mathcal{P}_1, \mathcal{P}_2) := \mathrm{con}(\mathcal{C}_\nabla \cup \mathcal{C}_\oplus)$.

Since the operator h_c is only defined for arguments having the same affine hull and lineality space, by requiring orthogonal forms we ensure that the result does not depend on the considered representations.

Note that the particular convex combination encoded by function $\oplus$ is deliberately left unspecified so as to allow for a very liberal definition of h_c that still possesses the required properties. For instance, in [7] it was argued that a good heuristics could be obtained by letting $\oplus$ compute a normed linear combination (i.e., a sort of average) of the chosen constraints. Another legitimate choice would be to "bless" one of the constraints in $\mathcal{C}_p$ and forget all the others. In both cases, by keeping just one constraint for each point p, we hopefully reduce the cardinality of the constraint system describing the result, so that it is more likely that condition (3) of Definition 4 will be met. Actually, this attempt at reducing the number of constraints is the main difference between the technique presented in Definition 5 and the extrapolation operator proposed in [29, Section 3.3], which could itself be included in the current framework as a more refined widening heuristics.

Third Technique: Evolving Points. Our third heuristic technique is a variant of the extrapolation operator '$\propto$' defined in [27]. The technique examines each new point p_2 of the polyhedron $\mathcal{P}_2$ as if it was obtained from each old point p_1 of the polyhedron $\mathcal{P}_1$: we say that p_2 is an evolution of p_1. The extrapolation is defined as continuing this evolution toward infinity, therefore generating the ray having direction $p_2 - p_1$. The new ray will subsume point p_2, so that it is likely that the convergence condition (4) of Definition 4 will be met. Notice that any ray that violates a constraint of the standard widening is dropped.

Definition 6. (Evolving Points) Let $\mathcal{P}_1, \mathcal{P}_2 \in \mathbb{CP}_n$ be such that $\mathcal{P}_1 \subset \mathcal{P}_2$ and $\mathrm{lin.space}(\mathcal{P}_1) = \mathrm{lin.space}(\mathcal{P}_2)$. For each $i = 1, 2$, consider a generator system $\mathcal{G}_i = (L_i, R_i, P_i)$ in orthogonal form such that $\mathcal{P}_i = \mathrm{gen}(\mathcal{G}_i)$ and let

$$R := \{ \boldsymbol{p}_2 - \boldsymbol{p}_1 \mid \boldsymbol{p}_1 \in P_1, \boldsymbol{p}_2 \in P_2 \setminus P_1 \}.$$

Then we define $h_p(\mathcal{P}_1, \mathcal{P}_2) := \mathrm{gen}\bigl((L_2, R_2 \cup R, P_2)\bigr) \cap (\mathcal{P}_1 \nabla \mathcal{P}_2)$.

Since the operator h_p is only defined for arguments having the same lineality space, by requiring orthogonal forms we ensure that the result does not depend on the particular generator system representations considered.

The difference with respect to the extrapolation operator '$\propto$' is that we do not require the two points to lie on the same 1-dimensional face of $\mathcal{P}_2$; moreover, the result of '$\propto$' may be less precise than the standard widening. Note that, as in the 'combining constraints' technique, it is possible to add just a single ray which is a convex combination of the rays in R instead of the complete set R; yielding a more precise widening technique. However, this technique and the one defined by the h_p operator are incomparable with respect to the '$\frown$' relation and one can fail the '$\frown$' convergence criteria when the other succeeds.

Fourth Technique: Evolving Rays. We now introduce a fourth widening heuristics that tries to extrapolate the way rays have evolved since the last iteration. The technique examines each new ray $\boldsymbol{r}_2$ of the polyhedron $\mathcal{P}_2$ as if it was generated by rotation of each old ray $\boldsymbol{r}_1$ of the polyhedron $\mathcal{P}_1$: we say that $\boldsymbol{r}_2$ is an evolution of $\boldsymbol{r}_1$. The extrapolation is defined as continuing this evolution until one or more of the non-null coordinates of ray $\boldsymbol{r}_2$ become zero. This way, it is likely that the convergence condition (5) of Definition 4 will be met. Intuitively, the new ray will reach one of the boundaries of the orthant where $\boldsymbol{r}_2$ lies, without trespassing it.

Definition 7. (evolve) *The function* evolve: $\mathbb{R}^n \times \mathbb{R}^n \to \mathbb{R}^n$ *is defined, for each* $\boldsymbol{v}, \boldsymbol{w} \in \mathbb{R}^n$, *as* evolve$(\boldsymbol{v}, \boldsymbol{w}) := \boldsymbol{v}'$, *where*

$$v'_i := \begin{cases} 0, & \text{if } \exists j \in \{1, \ldots, n\} \cdot (v_i \cdot w_j - v_j \cdot w_i) \cdot v_i \cdot v_j < 0; \\ v_i, & \text{otherwise.} \end{cases}$$

To understand this definition consider a pair of coordinates i and j and suppose that the vectors $\boldsymbol{v}$ and $\boldsymbol{w}$ are projected onto the two-dimensional plane defined by i (for the first coordinate) and j (for the second coordinate). Then, we identify the direction of the rotation of the vector $(v_i, v_j)^\mathrm{T}$ with respect to the vector $(w_i, w_j)^\mathrm{T}$ by using the well-known cross-product test [12, Chapter 35]; the direction is clockwise if cw $:= v_i \cdot w_j - v_j \cdot w_i > 0$ and anti-clockwise when cw < 0. Moreover, vector $(v_i, v_j)^\mathrm{T}$ lies inside the first or third quadrant when $q := v_i \cdot v_j > 0$ and it lies inside the second or fourth quadrant when $q < 0$. Then, the condition cw $\cdot q < 0$ states that the evolution is clockwise and $(v_i, v_j)^\mathrm{T}$ is in the second or fourth quadrant or the evolution is anti-clockwise and $(v_i, v_j)^\mathrm{T}$ is in the first or third quadrant: in all these cases, the evolution is toward the j

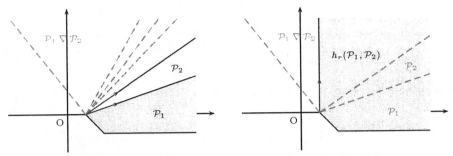

Fig. 2. The heuristics h_r improving on the standard widening

axis. Thus, for a fixed i, if there exists j such that the evolution is toward the j axis, then we define $v'_i = 0$. Otherwise, we let $v'_i = v_i$. We are now ready to define our last widening heuristics.

Definition 8. (Evolving Rays) *Let $\mathcal{P}_1, \mathcal{P}_2 \in \mathbb{CP}_n$ be such that $\mathcal{P}_1 \subset \mathcal{P}_2$ and* lin.space($\mathcal{P}_1$) = lin.space($\mathcal{P}_2$). *For each $i = 1, 2$, consider a generator system $\mathcal{G}_i = (L_i, R_i, P_i)$ in orthogonal form such that $\mathcal{P}_i = \text{gen}(\mathcal{G}_i)$ and let*

$$R := \{\, \text{evolve}(r_2, r_1) \mid r_1 \in R_1, r_2 \in R_2 \setminus R_1 \,\}.$$

Then we define $h_r(\mathcal{P}_1, \mathcal{P}_2) := \text{gen}\big((L_2, R_2 \cup R, P_2)\big) \cap (\mathcal{P}_1 \nabla \mathcal{P}_2)$.

Figure 2 shows an example where the 'evolving rays' technique is able to improve on the standard widening. It should be noted that the boundary of $\mathcal{P}_1 \nabla \mathcal{P}_2$ contains the intersection of the boundaries of $\mathcal{P}_1$ and $\mathcal{P}_2$, so that the 'combining constraints' technique is not applicable. Neither the 'evolving points' technique can be applied, since $\mathcal{P}_1$ and $\mathcal{P}_2$ have the same set of non-redundant points. Besides having the same affine hull and lineality space, polyhedra $\mathcal{P}_1$, $\mathcal{P}_2$ and $h_r(\mathcal{P}_1, \mathcal{P}_2)$, are defined by the same number of non-redundant constraints and points, so that $\mathcal{P}_1 \curvearrowright h_r(\mathcal{P}_1, \mathcal{P}_2)$ holds by condition (5) of Definition 4.

The New Widening. In order to use the above heuristic techniques in the general framework we have defined in the previous section, each of them needs to be an upper bound operator. This is trivial for the first technique. The same result holds, by construction, for the other three heuristics.

Proposition 2. *Let $\mathcal{P}_1, \mathcal{P}_2 \in \mathbb{CP}_n$, where $\mathcal{P}_1 \subset \mathcal{P}_2$, aff.hull($\mathcal{P}_1$) = aff.hull($\mathcal{P}_2$) and* lin.space($\mathcal{P}_1$) = lin.space($\mathcal{P}_2$). *Then, for each technique $h \in \{h_c, h_p, h_r\}$, $\mathcal{P}_2 \subseteq h(\mathcal{P}_1, \mathcal{P}_2) \subseteq \mathcal{P}_1 \nabla \mathcal{P}_2$.*

The new widening operator tries to apply the four heuristics, stopping as soon as we obtain a result which ensures convergence and actually improves on the standard widening. As far as the choice of the particular order of application is concerned, in principle, the more precise heuristic techniques should be tried before the others; thus, the 'do not widen' technique has to be tried first. A preliminary experimental evaluation (which is not reported here) has shown that better results are obtained if the 'combining constraints' technique is tried before the 'evolving points' and 'evolving rays' techniques, whereas the ordering of the latter two is almost immaterial.

Definition 9. (The $\hat{\nabla}$ Widening) *Let $\mathcal{P}_1, \mathcal{P}_2 \in \mathbb{CP}_n$, where $\mathcal{P}_1 \subset \mathcal{P}_2$. Then*

$$\mathcal{P}_1 \hat{\nabla} \mathcal{P}_2 := \begin{cases} \mathcal{P}_2, & \text{if } \mathcal{P}_1 \curvearrowright \mathcal{P}_2; \\ h_c(\mathcal{P}_1, \mathcal{P}_2), & \text{if } \mathcal{P}_1 \curvearrowright h_c(\mathcal{P}_1, \mathcal{P}_2) \subset \mathcal{P}_1 \nabla \mathcal{P}_2; \\ h_p(\mathcal{P}_1, \mathcal{P}_2), & \text{if } \mathcal{P}_1 \curvearrowright h_p(\mathcal{P}_1, \mathcal{P}_2) \subset \mathcal{P}_1 \nabla \mathcal{P}_2; \\ h_r(\mathcal{P}_1, \mathcal{P}_2), & \text{if } \mathcal{P}_1 \curvearrowright h_r(\mathcal{P}_1, \mathcal{P}_2) \subset \mathcal{P}_1 \nabla \mathcal{P}_2; \\ \mathcal{P}_1 \nabla \mathcal{P}_2, & \text{otherwise.} \end{cases}$$

It can be seen that $\hat{\nabla}$ is an instance of the framework proposed in the previous section: in particular, when applying the first heuristics, the omission of the applicability condition $\mathcal{P}_2 \subset \mathcal{P}_1 \nabla \mathcal{P}_2$ is a simple and inconsequential optimization. Thus the following result is a direct consequence of Theorem 3 and Proposition 2.

Proposition 3. *The $\hat{\nabla}$ operator is a widening at least as precise as ∇.*

Proposition 3 is not strong enough to ensure that the final results of upward iteration sequences using the new widening are *uniformly* more precise than those obtained by using the standard widening. It is well known, in fact, that the standard widening (and thus the new widening) is not a monotonic operator [19]. However, the experimental evaluation of the next section shows that, in practice, precision degradations are actually rare.

6 Experimental Evaluation

We have extended the *Parma Polyhedra Library* (PPL) [2,4], a modern C++ library for the manipulation of convex polyhedra, with a prototype implementation of the widening of Definition 9. In particular, the operator ⊕ used for 'combining constraints' is the simple (i.e., non-normed) average: as the library uses arbitrary precision integers, the computation of norms may generate constraints having huge coefficients and it is therefore avoided. The PPL has been integrated with the CHINA analyzer [1] for the purpose of detecting linear argument size relations [5]. Our benchmark suite consists of 361 Prolog programs, ranging from small synthetic benchmarks to real-world applications. They define 23279 predicates whose analysis with CHINA requires the direct use of a widening and about as many predicates for which no widening is used. In this respect, it must be noted that CHINA employs a sophisticated chaotic iteration strategy proposed in [8,9] that, among other benefits, greatly reduces the number of widenings' applications.[4] This is an important point, since it would be quite easy

---

[4] CHINA uses the recursive fixpoint iteration strategy on the weak topological ordering defined by partitioning of the call graph into strongly-connected subcomponents [9].

to improve on an iteration strategy applying widenings "everywhere or improperly" [8]. Also note that the polyhedra yielded by application of each of the two widening operators are strengthened by enforcing non-negativity constraints on all of the vector space dimensions, since the sizes of arguments cannot be negative: this further improvement is implemented by adopting the 'widening up to' technique of [24, 26]. The results of this experimental evaluation are summarized in Table 1, where each row corresponds to a different choice for the value of the extrapolation threshold k, controlling the delay before the applications of both the standard and the new widening operators.

Table 1. Precision and time comparisons

	Precision						Time			
	# programs			# predicates			std ∇_k		new $\hat{\nabla}_k$	
k (delay)	improve	degr	incomp	improve	degr	incomp	all	top 20	all	top 20
0	121	0	2	1340	3	2	1.00	0.72	1.05	0.77
1	34	0	0	273	0	0	1.09	0.79	1.11	0.80
2	29	0	0	222	0	0	1.16	0.83	1.18	0.84
3	28	0	0	160	0	0	1.23	0.88	1.25	0.89
4	25	0	2	126	2	0	1.32	0.95	1.34	0.95
10	25	0	0	124	0	0	1.82	1.23	1.85	1.24

The part of the table headed 'Precision' shows the obtained precision improvements and degradations (in the columns labeled 'improve' and 'degr', respectively), both in terms of the number of programs and the number of predicates affected; in the columns labeled 'incomp' we report those cases where incomparable results have been obtained. For $k = 0$, we observe a precision improvement on one third of the considered programs; not surprisingly, fewer improvements are obtained for higher values of k, but we still have an improvement on 7% of the benchmarks when considering $k = 10$. While confirming, as informally argued in [5], that for this particular analysis there is little incentive in using values of k greater than 4, our experiments show that the new widening captures growth patterns that do happen in practice and that for the standard widening (no matter how delayed) are out of reach. This is important since the results obtained in practice are, besides correctness, what really matters when evaluating widening operators. The experimentation also shows that the idea of delaying the widening [13] maintains its validity: even though the new widening is less sensitive to the amount of delay applied, delaying still improves some of the results.

The part of the table headed 'Time' shows the sum, over all the benchmarks, of the fixpoint computation times. This is expressed as a proportion of the time spent when using the standard widening with $k = 0$. Since smaller benchmarks may affect the outcome of this summarization, in the columns labeled 'top 20' we also show the same values but restricted to the 20 benchmarks whose analysis takes more time. It can be seen that the new widening has a negative, but relatively modest impact on efficiency, which anyway is smaller than the cost of increasing the value of k. When looking at these time results, it should be considered that we are comparing a prototype implementation of the new widening with respect to a rather optimized implementation of the standard widening. It is also important to remark that the good performance degradation observed for both widenings when increasing the value of k is essentially due to the iteration strategy employed by CHINA and should not be expected to automatically carry over to systems using other fixpoint computation techniques.

7 Conclusion

For the domain of convex polyhedra, the convergence of the fixpoint computation sequence has been typically obtained thanks to the widening operator proposed by Cousot and Halbwachs. Though remarkably precise, this operator does not fulfill the requirements of a number of applications in the fields of analysis and verification that are particularly sensitive to the precision of the deduced numerical information. In this paper, elaborating on an idea proposed in [7], we have defined a framework for the systematic specification of new widening operators improving on the precision of the standard widening. The framework allows any upper bound operator on the domain of convex polyhedra to be transformed into a proper widening operator, therefore ensuring the termination of the computation. We have instantiated the framework with a selection of extrapolation operators, some of which embody improvements of heuristics already proposed in the literature. A first experimental evaluation has yielded promising results.

Acknowledgments

We would like to express our gratitude to Frédéric Besson for his useful comments and observations on the ideas sketched in [7]; Fred Mesnard for the information and the discussions we had with him about the impact of precision on termination inference for Prolog programs; and the reviewers for their careful comments that helped us improve the paper.

References

1. R. Bagnara. *Data-Flow Analysis for Constraint Logic-Based Languages*. PhD thesis, Dipartimento di Informatica, Università di Pisa, Pisa, Italy, March 1997. Printed as Report TD-1/97.
2. R. Bagnara, P. M. Hill, E. Ricci, and E. Zaffanella. *The Parma Polyhedra Library User's Manual*. Department of Mathematics, University of Parma, Parma, Italy, release 0.4 edition, July 2002. Available at http://www.cs.unipr.it/ppl/.
3. R. Bagnara, P. M. Hill, E. Ricci, and E. Zaffanella. Precise widening operators for convex polyhedra. Quaderno 312, Dipartimento di Matematica, Università di Parma, Italy, 2003. Available at http://www.cs.unipr.it/Publications/.

4. R. Bagnara, E. Ricci, E. Zaffanella, and P. M. Hill. Possibly not closed convex polyhedra and the Parma Polyhedra Library. In M. V. Hermenegildo and G. Puebla, editors, *Static Analysis: Proceedings of the 9th International Symposium*, volume 2477 of *Lecture Notes in Computer Science*, pages 213–229, Madrid, Spain, 2002. Springer-Verlag, Berlin.
5. F. Benoy and A. King. Inferring argument size relationships with CLP($\mathcal{R}$). In J. P. Gallagher, editor, *Logic Program Synthesis and Transformation: Proceedings of the 6th International Workshop*, volume 1207 of *Lecture Notes in Computer Science*, pages 204–223, Stockholm, Sweden, 1997. Springer-Verlag, Berlin.
6. P. M. Benoy. *Polyhedral Domains for Abstract Interpretation in Logic Programming*. PhD thesis, Computing Laboratory, University of Kent, Canterbury, Kent, UK, January 2002.
7. F. Besson, T. P. Jensen, and J.-P. Talpin. Polyhedral analysis for synchronous languages. In A. Cortesi and G. Filé, editors, *Static Analysis: Proceedings of the 6th International Symposium*, volume 1694 of *Lecture Notes in Computer Science*, pages 51–68, Venice, Italy, 1999. Springer-Verlag, Berlin.
8. F. Bourdoncle. Efficient chaotic iteration strategies with widenings. In D. Bjørner, M. Broy, and I. V. Pottosin, editors, *Proceedings of the International Conference on "Formal Methods in Programming and Their Applications"*, volume 735 of *Lecture Notes in Computer Science*, pages 128–141, Academgorodok, Novosibirsk, Russia, 1993. Springer-Verlag, Berlin.
9. F. Bourdoncle. Sémantiques des langages impératifs d'ordre supérieur et interprétation abstraite. PRL Research Report 22, DEC Paris Research Laboratory, 1993.
10. T. Bultan, R. Gerber, and W. Pugh. Model-checking concurrent systems with unbounded integer variables: Symbolic representations, approximations, and experimental results. *ACM Transactions on Programming Languages and Systems*, 21(4):747–789, 1999.
11. M. A. Colón and H. B. Sipma. Synthesis of linear ranking functions. In T. Margaria and W. Yi, editors, *Tools and Algorithms for Construction and Analysis of Systems, 7th International Conference, TACAS 2001*, volume 2031 of *Lecture Notes in Computer Science*, pages 67–81, Genova, Italy, 2001. Springer-Verlag, Berlin.
12. T. H. Cormen, T. E. Leiserson, and R. L. Rivest. *Introduction to Algorithms*. The MIT Press, Cambridge, Mass., 1990.
13. P. Cousot. Semantic foundations of program analysis. In S. S. Muchnick and N. D. Jones, editors, *Program Flow Analysis: Theory and Applications*, chapter 10, pages 303–342. Prentice-Hall, Inc., Englewood Cliffs, New Jersey, 1981.
14. P. Cousot, editor. *Static Analysis: 8th International Symposium, SAS 2001*, volume 2126 of *Lecture Notes in Computer Science*, Paris, France, 2001. Springer-Verlag, Berlin.
15. P. Cousot and R. Cousot. Static determination of dynamic properties of programs. In B. Robinet, editor, *Proceedings of the Second International Symposium on Programming*, pages 106–130. Dunod, Paris, France, 1976.
16. P. Cousot and R. Cousot. Abstract interpretation: A unified lattice model for static analysis of programs by construction or approximation of fixpoints. In *Proceedings of the Fourth Annual ACM Symposium on Principles of Programming Languages*, pages 238–252, New York, 1977. ACM Press.
17. P. Cousot and R. Cousot. Abstract interpretation frameworks. *Journal of Logic and Computation*, 2(4):511–547, 1992.

18. P. Cousot and R. Cousot. Comparing the Galois connection and widening/narrowing approaches to abstract interpretation. In M. Bruynooghe and M. Wirsing, editors, *Proceedings of the 4th International Symposium on Programming Language Implementation and Logic Programming*, volume 631 of *Lecture Notes in Computer Science*, pages 269–295, Leuven, Belgium, 1992. Springer-Verlag, Berlin.
19. P. Cousot and N. Halbwachs. Automatic discovery of linear restraints among variables of a program. In *Conference Record of the Fifth Annual ACM Symposium on Principles of Programming Languages*, pages 84–96, Tucson, Arizona, 1978. ACM Press.
20. G. Delzanno and A. Podelski. Model checking in CLP. In R. Cleaveland, editor, *Tools and Algorithms for Construction and Analysis of Systems, 5th International Conference, TACAS'99*, volume 1579 of *Lecture Notes in Computer Science*, pages 223–239, Amsterdam, The Netherlands, 1999. Springer-Verlag, Berlin.
21. N. Dershowitz and Z. Manna. Proving termination with multiset orderings. *Communications of the ACM*, 22(8):465–476, 1979.
22. N. Dor, M. Rodeh, and S. Sagiv. Cleanness checking of string manipulations in C programs via integer analysis. In Cousot [14], pages 194–212.
23. N. Halbwachs. *Détermination Automatique de Relations Linéaires Vérifiées par les Variables d'un Programme*. Thèse de $3^{\text{ème}}$ cycle d'informatique, Université scientifique et médicale de Grenoble, Grenoble, France, March 1979.
24. N. Halbwachs. Delay analysis in synchronous programs. In C. Courcoubetis, editor, *Computer Aided Verification: Proceedings of the 5th International Conference*, volume 697 of *Lecture Notes in Computer Science*, pages 333–346, Elounda, Greece, 1993. Springer-Verlag, Berlin.
25. N. Halbwachs, Y.-E. Proy, and P. Raymond. Verification of linear hybrid systems by means of convex approximations. In B. Le Charlier, editor, *Static Analysis: Proceedings of the 1st International Symposium*, volume 864 of *Lecture Notes in Computer Science*, pages 223–237, Namur, Belgium, 1994. Springer-Verlag, Berlin.
26. N. Halbwachs, Y.-E. Proy, and P. Roumanoff. Verification of real-time systems using linear relation analysis. *Formal Methods in System Design*, 11(2):157–185, 1997.
27. T. A. Henzinger and P.-H. Ho. A note on abstract interpretation strategies for hybrid automata. In P. J. Antsaklis, W. Kohn, A. Nerode, and S. Sastry, editors, *Hybrid Systems II*, volume 999 of *Lecture Notes in Computer Science*, pages 252–264. Springer-Verlag, Berlin, 1995.
28. T. A. Henzinger, P.-H. Ho, and H. Wong-Toi. HYTECH: A model checker for hybrid systems. *Software Tools for Technology Transfer*, 1(1+2):110–122, 1997.
29. T. A. Henzinger, J. Preussig, and H. Wong-Toi. Some lessons from the HYTECH experience. In *Proceedings of the 40th Annual Conference on Decision and Control*, pages 2887–2892. IEEE Computer Society Press, 2001.
30. Z. Manna, N. S. Bjørner, A. Browne, M. Colón, B. Finkbeiner, M. Pichora, H. B. Sipma, and T. E. Uribe. An update on STeP: Deductive-algorithmic verification of reactive systems. In R. Berghammer and Y. Lakhnech, editors, *Tool Support for System Specification, Development and Verification*, Advances in Computing Sciences. Springer-Verlag, Berlin, 1999.
31. F. Mesnard and U. Neumerkel. Applying static analysis techniques for inferring termination conditions of logic programs. In Cousot [14], pages 93–110.
32. W. Pugh. A practical algorithm for exact array dependence analysis. *Communications of the ACM*, 35(8):102–114, 1992.

Cartesian Factoring of Polyhedra in Linear Relation Analysis

Nicolas Halbwachs, David Merchat, and Catherine Parent-Vigouroux

Vérimag*, Grenoble - France
{Nicolas.Halbwachs,David.Merchat,Catherine.Parent}@imag.fr

Abstract. Linear Relation Analysis [CH78] suffers from the cost of operations on convex polyhedra, which can be exponential with the number of involved variables. In order to reduce this cost, we propose to detect when a polyhedron is a Cartesian product of polyhedra of lower dimensions, i.e., when groups of variables are unrelated with each other. Classical operations are adapted to work on such factored polyhedra. Our implementation shows encouraging experimental results.

1 Introduction

Linear Relation Analysis [CH78,Hal79] is one of the very first applications of abstract interpretation [CC77], and remains one of the most powerful and effective techniques for analyzing properties of numerical programs. It was applied in various domains like compile-time error detection [DRS01], program parallelization [IJT91], automatic verification [HPR97,HHWT97] and formal proof [BBC+00,BBM97].

In its original setting, Linear Relation Analysis was designed to discover linear inequalities (or convex polyhedra) invariantly holding at each control point of a sequential program. These polyhedra are built by forward and/or backward propagation of predicates along the paths of the control graph of the program. These propagations involve the computation of classical operations over convex polyhedra: intersection, least upper bound (convex hull), affine transformation, projection, check for inclusion and emptiness, and widening to enforce termination. Moreover, it is very important that the representation of polyhedra be kept minimal. All these operations are easy, provided the *double-description* of polyhedra [MRTT53] is available: it consists in characterizing a polyhedron both as the set of solutions of a system of linear inequalities and as the convex hull of a finite system of generators (vertices and rays). Knowing both these representations also allows each of them to be minimized, i.e., discarding irrelevant

---

* Vérimag is a joint laboratory of Université Joseph Fourier, CNRS and INPG associated with IMAG.

(redundant) inequalities and generators. Several libraries for polyhedra manipulation are available [Wil93][1], [CL98][2], [HPR97], [BRZH02][3].

The problem with the double-description is that the size of each description can grow exponentially with the dimension of the space (number of variables): an n-dimensional hypercube is defined by $2n$ inequalities, but has 2^n vertices; the converse can happen, since the descriptions are completely dual.

As a consequence, the dimension of the space is an important limitation to the application of Linear Relation Analysis to real-life examples. In program verification, a classical way of decreasing the number of variables, consists of applying first a *program slicing* [Tip95]: it consists in analyzing variables dependencies to discard variables which cannot influence the property to be verified. However, precise slicing is not always easy, and the approach works only when the goal of the analysis is precisely known (e.g., a given property to verify) to be used as the source of the slicing.

In this paper, we propose a complementary approach to reduce the number of variables. It consists in detecting that a polyhedron can be factored as a Cartesian product of polyhedra in smaller dimensions. This situation, which occurs very often in real-life examples, means that the set of variables can be partitioned into subsets, such that variables belonging to different subsets are independent, i.e., not related by any inequality in the polyhedron. In order to take advantage of such factorings, they must be detected, and operations should be, as far as possible, performed on factored arguments.

Compared with slicing, our approach will detect variables independence, not in an absolute way, but with respect to the analysis which is performed: some variables may be related by the concrete semantics of the program, but these relations may be ignored by the Linear Relation Analysis, because of approximation. However, notice that in this paper, we consider factoring without additional loss of information. Of course, one could also decide to abstract away some relations in order to obtain a finer factoring and better performances.

2 Convex Polyhedra

2.1 The Double Description

Let $\mathcal{N}$ be either $\mathbb{R}$ or $\mathbb{Q}$. A closed convex polyhedron — or simply, a polyhedron — P in $\mathcal{N}^n$ can be characterized by a $m \times n$ matrix A and a m-vector B, such that

$$P = \{X \in \mathcal{N}^n \mid AX \leq B\}$$

---

[1] See also http://www.ee.byu.edu:8080/~wilde/polyhedra.html.
[2] See also http://icps.u-strasbg.fr/polylib/ and
   http://www.irisa.fr/polylib.
[3] See also http://www.cs.unipr.it/ppl/.

(A, B) is the *constraint description* of P. A polyhedron P can be also characterized by two finite sets $V = \{v_i\}$, $R = \{r_j\}$ of n-vectors, such that

$$P = \left\{ \sum_{i=1}^{|V|} \lambda_i v_i + \sum_{j=1}^{|R|} \mu_j r_j \;\bigg|\; \lambda_i \geq 0, \mu_j \geq 0, \sum_{i=1}^{|V|} \lambda_i = 1 \right\}$$

(V, R) is the *system of generators* of P [4]; V is the set of *vertices*, R is the set of *rays*. This description expresses that any point in P is the sum of a *convex combination* of vertices and a *positive combination* of rays. Fig. 1 illustrates this double description.

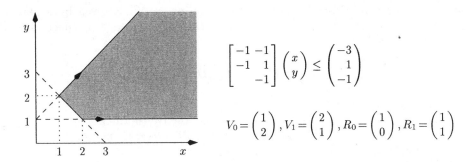

Fig. 1. Double description of a polyhedron

Chernikova's algorithm [Che68] improved by Leverge [LeV92,Wil93] performs the translation from one description to the other. An important feature of this algorithm is that the resulting description is minimal, in the sense that it does not contain any redundant element: A constraint, a vertex, or a ray is redundant if removing it does not change the polyhedron. In the example of Fig. 1, $x \geq 0$ would be a redundant constraint, $(2,2)$ would be a redundant vertex, and $(2,1)$ would be a redundant ray.

Notations: In the rest of the paper, we will generally assimilate a polyhedron with its system of constraints, for instance by noting $P \wedge P'$ the set of solutions of the conjunction of the constraints of P and P'. Notice that we will use this notation even if the constraints of P and P' do not involve the same set of variables, meaning that the conjunction concerns the union of the variables of P and P'.

2.2 Operations on Polyhedra

As soon as both descriptions are available, all operations needed for program analysis are available:

---

[4] The system of generators of the empty polyhedron is $(\emptyset, \emptyset)$.

Intersection: Let (A, B), (A', B') be the respective systems of constraints of P_1 and P_2, then $\left(\begin{bmatrix} A \\ A' \end{bmatrix}, \begin{pmatrix} B \\ B' \end{pmatrix} \right)$ (the concatenation, or conjunction, of the systems of constraints) is a system of constraints of $P \cap P'$. Of course, this conjunction can result in redundant constraints.

Convex hull: The convex hull is used as an approximation of union, which is not an internal operation on polyhedra (it does not preserve convexity). The convex hull of two polyhedra is the least convex polyhedron which contains both of them. Let (V, R), (V', R') be the respective systems of generators of P_1 and P_2, then $(V \cup V', R \cup R')$ is a system of generators of their convex hull, noted $P \sqcup P'$. Again, this system of generators is generally not minimal.

Affine transformation: An affine transformation in $\mathcal{N}^n$ is given by a pair (C, D), where C is a $n \times n$ matrix and D is a n-vector. The image of a polyhedron P by an affine transformation (C, D) is

$$CP + D = \{CX + D \mid X \in P\}$$

Then, if (V, R) is a system of generators of P, $(CV + D, CR)$ is a system of generators of $CP + D$. When C is invertible, the transformation can also be done on P's system of constraints, and the affine transformation preserves the minimality of both descriptions.

Existential quantification: We note $\exists x_j, P$ the results of eliminating the j-th variable in P by the *Fourier-Motzkin procedure*: it consists of replacing each constraint $A_i X \leq B$ where $A_{ij} > 0$ by its positive combinations with all constraints $A_k X \leq B$ where $A_{kj} < 0$ to get a null coefficient for X_j (i.e., $(A_{ij}.A_k - A_{kj}.A_i)X \leq (A_{ij}.B_k - A_{kj}.B_i))$. Existential quantification of x_j can be easily done, also, on systems of generators, simply by adding u_j and $-u_j$ as new rays, where u_j is the jth unit vector of $\mathcal{N}^n$.

Test for inclusion: Let (V, R) be a system of generators of P, and (A, B) be a system of constraints of P'. Then $P \subseteq P'$ if and only if $Av \leq B$, for all $v \in V$, and $Ar \leq 0$, for all $r \in R$.

Test for emptiness: A polyhedron is empty if and only if its set of vertices is empty.

Widening: The widening is used to extrapolate the limit of an increasing sequence of polyhedra. There is some freedom in defining such an operator, we use the one proposed in [Hal79]. Intuitively, the system of constraints of the widening $P \nabla P'$ is the subset of P's constraints still satisfied by P'. Now, since this definition relies on the system of constraints of P, which is not canonical in general, the actual definition is more complex: a constraint of $P \nabla P'$ is a constraint of P' which is *mutually redundant*[5] with a constraint of P (meaning that either it is a constraint of P, or it can *replace* a constraint of P without changing it). Here again, both descriptions are used to perform this operation.

---

[5] Two constraints are mutually redundant in a system of constraints if you can replace each of them by the other without changing the set of solutions.

3 Factoring of Polyhedra

Let I be a subset of $\{1\ldots n\}$. We note $P{\downarrow}I$ the projection of the polyhedron P on variables with indices in I (i.e., the result, in $\mathcal{N}^{|I|}$ of the existential quantification of all variables with indices outside I).

Let $(I_1, I_2, \ldots I_\ell)$ be a partition of $\{1\ldots n\}$. We say that a polyhedron P *can be factored according to* $(I_1, I_2, \ldots I_\ell)$ if and only if

$$P = P{\downarrow}I_1 \times P{\downarrow}I_2 \times \ldots P{\downarrow}I_\ell$$

A matrix A is *block-diagonalizable* according to a partition $(I_1, I_2, \ldots I_\ell)$ if for each of its row A_i there is one $k_i \in \{1..\ell\}$ such that $\{j \mid A_i^j \neq 0\} \subseteq I_{k_i}$.

Some obvious facts:

f1. for any polyhedron P, there is a greatest partition $(I_1, I_2, \ldots I_\ell)$ according to which P can be factored (possibly the trivial partition, with $\ell = 1$).

f2. for any matrix A, there is a greatest partition $(I_1, I_2, \ldots I_\ell)$ according to which A is block-diagonalizable (possibly the trivial partition, with $\ell = 1$).

f3. if (A, B) is the constraint description of a polyhedron P, and if A is block-diagonalizable according to a partition $(I_1, I_2, \ldots I_\ell)$, then P can be factored according to $(I_1, I_2, \ldots I_\ell)$ (the converse is not true, if (A, B) is not minimal). This gives an easy way to factor a polyhedron, and to get the constraint descriptions of its factors: each constraint (A_i, B_i) becomes a constraint of the factor P_{k_i}.

f4. For any pair (P, P') of polyhedra (resp., for any pair (A, A') of matrices) there is a greatest common partition (possibly the trivial partition) according to which both polyhedra can be factored (resp., both matrices are block-diagonalizable).

f5. Conversely, given a description of the factors $P_1, \ldots P_\ell$, one can easily obtain the corresponding description of $P = P_1 \times \ldots \times P_\ell$:
  - its system of constraints is just the conjunction of those of the factors;
  - its system of generators is obtained by composing together all the ℓ-tuples of vertices (resp., of rays) of the factors. This composition explains the explosion of the size of the systems of generators, since $|V| = \prod_{k=1}^\ell |V_k|$ and $|R| = \prod_{k=1}^\ell |R_k|$.

A similar treatment works also to obtain a description of P factored according to any partition rougher than $(I_1, I_2, \ldots I_\ell)$.

Example: Fig. 2 shows a factored polyhedron in 2 dimensions. In its minimal system of constraints:

$$\begin{bmatrix} -1 & 0 \\ 0 & 1 \\ 0 & -1 \end{bmatrix} \begin{pmatrix} x \\ y \end{pmatrix} \leq \begin{pmatrix} -1 \\ 2 \\ 0 \end{pmatrix}$$

the matrix is block-diagonal. Now, if the redundant constraint $2x \geq y$ is added, the matrix is non longer block-diagonalizable, and the factoring of the polyhedron is hidden.

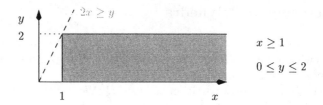

Fig. 2. A factored polyhedron

4 Easy Operations

Most of the operations mentioned in Section 2.2 can be easily applied componentwise to factored polyhedra. The operands need first to be factored in the same way (using *f4* and *f5* above). Moreover, in many cases, the result may be better factored than the operands, which can be done using *f2*.

Intersection. If P and P' are factored according to the same partition $(I_1, I_2, \ldots I_\ell)$, then so is $P \cap P' = P_1 \cap P'_1 \times P_2 \cap P'_2 \times \ldots \times P_\ell \cap P'_\ell$. It may be the case that $P \cap P'$ can be further factored (Fig. 3).

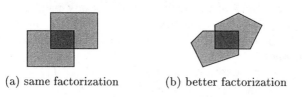

(a) same factorization (b) better factorization

Fig. 3. Intersection of factored polyhedra

Affine transformation. Let $X \mapsto CX + D$ be an affine transformation. If C is block-diagonalizable according to $(I_1, I_2, \ldots I_\ell)$, and P is factored according to the same partition, then so is $CP + D = C_{I_1}P_1 + D_{I_1} \times \ldots \times C_{I_\ell}P_\ell + D_{I_\ell}$. If C is not invertible, it can be the case that $CP + D$ can be further factored.

Widening. If P and P' are factored according to the same partition $(I_1, I_2, \ldots, I_\ell)$, then so is $P \nabla P' = P_1 \nabla P'_1 \times P_2 \nabla P'_2 \times \ldots \times P_\ell \nabla P'_\ell$. It may be the case (in fact, it happens very often) that $P \nabla P'$ can be further factored

Emptiness and inclusion. Let $P = P_1 \times P_2 \times \ldots \times P_\ell$. Then P is empty if and only if there exists $k \in \{1..\ell\}$ such that P_k is empty. If P and P' are factored according to the same partition $(I_1, I_2, \ldots I_\ell)$, then $P \subseteq P'$ if and only if, for all $k \in \{1..\ell\}$, $P_k \subseteq P'_k$.

5 The Convex Hull

The computation of the convex hull is more difficult. The convex hull of two factored polyhedra can be either less factored (Fig. 4.a) or as factored (Fig. 4.b), or even more factored (Fig. 4.c) than the operands.

(a) less factorization

(b) same factorization

(c) better factorization

Fig. 4. Convex hull of factored polyhedra

The goal is to get the factored result, when possible, in a decomposed way, and without penalizing the computation when the result is not factored. This can be achieved thanks to the following proposition:

Proposition 1. Let $P = P_1 \times P_2$ and $P' = P'_1 \times P'_2$ be two polyhedra factored according to the same partition. Let λ be a fresh variable and let us consider the polyhedra Q_1 and Q_2 defined by:

$$Q_1 = (P_1 \wedge \{\lambda = 0\}) \sqcup (P'_1 \wedge \{\lambda = 1\}) \quad Q_2 = (P_2 \wedge \{\lambda = 0\}) \sqcup (P'_2 \wedge \{\lambda = 1\})$$

Then,

- if λ is lower-bounded by a non constant expression in Q_1 — i.e., there is a constraint $E(X_1) \leq \lambda$ in the system of constraints of Q_1, where $E(X_1)$ is a non constant linear expression of X_1 — and upper-bounded by a non constant expression in Q_2, or conversely, the convex hull $P \sqcup P'$ is non longer factored, and can be computed as $\exists \lambda, Q_1 \wedge Q_2$;
- otherwise $P \sqcup P' = (\exists \lambda, Q_1) \times (\exists \lambda, Q_2)$.

Proof: By definition of the convex hull,

$$X \in P \sqcup P' \Leftrightarrow \exists Y \in P, Y' \in P', \lambda \in [0,1], \text{ such that } X = \lambda Y + (1-\lambda) Y'$$
$$\Leftrightarrow X = (X_1, X_2) \wedge \exists \lambda \in [0,1] \text{ such that}$$
$$\exists Y_1 \in P_1, Y'_1 \in P'_1, X_1 = \lambda Y_1 + (1-\lambda) Y'_1 \wedge$$
$$\exists Y_2 \in P_2, Y'_2 \in P'_2, X_2 = \lambda Y_2 + (1-\lambda) Y'_2$$
$$\Leftrightarrow X = (X_1, X_2) \wedge \exists \lambda \in [0,1] \text{ such that}$$
$$(X_1, \lambda) \in Q_1 \wedge (X_2, \lambda) \in Q_2$$

Now, the existential quantification of λ in the last system of constraints can only produce dependencies between previously independent variables in two cases:

- if there is some constraint $E(X_1) \leq \lambda$ in Q_1, and some constraint $\lambda \leq F(X2)$ in Q_2 — which will produce $E(X_1) \leq F(X_2)$;

– or, conversely, if there is some constraint $\lambda \leq E(X_1)$ in Q_1, and some constraint $F(X2) \leq \lambda$ in Q_2 — which will produce $F(X_2) \leq E(X_1)$;

where $E(X_1)$ and $F(X2)$ are non constant expressions. Otherwise, λ can be quantified separately in Q_1 and Q_2.
□

This result generalizes to multiple factorings:

Proposition. Let $P = P_1 \times \ldots \times P_\ell$ and $P' = P'_1 \times \ldots \times P'_\ell$ be two polyhedra factored according to the same partition. Let λ be a fresh variable and let us consider the polyhedra $(Q_k)_{k=1..\ell}$ defined by:

$$Q_k = (P_k \wedge \{\lambda = 0\}) \sqcup (P'_k \wedge \{\lambda = 1\})$$

Then, the partition of $P \sqcup P'$ is obtained from $(I_1, \ldots, I_\ell)$ by merging I_k and $I_{k'}$ whenever either λ is lower-bounded by a non constant expression in Q_k and upper-bounded by a non constant expression in $Q_{k'}$, or conversely. Let $(J_1, \ldots, J_h)$ be the resulting partition, each J_m being a union of some I_ks. Then

$$P \sqcup Q = R_1 \times R_2 \times \ldots \times R_h \text{ where } R_m = \exists \lambda, \underset{I_k \subseteq J_m}{\times} Q_k$$

6 Experimental Results

6.1 Operations on Factored Hypercubes

We first compared the performances of the operations in the best case, where operands are completely factored hypercubes (i.e., in fact, intervals). For intersection and widening[6], the results are, of course, excellent:

Intersection	Classical operations			Factored operations				
Dimension	10	11	12	13	10	20	30	40	50
Operation time	3"	13"	60"	4'36	0"02	0"03	0"03	0"04	0"07

Widening	Classical operations					Factored operations				
Dimension	8	10	12	14	16	10	20	30	40	50
Operation time	0"05	0"22	1"68	20"63	6'58"	0"01	0"02	0"04	0"06	0"07

Concerning the convex-hull, we made two series of experiments:

– the first one concerns the best case, where the result is still fully factored. The following table only gives the times of the classical convex hull, since the factored one gives non measurable times (less than 0.01 sec. in dimension 50): in dimension n, it performs n convex hulls of polyhedra with 2 variables (the current variable and the variable λ of Prop. 1).

---

[6] Operands are such that half of the constraints are kept by the widening.

Dimension	10	11	12	13	14	15	16
Classical	0"06	0"28	2"01	12"07	54"99	3'44"	15'27"

– the second series concerns the worst case, where the result is not factored at all:

Dimensions	10	11	12	13	14	15	16
Classical	0"09	0"48	3"81	21"89	1'35"	6'29"	25'54"
Factored	0"17	0"41	2"93	5"76	1'20"	5'50"	22'53

Notice that, even in this case, the factored operation is still better than the classical one. In addition with the same operations than in the previous case, it has to perform an existential quantification of λ, which appears to dominate largely in the overall cost.

6.2 Experiments in Program Analysis

Real experiments in program analysis are more difficult to conduct, for the following reason: our verification tool, NBAC [JHR99] performs much more than a simple analysis, since it deals with successive forward and backward analyses together with slicing and dynamic partitioning. As a consequence, the cost of polyhedra operations is not always prominent. Our experiments concerned parameterized problems, where the number of numeric variables can be easily increased without increasing the rest of the treatment. Let us show a few results:

Problem	car			
Dimension	4	5	6	7
Time without factoring	1"63	4"74	7"79	55'31"
Time with factoring	3"84	10"48	16"09	2'55"

Problem	Ntoggle			
Dimension	4	5	6	7
Time without factoring	1"39	2"01	3"40	44'51"
Time with factoring	3"21	4"60	7"71	16'32

Of course, these results should be taken with care, and further experiments must be conducted. However, all our experiments show that the factored version outperforms the classical one from a quite small dimension (less than 10, in general). We will start experiments in a completely different context, by linking the analyzer of [DRS03] with our library with factored operations.

7 Conclusion and Future Works

We presented an adaptation of classical operations on polyhedra to work on Cartesian products of polyhedra. This adaptation is straightforward, except in the case of the convex hull. The gain in performance is obvious — and spectacular

— when the arguments of the operations are factored in the same way. So the interest of the approach relies on the fact that, during an analysis, polyhedra are indeed factored in similar ways. It appears to be often the case, at least in the end of an analysis, after the application of the widening, which tends to suppress dependences between variables.

This work can be pursued in several directions. First, the fact that polyhedra are factored depends on the choice of variables. A simple variable change (e.g., a rotation) can make possible a factoring. The question is whether the detection of this fact can be done efficiently enough to make it worthwhile. An other improvement concerns the beginning of the analysis: as mentioned before, factoring is more likely to occur at the end, after one or several widenings. Now, at the beginning of an analysis, variables are tightly dependent; in fact, they are likely to satisfy linear equations. This suggests to look for an other way of saving variables, by early detection of these equations [Kar76] and elimination of variables. Of course, since each equation allows only one variable to be removed, this technique is less likely to produce spectacular improvements than polyhedra factoring.

References

[BBC+00] N. Bjorner, A. Browne, M. Colon, B. Finkbeiner, Z. Manna, H. Sipma, and T. Uribe. Verifying temporal properties of reactive systems: A STeP tutorial. *Formal Methods in System Design*, 16:227–270, 2000.

[BBM97] N. Bjorner, I. Anca Browne, and Z. Manna. Automatic generation of invariants and intermediate assertions. *Theoretical Computer Science*, 173(1):49–87, February 1997.

[BRZH02] R. Bagnara, E. Ricci, E. Zaffanella, and P. M. Hill. Possibly not closed convex polyhedra and the parma polyhedra library. In M. V. Hermenegildo and G. Puebla, editors, *9th International Symposium on Static Analysis, SAS'02*, Madrid, Spain, September 2002. LNCS 2477.

[CC77] P. Cousot and R. Cousot. Abstract interpretation: a unified lattice model for static analysis of programs by construction or approximation of fixpoints. In *4th ACM Symposium on Principles of Programming Languages, POPL'77*, Los Angeles, January 1977.

[CH78] P. Cousot and N. Halbwachs. Automatic discovery of linear restraints among variables of a program. In *5th ACM Symposium on Principles of Programming Languages, POPL'78*, Tucson (Arizona), January 1978.

[Che68] N. V. Chernikova. Algorithm for discovering the set of all solutions of a linear programming problem. *U.S.S.R. Computational Mathematics and Mathematical Physics*, 8(6):282–293, 1968.

[CL98] Ph. Clauss and V. Loechner. Parametric analysis of polyhedral iteration spaces. *Journal of VLSI Signal Processing*, 19(2), July 1998.

[DRS01] N. Dor, M. Rodeh, and M. Sagiv. Cleanness checking of string manipulations in C programs via integer analysis. In P. Cousot, editor, *SAS'01*, Paris, July 2001. LNCS 2126.

[DRS03] N. Dor, M. Rodeh, and M. Sagiv. CCSV: towards a realistic tool for statically detecting all buffer overflows in C. to appear in PLDI03, 2003.

[Hal79]   N. Halbwachs. Détermination automatique de relations linéaires vérifiées par les variables d'un programme. Thèse de troisième cycle, University of Grenoble, March 1979.
[HHWT97]   T. A. Henzinger, P.-H. Ho, and H. Wong-Toi. Hytech: A model checker for hybrid systems. *Software Tools for Technology Transfer*, 1:110–122, 1997.
[HPR97]   N. Halbwachs, Y.E. Proy, and P. Roumanoff. Verification of real-time systems using linear relation analysis. *Formal Methods in System Design*, 11(2):157–185, August 1997.
[IJT91]   F. Irigoin, P. Jouvelot, and R. Triolet. Semantical interprocedural parallelization: An overview of the PIPS project. In *ACM Int. Conf. on Supercomputing, ICS'91, Köln*, 1991.
[JHR99]   B. Jeannet, N. Halbwachs, and P. Raymond. Dynamic partitioning in analyses of numerical properties. In A. Cortesi and G. Filé, editors, *Static Analysis Symposium, SAS'99*, Venice (Italy), September 1999. LNCS 1694, Springer Verlag.
[Kar76]   M. Karr. Affine relationships among variables of a program. *Acta Informatica*, 6:133–151, 1976.
[LeV92]   H. LeVerge. A note on Chernikova's algorithm. RR. 635, IRISA, February 1992.
[MRTT53]   T. S. Motzkin, H. Raiffa, G. L. Thompson, and R. M. Thrall. The double description method. In H. W. Kuhn and A. W. Tucker, editors, *Contribution to the Theory of Games – Volume II*. Annals of Mathematic Studies, nr 28, Princeton University Press, 1953.
[Tip95]   F. Tip. A survey of program slicing techniques. *Journal of Programming Languages*, 3(3):121–189, September 1995.
[Wil93]   D. K. Wilde. A library for doing polyhedral operations. RR. 785, IRISA, December 1993.

Continuation-Based Partial Evaluation without Continuations

Peter Thiemann

Universität Freiburg, Germany
thiemann@informatik.uni-freiburg.de

Abstract. Continuation-based partial evaluation is an implementation technique for program specializers that allows generated code contexts to commute with specialization-time values. Thus it enables additional specialization-time computations. Its most general implementation known to date is based on the manipulation of continuations.

We show that a substitution monad provides an alternative implementation of the context manipulation performed by continuation-based partial evaluation. We prove its equivalence to the original continuation-based implementation. A type-based binding-time analysis that is augmented with effects provides static information about the generated code contexts. We prove the soundness of the resulting type and effect system with respect to our implementation and point out how a binding-time analysis extended with this effect information may avoid code duplication and enable the generation of more efficient generating extensions.

Keywords: Functional programming, partial evaluation, type systems.

1 Introduction

Partial evaluation [4,16] is an automatic program transformation that specializes a program with respect to known input data. Of particular interest is offline-partial evaluation, where each part of the program is annotated as either executable at specialization time or as generating specialized code. For example, in the program

power x n = if^s n ==^{s} 0 then (lift 1) else x *^{d} power x $(n -^s 1)$

the superscript s (*static*) indicates a specialization-time expression, whereas the superscript d (*dynamic*) indicates a run-time expression. The function lift converts the internal representation of a number into a constant expression (a syntax tree). In the example, running the program power x 2 yields the syntax tree

x * (x * 1)

The annotations may be added to the program manually or by means of a program analysis (binding-time analysis). In either case, a type system can be used to specify when an annotation is sound.

The binding-time analysis is an asset and a drawback at the same time. It is an asset because it clearly indicates which expressions are processed at specialization time (and which are not). It is also a drawback because some programs require non-trivial transformation (*binding-time improvements*) before they specialize well. Hence, some research has been geared towards automatizing these transformations and including them into partial evaluation systems [1, 8, 9, 17, 21].

Another option is to consider a language which makes binding times explicit [15, 25]. However, considerable effort and sometimes transformation is required to make programs specialize well in these approaches, too. Furthermore, neither of the approaches presently guarantees semantics preservation, nor do they consider the transformations outlined in the next two paragraphs.

The present work concerns continuation-based partial evaluation, which incorporates one of the most essential binding-time improvements for call-by-value functional programming languages. It was pioneered by Bondorf, Consel, and Danvy [1, 3] and later refined and explained by Danvy, Hatcliff, Lawall, and the present author [14, 17, 18]. The basic idea is that code may be generated interleaved with specialization-time computations. For example

$$\texttt{reset (lift } (17 +^s \texttt{let}^D \ x = e \texttt{ in } 4))$$

specializes to

$$\texttt{let } x = e \texttt{ in } 21$$

that is, the code generation for the surrounding dynamic context $\texttt{let } x = e \texttt{ in } [\ ]$ is interleaved with the specialization-time computation $17 + 4$. The $\texttt{reset}$ operator delimits the scope of the dynamic context by "capturing" the interleaved context and filling its hole with the value of its body, $\texttt{lift } 21$. It turns out [14, 18], that this feature is essential to guarantee semantics preservation when specializing programs with effects.

Danvy and Lawall [17] have proposed to extend generation of interleaved code to also include dynamic conditionals. Extending the previous example

$$\texttt{reset (lift } (17 +^s \texttt{if0}^D \ e \ 4 \ 25))$$

specializes to

$$\texttt{if0 } e \ 21 \ 42$$

that is, the computation $(17 + [\ ])$ is performed twice and the conditional floats to the top level of the expression. Again, the $\texttt{reset}$ delimits the scope of the dynamic context. This feature vastly simplifies "The Trick", a common binding-time improvement [8].

The first and to date most general implementation of interleaved code generation is in terms of a non-standard use of continuations, either in the source program [3] or in the implementation of the specializer [1, 17]. Later on, state-based implementations have been suggested [12, 24]. In those implementations, a reference cell collects dynamic variable bindings like the "$\texttt{let } x = e$" in the

Terms	$e ::= x \mid \lambda^b x.e \mid e@^b e \mid \text{let}^b\ x = e\ \text{in}\ e \mid$
	$c \mid \text{succ}^b\ e \mid \text{if0}^b\ e\ e\ e \mid \text{lift}\ e \mid \text{reset}\ e$
Binding times	$b ::= S \mid D \qquad S < D$
Types	$\tau ::= \text{int} \mid \rho \xrightarrow{t} \rho$
Annotated types	$\rho ::= (\tau, b)$
Effects	$t ::= \mathbf{1} \mid i(t,t) \mid l(t) \mid t \gg t \mid t \sqcup t$

Fig. 1. Two-level language

first example. An enclosing reset turns these bindings into let expressions. The reset is usually implicit in the specialization of the dynamic lambda.

The state-based implementation is less general than the continuation-based one because it cannot be easily extended to deal with the second example, the dynamic conditional. The problem is the duplication of the static computation, which cannot be simulated by just storing dynamic variable bindings.

In the present work, we start from a monadic specification for continuation-based partial evaluation and suggest an substitution-based direct-style implementation of the underlying monad that is as general as the continuation-based implementation. We show that our new implementation is equivalent to the standard implementation with continuations and develop a novel annotated type and effect system for two-level call-by-value lambda calculus that models interleaved code generation (as demonstrated with the let and if above) as a specialization-time effect. This type system may be used to optimize specialization by taking advantage of (the absence of) specialization-time effects. An extended version with proofs is available on the author's webpage[1].

Overview. In Sec. 2, we present a call-by-value two-level lambda calculus and a type and effect system specifying its static semantics. Section 3 specifies its dynamic semantics via a translation into the computational metalanguage augmented with code-generating operators. The translation requires some operations from the underlying monad and Sec. 4 states these requirements in the form of equational axioms and provides two implementations for the monad, one with continuations and another with substitutions. Section 5 argues informally that the two monads are equivalent. In Sec. 6, we prove type soundness for the two-level lambda calculus and in Sec. 7 we give some examples, how specialization may be optimized with the presented system. Section 8 discusses some related work and Section 9 concludes.

2 Two-Level Lambda Calculus

We consider an applied two-level call-by-value lambda calculus with built-in natural numbers. Its syntax is given in Fig. 1. Each subexpression except for

---

[1] http://www.informatik.uni-freiburg.de/~thiemann/papers/

$$t \sqcup t = t \tag{1}$$
$$t \sqcup t' = t' \sqcup t \tag{2}$$
$$t \sqcup (t' \sqcup t'') = (t \sqcup t') \sqcup t'' \tag{3}$$
$$\mathbf{1} \gg t = t \tag{4}$$
$$l(t') \gg t = l(t' \gg t) \tag{5}$$
$$i(t', t'') \gg t = i((t' \gg t), (t'' \gg t)) \tag{6}$$
$$(t' \gg t'') \gg t = t' \gg (t'' \gg t) \tag{7}$$
$$(t' \sqcup t'') \gg t = (t' \gg t) \sqcup (t'' \gg t) \tag{8}$$
$$l(t' \sqcup t'') = l(t') \sqcup l(t'') \tag{9}$$
$$i(t' \sqcup t'', t) = i(t', t) \sqcup i(t'', t) \tag{10}$$
$$i(t, t' \sqcup t'') = i(t, t') \sqcup i(t, t'') \tag{11}$$

Fig. 2. Algebraic properties of effects

variables, constants, `lift`, and `reset` expressions is annotated with a binding-time annotation b, which can be s (static) or d (dynamic). The computation rules are beta value reduction for static beta redexes and static `let` expressions, and delta reduction for static successors `succ` and testing for zero `if0`. The only non-standard expression is `reset` e and we will defer its explanation to Sec. 7.

The syntax of two-level types in Fig. 1 is standard [10], except for the addition of effects. Effects characterize the generation of interleaved code as exemplified by the `let x = e in ...` in the introduction. The effect **1** indicates that no such code is generated, $l(t)$ indicates that a `let x = e in e'` is generated where e and x are arbitrary and e' is described by t, $i(t_1, t_2)$ indicates an interleaved `if0 e e_1 e_2` with arbitrary e but branches e_1 and e_2 specified by t_1 and t_2, respectively. Of the remaining operations, effect union, $t_1 \sqcup t_2$, specifies interleaved code described by either t_1 or t_2 and $t_1 \gg t_2$ specifies sequential composition. Fig. 2 specifies the algebraic properties of the operations on effects. In essence, each effect can be simplified to a union of simple effects generated by **1**, $l(t)$, and $i(t', t'')$. The union operator can be floated to the top level using equations (8), (9), (10), and (11). Sequential composition $\gg$ can be pushed through towards **1**s using the equations (5), (6), and (7) and then eliminated by (4). The type and effect system presented in Fig. 3 for specifying binding times is new. It defines the validity of the judgement $\Gamma \vdash e : \rho \, ! \, t$, that is, in environment Γ, the two-level expression e has two-level type ρ and effect t. The typing part of the system is standard [26] and it relies on the inference system in Fig. 4 to specify a well-formedness criterion for types. The new ingredient is the effect part. It describes a specialization-time effect, that is, it yields additional information about the behavior of the two-level expression during specialization.

To illustrate the operations on effects, let us consider the rule for function application. It states that if specialization of e_1 and e_2 (in that order) generates

$$\frac{\vdash_{wft} \rho}{\Gamma, x : \rho \vdash x : \rho \,!\, 1} \qquad \Gamma \vdash c : (\text{int}, S) \,!\, 1$$

$$\frac{\Gamma \vdash e : (\text{int}, b) \,!\, t}{\Gamma \vdash \text{succ}^b \, e : (\text{int}, b) \,!\, t} \qquad \frac{\Gamma \vdash e : (\text{int}, S) \,!\, t}{\Gamma \vdash \text{lift} \, e : (\text{int}, D) \,!\, t}$$

$$\frac{\Gamma, x : \rho_2 \vdash e : \rho_1 \,!\, t \quad \rho = (\rho_2 \xrightarrow{t} \rho_1, b) \quad \vdash_{wft} \rho}{\Gamma \vdash \lambda^b x.e : \rho \,!\, 1} \qquad \frac{\Gamma \vdash e_1 : (\rho_2 \xrightarrow{t} \rho_1, b) \,!\, t_1 \quad \Gamma \vdash e_2 : \rho_2 \,!\, t_2}{\Gamma \vdash e_1 \,@^b\, e_2 : \rho_1 \,!\, t_1 \gg t_2 \gg t}$$

$$\frac{\Gamma \vdash e_1 : (\tau, S) \,!\, t_1 \quad \Gamma, x : (\tau, S) \vdash e_2 : \rho_2 \,!\, t_2}{\Gamma \vdash \text{let}^S \, x = e_1 \text{ in } e_2 : \rho_2 \,!\, t_1 \gg t_2}$$

$$\frac{\Gamma \vdash e_1 : (\tau, D) \,!\, t_1 \quad \Gamma, x : (\tau, D) \vdash e_2 : \rho_2 \,!\, t_2}{\Gamma \vdash \text{let}^D \, x = e_1 \text{ in } e_2 : \rho_2 \,!\, t_1 \gg l(t_2)}$$

$$\frac{\Gamma \vdash e_1 : (\text{int}, S) \,!\, t_1 \quad \Gamma \vdash e_2 : \rho \,!\, t_2 \quad \Gamma \vdash e_3 : \rho \,!\, t_3}{\Gamma \vdash \text{if0}^S \, e_1 \, e_2 \, e_3 : \rho \,!\, t_1 \gg (t_2 \sqcup t_3)}$$

$$\frac{\Gamma \vdash e_1 : (\text{int}, D) \,!\, t_1 \quad \Gamma \vdash e_2 : \rho \,!\, t_2 \quad \Gamma \vdash e_3 : \rho \,!\, t_3}{\Gamma \vdash \text{if0}^D \, e_1 \, e_2 \, e_3 : \rho \,!\, t_1 \gg i(t_2, t_3)}$$

$$\frac{\Gamma \vdash e : (\tau, D) \,!\, t}{\Gamma \vdash \text{reset} \, e : (\tau, D) \,!\, 1}$$

Fig. 3. Typing rules

$$\vdash_{wft} (\text{int}, b)$$

$$\frac{\vdash_{wft} (\tau_2, b_2) \quad \vdash_{wft} (\tau_1, b_1) \quad b \le b_1 \quad b \le b_2 \quad \text{if } b = D \text{ then } t = 1}{\vdash_{wft} ((\tau_2, b_2) \xrightarrow{t} (\tau_1, b_1), b)}$$

Fig. 4. Well-formedness of annotated types

interleaved code as described by t_1 and t_2, and if applying the value of e_1 to the value of e_2 generates interleaved code as described by the latent effect t, then the interleaved code generated by $e_1 @^b e_2$ starts as described by t_1, followed by t_2, and finally t. Similar reasoning applies to the static and the dynamic let expressions. In the latter, the explicit $l(\dots)$ stands for the let created by the expression itself (which is always interleaved, so that it can float out of static contexts). Since the outcome of the static conditional cannot be determined before specialization, the interleaved code is approximated by taking the union of the two effects. The dynamic conditional also generates its code interleaved by default and hence need not constrain the binding time of its branches[2].

---

[2] A thorough discussion of this feature is out of the scope of this paper but may be found in the literature [8,17].

```
𝒯⟦x⟧                      = return x
𝒯⟦λˢx.e⟧                  = return (λx.𝒯⟦e⟧)
𝒯⟦λᴰx.e⟧                  = newVar >>= λx.𝒯⟦e⟧ >>= λe'.return (LamExp x e')
𝒯⟦e₁@ˢe₂⟧                 = 𝒯⟦e₁⟧ >>= λf.𝒯⟦e₂⟧ >>= λv.f@v
𝒯⟦e₁@ᴰe₂⟧                 = 𝒯⟦e₁⟧ >>= λe'₁.𝒯⟦e₂⟧ >>= λe'₂.return (AppExp e'₁ e'₂)
𝒯⟦letˢ x = e₁ in e₂⟧      = 𝒯⟦e₁⟧ >>= λx.𝒯⟦e₂⟧
𝒯⟦letᴰ x = e₁ in e₂⟧      = 𝒯⟦e₁⟧ >>= λe'₁.newVar >>= λx.mlet x e'₁ 𝒯⟦e₂⟧
𝒯⟦c⟧                      = return c
𝒯⟦succˢ e⟧                = 𝒯⟦e⟧ >>= λv.return (succ v)
𝒯⟦succᴰ e⟧                = 𝒯⟦e⟧ >>= λe'.return (SuccExp e')
𝒯⟦if0ˢ e₁ e₂ e₃⟧          = 𝒯⟦e₁⟧ >>= λv₁.if0 v₁ 𝒯⟦e₂⟧ 𝒯⟦e₃⟧
𝒯⟦if0ᴰ e₁ e₂ e₃⟧          = 𝒯⟦e₁⟧ >>= λe'₁.mif e'₁ 𝒯⟦e₂⟧ 𝒯⟦e₃⟧
𝒯⟦lift e⟧                 = 𝒯⟦e⟧ >>= λv.return (ConExp v)
𝒯⟦reset e⟧                = mreset 𝒯⟦e⟧
```

Fig. 5. Translation into augmented metalanguage

The reset · expression is also a novelty of our presentation. As its typing rule specifies, it is applicable to any dynamic value (a syntax tree) and is used to flush the interleaved code by dumping it on top of that syntax tree. Its effect is empty, **1**, since all interleaved code is now part of the dynamic value.

As usual in an effect system [19], each function type carries a latent effect indicating the effect that is unleashed when the function is applied. The well-formedness judgement enforces the usual constraints on the binding-time annotations. In addition, it ensures that the application of a dynamic (run-time) function does not generate interleaved code.

3 Monadic Specification of Partial Evaluation

Effects have been abstracted and described using monads [11,28]. For that reason, we construct a monadic specification of partial evaluation, using special operators that exert the effects, mlet for $l(t)$ and mif for $i(t,t)$, or flush them, mreset. There is also a newVar operator for creating fresh variable names, which is left unspecified.

We specify the semantics of the two-level calculus by translation into a variant of Moggi's computational metalanguage [22], that is, the call-by-name lambda calculus augmented with the monadic return · and bind operations (·>>=·) plus the special newVar, mlet, mif, and mreset operators. There are also constructors for generating syntax trees for applied call-by-value lambda calculus.

For concreteness, we specify syntax trees and the operations in the form of Haskell definitions [13]. Here is the datatype for syntax trees.

```
type Var = String
data Exp =
```

```
  VarExp Var              -- variable
| ConExp String           -- constant
| SuccExp Exp             -- successor
| LamExp Var Exp          -- lambda
| AppExp Exp Exp          -- application
| LetExp Var Exp Exp      -- let
| IfExp  Exp Exp Exp      -- conditional
```

We capture the further requirements in a type class PEMonad, which states the required operations on a monad m, suitable for implementing partial evaluation, and their types.[3]

```
class Monad m => PEMonad m where
  mlet   :: Var -> Exp -> m a -> m a
  mif    :: Exp -> m a -> m a -> m a
  mreset :: m Exp -> m Exp
```

The type signatures show that

- mlet transforms a computation (its last argument) into a computation;
- mif transforms two computations into another computation;
- the type (and hence the binding time) of the body of the mlet as well as the type of the branches of the mif is *unconstrained*;
- mreset requires that its argument computation returns a syntax tree (*i.e.*, a dynamic value) and it returns a syntax tree, too.

The translation rules in Fig. 5 are reasonably straightforward. For the static constructs they correspond exactly to the standard monadic translation. As an example for a dynamic construct, we consider the translation of the dynamic lambda:

$$\mathcal{T}[\![\lambda^D x.e]\!] = \mathtt{newVar} \mathbin{>\!\!>\!\!=} \lambda x. \mathcal{T}[\![e]\!] \mathbin{>\!\!>\!\!=} \lambda e'.\mathtt{return}\ (\mathtt{LamExp}\ x\ e')$$

The translated term creates a fresh variable name and binds it to x, the bound variable of the translated lambda. In that environment, it specializes e, binds the result to e', and returns the syntax tree LamExp x e'. For understanding the rules, it is important to keep in mind that $\mathcal{T}[\![\cdot]\!]$ is a *translation*, that is, the x and e on both sides are *identical*.

To avoid clutter in the translation (and in the proofs) we assume that the type Var is a subset of the type Exp with VarExp being the injection function. The type-correct right-hand side for the dynamic lambda would be

$$\mathtt{newVar} \mathbin{>\!\!>\!\!=} \lambda x'.\mathtt{let}\ x\ =\ \mathtt{VarExp}\ x'\ \mathtt{in}\ \mathcal{T}[\![e]\!] \mathbin{>\!\!>\!\!=} \lambda e'.\mathtt{return}\ (\mathtt{LamExp}\ x'\ e')$$

and similarly in the translation of the dynamic let.

---

[3] A type class declares a group of overloaded functions. In the present case, the definitions are overloaded on a type constructor m where m is assumed to be a monad. The latter is indicated by the Monad m => constraint. It means that m supports the monadic operators unit, return :: a -> m a, and bind, (>>=) :: m a -> (a -> m b) -> m b, where the latter is an infix operator.

4 Monads for Partial Evaluation

Having constructed the monadic translation for the two-level lambda calculus, the next task is to define a suitable monad that supports the operations, mlet, mif, and mreset (and newVar). In fact, we will present two such monads. One of them is the continuation monad and its definitions correspond to the usual implementation of continuation-based partial evaluation [1,17]. The other monad is, perhaps surprisingly, a simple substitution monad. Nevertheless, as we will show in Sec. 4.3, both monads fulfill the expected laws for the new operations and we will use these laws in Sec. 5 to prove that the results of interpreting a translated two-level term in either monad are equivalent.

4.1 Continuation Monad

The type for the continuation monad is standard. Since we are defining a monad for partial evaluation, where the result is always a syntax tree, the type of answers is Exp. For technical reasons, Haskell requires the definition of a new data type C and a corresponding untagging operation unC.

```
data C a = C ((a -> Exp) -> Exp)
unC (C k) = k
```

The definitions for return and >>= are standard[4].

```
instance Monad C where
  return x = C (\ c -> c x)
  ma >>= f = C (\ c -> unC ma (\ x -> unC (f x) c))
```

Of course, the essence of continuation-based partial evaluation lies in the definitions of the PEMonad operators. The definitions below correspond to code fragments from Bondorf, Danvy, and Lawall [1,17]. In particular, note how the continuation is duplicated in the mif.

```
instance PEMonad C where
  mlet v e ma =
    C (\ c -> LetExp v e (unC ma c))
  mif e m1 m2 =
    C (\ c -> IfExp e (unC m1 c) (unC m2 c))
  mreset me =
    C (\ c -> c (unC me id))
```

---

[4] The notation \ x -> e is Haskell's syntax for a lambda abstraction.

An instance declaration introduces a binding for one specific case of a group of overloaded operators. The present declaration defines the operators of class Monad where m is the type constructor C. That is, it defines the operations return :: a -> C a and (>>=) :: C a -> (a -> C b) -> C b.

4.2 Substitution Monad

A computation of type S a in the substitution monad is a tree where the leaves hold the computed values of type a. Each inner nodes is either an L node, standing for an interleaved let expression, or an I node, standing for an interleaved if expression. The following datatype captures this intuition.

```
data S a = V a
         | L Var Exp (S a)
         | I Exp (S a) (S a)
```

The monadic operations are simple to specify. The return operation creates a trivial tree using the V constructor. The bind operation $m \mathop{>\!\!>\!\!=} f$ propagates f to each leaf of m, applies it to the value x found there, and pastes the resulting tree $f\ x$ in place of the leaf.

```
instance Monad S where
  return x = V x
  ma >>= f = case ma of
               V x        -> f x
               L v e s    -> L v e (s >>= f)
               I b s1 s2  -> I b (s1 >>= f) (s2 >>= f)
```

The operations of the PEMonad class are straightforward to implement, too. The mlet operation takes a variable name v, an expression e, and a tree ma. It constructs a new tree where the root is an L node with exactly those arguments. Similarly, the mif operation takes an expression e and two trees, m1 and m2, and applies the I constructor to these arguments. The mreset operation translates its argument tree into an expression by transforming each L node to a let expression, each I node to a conditional expression, and by stripping V nodes.

```
instance PEMonad S where
  mlet v e ma = L v e ma
  mif e m1 m2 = I e m1 m2
  mreset me =
    case me of
      V e        -> return e
      L v e me   -> mreset me >>= \ e' -> return (LetExp v e e')
      I b m1 m2  -> mreset m1 >>= \ e1 -> mreset m2 >>= \ e2 ->
                    return (IfExp b e1 e2)
```

Recall the example from the introduction with e a dynamic variable:

$$\texttt{reset}\ (\texttt{lift}\ (17 +^s \texttt{let}^D\ x\ =\ e\ \texttt{in}\ 4))$$

Translating this term to the metalanguage yields (after some simplification):

$$\texttt{mreset}\ (\texttt{mlet}\ x'\ e\ (\texttt{return}\ 4)) \mathop{>\!\!>\!\!=} \lambda v_2.\texttt{return}\ (17 + v_2)) \mathop{>\!\!>\!\!=} \lambda v.\texttt{return}\ (\texttt{ConExp} v)$$

Executing mlet and the first return yields

$$\text{mreset (L } x' \text{ e } 4 \text{>>= } \lambda v_2.\text{return } (17 + v_2)) \text{ >>= } \lambda v.\text{return (ConExp } v)$$

Due to the definition of >>=, the outstanding addition 17+ slips under the dynamic binding L x' ...:

$$\text{mreset (L } x' \text{ e } (17 + 4)) \text{ >>= } \lambda v.\text{return (ConExp } v)$$

Again, >>= allows the translation of lift to slip under the L:

$$\text{mreset (L } x' \text{ e (ConExp 21))}$$

Finally, mreset transforms the L into a let expression:

$$\text{LetExp } x' \text{ e (ConExp 21)}$$

4.3 Laws

Besides fulfilling the usual monad laws [29], a PEMonad must obey a number of additional laws. These laws characterize the interaction of mlet and mif with the >>= operator, as well as the interaction of mlet and mif with mreset.

The first two laws state that the mlet and mif operations are both associative with respect to >>=.

(MLB) mlet v e ma >>= f == mlet v e (ma >>= f)
(MIB) mif e m1 m2 >>= f == mif e (m1 >>= f) (m2 >>= f)

The next three laws state that the mreset operation absorbs an mlet or an mif at the price of generating the corresponding code.

```
(MRR)   mreset (return e)       == return e
(MRL)   mreset (mlet v1 e1 me)  == mreset me >>= \ e ->
                                   return (LetExp v1 e1 e)
(MRI)   mreset (mif e m1 m2)    == mreset m1 >>= \ e1 ->
                                   mreset m2 >>= \ e2 ->
                                   return (IfExp e e1 e2)
```

Lemma 1. *The laws (MLB), (MIB), (MRR), (MRL), and (MRI) hold in C and S.*

In addition, the mlet and mif operations for a PEMonad obey the monadic flattening laws on the level of generated syntax trees. To state these laws, we define two auxiliary operations, mmlet and mmif, that incorporate the computation of their first expression:

```
mmlet :: Var -> m Exp -> m a -> m a
mmif  :: m Exp -> m a -> m a -> m a

mmlet v me ma = me >>= \ e -> mlet v e ma
mmif me m1 m2 = me >>= \ e -> mif e m1 m2
```

Using these definitions, we can state flattening laws corresponding to the third monad law (associativity of let/bind), on the level of interleaved generated code.

```
mmlet v2 (mmlet v1 m1 m2) m3
        ==  mmlet v1 m1 (mmlet v2 m2 m3)
mmlet v (mmif m1 m2 m3) m4
        ==  mmif m1 (mmlet v m2 m4) (mmlet v m3 m4)
mmif (mmlet v m1 m2) m3 m4
        ==  mmlet v m1 (mmif m2 m3 m4)
mmif (mmif m1 m2 m3) m4 m5
        ==  mmif m1 (mmif m2 m4 m5) (mmif m3 m4 m5)
```

They also hold for both, S and C, and they are proven using (MLB) and (MIB).

4.4 New Variables

As stated before, we are not going to specify the newVar operation completely. However, we have to make some assumptions about it. Its type is

```
newVar :: PEMonad m => m Var
```

and its only effect is the generation of a fresh variable name. That is,

$$\text{newVar} == (\nu \text{x} \in \text{Var})\ \text{return x}$$

5 Equivalence of PE Monads

It turns out that the laws (MLB), (MIB), (MRR), (MRL), and (MRI) completely characterize the computational behavior of the operations of PEMonad. To make that formal, let λ_{PE} be the equational theory of the computational metalanguage (beta equivalence plus the three monad laws) augmented by delta rules for successor and if0 and the mentioned PEMonad laws.

We take equivalence of the two PEMonads introduced above to mean that, for each closed two-level lambda term e of type (τ, D), "running" the term $\mathcal{T}[\![e]\!]$ yields the same answer. Here are the definitions for running C and S computations.

```
runC :: C Exp -> Exp
runC me = unC (mreset me) id

runS :: S Exp -> Exp
runS se = let V x = mreset se in x
```

To (informally) demonstrate equivalence in λ_{PE}, observe that the laws (MLB) and (MIB) allow mlet and mif operations to float outside of >>= operations. That means, each translated term is equal to one where all the mlets and mifs, interspersed with newVars, are aggregated either at the top of the term or in the argument of mresets. After application of mreset at the toplevel, in runC or runS, and performing newVars, the laws (MRR), (MRL), and (MRI) enable all mlets and mifs to be removed. The resulting term does not contain monadic operators except return and >>=, hence its computed value is independent of the underlying monad.

6 Soundness

In this section, we connect the type system with the semantics. We shall argue in denotational style by first defining a semantics of a two-level type with effect and then proving type soundness by examining the translated term in the S monad. Since the simply-typed lambda calculus, the basis of our two-level calculus, is strongly normalizing, we state the semantics in terms of sets. In addition, we assume a standard semantics mapping $[\![\cdot]\!]$ that maps an expression, e, and a value environment, φ, to a value (see for example [20]). We make this more formal by defining the carriers of an appropriate Henkin model for the type language of the metalanguage.

Definition 1 (Types of the Metalanguage).

$$\sigma ::= \text{Int} \mid \text{Var} \mid \text{Exp} \mid \text{M } \sigma \mid \sigma \text{ -> } \sigma$$

Definition 2 (Semantic Values). *Let $[\![\text{Var}]\!]$ be the set of variable names. Let $[\![\text{Exp}]\!]$ be the set of expressions generated by the definition of Exp in Sec. 4. Let $[\![\text{Int}]\!]$ be the set of natural numbers.*
For each type σ, let

$$[\![\text{M } \sigma]\!] = \{V \, v \mid v \in [\![\sigma]\!]\}$$
$$\cup \{L \, x \, e \, m \mid x \in [\![\text{Var}]\!], e \in [\![\text{Exp}]\!], m \in [\![\text{M } \sigma]\!]\}$$
$$\cup \{I \, e \, m_1 \, m_2 \mid e \in [\![\text{Exp}]\!], m_i \in [\![\text{M } \sigma]\!]\}$$

For each types σ_2 and σ_1, let

$$[\![\sigma_2 \text{ -> } \sigma_1]\!] = [\![\sigma_1]\!]^{[\![\sigma_2]\!]}$$

that is, the set theoretic functions from $[\![\sigma_2]\!]$ to $[\![\sigma_1]\!]$.

Clearly, this family of carrier sets with set-theoretic function application satisfies the preconditions for a Henkin model. Now, we can define the semantics of an annotated type in terms of the Henkin model.

Definition 3 (Semantics of Annotated Types).

$$[\![\rho \,!\, 1]\!] = \{V \, v \mid v \in [\![\rho]\!]\}$$
$$[\![\rho \,!\, l(t)]\!] = \{L \, x \, e \, v \mid x \in [\![\text{Var}]\!], e \in [\![\text{Exp}]\!], v \in [\![\rho \,!\, t]\!]\}$$
$$[\![\rho \,!\, i(t_1, t_2)]\!] = \{I \, e \, v_1 \, v_2 \mid e \in [\![\text{Exp}]\!], v_i \in [\![\rho \,!\, t_i]\!]\}$$
$$[\![\rho \,!\, t_1 \sqcup t_2]\!] = [\![\rho \,!\, t_1]\!] \cup [\![\rho \,!\, t_1]\!]$$
$$[\![(\tau, D)]\!] = [\![\text{Exp}]\!]$$
$$[\![(\text{int}, S)]\!] = [\![\text{Int}]\!]$$
$$[\![(\rho_2 \xrightarrow{t} \rho_1, S)]\!] = \{f \mid (\forall x \in [\![\rho_2]\!]) \, f \, x \in [\![\rho_1 \,!\, t]\!]\}$$

It turns out that the translation $\mathcal{T}[\![\cdot]\!]$ is type preserving.

Theorem 1 (Translation Soundness). *Suppose that* $\Gamma \vdash e : \rho\,!\,t$. *Then* $\mathcal{T}[\![\Gamma]\!] \vdash \mathcal{T}[\![e]\!] : \mathtt{M}\,\mathcal{T}[\![\rho]\!]$ *in the simply-typed lambda calculus where*

- $\mathtt{M}$ *is a PEMonad (for instance,* $\mathtt{S}$ *or* $\mathtt{C}$*);*
- $\mathcal{T}[\![\Gamma]\!](x) = \mathcal{T}[\![\Gamma(x)]\!]$, *for all* $x \in \mathrm{dom}(\Gamma)$*;*
- $\mathcal{T}[\![(\tau, D)]\!] = \mathtt{Exp}$*;*
- $\mathcal{T}[\![(\mathtt{int}, S)]\!] = \mathtt{Int}$*;*
- $\mathcal{T}[\![(\rho_2 \xrightarrow{t} \rho_1, S)]\!] = \mathcal{T}[\![\rho_2]\!] \mathrel{\text{->}} \mathtt{M}\,\mathcal{T}[\![\rho_1]\!]$.

In other words, Theorem 1 establishes that each well-typed two-level lambda expression may be translated into a standard functional programming language (*e.g.*, Haskell or ML) and executed there to achieve specialization. Hence, the translation $\mathcal{T}[\![\cdot]\!]$ creates a *generating extension*, *i.e.*, a dedicated specializer for one particular two-level lambda expression. See the author's article [27] for more background information.

To prove type and effect soundness, we need an auxiliary lemma. It establishes that all types inferred by the inference system are well-formed.

Lemma 2. *Suppose that* $\Gamma \vdash e : \rho\,!\,t$ *and* $(\forall x \in \mathrm{dom}(\Gamma))\ \vdash_{\mathit{wft}} \Gamma(x)$. *Then* $\vdash_{\mathit{wft}} \rho$.

Proof. Standard induction on the derivation of $\Gamma \vdash e : \rho\,!\,t$.

Theorem 2 (Type and Effect Soundness). *Suppose that* $\Gamma \vdash e : \rho\,!\,t$ *and, for all* $x \in \mathrm{dom}(\Gamma)$, $\varphi(x) \in [\![\Gamma(x)]\!]$ *and* $\vdash_{\mathit{wft}} \Gamma(x)$. *Then* $[\![\mathcal{T}[\![e]\!]]\!]\varphi \in [\![\rho\,!\,t]\!]$.

Adding recursion to our framework would give rise to two complications. First, we would have to base the semantics on domains instead of sets. Second, we would have to add recursion in the form $\mu e.t$ to the language of effects. Both are standard [20, 23] and are elided here for the sake of conciseness.

7 Optimized Specification

The two-level calculus presented in Sec. 2 has one unusual feature compared to standard accounts (*e.g.*, in the text book [16] or in the papers about continuation-based partial evaluation [1, 17]). The expression `reset e` is usually not made explicit in the two-level language, but rather hidden in the translation of the dynamic versions of the binding constructs, $\mathtt{let}^D\ x\ =\ e\ \mathtt{in}\ \ldots$ and $\lambda^D x.\ldots$.

With our formal system, the `reset e` expression plays a clearly defined role. It coerces a dynamic two-level term with arbitrary effect into a two-level term without effect. Instead of integrating `reset ·` into the translation of $\lambda^D x.e$, the type system makes sure that the effect of e is **1** (that is, empty). This way, the binding-time analysis is free to place `reset ·` as early as possible (this avoids code duplication in specialized expressions and hence more efficient specialization) or to avoid placing reset · at all, if the type system infers that the effect is **1**, already.

Here are two examples that illustrate either point.

- Code duplication. Let $\Gamma(f_1) = \Gamma(f_2) = (\rho_2 \xrightarrow{1} \rho_1, D)$, $\Gamma(x) = (\text{int}, D)$, and $\Gamma(a) = \rho_2$. Then

$$\Gamma \vdash (\text{if0}^D \ x \ f_1 \ f_2)@^D a : \rho_1 \ ! \ i(1,1)$$

Specializing this code as it is would lead to duplicating the application and its argument a:

$$\text{if0}^D \ x \ (f_1@^D a) \ (f_2@^D a)$$

However, since both f_1 and f_2 are dynamic, the binding-time analysis may wrap the conditional into a reset · so that the effect of the term vanishes:

$$\Gamma \vdash (\text{reset} \ (\text{if0}^D \ x \ f_1 \ f_2))@^D a : \rho_1 \ ! \ 1$$

Specializing this code avoids the duplication:

$$(\text{if0} \ x \ f_1 \ f_2)@a$$

- Avoiding the placement of reset ·. Suppose that

$$\Gamma, x : \rho_2 \vdash e : \rho_1 \ ! \ 1$$

where $\vdash_{wft} (\rho_2 \xrightarrow{1} \rho_1, D)$ so that

$$\Gamma \vdash \lambda^D x.e : (\rho_2 \xrightarrow{1} \rho_1, D) \ ! \ 1$$

Observe that it is not necessary to insert a reset · on top of the lambda's body because the body's effect is empty. In contrast, a conventional continuation-based partial evaluator *always* insert a reset · in this place.

8 Related Work

Consel and Danvy [3] were the first to argue that the binding time of dynamic let expressions can be improved converting source programs to continuation-passing style.

Subsequently, Bondorf [1] discovered that the same binding-time improvement can be achieved by writing the partial evaluator in (not-quite) continuation-passing style. In fact, it is essential to deviate from standard continuation-passing style in the treatment of the dynamic let and lambda expressions.

Danvy and Lawall [17] showed that the non-standard handling of continuations in Bondorf's partial evaluator can be implemented using the control operators shift and reset [6] that provide compositional continuations. They also suggest to generalize the treatment of the dynamic let to the dynamic if.

Our mreset operator instantiates to the reset operator in their work as evident from the definition of mreset for the C monad. However, instead of employing the shift operator in its full generality, our PEMonad makes do with the mlet and mif operators (which could be implemented using shift).

It was later seen that the treatment of dynamic let expressions (first termed "let-insertion" [2]) enabled by continuation-based partial evaluation was essential to achieve a satisfactory and sound specialization for languages with computational effects [14, 18].

Recently, the work on type-directed partial evaluation for call-by-value languages [5, 12] has spread new interest on the implementation of let-insertion. In addition, work to define powerful and efficient online program generators has led to the discovery of a state-based implementation of let-insertion [24]. The latter work also proves the equivalence of their let-insertion to the continuation-based method using a type-indexed relation. However, their let-insertion does not scale to if-insertion in an obvious way and our correspondence is much more direct.

9 Conclusion

This work has two major contributions.

1. It presents a new and simple formalization and implementation of con-tinuation-based partial evaluation. This formalization is pleasingly easy to reason about and it is proven equivalent to the traditional one with continuations.
2. It presents a new type and effect system for two-level lambda calculus. This type system can form the basis for a binding-time analysis that constructs optimized generating extensions.

In future work, we would like to examine the connection to the state-based formulation of continuation-based partial evaluation and we would like to design and implement an actual binding-time analysis based on the type system presented in this work. It would also be interesting to compare the efficiency of our substitution-based implementation with the ones using continuations and state. The continuation-based approach is the most general but its efficiency depends crucially on the presence of efficiently implemented control operators (call/cc). The store-based approach imposes fewer demands on the language, but it is not clear how it can deal with conditionals. The effect system presented in this work would provide the means for optimizing the use of control operators and (potentially) eliminate them in favor of the more efficient store-based implementation where that is possible.

Acknowledgement

The comments of the reviewers helped to improve the presentation of the paper. Thanks to Tim Sheard for commenting on a draft of this paper.

References

1. Anders Bondorf. Improving binding times without explicit CPS-conversion. In *Proc. 1992 ACM Conference on Lisp and Functional Programming*, pages 1–10, San Francisco, California, USA, June 1992.
2. Anders Bondorf and Olivier Danvy. Automatic autoprojection of recursive equations with global variables and abstract data types. *Science of Computer Programming*, 16(2):151–195, 1991.
3. Charles Consel and Olivier Danvy. For a better support of static data flow. In John Hughes, editor, *Proc. Functional Programming Languages and Computer Architecture 1991*, number 523 in Lecture Notes in Computer Science, pages 496–519, Cambridge, MA, 1991. Springer-Verlag.
4. Charles Consel and Olivier Danvy. Tutorial notes on partial evaluation. In *Proceedings of the 1993 ACM SIGPLAN Symposium on Principles of Programming Languages*, pages 493–501, Charleston, South Carolina, January 1993. ACM Press.
5. Olivier Danvy. Type-directed partial evaluation. In *Proceedings of the 1996 ACM SIGPLAN Symposium on Principles of Programming Languages*, pages 242–257, St. Petersburg, Fla., January 1996. ACM Press.
6. Olivier Danvy and Andrzej Filinski. Representing control: A study of the CPS transformation. *Mathematical Structures in Computer Science*, 2:361–391, 1992.
7. Olivier Danvy, Robert Glück, and Peter Thiemann, editors. *Dagstuhl Seminar on Partial Evaluation 1996*, number 1110 in Lecture Notes in Computer Science, Schloß Dagstuhl, Germany, February 1996. Springer-Verlag.
8. Olivier Danvy, Karoline Malmkjær, and Jens Palsberg. Eta-expansion does The Trick. *ACM Transactions on Programming Languages and Systems*, 18(6):730–751, November 1996.
9. Dirk Dussart, Eddy Bevers, and Karel De Vlaminck. Polyvariant constructor specialization. In William Scherlis, editor, *Proc. ACM SIGPLAN Symposium on Partial Evaluation and Semantics-Based Program Manipulation PEPM '95*, pages 54–63, La Jolla, CA, June 1995. ACM Press.
10. Dirk Dussart, Fritz Henglein, and Christian Mossin. Polymorphic recursion and subtype qualifications: Polymorphic binding-time analysis in polynomial time. In Alan Mycroft, editor, *Proceedings of the 1995 International Static Analysis Symposium*, number 983 in Lecture Notes in Computer Science, pages 118–136, Glasgow, Scotland, September 1995. Springer-Verlag.
11. Andrzej Filinski. Representing layered monads. In Alexander Aiken, editor, *Proceedings of the 1999 ACM SIGPLAN Symposium on Principles of Programming Languages*, pages 175–188, San Antonio, Texas, USA, January 1999. ACM Press.
12. Andrzej Filinski. Normalization by evaluation for the computational lambda-calculus. In Samson Abramsky, editor, *Proc. of 5th Int. Conf. on Typed Lambda Calculi and Applications, TLCA'01*, number 2044 in Lecture Notes in Computer Science, pages 151–165, Krakow, Poland, 2001. Springer-Verlag.
13. Haskell 98, a non-strict, purely functional language. http://www.haskell.org/definition, December 1998.
14. John Hatcliff and Olivier Danvy. A computational formalization for partial evaluation. *Mathematical Structures in Computer Science*, 7(5):507–542, 1997.
15. John Hughes. Type specialisation for the λ-calculus; or, a new paradigm for partial evaluation based on type inference. In Danvy et al. [7], pages 183–215.
16. Neil Jones, Carsten Gomard, and Peter Sestoft. *Partial Evaluation and Automatic Program Generation*. Prentice-Hall, 1993.

17. Julia Lawall and Olivier Danvy. Continuation-based partial evaluation. In *Proceedings of the 1994 ACM Conference on Lisp and Functional Programming*, pages 227–238, Orlando, Florida, USA, June 1994. ACM Press.
18. Julia Lawall and Peter Thiemann. Sound specialization in the presence of computational effects. In *Proceedings of the Theoretical Aspects of Computer Software*, number 1281 in Lecture Notes in Computer Science, pages 165–190, Sendai, Japan, September 1997. Springer-Verlag.
19. John M. Lucassen and David K. Gifford. Polymorphic effect systems. In *Proc. 15th Annual ACM Symposium on Principles of Programming Languages*, pages 47–57, San Diego, California, January 1988. ACM Press.
20. John Mitchell. *Foundations for Programming Languages*. MIT Press, 1996.
21. Torben Æ. Mogensen. Evolution of partial evaluators: Removing inherited limits. In Danvy et al. [7], pages 303–321.
22. Eugenio Moggi. Notions of computations and monads. *Information and Computation*, 93:55–92, 1991.
23. Flemming Nielson, Hanne Riis Nielson, and Chris Hankin. *Principles of Program Analysis*. Springer Verlag, 1999.
24. Eijiro Sumii and Naoki Kobayashi. A hybrid approach to online and offline partial evaluation. *Higher-Order and Symbolic Computation*, 14(2/3):101–142, 2001.
25. Walid Taha and Tim Sheard. MetaML and multi-stage programming with explicit annotations. *Theoretical Computer Science*, 2000.
26. Peter Thiemann. A unified framework for binding-time analysis. In Michel Bidoit and Max Dauchet, editors, *TAPSOFT '97: Theory and Practice of Software Development*, number 1214 in Lecture Notes in Computer Science, pages 742–756, Lille, France, April 1997. Springer-Verlag.
27. Peter Thiemann. Combinators for program generation. *Journal of Functional Programming*, 9(5):483–525, September 1999.
28. Philip Wadler and Peter Thiemann. The marriage of monads and effects. *ACM Transactions on Computational Logic*, 4(1):1–32, January 2003.
29. Philip L. Wadler. Comprehending monads. In *Proceedings of the 1990 ACM Conference on Lisp and Functional Programming*, pages 61–78, Nice, France, 1990. ACM Press.

Loop Transformations for Reducing Data Space Requirements of Resource-Constrained Applications

Priya Unnikrishnan[1], Guangyu Chen[1], Mahmut Kandemir[1], Mustafa Karakoy[2], and Ibrahim Kolcu[3]

[1] CSE Department, Pennsylvania State University, University Park, PA 16802, USA
{unnikris,gchen,kandemir}@cse.psu.edu
[2] Department of Computing, Imperial College, London, SW7 2AZ, UK
m.karakoy@ic.ac.uk
[3] Computation Department, UMIST Manchester, M60 1QD, UK
ikolcu@co.umist.ac.uk

Abstract. Embedded computing platforms are often resource constrained, requiring great design and implementation attention to memory, power and heat related parameters. An important task for a compiler in such platforms is to simplify the process of developing applications for limited memory devices and resource constrained clients. Focusing on array-intensive embedded applications, this work explores how loop-based compiler optimizations can be used for increasing memory location reuse. Our goal is to transform a given application in such a way that the resulting code has fewer cases (as compared to the original code) where the lifetimes of array elements overlap. The reduction in lifetimes of array elements can then be exploited by reusing memory locations as much as possible. Our results indicate that the proposed strategy reduces data space requirements of ten resource constrained applications by more than 40% on the average.

1 Introduction

Loop nests have traditionally been considered as an important scope for optimization. This is because many applications spend bulk of their execution cycles in nested loops. In particular, array-intensive applications have recently received a lot of attention and many compiler techniques that target loop-level parallelism and data locality have been proposed and implemented (e.g., see Wolfe's book [28] for a comprehensive study of the subject). Most of these techniques try to re-order loop iterations and/or re-layout data structures in memory to improve performance.

Recent years have witnessed a tremendous growth in resource constrained systems. In contrast to mainstream general-purpose systems, these systems have limited computational power, limited amount of memory, and operate under battery power. An important problem in compiling applications to execute in resource constrained environments is to restructure code and/or data to make best use of the limited memory space available. This is a challenging problem because most programmers do not pay much attention to the data space requirements of their programs. In fact, straightforward implementation of many array-intensive applications can be very extravagant in memory usage. Consequently, the compiler needs to convert a resource-inefficient program to a resource-efficient one. Many resource constrained systems run one or few applications. For example, a processor embedded within an automobile executes the same application code over and over again. Consequently, the application's memory requirements directly dictate the memory requirements of the system; that is, the data and instruction memories are customized according to the application's memory requirements.

While traditional loop-based compiler techniques that target data-intensive scientific applications have been shown to improve performance (by improving data access pattern), they generally do "not" reduce data space requirements (as they either change just the execution order of loop iterations or just modify array layout storage in memory). Recently, several approaches from the embedded systems community have been proposed for reducing data space requirements by analyzing lifetimes of variables (e.g., [29,7,6]). The idea is that the variables whose lifetimes do not overlap can use the same memory location. While one might think that the algorithms developed for register allocation (e.g., [5]) can be used for this purpose, this is not as straightforward since working on an individual array element granularity (i.e., treating each array element as a distinct variable) can be difficult. Obviously, the success of any memory reuse technique depends largely on how the input code is structured; i.e., on the order in which the array elements are produced and consumed. Consequently, if the way that the application code is written does not present many opportunities for memory location reuse, there is very little that these approaches can do.

Goal: In this work, we focus on array-intensive resource constrained applications and explore how loop-based compiler optimizations can be used for increasing the effectiveness of memory location reuse techniques. Our goal is to transform a given application in such a way that the resulting code has fewer cases (as compared to the original code) where the lifetimes of array elements overlap. Note that many applications from the domain of embedded image/video processing are array intensive [6].

Contributions: In this paper, we make the following contributions:
• We present a strategy using which an optimizing compiler can increase the effectiveness of the memory reuse techniques proposed for memory-limited systems.
• We present experimental data showing the effectiveness of our strategy. Our results indicate that the proposed strategy reduces data space requirements of ten complete applications by more than 40% on the average.

Fig. 1. Three phases of memory space optimization

Big Picture and Related Work: Figure 1 shows where our approach fits in the overall memory space optimization process. Our strategy is a high-level (source-level) optimization technique and is complementary to the classical locality-enhancing techniques. It can be applied before locality-enhancing techniques to reduce the memory space requirement of the application being optimized. Alternately, it can also be combined with locality-enhancing techniques. In this work, our major contribution is reducing the lifetimes of array elements through loop transformations. This corresponds to the first block in Figure 1, and so far, has not taken much attention. We also present a strategy (in Section 4) to determine the real data memory requirements after our transformations (the second block in Figure 1). Once the memory requirement is determined, the code needs to be re-written (the third block in Figure 1). This process has been addressed in previous research (e.g., [7, 23]); so, in this paper, we do not consider it.

Previous work on storage space optimization mainly focused on the second and third blocks of Figure 1. Lefebvre and Feautrier [16] proposed a method for automatic storage management for loop-based parallel programs with affine references. They showed that parallelization by total data expansion can be replaced by partial data expansion without distorting the degree of parallelism. Grun et al [10] presented memory size estimation techniques for multimedia applications. Strout et al [23] introduced the universal occupancy vector which enables schedule-independent storage space optimization. Their objective is to reduce data space requirements of a given code without preventing subsequent locality optimizations from being performed. Wilde and Rajopadhye [26] investigated memory reuse by performing static lifetime computations of variables using a polyhedral model. Wolfe [28] defined an optimization method called the array contraction for vector architectures. Our work is different from these efforts as we focus on the first block in Figure 1, and demonstrate how linear loop transformations (i.e., the transformations that optimize each nest independently without changing the number of loops in a nest) can increase the effectiveness of the following two blocks in the figure.

The work done by Song et al [22] and Catthoor and his colleagues [6] showed how loop fusion can be used for minimizing data space requirements. Along similar lines, Fraboulet et al [8] also presented an algorithm to reduce the use of temporary arrays by loop fusion. They demonstrated that although the complexity of their algorithm is not polynomial, it is very efficient in practice. These studies are orthogonal to our approach discussed in this paper which focuses on linear transformations; two strategies can also be combined under a unified optimizer.

Thies et al [24] describe a unified general framework for scheduling and storage optimization. One of the problems that they address, namely, "choosing a store for a given schedule" is similar to the problem addressed in this paper. However, there are some imporant differences between these two studies. First, they formulate the problem and solve it using a general linear programming solver, which may not be viable for large applications. In contrast, we make use of existing loop transformation theory. Second, in performing a storage assignment, we can be more aggressive as we not consider parallel loop execution as an option. Third, we report extensive experimental results to demonstrate the success of our static analysis and optimization.

In the parallel processing area, memory expansion has been used as a means for enhancing parallelism [4, 18, 25]. Our work, in a sense, tries to achieve the opposite effect of these efforts as we focus on resource constrained systems rather than parallel environments.

Roadmap: The next section gives a high-level description of the problem we address. Section 3 discusses details of our optimization strategy. Section 4 presents a technique for determining the memory space requirements after our lifetime minimization strategy is applied. Section 5 concludes the paper with a summary of our major results.

2 Problem Definition

In a given nest, we define the *lifetime* of an array element as the difference (in loop iterations) between the time it is assigned (written) and the time it is last used (read). For a given array element a, the start of its lifetime is referred to as $\mathcal{S}(a)$, whereas the end of its lifetime is denoted using $\mathcal{E}(a)$ (both in terms of loop iterations). Using these definitions, the *lifetime vector* for this array element can be given as

$$s = \mathcal{E}(a) - \mathcal{S}(a),$$

where "-" denotes vector subtraction. Note that the lifetime of a is expressed as a vector as in general there might be multiple loops in the nest, and expressing lifetime as a vector allows the compiler to measure the impact of loop transformations on it. As an example, if an array element (that is accessed in a nest with two loops) is produced in iteration $(1 \quad 3)^T$ and consumed (i.e., last-read) in iteration $(4 \quad 5)^T$, its lifetime vector is $(4 \quad 5)^T - (1 \quad 3)^T = (3 \quad 2)^T$. In the rest of this presentation, when there is no confusion, we use the terms lifetime vector and lifetime interchangeably. It should be noted that before $\mathcal{S}(a)$ and after $\mathcal{E}(a)$ the memory location allocated to this array element can be used for storing another array element (which belongs to the same array or to a different array). Obviously, the shorter the difference between $\mathcal{S}(a)$ and $\mathcal{E}(a)$ the better; as it leaves more room for other array elements. Consider Figure 2 that shows

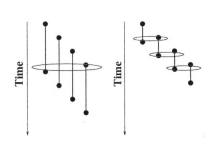

Fig. 2. Left: Lifetimes of four array elements. Right: Lifetimes after optimization

Algorithm I:
determine $s_m = max\{s_1, s_2, \cdots, s_W\}$
for $c_m = (0 \quad 0 \quad \cdots \quad 0 \quad 1)^T$
 while $c_m < s_m$ do
  for each combination of $c_1, c_2, \cdots, c_W$
   such that $c_m = max\{c_1, c_2, \cdots, c_W\}$ do
   determine a $\mathcal{T}$ such that
     $\mathcal{GT}^{-1} c_i = o - o_i$
   if $\mathcal{T}$ is legal do
    estimate memory space reduction R
    record $\mathcal{T}$ and R
   endif
  endfor
  select the next c_m
 endfor-while
select $\mathcal{T}$ with the maximum reduction R
apply $\mathcal{T}$ and transform the nest

Fig. 3. Algorithm for reducing memory space requirement of an array in a given nest

two example scenarios. Each vertical line in this figure represents the lifetime of an array element. On the left side, we have four array elements. Clearly, the lifetimes of these elements overlap (as indicated using an oval), hence there is no opportunity for memory location reuse. Suppose now that we somehow modified the lifetimes of these array elements to the one shown on the right side of the figure (e.g., using loop transformations [28]). We see that, at a given moment, only two lifetimes overlap. Consequently, we can work with only two memory locations instead of four. The rest of this paper discusses how loop transformations can be used for achieving this optimization in array-intensive applications.

However, reducing lifetimes of array elements does "not" guarantee memory location reuse. This is because in order to have memory location reuse, the lifetimes should be shortened such that the different elements can share the same memory location. As a result, it is important for the compiler to make sure that this happens (when lifetimes are reduced). For this purpose, in Section 4, we present an approach for estimating the memory space saving after our lifetime reduction strategy is applied. Using this approach, the compiler can check whether the lifetime reduction will really be beneficial; if not, the compiler may choose not to apply it.

3 Our Approach

3.1 Preliminaries

The loops in a C program surrounding any statement can collectively be represented using a column vector (called the "iteration vector")

$$I = (i_1 \quad i_2 \quad \cdots \quad i_n)^T,$$

where n is the number of the enclosing loops. Here, i_k is the kth loop index from top. The loop range (affine bounds) of these loops can be described by a system of inequalities which define the polyhedron $\mathcal{V}\boldsymbol{I} \leq \boldsymbol{v}$, where $\mathcal{V}$ is a $k \times n$ matrix and $\boldsymbol{v}$ is a k-entry vector. If all loop bounds are constants, then we have $k = 2n$ (i.e., one upper and one lower bound per loop). The integer values that can be taken on by $\boldsymbol{I}$ define the iteration space of the nest. Similarly, data (memory) layout of an array can also be represented using a polyhedron. This rectilinear polyhedron, called the index space, is delimited by array bounds, and each integer point in it, called an array index, is represented using an "index vector"

$$\boldsymbol{a} = \begin{pmatrix} a_1 & a_2 & \cdots & a_m \end{pmatrix}^T,$$

where m is the number of dimensions of the array.

Based on the iteration space and index space (data space) definitions, an array access (i.e, an array reference) can be defined as a mapping from iteration space to index space, and can be described as

$$\mathcal{G}\boldsymbol{I} + \boldsymbol{o}.$$

Assuming a nest with n loops that accesses an array of m dimensions, in the expression above, $\boldsymbol{I}$ denotes the iteration vector, $\mathcal{G}$ is an $m \times n$ matrix (called the "access matrix" or the "reference matrix"), and $\boldsymbol{o}$ is an m-entry constant vector (called the "offset vector") [28, 27, 17]. As an example, in a nest with two loops (i_1 and i_2), array reference $A[i_1 + 2][i_1 + i_2 - 3]$ can be represented as

$$\mathcal{G}\boldsymbol{I} + \boldsymbol{o} = \begin{pmatrix} 1 & 0 \\ 1 & 1 \end{pmatrix} \begin{pmatrix} i_1 \\ i_2 \end{pmatrix} + \begin{pmatrix} 2 \\ -3 \end{pmatrix}.$$

The application of a loop transformation represented by a square, non-singular matrix $\mathcal{T}$ can be accomplished in two steps [28]: (i) re-writing loop body and (ii) re-writing loop bounds. For the first step, assuming that $\boldsymbol{I}$ is the original iteration vector and $\boldsymbol{J} = \mathcal{T}\boldsymbol{I}$ is the new (transformed) iteration vector, each occurrence of $\boldsymbol{I}$ in the loop body is replaced by $\mathcal{T}^{-1}\boldsymbol{J}$ (note that $\mathcal{T}$ is invertible). In other words, an array reference represented by $\mathcal{G}\boldsymbol{I} + \boldsymbol{o}$ is transformed to $\mathcal{G}\mathcal{T}^{-1}\boldsymbol{J} + \boldsymbol{o}$. Determining the new loop bounds, however, is more complicated and, in general, may require the use of a technique such as Fourier–Motzkin elimination (a method for solving an affine system of inequalities [28, 3]). As an example, a loop nest that consists of i_1 (the outer loop) and i_2 (the inner loop) can be transformed into one with i_2 being the outer and i_1 being the inner using the following loop transformations matrix:

$$\mathcal{T} = \begin{pmatrix} 0 & 1 \\ 1 & 0 \end{pmatrix}.$$

One can see that application of a loop transformation changes the execution order of loop iterations. For example, applying the loop transformation represented by the matrix given above maps an original loop iteration $(3 \quad 5)^T$ to $(5 \quad 3)^T$. Also, any acceptable loop transformation should preserve the data dependences in the nest. If $\mathcal{D}$ is the data dependence matrix (i.e., a matrix for which each column is a dependence vector), after the loop transformation represented by $\mathcal{T}$, all columns of $\mathcal{T}\mathcal{D}$ should be lexicographically non-negative [28]. Wolfe [28] gives a detailed discussion of loop transformations. It should be emphasized that $\mathcal{G}\mathcal{T}^{-1}$ is the new access matrix after the transformation. Most of the proposed loop based techniques that target at enhancing data locality or parallelism can be cast as a problem of determining a $\mathcal{T}$ such that $\mathcal{G}\mathcal{T}^{-1}$ is in a desired form. While previous compiler work used loop transformations for improving data locality and loop-level parallelism, our work employs them for reducing the data space requirements of resource constrained programs. In our approach, when we determine a candidate loop transformation, we check whether it preserves data dependences in the code; if it does not, we try an alternate transformation as will be discussed later.

When the loop nest being optimized is imperfectly nested (i.e., there are statements sandwiched between loops), we first apply transformations to convert it to perfectly nested loops. There are at least two ways of achieving this. First, we can use classical transformations such as loop fission, loop distribution, and code sinking [28,19]. Alternately, we can try to embed the iteration spaces of individual statements into a common iteration space. For this purpose, the techniques proposed by Catthoor et al [6] or Ahmed et al [1] can be employed.

3.2 Assumptions

In this work, we focus on array-intensive applications that execute under memory space constraints. Many embedded image and video processing codes are array intensive [7,6]; they contain several loop nests operating on arrays of signals. We make the following assumptions:

• We assume that all array subscript expressions and loop bounds are "affine functions" of the enclosing loop indices and loop-invariant variables. Many previous compiler techniques proposed for array based applications work under this constraint [27, 19, 17, 13, 28]. This is because loop transformations are constrained by data dependences in the nest; the existence of non-affine expressions or indexed subscripts can make dependence analysis very difficult, and sometimes impossible. Fortunately, many array-intensive applications that run on resource constrained systems use only affine subscript expressions and loop bounds [7]. In addition, we also assume that, for a given array, all its elements have the same lifetime behavior (that is, their lifetimes can be characterized using the same set of lifetime vectors). Fortunately, the set of programs that can be handled under this assumption is the same set of programs where dependence vectors are constants. They constitute a large majority of array-based codes.

• When trying to reduce the lifetimes of array elements, we mainly focus on "uniformly generated references" as defined by Gannon et al [9]. Two array references $\mathcal{G}_1\boldsymbol{I}+\boldsymbol{o_1}$ and $\mathcal{G}_2\boldsymbol{I}+\boldsymbol{o_2}$ are said to be uniformly referenced if $\mathcal{G}_1 = \mathcal{G}_2$ even if $\boldsymbol{o_1} \neq \boldsymbol{o_2}$. That is, uniformly generated references have the same access matrix. This too is not a major limitation in our target domain, because many array references that appear in resource constrained applications are uniformly generated (e.g., stencil-type of computations that operate on images/video frames).

We also discuss how our strategy for deriving a suitable $\mathcal{T}$ can be modified when we have non-uniformly generated access matrices.

- For a given nested loop, we assume that it is in the single assignment form (i.e., each array element is assigned only once in the nest). While many codes fall into this category, there are also compiler techniques (e.g., [15, 18]) to bring those which are not in this form to this form. This is not a vital limitation for our approach, and we discuss what happens when we relax this constraint. Note, however, that we assume the single assignment rule only in per nest basis; that is, the same array element might be assigned multiple times in different nests.
- We assume that input-output arrays (called the "I/O arrays") are "not" space-reduced. An input array is one that contains the input data for the application, whereas an output array is the one that holds the final result. Our optimization targets all other arrays (called the non-I/O arrays) in the application being optimized. However, if one knows that an input array is not required beyond a certain program point, our approach can also take advantage of this.

In this paper, when we use notations such as $<, \leq, =, \geq,$ and $>$ with vectors, they denote "lexicographic comparisons." For example, for two vectors $\boldsymbol{x}$ and $\boldsymbol{y}$, $\boldsymbol{x} < \boldsymbol{y}$ means that $\boldsymbol{x}$ is lexicographically smaller than $\boldsymbol{y}$. That is, if $\boldsymbol{x} = (x_1 \ x_2 \ \cdots \ x_b)^T$ and $\boldsymbol{y} = (y_1 \ y_2 \ \cdots \ y_b)^T$, there exists at least a z (where $1 \leq z \leq b$) such that $x_j = y_j$ for all $1 \leq j \leq (z-1)$ and $x_z < y_z$.

3.3 Loop Transformations for Lifetime Reduction

Theory and Algorithm. In this section, we demonstrate how loop transformations can be used for reducing data space requirements. Since, as mentioned earlier in Section 3.1, a loop transformation changes the execution order of loop iterations (hence the order in which array elements are produced and consumed), it can be used to shorten the lifetimes of array elements. As an example, consider the following abstract loop nest, where vectors $\boldsymbol{I_l}$ and $\boldsymbol{I_u}$ denote the lower and upper loop bounds, respectively.

$$\begin{aligned}
&\text{for } \boldsymbol{I} = \boldsymbol{I_l}, \boldsymbol{I_u} \\
&\quad A[\mathcal{G}_1 \boldsymbol{I} + \boldsymbol{o_1}] = ... \\
&\quad ... = A[\mathcal{G}_2 \boldsymbol{I} + \boldsymbol{o_2}] ... \\
&\quad ... = A[\mathcal{G}_3 \boldsymbol{I} + \boldsymbol{o_3}] ...
\end{aligned}$$

Let us assume that, for a given loop iteration $\boldsymbol{I'}$ (where $\boldsymbol{I_l} \leq \boldsymbol{I'} \leq \boldsymbol{I_u}$), we have

$$\mathcal{G}_1 \boldsymbol{I'} + \boldsymbol{o_1} = \mathcal{G}_2(\boldsymbol{I'} + \boldsymbol{s_1}) + \boldsymbol{o_2} = \mathcal{G}_3(\boldsymbol{I'} + \boldsymbol{s_2}) + \boldsymbol{o_3}.$$

That is, a specific array element is written in iteration $\boldsymbol{I'}$ and read in iterations $\boldsymbol{I'} + \boldsymbol{s_1}$ and $\boldsymbol{I'} + \boldsymbol{s_2}$. Consequently, assuming that no other iteration accesses it, the lifetime of this element is $max\{s_1 + \boldsymbol{I'}, s_2 + \boldsymbol{I'}\} - \boldsymbol{I'}$, which is equal to $max\{s_1, s_2\}$. Suppose now that we transform this loop nest using a loop transformation matrix $\mathcal{T}$. In this case, the transformed nest looks like

$$\text{for } \boldsymbol{J} = \boldsymbol{J_l}, \boldsymbol{J_u}$$

$$A[\mathcal{G}_1 \mathcal{T}^{-1} \boldsymbol{J} + \boldsymbol{o}_1] = ...$$
$$... = A[\mathcal{G}_2 \mathcal{T}^{-1} \boldsymbol{J} + \boldsymbol{o}_2] ...$$
$$... = A[\mathcal{G}_3 \mathcal{T}^{-1} \boldsymbol{J} + \boldsymbol{o}_3] ...$$

Now, assuming that

$$\mathcal{G}_1 \mathcal{T}^{-1} \boldsymbol{J}' + \boldsymbol{o}_1 = \mathcal{G}_2 \mathcal{T}^{-1} (\boldsymbol{J}' + \boldsymbol{c}_1) + \boldsymbol{o}_2 = \mathcal{G}_3 \mathcal{T}^{-1} (\boldsymbol{J}' + \boldsymbol{c}_2) + \boldsymbol{o}_3$$

holds for a given $\boldsymbol{J}'$ for the same array element above, the new lifetime vector can be expressed as $max\{\boldsymbol{c}_1, \boldsymbol{c}_2\}$. As a result, such a transformation can be considered "beneficial" if

$$max\{\boldsymbol{c}_1, \boldsymbol{c}_2\} < max\{\boldsymbol{s}_1, \boldsymbol{s}_2\}.$$

An important question here is how to determine an appropriate loop transformation matrix $\mathcal{T}$ such that the condition above is satisfied. That is, since the original lifetime $max\{\boldsymbol{s}_1, \boldsymbol{s}_2\}$ is known, can we find a loop transformation such that the new lifetime vector is $max\{\boldsymbol{c}_1, \boldsymbol{c}_2\}$ and $max\{\boldsymbol{c}_1, \boldsymbol{c}_2\} < max\{\boldsymbol{s}_1, \boldsymbol{s}_2\}$? As discussed in Section 3.2, we are mostly interested in cases where $\mathcal{G}_1 = \mathcal{G}_2 = \mathcal{G}_3 = \mathcal{G}$ (i.e., the uniformly generated references). Therefore, for a given $\boldsymbol{c}_1$, in order to satisfy $\mathcal{G}\mathcal{T}^{-1}\boldsymbol{J}' + \boldsymbol{o}_1 = \mathcal{G}\mathcal{T}^{-1}(\boldsymbol{J}' + \boldsymbol{c}_1) + \boldsymbol{o}_2$, we need to have

$$\boldsymbol{o}_1 = \mathcal{G}\mathcal{T}^{-1}\boldsymbol{c}_1 + \boldsymbol{o}_2$$
$$\Longrightarrow \quad \mathcal{G}\mathcal{T}^{-1}\boldsymbol{c}_1 = \boldsymbol{o}_1 - \boldsymbol{o}_2$$

Similarly, for a given $\boldsymbol{c}_2$, to satisfy $\mathcal{G}\mathcal{T}^{-1}\boldsymbol{J}' + \boldsymbol{o}_1 = \mathcal{G}\mathcal{T}^{-1}(\boldsymbol{J}' + \boldsymbol{c}_2) + \boldsymbol{o}_3$, we need to have $\mathcal{G}\mathcal{T}^{-1}\boldsymbol{c}_2 = \boldsymbol{o}_1 - \boldsymbol{o}_3$. Based on these results, our algorithm (Algorithm I) for minimizing memory space requirements of a given array in a nest is shown in Figure 3.

In this algorithm, assuming that there are W read references ($\mathcal{G}\boldsymbol{I} + \boldsymbol{o}_i$ where $1 \leq i \leq W$) and one write reference ($\mathcal{G}\boldsymbol{I} + \boldsymbol{o}$) to the array, $\boldsymbol{s}_1, \boldsymbol{s}_2, \cdots, \boldsymbol{s}_W$ are the original lifetime vectors and $\boldsymbol{c}_1, \boldsymbol{c}_2, \cdots, \boldsymbol{c}_W$ are the lifetime vectors tried. A combination of these vectors is tried as long as

$$\boldsymbol{c}_m < \boldsymbol{s}_m,$$

where $\boldsymbol{c}_m = max\{\boldsymbol{c}_1, \boldsymbol{c}_2, \cdots, \boldsymbol{c}_W\}$ and $\boldsymbol{s}_m = max\{\boldsymbol{s}_1, \boldsymbol{s}_2, \cdots, \boldsymbol{s}_W\}$. In other words, this algorithm tries all alternative lifetime vector combinations (within the for-while construct) as long as the largest vector in a given combination is still smaller than the largest original lifetime vector. If an alternative leads to a legal loop transformation matrix $\mathcal{T}$, this matrix along with the memory space reduction it brings (called R in the algorithm) is recorded. To calculate the memory space reduction, we use the strategy discussed in Section 4. When all alternatives are tried, the one with the maximum memory reduction is selected, and the corresponding loop transformation is applied to the nest.

The table in Figure 4 gives the alternatives to be tried for an original lifetime vector of $(1\ 0\ 0\ 0)^T$ for an array with two read references and a write reference in a nest with four loops. The alternatives tried are numbered from 1 to 9. In

1	2	3
$\begin{pmatrix}0\\0\\0\\1\end{pmatrix};\begin{pmatrix}0\\0\\0\\1\end{pmatrix}$	$\begin{pmatrix}0\\0\\1\\0\end{pmatrix};\begin{pmatrix}0\\0\\0\\1\end{pmatrix}$	$\begin{pmatrix}0\\0\\0\\1\end{pmatrix};\begin{pmatrix}0\\0\\1\\0\end{pmatrix}$
4	5	6
$\begin{pmatrix}0\\0\\1\\0\end{pmatrix};\begin{pmatrix}0\\0\\1\\0\end{pmatrix}$	$\begin{pmatrix}0\\1\\0\\0\end{pmatrix};\begin{pmatrix}0\\0\\0\\1\end{pmatrix}$	$\begin{pmatrix}0\\1\\0\\0\end{pmatrix};\begin{pmatrix}0\\0\\1\\0\end{pmatrix}$
7	8	9
$\begin{pmatrix}0\\0\\0\\1\end{pmatrix};\begin{pmatrix}0\\1\\0\\0\end{pmatrix}$	$\begin{pmatrix}0\\0\\1\\0\end{pmatrix};\begin{pmatrix}0\\1\\0\\0\end{pmatrix}$	$\begin{pmatrix}0\\1\\0\\0\end{pmatrix};\begin{pmatrix}0\\1\\0\\0\end{pmatrix}$

Fig. 4. The candidate lifetime vectors for an array with two read references and a default lifetime vector of $s_m = (1\ 0\ 0\ 0)^T$

Algorithm II:

```
for each array i do
    determine s_{i,m} = max{s_{i,1}, s_{i,2}, ···, s_{i,W}}
endfor
for (c_{1,m}, c_{2,m}, ···, c_{t,m}) = (u, u, ···, u)
    while (c_{1,m}, c_{2,m}, ···, c_{t,m}) <
          (s_{1,m}, s_{2,m}, ···, s_{t,m}) do
        for each array i and each combination of
            c_{i,1}, c_{i,2}, ···, c_{i,W}
            such that
            c_{i,m} = max{c_{i,1}, c_{i,2}, ···, c_{i,W}} do
                determine a T such that for all i
                    G_i T^{-1} c_{i,1} = o_i − o_{i,1}
                    G_i T^{-1} c_{i,2} = o_i − o_{i,2}
                    ...
                    G_i T^{-1} c_{i,W} = o_i − o_{i,W}
                if T is legal do
                    estimate memory space reduction R
                    record T and R
                endif
                select the next (c_{i,1}, c_{i,2}, ···, c_{i,W})
                    for all i
        endfor
        select the next (c_{1,m}, c_{2,m}, ···, c_{t,m})
    endfor-while
    select T with the maximum reduction R
    apply T and transform the nest
```

Fig. 5. Algorithm for optimizing memory space requirements of multiple arrays

each alternative, the two lifetime vectors correspond to the two (write reference, read reference) pairs. Note that alternative 1 generates a $c_m = (0\ 0\ 0\ 1)^T$; alternatives 2, 3, and 4 generate a $c_m = (0\ 0\ 1\ 0)^T$; and alternatives 5, 6, 7, 8 and 9 generate a $c_m = (0\ 1\ 0\ 0)^T$, and that all these c_ms are better than $(1\ 0\ 0\ 0)^T$. The for-while loop in Algorithm I iterates over these three c_m vectors. For a given c_m vector, the inner for-loop in the algorithm tries different alternatives that give this c_m.

It should be emphasized that the algorithm in Figure 3 tries all possible alternatives for c_m as long as $c_m < s_m$, and among all alternatives, selects the one with the maximum reductions in the memory space requirements. Alternately, we can also stop the algorithm as soon as the first legal T matrix is found. This is reasonable as we try the potential c_m vectors in an ordered fashion, starting from the best candidate. In fact, our current implementation takes this approach to save compilation time.

The complexity of Algorithm I can be calculated as follows. Assuming $\mathcal{N}$ different nests in the application each with n loops (for simplicity) and that the original lifetime vector is the largest possible one (i.e., its first entry is non-zero), the maximum potential number of alternatives tried is $\mathcal{N}\sum_{k=1}^{n-1}(W(k^{W-1}-1)+1)$. Since we need to determine a loop transformation matrix (a process with a complexity of n^3) for each alternative, the overall complexity of the algorithm is $O(\mathcal{N}Wn^{W+2})$.

Example. In this subsection, we give an example to demonstrate how our approach works in practice. Let us consider the following loop nest (in a pseudo-language syntax):

$$\text{for } i_1 = 2, N$$
$$\quad \text{for } i_2 = 2, N$$
$$\quad\quad A[i_1][i_2] = ...$$
$$\quad\quad ... = A[i_1 - 1][i_2 - 1]$$

Here, we have

$$\mathcal{G} = \begin{pmatrix} 1 & 0 \\ 0 & 1 \end{pmatrix}; o_1 = \begin{pmatrix} 0 \\ 0 \end{pmatrix}; \text{ and } o_2 = \begin{pmatrix} -1 \\ -1 \end{pmatrix}.$$

By solving $\mathcal{G}I' + o_1 = \mathcal{G}(I' + s_1) + o_2$, we determine that $s_1 = (1 \ 1)^T$. Obviously, this is not a preferable lifetime (vector) as it crosses the iterations of the outermost loop in the nest. A preferable one would be $c_1 = (0 \ 1)^T$. From

$$\mathcal{G}\mathcal{T}^{-1}c_1 = o_1 - o_2,$$

we have

$$\begin{pmatrix} 1 & 0 \\ 0 & 1 \end{pmatrix} \mathcal{T}^{-1} \begin{pmatrix} 0 \\ 1 \end{pmatrix} = \begin{pmatrix} 0 \\ 0 \end{pmatrix} - \begin{pmatrix} -1 \\ -1 \end{pmatrix},$$

which gives us

$$\mathcal{T} = \begin{pmatrix} 1 & -1 \\ 0 & 1 \end{pmatrix}.$$

To see whether this transformation is legal (acceptable), we check the data dependences after the transformation. Since, in this nest, there exists a single data dependence with a dependence vector of $(1 \ 1)^T$, the transformed dependence vector is

$$\mathcal{T} \begin{pmatrix} 1 \\ 1 \end{pmatrix} = \begin{pmatrix} 1 & -1 \\ 0 & 1 \end{pmatrix} \begin{pmatrix} 1 \\ 1 \end{pmatrix} = \begin{pmatrix} 0 \\ 1 \end{pmatrix}.$$

Since this dependence vector is lexicographically positive, the transformation is legal [28]. Consequently, the transformed nest is as follows:

$$\text{for } i'_1 = 2 - N, N - 2$$
$$\quad \text{for } i'_2 = max\{2, 2 - i'_1\}, min\{N, N - i'_1\}$$
$$\quad\quad A[i'_1 + i'_2][i'_2] = ...$$
$$\quad\quad ... = A[i'_1 + i'_2 - 1][i'_2 - 1]$$

To illustrate how this transformation shortens the lifetimes of array elements, we concentrate on array element $A[8][3]$. In the original nest, the write is performed to this element in iteration $\mathcal{S}(A[8][3]) = (8 \ 3)^T$; the same element is read in iteration $\mathcal{E}(A[8][3]) = (9 \ 4)^T$; in other words, there are N iterations between the write and the read. On the other hand, after the transformation, the same array element is written in iteration $\mathcal{S}(A[8][3]) = (5 \ 3)^T$ and read in $\mathcal{E}(A[8][3]) = (5 \ 4)^T$, the next iteration. That is, the lifetime of this element after the transformation is only 1 iteration.

An important issue that deserves discussion here is the conflicting goals between optimizing data locality and reducing data memory requirements. A pure locality-enhancing technique would not apply any loop transformation to the original nest above (except maybe loop unrolling). This is because the data locality in the original nest is very good as it is; in fact, both the references shown above exhibit perfect spatial reuse in the innermost loop position (under row-major memory layout). While the loop transformation derived above helps to exploit the group temporal reuse between the two references, since the transformed code distorts the original spatial localities of both the references, it may not be preferable.

At this point, we want to discuss our choice of the lifetime vectors tried for reducing the lifetimes of the array elements. One might ask the question of why we are trying a lifetime vector such as $(0\ \ 1)^T$ instead of, say, $(0\ \ 2)^T$ or $(0\ \ 5)^T$. Obviously, nothing prevents the compiler from trying a vector such as $(0\ \ 2)^T$ or $(0\ \ 5)^T$. However, trying all possible (target) lifetime vectors is not feasible. Consequently, we should focus on a set of (lifetime) vectors that are really significantly different from each other. Note that $(0\ \ 1)^T$ and $(1\ \ 0)^T$ are very different from each other, as in the first of them the lifetime of the array element is within the iterations of the innermost loop, whereas in the second one the lifetime spans the entire inner loop. In comparison, the difference between $(0\ \ 1)^T$ and $(0\ \ 5)^T$ may not be that significant (depending on the loop bounds). In many array-intensive applications the loop bounds and original array sizes are very large. Therefore, in this work we only focus on vectors that are significantly different from each other. More specifically, the lifetime vectors we try have all 0 entries except for one entry which is 1. However, we should point out that in some cases it may not be possible to find a legal loop transformation that results in a lifetime vector $(0\ \ 1)^T$, but it might be possible to find a legal transformation for lifetime vector, say, $(0\ \ 5)^T$. Our experience shows that such cases do not occur very frequently (and, when they occur, they can be handled by modifying Algorithm I slightly).

3.4 Handling Non-uniform References

So far, we have focused mainly on uniformly generated references. In the following discussion, we show that our approach can also be used when array references are not uniformly generated. We consider the following abstract nest:

$$\text{for } I = I_l, I_u$$
$$A[\mathcal{G}_1 I + o_1] = ...$$
$$... = A[\mathcal{G}_2 I + o_2] ...$$

If we transform this nest using loop transformation matrix $\mathcal{T}$, we obtain the following transformed fragment:

$$\text{for } J = J_l, J_u$$
$$A[\mathcal{G}_1 \mathcal{T}^{-1} J + o_1] = ...$$
$$... = A[\mathcal{G}_2 \mathcal{T}^{-1} J + o_2] ...$$

Assuming that for two iterations J' and $J' + c_1$ the equality

$$\mathcal{G}_1 \mathcal{T}^{-1} J' + o_1 = \mathcal{G}_2 \mathcal{T}^{-1}(J' + c_1) + o_2$$

holds, we have

$$(\mathcal{G}_1 \mathcal{T}^{-1} - \mathcal{G}_2 \mathcal{T}^{-1}) J' = \mathcal{G}_2 \mathcal{T}^{-1} c_1 + (o_2 - o_1).$$

The difficulty with this expression is that it is a function of J'; this prevents us from carrying out an analysis similar to the one discussed in Section 3.3. Instead, we take the following approach. We first observe that ensuring $\mathcal{G}_1 \mathcal{T}^{-1} = \mathcal{G}_2 \mathcal{T}^{-1}$ will make the left hand side of the expression above $\mathbf{0}$. Then, we need to make sure that the right hand side expression also results in $\mathbf{0}$. The necessary condition for this is $\mathcal{G}_2 \mathcal{T}^{-1} c_1 = o_1 - o_2$. Consequently, we need to find a loop transformation matrix $\mathcal{T}$ such that both of the following equalities are satisfied:

$$\mathcal{G}_1 \mathcal{T}^{-1} = \mathcal{G}_2 \mathcal{T}^{-1}$$
$$\mathcal{G}_2 \mathcal{T}^{-1} c_1 = o_1 - o_2.$$

This means that in the non-uniformly generated references case, we impose more constraints on $\mathcal{T}$; consequently, finding a suitable loop transformation matrix is more difficult than the uniformly generated references case. Specifically, the first equality above is problematic. If both $\mathcal{G}_1$ and $\mathcal{G}_2$ are full rank matrices, this equality can be satisfied only when $\mathcal{G}_1 = \mathcal{G}_2$. On the other hand, if one of these matrices is full-rank while the other is not, this equality cannot be satisfied at all (as $\mathcal{T}^{-1}$ is of full-rank). Finally, if none of $\mathcal{G}_1$ and $\mathcal{G}_2$ is full-rank, then the equality in question may be satisfied depending on the actual entries of these matrices.

3.5 Multiple Arrays

When multiple arrays are accessed in a given nest, the loop transformation selected should be acceptable for all arrays; that is, to the extent possible, such a transformation should minimize the lifetimes of the elements of all the arrays accessed in the nest. This places more restrictions on selection of $\mathcal{T}$. Consider the following "transformed" loop nest which accesses two different arrays: A and B.

$$\text{for } J = J_l, J_u$$
$$A[\mathcal{G}_1 \mathcal{T}^{-1} J + o_1] = ...$$
$$B[\mathcal{G}_2 \mathcal{T}^{-1} J + o_2] = ...$$
$$... = A[\mathcal{G}_1 \mathcal{T}^{-1} J + o_3] ...$$
$$... = B[\mathcal{G}_2 \mathcal{T}^{-1} J + o_4] ...$$

Let us assume that (through this loop transformation) we would like to obtain a lifetime vector c_1 for array A and a lifetime vector c_2 for array B. So, we need to select a $\mathcal{T}$ such that both of the following equations are satisfied:

$$\mathcal{G}_1 \mathcal{T}^{-1} c_1 = o_1 - o_3$$
$$\mathcal{G}_2 \mathcal{T}^{-1} c_2 = o_2 - o_4$$

Note that each of these equations is similar to the one used for the single array case. An important question here is to decide on suitable c_1 and c_2. As before, these lifetime vectors should be smaller than the corresponding default (original) lifetime vectors; therefore, we try different lifetime vectors as long as they are smaller than the default lifetime vectors. A loop transformation can be considered beneficial if it brings some reduction in lifetimes of variables. To quickly decide whether a loop transformation is promising or not, we adopt the following strategy. Assuming that s_1 and s_2 are the original lifetime vectors for A and B respectively, the loop transformation matrix $\mathcal{T}$ which results in lifetime vectors c_1 and c_2 will be "beneficial" if

$$[(c_1 < s_1) \text{ and } (c_2 < s_2)] \text{ or } [(c_1 = s_1) \text{ and } (c_2 < s_2)]$$

$$\text{or } [(c_1 < s_1) \text{ and } (c_2 = s_2)].$$

As implied above, this is not perfectly accurate as in some cases even if we have $c_1 > s_1$ and $c_2 < s_2$, we may have some storage benefits depending on whether the lifetime reduction coming from array B is larger than the lifetime increase on array A. However, checking for this can only be done after determining the exact storage requirements. Instead, if any of the above conditions can be satisfied, it guarantees the storage benefits.

To illustrate how the compiler tries different lifetime vectors, we consider the abstract loop nest above and assume that $s_1 = (0\ 1\ 0)^T$ and $s_2 = (1\ 0\ 0)^T$. Consequently, the acceptable alternatives are

$$c_1 = (0\ 0\ 1)^T \text{ and } c_2 = (0\ 0\ 1)^T,$$
$$c_1 = (0\ 0\ 1)^T \text{ and } c_2 = (0\ 1\ 0)^T,$$
$$c_1 = (0\ 0\ 1)^T \text{ and } c_2 = (1\ 0\ 0)^T,$$
$$c_1 = (0\ 1\ 0)^T \text{ and } c_2 = (0\ 0\ 1)^T,$$
$$c_1 = (0\ 1\ 0)^T \text{ and } c_2 = (0\ 1\ 0)^T.$$

3.6 Putting It All Together

In this section, we present our compiler algorithm for optimizing multiple arrays. If we consider storage optimization for a single nest at a time (i.e., if we do not use multi-nest optimization), our compiler executes the algorithm given in Figure 5 (Algorithm II) *for each nest* in the code. In this algorithm, u denotes the constant vector $(0\ 0\ \cdots\ 0\ 1)^T$. This algorithm first determines, for each array i $(1 \leq i \leq t)$, its maximum (original) lifetime vector $s_{i,m}$. For simplicity, we assume that in the input code each array has $W + 1$ references: a write reference with access matrix $\mathcal{G}_i$ and offset vector o_i, and W read references, where the kth reference has an access matrix $\mathcal{G}_i$ and offset vector $o_{i,k}$. Our objective is to transform the input code so that we reduce the lifetime vectors for as many arrays as possible. The for-while construct in this algorithm tries different alternative lifetime vectors for arrays. To check for the best possible case, we first try the case when all lifetime vectors are $(0 \ 0 \ \cdots \ 0 \ 1)^T$. If we can find a $\mathcal{T}$ that satisfies these lifetime vectors, this $\mathcal{T}$ and the memory space reduction it brings (denoted using R in the algorithm) are recorded, and other alternatives are tried (within the for-while construct). Note that an alternative gives a potential lifetime vector for each array. However, from a given array's perspective, if there are multiple references to it (in the nest), there might be multiple ways to satisfy a given lifetime vector (see Section 3.3). Therefore, the inner for-loop in the algorithm tries all such alternatives. As an example, for a given array i, when we try a specific $c_{i,m}$, all combinations of $c_{i,1}, c_{i,2}, \cdots$, $c_{i,W}$ such that $c_{i,m} = max\{c_{i,1}, c_{i,2}, \cdots, c_{i,W}\}$ are tried. Note also that the constraints (equalities) in this algorithm that involve access matrices are written for all arrays. While, as in the single array case, this algorithm is written in such a way that all alternatives are tried before selecting a loop transformation matrix, in our current implementation, we stop when the first legal $\mathcal{T}$ is found. The complexity of Algorithm II is $O(2^t \mathcal{N} W n^{W+2})$ assuming $\mathcal{N}$ nests (each with n loops) and t arrays accessed in each nest (each with W read references in each nest). This is because the for-while construct iterates $2^t - 1$ times, and in each iteration, we perform a computation of the order of $O(\mathcal{N} W n^{W+2})$ complexity. In many applications the number of arrays accessed in a given nest (t) is small; so, the algorithm is expected to be fast in practice.

The algorithm above is written under the assumption that each array is accessed using uniformly generated references (i.e., a single $\mathcal{G}_i$ for array i in a given nest). If this is not the case, we can modify the algorithm by adding the necessary constraints (see Section 3.4) to Algorithm II. Specifically, assuming that $\mathcal{G}_{i,k}$ and $\mathcal{G}_{i,k'}$ are two different non-uniformly generated references to array i, we need to add $\mathcal{G}_{i,k}\mathcal{T}^{-1} = \mathcal{G}_{i,k'}\mathcal{T}^{-1}$ to the constraints that appear in the algorithm. In the following subsection, we show how this algorithm is extended to incorporate multi-nest optimization. If an array to be space-reduced is not in the SSA form, using the approach in [18], we can determine the last writes to its elements, and based on that, we can then apply our strategy. Alternately, we can first convert the code to the single assignment form, and then apply our strategy. The algorithm given in Figure 5 can also be extended to handle multiple nests at a time. For a discussion, we refer the reader to [11].

4 Determining Storage Requirement

Our strategy, as explained above, tries to reduce the lifetimes of array elements. However, to evaluate the impact of this on memory space requirements, we need to be able to estimate potential memory space requirement it brings. In this section, we demonstrate that lifetime vectors combined with single assignment rule (assumed for each nest) allows us to estimate the magnitude of savings in data memory space. In doing so, we also make use of the assumption that all elements of a given array have the same lifetime behavior (see Section 3.2).

Recall that if we have a lifetime vector c_1 (for a given array A with one write and one read reference), for a given element a_1 of array A, we have

$$a_1 = \mathcal{G} I_1 + o_1 = \mathcal{G}(I_1 + c_1) + o_2.$$

Here, I_1 is the iteration in which a_1 is written. Now, suppose that, for another element (a_2) of the same array, we have

$$a_2 = \mathcal{G}I_2 + o_1 = \mathcal{G}(I_2 + c_1) + o_2.$$

Assuming $I_2 > I_1$, in order to reuse the memory location used for a_1 for storing a_2, the following condition should be satisfied:

$$I_1 + c_1 < I_2.$$

That is, the last use of a_1 should be completed before the write operation to a_2 (this can easily be extended to the cases with multiple read references). It should be noted that after $I_1 + c_1$, the location allocated for a_1 can be reused by (one of) the other array elements that satisfy the above inequality. Only the elements for which the write operation occurs before or at $I_1 + c_1$ cannot use the memory location used for a_1. Then, if we find the number of such elements, we can estimate the maximum data storage requirements for the array in question. Since we assume single assignment to array elements within a given loop, the number of such array elements is (at most) the same as the number of iterations that are executed when we move from I_1 to $I_1 + c_1$. Now, let us assume that the number of iterations for loops $i_1, i_2, ..., i_n$ are $N_1, N_2, ..., N_n$, respectively, where i_1 is the outermost loop. Then, based on the discussion above, the maximum storage requirement can be estimated as

$$c_1^T \bullet \begin{pmatrix} N_2 N_3 ... N_{n-1} N_n \\ \vdots \\ N_{n-2} N_{n-1} N_n \\ N_{n-1} N_n \\ N_n \\ 1 \end{pmatrix},$$

where $\bullet$ denotes the dot product. This process can be repeated for each array in the code.

This approach handles only "intra-array memory reuse". That is, the memory reuse that takes place between the elements of the same array. It is also possible to exploit memory reuse opportunities between the elements that belong to different arrays. We term this type of memory reuse as the "inter-array memory reuse". In fact, an array B (which is different from the one we focused above) can also reuse the locations of the array above (A). However, B can also exploit its own intra-array reuse. Whether exploiting intra-array or inter-array reuse (for array B) is more beneficial depends on the lifetime vectors c_1 (for array A) and c_2 (for array B). In this paper, we focus on intra-array memory location reuse only, and do not consider inter-array memory reuse.

5 Concluding Remarks

With the proliferation of resource constrained systems, compiling applications under memory limitations has become an important problem. This work proposed a compiler strategy that uses loop transformations for reducing lifetimes of array elements in a given array-intensive application. Reducing lifetimes of array elements increases the effectiveness of the memory location reuse techniques. Our experimental results indicated that our approach is successful in reducing memory space requirements and improving data locality.

References

1. N. Ahmed, N. Mateev, and K. Pingali. Synthesizing transformations for locality enhancement of imperfectly-nested loop nests. In *Proc. International Conference on Supercomputing (ICS)*, May 2000.
2. S. P. Amarasinghe, J. M. Anderson, M. S. Lam, and C. W. Tseng. The SUIF compiler for scalable parallel machines. In *Proc. 7th SIAM Conference on Parallel Processing for Scientific Computing*, February, 1995.
3. C. Ancourt and F. Irigoin. Scanning polyhedra with DO loops. In *Proc. ACM Symp. on Principles of Prog. Lang. (POPL)*, June 1991.
4. D. Barthou, A. Cohen, and J-F. Collard. Maximal static expansion. In *Proc. 25th Annual ACM Symp. on Principles of Prog. Lang. (POPL)*, San Diego, CA, 1998.
5. P. Briggs. *Register Allocation via Graph Coloring*, PhD thesis, Rice University, Houston, TX, April 1992.
6. F. Catthoor, K. Danckaert, C. Kulkarni, E. Brockmeyer, P.G. Kjeldsberg, T. V. Achteren, and T. Omnes. *Data Access and Storage Management for Embedded Programmable Processors*, Kluwer Academic Publishers, 2002.
7. F. Catthoor et al. *Custom Memory Management Methodology – Exploration of Memory Organization for Embedded Multimedia System Design*. Kluwer Academic, 1998.
8. A. Fraboulet, K. Kodary, and A. Mignotte. Loop fusion for memory space optimization. In *Proc. 14th International Symposium on System Synthesis (ISSS)*, Montreal, Canada, September 30–October 3, 2001.
9. D. Gannon, W. Jalby, and K. Gallivan. Strategies for cache and local memory management by global program transformations. *Journal of Parallel and Distributed Computing (JPDC)*, 5:587–616, 1988.
10. P. Grun, F. Balasa, and N. Dutt. Memory size estimation for multimedia applications. In *Proc. CODES/CACHE*, 1998.
11. P. Unnikrishnan, G. Chen, M. Kandemir, M. Karakoy, and I. Kolcu. Loop Transformations for Reducing Data Space Requirements of Resource-Constrained Applications. *Technical Report of CSE Department, The Pennsylvania State University,,* 2002.
12. F. Irigoin and R. Triolet. Supernode partitioning. In *Proc. 15th Annual ACM Symp. on Principles of Programming Languages (POPL)*, pages 319–329, 1988.
13. M. Kandemir. A compiler technique for improving whole program locality. In *Proc. 28th Annual ACM Symposium on Principles of Programming Languages (POPL)*, London, UK, January, 2001.
14. K. Kennedy and K. S. McKinley. Maximizing loop parallelism and improving data locality via loop fusion and distribution. In *Proc. Workshop on Languages and Compilers for Parallel Computing (LCPC)*, pp. 301–321, Oregon, Aug 1993.
15. K. Knobe and V. Sarkar. Array SSA form and its use in parallelization. In *Proc. 15th Annual ACM Symposium on Principles of Programming Languages (POPL)*, pages 107–120, 1998.
16. V. Lefebvre and P. Feautrier. Automatic storage management for parallel programs. *Research report PRiSM 97/8*, France, 1997.

17. W. Li. *Compiling for NUMA Parallel Machines*. Ph.D. Thesis, Computer Science Department, Cornell University, Ithaca, New York, 1993.
18. D. E. Maydan, S. P. Amarasinghe, and M. S. Lam. Array dataflow analysis and its use in array privatization. In *Proc. Annual ACM Symposium on Principles of Programming Languages (POPL)*, pages 2–15, January 1993.
19. K. McKinley, S. Carr, and C.-W. Tseng. Improving data locality with loop transformations. *ACM Transactions on Programming Languages and Systems (TOPLAS)*, 18(4):424–453, July 1996.
20. MIPSpro Family of Compilers.
    http://www.sgi.com/developers/devtools/languages/mipspro.html.
21. W. Pugh and D. Wonnacott. An exact method for analysis of value-based array data dependences. In *Proc. 6th Workshop on Languages and Compilers for Parallel Computing (LCPC)*, Portland, Aug 1993.
22. Y. Song, R. Xu, C. Wang, and Z. Li. Data locality enhancement by memory reduction. In *Proc. 15th ACM International Conference on Supercomputing (ICS)*, June, 2001.
23. M. Strout, L. Carter, J. Ferrante, and B. Simon. Schedule-independent storage mapping in loops. In *Proc. ACM Conference on Architectural Support for Programming Languages and Operating Systems (ASPLOS)*, October, 1998.
24. W. Thies, F. Vivien, J. Sheldon, and S. Amarasinghe, A unified framework for schedule and storage optimization. In *Proc. the SIGPLAN Conference on Programming Language Design and Implementation*, Snowbird, UT, June, 2001.
25. P. Tu and D. Padua. Automatic array privatization. In *Proc. 6th Workshop on Languages and Compilers for Parallel Computing (LCPC)*, Lecture Notes in Computer Science, pages 500–521, Portland, OR, August 1993.
26. D. Wilde and S. Rajopadhye. Memory reuse analysis in the polyhedral model. *Parallel Processing Letters*, 1997.
27. M. Wolf and M. Lam. A data locality optimizing algorithm. In *Proc. ACM SIGPLAN 91 Conference on Programming Language Design and Implementation (PLDI)*, pages 30–44, June 1991.
28. M. Wolfe. *High Performance Compilers for Parallel Computing*, Addison-Wesley Publishing Company, 1996.
29. Y. Zhao and S. Malik. Exact memory size estimation for array computations without loop unrolling. In *Proc. ACM/IEEE Design Automation Conference (DAC)*, June 1999.

Code Compaction of Matching Single-Entry Multiple-Exit Regions*

Wen-Ke Chen, Bengu Li, and Rajiv Gupta

Dept. of Computer Science, The University of Arizona, Tucson, Arizona 85721

Abstract. With the proliferation of embedded devices and systems, there is renewed interest in the generation of compact binaries. Code compaction techniques identify code sequences that repeatedly appear in a program and replace them by a single copy of the recurring sequence. In existing techniques such sequences are typically restricted to single-entry single-exit regions in the control flow graph. We have observed that in many applications recurring code sequences form single-entry multiple-exit (SEME) regions. In this paper we propose a generalized algorithm for code compaction that first decomposes a control flow graph into a hierarchy of SEME regions, computes signatures of SEME regions, and then uses the signatures to find pairs of matching SEME regions. Maximal sized matching SEME regions are found and transformed to achieve code compaction. Our transformation is able to compact matching SEME regions whose exits may lead to a combination of identical and differing targets. Our experiments show that this transformation can lead to substantial reduction in code size for many embedded applications.

Keywords: Code compaction, single-entry-multiple-exit regions, control flow signature, predicated execution.

1 Introduction

In the embedded domain, often applications are required to fit in a limited amount of memory and their execution is required to be energy efficient. One avenue of reducing the memory needs of an application program is through the use of code size reduction techniques. Code size reduction can also lead to better instruction cache performance and hence yield energy savings during execution. There are two broad categories of code size reduction techniques: *code compaction* techniques that produce directly executable code and are implemented entirely in software (e.g., [2,4]); and *code compression* techniques that produce code that must be decompressed prior to execution (e.g., [3]). Techniques that rely on hardware support to generate compact binaries also exist [15,10,13,6]. This paper addresses the problem of *code compaction*.

---

* Supported by grants from IBM, Intel, and NSF grants CCR-0105355, CCR-0208756, CCR-0220334, and EIA-0080123 to the Univ. of Arizona.

Code Compaction Techniques. A commonly used approach to *code compaction* is the application of compiler based transformations which find recurring code sequences in an application and replace them by a single shared copy of the code sequence [16, 7, 17, 1, 2]. There are two commonly used transformations for removing repeated occurrences of a code sequence: *tail merging* [16, 7, 1] and *procedural abstraction* [17, 2]. If the recurring sequences appear along alternate paths immediately prior to a merge point in the control flow graph, *tail merging* is applied to replace multiple occurrences of the code sequence immediately before the merge point by a single occurrence of the code sequence following the merge point. If the control flow does not merge following the recurring code sequences, *procedural abstraction* is used. A procedure is created to contain the code sequence and this procedure is called from each point where the sequence occurs. Therefore, *procedural abstraction* introduces runtime overhead due to call and return while *tail merging* does not require this additional overhead.

An important aspect of the above code compaction transformations is the scope of code sequences to which the transformations are applied. Early works consider code sequences made up of a single basic block or a part (suffix) of a single basic block. More recent techniques have extended the transformations to consider code sequences that form *single-entry single-exit* (SESE) regions in the control flow graph. Moreover the code sequences need not be identical – as long as they can be made identical through renaming of variables (registers), the transformations can be applied. We will refer to such code sequences as *similar code sequences* and their corresponding control flow graph regions as *matching regions*. It should be noted that finding multiple instances of a single large matching region is better than finding several smaller matching regions. This is because while tail merging or a single application of procedural abstraction will be sufficient to compact the large regions, to individually compact the smaller subregions it contains will require multiple applications of procedural abstraction. The latter yields less compact code and introduces greater amount of call-return overhead.

Our Contribution. By studying several embedded benchmarks we have observed that often *similar* code sequences that appear in applications are larger than a basic block but they do not form matching SESE regions. Instead we have observed frequent presence of *similar single-entry multiple-exit* (SEME) regions. Moreover, the exits of the matching regions may lead to a combination of same and different program points. To take advantage of the above situations we require a generalized algorithm for identifying matching regions and a generalized transformation to handle the complexity of the exits associated with these regions.

In this paper we present a generalized algorithm for detecting matching SEME regions and a generalized tail merging transformation to compact such regions. The two key components of our algorithm are as follows:

- *Finding matching SEME regions.* There are several problems that we solve to find matching regions. First we construct a *region hierarchy graph* (RHG)

which represents a decomposition of the program into a hierarchy of SEME regions. Second we compute *signatures* of these regions. Finally using a combination of *signatures* and the *RHG* we search for SEME regions that match. Our approach to matching signatures naturally allows small differences to be present between the matched regions which can be effectively handled during the compaction transformation.
– *Generalized tail merging transformation.* The key to developing this transformation is an ability to compact matching SEME regions such that their exits lead to a combination of same and different target points in the control flow graph. By introducing a *distinguishing predicate*, which identifies the context in which a compacted region is being executed, we are able to efficiently handle transfer of control to different targets from corresponding exits of the matching regions. Thus, without using procedural abstraction, we are able to compact matching SEME regions with a combination of exits with same and different targets.

Before we present the details of the above algorithm in the subsequent sections, we illustrate the power of our approach in handling situations taken from benchmarks. The example in Fig. 1 is taken from one of the spec2000 benchmarks. It illustrates a situation in which two matching SEME regions, with three exits each, have all their exits leading to the same program point. Small amount of renaming is needed to make these regions identical and carrying out a more general form of tail merging for compaction as shown in Fig. 1. Thus not only is a large sequence of code reused, the overhead introduced by code compaction is minimal. What is important to note is that existing techniques will not handle this situation well – they will perform less compaction and introduce additional overhead. Since existing algorithms are based upon SESE regions, and the only SESE subregions in the SEME region are individual basic blocks, they will transform each pair of corresponding basic blocks separately. While the three basic blocks from which we exit the SEME region (3, 4, and 5) can be transformed using tail merging, the other two basic blocks (1 and 2) will be transformed using procedural abstraction which will introduce additional call-return overhead. Finally since the control structures of the SEME regions will stay in place, the conditional branches in the two regions at which basic blocks 1 and 2 terminate are not compacted at all. Thus, existing algorithms will achieve less compaction at greater overhead cost while our algorithm will perform much better by compacting the entire SEME region in a single application of a generalized tail merging transformation.

While in the above example the SEME regions shared a single identical target for all the exits, in general this may not be the case. Two such situations that we observed in benchmarks and are handled by us are illustrated in Fig. 2 and Fig. 3. In Fig. 2 after exiting region SEME(y), an extra statement S is executed and then the same program point is reached that is also the target of exits of region SEME(x). By introducing a conditional execution of S we carry out compaction as shown in the figure. In Fig. 3 we can see that pair of corresponding exits from matching regions lead to different targets (T_1 and T_2). In this case we

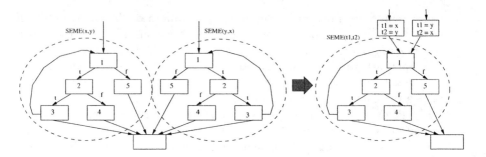

Fig. 1. spec2000::parser::parse.c::match()

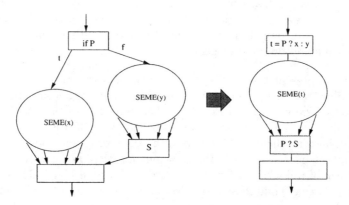

Fig. 2. spec2000::twolf::unetseg.c::unetseg()

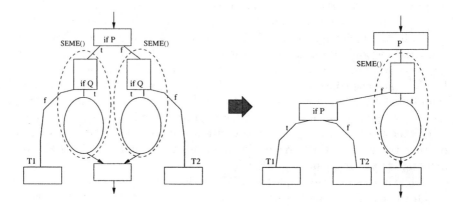

Fig. 3. MediaBench::mesa::clip.c::gl_viewclip_line()

introduce a conditional selection of the target at the corresponding exit following compaction. Both of the above examples are being essentially compacted using a common approach for handling differences between the matching SEME regions. We find a *distinguishing predicate* (denoted by P in our examples) which essentially will capture the context in which the compacted code sequence is being executed (i.e., if $SEME_1$ and $SEME_2$ are replaced by $SEME_{12}$, during an execution of $SEME_{12}$, P will indicate whether the execution corresponds to an execution of $SEME_1$ or $SEME_2$). Thus, P can be used to perform conditional execution of statements in the matching SEME regions that need to be handled differently. While in our examples a distinguishing predicate was already present in the program, if one is not present it is explicitly introduced by our transformation. These examples also illustrate that the transformation we use is essentially a generalized form of tail merging which incurs lower overhead than procedural abstraction. Clearly the large SEME regions present in the above examples will not be handled effectively by existing techniques as existing techniques can at best transform smaller SESE subregions using, in many cases, the more expensive procedural abstraction transformation.

Outline. The remainder of the paper is organized as follows. In section 2 we develop the *region hierarchy graph* that decomposes a program into a hierarchy of SEME regions. In section 3 we describe our algorithm for computing *signatures* and *finding matching SEME regions*. In section 4 we present the *generalized tail merging* transformation. Experimental results are presented in section 5 and concluding remarks are given in section 6.

2   Hierarchy of SEME Regions

Given a control flow graph (CFG), SEME regions can be formed in a number of ways. Therefore as a first step it is important that we find a systematic method for forming SEME regions. The approach we take is to develop a *region hierarchy graph* (RHG) which decomposes the program into a hierarchy of SEME regions. A hierarchical representation is needed because larger SEME regions are formed by combining smaller SEME regions. Using this graph we will be able to explore all possible SEME regions that can be formed for a given control flow graph.

While an algorithm for decomposing a program into a hierarchy of SESE regions exists [9], no such algorithm has been developed for SEME regions. Next we present an algorithm that we have developed for building a RHG for SEME regions. For this purpose we first construct the *control dependence graph* (CDG) [5] corresponding to the given CFG. Let us briefly review the structure of the CDG and then see why CDG is an appropriate choice for building the RHG.

A CDG partitions the program into *control dependence regions*. Corresponding to each control dependence region, it creates a special region node which directly points to all the basic blocks within that region. In addition, it points to other nested control dependence regions. We assume that nodes within a control dependence region are ordered from left to right according to the order in which they appear in the program with an earlier node always appearing to the left of a later node. The set of basic blocks that belong to the same control dependence region are *control equivalent*, i.e. the conditions under which they are executed are identical. Finally the internal nodes of a CDG are made up of two types of nodes: those created to represent control dependence regions and those that correspond to basic blocks ending with conditionals.

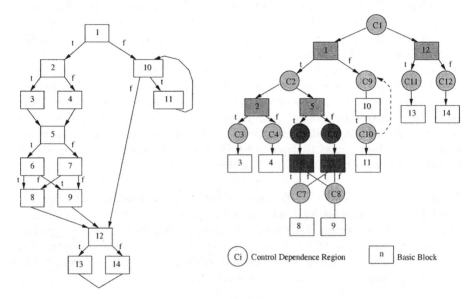

Fig. 4. Example control flow graph and its control dependence graph

Consider an example CFG and its corresponding CDG shown in Fig. 4. As we can see, nodes 1 and 12 belong to the same control dependence region C_1 because they are control equivalent. Internal nodes include control dependence region nodes C_1 through C_{12} and basic blocks ending at conditionals (i.e., nodes 1, 2, 5, 6, 7, 10, and 12).

Our motivation for using the CDG as the basis for computing the RHG is as follows. First CDG is already a hierarchical decomposition of the program such that each internal node of this graph represents a program region. Second, while each such region corresponds to a subgraph of the CFG which may have single or multiple entries and exits, it is easy to distinguish single entry regions from multiple entry regions. In particular if there does not exist any edge from outside the region to a node within the region (see Fig. 5) then the region has only one entry node which is the first basic block encountered during the *in order* traversal of the region subgraph in the CDG. For example, in Fig. 4 the regions C_5 and C_6 are multi-entry regions.

Given that we can classify each internal node of the CDG as representing either a multi-entry or single-entry region, we can further construct a region hierarchy graph whose nodes represent single-entry regions where each region may have one or more exits. Since each node in the RHG represents a single

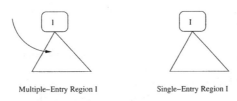

Fig. 5. Distinguishing single-entry regions from multiple-entry regions

entry region, the RHG is a tree. Next we define the RHG formally and present an algorithm for constructing it.

A *SEME region* R is denoted as $R = (n_{entry}, N)$ where n_{entry} is the *single entry node* of the region in the CFG formed by the nodes in N. Each control flow graph edge whose source node is in N, but the destination node does not belong to N, represents an *exit* from region R. If R has a single exit, then it represents a SESE region, i.e., by definition SEME regions subsume SESE regions.

Definition 1. A *region hierarchy graph* (RHG) is a tree in which each node represents a SEME region corresponding to the subgraph rooted at a single-entry node identified in the CDG. The children of a node $SEME_i$ in the RHG are the largest distinct SEME regions entirely contained within $SEME_i$.

The algorithm for constructing the RHG is given Fig. 6. The algorithm examines each internal node and if it represents a single entry region it constructs a region and adds it to the region set $\mathcal{RS}$. If the internal node is a basic block, it is the entry node for the region. If the internal node is a control dependence region node, then we keep taking the leftmost link till the first basic block is encountered. This basic block is the entry node. All basic blocks that are descendants of the internal node belong to the region. The construction of the RHG can be implemented efficiently through a single bottom-up traversal of the CDG and thus the runtime cost of building the RHG is proportional to the size of the CDG. The RHG corresponding to the CDG in Fig. 4 is shown in Fig. 6.

3 Searching for Matching SEME Regions

There are two problems that are addressed in this section: *searching* and *matching*. While there exist some previous work [11, 12] on identifying matching fragments, these techniques can not be applied directly to SEME matching. Given two SEME regions, matching is the process that finds out whether the two regions are *sufficiently similar* while searching is the process that selects pairs of SEME regions for matching and if they match, it iteratively expands and matches them to find larger matching regions. To carry out matching we define a method of computing *signatures* of SEME regions which are used as the basis of matching. This method is described first in the section. Following that we will show how RHG can be used to conveniently implement the search of matching SEME regions.

Input: A control flow graph (CFG) and its control dependence graph (CDG).
Output: A set of SEME regions, $\mathcal{RS}$.
definitions:
  backedges, $\mathcal{BE} = \{ (s,d) : (s,d) \in \text{CDG}$ is a loop back edge $\}$
  descendant set of an internal node $c \in \text{CDG}$,
    $\mathcal{DESCENDANT}(c) = \{\, n : \exists$ a path $c \to n$ in CDG which
                                 contains no edge from $\mathcal{BE}\,\}$
  reaching set of an internal node $c \in \text{CDG}$,
    $\mathcal{REACH}(c) = \{n : n$ is a basic block$; n \in \{c\} \cup \mathcal{DESCENDANT}(c)\,\}$
initialization:
  $\mathcal{RS} = \phi$
Algorithm:
  foreach internal node $c \in \text{CDG}$ in reverse topological order **do**
    if $\exists$ an edge (s,d) st $d \in \mathcal{DESCENDANT}(c)$ and $s \notin \{c\} \cup \mathcal{DESCENDANT}(c)$
    then– do nothing; c represents a multiple-entry region
    else – add region for c to $\mathcal{RS}$
        if c is a basic block **then**
          $\mathcal{RS} = \mathcal{RS} \cup \{(n_{entry} = c, \mathcal{REACH}(c))\}$
        else – c is a control dependence region node
          Let l be the first basic block reached by following leftmost links
            starting at $c \in \text{CDG}$
          $\mathcal{RS} = \mathcal{RS} \cup \{(n_{entry} = l, \mathcal{REACH}(l))\}$
        endif
    endif
  endfor

Fig. 6. SEME region hierarchy: Construction algorithm and example

Signatures. We use a pair of signatures to characterize a SEME region. The first level is the *control flow signature* (CFS) which simply captures the shape of the SEME region. If two SEME regions have the same control flow signature, then they must have the same shape, i.e. the regions contain identical number of nodes connected with each other by identical edges and the single entry as well as the exits are in corresponding positions. Once the control flow signatures of two regions match, a correspondence is established between the basic blocks of the two regions. At this point the second level signatures, which are essentially the *data flow signatures* (DFS) of each of the basic blocks, are compared. In the remainder of this discussion we will mainly concentrate on control flow signatures because data flow signatures of various kinds have already been developed by other researchers to match code sequences that extend across a complete basic block or that form a suffix of a basic block [7, 2]. These existing techniques also allow for differences that can be overcome using variable renaming.

Our algorithm for generating the control flow signature generates a serialization of the control flow graph in which all nodes, edges, label on edges, entry, and exits are included. The nodes are renamed before inclusion in this serialization. Thus, if two SEME regions have the same shape, they produce the same signature when processed by our signature generating algorithm.

Fig. 7 presents a function CFS(n, R) which when called with n being the entry node of region R, returns the CFS for region R. It carries out an *in order*

```
CFS (n, R = (n_e, N)) {
    if (AN(n) ≠ null) then
        if (n ∈ N) then
            return( (AN(n), in) )
        else
            return( (AN(n), out) )
        endif
    else
        if (n ∈ N) then
            AN(n) = count; count + +;
            if (Succ(n) = {n_s}) then
                return( (AN(n), in) o (−) o CFS(n_s, R) )
            elseif (Succ(n) = {n_t, n_f}) then
                return( (AN(n), in) o(T) o CFS(n_t, R) o (F) o CFS(n_f, R) )
            endif
        else
            AN(n) = *; return( (AN(n), out) )
        endif
    endif
}
main () {
    count = 0; CFS_R = CFS(n_entry, R = (n_entry, N));
}
```

Fig. 7. Computing the control flow signature of a region

traversal of the region R starting at the entry node such that no edge is visited twice. Each node in the region is assigned a new unique id/name $\mathcal{AN}(n)$ when it is visited for the first time prior to which all nodes are assigned a *null* id. All nodes and edges contained within the region are visited once. In addition all exit edges for the regions as well as the nodes outside the region to which the exit edges lead are also visited once. These outside nodes are assigned an $\mathcal{AN}(n)$ value of $*$. This is because, for our compaction transformation to be applicable, while the positions of exits of matching SEME regions must be the same, their targets need not be the same. The signature is made up of sequence of nodes and edges that are visited, in the order that they are visited. A visit to node n adds $(\mathcal{AN}(n), in)$ to the signature if n belongs to the region and $(\mathcal{AN}(n), out)$ if it is out of the region (i.e., it is a target of an exit edge). The traversal of an edge is indicated by adding $(-)$, (T), and (F) to the signature if the edge is not labeled, labeled true, and labeled false respectively. When two SEME regions generate the same signature, the $\mathcal{AN}$ values assigned to the nodes establish a correspondence between the nodes, edges and exits of the two regions. This information can then be used to match the data flow signatures of the corresponding nodes and carrying out the compaction transformation itself. The runtime cost of computing the signature is proportional to the size of the SEME region.

Fig. 8 illustrates the computation of the control flow signature of a region taken from the flow graph of Fig. 4. As we can see, the signature contains eight edges since the region contains six internal edges and two exit edges. The nodes that connect these edges are also a part of the signature. The signature constructed in this manner uniquely characterizes the SEME region.

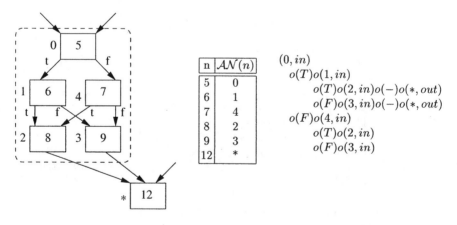

Fig. 8. CFS($R = (5, \{5, 6, 7, 8, 9\})$)

Search Strategy. Given the above method we can generate the signatures of all the SEME regions represented explicitly in the region hierarchy graph. However, if we simply find matching regions by comparing the signatures of these regions, we may only find small matching regions. This is because all SEME regions are not represented explicitly in the RHG. Consider the RHG of Fig. 9. Node 4 contains three regions 2, 1 and 3. While these contained regions represent disjoint SEME regions that together form region 4, they can be used to form other valid SEME regions composed of (2,1) and (1,3). Thus to find maximal matching regions we must consider both SEME regions that are explicitly and implicitly represented by the RHG.

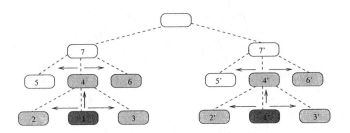

Fig. 9. Searching the RHG

To find a pair of matching regions we first find a pair of matching leaf regions. Then we gradually grow these regions as long as both can be expanded such that they still continue to match. The leaf regions are expanded by first attempting to incorporate their siblings to the left and then siblings to the right. If all siblings get incorporated, then we go to the parent and start expansion again. Thus this approach explores both SEME regions that are explicitly and implicitly represented by the RHG. It is important to once again note that this simple search is made possible because the RHG was constructed using the CDG. Siblings belong to the same control dependence region and hence can be joined to form larger SEME regions.

The algorithm given in Fig. 10 presents in detail the search process and matching process. While the algorithm is based upon our earlier descriptions of this section, there are a few things that are worth pointing out. First in the search algorithm $Matchleft*$ and $Matchright*$ continue to expand a region by respectively including left and right siblings till no more can be matched or none exist. During this matching process while the positions of the exits from the SEME regions are matched, their targets are not matched. This is because our transformation is powerful enough to compact similar SEME regions even when the targets of their exits are not the same. The second thing worth noting is that a call to $Match(R_1, R_2)$ returns the ratio of the code size that will be introduced (i.e., code to set up variables introduced by renaming and to initialize the distinguishing predicate that may be needed to express conditional execution in the transformed code) and the size of code that will be removed. If this ratio is no larger than a preset threshold value, then we consider the regions to match and worthy of compaction. The number of matches performed by the above algorithm, which bounds its runtime cost, is $O(n^2)$.

$\mathcal{LRS} = \{L : L \in RHG,\ st\ it\ contains\ no\ nested\ regions\}$
while $\exists\ R_1, R_2 \in \mathcal{LRS}$ st $CFS(R_1) = CFS(R_2)$ **do**
   if $Match(R_1, R_2) \leq Threshold$ **then**
     $\mathcal{R}_1 = \{R_1\};\ \mathcal{R}_2 = \{R_2\};$
     repeat
       if $\mathcal{R}_1 = Children(P_1)$ and $\mathcal{R}_2 = Children(P_2)$ **then**
         $\mathcal{R}_1 = \{P_1\};\ \mathcal{R}_2 = \{P_2\}$
       endif
       $\mathcal{OR}_1 = \mathcal{R}_1;\ \mathcal{OR}_2 = \mathcal{R}_2;$
       $(\mathcal{R}_1, \mathcal{R}_2) = Matchleft * (\mathcal{R}_1, \mathcal{R}_2);$
       $(\mathcal{R}_1, \mathcal{R}_2) = Matchright * (\mathcal{R}_1, \mathcal{R}_2);$
     until $\mathcal{OR}_1 = \mathcal{R}_1$ and $\mathcal{OR}_2 = \mathcal{R}_2;$
     $\mathcal{MRS} = \mathcal{MRS} \cup \{(\mathcal{R}_1, \mathcal{R}_2)\}$
   endif
endwhile

Match (R_1, R_2) {
   if $CFS(R_1) = CFS(R_2)$ **then**
     $Pred \leftarrow false;\ Rename \leftarrow \phi$
     foreach $b_1 \equiv b_2$ st $b_1 \in R_1$ and $b_2 \in R_2$ **do**
       if $DFS(b_1) = DFS(R_2)$ **then**
         $Rename \leftarrow Rename \cup diff(b_1, b_2)$
       else $Pred \leftarrow true$ **endif**
     endfor
     $ExtraI = ExtraI(Pred) + ExtraI(Rename)$
     return ($ExtraI/MaxI(R_1, R_2)$)
   endif
}

Fig. 10. Searching for matching regions

4 Generalized Tail Merging Transformation

Finally, given two matching SEME regions SEME(x) and SEME(y), we develop a transformation to compact the two regions. The transformation is pictorially illustrated in Fig. 11. There are three main components of this transformation. First a renamed version of the SEME region SEME(t) is constructed to replace SEME(x) and SEME(y). We do not discuss details of renaming as this is a known technique. Second the incoming edges of SEME(x) and SEME(y) are made the incoming edges of SEME(t). However, along these incoming edges additional code is introduced to carry out two functions: initializing variables introduced during *renaming* and initialization of the *distinguishing predicate* if one is needed. During execution of SEME(t), the value of the distinguishing predicate determines whether an execution of SEME(t) in the transformed code corresponds to an execution of SEME(x) or an execution of SEME(y) in the original code. Third the exits of the SEME(t) are connected.

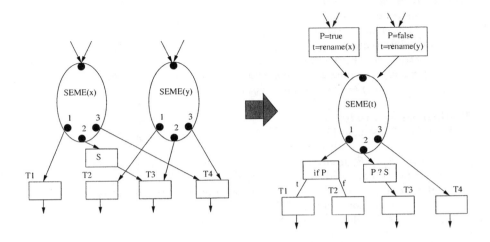

Fig. 11. Generalized tail merging

Three different situations arise when handling the exits which are illustrated in Fig. 11 by corresponding exits marked 3, 2, and 1. The targets of the pair of corresponding exits marked 3 in SEME(x) and SEME(y) are identical (T_4) and thus exit marked 3 in SEME(t) is connected to T_4. The exit marked 2 leads to target T_3 but there is a small difference between SEME(x) and SEME(y). There is an extra statement S between 2 in SEME(x) and T_3. This statement's execution is made conditional upon the predicate P (denoted by $P?S$) and 2 in SEME(t) is connected to T_3 via statement $P?S$. The targets of the pair of exits marked 1 lead to entirely different points in the program, i.e. T_1 and T_2. Therefore at the exit marked 1 in SEME(t) we place a condition that tests predicate P and based upon the outcome appropriately transfers control to either T_1 or T_2 as shown in Fig. 11. Detailed algorithm for carrying out the transformation is presented in Fig. 12.

From the above transformation we can see that it is essentially a generalization of tail merging so that we never have to make use of procedural abstraction. Like tail merging, when corresponding exits of matched regions lead to the same target point, the corresponding exit in the transformed code is simply connected to the same target. Thus, no additional branching overhead is introduced for this exit. In other situations, where targets are not the same or an extra block is present in one case, the distinguishing predicate is used to allow selection of the target or conditional execution of the extra statement. Thus, by introducing the distinguishing predicate we enable conditional execution possible and eliminate the need for using procedural abstraction. It should also be noted that if any two corresponding basic blocks in SEME(x) and SEME(y) differ, then they can also be merged and appropriately executed by testing predicate P. This form of conditional execution does not require introduction of explicit branches as modern processors such as Intel's IA64 support predicated execution of instructions.

Renamed SEME Region:
  Given matching regions SEME$(x_1, \cdots, x_n)$ and SEME$(y_1, \cdots, y_n)$
    Create renamed region SEME$(t_1, \cdots, t_n)$.
    Introduce renaming code along entry corresponding to SEME$(x_1, \cdots, x_n)$
      $(t_1, \cdots, t_n) \leftarrow rename(x_1, \cdots, x_n)$
    Introduce renaming code along entry corresponding to SEME$(y_1, \cdots, y_n)$
      $(t_1, \cdots, t_n) \leftarrow rename(y_1, \cdots, y_n)$

Distinguishing Predicate:
  Predicate P distinguishing an execution of SEME$(x_1, \cdots, x_n)$ from
    SEME$(y_1, \cdots, y_n)$ if needed iff:
    $\exists$ exits $E_1 \equiv E_2$ from SEME$(x_1, \cdots, x_n)$ and SEME$(y_1, \cdots, y_n)$
      which do not lead to the same target.
    if P does not naturally occur in the program, create P by introducing:
      $P = true$ along entry to SEME$(x_1, \cdots, x_n)$; and
      $P = false$ along entry to SEME$(y_1, \cdots, y_n)$.

Handling Exits:
  foreach pair of exits $E_x \equiv E_y$ from SEME$(x_1, \cdots, x_n)$ and SEME$(y_1, \cdots, y_n)$ **do**
    Let T_x and T_y be the targets of E_x and E_y;
    if $T_x = T_y$ **then**
      Connect corresponding exit E_t in SEME$(t_1, \cdots, t_n)$ to $T_x (= T_y)$
    elseif T_x *postdominates* T_y or T_y *postdominates* T_x via S **then**
      Connect corresponding exit E_t in SEME$(t_1, \cdots, t_n)$ via
        predicated execution of S, $P?S$ to the appropriate target (T_x or T_y)
    else
      Introduce the following test on P for selection of target:
        "*if P then goto T_x else goto T_y*"
    endif
  endfor

Fig. 12. Code compaction transformation algorithm

5 Experimental Results

We looked for benefits of applying our approach to functions from a few benchmark programs taken from the Mediabench [14] and MiBench [8] embedded suites and spec2000 suite. We found many instances of regions where our transformation is beneficial. Table 1 shows the characteristics of the matching regions that were compacted. It should be noted that in some functions SEME regions were found but since all exits went to same targets, distinguishing predicate was not needed. In other cases while the distinguishing predicate was needed, the regions were merely SESE regions. Finally in other cases both SEME regions were compacted and distinguishing predicate was also needed. Thus, the various elements of our generalized tail merging transformation plays an important role in the compaction of code for all these functions.

We computed the code sizes of these functions by compiling the original and transformed (i.e., compacted) source codes into ARM instructions. All benchmarks were compiled using gcc 2.95.2 with options -O2 -march=armv4. For

Table 1. Matching region characteristics

Benchmark:: Function	Characteristics
gsm:: LARp_to_rp	Distinguishing Predicate; SESE
gsm:: Long_term_analysis_filtering	Distinguishing Predicate; SESE
mesa:: update_pixel_logic	SEME
mesa:: gl_viewclip_line	Distinguishing Predicate; SEME
mesa:: gl_viewclip_polygon	Distibguishing Predicate; SEME
mesa:: gl_userclip_line	Distinguishing Predicate; SESE
mesa:: gl_userclip_polygon	Distinguishing Predicate; SESE
tiff-v3.5.4:: PackBitsEncode	SEME
sphinx:: sorted_id	SEME
twolf:: unetseg	Distinguishing Predicate; SEME
parse:: match	SEME
craft:: RepetitionDraw	Distinguishing Predicate; SESE
gzip:: inflate_codes	SEME
gzip:: inflate_dynamic	Distinguishing Predicate; SEME

comparison we also computed the code size reduction achieved by existing techniques that apply compaction transformations to SESE regions using branch and link instructions. Table 2 shows the resulting data for named functions taken from benchmarks. As we can see, the code size reductions are substantial in most cases. While our approach gave an average reduction of 24.96%, existing techniques provide an average reduction of 14.56% in code size.

Table 2. Code size reduction

Benchmark:: Function	Original Size	SEME		SESE	
		Size	Reduction(%)	Size	Reduction(%)
gsm:: LARp_to_rp	74	45	39.19	49	33.78
gsm:: Long_term_analysis_filtering	160	64	60.00	76	52.50
mesa:: update_pixel_logic	65	47	27.69	61	6.15
mesa:: gl_viewclip_line	818	666	18.58	674	17.60
mesa:: gl_viewclip_polygon	1326	982	25.94	1126	15.08
mesa:: gl_userclip_line	306	262	14.38	283	7.52
mesa:: gl_userclip_polygon	395	341	13.67	350	11.39
tiff-v3.5.4:: PackBitsEncode	150	121	19.33	139	7.33
sphinx:: sorted_id	83	46	44.58	61	26.56
twolf:: unetseg	1627	1588	02.40	1627	0.00
parse:: match	120	94	21.67	118	1.67
craft:: RepetitionDraw	60	41	31.67	54	10.00
gzip:: inflate_codes	310	260	16.13	284	8.39
gzip:: inflate_dynamic	458	393	14.19	431	5.90
average			24.96%		14.56%

6 Conclusions

In this paper we presented a generalized tail merging transformation which achieves two goals. First it enables application of code compaction to large SEME regions which cannot be compacted by a single application of existing transformations that function only for SESE regions. Second the use of distinguishing predicate enables the application of our tail merging style transformation in the presence of small differences between the matching regions. Existing techniques cannot handle SEME regions and thus in contrast they will rely upon multiple applications of the procedural abstraction transformation to SESE subregions of the SEME region. Therefore they will achieve less compaction and introduce greater runtime overhead due to calls and returns. Thus we are able to carry out greater degree of compaction with reduced compaction overhead.

References

1. K. Cooper and N. McIntosh, "Enhanced Code Compression for Embedded RISC Processors," *SIGPLAN Conference on Programming Language Design and Implementation* (PLDI), May 1999.
2. S. Debray, W. Evans, R. Muth, and B. De Sutter, "Compiler Techniques for Code Compaction," *ACM Transactions on Programming Languages and Systems* (TOPLAS), vol. 22, no. 2, pages 378-415, March 2000.
3. S. Debray and W. Evans, "Profile-Guided Code Compression," *SIGPLAN Conference on Programming Language Design and Implementation* (PLDI), pages 95-105, June 2002.
4. B. De Sutter, B. De Bus and K. De Bosschere, "Sifting out the Mud: low level C++ Code Reuse," *SIGPLAN Conference on Object-Oriented Programming Systems, Languages and Applications* (OOPSLA), pages 275-291, Seattle, Wanshington, November 2002.
5. J. Ferrante, K.J. Ottenstein, and J.D. Warren, "The Program Dependence Graph and Its Use in Optimization," *ACM Transactions on Programming Languages and Systems* (TOPLAS), vol. 9, no. 3, pages 319-349, 1987.
6. C. Fraser, "An Instruction for Direct Intepretation of LZ77-compressed Programs," Technical Report, Microsoft Research, MSR-TR-2002-90, September 2002.
7. C. Fraser, E. Myers, and A. Wendt, "Analyzing and Compressing Assembly Code," *ACM SIGPLAN Symposium on Compiler Construction* (CC), 1984.
8. M.R. Guthaus, J.S. Ringenberg, D. Ernst, T.M. Austin, T. Mudge, R.B. Brown, "MiBench: A Free, Commercially Representative Embedded Benchmark Suite," *IEEE 4th Annual Workshop on Workload Characterization* (WWC), Austin, TX, December 2001.
9. R. Johnson, D. Pearson, and K. Pingali, "The Program Structure Tree: Computing Control Regions in Linear Time," *SIGPLAN Conference on Programming Language Design and Implementation* (PLDI), pages 171-185, 1994.
10. D. Kirovski, J. Kin, and W. H. Mangione-Smith, "Procedure Based Program Compression," *30th Annual ACM/IEEE International Symposium on Microarchitecture* (MICRO), pages 204-217, 1997.
11. R. Komondoor and S. Horwitz, "Using Slicing to Identify Duplication in Source Code," *International Static Analysis Symposium* (SAS), pages 40-56, Paris, France, July 2001.

12. J. Krinke, "Identifying Similar Code with Program Dependence Graphs," *Working Conference on Reverse Engineering* (WCRE), pages 301-309, Stuttgart, Germany, October 2001.
13. A. Krishnaswamy and R. Gupta, "Profile Guided Selection of ARM and Thumb Instructions," *ACM SIGPLAN Joint Conference on Languages Compilers and Tools for Embedded Systems & Software and Compilers for Embedded Systems* (LCTES/SCOPES), pages 55-63, Berlin, Germany, June 2002.
14. C. Lee, M. Potkonjak, and W.H. Mangione-Smith, "Mediabench: A Tool for Evaluating and Synthesizing Multimedia and Communications Systems," *IEEE/ACM International Symposium on Microarchitecture* (MICRO), Research Triangle Park, North Carolina, December 1997.
15. C. Lefurgy, P. Bird, I.-C. Chen, and T. Mudge, "Improving Code Density Using Compression Techniques," *30th Annual ACM/IEEE International Symposium on Microarchitecture* (MICRO), pages 194-203, 1997.
16. W. Wulf, R. Johnson, C. Weinstock, S. Hobbs, and C. Geschke, "The Design of an Optimizing Compiler," American Elsevier, New York, 1975.
17. M. Zastre, "Compacting Object Code via Parameterized Procedural Abstraction," MS Thesis, University of Victoria, 1995.

Existential Heap Abstraction Entailment Is Undecidable*

Viktor Kuncak and Martin Rinard

Laboratory for Computer Science
Massachusetts Institute of Technology
Cambridge, MA 02139
{vkuncak,rinard}@lcs.mit.edu

Abstract. In this paper we study constraints for specifying properties of data structures consisting of linked objects allocated in the heap. Motivated by heap summary graphs in role analysis and shape analysis we introduce the notion of *regular graph constraints*. A regular graph constraint is a graph representing the heap summary; a heap satisfies a constraint if and only if the heap can be homomorphically mapped to the summary. Regular graph constraints form a very simple and natural fragment of the existential monadic second-order logic over graphs.

One of the key problems in a compositional static analysis is proving that procedure preconditions are satisfied at every call site. For role analysis, precondition checking requires determining the validity of implication, i.e., *entailment* of regular graph constraints.

The central result of this paper is the undecidability of regular graph constraint entailment. The *undecidability* of the *entailment* problem is surprising because of the simplicity of regular graph constraints: in particular, the *satisfiability* of regular graph constraints is *decidable*.

Our undecidability result implies that there is no complete algorithm for statically checking procedure preconditions or postconditions, simplifying static analysis results, or checking that given analysis results are correct. While incomplete conservative algorithms for regular graph constraint entailment checking are possible, we argue that heap specification languages should avoid second-order existential quantification in favor of explicitly specifying a criterion for summarizing objects.

Keywords: Shape Analysis, Typestate, Monadic Second-Order Logic, Type Checking, Program Verification, Graph Homomorphism, Post Correspondence Problem.

1 Introduction

Typestate Systems. Types capture important properties of objects in the program, reflecting not only the format of stored information but also the set of

---

* This research was supported in part by DARPA Contract F33615-00-C-1692, NSF Grant CCR00-86154, NSF Grant CCR00-63513, and the Singapore-MIT Alliance.

applicable operations and the intended use of the objects in the program. Types therefore help avoid programming errors and increase the maintainability of the program. In an imperative language, the properties of objects change over time. However, in traditional type systems, the type of the object does not change over the object's lifetime. This property of traditional types therefore limits the set of properties that they can express. It is therefore desirable to develop abstractions that change as the properties of objects change. A *typestate* is a system where types of objects change over time. A simple typestate system was introduced in [34]; more recent examples include [21, 14, 8, 9, 10, 33, 36, 11]. Similarly to [13], these typestate systems are a step towards the highly automated static checking of complex properties of objects.

One of the difficulties in specifying properties of objects in the presence of linked data structures is that a property of an object x may depend on properties of objects y that are linked to x in the heap. Some systems allow programmers to identify properties of an object x in terms of the properties of the objects y such that x references y. The idea that important properties of an object x depend on the the number and properties of objects z such that z references x was introduced in the role system [21].

Existential Semantics of Roles. To allow definitions of cyclic structures, in [21, Section 3.3] we have adopted the following semantics: a heap satisfies a set of properties if there *exists* some assignment of predicate names to heap objects such that the given local referencing constraints are satisfied. We call constraints defined in this way *role constraints*. The existential quantification over predicate names can be expressed in existential monadic second-order logic [12]. Role constraints explicitly specify constraints on incoming and outgoing fields of objects as well as inverse reference and acyclicity constraints. Role constraints encode may-reachability properties implicitly, through the reachability between summary nodes.

The Entailment Problem. One of the key problems for a compositional static analysis is checking that the precondition of a procedure is satisfied at every call site. In general, checking a precondition corresponds to verifying the validity of implication (entailment) of heap properties. In [21, Section 6.3.1] we present a *conservative* algorithm for checking the entailment of role constraints. In this paper we study the possibility of the existence of a *complete* sound algorithm for role constraint entailment. We argue that no such algorithm exists: the entailment problem is undecidable.

Regular Graph Constraints. What is interesting about our undecidability result is that the source of undecidability is a particularly weak fragment of role constraints. We call this fragment *regular graph constraints*. Regular graph constraints capture the problem of mutually recursive properties over potentially cyclic graphs, while abstracting from the details of the particular specification language. The only local properties expressible in regular graph constraints are points-to referencing relationships; unlike role constraints, regular graph constraints cannot express sharing, inverse reference or acyclicity properties. Despite this simplicity, the entailment of regular graph constraints turns out to be undecidable. The entailment of role constraints is therefore undecidable as well, and so is the entailment for any other constraints that can encode regular graph constraints. We thus hope that our study of regular graph constraints provides a useful guidance for researchers in choosing an appropriate abstraction for linked data structures.

A regular graph constraint is given by a graph G. A heap H satisfies the constraint iff there exists a graph homomorphism from H to G. The existential quantification over properties of objects is modeled in regular graph constraints as the existence of a homomorphism from H to G. Regular graph constraints allow specifying properties of graphs in some given class of graphs C. If C is the set of trees, regular graph constraints reduce to tree automata [35,6]; if C is the set of grids, the constraints reduce to domino systems [17]. We therefore view regular graph constraints as a natural generalization of constraints on trees and grids, a generalization that is much weaker than the monadic second-order logic (for which undecidability over non-tree-like domains is well known [7]).

In this paper we consider as the class C the set of *heaps*. Our notion of heap (Definition 2) is motivated by the garbage collected heap in programming languages such as Java or ML. Heaps contain a "root" node (which models the roots of the heap such as global and local variables), and a "null" node (the contents of null-valued fields). All nodes in the heap are reachable from the root (because unreachable nodes in a garbage collected heap may be ignored), and all edges are total functions from nodes to nodes (the functions are total because we consider null to be a graph node as well). We present our results for the case when the heap contains two kinds of fields, labeled "1" and "2". A model with two fields captures the essence of the heap entailment problem, while simplifying our presentation. Note that the entailment problem becomes easily decidable if each object has only one field, because all heaps become lists. On the other hand, if the objects are allowed to have more than two fields, our undecidability result directly applies by picking some two-element subset of the fields in the program.

Undecidability of Entailment. In Section 2.4 we show that there exists a simple and efficient algorithm that decides if a regular graph constraint is satisfiable. In contrast, the entailment problem for regular graph constraints is undecidable. We sketch this undecidability result in Section 3 as the main technical contribution of the paper (additional proof details are in [22]).

A common way of showing the undecidability of problems over graphs is to encode Turing machine computation histories [32] as a special form of graphs called *grids*. The difficulty with showing the undecidability of entailment of regular graph constraints is that regular graph constraints cannot define the subclass of grids among the class of heaps (otherwise the *satisfiability* of regular graph constraints over heaps would be undecidable, which is not the case). To show the *undecidability* of the *entailment* of regular graph constraints, we use constraints on both sides of the implication to restrict the set of possible counterexample models for the implication. For this purpose we introduce a new class of graphs called *corresponder graphs* (Section 3.2). Satisfiability of regular graph constraints over corresponder graphs can encode the existence of a solution of a Post correspondence problem instance, and is therefore undecidable. We give a method for constructing an implication such that all counterexamples for the validity of implication are corresponder graphs which satisfy a given regular graph constraint. This construction shows that the validity of the implication is undecidable. The main difficulty in the proof is a characterization of corresponder graphs using a finite set of allowed and disallowed homomorphic summaries (Section 3.4), a construction vaguely resembling the characterization of planar graphs in terms of forbidden minors [29].

Some Consequences. Regular graph constraints are closed under conjunction and, in certain cases, closed under disjunction (Section 2.3). Due to closure under conjunction, implication $P \Rightarrow Q$ is reducible to the equivalence $P \wedge Q \Leftrightarrow P$ of regular graph constraints. As a result, the equivalence of two regular graph constraints is also undecidable.

These results place limitations on the completeness of systems such as role analysis [21]. The implication problem for graphs naturally arises in compositional checking of programs whenever procedure preconditions or postconditions are given as regular graph constraints. The complete checking of procedure preconditions at call sites and procedure postconditions is therefore undecidable. Furthermore, it is impossible to build a complete checker for role analysis results if the only inputs to the checker are regular graph constraints expressing the set of heaps at every program point. Similarly, there is no complete procedure for semantically checking equivalence or subsumption of dataflow facts expressed as regular graph constraints; every conservative fixpoint algorithm must perform some unnecessary iterations in some cases.

Related Work. [27] shows the undecidability of alias analysis for programs with general control-flow, strengthening the consequence of Rice's theorem [28] to the case where all program statements are reachable. In contrast, our result shows that local analysis of a *single statement* is undecidable.

Most shape analysis algorithms are non-compositional [23, 5, 16, 30, 31] and many of them were originally used for program optimization. In such an analysis, the imprecision in heap property entailment can cause the analysis to perform some extra fixpoint iterations but may lead to a result that is sufficiently precise for program optimization. We choose a *compositional* approach to program analysis in [21] because it ensures the conformance of the program with respect to the design, increases the scalability of the analysis, and allows the analysis of incomplete programs. Our primary goal is program reliability, and the precision requirements needed to avoid spurious warnings about procedure precondition and postcondition violations seem more demanding than the requirements of analyses intended for program optimization. It is these precision requirements of the compositional analysis that motivate the study of the completeness of heap property entailment algorithms.

Several recent systems support the analysis of tree-like data structures [33,9, 36,15,24,3]. The restriction to tree-like data structures is in contrast to our notion of a heap, which allows nodes with in-degree greater than one. The presence of non-tree data structures is one of the key factors that make the implication of regular graph constraints undecidable. [1] suggests an alternative way to gain decidability. The logic L_r in [1] allows specifying reachability properties between local variables. What L_r does not allow is defining a set of nodes A using some reachability property and then stating further properties of objects in the set A.

Our experience with regular graph constraints indicates that unrestricted existential quantification over sets of objects quickly leads to heap abstractions whose comparison is undecidable. It is interesting to note that the existential quantification over disjoint sets of objects also occurs in [31], whenever an instrumentation predicate has the "unknown" truth value 1/2. An advantage of the approach in [31] is the existence of *abstraction predicates* that induce a canonical homomorphism for any given concrete heap. Case analysis and appropriate compatibility constraints [31, Page 265] can be used to sharpen the heap properties and eliminate 1/2 values; the implication of heap properties can then be approximated by combining sharpening with simple structural comparison of three-valued structures.

Elements of the first-order logic with transitive closure [31, 20] or first-order logic with inductive definitions [25], [19, Page 57] seem to be necessary for naturally expressing reachability properties. Reachability properties are in turn useful as a criterion for summarizing sets of objects, leading to potentially more intuitive semantics and the possibility of verifying stronger properties. We are therefore considering extending role definitions with regular expressions and exploring the possibility of translating role constraints into three-valued structures [31].

2 Regular Graph Constraints

In this section we define the class of graphs considered in this paper as well as the subclass of heaps as deterministic graphs with reachable nodes. We define the notion of regular graph constraints and show that satisfiability of the constraints over heaps is efficiently decidable. We also state some closure properties of regular graph constraints.

Preliminaries. If $r \subseteq A \times B$ and $S \subseteq A$, the *relational image* of set S under r is the set $r[S] = \{y \mid x \in S \land \langle x, y \rangle \in r\}$. A *word* is a finite sequence of symbols; if $w = a_1 \ldots a_n$ is a word then $|w|$ denotes the length n of w.

2.1 Graphs

We consider only directed graphs in this paper. Our graphs contain two kinds of edges, represented by relations s_1 and s_2. These relations represent fields of objects in an object-oriented program. The constant root represents the root of the graph. We use edges terminated at null to represent partial functions (and abstract representations of graphs containing partial functions).

Definition 1. *A graph is a relational structure*

$$G = \langle V, s_1, s_2, \mathsf{null}, \mathsf{root} \rangle$$

where

- *V is a finite set of nodes;*
- *$\mathsf{root}, \mathsf{null} \in V$ are distinct constants, $\mathsf{root} \neq \mathsf{null}$;*
- *$s_1, s_2 \subseteq V \times V$ are two kinds of graph edges, such that for all nodes x*

$$\langle \mathsf{null}, x \rangle \in s_i \text{ iff } x = \mathsf{null}$$

for $i \in 1, 2$.

Let $\mathcal{G}$ denote the class of all graphs.

An s_1-successor of a node x is any element of the set $s_1[\{x\}]$, similarly an s_2-successor of x is any element of $s_2[\{x\}]$. Note that there are exactly two edges originating from null. When drawing graphs we never show these two edges.

Definition 2. *A heap is a graph $G = \langle V, s_1, s_2, \mathsf{null}, \mathsf{root} \rangle$ where relations s_1 and s_2 are total functions and where for all $x \neq \mathsf{null}$, node x is reachable from root. Let $\mathcal{H}$ denote the class of all heaps.*

Example 3. We can define a heap representing list of length two by
$V = \{\mathsf{root}, x, \mathsf{null}\}$; $s_1 = \{\langle \mathsf{root}, x \rangle, \langle x, \mathsf{null} \rangle, \langle \mathsf{null}, \mathsf{null} \rangle\}$;
$s_2 = \{\langle \mathsf{root}, \mathsf{null} \rangle, \langle x, \mathsf{null} \rangle, \langle \mathsf{null}, \mathsf{null} \rangle\}$.

2.2 Graphs as Constraints

A regular constraint on a graph G is a constraint stating that G can be homomorphically mapped to another graph G'. The constraint satisfaction relation $\rightarrow$ corresponds to abstraction relation in program analyses, [26].

Definition 4. *We say that a graph G satisfies the constraints given by a graph G', and write $G \rightarrow G'$, iff there exists a homomorphism from G to G'.*

Homomorphism between directed graphs is a special case of homomorphism of structures [18, Page 5].

Definition 5. *A function $h : V \rightarrow V'$ is a homomorphism between graphs*

$$G = \langle V, s_1, s_2, \mathsf{null}, \mathsf{root} \rangle$$

and

$$G' = \langle V', s_1', s_2', \mathsf{null}', \mathsf{root}' \rangle$$

iff all of the following conditions hold:

1. *$\langle x, y \rangle \in s_i$ implies $\langle h(x), h(y) \rangle \in s_i'$, for all $i \in \{1, 2\}$*
2. *$h(x) = \mathsf{root}'$ iff $x = \mathsf{root}$*
3. *$h(x) = \mathsf{null}'$ iff $x = \mathsf{null}$*

If there exists a homomorphism from G to G', we call G a model for G'.

In shape analysis, a homomorphism corresponds to the abstraction function mapping heap objects to the summary nodes in a shape graph. We do not require homomorphism to be onto or to be injective.

We can think of a homomorphism $h : V \to V'$ as a coloring of the graph G by nodes of the graph G'. The color $h(x)$ of a node x restricts the colors of the s_1-successors of x to the colors in $s_1[\{h(x)\}]$ and the colors of the s_2-successors to the colors in $s_2[\{h(x)\}]$. For example, a graph G can be colored with k colors so that the adjacent nodes have different colors iff G is homomorphic to a complete graph without self-loops.

The identity function is a homomorphism from any graph to itself. Therefore, $G \to G$ for every graph G. A composition of homomorphisms is a homomorphism, so $\to$ is transitive.

There is an isomorphism ι between the set of regular graphs constraints and certain subset S of the set of closed formulas in second-order monadic logic. All formulas in S have the form $\exists X_1 \ldots \exists X_k \forall x \forall y.\psi$ where $X_1, \ldots, X_k$ denote sets of nodes, x, y denote individual nodes and ψ is quantifier-free [22, Page 4]. The isomorphism ι has the following property: $H \to G$ iff $H \models \iota(G)$ where $\models$ is the standard Tarskian semantics of monadic second-order logic formulas [7] expressing that the closed formula $\iota(G)$ is true in the model H. With the isomorphism ι in mind, we introduce constraints that are propositional combinations of regular graph constraints and correspond to propositional combinations of the corresponding formulas: $H \to G_1 \wedge G_2$ iff $H \to G_1$ and $H \to G_2$; $H \to G_1 \vee G_2$ iff $H \to G_1$ or $H \to G_2$; $H \to \neg G_1$ iff not $H \to G_1$. Similarly, if C is a class of graphs, we define the satisfiability over C corresponding to satisfiability of formula over a class of models C, and the validity of implication over C corresponding to the validity of implication of formulas over a class of models C.

Definition 6 (Satisfiability). *A graph G is satisfiable over the class of graphs C iff there exists a graph $H \in C$ such that $H \to G$. The satisfiability problem over the class of graphs C is: given a graph G, determine if G is satisfiable.*

Definition 7 (Implication). *We say that G_1 implies G_2 over the class of graphs C, and write $G_1 \leadsto_C G_2$, iff $(H \to G_1)$ implies $(H \to G_2)$ for all graphs $H \in C$. The* implication problem *(or* entailment problem*) for C is: given graphs G_1 and G_2, determine if $G_1 \leadsto_C G_2$.*

We say that a regular graph constraint G_1 is equivalent over C to a regular graph constraint G_2 (and write $G_1 \approx_C G_2$) iff for every $H \in C$, $H \to G_1$ iff $H \to G_2$. Note that $G_1 \sim_C G_2$ iff $C \models \iota(G_1) \Leftrightarrow \iota(G_2)$.

In this paper we consider $C = \mathcal{H}$ as the set of models of regular graph constraints; see Table 1 and [22] for the summary of satisfiability and entailment over different classes of graphs.

2.3 Closure Properties

In this section we give a construction for computing the conjunction of two graphs and a construction for computing the disjunction of two graphs. We use these constructions in Section 3.

Conjunction. We show how to use a Cartesian product construction to obtain a conjunction of two graphs G_1 and G_2.

Definition 8 (Cartesian Product). *Let* $G^1 = \langle V^1, s_1^1, s_2^1, \mathsf{null}^1, \mathsf{root}^1 \rangle$ *and* $G^2 = \langle V^2, s_1^2, s_2^2, \mathsf{null}^2, \mathsf{root}^2 \rangle$ *be graphs. Then* $G^0 = G^1 \times G^2$ *is the graph* $G^0 = \langle V^0, s_1^0, s_2^0, \mathsf{null}^0, \mathsf{root}^0 \rangle$ *such that* $\mathsf{null}^0 = \langle \mathsf{null}^1, \mathsf{null}^2 \rangle$, $\mathsf{root}^0 = \langle \mathsf{root}^1, \mathsf{root}^2 \rangle$,

$$V^0 = \{\mathsf{null}^0, \mathsf{root}^0\} \cup (V^1 \setminus \{\mathsf{null}^1, \mathsf{root}^1\}) \times (V^2 \setminus \{\mathsf{null}^2, \mathsf{root}^2\})$$

and

$$s_i^0 = \{\langle \langle x^1, x^2 \rangle, \langle y^1, y^2 \rangle \rangle \mid \langle x^1, y^1 \rangle \in s_i^1; \langle x^2, y^2 \rangle \in s_i^2\}$$

for $i \in \{1, 2\}$.

The proof of the following Proposition 9 is straightforward, see [22].

Proposition 9 (Conjunction via Product). *For every graph G, $G \to G_1 \times G_2$ iff ($G \to G_1$ and $G \to G_2$).*

Disjunction. Given our definition of graphs, there is no construction that yields disjunction of arbitrary graphs over the class of heaps [22, Example 26]. To ensure that we can find union graphs over the set of heaps, we simply require $s_2[\{\mathsf{root}\}] = \{\mathsf{null}\}$.

Definition 10 (Orable Graphs). *A graph* $G = \langle V, s_1, s_2, \mathsf{null}, \mathsf{root} \rangle$ *is orable iff for all* $x \in V$, $\langle \mathsf{root}, x \rangle \in s_2$ *iff* $x = \mathsf{null}$.

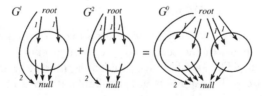

Fig. 1. Graph sum

Definition 11 (Graph Sum). *Let* $G^1 = \langle V^1, s_1^1, s_2^1, \mathsf{null}, \mathsf{root} \rangle$ *and* $G^2 = \langle V^2, s_1^2, s_2^2, \mathsf{null}, \mathsf{root} \rangle$ *be orable graphs such that* $V^1 \cap V^2 = \{\mathsf{null}, \mathsf{root}\}$. *Then* $G^0 = G^1 + G^2$ *is the graph* $G^0 = \langle V^0, s_1^0, s_2^0, \mathsf{null}, \mathsf{root} \rangle$ *where* $V^0 = V^1 \cup V^2$, $s_1^0 = s_1^1 \cup s_1^2$, *and* $s_2^0 = s_2^1 \cup s_2^2$ *(see Figure 1).*

The previous definition is justified by the following Proposition 12. The proof of Proposition 12 uses the fact that every non-null node in a heap is reachable from root, and the assumption $s_2[\{\text{root}\}] = \{\text{null}\}$ for orable graphs, see [22].

Proposition 12 (Disjunction via Sum). *Let G be a heap and G^1 and G^2 be orable graphs. Then $G \to G^1 + G^2$ iff $(G \to G^1$ or $G \to G^2)$.*

If G^1 and G^2 are orable graphs, then $G^1 \times G^2$ and $G^1 + G^2$ are also orable. In the sequel we deal only with orable graphs.

GraphCleanup:
Repeat the following two operations until the graph stabilizes:

  remove an unreachable node $v \neq$ null as well as edges incident with v
  remove a node x such that $s_1[\{x\}] = \emptyset$ or $s_2[\{x\}] = \emptyset$

Mark(x):

  if marked[x] then return, otherwise:
  marked[x] := true;
  pick a s_1-successor y of x; marked[$\langle x, y \rangle$] := true; mark(y)
  pick a s_2-successor z of x; marked[$\langle x, z \rangle$] := true; mark(z)

SatisfiabilityCheck:

  perform *GraphCleanup*;
  if the resulting graph G' does not contain root, then G is unsatisfiable;
  otherwise a heap satisfying G can be obtained as follows:
  let all graph nodes and edges be unmarked;
  Mark(root);
  return subgraph containing marked nodes and edges

Fig. 2. Satisfiability check for heaps

2.4 Satisfiability over Heaps

We next consider the satisfiability problem for a regular graph constraint G over the class $\mathcal{H}$ of all heaps. In the context of program checking, graph G denotes a property of the heap. The satisfiability problem is interesting in program checking for several reasons. If graph G is not satisfiable, it represents a contradictory specification. If G was supplied by the developer, it is likely that the specification contains an error. If G was derived by a program analysis considering several cases, then the case corresponding to G can be omitted from consideration because it represents no concrete heaps. Finally, satisfiability is easier than entailment, so it is natural to explore the satisfiability first.

Satisfiability of graphs over the class $\mathcal{H}$ of heaps is efficiently decidable by the algorithm in Figure 2. The goal of the algorithm is to find, given a graph G, whether there exists a heap H such that $H \to G$. Recall the property of a heap that every node has exactly one s_1 outgoing edge and exactly one s_2 outgoing edge. This property need not hold for G, so we cannot take $H = G$ to be the heap proving satisfiability of G. However, if G is satisfiable then G has a subgraph which is a heap. The algorithm in Figure 2 updates the current graph until it becomes a heap or *GraphCleanup* removes the root node. The correctness of the algorithm follows from the fact that *GraphCleanup* removes only nodes which are never in the range of any homomorphism (see [22] for a correctness proof).

3 Undecidability of Implication over Heaps

This section presents the central result of this paper: *The implication of graphs over the class of heaps $(\leadsto_\mathcal{H})$ is undecidable.* To understand the implication problem, observe first that the following Proposition 13 holds.

Proposition 13. *Let C be any class of graphs. Let $G \to G'$. Then $G \leadsto_C G'$.*

Proposition 13 provides a sufficient condition for the graph implication to hold and is a direct consequence of the transitivity of relation $\to$. The implication problem is difficult because the converse of Proposition 13 for $C = \mathcal{H}$ does not hold. For example, if G is a graph that contains some nodes that can never be an image of a homomorphism and G' is the result of eliminating these nodes, then it is not the case that $G \to G'$, although $G \approx G'$ and thus $G \leadsto G'$. Moreover, the undecidability of implication $\leadsto$ means that the incompleteness of $\to$ as an implication test is a fundamental one: $\to$ is a computable relation whereas $\leadsto$ is not computable. Preceding a $\to$ check with some computable graph-cleanup operation such as one in Figure 2 cannot yield a complete implication test.

3.1 The Idea of the Undecidability Proof

As we have seen in Section 2.4, the satisfiability problem of regular graph constraints over heaps $\mathcal{H}$ is decidable. On the other hand, there are subclasses of $\mathcal{H}$ that have an undecidable satisfiability problem. One such subclass is the class of grids. For grids, regular graph constraints correspond to tiling problems [17, 2], which are undecidable because they can represent Turing machine computation histories [32]. A smaller class can have a more difficult regular graph constraint satisfiability problem if it is not definable within the larger class using regular graph constraints. To show the undecidability of the implication problem, we therefore use constraints on *both sides* of the implication to describe a subclass CG of graphs over which the satisfiability problem is undecidable. We construct the class CG in such a way that we can represent the solutions of the Post Correspondence Problem instances as colorings of graphs in CG. (See [32, Page 183] for Post Correspondence Problem, PCP for short.) We call the elements of CG "corresponder graphs". We choose CG over the class of grids because it seems easier to use the presence and the absence of homomorphisms to characterize CG than to characterize the class of grids. The definition of Corresponder Graphs (Definition 15 and Figure 3) captures the essence of our construction: corresponder graphs need to be sufficiently rich to make Proposition 16 true, and sufficiently simple to make Proposition 17 true. Once we have proven Proposition 16 and Proposition 17, the following Theorem 14 yields the undecidability result which is the central contribution of this paper.

Theorem 14. *The implication of graphs is undecidable over the class of heaps.*

Proof. We reduce satisfiability of graphs over the class of corresponder graphs to the problem of finding a counterexample to an implication of graphs over the class of heaps. Given the reduction in Proposition 16, this establishes that the implication of graphs is undecidable.

Let G be a graph. Consider the implication

$$(G \times P) \leadsto_{\mathcal{H}} Q \qquad (1)$$

We claim that a heap H is a counterexample for this implication iff H is a corresponder graph such that $H \to G$.

Assume that H is a corresponder graph and $H \to G$. By Proposition 17, we have $H \to P$ and $\neg(H \to Q)$. We then have $H \to (G \times P)$. Since $\neg(H \to Q)$, we conclude that H is a counterexample for (1).

Assume now that H is a counterexample for (1). Then $H \to G \times P$ and $\neg(H \to Q)$. Since $H \to P$ and $\neg(H \to Q)$, by Proposition 17 we conclude that H is a corresponder graph. Furthermore, $H \to G$. ∎

3.2 Corresponder Graphs

Corresponder graphs are a subclass of the class of heaps. Figure 3 shows an example corresponder graph. To encode the matching of words in a PCP instance, a corresponder graph has an upper list of U-nodes and a lower list of L-nodes. These lists are formed using s_1 edges (drawn horizontally in Figure 3). The U-list nodes and L-list nodes are connected using s_2 edges (drawn vertically). These s_2 edges allow a coloring of a corresponder graph to express the matching of letters in words. A solution to a PCP instance is a list of indices of word pairs; our construction encodes this list by the colors of C-nodes of the corresponder graph. s_2 edges from C-nodes partition U-list nodes and L-list nodes into disjoint consecutive list segments. The coloring constraints along these s_2 edges ensure that a coloring of a sequence of U-nodes and a coloring of a sequence of L-nodes encode words from the same pair of the PCP instance. There are twice as many C-nodes as there are word pairs in a PCP instance, to allow an edge to both a U-node and an L-node. The lists of U-nodes and L-nodes in a corresponder graph both have the length $2n$ where the n is the length of the concatenated words in the solution of a PCP instance.

Definition 15 (Corresponder Graphs). *Let $k \geq 2$, $n \geq 2$, $0 = u_0 < u_1 < \ldots < u_{k-1} < n$, and $0 = l_0 < l_1 < \ldots < l_{k-1} < n$. A corresponder graph*

$$\mathsf{CG}(n, k, u_1, \ldots, u_{k-1}, l_1, \ldots, l_{k-1})$$

is a graph isomorphic to $G = \langle V, s_1, s_2, \text{null}, \text{root} \rangle$ where

$$V = \{\text{null}, \text{root}\} \cup \{C_0, C_1, \ldots, C_{2k-1}\}$$
$$\cup \{U_0, U_1, \ldots, U_{2n-1}\} \cup \{L_0, L_1, \ldots, L_{2n-1}\}$$

$s_1 = \{\langle \text{root}, C_0 \rangle\}$
$\cup \{\langle C_i, C_{i+1}\rangle \mid 0 \leq i < 2k-1\} \cup \{\langle C_{2k-1}, \text{null}\rangle\}$
$\cup \{\langle U_i, U_{i+1}\rangle \mid 0 \leq i < 2n-1\} \cup \{\langle U_{2n-1}, \text{null}\rangle\}$
$\cup \{\langle L_i, L_{i+1}\rangle \mid 0 \leq i < 2n-1\} \cup \{\langle L_{2n-1}, \text{null}\rangle\}$

$s_2 = \{\langle \text{root}, \text{null}\rangle\}$
$\cup \{\langle C_{2i}, U_{2u_i}\rangle \mid 0 \leq i < k\}$
$\cup \{\langle C_{2i+1}, L_{2l_i+1}\rangle \mid 0 \leq i < k\}$
$\cup \{\langle U_{2i}, L_{2i}\rangle \mid 0 \leq i < n\}$
$\cup \{\langle L_{2i+1}, U_{2i+1}\rangle \mid 0 \leq i < n\}$
$\cup \{\langle U_{2i+1}, \text{null}\rangle \mid i \in \{0, \ldots, n-1\} \setminus \{l_0, \ldots, l_{k-1}\}\}$
$\cup \{\langle U_{2i+1}, \text{root}\rangle \mid i \in \{l_0, \ldots, l_{k-1}\}\}$
$\cup \{\langle L_{2i}, \text{null}\rangle \mid i \in \{0, \ldots, n-1\} \setminus \{u_0, \ldots, u_{k-1}\}\}$
$\cup \{\langle L_{2i}, \text{root}\rangle \mid i \in \{u_0, \ldots, u_{k-1}\}\}$

We denote the set of all corresponder graphs $\mathsf{CG}(n, k, u_1, \ldots, u_{k-1}, l_1, \ldots, l_{k-1})$ by CG.

3.3 Satisfiability over Corresponder Graph Is Undecidable

Proposition 16. *Satisfiability of regular graph constraints over the class of corresponder graphs is undecidable.*

Proof. We give a reduction from PCP. Let $m \geq 2$ and let

$$\langle v_0, w_0\rangle, \langle v_1, w_1\rangle, \ldots, \langle v_{m-1}, w_{m-1}\rangle$$

be an instance of PCP where v_i, w_i are nonempty words

$$v_i = v_i^0 v_i^1 \ldots v_i^{p_i-1} \quad 0 \leq i \leq m-1$$
$$w_i = w_i^0 w_i^1 \ldots w_i^{q_i-1} \quad 0 \leq i \leq m-1$$

where $p_i = |v_i|$ and $q_i = |w_i|$. We construct a graph G such that there exists a corresponder graph G_0 with the property $G_0 \to G$ iff the PCP instance has a solution.

Consider a PCP instance $\langle c, bc\rangle, \langle ab, a\rangle$. Figure 3 illustrates how a corresponder graph G_0 with a homomorphism from G_0 to G encodes a solution of this PCP instance. Graph G constructed for this PCP instance is presented in Figure 4 using the monadic second-order logic formula $\iota(G)$.

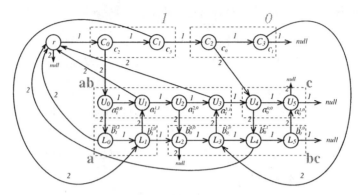

Fig. 3. An example corresponder graph with a homomorphism (coloring) that encodes the solution 1,0 of the PCP instance $\langle v_0, w_0 \rangle, \langle v_1, w_1 \rangle$ where $v_0 = \text{c}, v_1 = \text{ab}, w_0 = \text{bc}, w_1 = \text{a}$. The solution is the sequence of indices 1, 0 which is encoded by the fact that the C-nodes have colors $c_{2 \cdot 1}, c_{2 \cdot 1+1}$ followed by colors $c_{2 \cdot 0}, c_{2 \cdot 0+1}$. The four U-node colors $a_1^{0,0}, a_1^{1,1}, a_1^{2,0}, a_1^{3,1}$ encode the two positions in the word v_1. The two U-node colors $a_0^{0,0}, a_0^{1,0}$ encode the only position of the word v_0. Analogously, the two L-node colors $b_1^{0,1}, b_1^{1,0}$ encode the only position of the word w_1, whereas $b_0^{0,0}, b_0^{1,0}, b_0^{2,1}, b_0^{3,0}$ encode the two positions of the word w_0.

In general, define the components of $G = \langle V, s_1, s_2, \text{null}, \text{root} \rangle$ as follows. For every pair of words $\langle v_i, w_i \rangle$ in PCP instance introduce two nodes $c_{2i}, c_{2i+1} \in V$. These nodes summarize C-nodes of a corresponder graph. For every position v_i^j of the word v_i introduce nodes $a_i^{2j,0}$ and $a_i^{2j+1,0}$ and for every position w_i^j introduce nodes $b_i^{2j,0}$ and $b_i^{2j+1,0}$. The a-nodes summarize U-nodes and the b-nodes summarize the L-nodes of the corresponder graph. Introduce further the nodes $b_i^{2j,1}$ to encode the property of a U-node that the matching L-node is colored by some $a_j^{0,0}$ denoting the first position of a word. For analogous reasons introduce $a_i^{2j+1,1}$ nodes. Let

$$V = \{\text{null}, \text{root}\} \cup \{c_0, c_1, \ldots, c_{2m-1}\}$$
$$\cup \{a_i^{j,0} \mid 0 \leq i < m; 0 \leq j < 2p_i\} \cup \{b_i^{j,0} \mid 0 \leq i < m; 0 \leq j < 2q_i\}$$
$$\cup \{a_i^{2j+1,1} \mid 0 \leq i < m; 0 \leq j < p_i\} \cup \{b_i^{2j,1} \mid 0 \leq i < m; 0 \leq j < q_i\}$$

Define s_1 graph edges as follows.

The c_i nodes are connected into a list that begins with root; every c_{2i} is followed by c_{2i+1}. The pairs c_{2i}, c_{2i+1} for different i can repeat in the list any number of times and in arbitrary order. This list encodes colorings that represent PCP instance solutions.

The nodes representing word positions are linked in the order in which they appear in the word. The last position in a word can be followed by the first position of any other word, or by null. The nodes for the v_i words and the nodes

$\iota(G) \equiv \exists c_0, c_1, c_2, c_3, a_0^{0,0}, a_0^{1,0}, a_0^{1,1}, a_1^{0,0}, a_1^{1,0}, a_1^{1,1}, a_1^{2,0}, a_1^{3,0}, a_1^{3,1},$
$\quad b_0^{0,0}, b_0^{0,1}, b_0^{1,0}, b_0^{2,0}, b_0^{2,1}, b_0^{3,0}, b_1^{0,0}, b_1^{0,1}, b_1^{1,0}, \text{null}, \text{root}.$
$\quad \forall x, y. \text{ disjoint} \wedge \text{null}_{\text{def}} \wedge \text{root}_{\text{def}} \wedge$
$\quad (s_1(x,y) \Rightarrow C \wedge L_{v_0} \wedge L_{v_1} \wedge L_{v_0,v_1} \wedge L_{w_0} \wedge L_{w_1} \wedge L_{w_0,w_1}) \wedge$
$\quad (s_2(x,y) \Rightarrow I \wedge M_a \wedge M_b \wedge M_c \wedge T)$
$C \equiv (c_0(x) \Rightarrow c_1(y)) \wedge (c_2(x) \Rightarrow c_3(y)) \wedge$
$\quad (\text{root}(x) \vee c_1(x) \vee c_3(x) \Rightarrow c_0(y) \vee c_2(y) \vee \text{null}(y))$
$L_{v_0} \equiv a_0^{0,0}(x) \Rightarrow a_0^{1,0}(y) \vee a_0^{1,1}(y)$
$L_{v_1} \equiv (a_1^{0,0}(x) \Rightarrow a_1^{1,0}(y) \vee a_1^{1,1}(y)) \wedge (a_1^{1,0}(x) \vee a_1^{1,1}(x) \Rightarrow a_1^{2,0}(y)) \wedge$
$\quad (a_1^{2,0}(x) \Rightarrow a_1^{3,0}(y) \vee a_1^{3,1}(y))$
$L_{v_0,v_1} \equiv a_0^{1,0}(x) \vee a_0^{1,1}(x) \vee a_1^{3,0}(x) \vee a_1^{3,1}(x) \Rightarrow a_0^{0,0}(y) \vee a_1^{0,0}(y) \vee \text{null}(y)$
$\quad L_{w_0}, L_{w_1}, L_{w_0,w_1} \text{ analogous to } L_{v_0}, L_{v_1}, L_{v_0,v_1} \text{ with } b_k^{i,j} \text{ instead of } a_r^{p,q}$
$I \equiv (c_0(x) \Rightarrow a_0^{0,0}(y)) \wedge (c_1(x) \Rightarrow b_0^{1,0}(y)) \wedge (c_2(x) \Rightarrow a_1^{0,0}(y)) \wedge (c_3(x) \Rightarrow b_1^{1,0}(y))$
$M_a \equiv (a_0^{0,0}(x) \Rightarrow b_1^{1,0}(y)) \wedge (b_1^{1,0}(x) \Rightarrow a_1^{1,1}(y))$
$\quad M_b, M_c \text{ analogous to } M_a \text{ with positions for letter 'b' and 'c' instead of 'a'}$
$T \equiv (\text{root}(x) \vee a_0^{1,0}(x) \vee a_1^{1,0}(x) \vee a_1^{3,0}(x) \vee b_0^{0,0}(x) \vee b_0^{2,0}(x) \vee b_1^{0,0}(x) \Rightarrow \text{null}(y))$
$\quad \wedge (a_0^{1,1}(x) \vee a_1^{1,1}(x) \vee a_1^{3,1}(x) \vee b_0^{0,1}(x) \vee b_0^{2,1}(x) \vee b_1^{0,1}(x) \Rightarrow \text{root}(y))$

Fig. 4. Formula $\iota(G)$ for the graph G constructed for the PCP instance from Figure 3. disjoint denotes that all existentially quantified sets are disjoint. null_{def} and root_{def} define singleton sets contain null and root node, respectively. L_{v_0} connects colors that encode positions in word v_0, similarly for $L_{v_1}, L_{w_0}, L_{w_1}$. L_{v_0,v_1} allows any sequence $(v_0|v_1)*$ of words as U-node colors, analogously for L_{w_0,w_1}. Formula I connects each node representing the choice of word pair k to the first position of the word v_k and w_k. M_a connects word positions containing the letter a, similarly for M_b, M_c.

for the w_i words form disjoint lists along the s_1 edges.

$s_1 = \{\langle \text{root}, c_{2i}\rangle \mid 0 \leq i < m\} \cup \{\langle c_{2i}, c_{2i+1}\rangle \mid 0 \leq i < m\}$
$\quad \cup \{\langle c_{2i+1}, c_{2j}\rangle \mid 0 \leq i,j < m\} \cup \{\langle c_{2i+1}, \text{null}\rangle \mid 0 \leq i < m\}$
$\quad \cup \{\langle a_i^{2j,0}, a_i^{2j+1,\alpha}\rangle \mid 0 \leq i < m; 0 \leq j < p_i; \alpha \in \{0,1\}\}$
$\quad \cup \{\langle a_i^{2j+1,\alpha}, a_i^{2j+2,0}\rangle \mid 0 \leq i < m; 0 \leq j < p_i - 1;$
$\qquad \alpha \in \{0,1\}\}$
$\quad \cup \{\langle a_i^{2p_i-1,\alpha}, a_j^{0,0}\rangle \mid 0 \leq i,j < m; \alpha \in \{0,1\}\}$
$\quad \cup \{\langle a_i^{2p_i-1,\alpha}, \text{null}\rangle \mid 0 \leq i < m; \alpha \in \{0,1\}\}$
$\quad \cup \{\langle b_i^{2j,\alpha}, b_i^{2j+1,0}\rangle \mid 0 \leq i < m; 0 \leq j < q_i; \alpha \in \{0,1\}\}$
$\quad \cup \{\langle b_i^{2j+1,0}, b_i^{2j+2,\alpha}\rangle \mid 0 \leq i < m; 0 \leq j < q_i - 1;$
$\qquad \alpha \in \{0,1\}\}$
$\quad \cup \{\langle b_i^{2q_i-1,0}, b_j^{0,\alpha}\rangle \mid 0 \leq i,j < m; \alpha \in \{0,1\}\}$
$\quad \cup \{\langle b_i^{2q_i-1,0}, \text{null}\rangle \mid 0 \leq i < m\}$

Define s_2 graph edges as follows.

Every c_j edge points to the position at the beginning of the word. Even numbered nodes point to the a^0-positions; odd numbered nodes point to b^1-positions.

The a_i and b_j word positions are connected so that an a-node points to a b-node for even indices, whereas a b-node points to an a-node for odd indices. The s_2-edges from a-nodes to b-nodes propagate the information that the a-node denotes the first position of some word through the value 1 of index α of the color $b^{2l,\alpha}$. The $b_k^{2l,1}$ nodes have an s_2-edge to root whereas $b_k^{2l,0}$ nodes have an s_2-edge to null. This distinction ensures that every $a_i^{0,0}$-colored node has an incoming edge from a C-node; which implies that every word occurring in the sequence of words that color U-nodes of a corresponder graph is selected by some C-node.

$$s_2 = \{\langle \mathsf{root}, \mathsf{null} \rangle\}$$
$$\cup \{\langle c_{2i}, a_i^{0,0} \rangle \mid 0 \leq i < m\} \cup \{\langle c_{2i+1}, b_i^{1,0} \rangle \mid 0 \leq i < m\}$$
$$\cup \{\langle a_i^{0,0}, b_k^{2l,1} \rangle \mid 0 \leq i, k < m; 0 \leq l < q_k; v_i^0 = w_k^l\}$$
$$\cup \{\langle a_i^{2j,0}, b_k^{2l,0} \rangle \mid 0 \leq i, k < m; 0 < j < p_i; 0 \leq l < q_k;$$
$$v_i^j = w_k^l\}$$
$$\cup \{\langle b_k^{2l,0}, \mathsf{null} \rangle \mid 0 \leq k < m; 0 \leq l < q_k\}$$
$$\cup \{\langle b_k^{2l,1}, \mathsf{root} \rangle \mid 0 \leq k < m; 0 \leq l < q_k\}$$
$$\cup \{\langle b_k^{1,0}, a_i^{2j+1,1} \rangle \mid 0 \leq i, k < m; 0 \leq j < p_i; v_i^j = w_k^l\}$$
$$\cup \{\langle b_k^{2l+1,0}, a_i^{2j+1,0} \rangle \mid 0 \leq i, k < m; 0 \leq j < p_i;$$
$$0 < l < q_k; v_i^j = w_k^l\}$$
$$\cup \{\langle a_i^{2j+1,0}, \mathsf{null} \rangle \mid 0 \leq i < m; 0 \leq j < p_i\}$$
$$\cup \{\langle a_i^{2j+1,1}, \mathsf{root} \rangle \mid 0 \leq i < m; 0 \leq j < p_i\}$$

Claim. The PCP instance has a solution iff there exists a corresponder graph G_0 such that $G_0 \to G$.

This proof of this Claim is not very surprising because we have defined the notion of corresponder graphs to make it true. See [22] for details. ∎

3.4 Using Homomorphisms to Characterize Corresponder Graphs

In Section 3.2 we have defined corresponder graphs as a parameterized family $\mathsf{CG}(n, k, u_1, \ldots, u_{k-1}, l_1, \ldots, l_{k-1})$. In this section we give an alternative characterization of corresponder graphs, as a subclass of heaps that satisfies certain set of graph invariants. We chosen these invariants so that each invariant is expressible as a homomorphism to some graph or as an absence of a homomorphism to some graph. These graphs show that the class of corresponder graphs is definable as the set of heaps that are counterexamples for the implication of two specific regular graph constraints.

Proposition 17. *There exist graphs P and Q such that for every heap H, $H \to (P \land \neg Q)$ iff H is a corresponder graph.*

Proof Sketch. We take P to be the graph in Figure 5 and let $Q = Q_0 + \cdots + Q_{16}$. See Appendix for the figures of graphs $P, Q_0, \ldots, Q_{16}$ and [22] for more proof details.

($\Longleftarrow$) : If G_0 is a corresponder graph we show that $G_0 \to P$ and for all $0 \le i \le 16$ it is not the case that $G_0 \to Q_i$. To show $G_0 \to P$ we find a homomorphism mapping C-nodes to c-nodes, U-nodes to a-nodes and L-nodes to b-nodes. Showing $\neg(G_0 \to Q_i)$ is not difficult either (e.g. for Q_0 consider a homomorphic image of the s_1-path from root to null).

($\Longrightarrow$) : (This is the more difficult direction.) Assume $G_0 \to P$ and for all $0 \le i \le 16$ it is not the case that $G_0 \to Q_i$. We show that G_0 is a corresponder graph. While P ensures that G_0 has roughly the desired shape, the graphs Q_i ensure the remaining invariants that characterize corresponder graphs. The graphs Q_0 (Figure 6) Q_1 (Figure 7), Q_2 (Figure 8), and Q_3 (Figure 9) eliminate models of P that contain cycles of certain from. For example, if following s_1-edges in G_0 starting from root leads to a cycle, then G_0 must be homomorphic to Q_0 in Figure 9. In this way Q_0 ensures the property of corresponder graphs that following s_1-edges from root eventually leads to null.

The graphs Q_4 (Figure 10), Q_5 (Figure 11), Q_6 (Figure 12), and Q_9 (Figure 15) ensure that certain distinct paths in the graph G_0 commute (i.e. lead to the same node). The graphs Q_7 (Figure 13) and Q_8 (Figure 14) ensure that there is the same number of U and L-nodes in a model of P. The graphs Q_{10} (Figure 16) and Q_{11} (Figure 17) ensure that U or L nodes have an s_2 edge to root iff the U or L node in the same column has an s_2-edge from a C-node. The graph Q_{12} (Figure 18) ensures that if a node C_{2i} has an s_2-edge to a node U_{j_1}, and the node C_{2i+2} has an s_2-edge to U_{j_2}, then U_{j_1} occurs before U_{j_2} in the list of U-nodes. Similarly, Q_{13} (Figure 19) ensures that s_2-edges from C_{2i+1}-nodes to L-nodes are in the proper order.

Finally, graphs Q_{14} (Figure 20), Q_{15} (Figure 21) and Q_{16} (Figure 22) ensure that C-nodes have s_2 edges only to U and L-nodes, and that an L or U node can only have an edge to root, null, a U-node, or an L-node. ∎

Having shown Proposition 17 and Proposition 16, Theorem 14 follows.

4 Conclusion

We have proposed regular graph constraints as an abstraction of mutually recursive properties of objects in potentially cyclic graphs. Regular graph constraints are a natural generalization of tree automata and domino systems. We have shown that satisfiability of regular graph constraints is decidable over the domain of heaps. As a main result, we have shown that the implication of regular graph constraints is undecidable. The consequence of this result is that verifying that procedure preconditions are satisfied is undecidable for any system of constraints that subsumes regular graph constraints.

The fact that decidability of problems with regular constraints is sensitive to the choice of the class of graphs is summarized in Table 1. The table indicates that techniques for reasoning about different classes of graphs may be substantially different. We therefore expect that a good support for mechanized

Table 1. Decidability of regular graph constraints

class	satisfiability decidable	source	entailment decidable	source
graphs	yes	trivial	yes	easy
trees	yes	[35]	yes	[35]
grids	no	[17]	no	[17]
heaps	yes	present paper	no	present paper

reasoning about data structures will likely contain a set of specialized techniques for different classes of graphs corresponding to commonly used data structures.

Acknowledgements

We thank Chandrasekhar Boyapati, Yuri Gurevich, Patrick Lam, Andreas Podelski, and the participants of the Dagstuhl Seminar 03101 "Reasoning About Shape" for useful discussions. We thank Patrick Lam, Darko Marinov, Chandrasekhar Boyapati, and anonymous reviewers for useful comments on an earlier version of this paper.

References

1. Michael Benedikt, Thomas Reps, and Mooly Sagiv. A decidable logic for linked data structures. In *Proc. 8th European Symposium on Programming*, 1999.
2. Egon Börger, Erich Gräedel, and Yuri Gurevich. *The Classical Decision Problem*. Springer-Verlag, 1997.
3. Cristiano Calcagno, Luca Cardelli, and Andrew D. Gordon. Deciding validity in a spatial logic for trees. Submitted, September 2002.
4. Venkatesan T. Chakaravarthy and Susan B. Horwitz. On the non-approximability of points-to analysis. *Acta Informatica*, 38(8):587–598, June 2002.
5. David R. Chase, Mark Wegman, and F. Kenneth Zadeck. Analysis of pointers and structures. In *Proc. ACM PLDI*, 1990.
6. H. Comon, M. Dauchet, R. Gilleron, F. Jacquemard, D. Lugiez, S. Tison, and M. Tommasi. Tree automata techniques and applications. Available on: http://www.grappa.univ-lille3.fr/tata, 1997. release 1 October 2002.
7. Bruno Courcelle. The expression of graph properties and graph transformations in monadic second-order logic. In *Handbook of graph grammars and computing by graph transformations, Vol. 1 : Foundations*, chapter 5. World Scientific, 1997.
8. Manuvir Das, Sorin Lerner, and Mark Seigle. ESP: Path-sensitive program verification in polynomial time. In *Proc. ACM PLDI*, 2002.
9. Robert DeLine and Manuel Fähndrich. Enforcing high-level protocols in low-level software. In *Proc. ACM PLDI*, 2001.
10. S. Drossopoulou, F. Damiani, M. Dezani-Ciancaglini, and P. Giannini. Fickle: Dynamic object re-classification. In *Proc. 15th European Conference on Object-Oriented Programming*, LNCS 2072, pages 130–149. Springer, 2001.
11. Dawson Engler, Benjamin Chelf, Andy Chou, and Seth Hallem. Checking system rules using systemspecific, programmer-written compiler extensions. In *Proc. 4th USENIX Symposium on Operating Systems Design and Implementation*, 2000.

12. Ronald Fagin, Larry J. Stockmeyer, and Moshe Y. Vardi. On monadic NP vs monadic co-NP. *Information and Computation*, 120(1), 1995.
13. Cormac Flanagan, K. Rustan M. Leino, Mark Lilibridge, Greg Nelson, James B. Saxe, and Raymie Stata. Extended Static Checking for Java. In *Proc. ACM PLDI*, 2002.
14. Jeffrey S. Foster, Tachio Terauchi, and Alex Aiken. Flow-sensitive type qualifiers. In *Proc. ACM PLDI*, 2002.
15. Pascal Fradet and Daniel Le Metayer. Shape types. In *Proc. 24th ACM POPL*, 1997.
16. Rakesh Ghiya and Laurie Hendren. Is it a tree, a DAG, or a cyclic graph? In *Proc. 23rd ACM POPL*, 1996.
17. Dora Giammarresi and Antonio Restivo. Two-dimensional languages. In Grzegorz Rozenberg and Arto Salomaa, editors, *Handbook of Formal Languages Vol.3: Beyond Words*. Springer-Verlag, 1997.
18. Wilfrid Hodges. *Model Theory*, volume 42 of *Encyclopedia of Mathematics and its Applications*. Cambridge University Press, 1993.
19. Neil Immerman. *Descriptive Complexity*. Springer-Verlag, 1998.
20. Daniel Jackson. Alloy: A lightweight object modelling notation. Technical Report 797, MIT Laboratory for Computer Science, 2000.
21. Viktor Kuncak, Patrick Lam, and Martin Rinard. Role analysis. In *Proc. 29th ACM POPL*, 2002.
22. Viktor Kuncak and Martin Rinard. Typestate checking and regular graph constraints. Technical Report 863, MIT Laboratory for Computer Science, 2002. http://www.mit.edu/~vkuncak/papers/index.html.
23. James R. Larus and Paul N. Hilfinger. Detecting conflicts between structure accesses. In *Proc. ACM PLDI*, Atlanta, GA, June 1988.
24. Anders Møller and Michael I. Schwartzbach. The Pointer Assertion Logic Engine. In *Proc. ACM PLDI*, 2001.
25. Greg Nelson. Techniques for program verification. Technical report, XEROX Palo Alto Research Center, 1981.
26. Flemming Nielson, Hanne Riis Nielson, and Chris Hankin. *Principles of Program Analysis*. Springer-Verlag, 1999.
27. Ganesan Ramalingam. The undecidability of aliasing. *ACM Transactions on Programming Languages and Systems (TOPLAS)*, 16(5):1467–1471, 1994.
28. H. G. Rice. Classes of recursively enumerable sets and their decision problems. *Transactions of the American Mathematical Society*, 89:25–29, 1953.
29. Neil Robertson and Paul D. Seymour. Graph minors: A survey. In Ian Anderson, editor, *Surveys in Combinatorics Papers for the London Math. Soc. Lecture Note Series*, 1985.
30. Mooly Sagiv, Thomas Reps, and Reinhard Wilhelm. Solving shape-analysis problems in languages with destructive updating. *ACM TOPLAS*, 20(1):1–50, 1998.
31. Mooly Sagiv, Thomas Reps, and Reinhard Wilhelm. Parametric shape analysis via 3-valued logic. *ACM TOPLAS*, 24(3):217–298, 2002.
32. Michael Sipser. *Introduction to the Theory of Computation*. PWS Publishing Company, 1997.
33. F. Smith, D. Walker, and G. Morrisett. Alias types. In *Proc. 9th European Symposium on Programming*, Berlin, Germany, March 2000.
34. Robert E. Strom and Shaula Yemini. Typestate: A programming language concept for enhancing software reliability. *IEEE Transactions on Software Engineering*, January 1986.
35. Wolfgang Thomas. Languages, automata, and logic. In *Handbook of Formal Languages Vol.3: Beyond Words*. Springer-Verlag, 1997.
36. David Walker and Greg Morrisett. Alias types for recursive data structures. In *Workshop on Types in Compilation*, 2000.

Appendix: Regular Constraints that Characterize Corresponder Graphs

In this appendix we present the graphs $P, Q_0, \ldots, Q_{16}$ that characterize the class of corresponder graphs CG.

When presenting the graphs we use the following conventions. We use the label r to denote the root of the graph. We label the edges of the relation s_1 relation by 1 and the edges of s_2 by 2. Note that if a node has no outgoing edges, it would be useless in the graph in terms of specifying a set of models G_0. Every graph node in our graphs thus has least one outgoing edge for every label. However, to make the graph presentation clearer, if a node x has an outgoing edge with label a to every node in the graph, we simply *omit all a edges of node x* from the sketch. In particular, if a node has no outgoing edges in the graph sketch, it means that its outgoing edges are unconstrained. A double-headed arrow from node x to node y with label a denotes two single arrows, one from x to y and one from y to x, both labeled with a. We do not show the edge $\langle \text{root}, \text{null} \rangle \in s_2$ that is always present in an orable graph. We similarly do not show the edges originating from null. We sometimes display null several times in the same picture; all these occurrences denote the unique null node in the graph.

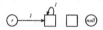

Fig. 6. Graph Q_0

Fig. 7. Graph Q_1

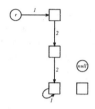

Fig. 8. Graph Q_2

Fig. 9. Graph Q_3

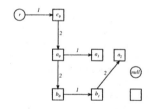

Fig. 10. Graph Q_4

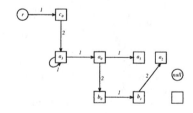

Fig. 11. Graph Q_5

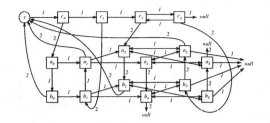

Fig. 5. Graph P

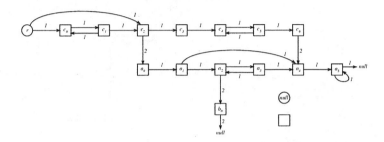

Fig. 18. Graph Q_{12}

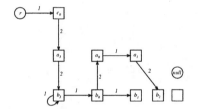

Fig. 12. Graph Q_6

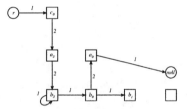

Fig. 14. Graph Q_8

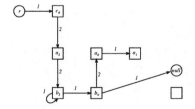

Fig. 13. Graph Q_7

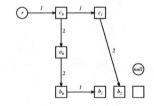

Fig. 15. Graph Q_9

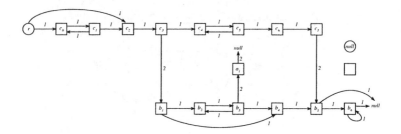

Fig. 19. Graph Q_{13}

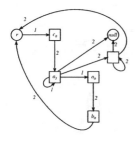

Fig. 16. Graph Q_{10}

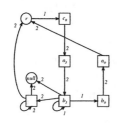

Fig. 17. Graph Q_{11}

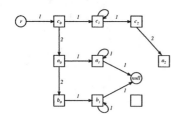

Fig. 20. Graph Q_{14}

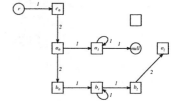

Fig. 21. Graph Q_{15}

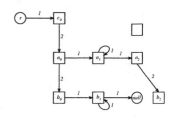

Fig. 22. Graph Q_{16}

Typestate Verification: Abstraction Techniques and Complexity Results

John Field[1], Deepak Goyal[2,*], G. Ramalingam[1], and Eran Yahav[3]

[1] IBM T.J. Watson Research Center
{jfield,rama}@watson.ibm.com
[2] IBM T.J. Watson Research Center*
[3] Tel Aviv University
yahave@post.tau.ac.il

Abstract. We consider the problem of *typestate verification* for *shallow* programs; i.e., programs where pointers from program variables to heap-allocated objects are allowed, but where heap-allocated objects may not themselves contain pointers. We prove a number of results relating the complexity of verification to the nature of the finite state machine used to specify the property. Some properties are shown to be intractable, but others which appear to be quite similar admit polynomial-time verification algorithms. Our results serve to provide insight into the inherent complexity of important classes of verification problems. In addition, the program abstractions used for the polynomial-time verification algorithms may be of independent interest.

In solving a problem of this sort, the grand thing is to be able to reason backward. ... In the everyday affairs of life it is more useful to reason forward.
–Sir Arthur Conan Doyle, *A Study in Scarlet.*

1 Introduction

The desire for more reliable software has led to increasing interest in extended static checking: statically verifying whether a program satisfies certain desirable properties. A technique that has received particular attention is that of finite state or *typestate* verification (e.g., see [27, 26, 21, 6, 8, 3, 9, 13, 12, 17, 1]). In this model, objects of a given type exist in one of finitely many *states*; the operations permitted on an object depend on the state of the object, and the operations may potentially alter the state of the object. The goal of typestate verification is to statically determine if the execution of a given program may cause an operation to be performed on an object in a state where the operation is not permitted.

Typestate verification can be used to check that objects satisfy certain kinds of temporal properties; e.g., that an object is not used before it is initialized, or that a file is not used after it is closed. In this paper, we will specify such

---

* Author's current affiliation: Calypto Design Systems Inc., dgoyal@calypto.com

properties using regular expressions or finite state automata that define the set of *valid* sequences of operations that can be performed on an object.

Our goal in this paper is to develop an initial understanding of how the difficulty of performing typestate verification relates to the *nature of the property being verified*. Among other things, we will show that not all finite state properties are equally hard to verify. For example, given a *shallow* program (where pointers from program variables to heap-allocated objects are allowed, but where heap-allocated objects may not themselves contain pointers), we show that verifying that a file is not read after it is closed can be done in *polynomial time*, while verifying that a file is not read before it is opened is *PSPACE-Complete*.

While there has been much progress on many aspects of automated program verification, we are not aware of any previous work relating the difficulty of typestate verification to properties of the finite state automaton. This work is part of a broader effort to develop efficient program verification techniques that are tailored to the property being verified [23].

Typestate Verification and Shallow Programs

In order to meaningfully compare the complexity of verification algorithms, we need to make some baseline assumptions about the precision of the analysis. In this paper, we will use the term *verification* to mean verification that is *precise* modulo the widely-used assumption that all paths in the program are feasible. Specifically, given a finite state property, a path in a program is said to be an *error path*, if execution along that path would cause an invalid sequence of operations to be performed on at least one *object* and the goal of typestate verification is to determine if a given program has any error path.

Typestate verification can be done in polynomial time if the program to be verified allows no inter-variable aliasing. Conversely, it is a straightforward consequence of previous results [18, 20] that if a program has *two or more* levels of pointers, typestate verification is PSPACE-hard[4]. In this paper, we therefore concentrate on understanding the class of *shallow* programs occupying a point in between these extremes.

Assume we wish to perform typestate verification for objects of a type T. A T-*shallow* program is a well-typed procedure-free program where all variables are pointers to T-typed objects, and whose statements are allocations (creation of a new object of type T), copy assignments (copying the value of a variable to another), or invocations of an operation on a variable. Note that shallow programs may contain multiple pointers to objects of type T, but allocated objects may not themselves contain T-pointers. In other words, pointers in shallow programs are *single-level* [20]. Our results also apply to programs that manipulate complex or recursive types where allocated objects contain pointers, *provided that those pointers cannot refer to objects of type T*. Programs that are shallow with respect to a given type, e.g. File, are not uncommon in practice.

---

[4] In the presence of recursive data structures, typestate verification is undecidable [19, 24].

Example: Verifying File Operations

Consider the problem of checking that a closed file is never read or closed again, which we will refer to as read*; close. In general, we will use regular expressions to designate sequences of *valid* operations on an object of a given type, where a sequence is valid iff it is a prefix of a string in the language defined by the regular expression.

The principal difficulty in doing precise verification arises from determining how *aliasing* interacts with operations on objects. Some prior work on typestate verification (e.g. [7]) has employed a two-step approach to the problem, in which an initial phase performs a conservative heap analysis of the program, and a subsequent phase uses the information from the heap analysis to do typestate analysis. However, we can see from the program fragments in Figure 1 that such an approach can sometimes lead to imprecise results. One can easily verify that in both Figures 1(a) and 1(b), all sequences of file operations on a given object are prefixes of read*; close; i.e., that no read ever follows a close.

However, consider a two-phase analysis in which the heap analysis is separate from the typestate analysis. In Fig. 1(a), a precise (and correct) heap analysis will determine that program variable z at program point s2 may point to the object created at s0 or the object created at s1. Furthermore, a precise typestate analysis will determine that the object created at s1 could be in a *closed* state at s2. A two-phase analysis must therefore erroneously conclude that the read could be performed on a closed file. Similarly, in Fig. 1(b), any conservative heap analysis would determine that objects created at program points s3 and s5 could reach the read statement at s4. In addition, a typestate analysis would also determine that the objects created at program points s3 and s5 could be in a closed state at s4. The analysis would, however, not be able to discover that f can never point to a closed object at s4, and would incorrectly indicate a possible error. In this paper we show that for a certain class of problems (including read*; close), it is possible to formulate a precise polynomial time verification algorithm for shallow programs.

```
s0 : x := new ();              s3 : f := new ();
s1 : y := new ();              while (?) {
z := y;                            s4 : f.read();
if (?) {                           if (?) {
    y.close();                         f.close();
    z := x;                            s5 : f := new ();
}                                  }
s2 : z.read();                 }
       (a)                            (b)
```

Fig. 1. Program fragments illustrating the effect of aliasing on typestate verification

Main Results

The main complexity results established in this paper are as follows (in all cases, we assume that programs are shallow):

- Verification is in P for omission-closed properties: a property is said to be omission-closed if every subsequence of a valid sequence is also a valid sequence. (Example: read*; close.)
- Verification is NP-Complete for acyclic programs (i.e., programs without loops) and PSPACE-complete for arbitrary programs for properties with a repeatable enabling sequence: a property is said to have a repeatable enabling sequence if there is an automaton state where a particular sequence γ of operations is invalid, but $\beta^+\gamma$ is valid. Example: open$^+$; read.
- An integer-valued function f is said to be a bound on the shortest error path length for a typestate property if every erroneous program of size n is guaranteed to have an error path of length $f(n)$ or less. If PSPACE is not equal to NP, then no polynomial bound exists for the shortest error path length for properties with a repeatable enabling sequence. (In other words, it may not be possible to find short, i.e., polynomial size error paths in the worst case.)
- Verification is in P for acyclic programs for almost-omission-closed properties: a property is said to be almost-omission-closed if there is an integer k such that every subsequence of a valid sequence of length greater than k is also valid. Example: open; read. Note that any property with only finitely many valid sequences is trivially almost-omission-closed.
- Verification is in P for almost-omission-closed properties that have a polynomial bound on the shortest error path length.
- A program is said to have a maximum aliasing factor of k if there is no path in the program that will produce an object pointed to by more than k different variables. Arbitrary finite state properties for programs of size n with a maximum aliasing factor of k may be verified in time $O(n^{k+1})$ for programs of size n.

The results above are summarized in Fig. 2 in terms of the properties of regular expressions which define the properties to be verified (the notation used there will be defined in Section 2).

The polynomial-time verification results summarized above use program abstractions that may be of independent interest—in particular, they may prove useful as the starting point for developing more general abstractions for non-shallow programs (e.g., in a manner similar to [23]). The bulk of the abstractions we use are *predicate abstractions* [15]; however we show in the sequel that the *vocabulary* of predicates used in a predicate abstraction can have a dramatic impact on the efficiency of the resulting analysis. Our predicate vocabularies are carefully designed to yield efficient analyses without sacrificing precision. In addition, in Section 5, we develop a novel *integer* abstraction, which is based on *counting* the number of program paths along which a simple property holds true; this in turn allows inferring whether a more complex property holds.

	Omission-Closed	Almost-Omission-Closed	Repeatable Enabling Seq	Other
E.g.	read*;close	open;read	open+;read	(lock;unlock)*
Defn.	$\forall \alpha\beta\gamma.$ $Valid(\alpha\beta\gamma)$ $\Rightarrow Valid(\alpha\gamma)$	$\exists k \forall \alpha\beta\gamma.(\|\alpha\beta\gamma\| \geq k \land Valid(\alpha\beta\gamma))$ $\Rightarrow Valid(\alpha\gamma)$	$\exists \alpha\beta\gamma.$ $Valid(\alpha\beta^+\gamma) \land$ $\neg Valid(\alpha\gamma)$	
Acyclic Pgms	P	P	NP-complete	?
Cyclic Pgms	P	Poly. Error Path $\Rightarrow$ P General: ?	PSPACE complete	?
Bounded Aliasing	P			

Fig. 2. Overview

Related Work

There has been significant recent interest in a variety of property verification techniques, many of them focusing on typestate verification. While significant progress has been made in improving the precision and efficiency of verification, developing verification techniques that are sufficiently precise and scalable to handle industrial-size applications for a wide variety of problems is still a challenge, and motivates our work here.

One of the open challenges in typestate verification is an adequate treatment of aliasing. Some approaches avoid the issue: e.g., the original work on typestate verification [27, 26] did not allow any aliasing; more recent work on typestate verification based on linear types [8] also restricts aliasing severely. Other approaches (e.g. [7]) perform alias analysis and typestate verification separately: an initial phase performs a conservative alias analysis for the program, and a subsequent phase uses the information from the alias analysis to do typestate verification. However, this can lead to imprecise results, as illustrated by the examples in Fig. 1.

A second challenge to practical verification is dealing with infeasible program paths. Das et al. [7] address this issue using efficient path-sensitive algorithms (which eliminate certain infeasible paths from consideration during analysis), but do not track certain additional information, e.g., aliasing, precisely. Our algorithms do not address the question of path sensitivity, but there could be merit in combining aspects of our approach with those that eliminate infeasible paths.

Several recent verification approaches [2, 16] combine predicate abstraction [15], counterexample-guided refinement of the predicate vocabulary [4], and exploration of the resulting abstract state space using model-checking. These techniques use symbolic and theorem-proving techniques to identify a set P of predicates relevant to the problem of interest, then model-check the resulting finite state system over a state space constructed from the powerset lattice $2^{P \to \{true, false\}}$. This process iterates with increasingly larger sets of predicates until a satisfactory result is obtained. In principle, these algorithms have the potential to avoid imprecision due to both aliasing and path infeasibility. However, the worst-case complexity of a *single* iteration is exponential in the number of predicates. By contrast, while most of the algorithms we present are based on abstractions by a set of predicates Q, our analysis is based on the function-space lattice $Q \rightarrow \{\textit{false}, \textit{maybe}\}$, and runs in time linear in the size of Q. This approach yields polynomial-time algorithms, while none of the techniques based on model-checking have a polynomial time worst-case complexity for the same problems (even though they may utilize a smaller number of predicates than our algorithm). Our selection of predicates ensures that the use of the smaller function space lattice results in no loss of precision, i.e., we ensure that our abstraction is *complete* (e.g., see [14]). Finally, the predicate abstractions we use are dependent solely on the nature of the typestate problem being verified, and do not require expensive predicate discovery at verification time.

Finally, we note that our lower bound results follow the tradition set by earlier complexity results due to Landi and Ryder [18], and Muth and Debray [20].

2 Terminology and Notation

In this section, we provide some basic definitions that we will use in the rest of the paper.

Definition 1 (Shallow Program). *A shallow program is a <Stmt> defined by the following context-free grammar, where the ? denotes a nondeterministic branch (i.e., an uninterpreted conditional). All variables <Var> in the language are references to objects of type T. All operations <Op> in the language are methods supported by type T.*

```
<Stmt> ::= <Var> := <Var>  |   <Var> := new()  |   <Var>.<Op>()
         | <Stmt>;<Stmt>  |   if (?) <Stmt> [ else <Stmt> ]
         | Label: <Stmt>  |   goto Label
```

We will make the simplifying assumption that when a program begins execution all program variables point to separate objects (i.e., initialized to non-aliased values), and all objects reside in their initial state. In other respects, the semantics of shallow programs is completely standard, and we will not formalize it here. We will, however, appeal to the intuitive notion of a *path* ρ through a program P (or P-path): a valid sequence of statements starting at P's entry.

In this paper, we will study safety properties of shallow programs. Although safety properties could be specified via temporal logics (e.g., LTL [5]), we will use finite automata or regular expressions to simplify the presentation. Formally:

Definition 2 (Prefix-Closed Safety Automaton). *A prefix-closed safety property $\mathcal{F}$ is represented by a finite state automaton (FSA) $\mathcal{F} = \langle \Sigma, \mathcal{Q}, \delta, \textit{init}, \mathcal{Q} \setminus \{\textit{err}\}\rangle$ where Σ is the automaton alphabet consisting of observable operations, $\mathcal{Q}$ is the set of automaton states, δ is the transition function mapping a state and an operation to a successor state, $\textit{init} \in \mathcal{Q}$ is a distinguished initial state,*

$err \in Q$ is a distinguished error state for which for every $\sigma \in \Sigma$, $\delta(err, \sigma) = err$, and all states in $Q \setminus \{err\}$ are accepting states. We say that q' is the successor of a state q on operation op when $\delta(q, \text{op}) = q'$. Given a sequence of operations $\alpha = \text{op}_1; \text{op}_2; \ldots; \text{op}_k$, we write $Valid_\mathcal{F}(\alpha)$ or $\alpha \in Valid_\mathcal{F}$ when α is accepted by $\mathcal{F}$, and we write $Invalid_\mathcal{F}(\alpha)$ when α is not accepted by $\mathcal{F}$.

For brevity, we will refer to safety properties using a regular expression representing the language accepted by an automaton, rather than specifying the automaton itself. When specifying a safety property using a regular expression, we will adopt the convention that a regular expression α denotes the *prefix closure* of the set of sequences of operations defined by α. For example, when we write read*;close we also consider ϵ (the empty sequence) and read to be valid sequences.

Example 1. Consider the property read*;close stating that a file may be read an arbitrary number of times before it is closed (and should never be read after it was closed and never be closed twice). The alphabet for this problem consists of two operations $\Sigma = \{\text{read}, \text{close}\}$. The FSA for this property is shown in Fig. 3.

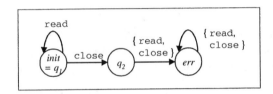

Fig. 3. A finite-state automaton for the property read*;close

When verifying a safety property represented by an automaton $\langle Q, init, err, \Sigma, \delta \rangle$ for a shallow program P, we will assume that each method name used in P is mapped to an element of Σ. Given this convention, we will use names of operations in Σ and methods in P interchangeably, i.e., we will say that a statement of the form x.op() invokes an operation op $\in \Sigma$. We can then relate method invocations to sequences of operations in Σ as follows:

Definition 3 (Operation Sequences for Objects). *Given a P-path ρ, $\mathcal{U}(\rho)$ denotes the set of object instances created during this execution, and for any object $o \in \mathcal{U}(\rho)$, $\rho[o]$ denotes the sequence of operations performed on o during execution of ρ.*

Given the definitions above, we can now formally describe the class of verification problems we wish to solve:

Definition 4 ($SV_\mathcal{F}$). *Given a safety property $\mathcal{F}$, the shallow verification problem for $\mathcal{F}$, $SV_\mathcal{F}$, determines for any shallow program P whether there exists a path P-path ρ such that $\rho[o] \in Invalid_\mathcal{F}$ for some $o \in \mathcal{U}(\rho)$.*

3 Omission-Closed Properties in Polynomial Time

In this section, we show that *omission-closed* properties can be verified in polynomial time.

Omission-Closed Properties

Informally, a property is omission-closed if the set of all valid sequences of operations is closed with respect to omissions: any sequence obtained by omitting one or more operations from a valid sequence of operations is also valid.

Definition 5. *A property represented by an automaton $\mathcal{F}$ is said to be* omission-closed *when for all sequences $\alpha, \beta, \gamma \in \Sigma^*$, $Valid_{\mathcal{F}}(\alpha\beta\gamma) \Rightarrow Valid_{\mathcal{F}}(\alpha\gamma)$.*

The following theorem presents alternative characterizations of omission-closed properties.

Theorem 1. *Given an automaton $\mathcal{F}$, the following are all equivalent, where all sequences are elements of Σ^*:*

(a) *For all sequences α, β, γ, $Valid_{\mathcal{F}}(\alpha\beta\gamma) \Rightarrow Valid_{\mathcal{F}}(\alpha\gamma)$.*
(b) *If ω_1 is a subsequence of ω_2, then $Valid_{\mathcal{F}}(\omega_2) \Rightarrow Valid_{\mathcal{F}}(\omega_1)$.*
(c) *There exists a finite set of* forbidden subsequences $\xi_1, \xi_2, \ldots, \xi_k$ *such that a sequence α is in $Invalid_{\mathcal{F}}$ iff α contains some ξ_i as a subsequence.*

Proof. The equivalence of (a) and (b) is straightforward. As for, (c), consider the forbidden subsequences ξ_i corresponding to the *acyclic* paths in the automaton $\mathcal{F}$ from the initial state to the error state. (For example, the forbidden subsequences for the automaton in Fig. 3 are $\xi_1 = $ close;read and $\xi_2 = $ close;close.) The result follows.

Background: Distributive Predicate Abstractions

The analysis we present will utilize a *predicate* abstraction that tracks the values of a set of predicates P defined on the concrete program-state. (We will use the term *program-state* to denote the state of the whole program in the concrete semantics, to distinguish it from a *state in a FSA specifying a property*.) For efficiency reasons, we will utilize an *independent attributes analysis* [22], an analysis that does not maintain the correlation between different predicate values. Specifically, the set of concrete program-states arising at a program point will be abstracted by a value in $P \to \{false, maybe\}$. We now summarize the conditions under which an *independent attributes analysis* can be used for a predicate abstraction without losing precision. Given a predicate φ and a statement St, we denote by $WP(St, \varphi)$ the weakest precondition of φ with respect to St [10].

Definition 6. *Given a finite set of predicates Base, we say that a finite set of predicates $\mathcal{P} = \{P_1, \ldots, P_k\}$ is a distributive WP-closure of Base when Base $\subseteq \mathcal{P}$ and for each predicate $P_i \in \mathcal{P}$, and for each statement St, $\mathrm{WP}(St, P_i) = P_{j_1} \vee \ldots \vee P_{j_m}$, such that for all $1 \leq g \leq m, P_{j_g} \in \mathcal{P}$. We also say that the set of predicates $\mathcal{P}$ is distributively WP-closed.*

Theorem 2. *Given a distributively WP-closed set of predicates $\mathcal{P}$ for a program Pgm, precise analysis (i.e., determining for every program point and every predicate in $\mathcal{P}$ whether there exists a path to the program point causing the predicate to be true) is possible in time $O(|\mathcal{P}||\mathrm{Pgm}|)$.*

Proof. Straightforward. E.g., the problem can be reduced to a reachability problem over a graph of size $O(|\mathcal{P}||Pgm|)$, as in the IFDS framework of [25].

A Polynomial Algorithm

We use a designated predicate *Error* that is *true* in a program-state if and only if the program-state contains an object in the error state *err*. We will now show that for omission-closed properties, a distributive WP closure of polynomial size can be constructed for $\{Error\}$. In general, a distributive WP closure for $\{Error\}$ needs to include predicates that refer to aliasing relationships among variables *as well as* the state of the objects pointed to by the variables. This motivates the following definition of a family of predicates.

Definition 7. *We write $In_\sigma(\mathtt{x})$ to denote the fact that the object pointed to by the variable $\mathtt{x}$ is in state $\sigma \in \mathcal{Q}$. Given any $S \subseteq \mathcal{Q}$, we use the shorthand $In_S(\mathtt{x}) \triangleq \bigvee_{\sigma \in S} In_\sigma(\mathtt{x})$ to denote that the object pointed to by the variable $\mathtt{x}$ is in one of the states in S.*

Definition 8. *Let A be a non-empty set of variables (in a given program), $S \subseteq \mathcal{Q}$ a set of states in $\mathcal{F}$. We use the predicate $\langle A, S \rangle$ to mean that all variables in A have the same value (are aliases), and the object referred to by variables in A is in one of the states in S. Formally,*

$$\langle A, S \rangle \triangleq \bigwedge_{\mathtt{x} \in A, \mathtt{y} \in A} (\mathtt{y} = \mathtt{x}) \wedge \bigwedge_{\mathtt{x} \in A} In_S(\mathtt{x})$$

The number of predicates of the form $\langle A, S \rangle$ is exponential in the number of program variables. However, not all predicates of this form are *relevant*, i.e. need to be in a distributive WP closure for $\{Error\}$. The key to obtaining a polynomial size distributive WP closure for $\{Error\}$ is to bound the size of the set A, for any relevant predicate $\langle A, S \rangle$ by a constant. We will do this in two steps. First, we will show that a predicate $\langle A, S \rangle$ is relevant only for certain $S \subseteq \mathcal{Q}$. Then, we will show that for each such set S, the predicate $\langle A, S \rangle$ is relevant for only A of cardinality less than a specific constant.

We first present an algorithm for determining which $S \subseteq \mathcal{Q}$ are relevant for verification. The algorithm shown in Fig. 4 is based on a backward traversal of the finite state automaton. The algorithm constructs a graph $\overleftarrow{\mathcal{F}} = (V_{\overleftarrow{\mathcal{F}}}, E_{\overleftarrow{\mathcal{F}}})$, where each vertex is a subset of $\mathcal{Q}$, and an edge $P \to S$ denotes that P is a pre-image of S for the transition function δ (see below).

Definition 9. Let $\overleftarrow{\delta}$ denote the reverse transition relation of $\mathcal{F}$, i.e., given a state $q \in \mathcal{Q}$, an operation $a \in \Sigma$, and a set of states $S \subseteq \mathcal{Q}$, $\overleftarrow{\delta}(q, a) \triangleq \{q' \in \mathcal{Q} | \delta(q', a) = q\}$, and $\overleftarrow{\delta}(S, a) \triangleq \bigcup_{q \in S} \overleftarrow{\delta}(q, a)$. For $S_1, S_2 \subseteq \mathcal{Q}$, S_2 is said to be a pre-image of S_1 if $\exists a \in \Sigma. \overleftarrow{\delta}(S_1, a) = S_2$.

```
V_F̄ = ∅;  E_F̄ = ∅;  workSet = {{err}};
while workSet ≠ ∅ {
    select and remove S from workSet;
    for each operation op ∈ Σ {
        P = δ̄(S, op);
        if P ∉ V_F̄ { V_F̄ = V_F̄ ∪ {P}; workSet = workSet ∪ {P}; }
        E_F̄ = E_F̄ ∪ {P → S};
    }
}
```

Fig. 4. Backwards exploration of the property automaton

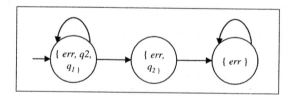

Fig. 5. The graph constructed by backward exploration of the automaton of Fig. 3.

Fig. 5 illustrates the graph constructed by backward exploration of the `read*;close` automaton shown in Fig. 3. We now establish a result about the graph $\overleftarrow{\mathcal{F}}$.

Theorem 3. *If $\mathcal{F}$ represents an omission-closed property, then for any $S \in V_{\overleftarrow{\mathcal{F}}}$, and any operation $a \in \Sigma$, $\overleftarrow{\delta}(S, a) \supseteq S$. Further, the graph $\overleftarrow{\mathcal{F}}$ is acyclic except for self-loops.*

Proof. For any $S \in V_{\overleftarrow{\mathcal{F}}}$ there exists a sequence of operations ξ such that S is the set of all states in which ξ is invalid (by construction). Now, $\overleftarrow{\delta}(S, a)$ is the set of all states in which $a\xi$ is invalid. Since $\mathcal{F}$ is omission-closed, $\overleftarrow{\delta}(S, a) \supseteq S$. Since any predecessor P of S must be a superset of S, it follows immediately that any cycle in the graph $\overleftarrow{\mathcal{F}}$ must be a self-loop. □

Fig. 6 and Fig. 7 present weakest-precondition equations for predicates of the form $\langle A, S \rangle$ and the special predicate *Error*. From these equations, we can determine which predicates are relevant for verification. The equations reveal two things. First, they show that it is sufficient if we restrict our attention to predicates of the form $\langle A, S \rangle$ where $S \in V_{\overleftarrow{\mathcal{F}}}$. Second, they show that a predicate $\langle A, P \rangle$ is relevant only if there is a relevant predicate $\langle B, S \rangle$ where S is a proper successor of P in the graph $\overleftarrow{\mathcal{F}}$ and B has cardinality at least $|A| - 1$. In other words, we need to only consider predicates of the form $\langle A, P \rangle$ where the cardinality of A is less than or equal to the length of the longest acyclic path from P to $\{err\}$ in $\overleftarrow{\mathcal{F}}$.

Stmt	WP(Stmt, $\langle A, S \rangle$)	
x := y	$\langle A[x \mapsto y], S \rangle$	
x := new ()	$\langle A, S \rangle$	if $x \notin A$
	false	if $x \in A \wedge A \neq \{x\}$
	true	if $A = \{x\} \wedge init \in S$
	false	if $A = \{x\} \wedge init \notin S$
x.op()	$\langle A, S \rangle$	if $\overleftarrow{\delta}(S, op) = S$
	$\langle A \cup \{x\}, \overleftarrow{\delta}(S, op) \rangle \vee \langle A, S \rangle$	if $\overleftarrow{\delta}(S, op) \supset S$
At program entry	true	if $|A| = 1 \wedge init \in S$
	false	if $|A| \neq 1 \vee init \notin S$

Fig. 6. WP equations for predicates of the form $\langle A, S \rangle$. We denote by $A[x \mapsto y]$ the set obtained by replacing any occurrence of x in A by y

Definition 10. *For any $S \in V_{\overleftarrow{\mathcal{F}}}$, define $dist(S)$ to be the number of edges in the longest acyclic path from S to $\{err\}$ in $\overleftarrow{\mathcal{F}}$. Given a program with a set of variables Vars, we define a set of predicates $\mathcal{P} = \{\langle A, S \rangle | S \in V_{\overleftarrow{\mathcal{F}}}, A \subseteq \text{Vars}, |A| \leq dist(S)\} \cup \{Error\}$.*

Theorem 4. *The set $\mathcal{P} \cup \{true, false\}$ is a distributively WP-closed set of predicates for $\{Error\}$.*

Proof. Follows from the above discussion.

Theorem 5. *If $\mathcal{F}$ is omission-closed, then $SV_{\mathcal{F}}$ is in P.*

Proof. Immediate from Theorem 4 and Theorem 2. Note that the cardinality of $\mathcal{P}$ is $O(|\textit{Vars}|^k)$, where *Vars* is the set of all variables in the program and k is the length of the longest acyclic path in $\overleftarrow{\mathcal{F}}$. (Note, from Theorem 3, that k is also bounded by the number of states in $\mathcal{F}$.) For example, `read*; close` verification can be done in time $O(|\textit{Vars}|^2 |Pgm|)$.

Stmt	WP(Stmt, $Error$)
x := y	$Error$
x := new ()	$Error$
x.op()	$Error$ if $\overleftarrow{\delta}(\{err\}, op) = \{err\}$ $\langle\{x\}, \overleftarrow{\delta}(\{err\}, op)\rangle \vee Error$ if $\overleftarrow{\delta}(\{err\}, op) \supset \{err\}$
At program entry	$false$

Fig. 7. WP equations for the predicate $Error$

Discussion

A logical formula can usually be simplified into a number of equivalent forms. Hence, a weakest-precondition can often be expressed in many ways. The form we chose to use in expressing weakest-preconditions above is critical to deriving a polynomial time verification algorithm. As an example, consider the read*; close example. The following is an alternative, correct, weakest-precondition equation, which says that an object in the err state is possible after x.close() iff either x points to an object in state q_2 or an object exists in the err state before the statement:

$$\text{WP}(\text{x.close()}, Error) = \langle\{x\}, \{q_2\}\rangle \vee Error. \tag{1}$$

The actual formulation we used

$$\text{WP}(\text{x.close()}, Error) = \langle\{x\}, \{err, q_2\}\rangle \vee Error \tag{2}$$

contains some redundancy. In particular, $\langle\{x\}, \{err, q_2\}\rangle$ is equivalent to $\langle\{x\}, \{err\}\rangle \vee \langle\{x\}, \{q_2\}\rangle$. But the disjunct $\langle\{x\}, \{err\}\rangle$ is redundant because it implies $Error$, another disjunct in our formula.

However, equation 2 is preferable to equation 1. In particular, we have seen that we can determine in polynomial time if $\langle\{x\}, \{err, q_2\}\rangle$ is possible at any program point. However, one can show that determining if $\langle\{x\}, \{q_2\}\rangle$ is possible at a program point is PSPACE-hard, adapting the proof we present in Section 4. Thus, unless PSPACE = P, a distributively WP-closed set containing $\langle\{x\}, \{q_2\}\rangle$ of polynomial size *does not exist!*

4 Repeatable Enabling Sequence Properties

In this section we show that verification of Repeatable Enabling Sequence properties (see Definition 11) is NP-complete for acyclic programs and PSPACE-complete in general.

Definition 11 (Repeatable Enabling Sequence Properties). *We say that a property represented by an automaton $\mathcal{F}$ is a repeatable enabling sequence* *property* if there exist sequences of operations α, β and γ such that the set of sequences $\alpha\beta^+\gamma$ are all valid but the sequence $\alpha\gamma$ is invalid. (The sequence β may be thought of as a repeatable sequence that enables γ.)

For example, the property open$^+$;read (see Figure 8) which requires that a read be preceded by one or more open operations is a repeatable enabling sequence property. (The more natural property open$^+$;read* is also a repeatable enabling sequence property, but we use open$^+$;read as the running example to contrast it with the omission-closed property read*;close.) We show that verification of repeatable enabling sequence properties is PSPACE-complete by reduction from the *simultaneously false* problem (see [20], [11]).

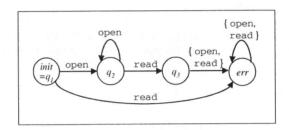

Fig. 8. An automaton for the property open$^+$;read

Definition 12. (Simultaneously False Problem) *Given a program P with an initial assignment of values (0 or 1) to a set $x_1, x_2, \ldots, x_n$ of boolean variables, where the program P contains only assignments (of constants or variables), conditionals or unconditional jumps, a* simultaneously false *problem for P is a problem of the form: is there an execution path from the entry point of P to a program point p such that $x_1 = 0, x_2 = 0, \ldots x_k = 0$ when control reaches p?*

Lemma 1. *(1) The simultaneously false problem for acyclic programs is NP-complete. (2) The simultaneously false problem for arbitrary programs is PSPACE-complete.*

Proof. See [20] and [11]. □

Let $\mathcal{F}$ be an automaton representing a repeatable enabling sequence property. We show that SV$_\mathcal{F}$ is PSPACE-hard by reduction from the simultaneously false problem. If α, β, γ are such that sequences $\alpha\beta^+\gamma$ are valid and sequence $\alpha\gamma$ is invalid, then β and γ must be non-empty (although α may be empty). Given an instance of the simultaneously false problem $x_1 = 0, x_2 = 0, \ldots, x_k = 0$ at program point p in a program P, we construct a program P' as follows. First, we create two objects Zero and One which support methods corresponding to the sequences $\alpha, \beta,$ and γ. Next, we copy program P into P' replacing every assignment of the form $\mathtt{x_i} = 0$ by $\mathtt{x_i} = \mathtt{Zero}$ and $\mathtt{x_i} = 1$ by $\mathtt{x_i} = \mathtt{One}$ respectively.

Then, at program point p, we insert the statement if (?) goto p₁. Let the sequence α be $a_1, a_2, \ldots, a_l$, let β be $b_1, b_2, \ldots b_m$, and let γ be $c_1, c_2, \ldots c_n$. We insert the following sequence of statements at the end.

```
            goto exit;
p₁ :    Zero.a₁(); Zero.a₂(); ...; Zero.a₁();
        One.a₁(); One.a₂(); ...; One.a₁();
        x₁.b₁(); x₁.b₂(); ...; x₁.bₘ();
        x₂.b₁(); x₂.b₂(); ...; x₂.bₘ();
        ...
        xₖ.b₁(); xₖ.b₂(); ...; xₖ.bₘ();
        One.c₁(); One.c₂(); ...; One.cₙ();
exit :
```

Note that control can reach program point p₁ only through the conditional branch statement if (?) goto p₁ (because of the statement goto exit; just before p₁).

Lemma 2. *Assuming that the sequences of operations β and γ are non-empty, the simultaneously false problem $x_1 = 0, x_2 = 0, \ldots x_k = 0$ at program point p in P returns true if and only if program P' violates the property represented by $\mathcal{F}$.*

Proof. Program P' creates only two objects $Zero$ and One. Note that the only sequence of operations performed on $Zero$ is $\alpha\beta^i$ where i is the number of variables in $x_1, x_2, \ldots, x_k$ that are aliased to $Zero$ at program point p. Thus, no illegal operation is ever performed on $Zero$. Similarly, the only sequence of operations performed on One is $\alpha\beta^j\gamma$ where j is the number of variables in $x_1, x_2, \ldots, x_k$ that are aliased to One at program point p. This sequence is invalid iff j can be 0. In other words, P' violates the property represented by $\mathcal{F}$ iff the simultaneously false problem $x_1 = 0, x_2 = 0, \ldots x_k = 0$ at program point p in P returns true. □

Theorem 6. *Consider a repeatable enabling sequence property represented by an automaton $\mathcal{F}$. $SV_{\mathcal{F}}$ is NP-complete for acyclic programs and PSPACE-complete for arbitrary (cyclic) programs.*

Proof. The proofs of NP-hardness and PSPACE-hardness of acyclic and arbitrary programs respectively follows from Lemmas 1 and 2 respectively. Lemma A1 in the Appendix shows that the problem of shallow verification for all safety properties represented by an automaton are in NP for acyclic programs and in PSPACE for arbitrary programs. □

Theorem 6 shows that verification of repeatable enabling sequence properties is difficult even for shallow programs. In fact, the situation is worse. We now show that even the shortest error paths may be of exponential size in the worst case.

Definition 13 (Error Path). *Let $\mathcal{F}$ be an automaton representing a property to be verified. We say that a path (possibly cyclic) in the control flow graph of*

P from the entry vertex to some vertex v is an error path if symbolic execution of the program along this path (ignoring the conditionals) exhibits a violation of the property associated with $\mathcal{F}$. The program P is said to be erroneous if there exists an error path in P. An integer-valued function f is said to be a bound on the shortest error path length if every erroneous program for size n is guaranteed to have an error path of length $f(n)$ or less.

Theorem 7. *If NP $\neq$ PSPACE, then there does not exist a polynomial bound on the shortest error path length for repeatable enabling sequence properties.*

Proof. The proof is given in the appendix. □

Theorem 7 suggests that it may not be possible to find short counterexample paths exhibiting the violation of properties like open$^+$; read. This is important to know because many approaches to verification (e.g., [3]) are inherently associated with the generation of a counterexample path that exhibits the violation of the property of interest. Theorem 7 suggests the possibility that even the shortest error path in the program may be of size exponential in the size of the program.

5 Verification by Counting

We have now seen that verification is intractable for repeatable enabling sequence properties and polynomial for omission-closed properties. Unfortunately, there are properties that fall into neither class. A simple example is the open; read property. Note that open; read is similar to open$^+$; read in that it requires that an object be opened before it can be read, but it differs from it in that an object cannot be opened multiple times. Does this make verification any easier?

5.1 The Intuition

The requirement that an object cannot be opened multiple times is a forbidden subsequence problem (where open; open is the forbidden subsequence) (see Theorem 1(c)). It follows that we can verify if the given program may open an object multiple times in polynomial time. Thus, open; read verification is polynomial-time equivalent to open$^+$; read verification of a program *guaranteed not to open any object more than once*. We will now show that, at least for acyclic programs, this added restriction (that an object can not be opened multiple times) does make polynomial time verification possible.

We first consider why read*; close verification is easy while open$^+$; read verification is not. Consider the following code fragment:

$\ldots$; p_1.open(); $\ldots$; p_k.open(); $\ldots$; q.read();

The open$^+$; read property will be violated if there is an execution path such that the value of q at the read statement is different from the values of *each p_i* at the corresponding open statements (assuming there are no open statements in the program other than those shown above). Determining if certain relationships can *simultaneously* exist among a potentially unbounded number of program variables is difficult.

In contrast, consider the following code fragment:

   ...; p$_1$.close(); ...; p$_k$.close(); ...; q.read();

The read*;close property will be violated here if there is an execution path such that the value of q at the read statement is equal to the value of *some* p$_i$ at the corresponding close statement. In other words, this requires *independent* answers to k different questions, each about the value of only *two* program variables. This turns out to be easy.

Let us now turn back to the earlier example above.

   ...; p$_1$.open(); ...; p$_k$.open(); ...; q.read();

If we now know that no object is opened twice, how can we exploit this for open$^+$;read (i.e., open;read) verification? For any given i, we know that it is easy to determine if q.read() statement may read the same object that is opened by the p$_i$.open() statement. Imagine that we can *count* the number of execution paths, n_i, along which this can happen, for each i. Adding up all the n_i would tell us how many times (i.e., along how many execution paths) the q.read() statement is a *valid* operation[5]. If this number does not equal the number of execution paths to the q.read() statement, then *there must be an execution path along which* q.read() *will read an unopened object!* Such indirect reasoning based on counting is the basis for the algorithm presented in this section.

Obviously, counting the number of paths is not feasible in the presence of cycles. In the rest of this section we will restrict our attention to acyclic, or loop-free, programs, and show how the above approach can be used for a class of verification problems.

5.2 Definitions

We start by formally defining the quantities we want to compute. Given some program P, consider a P-path ρ. Recall that $\mathcal{U}(\rho)$ denotes the set of object instances created in ρ, and for any $i \in \mathcal{U}(\rho)$, $\rho[i]$ denotes the sequence of operations performed on i. Let $\rho[\mathrm{p}]$ denote the value of variable p at the end of ρ. If s is a statement in the program, we will use s_{in} and s_{out} to denote the program points just before and just after the statement s.

Definition 14. *Let α denote a sequence of operations, π a program path, and Π_u the set of all paths from entry to a program point u. Define* $ct(\alpha, \pi) \triangleq |\{\, i \in \mathcal{U}(\pi) \mid \pi[i] = \alpha \,\}|$ *and* $ct(\alpha, u) \triangleq \sum_{\pi \in \Pi_u} ct(\alpha, \pi)$

---

[5] This is where we exploit the fact that no object is opened twice. Otherwise, adding up n_i will end up counting some paths multiple times.

We now define auxiliary counts of the form $\widehat{ct}(\langle X, \alpha \rangle, u)$, which we will subsequently use to compute $ct(\alpha, u)$, where X is a set of program variables. Informally, the set X will constrain the counting to the object instance pointed to by all variables in X. Second, while $ct(\alpha, u)$ counts *exact* matches for α, $\widehat{ct}(\langle X, \alpha \rangle, u)$ will count *subsequence* matches for α.

Definition 15. *Given two sequences α and β, let $\widehat{ct}(\alpha, \beta)$ denote the number of times α occurs as a (not necessarily contiguous) subsequence of β.*

$$\widehat{ct}(a_1...a_k, b_1...b_m) \triangleq |\{(i_1,...,i_k) \mid 1 \leq i_1 < ... < i_k \leq m \land a_1...a_k = b_{i_1}...b_{i_k}\}|$$

In the special case where α is the empty sequence, $\widehat{ct}(\alpha, \beta)$ is defined to be 1.

Definition 16. *Given a set of program variables X and a program path π, we define $\mathcal{U}(\pi, X) \triangleq \{i \in \mathcal{U}(\pi) \mid \forall p \in X.\pi[p] = i\}$. Essentially, if X is empty, then $\mathcal{U}(\pi, X)$ is $\mathcal{U}(\pi)$. If X is non-empty and all variables in X point to the same object i then $\mathcal{U}(\pi, X)$ is $\{i\}$. If all variables in X do not point to the same object, then $\mathcal{U}(\pi, X)$ is empty.*

Definition 17. *Let α denote a sequence of operations, π a program path, and Π_u the set of all paths from the entry vertex to a program point u. Then, define $\widehat{ct}(\langle X, \alpha \rangle, \pi) \triangleq \sum_{i \in \mathcal{U}(\pi, X)} \widehat{ct}(\alpha, \pi[i])$ and $\widehat{ct}(\langle X, \alpha \rangle, u) \triangleq \sum_{\pi \in \Pi_u} \widehat{ct}(\langle X, \alpha \rangle, \pi)$.*

Example 2. Consider the program shown below on the left. Let u denote the program point after the last statement y.read(). Let ρ_1 denote the path to u where the false branch of the if-statement is taken, and let ρ_2 denote the other path to u. The table on the right shows the values of the various quantities defined above. The fact that $ct(\text{read}, u)$ is non-zero indicates that the program contains a violation of the open; read property.

```
x := new ();
y := new ();
x.open();
if (?) {
    y.open();
}
x.read();
y.read();
```

X	α	$\widehat{ct}(\langle X, \alpha \rangle, \rho_1)$	$\widehat{ct}(\langle X, \alpha \rangle, \rho_2)$	$\widehat{ct}(\langle X, \alpha \rangle, u)$	$ct(\alpha, u)$
{x}	read	1	1	2	–
{x}	open; read	1	1	2	–
{y}	read	1	1	2	–
{y}	open; read	0	1	1	–
ϕ	read	2	2	4	1
ϕ	open; read	1	2	3	3

5.3 Counting Subsequences

We now show how the quantities defined above can be computed. Fig. 9 expresses the relationships that must hold between the $\widehat{ct}$ values at different program points.

Lemma 3. *For any sequence α and any acyclic program Pgm over a set of program variables Vars, $\widehat{ct}(\langle \phi, \alpha \rangle, u)$ can be computed for all program points u in polynomial time.*

Statement u	Equations	
	$\widehat{ct}(\langle X,\alpha\rangle,\text{entry}_{in})=\text{if }(|X|>1\text{ or }|\alpha|>0)\text{ then }0\text{ else }1$	
	$\widehat{ct}(\langle X,\alpha\rangle,u_{in})=\sum_{v\in\text{pred}(u)}\widehat{ct}(\langle X,\alpha\rangle,v_{out})$	
x := y	$\widehat{ct}(\langle X,\alpha\rangle,u_{out})=\widehat{ct}(\langle X-\{\,x\,\}\cup\{\,y\,\},\alpha\rangle,u_{in})$	(if x $\in X$)
	$\widehat{ct}(\langle X,\alpha\rangle,u_{out})=\widehat{ct}(\langle X,\alpha\rangle,u_{in})$	(if x $\notin X$)
x := new ()	$\widehat{ct}(\langle\{\,x\,\},\epsilon\rangle,u_{out})=\widehat{ct}(\langle\{\,x\,\},\epsilon\rangle,u_{in})$	
	$\widehat{ct}(\langle X,\alpha\rangle,u_{out})=0$	(if x$\in X$ and $(|X|>1$ or $|\alpha|>0))$
	$\widehat{ct}(\langle X,\alpha\rangle,u_{out})=\widehat{ct}(\langle X,\alpha\rangle,u_{in})$	(if x $\notin X$ and $X\neq\phi$)
x.f()	$\widehat{ct}(\langle X,\alpha\rangle,u_{out})=\widehat{ct}(\langle X,\alpha\rangle,u_{in})$	(when α is not of the form βf)
	$\widehat{ct}(\langle X,\alpha\rangle,u_{out})=\widehat{ct}(\langle X,\beta f\rangle,u_{in})+$	(where $\alpha=\beta f$)
	$\quad\widehat{ct}(\langle X\cup\{\,x\,\},\beta\rangle,u_{in})$	

Fig. 9. Equations for computing the number of subsequence matches. Note that, in general, the set X may be empty, or the sequence α may be the empty sequence ϵ, but the equations assume that both X and α can not be simultaneously empty. (We are not interested in the value of $\widehat{ct}(\langle\phi,\epsilon\rangle,u)$)

Proof. We compute the values of $\widehat{ct}(\langle\phi,\alpha\rangle,u)$ using the equations presented in Fig. 9. Note that computing $\widehat{ct}(\langle\phi,\alpha\rangle,u)$ at a program point u may transitively require computing the value of $\widehat{ct}(\langle X,\beta\rangle,v)$ at some vertex v, where β is a prefix of α, and X is a set of variables of cardinality at most $|\alpha|-|\beta|$. Hence, the number of values (or equations) we need to compute at any program point is $O(|\textit{Vars}|^{|\alpha|})$, where $\textit{Vars}$ is the set of all variables in the program. The result follows. □

5.4 Counting Exact Matches

Earlier we argued how we could compute the number of exact matches for read from the number of subsequence matches for read and the number of subsequence matches for open; read. We now present a generalization of this idea.

Lemma 4. *Let u denote any program point. We will use $\beta\succ\alpha$ to denote that β is a proper supersequence of α (i.e., that α is a proper subsequence of β). Then,*

$$ct(\alpha,u)=\widehat{ct}(\langle\phi,\alpha\rangle,u)-\sum_{\beta\succ\alpha}\widehat{ct}(\alpha,\beta)ct(\beta,u).$$

Proof. We will now show that $ct(\alpha,\pi)=\widehat{ct}(\langle\phi,\alpha\rangle,\pi)-\sum_{\beta\succ\alpha}\widehat{ct}(\alpha,\beta)ct(\beta,\pi)$ for any execution path π, from which the lemma follows immediately. Note that $ct(\alpha,\pi)$ counts exact matches for α in π, while $\widehat{ct}(\langle\phi,\alpha\rangle,\pi)$ counts occurrences of α as a subsequence in π. Now, consider any supersequence β of α. Every exact match for β in π will give us $\widehat{ct}(\alpha,\beta)$ subsequence matches for α. Hence, the above equality follows. □

A sequence α has infinitely many supersequences β. So, how can we make use of the above equation?

Definition 18. *A property represented by an automaton $\mathcal{F}$ is said to be* almost-omission-closed *if there exists an integer k such that for all sequences $\alpha, \beta, \gamma \in \Sigma^*$, if $|\alpha\beta\gamma|_{\dot{o}} k$ then $\text{Valid}_{\mathcal{F}}(\alpha\beta\gamma) \Rightarrow \text{Valid}_{\mathcal{F}}(\alpha\gamma)$.*

Let us refer to $(\alpha\gamma, \alpha\beta\gamma)$ as an omission-violation if $\alpha\beta\gamma$ is a valid sequence but $\alpha\gamma$ is not. An omission-closed property is one with no omission-violations. An almost-omission-closed property is one with only finitely many omission-violations. Note that open;read is an example of a verification problem where there is only one omission-violation, namely read is invalid but open;read is valid. We will now establish the following.

Theorem 8. *If $\mathcal{F}$ represents an almost-omission-closed property, then $\text{SV}_{\mathcal{F}}$ for acyclic programs is in P.*

Proof. Consider any α that is invalid. Then, any supersequence β of α of length $k+1$ must be a forbidden subsequence. Hence, we can check a program in polynomial time to see if it contains any such β. If it does, we can stop since the program does not satisfy the required property. Otherwise, we count the number of subsequence matches in the program for α and every supersequence β of α of size k or less. We can then compute the exact match count using Lemma 4. □

5.5 Verification of Programs with Loops?

How can we adapt the ideas described above to verify programs with loops? Given an almost-omission-closed property, if we can come up with a polynomial bound $p(n)$ on the length of the shortest error path, then we can "unroll" loops in a given program P sufficiently to generate a corresponding loop-free program P' that includes all paths of length $p(n)$ or less in P, and apply the preceding verification algorithm to P'. (Definition 20 in the appendix shows how such unrolling can be done.) This gives use the following theorem.

Theorem 9. *If $\mathcal{F}$ represents an almost-omission-closed property with a polynomial bound on the shortest error path length, then $\text{SV}_{\mathcal{F}}$ is in P.*

Unfortunately, we have not been able to identify polynomial bounds on the shortest error path length for almost-omission-closed properties. We conjecture that such polynomial bounds exist, at least for the open;read property.

6 Polynomial Time Verification for Programs with Limited Aliasing

In Section 4 we saw that, unless P = NP, verification of repeatable enabling sequence properties will require exponential time *in the worst-case*. Is it, however, possible to design verification algorithms that are efficient *in practice*, e.g., by exploiting properties of programs that arise in practice? For example, one seldom sees programs in which a very large number of variables point to the same object at a program point. In this section we present a verification algorithm motivated by this observation. The algorithm runs in time $O(|Pgm|^{k+1})$, where $|Pgm|$ is the size of the program and k is the maximum aliasing factor of the program: a program is said to have a maximum aliasing factor of k if there is no path in the program that will produce an object pointed to by more than k different variables. Unlike the polynomial solutions of previous sections, the algorithm presented here works for any typestate property.

We note that naive verification algorithms do not achieve the above complexity, i.e. they may take exponential time even for programs with a maximum aliasing factor of 2. In particular, consider the obvious abstraction where the program-state is represented by a partition of the program variables into equivalence classes (of variables that are aliased to each other), with a finite state associated with each equivalence class. The number of such program-states that can arise at a program point is exponential in the number of program variables even for programs with a maximum aliasing factor of 2.

Our algorithm uses predicates of the form $[A, S]$ defined below.

Definition 19. *Let $A \subseteq \text{Vars}$ be a non-empty set of program variables, and $S \subseteq Q$ a set of states of $\mathcal{F}$.*

$$[A, S] = \bigwedge_{x \in A, y \in A} (y = x) \wedge \bigwedge_{x \in A, z \in \text{Vars} \setminus A} (z \neq x) \wedge \bigwedge_{x \in A} In_S(x) \;)$$

When S contains a single state $\sigma \in Q$, we write $[A, \sigma]$, rather than $[A, \{\sigma\}]$.

Intuitively, a predicate $[A, S]$ means that all variables in A have the same value (are aliases), every variable not in A has a different value from the variables in A, and the object referred to by variables in A is in one of the state of S. The difference between $[A, S]$ and $\langle A, S \rangle$ (Definition 8) is noteworthy. The non-aliasing conditions are implicitly represented in $[A, S]$ by assuming that every variable not in A has a different value from the variables in A, whereas in $\langle A, S \rangle$, the variables not in A may or may not be aliased to the variables in A.

Fig. 10(b) presents our verification algorithm that computes, for all program points, the set of predicates of the form $[A, \sigma]$ that may-be-true at the program point. (A predicate p is said to be may-be-true at a program point u iff there exists a path to u such that execution along that path will cause p to become true.) The algorithm is based on a standard iterative collecting interpretation algorithm. The function $flow(\text{St})(\varphi)$, defined in Fig. 10(a), identifies the set of predicates that may-be-true after statement St given a predicate φ that may-be-true before statement St. For any program point l, $Succ(l)$ denotes the successors of l.

Theorem 10. *The algorithm of Fig. 10 precisely computes the set of predicates $[A, S]$ that may hold at any program point in time $O((\sum_{1 \leq i \leq k} \binom{n}{i}) * |Pgm|) = O(n^k * |Pgm|)$ where k is the maximum number of variables aliased to each other*

Statement	flow(Statement)$([A,\sigma])$
x := y	$\{[A \cup \{x\}, \sigma]\}$ if $y \in A$
	$\{[A \setminus \{x\}, \sigma]\}$ if $y \notin A$
x := new()	$\{[\{x\}, init], $ if $x \in A$
	$[A \setminus \{x\}, \sigma]\}$
	$\{[A, \sigma]\}$ if $x \notin A$
x.op()	$\{[A, \delta(\sigma, op)]\}$ if $x \in A$
	$\{[A, \sigma]\}$ if $x \notin A$

(a)

```
workList = {}
for each program point l
    results(l) = {}
    for each program variable x_i
      add (entry, [x_i, {init}]) to workList
while workList ≠ ∅ {
    remove (l, ψ) from workList
    for each ψ' ∈ flow(stmt_l)(ψ) {
      for l' ∈ Succ(l) {
        if ψ' ∉ results(l') {
          results(l') = results(l') ∪ {ψ'}
          add (l', ψ') to workList
} } } }
```

(b)

Fig. 10. An iterative algorithm using predicates of the form $[A, S]$

at any point in the program Pgm, and $n = |\text{Vars}|$ is the number of program variables.

The proof of the theorem appears in the Appendix. Though the worst-case complexity of the algorithm is exponential, the exponential factor k is expected to be a small constant for typical programs, since the number of pointers simultaneously pointing to the same object is expected to be small (and significantly smaller than $|\text{Vars}|$).

Note that using the set of predicates defined in Definition 19 is not sufficient to achieve the desired complexity. The style of "forward propagation" used by our algorithm is also essential, as it ensures that the cost of analysis is proportional to the number of predicates that may-be-true (rather than the number of total predicates, as is the case with alternative analysis techniques).

7 Open Problems

In this paper we have shown that verification of omission-closed properties is in P and that verification of repeatable enabling sequence properties is NP-complete for acyclic programs and PSPACE-complete in general. We have shown that verification of almost-omission-closed properties is in P for acyclic programs. However, many questions still remain open. E.g., we do not know if verification of almost-omission-closed properties is in P for cyclic programs. Moreover there are properties which do not lie in any of these classes. E.g., consider the property open; read* which generalizes open; read by allowing any number of read operations. We can adapt the *counting* method of Section 5 to show that verification of open; read* is in P for acyclic programs. However, we have not been able to formulate such a result for a general class of properties that includes open; read*. Finally, there are also other properties such as (lock; unlock)* (any number of alternating lock and unlock operations) for which we have neither been able to show a polynomial bound, nor show an NP-hardness result.

References

1. K. Ashcraft and D. Engler. Using programmer-written compiler extensions to catch security holes. In *Proc. IEEE Symp. on Security and Privacy*, Oakland, CA, May 2002.
2. T. Ball, R. Majumdar, T. Millstein, and S. Rajamani. Automatic predicate abstraction of C programs. In *Proc. ACM Conf. on Programming Language Design and Implementation*, pages 203–213, June 2001.
3. T. Ball and S. K. Rajamani. Automatically validating temporal safety properties of interfaces. In *SPIN 2001: SPIN Workshop*, LNCS 2057, pages 103–122, 2001.
4. E. Clarke, O. Grumberg, S. Jha, Y. Lu, and H. Veith. Counterexample-guided abstraction refinement. In *CAV'00*, July 2000.
5. E. Clarke, O. Grumberg, and D. Peled. *Model Checking*. MIT Press, 1999.
6. J. Corbett, M. Dwyer, J. Hatcliff, C. Pasareanu, Robby, S. Laubach, and H. Zheng. Bandera: Extracting finite-state models from Java source code. In *Proc. Intl. Conf. on Software Eng.*, pages 439–448, June 2000.
7. M. Das, S. Lerner, and M. Seigle. ESP: Path-sensitive program verification in polynomial time. In *Proc. ACM Conf. on Programming Language Design and Implementation*, pages 57–68, Berlin, June 2002.
8. R. DeLine and M. Fähndrich. Enforcing high-level protocols in low-level software. In *Proc. ACM Conf. on Programming Language Design and Implementation*, pages 59–69, June 2001.
9. R. DeLine and M. Fähndrich. Adoption and focus: Practical linear types for imperative programming. In *Proc. ACM Conf. on Programming Language Design and Implementation*, pages 13–24, Berlin, June 2002.
10. E. W. Dijkstra. *A Discipline of programing*. Prentice-Hall, 1976.
11. J. Field, D. Goyal, G. Ramalingam, and E. Yahav. Shallow finite state verification. Technical Report RC22673, IBM T.J. Watson Research Center, Dec. 2002.
12. C. Flanagan, K. R. M. Leino, M. Lillibridge, G. Nelson, J. B. Saxe, and R. Stata. Extended static checking for java. In *Proc. ACM Conf. on Programming Language Design and Implementation*, pages 234–245, Berlin, June 2002.
13. J. S. Foster, T. Terauchi, and A. Aiken. Flow-sensitive type qualifiers. In *Proc. ACM Conf. on Programming Language Design and Implementation*, pages 1–12, Berlin, June 2002.
14. R. Giacobazzi, F. Ranzato, and F. Scozzari. Making abstract interpretations complete. *Journal of the ACM*, 47(2):361–416, 2000.
15. S. Graf and H. Saidi. Construction of abstract state graphs with PVS. In *In Proceedings of the 9th Conference on Computer-Aided Verification (CAV'97)*, pages 72–83, Haifa, Israel, June 1997.
16. T. A. Henzinger, R. Jhala, R. Majumdar, and G. Sutre. Lazy abstraction. In *Symposium on Principles of Programming Languages*, pages 58–70, 2002.
17. V. Kuncak, P. Lam, and M. Rinard. Role analysis. In *Proc. ACM Symp. on Principles of Programming Languages*, Portland, January 2002.

18. W. Landi and B. G. Ryder. Pointer-induced aliasing: A problem classification. In *Proc. ACM Symp. on Principles of Programming Languages*, pages 93–103, New York, NY, 1991. ACM Press.
19. W. Landi. Undecidability of static analysis. *ACM Letters on Programming Languages and Systems*, 1(4):323–337, December 1992.
20. R. Muth and S. Debray. On the complexity of flow-sensitive dataflow analyses. In *Proc. ACM Symp. on Principles of Programming Languages*, pages 67–80, New York, NY, 2000. ACM Press.
21. G. Naumovich, L. A. Clarke, L. J. Osterweil, and M. B. Dwyer. Verification of concurrent sofware with FLAVERS. In *Proc. Intl. Conf. on Software Eng.*, pages 594–597, May 1997.
22. F. Nielson, H. R. Nielson, and C. Hankin. *Principles of Program Analysis*. Springer-Verlag, 2001.
23. G. Ramalingam, A. Warshavsky, J. Field, D. Goyal, and M. Sagiv. Deriving specialized program analyses for certifying component-client conformance. In *Proc. ACM Conf. on Programming Language Design and Implementation*, volume 37, 5 of *ACM SIGPLAN Notices*, pages 83–94, New York, June 17–19 2002. ACM Press.
24. G. Ramalingam. The undecidability of aliasing. *ACM Transactions on Programming Languages and Systems*, 16(5):1467–1471, 1994.
25. T. Reps, S. Horwitz, and M. Sagiv. Precise interprocedural dataflow analysis via graph reachability. In *Proc. ACM Symp. on Principles of Programming Languages*, pages 49–61, 1995.
26. R. E. Strom and D. M. Yellin. Extending typestate checking using conditional liveness analysis. *IEEE Trans. Software Eng.*, 19(5):478–485, May 1993.
27. R. E. Strom and S. Yemini. Typestate: A programming language concept for enhancing software reliability. *IEEE Trans. Software Eng.*, 12(1):157–171, 1986.

A Proofs

Lemma A1 *For any automaton $\mathcal{F}$, $SV_{\mathcal{F}}$ is in NP for acyclic programs and in PSPACE for arbitrary programs.*

Proof: $SV_{\mathcal{F}}$ is in NP for acyclic programs since we can non-deterministically choose a path through the program and check to see if any object reaches the error state during execution along that path. To show that $SV_{\mathcal{F}}$ for an arbitrary program P is in PSPACE, we construct a non-deterministic multi-tape polynomial-space-bounded Turing Machine M to solve the problem. M simulates input program P, non-deterministically choosing the branch to take at branch points. Let us refer to objects pointed to by the variables in P as *live* objects. M keeps track of which variables point to which (live) objects, and tracks the finite-state of each live object. The space needed to maintain this information is trivially bounded by a polynomial in the size of program P. If any of the relevant objects goes into the error state during simulation, M halts and signals the possibility of an error. Conversely, if there is a path that causes one of the objects to go into the error state, then M can guess this path and will halt signalling the error.

Definition 20. *Consider the control-flow-graph $G_P = (V_P, E_P)$ of program P. Let $G'_P = (V_P, E'_P)$ denote the acyclic graph obtained from G_P by removing all back-edges. We define Unroll(G_P, n) to be the acyclic graph obtained by making $n+1$ copies of G'_P (called $G'_P(1), G'_P(2), \ldots G'_P(n+1)$ respectively), and for every back-edge (u, v) in G_P, adding an edge from vertex u in $G''_P(i)$ to vertex v in $G''_P(i+1)$ for all i from 1 to v. More formally Unroll$(G_P, n) = (V^*, E^*)$ where*

$$V^* = \{\,(v, i) \mid v \in V_P,\ 1 \le i \le n+1\,\}$$
$$E^* = \{\,[(u, i), (v, i)] \mid [u, v] \in E'_P,\ 1 \le i \le n+1\,\} \cup$$
$$\{\,[(u, i), (v, i+1)] \mid [u, v] \in E_P - E'_P,\ 1 \le i \le n\,\}$$

It is easy to verify that Unroll(G_P, v) is acyclic contains every path of length v or less in G_P.

Proof of Theorem 7.

Let $\mathcal{F}$ be the finite state automaton associated with the repeatable enabling sequence property. From Theorem 6 it follows that verification of $\mathcal{F}$ for acyclic programs is in NP and for arbitrary (cyclic) programs is PSPACE-hard. We prove Theorem 7 by showing that if there is a polynomial bound on the shortest error path, then the verification problem for cyclic programs can be polynomial-time reduced to the verification problem for acyclic programs, which would imply that NP = PSPACE.

Let $p(n)$ denote a polynomial bound on the size of the shortest error path where n denotes the size of the program. Given an arbitrary program P with control flow fraph G_P, we construct the acyclic program Unroll$(G_P, p(n))$ which is acyclic and contains all paths of length $p(n)$ or less in G_P. The size of Unroll$(G_P, p(n))$ and the time taken to construct it are both polynomial in n. Thus, the problem of verification of G_P is polynomially reduced to the problem of verifying Unroll$(G_P, p(n))$, which is a contradiction.

Proof of Theorem 10.

The proof that the algorithm computes the precise solution is straightforward and requires showing that $\cup_{\varphi \in P} flow(\texttt{St})(\varphi)$ computes a precise abstract transfer function for statement St with respect to the set of predicates P, and that this is a distributive function.

We now establish the complexity of the algorithm. Assume that the maximal size of an alias-set occurring in the program is k. The algorithm may generate predicates of the form $[A, S]$ for all subsets of any size up to k of program variables Vars. The number of predicates that may have a *true* value in a program point is therefore $O(\sum_{1 \le i \le k} \binom{n}{i})$ where $n = |\textit{Vars}|$ (we treat the number of FSM states as a constant). The complexity of the chaotic iteration algorithm of Fig. 10 is therefore $O((\sum_{1 \le i \le k} \binom{n}{i}) * |Pgm|)$. The expression is also bounded by $O(n^k * |Pgm|)$. The above assumes that the step of computing $flow(\texttt{stmt}_l)(\psi)$ takes constant time.

Static Analysis of Accessed Regions in Recursive Data Structures

Stephen Chong and Radu Rugina

Computer Science Department
Cornell University, Ithaca, NY 14853
{schong,rugina}@cs.cornell.edu

Abstract. This paper presents a heap analysis algorithm that characterizes how programs access regions within recursive data structures, such as sublists within lists or subtrees within trees. The analysis precisely computes cyclicity, reachability, and heap access region information for programs with destructive updates.

The algorithm uses a shape graph abstraction of the heap that identifies connected, single-entry heap regions, whose entries are directly accessible from the stack. The edges of the shape graphs encode reachability information. This yields a more compact heap representation compared to the existing abstractions, making the analysis more efficient. Furthermore, the algorithm expresses heap access information using labels on the nodes of the shape graphs. The labels characterize the concrete locations that abstract nodes represent and make it possible to compare the sets of concrete locations modeled by nodes in different shape graphs. The labels allow the analysis to express the heap access information with respect to the nodes at a particular program point, for instance at the beginning of the current procedure. Our analysis is able to precisely and efficiently compute heap access region information for complex heap manipulations such as a recursive quicksort program that sorts a list in-place, using destructive updates.

1 Introduction

Programs often build and manipulate dynamic structures such as trees or lists. To check or enforce the correct construction and manipulation of dynamic heap structures, the compiler must automatically discover invariants that characterize the structure (or shape) of the heap in all of the possible executions of the program; such algorithms are usually referred to as shape analysis algorithms. In the past decades, researchers have developed a number of shape analysis algorithms that identify various properties of the heap, including aliasing, sharing, cyclicity, or reachability. Such properties allow the compiler to distinguish between various heap structures, for instance between acyclic and cyclic lists, or between trees, DAGs, and arbitrary graphs. However, none of the existing algorithms aim at characterizing the heap regions accessed by statements and procedures in the program.

This paper presents an analysis that extracts information about which heap regions the program accesses. Our analysis uses a heap abstraction which is able to distinguish between different regions within the same heap structure, such as different sublists and different subtrees. At the same time, it can accurately compute cyclicity and reachability information for each of these heap regions in the presence of destructive updates. Unlike any of the existing analyses with similar degrees of precision, the analysis relates the concrete locations modeled by abstractions at different program points. This enables the analysis to characterize, for instance, the heap locations accessed by the whole execution of a procedure in terms of the abstraction at the beginning of the procedure.

Some existing shape analyses [3, 17] can also compute regions, cyclicity, and reachability for programs with destructive updates. However, they cannot compare the concrete heap locations represented by nodes from different shape graphs. Therefore they cannot characterize the heap regions accessed by program fragments such as procedures.

Moreover, our analysis uses a different abstraction which results in fewer and smaller shape graphs compared to the existing analyses. For list traversals, those algorithms analyze a number of shape graphs that is exponential in the number of the pointers that point in the middle of the list. For instance, in the quicksort program presented in the following section, the existing analyses would analyze 24 shape graphs at the program point at the beginning of the main loop, each of the shape graphs having as many as 9 nodes. In contrast, our analysis processes only 2 shape graphs, having at most 5 nodes each.

Like most static analyses, we use a finite heap abstraction, consisting of summary nodes to approximate unbounded numbers of concrete heap locations. In our abstraction, all of the nodes in the shape graph are summary nodes; each of these nodes represent a *connected, single-entry heap region*, whose entry points are directly accessible from the stack. We refer to the heap locations directly pointed to by stack variables as *root locations*. Hence, the concrete locations in a summary node can only be reached through the root of that node; they are essentially "owned" by the root. For instance, during a list traversal, our analysis represents the list elements already traversed and the elements not yet traversed using two different summary nodes; each of them represents a single-entry, connected heap region. Similar to the existing shape analyses [15], we distinguish between the roots based on which stack variables point to them.

Our analysis keeps track of two properties for this abstraction: cyclicity for nodes and reachability for edges. If a summary node is cyclic, then there is a cycle consisting only of locations represented by that node. Reachability for an edge in the shape graph means that the target node is reachable from its source node. Keeping track of reachability is important because all of the summary nodes represent connected heap regions. We use three valued logic to describe these properties and track when they must hold, when they may hold, and when they definitely don't hold.

We have developed a precise specification of an algorithm in the form of a dataflow analysis. The dataflow information describes the above abstraction and the above cyclicity and reachability properties for nodes and edges. To accurately model destructive updates, the analysis uses standard techniques such as *materialization* and *summarization* of nodes [15]. However, these operations are significantly more complex for our abstraction, because our abstraction must correctly approximate the reachability of nodes. We emphasize that the analysis can only precisely summarize a node when the reachability on its incoming edge is "must" information, i.e., when the summarized node is definitely reachable from its predecessor. Another important aspect of our analysis is that a statement which traverses an edge always makes it a "must" edge, even if the edge was only a "may" edge before that statement.

This paper makes the following contributions:

- **Analysis Problem**. It identifies a new analysis problem, that of computing the heap regions that statements and procedures in the program may access;
- **Heap Abstraction**. It presents a new heap abstraction, where summary nodes represent connected, single-entry heap regions and edges contain reachability information. The abstraction uses node labels to relate the concrete locations that abstract nodes in different shape graphs represent;
- **Shape Analysis**. It presents an algorithm which computes shape information using this abstraction. It gives a precise, formal definition of the algorithm;
- **Theoretical Properties**. It gives formal results showing that the analysis algorithm is sound and is guaranteed to terminate.

The remainder of the paper is organized as follows. Section 2 presents an example. Section 3 presents the shape analysis algorithm and the computation of accessed regions. Finally, Section 4 discusses related work.

2 Example

Figure 1 presents an example of a program that our analysis is designed to handle. This is a quicksort program which recursively sorts a list region (i.e. a sublist) in-place, using destructive updates. For this program we want to automatically check that the two recursive calls access disjoint regions of the list. We first describe the execution of this program and then we discuss the analysis information required to check this property.

2.1 Program Execution

At each invocation, the function `quicksort` sorts a sublist, consisting of all the list elements between `first` and `last`, exclusively (i.e. not including `first` and `last`). At the end of the invocation, `first->next` will point to the first element in the sorted sublist, and the `next` field of the last element in the sorted sublist will point to `last`. When the function is first invoked, `first` must be not NULL, different to `last`, and the element pointed to by `last` must be reachable from

```
1  typedef struct cell {
2    int val;
3    struct cell *next;
4  } list;
5
6
7  void quicksort(list *first, list *last) {
8    list *mid, *crt, *prev;
9
10   mid = prev = first->next;
11   if (mid == last)   return;
12
13   crt = prev->next;
14   if (crt == last) return;
15
16   while(crt != last) {
17     if (crt->val > mid->val) {
18       /* append to "greater than" part */
19       prev = crt;
20     } else {
21       /* prepend to "less than" part */
22       prev->next = crt->next;
23       crt->next = first->next;
24       first->next = crt;
25     }
26     crt = prev->next;
27   }
28
29   quicksort(first, mid);
30   quicksort(mid, last);
31 }
```

Fig. 1. Quicksort on lists

first. We consider that NULL is always reachable from first, so last can be NULL.

The function first looks for the base cases of the computation, where the sublist has at most one element (lines 11 and 14). If the argument sublist has at least two elements, the function sorts the sublist according to the standard quicksort algorithm. The variable mid represents the pivot and is initialized (line 10) to point to the next element after first. To partition the sublist with respect to the pivot's value, the program traverses the list with two pointers, prev and crt. During the traversal, the list region between first and mid contains the elements less than or equal to the pivot, and the list region between mid and crt contains the elements greater than the pivot.

Finally, the program recursively sorts the two partitions (lines 29, 30); each of these calls sorts its partition in-place.

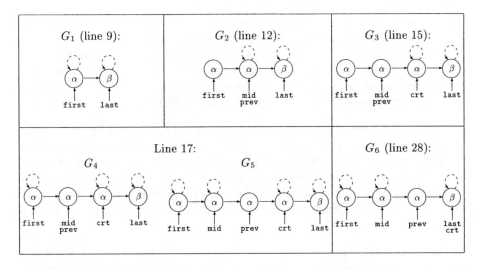

Fig. 2. Abstract shape graphs at selected program points for example

2.2 Required Analysis Information

To determine that the recursive calls to quicksort access disjoint regions of the list, the analysis must extract the following key pieces of information:

1. *Regions.* The analysis must use an abstraction that distinguishes between different regions of the list. For instance, the analysis must distinguish between the list regions from first to mid, from mid to prev, and from crt to last. The abstraction must thus use different summary nodes for each of these regions.
2. *Cyclicity Information.* The analysis must accurately determine that the program preserves listness. That is, it must establish that the sorting function produces an acyclic list whenever it starts with an acyclic list. In particular, it must determine that the destructive updates that move elements into the "less than" partition (lines 22-24) preserve the listness property.
3. *Reachability Information.* The analysis must precisely determine that the different list regions are reachable from one to another.
4. *Access Information.* The analysis must determine what list regions each invocation of quicksort accesses. It must give a precise characterization of the accessed heap location, with respect to the summary nodes at the beginning of the function.

Figure 2 shows the abstraction that our analysis computes at several key points in the program. This abstraction precisely captures the above pieces of information. All of the nodes in the graphs are not cyclic. The solid edges are "must" reachable, and the dashed edges are "may" reachable.

The graph G_1 shows the abstract shape graph at the beginning of the function, which consists of all heap nodes reachable from the function arguments, first and last. The abstraction consists of two summary nodes. The summary node pointed to by first represents the list elements between first, inclusively, and last, exclusively. The summary node pointed to by last represents the elements at the tail of the list. Each of these sets of list elements is a connected, single-entry heap region, whose entry point is directly accessible from the stack. These summary nodes represent disjoint regions within the same list structure.

Our analysis computes the accessed heap regions for the function quicksort, with respect to the shape information at the beginning of the function (i.e. G_1). Therefore, the analysis assigns different labels, α and β, to the summary nodes in G_1. These labels model the concrete heap locations that these abstract nodes represent *at the beginning of the function*. Then, at each point in the function body, the analysis expresses concrete locations for summary nodes in terms of the labels α and β.

The graph G_2 shows the abstract information at line 12. The assignment traverses the next selector of the element pointed to by first and assigns the resulting value to both mid and prev. Since the summary node pointed to by first has two outgoing edges, the analysis must consider both possibilities. In the first case, the analysis traverses the outgoing edge between the two nodes; as a result, the second node will be pointed to by the set {mid, prev, last}. The analysis then removes this node using the test condition at line 11. In the second case, the analysis traverses the self edge: it performs materialization and creates a new node. As part of the materialization, the analysis assigns label α to the newly created node, because it models a subset of the concrete locations that the node before materialization modeled. Note that during materialization, the analysis transforms the "may" self edge of first into a "must" reachable edge between first and {mid, prev}.

Figure 2 also shows the fixed-point information that the analysis computes at the beginning of the loop, at line 17. This fixed-point solution consists of two shape graphs, G_4 and G_5, which represent the two possible heap configurations at this point: G_4 shows the case where mid and prev point to the same location, that is, when the "greater than" partition is empty; and G_5 describes the case where the "greater than" partition contains at least one element, and thus mid and prev point to different list regions.

We emphasize that the previous shape analysis algorithms [3, 17] would produce a much larger number of possible configurations at this point. Essentially, each of the summary nodes with self edges creates two alternatives for those analyses; the total number of possible shape graphs for those algorithms is exponential in the number of traversing pointers with self edges: 2^3 for G_4 and 2^4 for G_5, which means 24 shape graphs. Moreover, those shape graphs would contain multiple nodes because they distinguish between heap locations pointed to by stack variables, and locations pointed to only by heap locations. For each of the nodes with self edges in G_4 and G_5, those analyses would create one more node, so the shape graphs would have up to 9 nodes.

2.3 Computing Heap Access Regions

The analysis can now use all of the computed shape information with labels to determine that the two recursive calls access disjoint regions of the list. First, the analysis inspects every indirect assignment of the form x->next = y in the body of the function, i.e. the assignments at lines 22-24. It then uses the shape graphs at those points and establishes that all those accesses update concrete heap locations represented by α. In other words, the function body only accesses elements owned by its first parameter. Interprocedural analysis of the two recursive calls determines that the heap access region for the whole execution of quicksort, including the recursive invocations, is the set of concrete locations represented by α.

The analysis can then use the computed access region for the whole execution of quicksort to determine that the two recursive calls access disjoint sublists. A compiler could use this information to automatically parallelize this program and execute the recursive calls concurrently.

2.4 Detecting Potential Bugs

The analysis is able to help in the detection of potential bugs. Suppose the second recursive call (line 30) is incorrectly invoked with quicksort(mid, last->next). In that case, the input shape graphs at each program point would be unchanged. However, the analysis would detect that the access region for the whole execution of quicksort is $\{\alpha, \beta\}$. Using this information at the recursive calls, the analysis will determine that both calls may access the tail of the list. Thus, it can no longer conclude that the two recursive calls access disjoint list regions.

Alternatively, consider if the programmer incorrectly writes the loop test condition at line 16 as prev != last. As a result, the analysis will compute two more possible shape graphs at the beginning of loop body; in each of these, crt points to the summary node labelled with β. Therefore, when the analysis inspects the assignment crt->next = first->next, it will determine that this statement writes a heap location represented by β. As a result, the analysis will compute an access region $\{\alpha, \beta\}$ for quicksort and will report that the two recursive calls may access the same list elements.

Although both of the above situations are bugs, in general such messages may be false positives, because the analysis is conservative. Nonetheless, when the analysis computes access region information different than a given specification, the programmer can treat it as an indication of a potential bug in the program.

3 Algorithm

This section presents the analysis algorithm. Although the algorithm computes shape graphs, label information, and accessed regions at the same time, we discuss them separately for clarity in presentation. We first show the basic intra-procedural algorithm which computes shape graphs. We then present how the algorithm keeps track of labels and how it computes the accessed heap regions. Finally, we describe the inter-procedural analysis algorithm.

3.1 Shape Analysis.

We formulate our shape analysis algorithm as a dataflow analysis which computes a shape graph at each program point. This section defines the dataflow information, the meet operator, and the transfer functions for statements.

We assume that that the program is preprocessed to a form where each statement is of one of the following six forms: x = NULL, x = y, x = malloc(), x->n = NULL, x seln = y, or x = y->n. Without loss of generality, we assume that each variable update x = ... is preceded by a statement x = NULL and that each selector update x->n = y is preceded by x->n = NULL. We assume that n is the unique selector name in the program.

Our algorithm expresses the shape information using predicates in three-valued logic [16], which consists of truth values 0 (false), 1 (true), and 1/2 (unknown). We use the standard three-valued order and operators: the conjunction $t \wedge_3 t' = min(t,t')$; the disjunction $t \vee_3 t' = max(t,t')$; the partial order $t \sqsubseteq_3 t'$ for $t = t'$ or $t' = 1/2$; and the meet $t \sqcup_3 t'$ equal to t if $t = t'$ and $1/2$ otherwise. We explicitly use subscript 3 when we refer three-valued operators, and we don't use any subscripts for the standard, two-valued operators.

Concrete Heaps. Concrete heaps represent the statically unbounded set of concrete heap locations and the points-to relations between them. We formalize concrete heaps as follows. Let V_s be the set of stack variables in the program. A concrete heap is a triple (L_h, E_s, E_h) consisting of:

- A set L_h of heap locations;
- A set $E_s \in V_s \times L_h \to \{0,1\}$ of edges from stack variables to heap locations;
- A set $E_h \in L_h \times L_h \to \{0,1\}$ of edges from heap locations to heap locations;

For edges, a value 1 indicates the presence of the edge in the concrete heap; a value 0 indicates its absence. We then consider two predicates which characterize the paths in this graph: $P(v,l)$ indicates if there is a path in the concrete heap between the variable $v \in V_s$ and the concrete location $l \in L_h$; and $Q(v,l',l)$ indicates that there is a path in the concrete heap between variable $v \in V_s$ and location $l \in L_h$ which doesn't contains the location $l' \in L_h$.

For each set of stack variables $X \subseteq V_s$, $X \neq \emptyset$, we define the *heap root* l_X^c as the heap location pointed to exactly by the variables in X: $Es(x, l_X^c) \Leftrightarrow x \in X$. We also define the set n_X^c of *nodes owned by* X as the concrete locations that can only be reached from l_X^c, and only on paths that don't traverse other roots:

$$n_X^c = \{\, l \mid \forall x \in X \,.\, P(x,l) \wedge \forall y \notin X \,.\, \neg Q(y, l_X^c, l)\,\}$$

Finally, for $X = \emptyset$ we define the set n_ϕ^c of all heap locations reachable from the stack, but not owned by any set X of variables. These are heap locations reachable from the stack through different roots. We emphasize that all of the sets n_X^c represent disjoint sets of concrete heap locations. Also, each of the sets n_X^c, $X \neq \emptyset$ are connected, single-entry subgraphs of the concrete heap, with entry node l_X^c; however, n_ϕ^c is not a single-entry subgraph, and is not connected either.

Dataflow Information. Let $L_a = \{\, n_X \mid X \subseteq V_s \,\}$ be a set of abstract heap nodes, where each node n_X models the concrete heap locations in n_X^c. The dataflow information of our analysis is an *abstract shape graph* $G = (N, E, C)$, where:

- $N \subseteq L_a$ is the set of nodes;
- $E : N \times N \to \{0, 1/2, 1\}$ is the set of edges with reachability information.
- $C : N \to \{0, 1/2, 1\}$, the cyclicity information on nodes.

The above predicates have the following meaning. If $E(n,m) = 1$, the edge between n and m is definitely reachable (i.e., the locations in m are definitely reachable from the locations in n); if $E(n,m) = 1/2$, the edge is possibly reachable; otherwise, it doesn't exist. The cyclic predicate $C(n)$ is 1 if there definitely is a cycle in the concrete heap structure modeled by n; it is $1/2$ if there may be a cycle; and it is 0 if there definitely isn't any cycle. The predicate C refers to internal cycles, consisting only of locations modeled by n. We denote by A the set of all abstract shape graphs.

We graphically represent nodes n with $C(n) \neq 0$ with double circles; definitely reachable edges with solid lines; and possibly reachable edges with dashed lines. Finally, we omit n_ϕ if it has no incoming or outgoing edges to other abstract nodes. The shape graphs from Figure 2 use this graphical representation.

The *abstraction function* δ characterizes the relation between concrete heaps and abstract shape graphs. Given a concrete heap (L_h, E_s, E_h), we define its abstraction $(N, E, C) = \delta(L_h, E_s, E_h)$ as follows:

$$N = \{\, n_X \mid n_X^c \neq \emptyset \,\} \cup \{\, n_\phi \,\}$$
$$E(n_X, n_Y) = \bigvee \{\, E_h(l_x, l_y) \mid l_x \in n_X^c, l_y \in n_Y^c \,\}$$
$$C(n_X) = \begin{cases} 1 \text{ if } \exists l_1, \ldots, l_k \in n_X^c \,.\, E_h(l_k, l_1) \wedge \bigwedge \{E_h(l_i, l_{i+1}) \mid 1 \leq i < k\} \\ 0 \text{ otherwise} \end{cases}$$

The node n_ϕ models a subgraph of the heap which is not connected and may have multiple entries. Intuitively, n_ϕ contains imprecise shape information and the analysis uses it as a fallback mechanism to conservatively handle the case of shared structures.

Merge Operation. The dataflow analysis merges shape graphs at each control-flow point in the program. The merge operation is non-trivial in our abstraction, because it must account for the following scenario. Consider two abstract graphs G_1 and G_2 that we want to merge. Also consider that one of these graphs contains a definitely reachable edge (n, m), but the other graphs contains only the target node m. In this case, m is not reachable from n in the second graph, so the analysis must conclude that (n, m) is possibly reachable in the merged graph. The following merge operation precisely captures this behavior. If $G_1 = (N_1, E_1, C_1)$

and $G_2 = (N_2, E_2, C_2)$, the merged graph is $G_1 \sqcup G_2 = (N, E, C)$, where:

$$N = N_1 \cup N_2$$

$$C(n) = \begin{cases} C_1(n) \vee_3 C_2(n) & \text{if } n \in N_1 \cap N_2 \\ C_1(n) & \text{if } n \notin N_2 \\ C_2(n) & \text{if } n \notin N_1 \end{cases}$$

$$E(n,m) = \begin{cases} E_1(n,m) \sqcup_3 E_2(n,m) & \text{if } \{n,m\} \subseteq N_1 \cap N_2 \\ 1 & \text{if } (E_1(n,m) = 1 \wedge m \notin N_2) \vee (E_2(n,m) = 1 \wedge m \notin N_1) \\ 0 & \text{if } (n \notin N_1 \vee m \notin N_1) \wedge (n \notin N_2 \vee m \notin N_2) \\ 1/2 & \text{otherwise} \end{cases}$$

In general we may have abstract shape graphs containing nodes n_X and n_Y such that X and Y each include a stack variable $x \in V_s$. Clearly, in no execution of the program can there coexist a concrete heap location from n_X^c with one from n_Y^c. We say that a graph G is *incompatible* if it contains two nodes n_X and n_Y such that $X \neq Y \wedge X \cap Y \neq \emptyset$. Given s shape graph G, we say that G' is a *possible configuration* if it is a maximal compatible subgraph of G. We use the term "maximal subgraph" relative to the partial order relation induced by the merge operator defined above. Finally, we denote by *Confs* (G) the set of all possible configurations of a graph G.

Case: x = malloc()	Case: x = y
$N' = N \cup \{n_{\{x\}}\}$ $C'(n) = \begin{cases} 0 & \text{if } n = n_{\{x\}} \\ C(n) & \text{otherwise} \end{cases}$ $E'(n,m) = \begin{cases} 0 & \text{if } n_{\{x\}} \in \{n,m\} \\ E(n,m) & \text{otherwise} \end{cases}$	$N' = \{f(n) \mid n \in N\}$ $C'(n) = C(f^{-1}(n))$ $E'(n,m) = E(f^{-1}(n), f^{-1}(m))$ $f : N \to N'$ $f(n_Y) = \begin{cases} n_{Y \cup \{x\}} & \text{if } y \in Y \\ n_Y & \text{otherwise} \end{cases}$
Case: x->next = NULL	Case: x->next = y
$N' = N$ $C'(n_X) = \begin{cases} 0 & \text{if } x \in X \\ C(n_X) & \text{otherwise} \end{cases}$ $E'(n_X, n_Y) = \begin{cases} 0 & \text{if } x \in X \\ E(n_X, n_Y) & \text{otherwise} \end{cases}$	$N' = N$ $C'(n_Z) = \begin{cases} 1 & \text{if } \{x,y\} \subseteq Z \\ C(n_Z) & \text{otherwise} \end{cases}$ $E'(n_X, n_Y) = \begin{cases} 1 & \text{if } x \in X \wedge y \in Y \\ E(n_X, n_Y) & \text{otherwise} \end{cases}$
Case: x = null, if $n_{\{x\}} \notin N$	
$N' = \{g(n) \mid n \in N\}$ $C'(n) = C(g^{-1}(n)), \forall n \in N$ $E'(n,m) = E(g^{-1}(n), g^{-1}(m))$ $g : N \to N'$ $g(n_Z) = n_{Z-\{x\}}$	

Fig. 3. Transfer function $[\![s]\!]_{\text{conf}}(N, E, C) = (N', E', C')$ for simple cases

$N' = N - \{n_{\{x\}}\}$ $C'(n) = C(n) \vee_3 (S(n, n_{\{x\}}) \wedge_3 C(n_{\{x\}})) \vee_3$ $\qquad (S(n, n_{\{x\}}) \wedge_3 E(n, n_{\{x\}}) \wedge_3 E(n_{\{x\}}, n))$ $E'(n, m) = E(n, m) \vee_3$ $\qquad (S(n, n_{\{x\}}) \wedge_3 E(n_{\{x\}}, m)) \vee_3$ $\qquad (S(n, n_{\{x\}}) \wedge_3 m = n) \vee_3$ $\qquad (S(n_\phi, n_{\{x\}}) \wedge_3 m = n_\phi \wedge_3 E(n, n_{\{x\}})) \vee_3$ $\qquad (S(n, n_\phi) \wedge_3 E(n_\phi, m))$
$S(n, m) = \begin{cases} 1 & \text{if } E(n, m) = 1 \wedge (\forall n' \notin \{n, m\} \,.\, E(n', m) = 0) \\ 1/2 & \text{if } E(n, m) \in \{1, 1/2\} \wedge \\ & \quad (\forall n' \notin \{n, m\} \,.\, E(n', m) \in \{0, 1/2\}) \wedge \\ & \quad (E(n, m) \neq 1 \vee \exists n' \neq m \,.\, E(n', m) = 1/2) \\ 0 & \text{otherwise} \end{cases}$
$S(n_\phi, m) = \begin{cases} 1/2 & \text{if } \exists n, n' \,.\, n \neq n' \wedge E(n, m) \neq 0 \wedge E(n', m) \neq 0 \\ 0 & \text{otherwise} \end{cases}$
$S(n, n_\phi) = \begin{cases} 1/2 & \text{if } E(n_{\{x\}}, n_\phi) \neq 0 \wedge E(n, n_\phi) \neq 0 \wedge (\forall n' \neq n_{\{x\}} \,.\, E(n', n_{\{x\}}) \neq 1) \\ 0 & \text{otherwise} \end{cases}$

Fig. 4. Transfer function for x=NULL, when $n_{\{x\}} \in N$, which performs summarization. The predicate $S(n, m)$ evaluates to 1 in the case of precise summarization of m into n and 1/2 for imprecise summarization

$$[\![x = y\text{->}n]\!]_{\text{conf}}(G) = \bigsqcup_{E(n_Y, p) \neq 0} G_p \quad (\text{where } y \in Y)$$

Case: $p = n_Y$ (**materialization on self edge**)
$N_p = N \cup \{n_{\{x\}}\} \cup \{n_{Y \cup \{x\}} \mid C(n_Y) \neq 0\}$
$C_p(n) = \begin{cases} 0 & \text{if } n = n_Y \\ C(n_Y) & \text{if } n = n_{\{x\}} \vee n = n_{Y \cup \{x\}} \\ C(n) & \text{otherwise} \end{cases}$
$E_p(n, m) =$
$= \begin{cases} E(n, m) & \text{if } n \notin \{n_Y, n_{\{x\}}, n_{Y \cup \{x\}}\} \\ 1 & \text{if } n = n_Y \wedge m = n_{\{x\}} \\ 0 & \text{if } n = n_Y \wedge m \neq n_{\{x\}} \\ E(n_Y, m) & \text{if } n = n_{\{x\}} \wedge m \notin \{n_{\{x\}}, n_Y\} \\ 1/2 & \text{if } n = n_{\{x\}} \wedge m = n_{\{x\}} \\ 1/2 \wedge_3 C(n_Y) & \text{if } n = n_{\{x\}} \wedge m = n_Y \\ 1 & \text{if } m = n = n_{Y \cup \{x\}} \\ E(n_Y, m) & \text{if } m \neq n = n_{Y \cup \{x\}} \end{cases}$

Case: $p \neq n_Y$ and $p \neq n_\phi$
$N_p = \{h(n) \mid n \in N\}$
$C_p(n) = \begin{cases} 0 & \text{if } n = n_Y \\ C(h(n)) & \text{otherwise} \end{cases}$
$E_p(n, m) =$
$\begin{cases} E(h^{-1}(n), (h^{-1}(m)) & \text{if } n \neq n_Y \\ 1 & \text{if } n = n_Y \wedge m = p \\ 0 & \text{if } n = n_Y \wedge m \neq p \end{cases}$
where:
$h(n) = \begin{cases} n_{Z \cup \{x\}} & \text{if } p = n_Z \\ n & \text{otherwise} \end{cases}$

Fig. 5. Transfer function for x = y->n, which performs materialization. We obtain each graph $G_p = (N_p, E_p, C_p)$ by following one edge, from n_Y to p

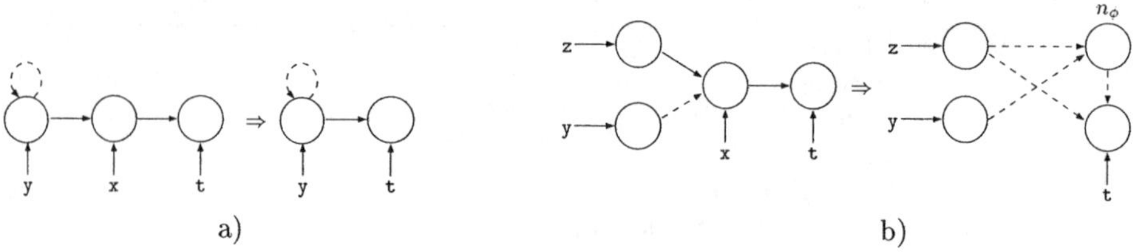

Fig. 6. Summarization for x = NULL: a) precise summarization, b) imprecise summarization

Transfer Functions. For each statement s in the program, we define a transfer function $[\![s]\!] : A \to A$, which describes how the statement modifies the input abstract shape graph. The analysis first splits the input graph G into all of the possible configurations in $Confs(G)$. It then analyzes each configuration separately. At the end, it merges the result for each configuration. Figures 3, 4, and 5 present the full definition of the transfer functions $[\![s]\!]_{\text{conf}}$ that the algorithm uses to analyze each configuration.

Figure 3 shows the transfer function for statements x = malloc(), x = y, x->n = NULL, x->n = y, and x = NULL when $n_{\{x\}} \notin N$. These equations use two helper functions f and g, which are invertible because the input graph G is compatible. Hence, f^{-1} and g^{-1} are well-defined.

The materialization and summarization of nodes is significantly more complex. Figure 4 presents the equations for the summarization of nodes, which takes place for a statement x=NULL, when $n_{\{x\}} \in N$. The analysis can precisely summarize the node $n_{\{x\}}$ into the node that y points to only if there a single incoming edge to $n_{\{x\}}$, and that edge is definitely reachable. Figure 6(a) shows this case. If there are multiple incoming edges to $n_{\{x\}}$, and more than two are definitely reachable edges, then the analysis summarizes $n_{\{x\}}$ into n_ϕ. Finally, if there are multiple incoming edges to $n_{\{x\}}$, and at most one is a definitely reachable edge, then the analysis must summarize $n_{\{x\}}$ both into n_ϕ and into the nodes that point to $n_{\{x\}}$ using definitely reachable edges. Figure 6(b) shows a case of imprecise summarization.

Figure 5 presents the transfer functions for an assignment x = y->n. Consider that n_Y is a node such that $y \in Y$. If n_Y has multiple outgoing edge, the variable x may traverse any of them during the execution of this statement. The algorithm analyzes each of these situations separately and then merges the results together. When traversing a self edge of n_Y, the analysis performs a materialization: it "extracts" one location from n_Y and creates the abstract node $n_{\{x\}}$ to model the remaining locations. If the node n_Y may have cycles, the analysis performs an imprecise materialization and adds back edges to n_Y. Otherwise, the analysis performs a precise materialization and doesn't create spurious back edges.

3.2 Formal Results

We summarizes the main theoretical results for our abstraction and and our analysis in the following theorems. We show that the meet operation is well-defined, the transfer functions are monotonic, and the analysis is sound. We use $[\![s]\!]_c$ to denote the concrete semantics of s. Because the analysis lattice has finite height, the monotonicity of the transfer functions implies that the analysis is guaranteed to terminate.

Theorem 1. *The merge operation $\sqcup$ is idempotent, commutative, and associative.*

Theorem 2. *For all statements s, the transfer function $[\![s]\!]$ is monotonic.*

Theorem 3 (Soundness). *If H_c is a concrete heap, then for all statements s we have $\delta([\![s]\!]_c(H_c)) \sqsubseteq [\![s]\!](\delta(H_c))$, where δ is the abstraction function defined in Section 3.1.*

3.3 Node Labels

This section presents the algorithm for computing accessed heap regions for statements and procedures in the program. The main difficulty when computing the accessed heap regions in our abstraction is that the same node may represent different concrete heap locations in different shape graphs. This makes it difficult to summarize heap accesses at different program points. In particular, it makes it difficult to summarize the heap accesses for each procedure in the program.

Our algorithm overcomes this difficulty using *node labels* to record information about the concrete heap locations that each abstract node represents. At the beginning of each procedure, the analysis assigns fresh labels to each node in the shape graph. Each label represents the set of concrete locations that the corresponding node models in the initial shape graph. During the analysis of individual statements, the algorithm computes, for each node and at each program point, the set of labels that describe the concrete locations that the node currently models. Finally, for each statement that reads or writes a heap location, the algorithm records the labels of the node being accessed by the statement. The analysis can therefore summarize the heap locations accessed by the whole execution of each procedure as a set of labels.

For allocation statements, the analysis uses one label per allocation site to model all of the heap cells allocated at this site in the current execution of the enclosing procedure. For an allocation site s, we denote by α_s the label for this site. We denote by *Lab* be the set of all labels in the analysis. This set consists of allocation site labels and fresh labels at the beginning of procedures. Within each procedure, different labels model disjoint sets of concrete heap locations.

Our analysis algorithm computes the shape graphs, node labels, and the access regions simultaneously. It uses an extended shape graph abstraction which incorporates information about labels and accessed regions. An extended shape graph is a tuple (N, E, C, L, R, W), where N, E, and C are the same as before,

Statement	New Labels	Statement	New Labels
x = malloc()	$L'(n) = \begin{cases} L(n) \text{ if } n \in N \\ \alpha_s \quad \text{ if } n = n_{\{x\}} \end{cases}$	x = y	$L'(n) = L(f^{-1}(n))$
x = NULL $(n_{\{x\}} \in N)$	$L'(n) = \begin{cases} L(n) \cup L(n_{\{x\}}) \text{ if } S(n, n_{\{x\}}) \neq 0 \\ L(n) \quad\quad\quad\quad \text{ if } S(n, n_{\{x\}}) = 0 \end{cases}$	x = NULL $(n_{\{x\}} \notin N)$	$L'(n) = L(g^{-1}(n))$
		x->n = NULL x->n = y	$L' = L$
x = y->n $(p = p_Y)$	$L'(n) = \begin{cases} L(n) \quad \text{ if } n \in N \\ L(n_Y) \text{ if } n = n_{\{x\}} \\ L(n_Y) \text{ if } n = n_{Y \cup \{x\}} \end{cases}$	x = y->n $(p \neq p_Y, n_\phi)$	$L'(n) = L(h^{-1}(n))$

Fig. 7. Equation for computing label sets, using the summarization predicate S and the functions f, g, and h defined in Figures 3, 4, and 5

$L : N \to \mathcal{P}(Lab)$ represents the label information for nodes, and $R, W \subseteq Lab$ characterize the heap locations that have been read and written from the beginning of the enclosing procedure. The merge operation is the pointwise union for labels and read and write sets. That is, if $G_1 = (N_1, E_1, C_1, L_1, R_1, W_1)$ and $G_2 = (N_2, E_2, C_2, L_2, R_2, W_2)$, then the merged graph is $G_1 \sqcup G_2 = (N, E, C, L, R, W)$, where N, E, and C are computed as before, $R = R_1 \cup R_2$, $W = W_1 \cup W_2$, and $L = \{L_1(n) \mid n \in N_1\} \cup \{L_2(n) \mid n \in N_2\}$.

Figure 7 shows how the analysis computes the labels for each statement. For an allocation statement s, the analysis assigns the label α_s of that allocation site to the newly created node. During summarization the analysis adds the labels of the summarized node to the set of labels of the node which gets summarized into. During materialization, the newly created node inherits the labels from the node on which the materialization has been performed.

Finally, the analysis computes the locations being read and written by each statement in a straightforward manner. For each heap update x->n = NULL or x->n = y, the analysis augments the set of written locations with the labels of all the nodes x points to: $W' = W \cup \bigcup_{x \in X} L(n_X)$. Similarly, for each assignment x = y->n, the analysis augments the set of read locations with the labels of all the nodes y points to: $R' = R \cup \bigcup_{y \in Y} L(n_Y)$. In all of the other cases, the sets of locations being read or written remain unchanged.

3.4 Interprocedural Analysis

Our algorithm performs a context-sensitive inter-procedural analysis to accurately compute shape information for procedure calls. At each call site, the algorithm maps the current analysis information into the name space of the invoked procedure, analyzes the procedure, then unmaps the results back into the name space of the caller. This general mechanism is similar to existing inter-procedural pointer analyses [4, 18, 14]. However, our mapping and unmapping processes are different than in pointer analysis because they operate on a different abstraction. In particular, our analysis maps and unmaps shape graphs, node labels, and read and write sets. Like existing context-sensitive pointer analyses, our algorithm caches the analysis results every time it analyzes a procedure. At each call site, the analysis sets up the calling context and look this context up in the cache to determine if an analysis result is available for this context. If so, it uses the results of the previous analysis of the procedure. Otherwise, it analyzes the caller in the new context.

Mapping and Unmapping. The mapping process sets up the calling context for the invoked procedure. Consider a call statement $f(a_1, \ldots, a_n)$ which invokes procedure f. Without loss of generality, we assume that each of the actual arguments $a_1, \ldots, a_n$ are local variables in the caller's environment. Let $p_1, \ldots, p_n$ be the formal parameters of the invoked procedure f. If the analysis information at the call site is $G = (N, E, C, L, R, W)$, the mapping process builds the input context G_i for the invoked procedure f as follows:

- It first partitions the nodes N of G into two sets: N_r, representing the nodes reachable from the actual parameters $a_1, \ldots, a_n$ at the call site, and $N_u = N - N_r$, representing the nodes unreachable from the actual parameters. Let G_r be the subgraph of G restricted to the nodes in N_r, and G_u be the unreachable subgraph of G, restricted to the nodes in N_u. The analysis proceeds with G_r to set up the calling context; it recovers the unreachable subgraph G_u later, during the unmapping.
- It then removes all of the local variables, except for the actual arguments, from the shape graph G_r and produces a new graph G'_r. For this, the analysis performs assignments x = NULL for each variable x which is not an actual parameter. During the removal of local variables, the analysis constructs a node map $m : N'_r \to \mathcal{P}(N_r)$ that records, for each node in G'_r, which nodes of G_r it represents.
- The analysis re-labels each node in G'_r with a fresh label and produces a new graph G''_r. It records the re-labeling information using a function $l : Lab \to N'_r$ such that $l(\alpha')$ represents the node of N'_r which has been re-labeled with α'.
- Finally, the analysis replaces each actual parameter a_i in G''_r with the corresponding formal parameter p_i, and produces the graph $G_i = (N_i, E_i, C_i, L_i, \emptyset, \emptyset)$, which is the calling context for the invoked procedure f.

Next, the analysis uses the constructed calling context G_i to determine the output graph $G_o = (N_o, E_o, C_o, L_o, R_o, W_o)$. The analysis computes G_o either by re-using a previous analysis for this context from the cache, or by analyzing the invoked function f. Further, the analysis unmaps the output graph G_o and computes the graph G' in the caller's analysis domain, at the program point right after the call. The unmapping process consists of the following steps:

- The analysis replaces each formal parameter p_i with the corresponding actual parameter a_i at the call site, and produces a graph $G'_o = (N'_o, E'_o, C'_o, L'_o, R_o, W_o)$. Here we assume that the formal parameters are never modified in the procedure body. Hence, they point to the same location throughout the procedure. One can relax this condition using temporary variables and assignments which copy the initial values of the formal parameters into these temporary variables.

- Next, the analysis replace nodes in G'_o with nodes from the reachable subgraph G_r before the call; it produces a new graph $G'''_o = (N'''_o, E'''_o, C'''_o, L'''_o, R'''_o, W'''_o)$. Intuitively, the analysis recovers the caller's local information, which has been removed during the mapping process.

  The algorithm computes the shape information N'''_o, E'''_o, C'''_o, and L'''_o as follows. For each node $n' \in N'_o$, it examines the following possibilities:
  - if $L'_o(n') = \{\alpha'\}$ and $\alpha' \notin R_o \cup W_o$: the region α' was neither read nor written by the execution of f. It means that the internal structure of this region has not been modified by the call, and no pointers into the middle of this structure have been created. It is therefore safe to replace the node labeled with α' in G'_o with its corresponding subgraph from G_r, consisting of all the nodes in $m(l(\alpha'))$.
  - if $L'_o(n') = \{\alpha'\}$, $\alpha' \in R_o \cup W_o$, $\alpha' \notin L'_o(n'')$, $\forall n'' \neq n'$, $|m(l(\alpha'))\}| = 1$: the heap structure represented by the region α' may have been read or written, but it represents exactly one node in both G_r and G'_o. The analysis can safely replace the node n' with the unique node n of $m(l(\alpha'))$.
  - Otherwise, the heap structure represented by region node n' may have been modified or represents multiple nodes in G_r. The analysis conservatively replaces n' with all of the nodes in $\bigcup \{m(l(\alpha')) \mid \alpha' \in L'_o(n')\}$, adds edges between any two of these nodes, and makes all of the nodes cyclic.

  The analysis computes the access region information R'''_o and W'''_o as follows:

  $$R'''_o = R \cup \bigcup \{L_r(n) \mid n \in m(l(\alpha')) \land \alpha' \in R_o\}$$
  $$W'''_o = W \cup \bigcup \{L_r(n) \mid n \in m(l(\alpha')) \land \alpha' \in W_o\}$$

  where L_r is the label map of subgraph G_r.
- Finally, the analysis adds back the unreachable subgraph G_u into G'''_o. The resulting graph G' represents the shape graph at the program point after the call.

Although the mapping and unmapping process is conservative, it may be imprecise for regions modified by the callee. In particular, the unmapping process imprecisely restores the local variables of the caller when these variables belong to regions modified by the invoked procedure. To reduce this kind of imprecision, our analysis performs *early nullification*: it runs a dead variable analysis, identifies the earliest points where local variables are guaranteed to be dead, and inserts nullifying statements x = NULL for such variables at these program points. This technique reduces the amount of local information and improves the efficiency and the precision of our algorithm.

Figure 8 shows the shape graphs that the analysis constructs during maping and unmapping for the first recursive call site in the quicksort example from Section 2. Using early nullification, the analysis inserts the statements prev = NULL and crt = NULL before the first call. These statements yield the graph G in Figure 8 at the call site. During the mapping process, the analysis derives the label map $l : \{\alpha' \mapsto n_{\{\texttt{first}\}}, \beta' \mapsto n_{\{\texttt{mid}\}}\}$ and the node map

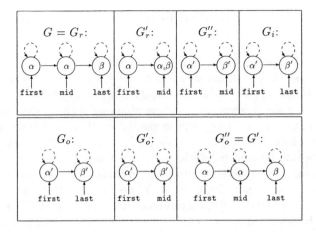

Fig. 8. Abstract shape graphs for mapping and unmapping processes for example

$m : \{n_{\{\text{first}\}} \mapsto \{n_{\{\text{first}\}}\}, n_{\{\text{mid}\}} \mapsto \{n_{\{\text{mid}\}}, n_{\{\text{last}\}}\}\}$. During the unmapping process, the analysis starts with the output G_o, whose heap access information indicates that only the first node has been read and written: $R_o = \{\alpha'\}, W_o = \{\alpha'\}$. The analysis can accurately replace the node $n_{\{\text{mid}\}}$ of G_o with the subgraph of G_r consisting of nodes $n_{\{\text{mid}\}}$ and $n_{\{\text{last}\}}$, because the label β' in G'_o denotes a region that hasn't been read or written by the invoked procedure. The resulting graph $G''_o = G'$ represents the information after the call.

Recursive Procedures. For the analysis of recursive procedures, our algorithm uses a standard fixed-point approach [14]. For each calling context G_i, the analysis maintains a best analysis result G_o for that context. The analysis initializes the best result G_o to the bottom element in the analysis domain, which is a graph with an empty set of nodes and empty sets of read and written locations. During the analysis of the program, the algorithm creates a stack of analysis contexts that models the call stack in the execution of the program. Whenever the analysis encounters an invoked procedure already on the stack, with the same calling context, it uses its current best analysis result for that context. When the algorithm finishes the analysis of a procedure and computes a new analysis result, it merges this result with the current best analysis result for that calling context. If the current best result changes, the algorithm re-analyzes all of the dependent analyses. The process continues until it reaches a fixed point.

4 Related Work

Early approaches to shape analysis [10, 1] propose graph abstractions of the heap based on allocation sites: each summary node in the shape graph represents all of the heap locations allocated at a certain site. Because of the abstraction based on allocation sites, these algorithms are imprecise in the presence of destructive updates.

A number of approaches to shape analyses have used access paths in the form of regular expressions to describe reachability of heap locations from the stack. Larus and Hilfinger present a dataflow analysis algorithm which computes access paths [11]. Other approaches use matrices of access paths to describe the reachability information [9, 8]. They propose algorithms that use the computed access paths to determine whether structures pointed to by different stack locations always access different heap locations, and use this information to parallelize applications that manipulate recursive heap structures. Researchers have also proposed language support for heap structures: in the Abstract Description of Data Structures (ADDS) [7], programmers can specify properties such as disjointness or backward pointers, and the compiler then uses analysis techniques based on access path matrices to check these properties. Deutsch [2] proposes a shape analysis which expresses aliasing using pairs of symbolic access paths. The analysis can parameterize the computed symbolic alias pairs, and show, for instance, that a list copy program produces a list whose elements are aliased with the corresponding elements of the original list.

Similar approaches use matrices of Booleans to express reachability information [5, 6]. For instance, the interference matrix indicates whether there may be heap locations reachable from different stack locations; and the direction matrix indicates if the heap location pointed to by a stack variable may be reachable from the heap location pointed to by another variable. The analysis uses the reachability information in these matrices to distinguish between trees, DAGs, and arbitrary graphs.

A more sophisticated analysis proposes a shape graph abstraction of the heap which distinguishes between heap locations depending on the stack variables that point to them [15]. This approach keeps track of the sharedness of summary nodes to identify acyclic lists or tree structures. The algorithm also introduces two key techniques that allow the analysis to compute accurate heap information: summarization into and materialization from summary nodes. Using these techniques, the analysis is able to determine that an in-place list reversal program preserves listness. Later analyses [17, 3] extend this algorithm with reachability information and thus are able to distinguish between sub-regions of the same heap structure. However, none of these algorithms is able to summarize heap access information for the whole execution of each procedure in the program.

More recently, researchers have proposed the use of three valued logic to express heap properties [16]. They propose a general framework which allows to express the heap abstraction using three valued logic formulas and show that existing analyses are instances of this framework. Subsequent work shows how to apply this framework to check the correctness of an insertion sort algorithm [12], and how to extend this framework for interprocedural analysis [13].

References

1. D. Chase, M. Wegman, and F. Zadek. Analysis of pointers and structures. In *Proceedings of the SIGPLAN'90 Conference on Program Language Design and Implementation*, White Plains, NY, June 1990.
2. A. Deutsch. Interprocedural may-alias analysis for pointers: Beyond k-limiting. In *Proceedings of the SIGPLAN'94 Conference on Program Language Design and Implementation*, Orlando, FL, June 1994.
3. N. Dor, M. Rodeh, and M. Sagiv. Checking cleanness in linked lists. In *Proceedings of the 8th International Static Analysis Symposium*, Santa Barbara, CA, July 2000.
4. M. Emami, R. Ghiya, and L. Hendren. Context-sensitive interprocedural points-to analysis in the presence of function pointers. In *Proceedings of the SIGPLAN'94 Conference on Program Language Design and Implementation*, Orlando, FL, June 1994.
5. R. Ghiya and L. Hendren. Connection analysis: A practical interprocedural heap analysis for C. In *Proceedings of the Eighth Workshop on Languages and Compilers for Parallel Computing*, Columbus, OH, August 1995.
6. R. Ghiya and L. Hendren. Is is a tree, a DAG or a cyclic graph? A shape analysis for heap-directed pointers in C. In *Proceedings of the 23rd Annual ACM Symposium on the Principles of Programming Languages*, St. Petersburg Beach, FL, January 1996.
7. L. Hendren, J. Hummel, and A. Nicolau. Abstractions for recursive pointer data structures: Improving the analysis and transformation of imperative programs. In *Proceedings of the SIGPLAN '92 Conference on Program Language Design and Implementation*, San Francisco, CA, June 1992.
8. L. Hendren, J. Hummel, and A. Nicolau. A general data dependence test for dynamic, pointer-based data structures. In *Proceedings of the SIGPLAN'94 Conference on Program Language Design and Implementation*, Orlando, FL, June 1994.
9. L. Hendren and A. Nicolau. Parallelizing programs with recursive data structures. *IEEE Transactions on Parallel and Distributed Systems*, 1(1):35–47, January 1990.
10. N. Jones and S. Muchnick. A flexible approach to interprocedural data flow analysis and programs with recursive data structures. In *Conference Record of the 9th Annual ACM Symposium on the Principles of Programming Languages*, Albuquerque, NM, January 1982.
11. J. Larus and P. Hilfinger. Detecting conflicts between structure accesses. In *Proceedings of the SIGPLAN'88 Conference on Program Language Design and Implementation*, Atlanta, GA, June 1988.
12. T. Lev-ami, T. Reps, M. Sagiv, and R. Wilhelm. Putting static analysis to work for verification: A case study. In *2000 International Symposium on Software Testing and Analysis*, August 2000.
13. N. Rinetzky and M. Sagiv. Interprocedural shape analysis for recursive programs. In *Proceedings of the 2001 International Conference on Compiler Construction*, Genova, Italy, April 2001.
14. R. Rugina and M. Rinard. Pointer analysis for multithreaded programs. In *Proceedings of the SIGPLAN'99 Conference on Program Language Design and Implementation*, Atlanta, GA, May 1999.
15. M. Sagiv, T. Reps, and R. Wilhelm. Solving shape-analysis problems in languages with destructive updating. *ACM Transactions on Programming Languages and Systems*, 20(1):1–50, January 1998.

16. M. Sagiv, T. Reps, and R. Wilhelm. Parametric shape analysis via 3-valued logic. In *Proceedings of the 26th Annual ACM Symposium on the Principles of Programming Languages*, San Antonio, TX, January 1999.
17. R. Wilhelm, M. Sagiv, and T. Reps. Shape analysis. In *Proceedings of the 2000 International Conference on Compiler Construction*, Berlin, Germany, April 2000.
18. R. Wilson and M. Lam. Efficient context-sensitive pointer analysis for C programs. In *Proceedings of the SIGPLAN'95 Conference on Program Language Design and Implementation*, La Jolla, CA, June 1995.

Establishing Local Temporal Heap Safety Properties with Applications to Compile-Time Memory Management

Ran Shaham[1,2], Eran Yahav[1], Elliot K. Kolodner[2], and Mooly Sagiv[1]

[1] School of Computer Science, Tel-Aviv University, Tel-Aviv, Israel
{rans,yahave,sagiv}@math.tau.ac.il
[2] IBM Haifa Research Laboratory, Haifa, Israel
kolodner@il.ibm.com

Abstract. We present a framework for statically reasoning about temporal heap safety properties. We focus on *local temporal heap safety properties*, in which the verification process may be performed for a program object independently of other program objects. We apply our framework to produce new conservative static algorithms for compile-time memory management, which prove for certain program points that a memory object or a heap reference will not be needed further. These algorithms can be used for reducing space consumption of Java programs. We have implemented a prototype of our framework, and used it to verify compile-time memory management properties for several small, but interesting example programs, including JavaCard programs.

1 Introduction

This work is motivated by the need to reduce space consumption, for example for memory-constrained applications in a JavaCard environment. Static analysis can be used to reduce space consumption by identifying source locations at which a heap-allocated object is no longer needed by the program. Once such source locations are identified, the program may be transformed to directly free unneeded objects, or aid a runtime garbage collector collect unneeded objects earlier during the run.

The problem of statically identifying source locations at which a heap-allocated object is no longer needed can be formulated as a local temporal heap safety property — a temporal safety property specified for each heap-allocated object independently of other objects.

The contributions of this paper can be summarized as follows.

1. We present a framework for verifying local temporal heap safety properties of Java programs.
2. Using this framework, we formulate two important compile-time memory management properties that identify when a heap-allocated object or heap reference is no longer needed, allowing space savings in Java programs.

3. We have implemented a prototype of our framework, and used it as a proof of concept to verify compile-time memory management properties for several small but interesting example programs, including JavaCard programs.

1.1 Local Temporal Heap Safety Properties

This paper develops a framework for automatically verifying *local temporal heap safety properties*, i.e., temporal safety properties that could be specified for a program object independently of other program objects. We assume that a safety property is specified using a *heap safety automaton* (HSA), which is a deterministic finite state automaton. The HSA defines the valid sequences of events that could occur for a single program object.

It is important to note that our framework implicitly allows infinite state machines, since the number of objects is unbounded. Furthermore, during the analysis an event is triggered for a state machine associated with an object. Thus, precise information on heap paths to disambiguate program objects is crucial for the precise association of an event and its corresponding program object's state machine.

In this paper, we develop static analysis algorithms that verify that on all execution paths, all objects are in an HSA accepting state. In particular, we show how the framework is used to verify properties that identify when a heap-allocated object or heap reference is no longer needed by the program. This information could be used by an optimizing compiler or communicated to the runtime garbage collector to reduce the space consumption of an application. Our techniques could also be used for languages like C to find a misplaced call to free that prematurely deallocates an object.

1.2 Compile-Time Memory Management Properties

Runtime garbage collection (GC) algorithms are implemented in Java and $C^{\#}$ environments. However, GC does not (and in general cannot) collect all the garbage that a program produces. Typically, GC collects objects that are no longer reachable from a set of *root* references. However, there are some objects that the program never accesses again and therefore not needed further, even though they are reachable. In previous work [28, 31] we showed that on average 39% of the space could be saved by freeing reachable unneeded objects. Moreover, in some applications, such as those for JavaCard, GC is avoided by employing static object pooling, which leads to non-modular, limited, and error-prone programs.

Existing compile-time techniques produce limited saving. For example, [1] produces a limited savings of a few percent due to the fact that its static algorithm ignores references from the heap. Indeed, our dynamic experiments indicate that the vast majority of savings require analyzing the heap.

In this paper, we develop two new static algorithms for statically detecting and deallocating garbage objects:

Free analysis . Statically identify source locations at which it is safe to insert a free statement in order to deallocate a garbage element.

Assign-null analysis. Statically identify source locations at which it is safe to assign null to heap references that are not used further in the run.

The assign-null analysis leads to space saving by allowing the GC to collect more space. In [31] we conduct dynamic measurements that show that assigning null to heap references immediately after their last use has an average space-saving potential of 15% beyond existing GCs. Free analysis could be used with runtime GC in standard Java environments and without GC for JavaCard.

Both of these algorithms handle heap references and destructive updates. They employ both forward (history) and backward (future) information on the behavior of the program. This allows us to free more objects than reachability based compile-time garbage collection mechanisms (e.g., [17]), which only consider the history.

1.3 A Motivating Example

Fig. 1 shows a program that creates a singly-linked list and then traverses it. We would like to verify that for this program a `free y` statement can be added immediately after line 10. This is possible because once a list element is traversed, it cannot be accessed along any execution path starting after line 10. It is interesting to note that even in this simple example, standard compile-time garbage collection techniques (e.g., [17]) will not issue such a free statement, since the element referenced by y is reachable via a heap path starting from x. Furthermore, integrating limited information on the future of the computation such as liveness of local reference variables (e.g., [1]) is insufficient for issuing such free statement. Nevertheless, our analysis is able to verify that the list element referenced by y is no longer needed, by investigating all execution paths starting at line 10.

In order to prove that a free statement can be added after line 10, we have to verify that all program objects referenced by y at line 10 are no longer needed on execution paths starting at this line. More specifically, for every execution path and every object o, we have to verify that from line 10 there is no use of a reference to o. In the sequel, we show how to formulate this property as a heap safety property and how our framework is used to successfully verify it.

1.4 A Framework for Verifying Heap Safety Properties

Our framework is conservative, i.e., if a heap safety property is verified, it is never violated on any execution path of the program. As usual for a conservative framework, we might fail to verify a safety property which holds on all execution paths of the program.

Assuming the safety property is described by an HSA, we instrument the program semantics to record the automaton state for every program object. First-order logical structures are used to represent a global state of the program.

```
    class L { // L is a singly linked list
      public L    n;   // next field
      public int val; // data field
    }
    class Main { // Creation and traversal of a singly-linked list
      public static void main(String args[]) {
        L x, y, t;
[1]     x = null;
[2]     while (...) { // list creation
[3]       y = new L();
[4]       y.val = ...;
[5]       y.n = x;
[6]       x = y;
        }
[7]     y = x;
[8]     while (y != null) {         // list traversal
[9]       System.out.print(y.val);
[10]      t = y.n;
[11]      y = t;
        }
      }
    }
```

Fig. 1. A program for creating and traversing a singly linked list

We augment this representation to incorporate information about the automaton state of every heap-allocated object.

Our abstract domain uses first-order 3-valued logical structures to represent an abstract global state of the program, which represent several (possibly an infinite number of) concrete logical structures [26]. We use *canonic abstraction* that maps concrete program objects (i.e., individuals in a logical structure) to abstract program objects based on the properties associated with a program object. In particular, the abstraction is refined by the automaton state associated with every program object.

For the purpose of our analyses one needs to: (i) consider information on the history of the computation, to approximate the heap paths, and (ii) consider information on the future of the computation, to approximate the future use of references. Our approach here uses a forward analysis, where the automaton maintains the temporal information needed to reason about the future of the computation.

In principle we could have used a forward analysis identifying heap-paths integrated into a backward analysis identifying future uses of heap references [30]. However, we find the cost of merging forward and backward information too expensive for a heap analysis as precise as ours.

1.5 Outline

The rest of this paper is organized as follows. In Section 2, we describe heap safety properties in general, and a compile-time memory management property of interest — the free property. Then, in Section 3, we give our instrumented concrete semantics which maintains an automaton state for every program object. Section 4 describes our property-guided abstraction and provides an abstract semantics. In Section 5, we describe an additional property of interest —

the assign-null property, and discuss efficient verification of multiple properties. Section 6 describes our implementation and empirical results. Related work is discussed in Section 7.

2 Specifying Compile-Time Memory Management Properties via Heap Safety Properties

In this section, we introduce heap safety properties in general, and a specific heap safety property that allows us to identify source locations at which heap-allocated objects may be safely freed.

Informally, a heap safety property may be specified via a heap safety automaton (HSA), which is a deterministic finite state automaton that defines the valid sequences of events for a single object in the program. An HSA defines a prefix-closed language, i.e., every prefix of a valid sequence of events is also valid. This is formally defined by the following definition.

Definition 1 (Heap Safety Automaton (HSA)).
A heap safety automaton $A = \langle \Sigma, Q, \delta, \text{init}, F \rangle$ is a deterministic finite state automaton, where Σ is the automaton alphabet which consists of observable events, Q is the set of automaton states, $\delta : Q \times \Sigma \to Q$ is the deterministic transition function mapping a state and an event to a single successor state, $\text{init} \in Q$ is the initial state, $\text{err} \in Q$ is a distinguished violation state (the sink state), for which for all $a \in \Sigma$, $\delta(\text{err}, a) = \text{err}$, and $F = Q \setminus \{\text{err}\}$ is the set of accepting states.

In our framework, we associate an HSA state with every object in the program, and verify that on all program execution paths, all objects are in an accepting state. The HSA is used to define an instrumented semantics, which maintains the state of the automaton for each object. The automaton state is *independently* maintained for every program object. However, the same automaton is used for all program objects.

When an object o is allocated, it is assigned the initial automaton state. The state of an object o is then updated by automaton transitions corresponding to events associated with o, triggered by program statements.

We now formulate the free property, which allows us to issue a free statement to reclaim objects unneeded further in the run. In the sequel, we make a simplifying assumption and focus on verification of the property for a single program point. In Section 5.2 we discuss a technique for efficient verification for a set of program points.

Definition 2 (Free Property $\langle pt, \text{x} \rangle$). *Given a program point pt and a program variable x, a free property $\langle pt, \text{x} \rangle$ states that the references to an object referenced by x at pt are not used further on execution paths starting at pt. Therefore, it is safe to issue a **free** x statement immediately after pt.*

The free property allows us to free an object that is not needed further in the run. Interestingly, such an object can still be reachable from a program variable through a heap path. For expository purposes, we only present the free property for an object referenced by a program variable. However, this free property can easily handle the free for an object referenced through an arbitrary reference expression exp, by introducing a new program variable z, assigned with exp just after pt, and verifying that free z may be issued just after the statement z = exp.

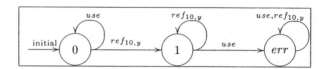

Fig. 2. A heap safety automaton $A_{10,y}^{free}$ for free y at line 10

Example 1. Consider the example program of Fig. 1. We would like to verify that a free y statement can be added immediately after line 10, i.e., a list element can be freed as soon as it has been traversed in the loop. The HSA $A_{10,y}^{free}$ shown in Fig. 2 represents the free property $\langle 10, y \rangle$. States 0 and 1 are accepting, while the state labelled *err* is the violation state. The alphabet of this automaton consists of two events associated with a program object o: (i) *use*, which corresponds to a use of a reference to o, and (ii) $ref_{10,y}$, which is triggered when program execution is immediately after execution of the statement at line 10 and y references o.

The HSA is in an accepting state along an execution path leading to the program exit iff o can be freed in the program after line 10. Thus, when on all execution paths, for all program objects o, only accepting states are associated with o, we conclude that free y can be added immediately after line 10.

First, when an object is allocated, it is assigned the initial state of $A_{10,y}^{free}$ (state 0). Then, a use of a reference to an object o (a *use* event) does not change the state of $A_{10,y}^{free}$ for o (a self-loop on state 0). When the program is immediately after line 10 and y references an object o ($ref_{10,y}$ event), o's automaton state is set to 1. If a reference to o is used further, and o's automaton state is 1 the automaton state for o reaches the violation state of the automaton. In that case the property is violated, and it is not possible to add a free y statement immediately after line 10 since it will free an object that is needed later in the program. However, in the program of Fig. 1, references to objects referenced by y at line 10 are not used further, hence the property is not violated, and it is safe to add a free y statement at this program point. Indeed, in Section 4 we show how the *free* $\langle 10, y \rangle$ property is verified.

An arbitrary free property is formulated as a heap safety property using an HSA similar to the one shown in Fig. 2 where the program point and reference expression are set accordingly.

It should be noted that in Java, free statements are not supported. Therefore, we assume that equivalent free annotations are issued, and could be exploited by the run-time environment. For example, a Java Virtual Machine (JVM) may include an internal free function, and the Just-In-Time (JIT) compiler (which is a run-time compiler included in the JVM) computes where calls to the function can be added.

3 Instrumented Concrete Semantics

We define an instrumented concrete semantics that maintains an automaton state for each heap-allocated object. In Section 3.1, we use first-order logical structures to represent a global state of the program and augment this representation to incorporate information about the automaton state of every heap-allocated object. Then in Section 3.2, we describe an operational semantics manipulating instrumented configurations.

3.1 Representing Program Configurations Using First-Order Logical Structures

The global state of the program can be naturally expressed as a first-order logical structure in which each individual corresponds to a heap-allocated object and predicates of the structure correspond to properties of heap-allocated objects. In the rest of this paper, we work with a fixed set of predicates denoted by P.

Definition 3 (Program Configuration). *A program configuration is a 2-valued first-order logical structure $C^\natural = \langle U^\natural, \iota^\natural \rangle$ where:*

- $U^\natural$ *is the universe of the 2-valued structure. Each individual in $U^\natural$ represents an allocated heap object.*
- $\iota^\natural$ *is the interpretation function mapping predicates to their truth-value in the structure, i.e., for every predicate $p \in P$ of arity k, $\iota^\natural(p): U^{\natural^k} \to \{0, 1\}$.*

Table 1. Predicates for partial Java semantics

Predicates	Intended Meaning
$at[pt]()$	program execution is immediately after program point pt
$x(o)$	program variable x references the object o
$f(o_1, o_2)$	field f of the object o_1 points to the object o_2
$s[q](o)$	the current state of o's automaton is q

We use the predicates of Table 1 to record information used by the properties discussed in this paper. The nullary predicate $at[pt]()$ records the program location in a configuration and holds in configurations in which the program is immediately after line pt. The unary predicate $x(o)$ records the value of a reference variable x and holds for the individual referenced by x. The binary predicate

$f(o_1, o_2)$ records the value of a field reference, and holds when the field f of o_1 points to the object o_2.

Predicates of the form $s[q](o)$ (referred to as *automaton state predicates*) maintain temporal information by maintaining the automaton state for each object. Such predicates record history information that is used to refine the abstraction. The abstraction is refined further by predicates that record spatial information, such as *reachability* and *sharing* (referred to as *instrumentation predicates* in [26]).

In this paper, program configurations are depicted as directed graphs. Each individual of the universe is displayed as a node. A unary predicate $p(o)$ which holds for an individual (node) u is drawn inside the node u. Predicates of the form $x(o)$ are shown as an edge from the predicate symbol to the node in which it holds since they can only hold for a single individual. The name of a node is written inside the node using an *italic* face. Node names are only used for ease of presentation and do not affect the analysis. A binary predicate $p(u_1, u_2)$ which evaluates to 1 is drawn as directed edge from u_1 to u_2 labelled with the predicate symbol. Finally, a nullary predicate $p()$ is drawn inside a box.

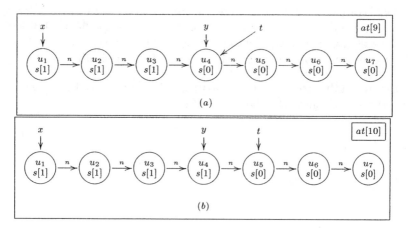

Fig. 3. Concrete program configurations (a) before — and (b) immediately after execution of t = y.n at line 10

Example 2. The configuration shown in Fig. 3(a) corresponds to a global state of the program in which execution is immediately after line 9. In this configuration, a singly-linked list of 7 elements has been traversed up to the 4-th element (labelled u_4) by the reference variable y, and the reference variable t still points to the same element as y. This is shown in the configuration by the fact that both predicates $y(o)$ and $t(o)$ hold for the individual u_4. Directed edges labelled by n correspond to values of the n field. The nullary predicate $at[9]()$ shown in a box in the upper-right corner of the figure records the fact that the program is immediately after line 9. The predicates $s[0](o)$ and $s[1](o)$ record which objects are in state 0 of the automaton and which are in state 1. For example, the individual u_3 is in automaton state 1 and the individual u_4 is in automaton state 0.

Maintaining Individual Automaton State. Given a heap safety property represented as an HSA $A = \langle \Sigma, Q, \delta, init, F \rangle$, we define the unary predicates $\{s[q](o) : q \in Q\}$ to track the state of the automaton for every heap-allocated object. In Section 3.2 we describe how these predicates are updated.

3.2 Operational Semantics

Program statements are modelled by generating the logical structure representing the program state after execution of the statement. In [26] it was shown that first-order logical formulae can be used to formally define the effect of every statement. In particular, first-order logical formulae are used to model the change of the automaton state of every affected individual, reflecting transition-updates in an ordered sequential manner.

In general, the operational semantics associates a program statement with a set of HSA events that update the automaton state of program objects. The translation from the set of HSA events to first-order logical formulae reflecting the change of the automaton state of every affected individual is automatic. We now show how program statements are associated with $A_{pt,x}^{free}$ events. For expository purposes, and without loss of generality, we assume the program is normalized to a 3-address form. In particular, a program statement may manipulate reference expressions of the form x or x.f.

Object Allocation. For a program statement x = new C() for allocating an object, a new object o_{new} is allocated, which is assigned the initial state of the HSA, i.e., we set the predicate $s[init](o_{new})$ to 1.

Example 3. Consider the HSA $A_{10,y}^{free}$ of Example 1. For this HSA we define a set of predicates $\{s[0](o), s[1](o), s[err](o)\}$ to record the state of the HSA individually for every heap-allocated object. Initially, when an object o is allocated at line 3 of the example program, we set $s[0](o)$ to 1, and other state predicates of o to 0.

Use Events. Table 2 shows the use events fired by each kind of a program statement, where (i) a use of x in a program statement updates the automaton state of the object referenced by x with a *use* event, and (ii) a use of the field f of the object referenced by x in a program statement updates the automaton state of the object referenced by x.f with a *use* event. For example, the statement x = y.f triggers use events for y and $y.f$, which update the automaton state of the object referenced by y with a *use* event, and update the automaton state of the object referenced by y.f with a *use* event. The order in which use events are triggered does not matter. However, in general, the order should be consistent with the HSA.

$ref_{pt,x}$ **Events.** For a free property $\langle pt, x \rangle$, the corresponding automaton $A^{free}_{pt,x}$ employs $ref_{pt,x}$ events in addition to *use* events. A $ref_{pt,x}$ event is triggered to update the automaton state of the object referenced by x when the current program point is *pt*. This event is triggered only after the *use* events corresponding to the program statement at *pt* are triggered.

Table 2. Use events triggered by program statements

statement	use events are triggered for an object referenced by
x = y	y
x = y.f	$y, y.f$
x.f = null	x
x.f = y	x, y
x binop y	x, y

Example 4. Fig. 3 shows the effect of the t = y.n statement at line 10, where the statement is applied to the configuration labelled by (a). First, this statement updates the predicate $t(o)$ to reflect the assignment by setting it to 1 for u_5, and setting it to 0 for u_4. In addition, it updates the program point by setting $at[10]()$ to 1 and $at[9]()$ to 0. Then, 2 *use* events followed by a $ref_{10,y}$ event are triggered: (i) *use* of the object referenced by y, causing the object u_4 to remain at automaton state 0, i.e., $s[0](u_4)$ remains 1; (ii) *use* of the object referenced by y.n, causing the object u_5 to remain at automaton state 0, i.e., $s[0](u_5)$ remains 1; and (iii) the event $ref_{10,y}$ for the object referenced by y, causing the object u_4 to change its automaton state to 1, i.e., setting the predicate $s[1]$ to 1 for u_4, and setting the predicate $s[0]$ to 0. After applying the above updates we end up with the logical structure shown in Fig. 3(b), reflecting both the changes in the store, and the transitions in the automaton state for program objects.

4 An Abstract Semantics

In this section, we present a conservative abstract semantics [10] abstracting the concrete semantics of Section 3. In Section 4.1, we describe how abstract configurations are used to finitely represent multiple concrete configurations. In Section 4.2, we describe an abstract semantics manipulating abstract configurations.

4.1 Abstract Program Configurations

We conservatively represent multiple concrete program configurations using a single logical structure with an extra truth-value 1/2 which denotes values which may be 1 and may be 0.

Definition 4 (Abstract Configuration). *An* abstract configuration *is a 3-valued logical structure* $C = \langle U, \iota \rangle$ *where:*

- U *is the universe of the 3-valued structure. Each individual in U represents possibly many allocated heap objects.*
- ι *is the interpretation function mapping predicates to their truth-value in the structure, i.e., for every predicate $p \in P$ of arity k, $\iota(p): U^k \to \{0, 1/2, 1\}$. For example, $\iota(p)(u) = 1/2$ indicates that the truth value of p may be 1 for some of the objects represented by u and may also be 0 for some of the objects represented by u.*

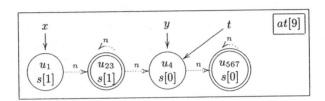

Fig. 4. An abstract program configuration representing the concrete configuration of Fig. 3(a).

We allow an abstract configuration to include a *summary node*, i.e., an individual which corresponds to one or more individuals in a concrete configuration represented by that abstract configuration. Technically, we use a designated unary predicate sm to maintain summary-node information. A summary node u has $sm(u) = 1/2$, indicating that it may represent more than one node.

Abstract program configurations are depicted by enhancing the directed graphs from Section 3 with a graphical representation for 1/2 values: a binary predicate $p(u_1, u_2)$ which evaluates to 1/2 is drawn as dashed directed edge from u_1 to u_2 labelled with the predicate symbol, and a summary node is drawn as circle with double-line boundaries.

Example 5. The abstract configuration shown in Fig. 4 represents the concrete configuration of Fig. 3(a). The summary node labelled by u_{23} represents the linked-list items u_2 and u_3, both having the same values for their unary predicates. Similarly, the summary node u_{567} represents the nodes u_5, u_6, and u_7.

Note that this abstract configuration represents many configurations. For example, it represents any configuration in which program execution is immediately after line 10 and a linked-list with at least 5 items has been traversed up to some item after the third item.

Embedding. We now formally define how configurations are represented using abstract configurations. The idea is that each individual from the (concrete) configuration is mapped into an individual in the abstract configuration. More generally, it is possible to map individuals from an abstract configuration into an individual in another less precise abstract configuration. The latter fact is important for our abstract transformer.

Formally, let $C = \langle U, \iota \rangle$ and $C' = \langle U', \iota' \rangle$ be abstract configurations. A function $f: U \to U'$ such that f is surjective is said to *embed C into C'* if for each predicate p of arity k, and for each $u_1, \ldots, u_k \in U$ one of the following holds:

$$\iota(p(u_1, \ldots, u_k)) = \iota'(p(f(u_1), \ldots, f(u_k))) \text{ or } \iota'(p(f(u_1), \ldots, f(u_k))) = 1/2$$
$$and$$
$$\text{for all } u' \in U' \text{ s.t. } |\{u \mid f(u) = u'\}| > 1 : \iota^{S'}(sm)(u') = 1/2$$

One way of creating an embedding function f is by using *canonical abstraction*. Canonical abstraction maps concrete individuals to an abstract individual based on the values of the individuals' unary predicates. All individuals having the same values for unary predicate symbols are mapped by f to the same abstract individual. Only summary nodes (i.e., nodes with $sm(u) = 1/2$) can have more than one node mapped to them by the embedding function.

Note that since automaton states are represented using unary predicates, the abstraction is refined by the automaton state of each object. This provides a simple property-guided abstraction since individuals at different automaton states are not summarized together. Indeed, adding unary predicates to the abstraction increases the worst-case cost of the analysis. However, as noted in [26] in practice this abstraction refinement often decreases significantly the cost of the analysis. Finally, our analysis is relational, allowing multiple 3-valued logical structures at a single program point, reflecting different behaviors.

4.2 Abstract Semantics

Implementing an abstract semantics directly manipulating abstract configurations is non-trivial since one has to consider all possible relations on the (possibly infinite) set of represented concrete configurations.

The *best* conservative effect of a program statement [10] is defined by the following 3-stage semantics: (i) a concretization of the abstract configuration is performed, resulting in all possible configurations *represented* by the abstract configuration; (ii) the program statement is applied to each resulting concrete configuration; (iii) abstraction of the resulting configurations is performed, resulting with a set of abstract configurations *representing* the results of the program statement.

Example 6. Fig. 5 shows the stages of an abstract action: first, concretization is applied to the abstract configuration resulting with an infinite set of concrete configuration represented by it. the program statement update is then applied to each of these concrete configurations. Following the program statement update, automaton transition updates are applied as described in Section 3.2. That is, at first *use* events are triggered to update the automaton states of the objects referenced by y and y.n. Then, a $ref_{10,y}$ event is triggered to update the automaton state of the object referenced by y. Finally, after all transition updates

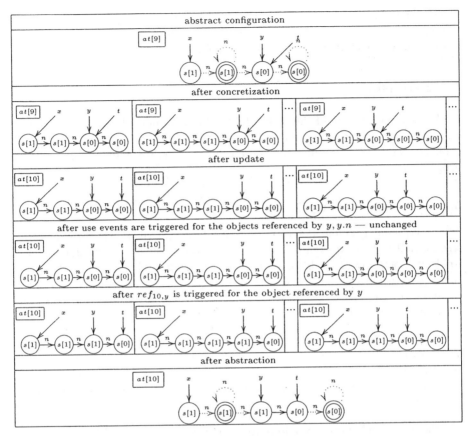

Fig. 5. Concretization, predicate-update, automaton transition updates, and abstraction for the statement t = y.n in line 10

have been applied, the resulting concrete configurations are abstracted resulting with a finite representation.

Our prototype implementation described in Section 6.1 operates directly on abstract configurations using *abstract transformers*, thereby obtaining actions which are more conservative than the ones obtained by the best transformers. Interestingly, since temporal information is encoded as part of the concrete configuration via automaton state predicates, the soundness of the abstract transformers is still guaranteed by the *Embedding Theorem* of [26]. Our experience shows that the abstract transformers used in the implementation are still precise enough to allow verification of our heap safety properties.

When the analysis terminates, we verify that in all abstract configurations, all individuals are associated with an accepting automaton state, i.e., in all abstract configurations, for every individual o, the predicate $s[err](o)$ evaluates to 0.

The soundness of our abstraction guarantees that this implies that in all concrete configurations, all individuals are associated with an accepting automaton state, and we conclude that the property holds.

5 Extensions

In this section, we extend the applicability of our framework by: (i) formulating an additional compile-time memory management property — the assign-null property; and (ii) extending the framework to simultaneously verify multiple properties.

5.1 Assign-Null Analysis

The assign-null problem determines source locations at which statements assigning null to heap references can be safely added. Such null assignments lead to objects being unreachable earlier in the program, and thus may help a runtime garbage collector collect objects earlier, thus saving space. As in Section 2, we show how to verify the assign-null property for a single program point and discuss efficient verification for a set of program points in Section 5.2.

Definition 5 (Assign-Null Property $\langle pt, \text{x}, \text{f} \rangle$). *Given a program point pt, an arbitrary reference expression* x, *and a reference field* f, *an assign-null property $\langle pt, \text{x}, \text{f} \rangle$ states that a reference* x.f *at pt is not used further before being redefined on execution paths starting at pt. Therefore, it is safe to add an* x.f = null *statement immediately after pt.*

The assign-null property allows us to assign null to a dead heap reference. As in the free property case, our assign-null property can also handle arbitrary reference expressions by introducing a new program variable t, assigned with exp just after a program point pt.

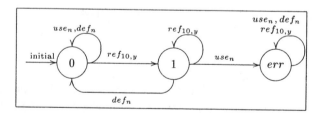

Fig. 6. A heap safety automaton $A^{an}_{10,y,n}$ for assign null to $y.n$ at 10

Example 7. Consider again the example program of Fig. 1. We would like to verify that a y.n = null statement can be added immediately after line 10, i.e., a reference connecting consecutive list elements can be assigned null as soon as it is traversed in the loop. The HSA $A^{an}_{10,y,n}$ shown in Fig. 6 represents the assign-null $\langle 10, y, n \rangle$ property. The alphabet of this automaton consists of the following events for an object o: (i) use_n, which corresponds to a use of the field n of the object; (ii) def_n, which corresponds to a definition of the field n of the object; (iii) $ref_{10,y}$, which is triggered when program execution is immediately after execution of the statement in 10 and y references the object o. Our implementation verifies assign-null $\langle 10, y, n \rangle$ property, by applying the framework with $A^{an}_{10,y,n}$ to the example program. Notice that this automaton contains a back arc and thus is more complex than the one for the free property.

An arbitrary assign-null property is formulated as a heap safety property using an HSA similar to the one shown in Fig. 6 where the program point, variable and field names are set accordingly.

5.2 Simultaneous Verification of Multiple Properties

So far we showed how to verify the free and assign-null properties for a single program point. Clearly, in practice one wishes to verify these properties for a set of program points without repeating the verification procedure for each program point. Our framework supports simultaneous verification of multiple properties, and in particular verification of properties for multiple program points. Assuming $HSA_1, \ldots, HSA_k$ describe k verification properties, then k automaton states $s_1, \ldots, s_k$ are maintained for every program object, where s_i maintains an automaton state for HSA_i. Technically, as described in Section 3, a state s_i of an individual o is represented by automaton state predicates $s_i[q](o)$, where q ranges over the states of HSA_i. The events associated with the automata $HSA_1, \ldots, HSA_k$ at a program point are triggered simultaneously, updating the corresponding automaton state predicates of individuals.

Interestingly, if we limit our verification of free $\langle pt, x \rangle$ properties to ones where x is used at pt (i.e., x is used in the statement at pt), then the following features are obtained: (i) an object is freed just after it is referenced last, i.e., exactly at the earliest time possible, and (ii) an object is freed "exactly once", i.e., there are no redundant frees of variables referencing the same object.

A similar choice for assign-null properties assigns null to a heap reference immediately after its last use. The motivation for this choice of verification properties comes from our previous work [31], showing an average of 15% potential space savings beyond a run-time garbage collector if a heap reference is assigned null just after its last use. However, we note that our framework allows verification of arbitrary free and assign-null properties, which may yield further space reduction. In fact, in [31] we show an average of 39% potential space savings beyond a run-time garbage collector assuming complete information on the future use of heap references.

6 Empirical Results

We implemented the static analysis algorithms for verifying free and assign-null properties, and applied it to several programs, including JavaCard programs.

Our benchmarks programs were used as a proof of concept, thus we did not measure the total savings obtained by our analysis. In particular the benchmarks provide three kinds of proof of concept: (i) we use small programs manipulating a linked-list to demonstrate the precision of our technique; (ii) we demonstrate how our techniques could be used to verify/automate manual space-savings rewritings. In particular, in our previous work [29] the code of the javac Java compiler was manually rewritten in order to save space. Here, we verify the manual rewritings in javac, which assign null to heap references, by applying our prototype implementation to a Java code fragment emulating part of the Parser facility of javac; (iii) we demonstrate how our techniques could play an important role in the design of future JavaCard programs. This is done by rewriting existing JavaCard code in a more modular way, and showing that our techniques may be used to avoid the extra space overhead due to the modularity.

6.1 Implementation

Our implementation consists of the following components: (i) a front-end, which translates a Java program (.class files) to a TVLA program [21]; (ii) an analyzer, which analyzes the TVLA program; (iii) a back-end, which answers our verification question by further processing of the analyzer output.

The front end (J2TVLA), developed by R. Manevich, is implemented using the Soot framework [33]. The analyzer, implemented using TVLA, includes the implementation of static analysis algorithms for the free and assign-null property verification. TVLA is a parametric framework that allows the heap abstractions and the abstract transformers to be easily changed. In particular, for programs manipulating lists we obtain a rather precise verification algorithm by relying on spatial instrumentation predicates, that give sharing, reachability and cyclicity information for heap objects [26]. For other programs, allocation-site information for heap objects suffices for the verification procedure. In both abstractions interprocedural information is computed [24]. Finally, our implementation allows simultaneous verification of several free or assign-null properties, by maintaining several automaton states per program object.

The back-end, implemented using TVLA libraries, traverses the analysis results, i.e., the logical structures at every program point, and verifies that all individuals are associated with an accepting state. For a single property, we could abort the analyzer upon reaching a non-accepting state on some object and avoid the back-end component. However, in the case of simultaneous verification of multiple safety properties, this would not work and the back-end is required.

6.2 Benchmark Programs

Table 3 shows our benchmark programs. The first 4 programs involve manipulations of a singly-linked list. DLoop, DPairs involve a doubly-linked list manipulation. small javac is motivated by our previous work [29], where we manually

Table 3. Analysis cost for the benchmark programs. Space is measured in MB, and time is measured in seconds

Program	Description	Free		Assign Null	
		space	time	space	time
Loop	the running example	1.71	1.93	1.37	1.76
CReverse	constructive reverse of a list	3.03	5.17	2.58	4.79
Delete	delete an element from a list	5.33	19.66	4.21	13.84
DLoop	doubly linked list variant of Loop	2.09	2.91	1.75	2.68
DPairs	processing pairs in a doubly-linked list	2.76	5.01	2.54	4.86
small javac	emulation of javac's parser facility	N/A	N/A	16.02	43.84
JavaPurse' slice	a JavaCard simple electronic purse	56.3	979	56.15	991
GuessNumber' slice	a JavaCard distributed guess number game	9.99	17.3	N/A	N/A

rewrite the code of the javac compiler, issuing null assignments to heap references. We can now verify our manual rewriting by applying the corresponding assign-null properties to Java code emulating part of the Parser facility in javac.

The last two benchmarks are JavaCard programs. JavaPurse is a simple electronic cash application, taken from Sun JavaCard samples [18]. In JavaPurse a fixed set of loyalty stores is maintained, so every purchase grants loyalty points at the corresponding store. GuessNumber [23] is a guess number game over mobile phone SIM cards, where one player (using a mobile phone) picks a number, and other players (using other mobile phones) try to guess the number.

Due to memory constraints, JavaCard programs usually employ a static allocation regime, where all program objects are allocated when the program starts. This leads to non-modular and less reusable code, and to more limited functionality. For example, in the GuessNumber program, a global buffer is allocated when the program starts and is used for storing either a server address or a phone number. In JavaPurse, the number of stores where loyalty points are granted is fixed.

A better approach that addresses the JavaCard memory constraints is to rewrite the code using a natural object-oriented programming style, and to apply static approaches to free objects not needed further in the program. Thus, we first rewrite the JavaCard programs to allow more modular code in the case of GuessNumber, and to lift the limitation on the number of stores in JavaPurse. Then, we apply our free analysis to the rewritten code, and verify that an object allocated in the rewritten code can be freed as soon it is no longer needed. In JavaPurse we also apply our assign null analysis and verify that an object allocated in the rewritten code can be made unreachable as soon it is no longer needed (thus, a run-time garbage collector may collect it). Concluding, we show that in principle the enhanced code bears no space overhead compared to the original code when the free or the assign-null analysis is used.

6.3 Results

Our experiments were done on a 900 Mhz Pentium-III with 512 MB of memory running Windows 2000. Table 3 shows the space and time the analysis takes. In Loop we verify our free ⟨10, y⟩ and assign-null ⟨10, y, n⟩ properties. For CReverse we verify an element of the original list can be freed as soon it is copied to the reversed list. In Delete we show an object can be freed as soon it is taken out of the list (even though it is still reachable from temporary variables). Turning to our doubly linked programs, we also show objects that can freed immediately after their last use, i.e., when an object is traversed in the loop (DLoop), and when an object in a pair is not processed further (DPairs). We also verify corresponding null-assignments that make an object unreachable via heap references as soon these references are not used further.

For small javac we verify that heap references to large objects in a parser class may be assigned null just after their last use. Finally, for scalability reasons we analyze slices of rewrritten JavaCard programs. Our current implementation does not include a slicer, thus we manually slice the code. Using the sliced programs we verify that objects allocated due by our rewritings, can be freed as soon they are not needed.

7 Related Work

One of the main difficulties in verifying local temporal heap safety properties is considering the effect of aliasing in a precise-enough manner. Some of the previous work on software verification allows universally quantified specifications similar to our local heap safety properties (e.g., [4, 9]). We are the first to apply such properties to compile-time memory management and to employ a high-precision analysis of the heap.

ESP [11] uses a preceding pointer-analysis phase and uses the results of this phase to perform finite-state verification. Separating verification from pointer-analysis may generally lead to imprecise results.

Some prior work used automata to dynamically monitor program execution and throw an exception when the property is violated (e.g.,[27, 8]). Obviously, dynamic monitoring cannot verify that the property holds for all program executions.

Recoding history information for investigating a particular local temporal heap safety property was used for example in [16, 25] (approximating flow dependencies) and [20] (verification of sorting algorithms). The framework presented here generalizes the idea of recording history information by using a heap safety automaton.

Our free property falls in the *compile-time garbage collection* research domain, where techniques are developed to identify and recycle garbage memory cells at compile-time. Most work has been done for functional languages [5, 17, 12, 14, 19]. In this paper, we show a free analysis, which handles a language with destructive updates, that may reclaim an object still reachable in the heap, but not needed further in the run.

Escape analysis (e.g., [7]), which allows stack allocating heap objects, has been recently applied to Java. In this technique an object is freed as soon as its allocating method returns to its caller. While this technique has shown to be useful, it is limited to objects that do not escape their allocating method. Our technique applies to all program objects, and allows freeing objects before their allocating method returns.

In region-based memory management [6, 32, 2, 13], the lifetime of an object is predicted at compile-time. An object is associated with a memory region, and the allocation and deallocation of the memory region are inferred automatically at compile time. It would be interesting to instantiate our framework with a static analysis algorithm for inferring earlier deallocation of memory regions.

Liveness analysis [22] may be used in the context of a run-time to reduce the size of the root set (i.e., ignoring dead stack variables and dead global variables) or to reduce the number of scanned references (i.e., ignoring dead heap references). In [3, 1, 15] liveness information for root references is used to reclaim more space.

In [31] we conduct dynamic measurements estimating the potential space savings achieved by communicating the liveness of stack variable references, global variables references and heap references to a run-time garbage collector. We conclude there that heap liveness information yields a potential for space savings significantly larger than the one achieved by communicating liveness information for stack and global variables. One way of communicating heap liveness information to a run-time GC is by assigning null to heap references. In this paper we present a static analysis algorithm for assigning null to heap references.

8 Conclusion

In this paper we present a framework for statically reasoning about local temporal heap safety properties. This framework is instantiated to produce two new static analysis algorithms for calculating the liveness of heap objects (free property) and heap references (assign-null property). Our initial experience shows evidence for the precision of our techniques, leading to space savings in Java programs. In the future we intend to apply our techniques to more "real-world" programs by integrating a code slicer and cheaper pointer analysis algorithms. It may be also interesting to explore opportunites for deallocating space using richer constructs than **free exp**. For example, using a new **free-list** construct for deallocating an entire list.

Acknowledgements

We would like to thank Giesecke & Devrient, Munich for their assistance and financial support. We would like to thank Roman Manevich and Thomas Stocker for many insights contributing to this research. Finally, we thank Nurit Dor for providing useful comments on earlier drafts of this paper.

References

1. O. Agesen, D. Detlefs, and E. Moss. Garbage Collection and Local Variable Type-Precision and Liveness in Java Virtual Machines. In *Prog. Lang. Design and Impl.*, June 1998.
2. M. F. Alexander Aiken and R. Levien. Better static memory management: Improving region-based analysis of higher-order languages. In *Prog. Lang. Design and Impl.*, June 1995.
3. A. W. Appel. *Compiling with Continuations*, chapter 16, pages 205–214. CUP, 1992.
4. T. Ball and S. Rajamani. SLIC: A Specification Language for Interface Checking (of C). Technical Report MSR-TR-2001-21, MSR, 2001.
5. J. M. Barth. Shifting garbage collection overhead to compile time. *Commun. ACM*, 20(7):513–518, 1977.
6. L. Birkedal, M. Tofte, and M. Vejlstrup. From region inference to von neumann machines via region representation inference. In *Symp. on Princ. of Prog. Lang.*, pages 171–183, 1996.
7. B. Blanchet. Escape analysis for object oriented languages. application to Java^{tm}. In *Conf. on Object-Oriented Prog. Syst., Lang. and Appl.*, Denver, 1998.
8. T. Colcombet and P. Fradet. Enforcing trace properties by program transformation. In *Proc. of 27th POPL*, pages 54–66, Jan. 19–21, 2000.
9. J. Corbett, M. Dwyer, J. Hatcliff, C. Pasareanu, R. Shawn, and L. Hongjun. Bandera: Extracting finite-state models from Java source code. In *Proc. 22nd ICSE*, June 2000.
10. P. Cousot and R. Cousot. Systematic design of program analysis frameworks. In *Symp. on Princ. of Prog. Lang.*, New York, NY, 1979. ACM Press.
11. M. Das, S. Lerner, and M. Seigle. ESP: Path-sensitive program verification in polynomial time. In *Prog. Lang. Design and Impl.*, pages 57–68, Berlin, June 2002.
12. I. Foster and W. Winsborough. Copy avoidance through compile-time analysis and local reuse. In *Proceedings of International Logic Programming Sympsium*, pages 455–469, 1991.
13. N. Hallenberg, M. Elsman, and M. Tofte. Combining region inference and garbage collection. In *Prog. Lang. Design and Impl.*, pages 141–152, Berlin, 2002.
14. G. W. Hamilton. Compile-time garbage collection for lazy functional languages. In *Memory Management, International Workshop IWMM 95*, 1995.
15. M. Hirzel, A. Diwan, and A. L. Hosking. On the usefulness of type and liveness accuracy for garbage collection and leak detection. In *Trans. on Prog. Lang. and Syst.*, 2002.
16. S. Horwitz, P. Pfeiffer, and T. Reps. Dependence analysis for pointer variables. In *Prog. Lang. Design and Impl.*, pages 28–40, New York, NY, 1989. ACM Press.
17. K. Inoue, H. Seki, and H. Yagi. Analysis of functional programs to detect run-time garbage cells. *Trans. on Prog. Lang. and Syst.*, 10(4):555–578, Oct. 1988.
18. Java card 2.2 development kit. Available at java.sun.com/products/javacard.
19. R. Jones. *Garbage Collection. Algorithms for Automatic Dynamic Memory Management.* John Wiley and Sons, 1999.
20. T. Lev-Ami, T. W. Reps, R. Wilhelm, and S. Sagiv. Putting static analysis to work for verification: A case study. In *ISSTA*, pages 26–38, 2000.
21. T. Lev-Ami and M. Sagiv. TVLA: A framework for kleene based static analysis. In *Static Analysis Symposium*. Springer, 2000.

22. S. Muchnick. *Advanced Compiler Design and Implementation.* Morgan Kaufmann, 1997.
23. Oberthur card systems. http://www.oberthurcs.com.
24. N. Rinetzky and M. Sagiv. Interprocedural shape analysis for recursive programs. *Lecture Notes in Computer Science*, 2027:133–149, 2001.
25. J. Ross and M. Sagiv. Building a bridge between pointer aliases and program dependences. In *Proceedings of the 1998 European Symposium On Programming*, Mar. 1998.
26. M. Sagiv, T. Reps, and R. Wilhelm. Parametric shape analysis via 3-valued logic. *ACM Transactions on Programming Languages and Systems (TOPLAS)*, 24(3):217–298, 2002.
27. F. Schneider. Enforceable security policies. *ACM Transactions on Information and System Security*, 3(1):30–50, Feb. 2000.
28. R. Shaham, E. K. Kolodner, and M. Sagiv. Automatic removal of array memory leaks in java. In *Int. Conf. on Comp. Construct.* Springer, Apr. 2000.
29. R. Shaham, E. K. Kolodner, and M. Sagiv. Heap profiling for space-efficient java. In *Prog. Lang. Design and Impl.* ACM, June 2001.
30. R. Shaham, E. K. Kolodner, and M. Sagiv. Backward shape analysis to statically predict heap behavior. Unpublished manuscript, 2002.
31. R. Shaham, E. K. Kolodner, and M. Sagiv. Estimating the impact of heap liveness information on space consumption in java. In *Int. Symp. on Memory Management.* ACM, 2002.
32. M. Tofte and J.-P. Talpin. Implementation of the typed call-by-value lambda-calculus using a stack of regions. In *Symp. on Princ. of Prog. Lang.*, pages 188–201, 1996.
33. R. Vallée-Rai, L. Hendren, V. Sundaresan, E. G. P. Lam, and P. Co. Soot - a java optimization framework. In *Proceedings of CASCON 1999*, pages 125–135, 1999.

Author Index

Abadi, Martín	316	Liblit, Ben	273
Aiken, Alex	273	Lin, Calvin	214
		Logozzo, Francesco	37
Bagnara, Roberto	337	López-García, Pedro	127
Baldan, Paolo	255		
Besson, Frédéric	19	Ma, Di	109
Blanchet, Bruno	316	Majumdar, Rupak	109
Boyland, John	55	McMillan, Ken L.	336
Bueno, Francisco	127	Merchat, David	355
		Minamide, Yasuhiko	153
Carlsson, Richard	73	Møller, Anders	1
Chatterjee, Krishnendu	109	Monniaux, David	237
Chen, Guangyu	383		
Chen, Wen-Ke	401	Palsberg, Jens	109
Chong, Stephen	463	Parent-Vigouroux, Catherine	355
Christensen, Aske Simon	1	Puebla, Germán	127
Engler, Dawson	295	Ramalingam, G.	439
		Reps, Thomas	189
Field, John	439	Ricci, Elisa	337
		Rinard, Martin	418
Goyal, Deepak	439	Rugina, Radu	463
Gupta, Rajiv	401		
Guyer, Samuel Z.	214	Sagiv, Mooly	483
		Sagonas, Konstantinos	73
Halbwachs, Nicolas	355	Schwartzbach, Michael I.	1
Henzinger, Thomas A.	109	Schwoon, Stefan	189
Hermenegildo, Manuel V.	127	Shaham, Ran	483
Hill, Patricia M.	337	Simone, Robert de	91
Jensen, Thomas	19	Tardieu, Olivier	91
Jha, Somesh	189	Thiemann, Peter	366
Kandemir, Mahmut	383	Unnikrishnan, Priya	383
Karakoy, Mustafa	383		
König, Barbara	255	Wilhelmsson, Jesper	73
König, Bernhard	255		
Kolcu, Ibrahim	383	Yahav, Eran	483
Kolodner, Elliot	483	Yang, Hongseok	171
Kremenek, Ted	295	Yelick, Katherine	273
Kuncak, Viktor	418	Yi, Kwangkeun	171
Lee, Oukseh	171	Zaffanella, Enea	337
Li, Bengu	401	Zhao, Tian	109

Lecture Notes in Computer Science

For information about Vols. 1–2592

please contact your bookseller or Springer-Verlag

Vol. 2593: A.B. Chaudhri, M. Jeckle, E. Rahm, R. Unland (Eds.), Web, Web-Services, and Database Systems. Proceedings, 2002. XI, 311 pages. 2003.

Vol. 2594: A. Asperti, B. Buchberger, J.H. Davenport (Eds.), Mathematical Knowledge Management. Proceedings, 2003. X, 225 pages. 2003.

Vol. 2595: K. Nyberg, H. Heys (Eds.), Selected Areas in Cryptography. Proceedings, 2002. XI, 405 pages. 2003.

Vol. 2596: A. Coen-Porisini, A. van der Hoek (Eds.), Software Engineering and Middleware. Proceedings, 2002. XII, 239 pages. 2003.

Vol. 2597: G. Păun, G. Rozenberg, A. Salomaa, C. Zandron (Eds.), Membrane Computing. Proceedings, 2002. VIII, 423 pages. 2003.

Vol. 2598: R. Klein, H.-W. Six, L. Wegner (Eds.), Computer Science in Perspective. X, 357 pages. 2003.

Vol. 2599: E. Sherratt (Ed.), Telecommunications and beyond: The Broader Applicability of SDL and MSC. Proceedings, 2002. X, 253 pages. 2003.

Vol. 2600: S. Mendelson, A.J. Smola, Advanced Lectures on Machine Learning. Proceedings, 2002. IX, 259 pages. 2003. (Subseries LNAI).

Vol. 2601: M. Ajmone Marsan, G. Corazza, M. Listanti, A. Roveri (Eds.) Quality of Service in Multiservice IP Networks. Proceedings, 2003. XV, 759 pages. 2003.

Vol. 2602: C. Priami (Ed.), Computational Methods in Systems Biology. Proceedings, 2003. IX, 214 pages. 2003.

Vol. 2603: A. Garcia, C. Lucena, F. Zambonelli, A. Omicini, J. Castro (Eds.), Software Engineering for Large-Scale Multi-Agent Systems. XIV, 285 pages. 2003.

Vol. 2604: N. Guelfi, E. Astesiano, G. Reggio (Eds.), Scientific Engineering for Distributed Java Applications. Proceedings, 2002. X, 205 pages. 2003.

Vol. 2606: A.M. Tyrrell, P.C. Haddow, J. Torresen (Eds.), Evolvable Systems: From Biology to Hardware. Proceedings, 2003. XIV, 468 pages. 2003.

Vol. 2607: H. Alt, M. Habib (Eds.), STACS 2003. Proceedings, 2003. XVII, 700 pages. 2003.

Vol. 2609: M. Okada, B. Pierce, A. Scedrov, H. Tokuda, A. Yonezawa (Eds.), Software Security – Theories and Systems. Proceedings, 2002. XI, 471 pages. 2003.

Vol. 2610: C. Ryan, T. Soule, M. Keijzer, E. Tsang, R. Poli, E. Costa (Eds.), Genetic Programming. Proceedings, 2003. XII, 486 pages. 2003.

Vol. 2611: S. Cagnoni, J.J. Romero Cardalda, D.W. Corne, J. Gottlieb, A. Guillot, E. Hart, C.G. Johnson, E. Marchiori, J.-A. Meyer, M. Middendorf, G.R. Raidl (Eds.), Applications of Evolutionary Computing. Proceedings, 2003. XXI, 708 pages. 2003.

Vol. 2612: M. Joye (Ed.), Topics in Cryptology – CT-RSA 2003. Proceedings, 2003. XI, 417 pages. 2003.

Vol. 2613: F.A.P. Petitcolas, H.J. Kim (Eds.), Digital Watermarking. Proceedings, 2002. XI, 265 pages. 2003.

Vol. 2614: R. Laddaga, P. Robertson, H. Shrobe (Eds.), Self-Adaptive Software: Applications. Proceedings, 2001. VIII, 291 pages. 2003.

Vol. 2615: N. Carbonell, C. Stephanidis (Eds.), Universal Access. Proceedings, 2002. XIV, 534 pages. 2003.

Vol. 2616: T. Asano, R. Klette, C. Ronse (Eds.), Geometry, Morphology, and Computational Imaging. Proceedings, 2002. X, 437 pages. 2003.

Vol. 2617: H.A. Reijers (Eds.), Design and Control of Workflow Processes. Proceedings, 2002. XV, 624 pages. 2003.

Vol. 2618: P. Degano (Ed.), Programming Languages and Systems. Proceedings, 2003. XV, 415 pages. 2003.

Vol. 2619: H. Garavel, J. Hatcliff (Eds.), Tools and Algorithms for the Construction and Analysis of Systems. Proceedings, 2003. XVI, 604 pages. 2003.

Vol. 2620: A.D. Gordon (Ed.), Foundations of Software Science and Computation Structures. Proceedings, 2003. XII, 441 pages. 2003.

Vol. 2621: M. Pezzè (Ed.), Fundamental Approaches to Software Engineering. Proceedings, 2003. XIV, 403 pages. 2003.

Vol. 2622: G. Hedin (Ed.), Compiler Construction. Proceedings, 2003. XII, 335 pages. 2003.

Vol. 2623: O. Maler, A. Pnueli (Eds.), Hybrid Systems: Computation and Control. Proceedings, 2003. XII, 558 pages. 2003.

Vol. 2624: H.G. Dietz (Ed.), Languages and Compilers for Parallel Computing. Proceedings, 2001. XI, 444 pages. 2003.

Vol. 2625: U. Meyer, P. Sanders, J. Sibeyn (Eds.), Algorithms for Memory Hierarchies. Proceedings, 2003. XVIII, 428 pages. 2003.

Vol. 2626: J.L. Crowley, J.H. Piater, M. Vincze, L. Paletta (Eds.), Computer Vision Systems. Proceedings, 2003. XIII, 546 pages. 2003.

Vol. 2627: B. O'Sullivan (Ed.), Recent Advances in Constraints. Proceedings, 2002. X, 201 pages. 2003. (Subseries LNAI).

Vol. 2628: T. Fahringer, B. Scholz, Advanced Symbolic Analysis for Compilers. XII, 129 pages. 2003.

Vol. 2631: R. Falcone, S. Barber, L. Korba, M. Singh (Eds.), Trust, Reputation, and Security: Theories and Practice. Proceedings, 2002. X, 235 pages. 2003. (Subseries LNAI).

Vol. 2632: C.M. Fonseca, P.J. Fleming, E. Zitzler, K. Deb, L. Thiele (Eds.), Evolutionary Multi-Criterion Optimization. Proceedings, 2003. XV, 812 pages. 2003.

Vol. 2633: F. Sebastiani (Ed.), Advances in Information Retrieval. Proceedings, 2003. XIII, 546 pages. 2003.

Vol. 2634: F. Zhao, L. Guibas (Eds.), Information Processing in Sensor Networks. Proceedings, 2003. XII, 692 pages. 2003.

Vol. 2636: E. Alonso, D, Kudenko, D. Kazakov (Eds.), Adaptive Agents and Multi-Agent Systems. XIV, 323 pages. 2003. (Subseries LNAI).

Vol. 2637: K.-Y. Whang, J. Jeon, K. Shim, J. Srivastava (Eds.), Advances in Knowledge Discovery and Data Mining. Proceedings, 2003. XVIII, 610 pages. 2003. (Subseries LNAI).

Vol. 2638: J. Jeuring, S. Peyton Jones (Eds.), Advanced Functional Programming. Proceedings, 2002. VII, 213 pages. 2003.

Vol. 2639: G. Wang, Q. Liu, Y. Yao, A. Skowron (Eds.), Rough Sets, Fuzzy Sets, Data Mining, and Granular Computing. Proceedings, 2003. XVII, 741 pages. 2003. (Subseries LNAI).

Vol. 2641: P.J. Nürnberg (Ed.), Metainformatics. Proceedings, 2002. VIII, 187 pages. 2003.

Vol. 2642: X. Zhou, Y. Zhang, M.E. Orlowska (Eds.), Web Technologies and Applications. Proceedings, 2003. XIII, 608 pages. 2003.

Vol. 2643: M. Fossorier, T. Høholdt, A. Poli (Eds.), Applied Algebra, Algebraic Algorithms and Error-Correcting Codes. Proceedings, 2003. X, 256 pages. 2003.

Vol. 2644: D. Hogrefe, A. Wiles (Eds.), Testing of Communicating Systems. Proceedings, 2003. XII, 311 pages. 2003.

Vol. 2645: M.A. Wimmer (Ed.), Knowledge Management in Electronic Government. Proceedings, 2003. XI, 320 pages. 2003. (Subseries LNAI).

Vol. 2646: H. Geuvers, F, Wiedijk (Eds.), Types for Proofs and Programs. Proceedings, 2002. VIII, 331 pages. 2003.

Vol. 2647: K.Jansen, M. Margraf, M. Mastrolli, J.D.P. Rolim (Eds.), Experimental and Efficient Algorithms. Proceedings, 2003. VIII, 267 pages. 2003.

Vol. 2648: T. Ball, S.K. Rajamani (Eds.), Model Checking Software. Proceedings, 2003. VIII, 241 pages. 2003.

Vol. 2649: B. Westfechtel, A. van der Hoek (Eds.), Software Configuration Management. Proceedings, 2003. VIII, 241 pages. 2003.

Vol. 2651: D. Bert, J.P. Bowen, S. King, M, Waldén (Eds.), ZB 2003: Formal Specification and Development in Z and B. Proceedings, 2003. XIII, 547 pages. 2003.

Vol. 2652: F.J. Perales, A.J.C. Campilho, N. Pérez de la Blanca, A. Sanfeliu (Eds.), Pattern Recognition and Image Analysis. Proceedings, 2003. XIX, 1142 pages. 2003.

Vol. 2653: R. Petreschi, Giuseppe Persiano, R. Silvestri (Eds.), Algorithms and Complexity. Proceedings, 2003. XI, 289 pages. 2003.

Vol. 2656: E. Biham (Ed.), Advances in Cryptology – EUROCRPYT 2003. Proceedings, 2003. XIV, 649 pages. 2003.

Vol. 2657: P.M.A. Sloot, D. Abramson, A.V. Bogdanov, J.J. Dongarra, A.Y. Zomaya, Y.E. Gorbachev (Eds.), Computational Science – ICCS 2003. Proceedings, Part I. 2003. LV, 1095 pages. 2003.

Vol. 2658: P.M.A. Sloot, D. Abramson, A.V. Bogdanov, J.J. Dongarra, A.Y. Zomaya, Y.E. Gorbachev (Eds.), Computational Science – ICCS 2003. Proceedings, Part II. 2003. LV, 1129 pages. 2003.

Vol. 2659: P.M.A. Sloot, D. Abramson, A.V. Bogdanov, J.J. Dongarra, A.Y. Zomaya, Y.E. Gorbachev (Eds.), Computational Science – ICCS 2003. Proceedings, Part III. 2003. LV, 1165 pages. 2003.

Vol. 2660: P.M.A. Sloot, D. Abramson, A.V. Bogdanov, J.J. Dongarra, A.Y. Zomaya, Y.E. Gorbachev (Eds.), Computational Science – ICCS 2003. Proceedings, Part IV. 2003. LVI, 1161 pages. 2003.

Vol. 2663: E. Menasalvas, J. Segovia, P.S. Szczepaniak (Eds.), Advances in Web Intelligence. Proceedings, 2003. XII, 350 pages. 2003. (Subseries LNAI).

Vol. 2665: H. Chen, R. Miranda, D.D. Zeng, C. Demchak, J. Schroeder, T. Madhusudan (Eds.), Intelligence and Security Informatics. Proceedings, 2003. XIV, 392 pages. 2003.

Vol. 2667: V. Kumar, M.L. Gavrilova, C.J.K. Tan, P. L'Ecuyer (Eds.), Computational Science and Its Applications – ICCSA 2003. Proceedings, Part I. 2003. XXXIV, 1060 pages. 2003.

Vol. 2668: V. Kumar, M.L. Gavrilova, C.J.K. Tan, P. L'Ecuyer (Eds.), Computational Science and Its Applications – ICCSA 2003. Proceedings, Part II. 2003. XXXIV, 942 pages. 2003.

Vol. 2669: V. Kumar, M.L. Gavrilova, C.J.K. Tan, P. L'Ecuyer (Eds.), Computational Science and Its Applications – ICCSA 2003. Proceedings, Part III. 2003. XXXIV, 948 pages. 2003.

Vol. 2670: R. Peña, T. Arts (Eds.), Implementation of Functional Languages. Proceedings, 2002. X, 249 pages. 2003.

Vol. 2674: I.E. Magnin, J. Montagnat, P. Clarysse, J. Nenonen, T. Katila (Eds.), Functional Imaging and Modeling of the Heart. Proceedings, 2003. XI, 308 pages. 2003.

Vol. 2675: M. Marchesi, G. Succi (Eds.), Extreme Programming and Agile Processes in Software Engineering. Proceedings, 2003. XV, 464 pages. 2003.

Vol. 2676: R. Baeza-Yates, E. Chávez, M. Crochemore (Eds.), Combinatorial Pattern Matching. Proceedings, 2003. XI, 403 pages. 2003.

Vol. 2678: W. van der Aalst, A. ter Hofstede, M. Weske (Eds.), Business Process Management. Proceedings, 2003. XI, 391 pages. 2003.

Vol. 2679: W. van der Aalst, E. Best (Eds.), Applications and Theory of Petri Nets 2003. Proceedings, 2003. XI, 508 pages. 2003.

Vol. 2686: J. Mira, J.R. Álvarez (Eds.), Computational Methods in Neural Modeling. Proceedings, Part I. 2003. XXVII, 764 pages. 2003.

Vol. 2687: J. Mira, J.R. Álvarez (Eds.), Artificial Neural Nets Problem Solving Methods. Proceedings, Part II. 2003. XXVII, 820 pages. 2003.

Vol. 2692: P. Nixon, S. Terzis (Eds.), Trust Management. Proceedings, 2003. X, 349 pages. 2003.

Vol. 2694: R. Cousot (Ed.), Static Analysis. Proceedings, 2003. XIV, 505 pages. 2003.

Vol. 2701: M. Hofmann (Ed.), Typed Lambda Calculi and Applications. Proceedings, 2003. VIII, 317 pages. 2003.

Vol. 2706: R. Nieuwenhuis (Ed.), Rewriting Techniques and Applications. Proceedings, 2003. XI, 515 pages. 2003.

Vol. 2707: K. Jeffay, I. Stoica, K. Wehrle (Eds.), Quality of Service – IWQoS 2003. Proceedings, 2003. XI, 517 pages. 2003.